D0909365

Ronald Reagan in Hollywood explores the relationship between the motion picture industry and American politics through the prism of Reagan's film career at Warner Bros. During the Great Depression, World War II, and the postwar era, the Hollywood film industry served as a "grand, worldwide propaganda base" for those who wanted to use movies to influence attitudes about patriotism, national defense, communism, the welfare state, race, sex, and civil liberties. Reagan thrived in this environment. During his years in Hollywood, from 1937 to 1952, he formed many of the ideas that he later carried into his presidency. Not merely a star, Reagan simultaneously became an articulate industry spokesperson and skilled propagandist, playing an important role in "the battle . . . to capture the minds" of humanity in the struggle against communism. By the time he left Warner Bros. in 1952, Reagan had abandoned his New Deal liberalism and had become a militant anticommunist.

Based on interviews with President Reagan and others, formerly secret FBI files, and material from more than 150 archival collections, *Ronald Reagan in Hollywood* is the most comprehensive book on this subject, providing an incisive analysis of Reagan's important formative years.

RONALD REAGAN IN HOLLYWOOD

Cambridge Studies in the History of Mass Communications

General Editors:

Kenneth R. M. Short, University of Houston
Garth Jowett, University of Houston

Advisory Board:

Erik Barnouw, Professor Emeritus, Columbia University
Lord Asa Briggs, Worcester College, University of Oxford
Thomas Cripps, Morgan State University
Everette Dennis, Gannett Center for Media Studies, Columbia University
Jean-Noël Jeanneny, University of Paris
Frederick Kahlenberg, University of Mannheim

Published Titles:

*Hollywood's Overseas Campaign: The North Atlantic Movie Trade,
1920–1950,* by Ian Jarvie
Cinema and Soviet Society, 1917–1953, by Peter Kenez

For Bev and Will

CONTENTS

PREFACE

The following pages set out an extraordinary story, that of the rise of Ronald Reagan from an obscure if ambitious youth in the Midwest to a Hollywood star who developed a remarkable talent for politics. Many actors have taken an interest in politics, but Reagan had the ability to take his fascination far beyond anything achieved by other Hollywood personalities. His political apprenticeship occurred during the fifteen years – from 1937 to 1952 – when he worked as a contract player for Warner Bros. Pictures, a period that stretched from the Great Depression, through World War II, and into the first years of the Cold War.

Reagan came to the West Coast in the middle of the Great Depression as a virtual unknown, seeking fame and fortune. These he soon found after signing with Warner Bros. By the time America entered World War II he had already reached movie stardom and had a weekly salary that had risen to heights beyond anything that seemed possible during his boyhood in central Illinois. But he found something more than renown and wealth in Hollywood; he discovered issues – fighting issues, he believed.

And so much of this work is not only about Reagan but also about those issues that changed his life and made a difference, it is fair to say, in the lives of many Americans. By focusing on what has been called the "battle of ideas," the conflict over what social and political principles actors and movies would represent, and by using Reagan's career as its focal point, this book explores the relationship between the motion picture industry and American politics. At first blush this may appear an odd topic, given the apparent superficiality of Hollywood in general and of Reagan's pictures in particular. Yet if one looks behind the films to how they were made and examines the organizations to which Reagan belonged, one immediately sees the influence of politics. Few people associated with movie making during this era doubted the ability of motion pictures to alter attitudes and behavior.

Certainly Reagan was no exception in this regard. For him, cinema was more than society's mirror; it was a platform. As he came to think of himself as more than an entertainer, so he also came to see Hollywood as a "grand world-wide propaganda base." By 1952, he considered himself engaged in a "great ideological struggle" to "capture the minds" of humanity.[1]

It is impossible to set out Reagan's political education without showing its close association with the movie industry and especially the Warner Bros. studio, where from the outset the actor found himself immersed in the Warners' own preoccupation with politics. The Warner family had come from Poland at the turn of the century, and the brothers Jack and Harry never forgot their own success in America. During the Great Depression they developed a reputation for being pro-Roosevelt and socially conscious. As Jews, they also became alarmed at what they saw occurring in Nazi Germany. They feared what a Europe dominated by Adolf Hitler might mean and became obsessed with the possibility of subversion in the United States. Often they made their films conveniently topical, and while they were always sensitive to what might hurt the box office, they did not hesitate to use their pictures in ways they hoped might influence opinion – this despite frequent difficulties with censors, pressure groups, and government officials. By the late 1930s, military preparedness and patriotism had become important themes for the Warners. The former notion was controversial before Pearl Harbor, but the Warners discovered that their enemies could not easily object to the latter. Reagan, who at the time was himself a New Deal Democrat, had to find his place within the Warners' scheme of things, and he quickly did so. He could hardly have ignored this introduction to politics.

To be sure, the Warners remained a presence in Reagan's life throughout this entire period, but the actor also had many opportunities outside of the studio to learn about politics. During World War II he worked as a propagandist for the Army Air Force in a unit that Jack Warner lobbied General Henry "Hap" Arnold to establish. Reagan spent the war in California, most of the time stationed at Culver City, thanks in no small part to Warner's influence. Reagan's work in propaganda is interesting, too, because it placed him under the command of Arnold, a leading advocate of American air power. After the war Reagan joined several political organizations, made fewer films, and rapidly became a force in Hollywood politics. The sources from which to study Reagan's activities become richer after 1945 and reveal his metamorphosis from a follower of Franklin D. Roosevelt to industry spokesperson and anticommunist. His emerging conservatism is therefore a theme in these pages. He came into his own with the Screen Actors Guild, where he gained national recognition as president. As a leader in the Motion Picture Industry Council he became an industry advocate, skilled in public relations and public speaking, at ease with crowds, cameras, celebrities, and politicians. Not only did he benefit from Hollywood's publicity, he learned how to use it. He rose to leadership in an industry fueled by money, power, and sex –

a place also of labor violence, anticommunism, economic insecurity, and personal and professional crises. It was an atmosphere hostile to social experiment and political risk-taking.

By examining this period it is the author's hope that the reader will gain greater insight into Reagan's development as a political leader and into Hollywood's place in the American political system. Understanding this early environment and Reagan's success in it shows that later, when he ran for public office, he was often underestimated by those who said that he was merely an actor. Here was the crucible in which began to form many of the ideas that Reagan would carry into the White House a generation or so later. This is not to argue that a direct line necessarily existed between these years and the positions later taken by Reagan as governor and president. After all, almost three decades elapsed between the time Reagan left Warner Bros. and assumed the United States presidency. But one finds in this earlier era that Hollywood divided over many of the same issues that separated Americans during the 1980s – matters involving communism, liberalism, welfare, the revival of patriotism, national defense, the role of Judeo-Christianity in entertainment and politics, women and the family, sexual behavior, anti-Semitism and ethnicity, racism and civil rights, the use of history, and freedom of expression, to name a few. A broad consistency existed between many of the views (although not all) that came to dominate Reagan's early world and those he later espoused as an elected leader. And just as this was a formative time for Reagan, so too was it an important period for Hollywood and its place in society. It was a time when actors aspired to respectability and became sought-after participants in politics. Reagan had much to do with these developments.

This book does not downplay the importance to Reagan of being a movie actor. It is noteworthy that from his days as a youth, steeped in the verities of the Christian Church and small-town life, acting was a way of learning for him. During his screen career, which spanned the years from 1937 to 1964, Reagan made fifty-three feature films. He appeared in forty-six of those pictures between 1937 and 1952, and of those movies, forty-one were made by Warner Bros.[2] He left behind a more visible record before entering elective office than any other American president. Understanding his roles, the public image that the studio created for him, and how his movies were put together reveals a good deal about his early world. But Reagan's Hollywood experiences involved much more than performing in films, and the movies served only as a starting point for this book, which is based on a wide array of sources, including interviews, FBI files released under the Freedom of Information Act, and, most important, materials from more than 150 collections in archives scattered around the country.

A word is in order about the organization of this book. The chapters that follow move forward in a broadly chronological fashion, but they have also been constructed around different themes. As a result, readers will find that as chapters consider new topics they revisit earlier periods. Chapters 1 through 9 carry the story through the end of World War II. Chapters 10 through 19 deal with the years from late 1945 through roughly 1952.

This work ends in the early 1950s because after that time documentation diminishes sharply. The year 1952 is a logical concluding point for other reasons: that year Reagan married the actress Nancy Davis, ended his association with Warner Bros., stepped down after five consecutive terms as president of the Screen Actors Guild, and soon thereafter went into television as host of a program known as "General Electric Theater." A little more than a decade later the politics first of California, then of the entire United States, beckoned to him.

During the past eight years I have been fortunate to have had the help of many friends and colleagues in preparing this book. I especially want to thank Merle Curti, the late Frank Freidel, Arthur Hove, Richard S. Kirkendall, Beatrice Rehl, and K. R. M. Short for reading the entire manuscript and offering valuable advice. Others who read parts of the work and made helpful recommendations were Terry Anderson, Thomas Cripps, Jerry Durham, Ian Jarvie, George Juergens, John Pauley, Janice Radway, Donald Ritchie, and Dwight Teeter. I am also grateful for the encouragement I received in the early stages of this work from Maurice Baxter, Robert Gunderson, Charles Jelavich, Martin Ridge, the late Boyd C. Shafer, and David Trask.

I am particularly indebted to my colleagues at the University of Wisconsin in Madison who read and commented on sections of this book or who otherwise shared their knowledge about topics related to this study. They include Raymond Anderson, Tino Balio, James L. Baughman, William Blankenburg, Allan Bogue, Paul Boyer, Steven Chafee, Edward (Mac) Coffman, John Cooper, Donald Crafton, Robert Dreschel, William Hachten, Robert Hawkins, Jacqueline Hitchon, Stanley Kutler, Robert McChesney, Jack McLeod, Harold L. Nelson, Chuck Salmon, Clay Schoenfeld, and MaryAnn Yodelis Smith. Bruce Evensen provided several insights into Hollywood and filmmaking. Students in my seminars – Carolyn Bronstein, Richard Digby-Junger, Andrew Feldman, Genevieve McBride, Christine Moore – also made contributions. James Fosdick, Shiela Reaves, John Schuon, Robert Ostrom, Roy Cadwell, Steve Westerman, Tom Grimes, and Michael McCauley helped with audiovisual equipment. Among those who assisted in typing or copy editing were Sue Dewane, Cary Groner, Linda Henzl, Mary Kuusisto, Eric Newman, Jeanne Niederklopfer, Sandra Ott, Cindy Schkirkie, and Brenda Weiss.

Several people – Gregory Black, David Culbert, the late Burris Dickinson, Garth Jowett, Clayton Koppes, Lary May, Nigel Mace, Roger Newman, Kurt Ritter, Michael Rogin, Spencer Weart – who were working on related themes were kind enough to share research with me. My thanks, too, to the staffs of the *Journal of American History, American Quarterly, American Journalism, Journal of Negro History,* and *Presidential Studies Quarterly,* where portions of this research have been published.

Many people shared their recollections about the people or events discussed in this book. I particularly found helpful conversations with Ronald Reagan, the late Helen Cleaver, Margaret (Cleaver) Gordon, Dorothy (Bovey) Potterveld, Fred Goodwin, Thomas Israel, Don Littlejohn, Salene Walters Lamm (aka Betty Flo Walker), and William ("Bill") Walker. I wish to thank Bob Tyrrell and Cathy Goldberg for helping to arrange the conversation with former President Reagan.

The research into the primary documents on which this book is based would have been severely hindered without the assistance of numerous people, many of them archivists, curators, and librarians. This study began and in some ways ended in the film archive and manuscript holdings at the State Historical Society of Wisconsin in Madison. I found no more helpful staff or more pleasant working conditions than here. I am particularly grateful to R. David Myers, Harry Miller, Maxine Flexner-Ducey, James Danky, and their staffs for their unfailing assistance. Work in the vast Warner Bros. archives would have been impossible without the help of Robert Knutson, and especially Leith Adams and Ned Comstock at the University of Southern California, as well as Mary Ann Jensen at Princeton University. Sam Gill and his staff made many valuable suggestions about using the collections in the Margaret Herrick Library in Beverly Hills. Kim Fellner, Mark Locher, and Tony Phipps helped me gain access to the minutes of the Screen Actors Guild board meetings. I profited greatly from Irwin Mueller's knowledge of the collections in the Harry S Truman Library in Independence, Missouri. My research into Ronald Reagan's early involvement with the Disciples of Christ was aided by the Rev. Tom Shepherd of the Dixon First Christian Church in Illinois and Ron Marlow, also of Dixon; Dr. (Rev.) Benjamin Moore, Peggy Owen Clark, and Dorothy Ketcham of the Hollywood–Beverly Christian Church in Hollywood; Dr. James Seale at the Disciples of Christ Historical Society in Nashville, Tennessee; and Robert W. Brown at Culver-Stockton College in Canton, Missouri.

Others who were helpful included Mary Bell Burch at the Indiana State Library in Indianapolis; David L. Blackmer of the Kiwanis International in Indianapolis; Rebecca Campbell Cape at the Lilly Library at Indiana University, Bloomington; Charles Lamb and Sharon K. Sumpter at the Archives of the University of Notre Dame; David S. Bainbridge at the Northern Indiana Historical Society, South Bend; Dwight M. Miller, Dale Meier, and Jennifer Pedersen at the Herbert Hoover Library in West Branch, Iowa; Raymond Teichman at the Franklin D. Roosevelt Library in Hyde Park, New York; Edward J. Reese, Will Mahoney, John E. Taylor, and Kathie Nicastro at the National Archives in Washington, D.C.; Emil Moschella, Susan Falb, Perry Baker, and Helen Ann Near at the Freedom of Information Section, U.S.

Department of Justice, Washington, D.C.; Jennie D. Guilbaud and Frederick
Pernell at the National Archives and Record Service in Suitland, Maryland;
Jeff Flannery in the Manuscript Division of the Library of Congress; Jo
Foster at Eureka College, Eureka, Illinois; Mike Chapman, Shawn Sensiba,
and William Shaw of the *Dixon Telegraph* in Dixon, Illinois; Mary Ellen
Jones at the Bancroft Library at the University of California, Berkeley; James
D'Arc at the Harold B. Lee Library, Brigham Young University; Steven
Bergren at the Palmer School in Davenport, Iowa; Nancy Merz of the Jesuit
Missouri Province Archives in St. Louis; Glenn Mason and Laura Arksey at
the Eastern Washington State Historical Society in Spokane; David Koch at
the Morris Library at Southern Illinois University in Carbondale; Joseph A.
Lane, Robert N. Wilson, and William R. Paris at the Court of Appeals,
Second Appellate, State of California, Los Angeles; Sarah Cooper and Mary
Tyler, the Southern California Library for Social Studies and Research, Los
Angeles; William Frank, the Huntington Library, San Marino, Calif.; Pruda
Lood, Hoover Institution Archives, Stanford University; Alva Moore Steven-
son, University Research Library, UCLA; Lou Ellen Kramer, UCLA Film and
Television Archive, UCLA; and Walter Hoffman, World Federalist Associa-
tion, Washington, D.C.

Finally, I owe a special thank you to two people, not only for their editorial
insights but also for their unfailing support. As in my earlier work, I am once
more indebted to Robert Ferrell, who provided numerous ideas for improving the manuscript. Beverly Vaughn was my most exacting and constructive
critic, making suggestions that led to major improvements in each chapter.
Whatever the shortcomings of this book, they would have been much greater
without the counsel of these two people.

PART ONE

THE MAKING OF A STAR

1

DIXON

There was the life that has shaped my body and mind for all the years to come after.

Ronald Reagan

One thing I do know – all the hours in the old church in Dixon (which I didn't appreciate at the time) and all of Nelle's faith have come together in a kind of inheritance without which I'd be lost and helpless.

Ronald Reagan to the Reverend and
Mrs. Ben H. Cleaver, 1973

Although it was almost midnight when the train pulled into the Frisco Depot in Springfield, Missouri, in early June 1952, more than seven hundred people were waiting to see the star of a new film called *The Winning Team*. The movie was about the baseball pitcher Grover Cleveland Alexander and was the last motion picture Ronald Reagan made for the Warner Bros. studio. From the back of a railway car Reagan and his new wife, actress Nancy Davis, smiled and waved, obviously pleased with the reception.

At forty-one, Reagan, while no longer a matinee idol, was still youthful enough to play an athlete on screen. In real life he was amiable and charming, and he possessed an ability to make people feel comfortable in his presence. He had an "easy-going, neighborly way about him," a Springfield newspaper reported. He and his wife seemed like "regular folk" – gracious, friendly, eager to please.[1]

It was unusual for Hollywood films to premiere in Springfield and for movie stars to visit there, but a more famous figure upstaged the Reagans. President Harry S Truman arrived the following afternoon for a reunion with the 35th Infantry Division, the unit in which he had served during World War I. When the president's plane landed at the airport, between five thousand and ten thousand people met him, and as he drove into the city another hundred thousand lined the streets shouting, "We want you again!"[2]

Reagan and Truman were not strangers. During the 1948 campaign the actor had tried to mobilize Hollywood for the president, introducing him at a rally in Los Angeles. More than a year later, as head of the Screen Actors Guild, he had met with Truman in the White House. Three years after that, in Springfield, he played master of ceremonies at the President's Ball.

However, things were different in 1952. The president's popularity had declined as casualties mounted in Korea. He would not seek reelection. Reagan, for his part, would not have supported Truman had he run. He had moved away from New Deal liberalism toward the Republican Party's candidate, Dwight D. Eisenhower.[3] By this time Reagan had become a political figure in his own right. He was a formidable speaker, and friends were encouraging him to run for office.

In 1952, though, hardly anyone could have predicted that Reagan would one day occupy the White House. As an actor he belonged to a group of people considered by many Americans to be less than admirable. Reagan himself had echoed the truism, only a month before coming to Springfield, that less than a generation earlier people in his profession "could not even be buried in the churchyard."[4] He was sensitive to charges that actors were not respectable. Part of his work as president of the Screen Actors Guild amounted to defending the acting profession. "We're all from places like Illinois and Indiana and Missouri," he told an audience in Springfield, "and we're trying to be good citizens."[5]

Truman was now skeptical of Reagan. Reagan's marriage to actress Jane Wyman had recently ended in divorce. He had remarried only three months before, and his new wife was more than three months pregnant. The Trumans kept the Reagans at arm's length. The president had been scheduled to attend a private showing of *The Winning Team* but skipped the film to receive visitors at his hotel. He considered inviting the Reagans for dinner but after some thought concluded that he did not want any "Hollywood riffraff."[6]

The Springfield episode is interesting. That the president would dismiss the Reagans so casually, and that Reagan himself felt defensive about his profession suggest that an important change occurred between then and our own time in the level of respect accorded entertainers. Reagan helped bring about this change in attitude. The union between the entertainment industry and political power, of course, reached its peak during his presidency less than three decades later. Truman underestimated Reagan, especially if he assumed that the actor was like many other performers – long on personality but short on character. Reagan did not fit this stereotype. To understand why, it is first helpful to examine his Midwestern origins.

Ronald Wilson Reagan was born on February 6, 1911, in a little Illinois locality named Tampico, the heart of that state's farm country. Its business

district comprised a single block of buildings where farmers came to buy
supplies and store grain in the elevator between two railroad lines. His father,
Jack, managed the general store across from the elevator. Tampico was a
typical Midwestern small town. Dutch (as a boy Ronald had asked family
and friends to call him Dutch because he thought it more masculine than
Ronald) and his brother, Neil (friends called him Moon), played on a Civil
War cannon in the park and competed to see who could stay on the monu-
ment longest.[7]

But Dixon, Illinois, was where Ronald Reagan grew up. With a population
of ten thousand, it was several times larger than Tampico and seemed like a
city. The future president was nine when the family moved to 816 Hennepin
Avenue. He lived in Dixon twelve years. "There was the life that has shaped
my body and mind for all the years to come after," he later wrote. "Going on
reading binges in the public library or in the park. Waiting and hoping for the
winter freeze without snow so that we could go skating on the Rock River – a
rink two hundred yards wide and endlessly long, as clear and smooth as
glass – the trick of skating for miles against the wind and then spreading the
coat and for the pleasure of letting the wind blow you back." Then "the long
thoughts of spring, the pain with the coloring of the falling leaves in the
autumn."[8]

It was a time when after sunset there was not much to do. The radio was a
novelty. Virtually every evening except when the family attended movies,
Reagan's mother read aloud at the kitchen table, flanked by her sons, with a
pan of buttered popcorn between them (there was also a supply of apples and
salted crackers). His father perused a newspaper at the other end. Nelle
Reagan traced each line of the book so the children could follow. Before her
younger son entered first grade at age five, he could recognize enough words
to read a newspaper.[9]

On December 27, 1920, the boy obtained card 3695 at the public library,
which entitled him to check out books. He recalled visiting this "house of
magic" once or twice a week, by foot after dinner, down Hennepin Avenue,
past South Central School, up the hill. When the family moved across the
river, he crossed the Galena Avenue bridge and walked through town. He
remembered his reading as largely undisciplined but focused on "heroes who
lived by standards of morality and fair play." Whenever he discovered a hero
he liked, he read everything he could about him. Such stories left him with an
"abiding belief in the triumph of good over evil."[10]

He discovered *King Arthur* and knights in armor and liked the Rover Boys.
Later a book entitled *Northern Trails* instilled awareness of nature and
wildlife. When he played football he read *Frank Merriwell at Yale*. He was
fascinated not only by Edgar Rice Burroughs's *Tarzan* novels but also by
Burroughs's science fiction, such as *John Carter: Warlord of Mars* and other
tales about Carter's travels. Then came a period in which he enjoyed Zane
Grey as well as *Sherlock Holmes, Horatio Alger, The Count of Monte Cristo,*

Last of the Mohicans, and *The Printer of Udell.* The latter work impressed him when he was eleven or twelve because of the qualities of the main character, and was influential in his decision to join the Christian Church.[11]

Reading was not confined to books. The *Evening Telegraph* provided a window on national and international events. The paper offered but a narrow opening controlled by publisher B. F. Shaw.

To a latter-day reader the *Evening Telegraph* affords an interesting view of life in Dixon. It publicized such heroes as Charles A. Lindbergh. As a teenager, Reagan followed the aviator's exploits from the time of the take-off for Paris in May 1927. Lindbergh flew over Dixon in the *Spirit of St. Louis* a few months later, in August (the Chamber of Commerce had invited him to pass over on his way to Milwaukee). When he arrived he pitched out an orange sack, retrieved by a nine-year-old in the huge crowd below, that contained a message that the Dixon Trust & Savings Bank posted in its window. It called for an expansion of commercial aviation, urging air mail service and airports. If these recommendations were followed, it promised, the United States would thus take "its rightful place . . . as the world leader in commercial flying."[12]

The *Evening Telegraph* chronicled Lindbergh's activities thereafter. Early in 1928, Dixon residents posted two thousand letters to be carried by the Lone Eagle. Lindbergh figured prominently in Reagan's high school graduation ceremony, where a speaker talked about "Making Dreams Come True" and described the hero as the kind of dreamer who had attracted worldwide attention.[13]

Interestingly, in little more than a dozen years Dixon would give Reagan himself a hero's reception that rivaled that of Lindbergh, one given detailed coverage by the *Evening Telegraph.* Reagan would return as a movie star in the role of a pilot, his picture displayed in advertising with those of Lindbergh and other aviation heroes. Moreover, during World War II, he would promote a crusade for flying similar to Lindbergh's.

The *Evening Telegraph* became a medium through which businessmen promoted the city and free enterprise. If its pages were any indication, city leaders placed their faith in such boosterism. Shaw and assistants also endorsed such views. During Reagan's years in high school the *Evening Telegraph* revealed faith in progress, democracy, technology, mobility, patriotism, and corporate growth. Misgivings that corporatism, factory life, and concentrated capital might erode liberty seemed out of place. This was "An Age of Hope," an editorial proclaimed, refuting Clarence Darrow, who had said wealth destroyed liberty. Americans were "erecting an entirely new civilization" that had "completely reversed some of the most fundamental tenets of all other cultures." They were building a culture that was unlike "any culture that ever appeared before." This new society sought the "removal from the path of every man of every material discomfort that science or machinery can conquer." This "revolution" had not been perfected, but the average working man in America had more comforts than the wealthy man of only a generation earlier. This era was neither a time when the "vision of spiritual freedom" would be lost nor an age for Darrow's pessimism. Americans stood at the dawn of a new era that could not be "measured by the old yard-sticks. . . . The gleaming skyscrapers of our great cities are symbolic of the shining white cities of brotherhood for which we are even now laying the foundations."[14]

Other experiences filled Reagan's early life. His passion was sports. At eleven he was a drum major in the boys' band. Poor eyesight made baseball difficult and left "feelings of inferiority and lack of self-confidence," he recalled. "I was always the last chosen for a side in any game." Football captured Reagan's interest. By the time he reached high school he was eager but small – 5'3" and 108 pounds. He played in a division for smaller players at first. But by his senior year he had grown to 151 pounds and kicked off for the varsity, earning a letter wearing jersey number 33.[15]

In Dixon, as in other such communities, football was more than a game; it offered lessons in living. The gospel of sports as a developer of character and citizenship – a theme of one of Reagan's best-known films, *Knute Rockne – All American* (1940) – was part of the Dixon experience. During his senior year the squad won only two games. Dixon lost its opener to Mendota, 25 to 0. Things went from bad to worse the following week when the Rock Falls team "romped through the line almost at will," running up thirty-eight points against Dixon in what the *Evening Telegraph* called one of the "poorest" games played on the local field in two years. On Thanksgiving Day the team lost 34 to 0 to the league champions, Sterling High. Before the Sterling game the Kiwanis Club invited the squad to lunch to hear an inspirational speaker, a former captain of the 1910 Cornell University team who had become an attorney in a nearby community. Fred Gardner spoke about sportsmanship and athletics, and declared that high school and college football offered the best-known way for building Americans. Training under qualified coaches would do more for their later lives, he said, than any course in Latin or Greek.[16]

Reagan came to see many virtues in football, and generally in sports, not least of which was that they served to combat racial prejudice. "I can't help but point out my conviction," he said in 1965, "that among the extremists you'll find no one who ever participated in athletics on a team that numbered among its personnel both Negroes and whites." His home life reinforced this idea. When his mother entertained the team in her house, a black player on the squad, Wink McReynolds, was always included. During Reagan's last year at Eureka College the football team came to Dixon, where it practiced and stayed the evening. When the local hotel owner refused to house the team's two black players – starting center Franklin Burkhardt and reserve tackle Jim Rattan – Reagan's parents put them up.[17]

If Reagan was almost too small for football, he did excel as a swimmer.

When Dixon held its first annual water carnival on Labor Day, 1928, he won the 220-yard river swim. More important than any competitive feat, though, was the stature he achieved as a lifeguard at nearby Lowell Park. In this respect the *Evening Telegraph* helped to make Reagan a hometown hero by reporting his exploits as a lifeguard (as it later related his successes as an announcer and movie actor). On the evening of August 2, 1928, he pulled a local man from the "jaws of death" to record his twenty-fifth save. His fifty-first save came in June 1931, his seventy-first in July 1932.[18]

★★★

The values that Ronald Reagan later took into the American presidency came from many sources, as do values that all people use to order their lives, but it does seem clear that they derived in important ways from two individuals. One was the future president's mother, Nelle. The other was the minister of the First Christian Church in Dixon, the Reverend Ben Hill Cleaver.[19]

As for the importance of Reagan's mother, Nelle, there hardly can be any doubt. The later president's adopted son Michael has recalled how Nelle "instilled a Christian attitude in the entire family." She assumed the responsibility for Ronald's religious training, taking him first to Sunday school, and when he was older, to the adult services. "I was raised to believe that God has a plan for everyone and that seemingly random twists of fate are all part of His plan," Reagan reminisced. "From my mother, I learned the value of prayer."[20]

Ronald and his brother Neil were baptized in 1922. Their baptisms were among the first performed in the church's building, dedicated three days earlier. Whereas Neil later joined Dixon's Catholic church and removed his name from First Christian's rolls, Ronald retained membership until he transferred it to the Hollywood–Beverly Christian Church in 1940.[21]

Nelle Wilson Reagan was born near Morrison in northwestern Illinois in 1884, and met Jack Reagan in nearby Fulton, Missouri. In 1904 the two married in the town's Catholic church. Jack was not nearly as serious about religion, and attended mass irregularly. For Nelle, religion was indispensable, and on Easter Sunday, 1910, she became a member of the Church of Christ in Tampico, where the Reagans then were living. After several years and a series of moves to Chicago, Galesburg, and Monmouth, they returned to Tampico, and thence to Dixon.[22]

When the family moved to Dixon, Nelle became quite active in the church. She believed in tithing and "could even put it on an almost selfish basis," her son recalled, "by guaranteeing that the Lord would make your 90 per cent twice as big if you made sure He got His tenth." The Reagan family income in the mid- and late 1920s was meager.[23] She made her contribution in other ways. For eighteen years she taught the True Blue Class in Sunday school, made up of twenty-five adult women. She was song director for the choir. She belonged to the Women's Missionary Society and headed the committee on missions. She revealed talent as a dramatic reader and gave readings to church groups in Dixon. She was a leader in convincing the congregation to build a parsonage for the Cleavers.[24]

To friends Nelle was "a lovely woman who gave of herself in service to others," surely "a practicing Christian if ever there was one." She was small in stature, had blue eyes, and was soft-spoken. Church members recalled her as cheerful and kind. Where her husband Jack was a skeptic, she was an optimist who considered people essentially good. From Nelle, her son Ronald learned "how to have dreams and believe I could make them come true."[25]

Nelle Reagan's Christian charity extended to the community; she visited hospital patients and prisoners in the local jail. On at least one occasion after she followed her son to Hollywood, she wrote the White House asking Eleanor Roosevelt to intervene on behalf of an Illinois man who sought treatment at Warm Springs, Georgia. In California she made a point of calling on patients at an impoverished tuberculosis sanitarium, bringing celebrities, together with movies supplied by her son. "I'm no society lady," she explained. "I don't spend my time at social gatherings, my time is devoted to God's work."[26]

Reagan's early training in religion was a testimony to the influence of his mother, to be sure, and also to that of his minister, Ben Cleaver. Reagan met Cleaver almost as soon as his family came to Dixon from Tampico in 1921. An attraction developed between the youthful Ronald and Cleaver's daughter. Margaret (Mugs) Cleaver was by all accounts witty, intelligent, and altogether delightful. According to her sister Helen, Dutch fell head over heels – a "genuine attraction" that lasted until 1934. "I was sure," Reagan wrote afterward, "she was going to be my wife." In the end, though, Margaret returned his engagement ring. Because of Mugs, Dutch found himself in proximity to Ben Cleaver, and in many ways the minister became a second father. "He was as close to being a 'minister's kid' as one can be without actually moving into the rectory," one of Reagan's biographers has written. "Naturally, he was *often* in our home," Helen remembered, "and felt the influence of father's guidance during those formative years." Cleaver advised him, helped get him into college, even taught him how to drive a car. Years later Reagan acknowledged his debt. "You were all so much a part of my life and had so much to do with charting my course," he wrote Helen after her father's death in 1975.[27]

Cleaver found the Christian Church, the denomination in which Reagan grew up, made to his liking. Known also as the Disciples of Christ, it traced its beliefs to the years after the American Revolution and to the leadership of Thomas and Alexander Campbell. Members followed the teachings of the New Testament. The denomination originated in rural America and flourished on the frontier. When Cleaver began his ministry, almost all the membership was in small communities in the South and Middle West; more than half the members lived in Kentucky, Illinois, Ohio, and Indiana. Membership was strong in Tennessee, Missouri, Iowa, Kansas, and Texas, as well.[28] The Dixon Christian Church opened communion to "all believers in Christ" and sought to keep services simple and understandable. It tried to foster an "undenominational spirit" that encouraged fellowship with other Christian groups.[29]

When Cleaver (he had been named after the Georgia senator, Ben Hill) entered the ministry, the Disciples reflected the beliefs of pioneers, Anglo-Saxons who lived in the Midwest and South. They shared views held by many other Americans at the turn of the century – belief in Providence, faith in progress, a nationalistic spirit that equated the country's interests with God's will and occasionally explained America's mission in millennialistic terms. They believed in Anglo-Saxon superiority. They revered farmers and laborers and were against big cities and the immoral people who lived there.[30]

Although some followers warned about the dangers of affluence, most shared a desire for money and believed that hard work combined with Christian honesty would bring it. Many of them admired the wealthy and courted businessmen, who often became influential members of the church. Most felt comfortable with laissez-faire capitalism.[31]

Like many Disciples, Cleaver feared urban secularism. This did not mean that he was provincial. He could read Hebrew and classical Greek, and he briefly attended the University of Chicago, although he apparently disagreed with the church's "liberal element" there.[32] Nevertheless, he appears to have accepted the Disciples' comparatively liberal understanding of human nature, sin, and redemption. Although believing people sinful and in need of salvation, the Disciples did not accept the view that original sin had totally corrupted human nature. Free will and intelligence enabled a person to gain grace.[33]

Cleaver preferred a small church in a rural setting. He thought the impersonalization of large city churches undermined Christianity. Religion depended on a strong relation between the local pastor and his congregation.[34] When he assumed the Dixon ministry at age forty-one, he had been a pastor for more than eighteen years in small communities in Missouri and Illinois, and Dixon was his tenth church. He remained in Dixon almost nine years, longer than any of his predecessors, finally resigning to take a church in Eureka, Illinois, where he served from 1931 to 1935.[35]

At first he had problems in Dixon. He was not a good speaker and he worried that he could not inspire the young. Some members thought him "too intellectual." He overcame such shortcomings, however, and was remembered as a superb organizer who was hard-working, conscientious, and well liked. The congregation held him in special regard because of his dedication. When the janitor became ill, he took over the duties. When the Great

Depression made it impossible for the church to meet its budget, he insisted the debt be retired first and he be paid last.[36]

The church of Reagan's youth joined religion with social and political issues, and here lay a source of some of the future president's ideas. The brotherhood of man was part of the First Christian Church's creed, and Nelle Reagan took the notion to heart. In early 1928 she read to her Dixon Sunday school class an essay about black Christians that she entitled "Negro Disciples and Their Contribution." She was "absolutely color blind when it came to racial matters," Reagan recalled. Her motto was "Judge everyone by how they act, not what they are."[37]

In this regard, Nelle was "way ahead of her time." At least a few members of the Dixon congregation belonged to the Ku Klux Klan and one of Reagan's contemporaries remembered parades and burning crosses. For the most part the Dixon Klansmen were against Catholics. Only a few blacks lived in Dixon during the 1920s and none attended the Christian Church. Few Disciples had given up the idea of black inferiority.[38] Moreover, belief in Anglo-Saxon superiority was an ingredient in the Disciples' zeal to spread Christianity. Dixon church members heard about the work of missionaries with "the warring tribes of the wild country of Africa," and about "the strange customs of a heathen people."[39]

Cleaver's racial attitudes during this period were of restrained sympathy. His family had come from Kentucky and settled in northeastern Missouri in 1818 in an area that became Ralls County. North of the confluence of the Missouri and Mississippi rivers, west of Illinois and south of Hannibal, it was part of Little Dixie. Of the people in Ralls County in 1840, one in four was a slave, and Cleaver's grandfather Thomas had been among the slave owners. Ben Cleaver believed that the New Testament – at least Paul and Timothy's epistle to Philemon – neither condemned nor sanctioned slavery. He knew that before the Civil War almost every church in Ralls County had blacks on the rolls "with a certain door for admittance, and seating space." Blacks later were dispatched to their own churches. Years afterward he was deeply embarrassed. "I bow my head in shame at recollection of no 'County Meeting,' during my four or five years as Secretary, when either of our two Negro Congregations was ever mentioned," he wrote in 1965. During retirement in southeast Missouri he was among the few whites in Cape Girardeau to join the National Association for the Advancement of Colored People.[40]

Another concern of the era was how to treat the poor, and in this regard members of the Christian Church disagreed. Almost all acknowledged that they should aid the needy, but whether it was better to rely on individual, congregational, or government programs was a point of contention. Most Disciples emphasized individual responsibility. Those who admired wealth or were otherwise conservative equated poverty with sin. Many argued that the poor needed moral redemption more than material relief. Charity developed slowly among members of the church, and most of it went to helping orphans. Nelle and Margaret Cleaver took part in this activity. Nelle participated in a Benevolence Institute. In 1927 Mugs helped the church's Triangle Club prepare a package of dolls for a St. Louis orphanage.[41]

Attitudes toward the poor related to the way many in the congregation thought of the necessity of making a living. The Dixon church esteemed local businessmen. In this respect it was perhaps part of a larger pattern of boosterism. Because many members were merchants, the congregation invited such speakers as the "big-bodied, big-souled business man and preacher" from Rockford, who gave a talk to the Bible School entitled "How to Do the Most and Live the Happiest." The church opened its parlors to the Kiwanis Club and even offered instruction in business etiquette. The youthful Reagan most likely shared this respect for businessmen. As vice president in charge of entertainment for the YMCA's Hi-Y Club in 1928 he often invited them to be guest speakers.[42]

For Cleaver, though, in his role as minister, worldly accomplishment was not enough. He told his congregation as much in early 1926 when he said that "spiritual values escape the foot-rule and adding-machine. Of greater importance than full treasuries and receipted accounts are clean hearts . . . filled with faith," and "transformed lives." It was good that members rejoiced over their business accomplishments, he said, but added that they should "covet a like high rank for our congregation as a believing, worshipping, and Christ-honoring body of disciples." "[We] must never allow ourselves to trust to our gifts of money and even of time and service" as a replacement for reverence. The object, he said, was to increase one's "conscience on stewardship" and "loyal adherence to church standards of conduct and doctrine," not to rely solely on "mercantile ways of raising money."[43]

Given the attitudes about businessmen, it should not be surprising that the Christian Church provided a foundation for Reagan's later anticommunism and hostility to the welfare state. Most members associated socialism with anarchy and denounced bolshevism "as tyrannical, immoral, and anti-Christian."[44] By implication it can be assumed that Cleaver was in accord with these sentiments. In a biography he prepared of his father, he revealed his own skepticism about social experimentation. His father had once traveled thirty miles on horseback to hear Alexander Campbell speak in a crowded courtroom in New London, Missouri. Campbell had gained prominence for debating Robert Owen, "the British–Welsh Atheist Philanthropist," whom Cleaver described as the founder of "a sort of communist colony" in New Harmony, Indiana, that "opposed all religions." Reports of the debate, which occurred in Cincinnati, attracted wide attention. The New

London talk made a deep impression on Cleaver's father, who remembered it "as one of the best he ever heard."[45] Ben took the lesson to heart and saw a linkage between the New Harmony experiment and twentieth-century bolshevism. But he was troubled by more than communism. He was also unenthusiastic about the New Deal. During Roosevelt's first term, when Reagan considered himself an enthusiastic New Dealer, Cleaver told his young friend that Americans "could not spend our way into prosperity."[46]

The religion of Reagan's youth naturally valued patriotism. Love of country and devotion to Christianity were not synonymous, but often converged. The Women's Missionary Society united Christianity and patriotism, with the latter first, opening meetings by singing "America," which was followed by the Lord's Prayer. The programs at Reagan's Hi-Y Club opened with "America" and a prayer, followed by an inspirational talk. In 1928, Ash Wednesday and Washington's birthday fell on the same date and the program committee arranged for a minister to talk about Lent while a high school teacher discussed Washington's youth. Cleaver used Lincoln's memory to support temperance, preached "Maintaining Faith in Our Leaders," and prayed for the country's fallen heroes.[47]

Cleaver's church did not neglect questions of war and peace. It is likely that the religion of Reagan's youth easily endorsed the use of national power. Christian Endeavor, the congregation's youth group, considered "What Should Be the Christian's Attitude Toward War?" Reagan's later opinions about pacifism perhaps began to emerge from such discussion. Although Cleaver admired the nonviolent philosophy of Mohandas K. Gandhi, he advised caution. He warned of "much 'slush' among Christians these days over the great and admirable characters outside the church." Gandhi may have been "a good man" but he had rejected Christianity while at Oxford and later in South Africa.[48]

Lastly the Disciples maintained that brotherhood, charity, enterprise, and patriotism depended on character. To this end the Dixon church counseled proper conduct for young adults.

Many church members associated poverty with alcohol, a sensitive topic in the Reagan household. Reagan remembered his father as "a restless man, burning with ambition to succeed," one who "might have made a brilliant career out of selling" had he not "lived in a time – and with a weakness – that made him a frustrated man." He understood "occasional absences or the loud voices in the night" and poignantly recalled when, at age eleven, he discovered his father lying drunk on the front porch, "arms spread out as if he were crucified – as indeed he was – his hair soaked with melting snow, snoring as he breathed." He never told his mother about this episode. But Nelle knew better than her son about Jack's drinking. She tried to explain to him and his brother that alcoholism was an illness and they should never condemn their father "for something that was beyond his control."[49] Nev-

ertheless, he was troubled enough to discuss the problem with friends. Later
he told others that finding his father on the front porch "marked a turning
point in his life."[50] During his senior year in high school he wrote of life as

a struggle
full of sorrow and pain.
A life that warps and breaks us,
And we try to run through it again.[51]

Christian Church members were aware of a "problem" in the Reagan household. Ben Cleaver was a vocal proponent of the Eighteenth Amendment.
Indeed, if he was "overboard" on any issue, it was temperance; he had no
sympathy for anyone who indulged. Some of Nelle's acquaintances discreetly
suggested she get a divorce, but she recoiled from this advice and spoke
against divorce in her Sunday school class. Dutch vainly tried to keep his
father's problem secret from Mugs, fearing it would end the couple's
romance.[52]

After leaving Dixon, the young Reagan disregarded some of these warn-
ings about drinking. Once he left for Iowa to work in a radio station, he
experimented with liquor. For years his picture was mounted behind the bar
at a hangout in Des Moines called Cy's Moonlight, where he and Neil drank
"near beer" spiked with alcohol. One particularly bad hangover, though,
convinced him moderation was best. "I decided if that's what you get for
drinking – a sense of helplessness – I didn't want any part of it."[53]

How to raise children was understandably a concern for the First
Christian Church. In 1928 the Ladies' Aid Society, of which Nelle was a
member, put out a *Hostess Reference Book*. Filled with recipes and advertising, it was interesting for its 150 rules governing the etiquette of children, of
relations between the sexes, and of businessmen. It emphasized personality,
but unlike many early twentieth-century success manuals it divorced neither
personality from character nor image from substance. Success required more
than becoming "an empty vessel to be filled and refilled according to the
expectations of others and the needs of the moment." It assumed Christian
faith. Developing and maintaining a good reputation in the community was
paramount. If growing up in Dixon involved picnics and swimming, football
and acting, the manual included restrictions that to latter-day observers seem
confining. Nevertheless, there was something poignant in this code, promul-
gated by mothers whose own opportunities had been limited, who were
uncertain, perhaps fearful, of the world their children would live in.[54]

The guidebook was nothing if not explicit. Children were to be obedient,
deferent to elders, and "clean and neat looking at all times." Being known
for respecting one's parents was "a reputation every child should cherish."
Obedience was a virtue. "Never do anything when forbidden by your elders," the pamphlet told the child. "Never talk back to older people, espe-

cially to your mother and father" and "never argue with your elders" because "they know best." It urged attention to demeanor. "Talk in a low, even voice," it suggested. Such behavior denoted refinement. Always "be pleasant to all with whom you come in contact. . . . Never know more about the subject discussed than the other fellow. A know-it-all is the most unwelcome person in the world and has few friends." And even if one did not have good clothes, "there can be no excuse for not being clean" because soap and water were in the "reach of all."

Personality was an invaluable asset in becoming "real, popular and respected." It developed in many ways, but table manners were considered the most important. "The study and training of table etiquette should be part of the very foundation upon which the young people receive their education and is just as necessary as Mathematics, Spelling and English," according to the women of the Dixon Christian Church. "Never keep your lips apart when chewing. . . . Never eat chicken with your fingers." And "never brush up the crumbs on the table or gather up the dishes," young people learned. "That is the maid's job." The list of "nevers" numbered several dozen.

The booklet prescribed the ideal relation between the sexes. Men should be chivalrous. A gentleman's first date with a young woman should be at her house to meet her family, and the best time for formal calls was between 3:00 and 5:00 P.M. He should not hold her arm when walking. And when a man and woman met by chance, it was the lady's place to speak first.[55]

Admittedly it is difficult to gauge the influence of all the advice received by young people in Dixon during Reagan's time. If read in isolation, Margaret Cleaver pointed out, the handbook circulated by the Ladies Aid left an impression that she, Dutch, and their friends were "more quaint than we really were." Margaret's sister Helen questioned the depth of Reagan's commitment to the Disciples' doctrine. He occasionally attended church "but was far from any great feeling for it," she believed.[56] Reagan wrote that he spent more time in church looking at Mugs than listening to sermons. Still, what he heard from Cleaver and from his mother must have been difficult to cast off. Years later, when he had become governor and president, he strongly endorsed a few fundamental principles. "One thing I do know," he told the Cleavers in 1973, was that "all the hours in the old church in Dixon (which I didn't appreciate at the time) and all of Nelle's faith have come together in a kind of inheritance without which I'd be lost and helpless." At many points the positions taken by the Disciples of Reagan's youth coincided with the words, if not the beliefs, of the latter-day Reagan.[57]

Reagan could have done far worse than to have taken advice from Ben Cleaver and his mother. In later years Cleaver and Reagan disagreed over international issues and Reagan turned a deaf ear to the minister's admonitions about wealth. But the minister was a presence in helping Reagan draw his future and the two remained warm friends. He was a "wonderful man,"

Reagan recalled shortly after leaving the White House, and had been a "great influence." All the while, Nelle provided stability for a shaky family. Devoted to Christian brotherhood and charity, she took her strength from faith. It was fitting that in 1981, as her son took the oath of his nation's highest office, his hand rested on Nelle's tattered Bible.[58]

2

LEARNING TO COMMUNICATE

There is no better way to learn than through seeing. The ideal way to
study History would be to visit the world's famous spots, and get the setting and facts at the same time. Since this is impossible for all, an
excellent substitution can be found in dramatization and pageant work.

Margaret Cleaver, 1928[1]

Developing an ability to communicate lay at the center of Ronald Reagan's
early education, and it was seldom separate from entertainment. Part of the
experience called for learning how to talk in front of people. At age fifteen he
was one of two leaders in the Easter sunrise prayer service, and he occasionally led Christian Endeavor, his church's group of young people that met on
Sunday evenings. At seventeen he served as toastmaster at the district
Christian Endeavor meeting in the Congregational Church in Moline.[2] During these years Reagan discovered acting. He found "a new, wonderful
world, possibly more fascinating than any other." It perhaps was another
opportunity to play hero. By the time he reached high school he knew that
being on stage helped him shed his "feelings of insecurity."[3]

Entertainment was always a concern for Dixon's elders, for its boundaries
were defined by morality. New forms of music and dance as well as movies
had invaded town life by the late 1920s. Dancing was especially troublesome. When Dutch and Mugs were in eighth grade and the Elks Club held its
annual dance for children of members, it took more than a little effort to
convince Ben Cleaver that Margaret should be allowed to attend. The
Christian Church prescribed conduct on the ballroom floor. It was not uncommon for churches of that generation to suspend people from membership for dancing.[4]

Motion pictures were likewise a source of worry, although they held the
possibility for being a positive force. During his youth Reagan was an avid
moviegoer. For thirty-five cents he entered Dixon's segregated theater where

17

he watched Tom Mix or Wallace Beery and saw a five-act vaudeville show accompanied by a nine-piece orchestra and a $15,000 pipe organ.[5] Cleaver took what one might describe as a middle position in regard to motion pictures. He appreciated a good time and "thoroughly enjoyed a good movie," his daughter remembered, but he believed there had "always been good and bad movies." Christian Endeavor discussed "What's Wrong and What's Right with the Movies?" Cleaver objected to "innuendo" and "ugliness." He saw no need for Sunday movies, and he joined other ministers to close them down.[6] Interestingly, Nelle Reagan emphasized the potential of movies for good. In 1927 the Women's Missionary Society discussed a united Christian world made possible by modern communication. She explained how movies, combined with newspapers, radio, steamships, and airplanes, made nations interdependent. Here were instruments "to apply the spirit of Jesus to all . . . human relationships." They made possible the extension of one's "personal circle to world-wide fellowship," curing "war, crime and sin of every kind." The group agreed that in Christ there was no east or west, only the brotherhood of man, "drawing the world together with an increasing sense of common need and common purpose." Great leadership meant that "glorious vision" to view the world "as one great neighborhood, one great fellowship of love."[7]

Nelle's optimism about the movies probably related to the way she thought about acting and public speaking. Both the Reagans and Cleavers looked on public speaking and acting as ways of learning. During high school graduation ceremonies in June 1928, Reagan listened to a speech about the importance of acting from an individual whose words he took seriously. As president of the class, Margaret Cleaver said the modern world was a "social world. Every person, to be the fullest success, must be able to mingle with people." In a society filled with clubs and civic organizations the person with the most contacts stood the best chance to succeed. The high school should set up a course in public speaking and dramatics, she thought. If one wished to study history, the ideal way to do so would be "to visit the world's famous spots, and get the setting and facts at the same time." Because such travel was impossible for most people, an "excellent substitute" was "dramatization and pageant work." Education involved more than absorbing facts, Margaret said, most of which students forgot anyway. It was equally important to understand how to tell facts to another person, "how to convey an idea clearly and forcefully, and, in general, how to conduct oneself before an audience." If facts from books perished, Mugs concluded, "ease and poise" were things one could never lose.[8]

Acting was part of Reagan's family experience. In Tampico, Jack and Nelle had formed a small dramatic group that put on plays in the "Opera House,"

a second-floor room with a stage and folding chairs above the town bank. On a good evening they might draw a hundred people. Four-month-old Neil, face covered with calcimine, made his debut there as a dying infant in *The Dust of the Earth*. Nelle and her younger son took performing seriously. She was the "dean of dramatic recitals for the countryside," the younger son reminisced. "It was her sole relaxation from her family and charitable duties; she executed it with the zest of a frustrated actress. She recited classic speeches in tragic tones, wept as she flung herself into the more poignant, if less talented, passages of such melodramas as *East Lynne,* and poured out poetry by the yard." She was an amateur playwright, as well. When Ronald was old enough, she pressed him "into protesting service – usually as the thing in a sheet at the Sunday School pageant with a character name such as 'The Spirit of Christmas Never Was.'"[9]

Then there was a high school English teacher and dramatics coach, Bernard J. Frazer. Small, thin, unpretentious, yet "manly," he had a way of leading students into performances, making them think about roles. He encouraged them to consider their character's motives. He liked Reagan's presence and considered him his best student.[10]

In high school Reagan became president of the Dramatics Club. He and Margaret Cleaver had the leads in Philip Barry's *You and I.* The *Evening Telegraph* liked their enthusiasm in a one-act play, *The Pipe of Peace,* performed before the Dixon Women's Club. Dutch and Mugs also appeared in George Bernard Shaw's *Captain Applejack,* in which Reagan played the villain ("I learned that heroes are more fun," he said).[11]

Reagan's interest in acting increased during his years at Eureka College, in the nearby town of the same name (the school was run by the Disciples of Christ). Tuition was $180 a year. Reagan began there in 1928. He managed a scholarship that paid half his tuition, and washing dishes paid for board. He later took a loan from the Strong Foundation. He found the college attractive, in part, because one of his grade school football heroes, Garland Waggoner (son of the Dixon minister who preceded Cleaver), went there. Maybe even more important was that Margaret also attended Eureka.[12]

At Eureka College he acquired a modest recognition as an actor. While on vacation during his freshman year he and the Cleavers attended a production of *Journey's End* (1929) by R. C. Sherriff, performed by a touring company. "I was drawn to the stage that night as if it were a magnet, astonished by the magic of an ordinary man convincing an audience that he was someone else. . . . War-weary, young but bitterly old Captain Stanhope carried me into a new world," Reagan remembered.[13] At Eureka he and Margaret appeared in A. A. Milne's absurd comedy *The Dover Road,* and Reagan played the brother-hero in *The Brat,* a reworking of Shaw's *Pygmalion.* But it was in Edna St. Vincent Millay's *Aria da Capo,* an antiwar play, that he achieved more than local attention. Led by Eureka's drama teacher Ellen Marie

Johnson, the school's cast, which included Margaret, took the one-act play to a competition at Northwestern University, where they won third place. Reagan was one of six actors given honorable mention, and the head of Northwestern's drama department asked him if he had ever thought of the stage as a career. By early 1932 the college yearbook, *The Prism,* commented that Reagan "made one actually feel the hypnotic power" that his character was supposed to possess.[14]

Mugs, however, did not want to devote her life to acting. She was an honor student. "Hollywood was never my cup of tea," she explained. She and Reagan grew apart. After graduation, she taught in a small high school, traveled, and fell in love with a foreign service officer. Her decision to marry someone else "shattered me," Reagan wrote years later.[15]

As a church school in a small community, Eureka faced troubled financial times, and it was from efforts by the school to solve this problem that Reagan got a taste of politics through participation in a student strike. The college had an endowment of $658,000, most of which came from Disciples churches in the state, the remainder from the Rockefeller-backed General Education Board. Within a hundred-mile radius of Eureka were nineteen colleges and two junior colleges. Unless Eureka cut expenses, its president Bert Wilson reasoned, it could not compete. He proposed to consolidate departments and dismiss part of the faculty. The issue came to a crisis just before Thanksgiving, 1928, during Reagan's freshman year.[16]

The faculty resisted the president's proposed moves. Most of the student body, antagonistic toward Wilson even before his reorganization scheme, signed a petition demanding he resign. Newspaper stories suggested he was incompetent and immoral. Rumor circulated that he had mismanaged funds.[17]

Wilson offered his resignation but the board of trustees refused it. Students, backed by the alumni, then accused him of lacking faith in the school. When the trustees again refused to accept the resignation a few days later, students assembled at midnight in the chapel and voted to strike. The board finally accepted Wilson's decision to step down.[18]

As a freshman Reagan was hardly the leader of the anti-Wilson forces, but he was the speaker who made the motion to strike. "It had been decided that the motion for putting our plan into effect should be presented by a freshman," he remembered, "because the charge could be made that upper classmen had a selfish interest." As one of the other student leaders recalled, "We put Reagan on because he was the biggest mouth of the freshman class; he was a cocky s.o.b., a loud talker."[19]

Reagan later implied that the students engineered Wilson's downfall. Others, such as former president of the college, Burris Dickinson, had a different view. "It wasn't a student strike," he maintained, "it was a faculty strike." The faculty, he said, had used the students.[20]

For Reagan the strike speech was intoxicating:

I'd been told that I should sell the idea so there'd be no doubt of the outcome. I reviewed the history of our patient negotiations with due emphasis on the devious manner in which the trustees had sought to take advantage of us. I discovered that night that an audience has a feel to it and, in the parlance of the theater, that audience and I were together. When I came to actually presenting the motion there was no need for parliamentary procedure: they came to their feet with a roar – even the faculty members present voted by acclamation. It was heady wine. Hell, with two more lines I could have had them riding through 'every Middlesex village and farm' – without horses yet.[21]

The strike and Wilson's subsequent resignation had beneficial results, Reagan judged. Campus spirit blossomed, and the faculty become more attentive to the students.[22]

What sort of student was Reagan? Participating in the strike may have been educational, but hardly revealed his study habits. "He absolutely hated to study," a close friend recalled. A fan magazine biography in 1943 perhaps captured the undergraduate: "As a student, he continued to get by, though he had to change majors twice before hitting one that didn't hamper his extracurricular activities. Recalling his painless theme-writing for B. J. [Frazer], he first picked English, but dropped it abruptly as Chaucer edged into the scene. History would have been all right except for the profs, who expected you to learn the book by heart. In the end he got stuck with something called economics and sociology. A knack for cramming the semester's work into one sleepless week, plus imagination, took him through the exams."[23]

Reagan had briefly considered attending the University of Wisconsin on a rowing scholarship and it is interesting to speculate what might have happened had he majored in economics and sociology there, where he could have been exposed to such excellent scholars as John R. Commons. At Eureka he likely encountered dedicated teachers. There economics and sociology were taught by Alexander Gray, who had studied at the universities of Toronto and Michigan, and at Yale. Among courses for the major were choices between Criminology and Charities as well as between Social Problems and Principles of Sociology. In economics, students could take classes on Unemployment, Life Insurance, and Investments. In addition, "Daddy" Gray – as the students called him – was the school's librarian and occasionally recommended books for students to take on vacation such as Valeriu Marcu's *Lenin* (1929), which Gray described as the "biography of a great man."[24]

Reagan took part in a wide range of extracurricular activities. Football enthralled him. He earned four letters under coach Ralph (Mac) McKenzie, a former star. He improved steadily (the 1931 yearbook noted that "he never gives up when the odds are against him" and the next year described him as "one of the best offensive guards on the squad"). He was among the school's best swimmers and taught swimming during his junior and senior years. He hoped to play basketball but settled for being a cheerleader when at the first practice he saw the quality of players. At the behest of Ben Cleaver, he taught Sunday school (although he often talked more about football than the Bible). He was president of the student senate, which directed student activities and elections, and of the Booster Club.[25]

Reagan's accomplishments at Eureka were impressive. To have attended college when neither of his parents had gone beyond grade school, and to have graduated during the Great Depression, was no small achievement. Eureka allowed Reagan to participate in dramatics, athletics, student politics, community affairs, and along the way, to develop social skills.

He omitted scholarship, however, hence missing the mental flexibility and discipline that would have resulted from a program of challenging, intensive, and sustained study – something impossible to achieve from the occasional week of cramming. He gave the impression of a "hail-fellow-well-met" who always had many friends. But he "never had vast intellectual abilities," one of those friends remembered, and "certainly was no scholar. . . . I knew he would be a success but certainly didn't think of him as presidential material at the time." The 1932 yearbook captioned his picture, "The time never lies heavily upon him; it is impossible for him to be alone."[26]

★★★

Graduation in 1932 hardly guaranteed success. Because of the depression, few opportunities existed for graduates. The Reagans suffered with everyone. Neil lost his job when the Dixon cement plant closed. Nelle worked in a dress shop for fourteen dollars a week. Jack, unable to find work in Dixon, eventually managed to get a job as a traveling shoe salesman and for a time had to live in Springfield. The family could not afford the rent on their house and moved to an apartment; Nelle once borrowed fifty dollars from her son Ronald to buy groceries. On Christmas Eve, 1931, Jack received a special-delivery letter informing him that he had been fired. It was, he lamented, "a hell of a Christmas present."[27]

The depression destroyed the dreams of Reagan's father. Jack had aspired to own the best shoe shop outside Chicago but wound up having to settle for a "grim, tiny hole-in-the-wall" store in a poor section on the outskirts of Springfield, with "garish orange paper ads plastered over the windows and front and one cheap bench with iron armrests to separate the customers, if there was more than one at a time." Once, while on a trip with the Eureka football team, Dutch visited his father and saw where he worked. "I thought of the hours he'd spent when we were boys talking about the grand shoe store he dreamed of opening one day," he remembered. "My eyes filled and I looked away."[28]

The son was unsure about what to do. "I'll never be satisfied with a $60-a-week job," he told friends. He wanted to go into show business, but how to get started? Hollywood seemed "as inaccessible as outer space." Few people offered encouragement. "Quit chasing rainbows," he was advised, "Dixon has jobs." His college fraternity brothers laughed at his plans but he boasted to them after graduation that if he was not earning $5,000 annually within five years he would consider college a waste. A yearly salary of $5,000 was to him at that time "the novelist's way of describing a man as eminently successful."[29]

One person who did offer encouragement was a Kansas City businessman, Sid Altschuler, whose wife had grown up in Dixon. The family returned there each summer, and Reagan had taught their daughters how to swim. Altschuler told him that radio was a sound business with hundreds of opportunities.[30]

Breaking into radio was not easy. The young Reagan hitchhiked to Chicago expecting to talk his way into one of the major stations, only to return home discouraged and with swollen feet. But at one interview he had been told to try a smaller station, and so he went to Davenport, Iowa, seventy-five miles from Dixon, where a crusty character with a Scottish brogue named Peter MacArthur took a liking to him.

After an audition at station WOC, MacArthur hired him to do a play-by-play of the Iowa–Minnesota football game. "Reagan, a grand footballer and letter man, knew what it was all about," Davenport's *Democrat and Leader* said the next morning. "His crisp account of the muddy struggle sounded like a carefully written story . . . and his quick tongue seemed to be as fast as the plays." He did the rest of Iowa's games. When one of WOC's staff announcers quit, Reagan replaced him, full-time, at $100 a month, which enabled him to give support to his family and begin repaying a loan he had taken while at Eureka.[31]

At WOC, Reagan entered the peculiar world of Colonel B. J. Palmer. WOC stood for World of Chiropractic. Palmer had purchased a station from a radio operator in Rock Island, Illinois, and moved it to Davenport in 1921, where it broadcast weather reports, farm news, and stock market information. Palmer conducted a school for chiropractors founded by his father, D. D. Palmer, and housed the station on the fourth floor of the college's administration building. B. J. also acquired the much larger WHO in Des Moines, which became a Midwest NBC affiliate.[32]

Palmer enjoyed boasting about WOC. He said it was the "strongest, loudest and clearest radio-phone installation in America," and that it held a world's record for long-distance transmission. It had been heard in Stockholm, Paris, Rome, and Manila. Explorers who traveled to the North Pole in 1923 listened regularly, Palmer claimed. He speculated that the reason his station could be heard so far away was that its ground was attached to the city water mains, which emptied into the Mississippi River. "Many now believe that the ground is the real antenna and that the air antenna is the counterpoise," he said. "If that is true then WOC has the best possible antenna, miles long and plenty wide."[33]

Palmer was a salesman, a raconteur, and, if one accepts his son's evaluation, a genius who could have become a showman equal to P. T. Barnum. He was a striking figure with full beard and flowing, collar-length hair, which he washed only annually but combed constantly and kept in place with a shoestring. He drank little but chain-smoked cheap cigars that were manufactured in West Davenport. He slept with his head facing the North Pole so that the earth's currents could "flow properly through his body." On hot summer nights before retiring to his screened-in porch, he soaked his nightshirt in cold water so that the evening breezes would cool his body.

Palmer was a believer in chiropractic, which taught that by relieving spinal pressure the chiropractor cured the body in a way medicines could not. Hanging eerily from the ceiling on the third floor of his house atop the Brady Street hill was a "world famous collection of spines," skeletons gathered by him and his father.[34]

Palmer was an apostle of advertising. One of his favorite lectures, which he delivered hundreds of times, was on salesmanship. "Sell yourself in all your business approaches," he told listeners. He liked homilies: "Get the big idea and all else follows." "Early to bed, early to rise; Work like hell – and advertise." "The more you tell the quicker you sell." Radio was by far the best medium for selling, he believed, and he drilled his announcers in radio salesmanship. "Smile your voice!" Be conversational and personal, use showmanship, he told employees at WOC and WHO.[35]

The inexperienced Reagan had an inauspicious beginning at WOC. He had performance problems, reading from advertisers' scripts in a manner that so exasperated the sponsors that WOC fired him. Unable to find a suitable replacement, however, the station took him back.[36]

As WOC grew it began to offer live entertainment, and Palmer turned the music room in his mansion into a studio. He purchased an Aeolian pipe organ and Chickering piano. During broadcasts an assistant drew curtains at the studio's southern end to eliminate outside distractions, although Palmer admitted it was difficult for artists to be at their best "with nothing more appreciative in sight than a queer looking Bird Cage on a pedestal."[37] This led to one of WOC's strangest broadcasts. The Palmers owned a Saint Bernard named Big Ben, much beloved by B. J.'s son. On one of the family's trips abroad the dog died; B. J. had it stuffed, mounted, and placed under the piano, where it often slept. Performers accustomed to seeing Big Ben under the piano paid little attention. One evening a female vocalist, wife of a Davenport civic leader, was well into a rendition of "Nearer My God to Thee" when she looked down on Big Ben. She shrieked, "MY GOD, HE'S DEAD!" The program continued without an explanation; B. J. eventually printed an account of what had happened and mailed it to inquirers.[38]

Reagan improved steadily, and Palmer came to like him. Under MacArthur's tutelage he was soon promoted and working at WHO. By October 1933, Dixon residents read in the *Evening Telegraph* that Reagan was fast gaining renown as a sports broadcaster and that a large advertiser sponsored his weekly sports program every Saturday evening. Months later the paper told readers that he had become one of the country's "outstanding sports announcers." His success helped Neil obtain a job with WOC, where he became the station's program manager.[39]

In Des Moines, Reagan started out by primarily covering sports, both as an announcer and a newspaper columnist. He interviewed celebrities, announced college football games and track meets, and reconstructed – he later estimated – six hundred big league baseball games as they came into the station over the telegraph. He soon had a program on WHO, the Teaberry Sports Review, twice each day, before dinner at 5:25 P.M. and later at 10:10 P.M. His column, "Around the World of Sports with Dutch Reagan," appeared in the Des Moines Dispatch between June 1935 and early 1937. In 1936, the station assigned him to cover the spring training of the Chicago Cubs and White Sox at Catalina Island.[40]

Reagan characterized himself as a "visualizer for the armchair quarterback." He admired the athletes whose exploits he reported. As an announcer he learned to use words to conjure images of far-away action, an illusion of reality. He was not present at most of the baseball games he broadcast, recreating instead the reports relayed to him by a telegraph operator. His reporting of the Cubs–Cardinals game in which the wire went dead and he had a batter foul off pitches for almost seven minutes was an episode he would recount many times.[41]

During his time in Des Moines, Reagan became a local celebrity. He often spoke at civic events, appeared at fairs, promoted businesses, and made his first films as a narrator for local editions of newsreels. His voice could occasionally be heard well beyond the Midwest. He once chatted on the air with the British-born movie star Leslie Howard, participating in a fund-raising appeal for flood victims. Howard's plea and Reagan's introduction went out over WHO's fifty-kilowatt transmitter and was picked up far into the Pacific, where sailors on a British steamer took up a collection on behalf of the victims.[42]

Reagan's chance at Hollywood came in early 1937 when he accompanied the Chicago Cubs to spring training on Catalina Island. While there he called an acquaintance, the actress-singer Joy Hodges, whom he had interviewed on WHO. She was from Des Moines. Impressed by his good looks, she introduced him to her agent, George Ward, who worked for the Meiklejohn Agency. Ward saw that Reagan could be marketed as the "likeable, clean-cut American" type.[43] He scheduled two screen tests. Strangely, this marvelous opportunity was almost lost. The first test, to have taken place at Paramount, never materialized because Reagan had to broadcast a Cubs exhibition game in the afternoon; when the studio kept him waiting, he walked out. Ward set up the second test with the casting director at Warner Bros., Max Arnow. Reagan had been scheduled to return home on the train next day. At this juncture lightning struck, perhaps because of his decision to go back to Iowa without waiting to see how the screen test had turned out. As he recalled, "Hollywood just loves people who don't need Hollywood." The Meiklejohn Agency wired that Jack Warner was offering a seven-year contract with one-year options beginning at $200 a week, a substantial sum for most people in 1937.[44]

When he left Iowa for Hollywood in 1937, WHO listeners tuned in to a broadcast of the farewell party. Testimonials came from Iowa's state treasurer, Des Moines's mayor and park commissioner, and WHO's president, all of whom used superlatives to extol the young announcer's virtues. Reagan confessed that perhaps for the first time he had been "rendered speechless." Nevertheless, an acquaintance also recalled that Reagan was ecstatic after he signed with Warner Bros. and that he "held court for several hours, sitting on his desk, jubilant, excited, euphoric, accepting everyone's congratulations, mesmerizing all of us with the tales of his Hollywood adventure then, and those yet to be." Shortly afterward, the staff at WHO bade him farewell at Cy's Moonlight Inn.[45]

3

FROM RAGS TO RICHES

It's a tough racket but when you consider the rewards you're shooting at – fame such as couldn't be won in any other profession and wealth that mounts to dizzying heights – it's worth the chances you take.
Ronald Reagan, 1937

Ronald Reagan left Des Moines in a "cloud of dust," as he recalled, in late May 1937. He was supposed to report to Warner Bros. by June 1. As he headed for California he was nervous, he admitted, and "not a little bit scared. . . . I'd had the same sort of a feeling that a man must have in death row. . . . He knows he has to walk up the scaffold and take it in the neck, and is anxious to get it over with as quickly as possible." He wasted no time in his new convertible. "I got a cramp in my foot," he later told fans in Des Moines, "and somehow or other couldn't get it off the gas pedal." On the last leg of the journey he crossed the scorching desert at midday and at sunset approached Los Angeles along a stretch of highway from San Bernardino where the air was filled with the fragrance of orange blossoms. He pulled up to the Biltmore Hotel so exhausted he "could hardly wobble."[1]

For most Americans the Hollywood that Reagan encountered was a "never-never land of sunny skies, Sleeping Beauties, and ivory towers," populated by "rich children" who were "politically indifferent, innocent, and ignorant." Behind this facade, though, the movie colony had a serious side. Producers and writers as well as actors and actresses were taking stands on issues, international and domestic. The Spanish Civil War divided Americans – and Hollywood; Adolf Hitler had repudiated the Treaty of Versailles and was rearming Germany; the Japanese were fighting in China. President Franklin D. Roosevelt had started his second term, and although the New Deal initiated programs that would alter the United States in many ways, Americans remained in the midst of the Great Depression.[2]

27

It was difficult, if not impossible, to escape politics in Hollywood. Current events dominated conversation at Hollywood parties; members of the film colony formed committees to assist Poland and Britain, to defeat Hitler and fascism; politics became a sort of "oasis in the intellectual desert." "Nobody goes to anyone's house any more to sit and talk and have fun," a commentator wrote in early 1937. "There's a master of ceremonies and a collection basket, because there are no gatherings now except for a Good Cause."[3]

Warner Bros. was attuned to these developments. But in the spring of 1937, Reagan was largely oblivious to them. He had never been outside the Midwest. He "wasn't mad at anyone," he later said, and came to Hollywood with the "light rosy glow" of someone about to become a movie actor.[4]

The immediate difficulty was to get the studio to take him seriously. Executive producer Hal Wallis considered him a "hick radio announcer." Warner Bros. put him to work in B films, the low-budget movies that usually accompanied the more expensive A pictures in a double feature.[5]

Those in charge of casting had to decide what roles he could play. They considered him for a movie about gold mining in northern California but director Michael Curtiz rejected him because he did not look old enough. The studio decided to take advantage of Reagan's broadcasting experience and cast him as a radio announcer in his first film *Love Is on the Air*. He appeared briefly in the same role in *Hollywood Hotel* and in *Boy Meets Girl*, a movie that featured two stars, James Cagney and Pat O'Brien. He gave a brief impersonation of a racing announcer in *Going Places*. The studio scheduled him to emcee the premier of *The Life of Emile Zola*. He regarded these roles as a "safe haven in strange seas" but found himself grasping the microphone "like grim death to a sick cat." Despite nervousness, though, he demonstrated enough ability in *Love Is on the Air* to convince at least one critic not to typecast him as a radio announcer.[6]

This first period provided an apprenticeship in how to conduct himself before audiences, microphones, and cameras. He learned how to give his voice personality, how to convey moods, how to "create an illusion with words as well as action." He discovered that when he went before the camera he was "surrounded by a wall of light and . . . couldn't see anyone." "It gave me," he wrote, "a feeling of privacy that completely dispelled any nervousness I might have expected." He observed that "automatically, I snapped into my well-rehearsed role and forgot all about the camera, the lights and everything but the part." He learned how to dramatize historical and current events.[7]

Reagan's life at this time affirmed the rags-to-riches theme. By going first into radio and then motion pictures, he entered fields that had flourished even during the depression. Offering opportunity to achieve fame, they thrived because they gave escape from ordinary existence. "In the dark days of the depression," Will Hays said, theater doors became "magic portals" and movies became "a great refuge for humanity." As the lyrics from one of Reagan's early pictures said, and as the actor would learn, Hollywood "makes your dreams come true."[8]

Warner Bros. used the rags-to-riches theme, and a number of Reagan's early pictures dealt with people who rose to acclaim. *Hollywood Hotel* (1938), *Cowboy From Brooklyn* (1938), *Going Places* (1939), and *Naughty but Nice* (1939) were musicals starring Dick Powell. Others played on the theme, as well. *Sergeant Murphy* (1938) was a story about an army private and his horse overcoming one-hundred-to-one odds to gain victory at the Grand National. *An Angel From Texas* (1940) featured Reagan and his wife, Jane Wyman, but Eddie Albert stole the show as a country boy who, with help of a wealthy backer (Wyman), inadvertently created a successful play. Warner Bros. told theater managers to emphasize the Cinderella motif. In *Million Dollar Baby* (1941), Priscilla Lane played a lowly working girl with dreams who received a gift of $1 million from a wealthy widow.[9]

With the exceptions of *Sergeant Murphy* and *Million Dollar Baby,* Reagan had short appearances or supporting roles in these early pictures. In *Hollywood Hotel* he was not even listed in the credits, although he appeared briefly as an announcer. In *Million Dollar Baby* he portrayed Lane's boyfriend but was miscast because he appeared as a pianist (director Curtis Bernhardt remarked that he was "without any musical feeling and sense" whatsoever), and because his character was cynical about the value of wealth.[10]

Not all of Reagan's early films, it should be noted, showed people rising from meager circumstance. A few emphasized class distinctions. In *Dark Victory,* Bette Davis was a rich heiress who chose to fall in love with her doctor rather than her stablehand (played by Humphrey Bogart). In *Angels Wash Their Faces* (1939) the scenario suggested a set of laws for the well-to-do, another for the poor. In *Kings Row* (1942), Reagan's Drake McHugh moved to the poor side of town when his fortune was embezzled. *Juke Girl* (1942) showed class conflict between migrant farmers and wealthy packers.

Reagan's career during the late 1930s suggested that class need not be a barrier. His own fortunes seemed to parallel the characters in many of Warner Bros.' more upbeat movies. He realized, though, that this world could vanish if the studio decided not to renew his option, and he sought to prepare himself. After finishing *Sergeant Murphy,* his second starring role, he could say he had been an actor, he told newspaper readers in Des Moines.[11]

So he enjoyed it while he could. Returning home after an all-night shooting session, he saw his first California sunrise. "And boy, when it comes up over the rise of mountains that hedge in Hollywood on the east, with the misty clouds radiating all the colors of the rainbow, it's something to write home about." In a series of articles published in the *Des Moines Register* he told of dining at expensive restaurants that had "more varieties of appetizers than I ever imagined existed" and of consuming plates heaped "high with bits of ham, pickled fish, spiced meats and goodness knows what else." Afterward, he related, "you feel so comfortable that you purr like a cat and don't give a whoop." Equally impressive were the shops and nightclubs along the strip near Sunset Boulevard.[12]

He was impressed with other "famed beauty spots" in California, notably Santa Barbara, which had "attracted more wealthy people from the east than any other community in America." Here lived "more millionaires to the square mile" than Iowa had cornfields. "There are scores of magnificent estates with elaborate stables and armies of retainers."[13]

Hollywood was fantasy. It was, he said, a place where there were "so many astonishing things" that "you accept even the most preposterous things as a matter of course." It was a "tough racket," he said, "but when you consider the rewards you're shooting at – fame such as couldn't be won in any other profession and wealth that mounts to dizzying heights – it's worth the chances you take."[14]

During the summer of 1937 there were thus indications that the self-deprecating actor might succeed, and by October he could tell Iowa readers that the studio had decided to pick up his option for another six months. Warner Bros.' publicity let it be known that he had been "discovered . . . in true movie hero fashion" and director Lloyd Bacon had dubbed him Iowa's Pride (after the well-known ham). His editor in Iowa apparently had confidence, labeling his articles "The Making of a Movie Star."[15]

Warner Bros. kept Reagan busy, as it did all its promising young performers. As a contract player under the studio system, he found his life carefully regulated. The studio controlled his public appearances. He had little say in selecting films. He worked on as many as three pictures at once. After *Love Is on the Air* in 1937, he appeared in eight pictures in 1938, eight in 1939, and six more in 1940. Of his fifty-three feature films, he made thirty before he entered military service in April 1942. He had starring or leading roles in slightly more than half of these first thirty pictures, most (but not all) of which were B movies. In addition to filmings, his work often required lengthy sessions before cameras to create publicity stills. Touring Los Angeles with the actress Margaret Lindsay, he recalled, "the cameraman caught up with us and our holiday was over. We had to do our tricks while he snapped his camera." Seeking shots that would "make the hearts of the young beat a bit faster," the studio was creating a persona.[16]

In measuring Reagan's rise to stardom, one should not underestimate the power of public relations. The exposure Reagan received at Warner Bros. extended well beyond his movies. Under the studio system of the 1930s, films bore the mark of the company that made them. A marketing, advertising, distribution, and exhibition network gave movies a nationwide and often worldwide circulation. Warner Bros. had several hundred theaters in the United States and offices in more than thirty countries. The studio told theater managers how to exploit films in recommendations that ranged from lobby displays, local newspaper stories, and radio programs, to publicity stunts aimed at involving the entire community. Gossip columns and fan magazines, if not controlled by the studios, supported the industry. The young Reagan, therefore, benefited from publicity in several media in addition to film.[17]

No gossip columnist helped Reagan more during these early years than did Louella Parsons, who was, in David Niven's words, "short, dumpy, and dowdy, with large brown eyes and a carefully cultivated vagueness of smile and manner." By coincidence, she also had come from Dixon, several years earlier. Niven, not a Parsons fan, remembered that she was a "Catholic, married three times, first to a real estate man, secondly to a riverboat captain, and thirdly to a doctor who specialized in venereal diseases." Parsons loved the spotlight. She and Reagan had minor parts in *Hollywood Hotel*. She was not a particularly good writer and aptly entitled her memoirs *The Gay Illiterate*. But she had credibility. She "could be so drunk at an interview one would swear she had already passed out," director Edward Dmytryk recalled. Yet in her next column, "everything was there – ungrammatical perhaps, but never out of context."[18]

In late 1939, Parsons took Reagan and several other young performers, including Jane Wyman, on a tour that started in Santa Barbara and covered San Francisco, Philadelphia, New York, Washington, and Chicago. By this time Reagan and Wyman were engaged. They had met on the set of *Brother Rat* and dated during the making of *Brother Rat and a Baby* – after Wyman had divorced her first husband, Myron Futterman. Warner Bros.' publicity department played the romance to the hilt, announcing that the "athletic" Reagan had been "wooing the blonde Miss Wyman" and had given her a 52-carat amethyst ring (Wyman's birthstone). The couple told Reagan's parents and the studio about their plans. Parsons was allowed to break the news to the public.[19]

The three months of barnstorming, which ended in Chicago in January 1940, proved modestly successful. Reagan did well, and *Variety* found him "very personable, deft and obviously at home on a stage." Five months later the Reverend Cleveland Kleihauer of the Hollywood–Beverly Christian Church married Reagan and Wyman in Glendale, California.[20]

Parsons liked the couple and publicized them as all-American (an image also reinforced by pictures of the Reagans that appeared in fan magazines). Parsons was "pretty much a fixture in our household during the early years of my childhood," remembered Maureen Reagan, who called her Aunt Lolly. To have Parsons in one's corner was a boost to any performer. In addition to her having a regular radio program, her columns were carried by the Hearst chain.[21]

Reagan first met Jack Warner while on the air at the studio's radio station, KFWB. It was a surprise encounter. He was in the midst of "turning on the old personality," when he realized Warner was standing at his side. "No matter what anyone accuses me of saying," he told fans in Iowa, "I'll plead guilty because I have no idea what I gabbled."[22]

Warner and his brother Harry were first and foremost businessmen. But more than most Hollywood executives, they took interest in domestic and international issues. They "thought politically" and "had political motivation, intent, and drive," so the screenwriter Paul Jarrico observed. Their studio developed a reputation for social consciousness, and the Warners supported President Roosevelt, sometimes enthusiastically. Politics was never far beneath the surface in many of their films. A part of Warner Bros.' entertainment during the depression, and several of Reagan's early movies, dramatized social conditions, dealt with crime and its causes, or treated questions of war and peace. From such pictures Reagan's early screen persona began to emerge.[23]

The Warners approached politics differently. Harry, the older brother and studio president, ran financial affairs from the company's New York office. Born in Poland in 1881, he had come to the United States with the Jewish immigrants who fled Eastern Europe in the aftermath of Czar Alexander II's assassination. In America he worked as a cobbler and bicycle repairman before he and another brother, Sam, opened a theater, the Bijou, in a remodeled store in New Castle, Pennsylvania. Harry, not Jack, evidently first decided that the Warners should support Roosevelt during the 1932 presidential campaign.[24]

Harry's unpretentious appearance disguised a volatile and combative personality. *Fortune* described him as "a small, strong, swarthy man with a deceptive cupid's bow mouth and a vague resemblance to George Arliss." He was, the magazine said, "willful and a worrier, constantly preoccupied with his own thoughts." In a crowd, Frederick Van Ryn commented, Warner in his blue doubled-breasted suit might have passed "for a retired business man living on a modest income." To Warner Bros.' star Pat O'Brien, Harry seemed "the silent watching type" who "wore a public humility like good tailoring." Yet it was not uncommon for disagreements to degenerate into shouting matches – "ferocity came naturally" to him.[25]

The older Warner brother was a moralist who apparently had "a profound urge to stamp his feelings on the world as well as on his family." He claimed that the educational potential of film had first attracted him to talking movies and that his two interests were morality and business. All Warner Bros. movies, he asserted, "have some moral lesson." Motion pictures, he declared, present "right and wrong, as the Bible says. By showing both right and wrong we teach the right." Those lessons, he liked to think, carried over into his personal life. "I am of Hollywood and yet I have managed to remain married to the same woman for the last thirty-four years," he announced in 1941. One senses that he disapproved of the life-style led by his younger brother Jack, who divorced his first wife. Harry often thought of employees as an extended family, and they viewed him as "a benevolent family tyrant." On the Warner Bros.' lot, Harry and Reagan occasionally exchanged pleasantries. The producer recognized Reagan from his films but for some time confused him with another actor and persisted in calling him Phil.[26]

Harry believed that business, entertainment, and public responsibility were joined. As businessmen, he said toward the end of World War II, "we try to make pictures that will make money for our company and exhibitors. As members of the entertainment industry, we try to make pictures that will provide pleasure and recreation for those who seek it. As Americans, we try to make pictures which will be a force for good . . . and which will advance the public interest and welfare." Movies could at once be entertaining, informative, and "carry the message of democracy." The studio adopted the motto "combining good citizenship with good picture making."[27]

Jack Warner was vice president in charge of production, and lived in California, where the pictures were produced. More than his older brother, he had his finger on the pulse of Hollywood. He approved scripts before they were turned into movies, although he confessed to being a "slow reader" who routinely skipped pages if there was no action. The extroverted Jack seemed "always smiling through a tan, under thin oiled hair," and once described himself as a "court jester" at the Roosevelt White House; but he was also an aggressive executive who "was a hard man to outtalk." Some employees, such as O'Brien, thought of him as the personification of "naked studio power," a person who took sadistic pleasure in avenging himself on actors. Others thought him a phony, unsuited to be a tyrant. "Harry was a bull," his one-time son-in-law and Warner Bros. employee Milton Sperling recalled. Jack was devious and "a frightened man." Lauren Bacall remembered him as "one of the most ill-at-ease human beings I'd ever encountered," although her husband Humphrey Bogart had a more generous assessment. "Jack's not a bad guy," Bogart told her, "he's just so uncomfortable with everyone. He has to make jokes to prove he's regular."[28]

Whatever Jack's shortcomings, he had confidence in his ability to anticipate public opinion. "During my 30 years in the motion picture business," he once boasted to Lieutenant General Henry H. Arnold, "I have been able to foresee trends of many kinds and therefore a great many of our pictures have been of a topical nature that have preceded these trends." Whereas Harry could be moralistic, Jack seemed amoral. "If a thing worked, it was moral," Jack Jr. recalled of his father.[29]

By the late 1930s the Warners had reason for interest in politics, for demonstrating allegiance to the United States, and for wanting to help President Roosevelt. As sons of Jewish immigrants from Poland, they were deeply apprehensive about the power of Germany and the rising European tide of anti-Semitism. They sensed the United States might not be immune from such intolerance.[30]

Then there were the economic and legal challenges facing the studio. Warner Bros. had only begun to recover financially from the depression when their markets abroad appeared to be in jeopardy. In July 1934, they shut their German theaters because of anti-Semitic restrictions.[31] Other countries imposed quotas on American films. The war that began in September 1939 threatened their most lucrative theaters in Britain because of bombings and blackouts. At home, the Justice Department in early 1935, and again in July 1938, charged Warner Bros. and other studios with violation of the Sherman Antitrust Act, claiming they dominated production and distribution and divided territories to eliminate competition. Defending themselves from such litigation would prove emotionally and financially draining.[32] After war was declared in Europe in 1939, Harry did not hesitate to write to President Roosevelt for help, pleading for the government to pull back from its antitrust suit at least until the situation abroad had been settled.[33]

Weighing these factors, one should not underestimate the Warners' political activism and their alarm over anti-Semitism. Jack Warner donated to the United Jewish Appeal and served as its chairman in 1927. Harry, initially skeptical, became a supporter. The Warners supported efforts to aid Jewish refugees, whose plight moved Harry who sent a telegram to Jack in London, asking the latter to speak with Ambassador Joseph P. Kennedy about the Jewish problem and urging him to secure British support for the Balfour Declaration.[34]

The Warners welcomed people who fled Hitler. They had the ambition, according to publicity, to make Hollywood a "veritable Periclean Greece."[35] In early April 1938, Jack and Ann Warner gave a hundred-dollar-a-plate dinner at their house to raise money for refugees. The guest of honor was Thomas Mann, the exiled Nobel Prize author, then on a lecture tour. Mann condemned Hitler as a person whose very conception had been "a catastrophe – a fiend fighting fiercely against time toward an inevitable doom." He denounced capitalistic England for appeasement.[36] Democratic America, he said, was the last stronghold of culture; it must discover a way to combat fascism, which was led by "moral and spiritual paupers" whose existence depended totally on force. Fascism appealed to European youth "through the sheer sensation of novelty and excitement," robbing it of any noble purpose, leaving it a "stupefied, broken-down instrument of war," he explained. "Freedom must find its own virility and go forth with armor to defend that freedom from its mortal enemies." The task would not be easy because democracy had "grown stale."[37] Mann's words made a strong impression on Jack Warner, although neither he nor Harry needed further convincing about fascism. Both publicly and privately, they inveighed against Hitler and used such influence as they possessed to counter his power.[38]

To appreciate the environment that Reagan entered when he arrived in Hollywood, it is worth dwelling on the Warners' politics during this time. Harry launched a campaign to eliminate German subjects from American newsreels and forbade Warner theaters to show clips from the Joe Louis–Max Schmeling heavyweight boxing match of June 1936. By late 1937 *Fortune* magazine noted he had become "violently anti-Nazi." In September 1938, Harry spoke to leaders of the American Legion and declared that Americans would "stand, alone, if necessary, in support of true democratic government and against the hates and *prejudices* of a world gone mad." In late 1938 the Warners supported the Hollywood Committee of Fifty-Six, a group of producers, directors, writers, and stars that advocated severing economic relations with Germany. In early February 1939, Jack confided to his friend, Anada (Doc) Salomon, Warner Bros.' Great Britain studio manager, that the "madman" Hitler had to be stopped and told his son, Jack Warner, Jr., that war with Germany was inevitable.[39]

All the while the Warners were intensely patriotic. They sought to demonstrate their loyalty before such groups as the American Legion. The Legion, Harry said, was "the watchdog of democracy – the guardian of equal rights for all," and "the bulwark of true Americanism." What the United States needed, he told the legion's leaders in September 1938, was a patriotic revival, "a renewed consciousness of our national life," and "more flag waving." In this spiritual reawakening, Americanism played a central role. "I tell you, Catholic, Protestant, Jew, or whatever faith you may observe," he said, "we must all be Americans first, last and always." Americanism was grounded in freedom of thought and worship, symbolized and "guaranteed by the American flag." Americanism was antifascist as well as anticommunist. The movie industry "has no sympathy with Communism, Fascism, Nazism, or any 'ism' other than Americanism," Warner said. He expressed the same sentiment to his employees. "We don't want anybody employed by our company," he told his workers in early June 1940, "who belongs to . . . communist, fascistic or any other un-American organization."[40]

The Warners believed motion pictures not only could but should influence opinion. "Through our medium we can reach from 40,000,000 to 70,000,000 with a single picture," Jack boasted in early 1939. Shortly thereafter Harry wrote in the *Christian Science Monitor* about film's "implied duties to ethics, patriotism, and the fundamental rights of individuals." Movies, he said, were "the most universally understood medium ever devised." Hollywood producers shared responsibility to promote tolerance and fair play with churches, schools, and service organizations. Harry told the Ancient Order of Hibernians that motion pictures could "be used as one of the most effectual means of exposing the plots against the United States, and of glorifying and sustaining our love of country and pride in its institutions." In another speech he asserted that the world looked "upon America as the strong frontier of democracy because the motion picture has given . . . a true conception of our institutions and our life here."[41]

So from the beginning of Reagan's motion picture career, movies were intended to provide more than entertainment. In addition to placing him in stories that reinforced the rags-to-riches theme, Warner Bros. put him in social commentary pictures dealing with such issues as political corruption, journalistic ethics, insurance fraud, the criminal probation system, urban poverty and juvenile delinquency, the status of migrant farmers, counterfeiting, illegal aliens, and international terrorism.[42] Several early pictures promoted Americanism, defense, and national unity. It was not uncommon for Warner Bros. to cooperate with the United States military as well as other branches of the government.

The Warners promoted patriotism and preparedness in their films in at least three ways. First, their pictures warned about spies and saboteurs.[43] Second, in "defense of democracy" they used history, hoping that their versions of the past would offer ideals around which Americans could unite. "The visual power of the screen is tremendous," Jack Warner said in January 1939, "and we propose to use it to acquaint Americans with their heritage." Finally, they intended to glorify government agents, to dignify military service, and after the war began in Europe that September, to urge support for the British.[44]

Several of Reagan's early pictures fell into these categories. By the time he entered military service, eleven of his films could be characterized as pro-preparedness. Indeed, a characteristic of the idealized persona created for Reagan was that he was a patriotic man of action: an athlete, a government agent, or a soldier.[45]

★★★

By 1940, three years after leaving Des Moines, Reagan's movie career was ascending. Audiences liked him, and he got along well with Jack Warner. The studio exercised the final option on his original contract and raised his salary to $600 a week. The Audience Research Institute examined the marquee value of sixty newcomers in Hollywood and predicted that within three years Reagan would be among the top ten in ability to sell movie tickets.[46]

Warner Bros. elevated Reagan to "star" status early in 1941. Some months later, in late August, Reagan signed a new agreement, a three-year contract at $1,650 a week. The document had two options. At the end of three years the studio could extend it for another three at $3,000 per week. A final option, for one year, would pay $5,000 weekly. Reagan told Warner he was delighted. He and his wife began construction of a new house.[47]

Roles also improved and in 1940 Reagan had important parts in such A films as *Knute Rockne – All American* and *Santa Fe Trail*. The next year he had leading roles in *Million Dollar Baby, Nine Lives Are Not Enough,* and *International Squadron*. The studio lent him to MGM, where he performed with Wallace Beery and Lionel Barrymore in *The Bad Man* (1941). Shortly after the new contract, he began work on what many critics have considered his best screen performance, as Drake McHugh in *Kings Row*. Following that film he starred with Ann Sheridan in *Juke Girl* and in 1942 costarred in *Desperate Journey*.

By the middle of 1941, a Gallup survey ranked him in the top 100 stars, in 82nd place. Although his ranking soon fell to 91st, by the following January he tied for 74th place with Laurence Olivier. Gallup estimated that in early 1942, Reagan made $52,000 per film, this when the country's top box office draw, Clark Gable, earned $210,000 per picture and Errol Flynn, Warner Bros.' leading man, made $157,000.[48]

Reagan's appeal was especially strong with theatergoers under eighteen. He was slightly more attractive to women than men in 1940 and 1941, although by January 1942, those who liked his films were about evenly divided by sex. He was a little more popular in cities with fewer than a hundred thousand people, and with those labeled as prosperous, upper-middle class, and poor, than in large metropolitan areas or with those considered middle class. Of people polled who said the name on a marquee made a difference, one in ten said he or she would go to a film just to see Reagan (those who would buy a ticket just to see Flynn ran between 30 and 40 percent). Reagan's marquee value rose sharply during the first half of 1942. In April, after *Kings Row,* 18 percent said they would buy a ticket after seeing Reagan's name. The percentage climbed to 21 in May and June after he costarred with Ann Sheridan ("another Warner star on the way up") in *Juke Girl* and reached 24 percent in July – all this after he entered military service.[49]

This remarkable rise, which would have seemed improbable if he had looked toward it in 1937, owed something to his good looks and engaging manner. His image was partly that of "Mr. Average Guy on the bright side," and partly that of a courageous and even heroic man of action. He was "no Adonis," the fan magazines said, but rather substituted "crinkly eyes and a wide grin for glamour." He was "the clear-eyed, clean-thinking young American in uniform. You can see a montage of American Background when you look at him – debating teams, football, ski parties, summer jobs in a gas station, junior proms, fraternity pin on his best girl's sweater, home for Christmas, home for Easter. Your mother would approve of him. Your dad would talk politics with him while you dressed."[50]

Modesty was part of the personality. "I'm no Flynn or Boyer and well I know it," he admitted. "Mr. Norm is my alias." In order "to make yourself important," he said, you needed to "love what you are doing," believe it important, and have confidence "you can get to the top." You did not, he added, have to "stand out from your fellow men in order to make your mark in the world. Average will do it."[51]

In addition to this picture of Reagan as the boy next door, the studio created a heroic Reagan. One facet of this persona was the athletic hero. The athletic image, persistent even into Reagan's presidency, emerged from the moment he arrived in Hollywood. Promoting his first film, *Love Is on the Air* (1937), the studio had billed the newcomer as an "all around athlete . . . broad-shouldered and with a slender waistline, . . . proficient in almost every sport." An "expert marksman and horseman," he held a "commission as a reserve officer in the U.S. Cavalry, steeplechase riding being his favorite exercise." The studio later exploited this background to make him believable as the legendary George Custer. It stressed his football experience, and of course he was memorable as the all-American football player George Gipp. Warner Bros. played up his experience as a lifeguard, noting that a "fallen tree trunk on the banks of the Rock River at Dixon, Illinois, holds the indelible record of 77 persons saved from drowning by Ronald Reagan." Studio publicity emphasized that he had been a sports announcer and suggested he had played baseball and other sports.[52] Another aspect of the heroic Reagan was the government agent and military hero. Then, too, there was the image of Reagan as the ordinary soldier. By 1942, a fan magazine reported, this "full-blooded American" was "now . . . in the Army along with your brother Joe."[53]

As America entered World War II the future looked bright. Warner Bros. considered him a "very talented artist" who had developed rapidly into a star assigned to the studio's top productions. That he costarred with Flynn in *Desperate Journey*, his last picture before active duty, shows that studio decision makers thought well of him.[54]

This, then, was an auspicious time to make Reagan more attractive to Midwestern fans, and so during the late summer of 1941 the studio helped arrange a homecoming. As it happened, Dixon's leaders had decided to honor Parsons with a Louella Parsons Day. She suggested that Reagan be invited too. Warner Bros. executives thought it a good idea, and took the opportunity to stage an extravaganza that premiered a new Reagan film called *International Squadron*, about a Yank in the Royal Air Force. Reagan, then working on *Kings Row*, received permission to participate.

On the last weekend of summer 1941, with a touch of autumn chill hanging in the air over Rock River Valley, more than fifty thousand people crowded into Dixon to welcome the two returning celebrities. They assembled along the town's main boulevard, Galena Street, which was then lined with elm trees. Nelle accompanied her son (Reagan's father had recently died). Ben Cleaver and wife, then living in Missouri, also returned.[55]

The pageantry not only captivated the spectators but enthralled its stars. Parsons later said it seemed "to spin in my memory like a happy but dizzy dream." It began with a ten-block parade, "the longest and loudest in the town's 109-year history," with five bands and fifteen floats. As newsreel cameramen photographed onlookers, hundreds of people with cameras in the crowd took their own pictures. Other stars whom Midwesterners had only seen on movie screens – Bob Hope, Joe E. Brown, Ann Rutherford, George Montgomery, Bebe Daniels, Ben Lyon – were there. With the luminaries in convertibles, the procession made its way past Geisenheimer's Dry Goods Store, where Parsons once had bought clothes, and by the establishment where Dutch Reagan's father had sold shoes. Parsons was overcome with emotion.[56]

Two hundred guests assembled for lunch on the riverfront lawn of Myrtle Walgreen's estate, Hazelwood, and the entourage dedicated the Louella Parsons Wing of the town hospital. A congratulatory telephone call arrived from Parsons's employer, Hearst. A banquet at the Masonic temple followed, then the premier of Reagan's film at the Dixon Theater, and finally a Hollywood Ball in the armory where the seventeen-year-old queen of Rock River, escorted by Reagan, received a bouquet of red roses from Parsons.

The event surpassed the excitement Lindbergh had generated fourteen years earlier. "Here were a one-time $5-a-week reporter and a lifeguard who achieved what Dixon and all one-hundred-percent hero-worshipping Americans dream of," Hearst's *Chicago Herald-American* reported. This "slice of Americana in the heart of the country where a simple beginning is a stepping stone to success" testified that even in depression America, the success ethic was alive and well. Parsons's and Reagan's stories were rags-to-riches, "as typically American as Sunday supplement heroes."[57]

The afternoon of the last day, Sunday, Reagan and Parsons did two radio programs, one nationwide over the Columbia Broadcasting System. CBS's Chicago affiliate introduced Reagan as master of ceremonies. He called the festivity a "dream which probably every boy has at some time – that of coming home and being acclaimed by the home folks."[58]

In this festive homecoming of long ago a small-town boy had returned as a symbol of success. Family, church, and community life had produced him. He grew up in a community where boosterism, hard work, confidence in science and industry, faith in progress and belief that one could rise from humble circumstances all were strong. Reagan's fame was first spread by the local paper, which carried stories about exploits as lifeguard and radio announcer. His all-American image was magnified by Hollywood and by the Hearst press in Parsons's columns. His return to Dixon confirmed that even during the depression it was possible for an American to succeed.

4

REFORM

There have been altogether too many pictures made by these Reds, Pinks, and Punks in which the communist doctrine was surreptitiously spread.
William Randolph Hearst to
Jack L. Warner, April 22, 1937

In Reagan's films of the late 1930s he was often a crime fighter and champion of the underdog, and the question arises as to whether the studio idealistically cast him in this role or did so simply because it was convenient. The answer is a little of both. The Warners were interested in reform. At the same time reform was a theme that did well at the box office.

The Warners achieved a reputation during this period for being liberal, and in many respects they were.[1] But the Warners' standing as reformers needs qualification. They had been "faithful Republicans" until they became disillusioned with President Herbert Hoover during the depression. Jack knew little about Franklin D. Roosevelt when Harry summoned Jack to the New York office one day in 1932. There, in the company of James A. Farley and several other power brokers, Harry asked his brother to campaign for Roosevelt, then the governor of New York. After Roosevelt's nomination Jack organized fifty film executives and producers into a Roosevelt-for-president committee. He used his studio's Hollywood radio station, KFWB, to organize a rally in the Los Angeles Coliseum attended by 175,000 people. He made it a point to meet the candidate; when Roosevelt was traveling from San Francisco to Los Angeles, Warner boarded the train at Santa Barbara and during the two-hour trip struck up a friendship that lasted until Roosevelt's death in 1945.[2]

From the beginning, however, the Warners' warmth toward the Roosevelts – and their enjoyment of the prestige that came with having the president of the United States as a friend – probably exceeded their fervor for the New Deal. True, the president drafted Jack to serve without compensa-

40

tion as an official of the National Recovery Administration in California, and Jack did so "cheerfully." He was a member of the recovery board and later chaired the state's advisory board, at which time he reported to the former muckraker and World War I propagandist, George Creel, in San Francisco. But his brother, Harry, balked at efforts to regulate the movie industry, especially on such matters as maximum hours and minimum wages. The studio had to be prodded into complying with the National Industrial Recovery Act.[3]

There were other problems. Whatever enthusiasm the Warners had for New Deal programs was dampened by litigation under the Sherman Anti-trust Act in early 1935, when in St. Louis and later in New York, government attorneys indicted Warner Bros., Paramount, and RKO, charging conspiracy in restraint of trade, and threatening jail sentences and fines. When the Warners' father died in 1935, his sons attributed his death in part to the antitrust proceedings. The government sued the brothers for taxes owed on sale of stock owned by their father. Convinced they were targets of harassment, they did not contribute to the president's reelection campaign in 1936. Two years later the government again indicted the Warners, together with Twentieth Century Fox producers, also under the Sherman Act.[4]

Despite antitrust litigation that continued for the remainder of the decade, the Warners began to renew their friendship with Roosevelt after Reagan arrived in Hollywood. They did so in large measure, one may speculate, because of the worsening international situation.

As for Reagan's politics, he had come from a Democratic family and by his own description was at the time "a near hopeless hemophilic liberal" who "bled for causes." It seemed natural that the studio should give him roles as a crusading reporter, an idealistic lawyer, a tomato farmer who defended the little man against the impersonal forces of society. He had little choice but to take what the studio meted out anyway and was not inclined to argue over his roles. He did not see national and international issues with the same fervor as did his employers. It was easy for him to keep his politics at the time because the Warners required few, if any, adjustments.[5]

Warner Bros. continued to make films about social issues into the early 1940s. The studio seemed eager to focus attention on impoverishment and slums. "The causes of crime," Harry maintained in February 1936, "are what they always have been, poverty, neglect and bad environment."[6]

There were several reasons for this emphasis. Civic-mindedness may have been one. But there was another, perhaps less obvious. Throughout the 1920s and 1930s the film industry stood accused of being a cause of crime, what with the movies' frequent exploitation of sex and violence. Critics charged that pictures presented the young with "false leaders." Theaters had been under attack as breeding grounds for delinquency. Social scientists appeared to establish moving pictures as providing the nation's youth with poor role models, a serious charge when gangsters were attaining folk hero status. The Payne Fund Studies, twelve investigations published in 1933, had helped convince many people that films left a deep psychological impression and "created an undesirable and dangerous socializing force."[7] The journalist Henry James Forman popularized these studies in the notion of "moviemade criminals." Critics urged state and federal legislation.[8]

Hollywood executives tried to deflect government censorship at every level – local, state, and national – through self-regulation. In the early 1920s they created the Motion Picture Producers and Distributors of America (MP-PDA) and engaged Will Hays as its first president. In 1930 they adopted a Production Code designed to satisfy critics, one of the rules of which prohibited scenes that provoked sympathy for criminals.

Several developments then altered the way in which Hollywood treated crime and other social problems and influenced virtually all of Reagan's early motion pictures. In 1934 the Roman Catholic Legion of Decency was created, which eventually organized seven to nine million Catholics to boycott offensive films.[9] That same year the producers established the Production Code Administration (PCA) as an arm of the MPPDA to strengthen enforcement of the code. Under its administrator, Joseph I. Breen, the PCA censored scripts as films were produced, this in a time well before the United States Supreme Court ruling in 1952 accorded cinema protection under the First Amendment. Finally, in late 1934, President Roosevelt's attorney general, Homer S. Cummings, called a national conference on crime, which organized civic, religious, youth, and law enforcement groups into a nationwide campaign.

Attacks on the industry at this time placed producers on the defensive. The Legion's threat to boycott offending films augmented the code's enforcement machinery at a time when such studios as Warner Bros. had been weakened financially by the depression. The Payne Fund Studies – dubbed the "painful studies" by Hays's staff – sent the MPPDA president scrambling for rebuttals. Experts to whom Hays turned tried to discredit the findings on psychological and sociological grounds, while others, such as the University of Chicago philosopher Mortimer Adler, attacked them for philosophical reasons.[10]

The Warners thereupon launched a counteroffensive against the idea that movies caused antisocial behavior. The object was to convince the American public that movies were a deterrent to crime. One tactic, seen in promotional campaigns for later Reagan films, was to encourage audiences to cooperate with local law enforcement officials. A second called for studio cooperation with the government and production of films that glorified law enforcement agents. A third involved taking advantage of attention focused by the depression and the New Deal on the social origins of crime and poverty. "People who spend their time fighting the pictures could spend it better fighting the slums," Harry Warner announced at an annual luncheon conference of the National Board of Review of Motion Pictures. "Criminals breed in poverty-stricken slum districts, not in moving picture theatres," he maintained.[11]

Although Harry attempted to divert attention from films as a source of crime, there were limits as to how far the studio could go in advocating reform. Publishers such as Hearst presented special obstacles. An episode involving the studio's leading male star, Errol Flynn, revealed Hearst's influence. On the same day, April 15, 1937, that the *Hollywood Reporter* ran a brief item announcing that Warner Bros. had signed an Iowa broadcaster named Ronald Reagan, it carried another story about Flynn, then in Spain, that created an uproar.

The circumstances suggested that politics during the late 1930s were risky for performers and could be fatal to their careers, particularly if they involved communism. The Spanish Civil War had become a cause célèbre for Hollywood activists, intellectuals, and publicity seekers during the late 1930s. In the spring of 1937, Flynn traveled to Spain reportedly with $1.5 million that he, James Cagney, and Frederic March had helped raise for the Loyalist cause. He became embroiled in controversy when the *Hollywood Reporter* published a story datelined Barcelona revealing he was a guest of the Spanish government and had been traveling with a Dr. Hermann F. Erben, a "well known member of the American Communist Party." Asked why he had come to Spain, according to the *Reporter,* the actor said he was there because of "the confusing news and the fact that all the American press is in the hands of powerful 'trusts.'" He had undertaken the trip "to see with my own eyes what is really happening and write a series of articles for publication."[12]

Although the purpose of Flynn's trip remains a mystery (it turned out that Erben was a Nazi, not a communist), it is clear that Hearst exploited the situation to pressure Warner Bros.[13] Fear that Hearst would launch an all-out attack against Flynn caused panic at the studio. As Flynn sailed home on the *Queen Mary,* Jack Warner radioed him not to make any statements or give any interviews. He instructed Charlie Einfeld in the New York office to meet the actor on the docks and do everything to "muzzle Flynn until you get a crack at him at the hotel or the home office." Moreover, Warner said, "Do not mince words with him."[14]

The incident threatened to ruin Flynn's career after what had been an expensive studio buildup. The situation was not lost on Jack Warner. "If any more stuff comes out in the American papers like this the public certainly won't want him," he shuddered. "He must be made to understand that we are in a neutral business and in a neutral country and we do not want anyone who is in the public spotlight like he is giving out statements about collecting money which immediately shows he is on the side of the Communists." Public reaction jeopardized a new film, *The Prince and the Pauper,* in which Warner Bros. had invested $1 million. Grad Sears of the sales department wired that he was "getting terrific repercussions from story carried in Hearst

papers accusing Flynn of being communist." He was having difficulty booking the film because the stories were "definitely breaking down" Flynn's
heroic image.[15]

Warner made every effort to appease Hearst, and the publisher agreed that
Flynn had been unjustly criticized and promised to interview the actor. But
Hearst made clear that he was pleased that such groups as the Knights of
Columbus, the American Legion, and the Veterans of Foreign Wars were
"taking cognizance of communistic pictures and communistic utterances.
There have been altogether too many pictures made by these Reds, Pinks,
and Punks in which the communist doctrine was surreptitiously spread."[16]

The Hays Office was also highly sensitive to criticism and never more so
than when it involved communism. Fearing that subversive ideas would
infiltrate films, Hays and Breen often went beyond the production code to
establish "industry policy" on such matters. A 1934 memorandum revealed
how they applied the code. Breen insisted on "nothing subversive of the
fundamental law of the land and of duly constituted authority." Banned
from the screen was communist propaganda.[17]

Breen's anticommunism derived from his Catholicism and from the fact
that after the First World War he had been arrested by bolsheviks in Hungary
and sentenced to death before being released. He became troubled by the
subversive nature of many scripts and warned of "subtle" efforts *to capture
the screen of the United States for Communistic propaganda purposes.*" He
saw a movement in Hollywood to inject communist propaganda into films.
The source was the screenwriters, he concluded, as well as performers, directors, and producers who formed the Hollywood Anti-Nazi League. The
League, Breen noted, was defaming Franco while "glorifying the Communistic 'loyalists'" in the Spanish Civil War. "Most of the agitators are Jews," he
claimed, "with a sprinkling of non-Jewish labor leaders," all of whom talked
much about "social equality," "the square deal," and "social justice."[18]
Breen wholeheartedly endorsed Pope Pius VI's encyclical on atheistic communism, in which the pope expressed "hope that the fanaticism with which
the sons of darkness work day and night at their materialistic and atheistic
propaganda will, at least, serve the holy purpose of stimulating the sons of
light to a like and even greater zeal for the honor of the Divine Majesty."[19]

Communism was one thing; social experimentation was another. Nevertheless, the Production Code Administration also discouraged the latter in
films. As run by the Republican Hays and his lieutenant Breen, the PCA had
become an agency that not only defended family, church, and state, but
protected capitalism.

How Hays and Breen influenced movie entertainment can be seen by
looking at what happened to the script of *Black Fury*, a Warner Bros. film
about coal mining that appeared before Reagan came to Hollywood. The
story indicted mine owners for the terrible working conditions of their employees. When owners learned of this picture and objected, Hays intervened

to have the studio change dialogue so the movie would show the miners' condition improving and imply that workers had little to complain about. Breen did not want the film to show company property destroyed and warned the studio about encouraging labor unrest. Hays often justified such intervention on the ground that industry policy prevented Hollywood from unfairly portraying another profession. Noteworthy, too, is that both Hays and Breen had a personal stake in this controversy. Hays was part owner of a coal mine in southern Indiana and Breen, before he headed the PCA, had handled public relations for the Peabody Coal Company in Chicago.[20]

The PCA protected the screen characterizations of the American justice system, as well as images of authority figures. It was permissible to show a corrupt city official, judge, or police officer, but Hays and Breen insisted that these cases be isolated, not indictments against city government, the legal system, or law enforcement officers in general. Some Reagan films reflected cynicism about city government and its legal structure, suggesting that extra-legal means were necessary to apprehend villains, and pictured juveniles involved in crime, all of which troubled Breen.[21]

Like the Warners, Reagan showed sympathy with social reform during the 1930s. In Dixon, Jack Reagan had been an outspoken Democrat in a solidly Republican area. After Roosevelt's election in 1932, he was put in charge of the local Works Progress Administration, where he dispensed food to the unemployed. His son believed that the New Deal served a good purpose. "There was no bureaucracy at Jack's level," the younger Reagan recalled, and "every week the line would form – not bums or strangers but friends, fathers of kids I'd gone to school with." Under Jack's leadership, "parks were created out of brush and swamp riverbanks, bridges over the river, and even a hangar at the new airport."[22] The son "idolized" Roosevelt and by his own account followed him "blindly." "I was a child of the Depression," he once told Maureen, "a Democrat by upbringing, and very emotionally committed to FDR." Following his father, he had voted for Democrats in every election. In Des Moines he occasionally imitated Roosevelt's fireside chats for WHO employees, and was thrilled in 1936 to see the president's limousine drive by the station.[23]

But Reagan did not have much opportunity to act out his opinions in the pictures to which the studio assigned him. Films were collaborative endeavors, the result of work by many people including writers, directors, producers, advertising specialists, and censors. They offered limited opportunity for a performer to interject opinions about reforming society. An occasional opening did exist for a thoughtful actor such as Edward G. Robinson, who made several pictures for Warner Bros. The nature of the medium made it difficult to deliver a message, Robinson told University of Illinois sociologist Donald R. Taft in 1938. "While all pictures have to be made from the primary standpoint of entertainment," he said, "every now and then there is an opportunity to combine entertainment with larger implications that 'point up' social aspects and encourage social awareness. . . . At such times there has been no formulated social thesis or anything resembling a syllabus but I have tried to seize certain elements of the story through which a social point could be made logically and convincingly." While it might not always be possible to resolve problems or analyze their "deeper causes," it was possible to create "a mood favorable to the best work that our social and law enforcing agencies are doing."[24]

Reagan was not in Robinson's league when it came to dramatizing social issues. His films were usually minor variations of successful A films that the studio had made with such box office stars as Robinson, Cagney, and Pat O'Brien. There is little evidence that Reagan gave thought to how he could use film to reform society.

Reagan did often play a heroic figure whose faith in American values seldom faltered. In three pictures he portrayed a character that helped authorities unravel crimes. In *Love Is on the Air* and *Nine Lives Are Not Enough* (1941) he was a "jet-propelled" reporter who assisted police in solving local murders.[25] In *Accidents Will Happen* (1938) he played an insurance adjuster who, though falsely accused of aiding a phony claims scheme, worked with investigators to bring racketeers to justice. In several pictures he portrayed either a defense lawyer or prosecuting attorney. In *Girls on Probation* (1938), about the criminal probation system, Reagan as an attorney fell in love with a woman falsely imprisoned. *Hell's Kitchen* (1939) and *Angels Wash Their Faces* (1939), about wayward youth, showed juvenile delinquency was a result of life in slums and privately owned correctional homes. As a lawyer in the former film, and a deputy district attorney in the latter, he defended delinquent boys, who were portrayed as victims of their environment. In *Juke Girl* (1942) he starred as a migrant farmer who stood up to a monopolistic buyer, was falsely accused of murder, and threatened with mob violence.[26]

A screen image was beginning to emerge. Despite his "wised-up and smart-cracking exterior," Reagan possessed the "heart of a Boy Scout" – and the naïveté. In both *Love Is on the Air* and *Nine Lives Are Not Enough,* he was eventually acclaimed a hero and rewarded with a better job – in the case of the latter film by becoming owner of his former paper. One device that the studio used to reinforce his heroic stature was to show on-screen a fictitious newspaper headline hailing Reagan as a hero.[27]

Reagan's character was most clearly a reformer in *Love Is on the Air,* somewhat less so in *Nine Lives Are Not Enough.* The connection with social consciousness was more tenuous in *Accidents Will Happen.* That movie appeared as an endorsement of the New Deal's campaign against crime. But if one examines the economic realities at Warner Bros. at this time, one can see that inspiration for the film, which dealt with insurance fraud, may well have come from the fact that in 1938 the studio had turned to insurance companies for financial backing. Small wonder that this picture, in addition to *Girls on Probation* and *Angels Wash Their Faces,* which also showed schemes to cheat insurance companies, warned audiences about such fraud.[28]

The early Reagan films were politically inoffensive. In *Love Is on the Air, Nine Lives Are Not Enough,* and *Accidents Will Happen,* Reagan's character, although not part of the legal system, helped authorities solve crimes. In other films his roles as an attorney made him part of the legal structure. The pictures examined causes of antisocial behavior. *Girls on Probation, Angels Wash Their Faces,* and *Hell's Kitchen* dealt most forthrightly with the social origins of crime and criminal rehabilitation. They told of people who were victims of either an imperfect legal or social system. Their central characters, who came from an urban world, were poor and disadvantaged. In each picture individuals found themselves confronting near-overwhelming odds.

Girls on Probation, based on a screenplay by Crane Wilbur, justified probation as a "humane system which tempers justice with mercy." Reagan played a young lawyer who rose to assistant district attorney. The story centered on a poor woman of immigrant parents who ran afoul of the law, was sent to prison, then paroled in custody of a probation officer. At one level *Girls on Probation* was an endorsement of probation and an exoneration of the legal system, because Reagan's character and the parole officer provided the heroine with support and demonstrated that those associated with the system could be humane. On another level, however, the film was critical of American justice. The story portrayed the heroine, estranged from her Old World father, as a casualty of a family structure out of place in America. She was primarily a victim of an impersonal legal system and did not have criminal intentions. At the end she was not so much rehabilitated as vindicated, a point driven home by the fact that Reagan's character, who represented social respectability, planned to marry her.[29]

Reagan appeared as a compassionate hero in *Angels Wash Their Faces* and *Hell's Kitchen,* two B films where the idea of criminal rehabilitation again figured in the plot. Both pictures focused on urban poverty and juvenile delinquency, and both offered a gloomy assessment of social institutions. Once more Reagan played an attorney supportive of the disadvantaged. *Angels Wash Their Faces,* about youth from the slums, drew a cynical picture of city government and the legal system. *Hell's Kitchen* was set in a variation of the reform school – the institution for homeless boys. Both pictures sought to capitalize on two 1938 films, *Angels With Dirty Faces* and *Crime School,* and Warner Bros. suggested something was amiss in society. Reagan's films, which opened in 1939, seemed to condone citizens who took matters into their own hands to rectify injustice – even if it meant vigilantism. But they did not take their social message very far.[30]

Some of the Reagan films had more than just a veneer of social consciousness. *Angels Wash Their Faces* was a follow-up to *Crime School,* and its title, scenario, and performers resembled *Angels With Dirty Faces.* As in *Angels With Dirty Faces, Angels Wash Their Faces* starred Ann Sheridan and the Dead End Kids (they had gotten their name from the 1937 Goldwyn film *Dead End),* who once more were on the margin of society, struggling to survive in a slum. Opening scenes panned the "squalid tenements over a narrow, dark canyon cluttered with push-carts, jumbled trash and filth of broken boxes, garbage and slum children; a teeming humanity swirling in and around . . . bargaining in a dozen strange tongues for its meagre scraps of existence." From rusty fire escapes of dilapidated buildings flew "banners of the slums – the patched sheets, the torn washing, the soggy mattresses and pillows put out to air." This approach undoubtedly came from writer John Wexley, a veteran of the Workers' Theater. Wexley had done the screenplay for *Angels With Dirty Faces* and hoped his script would expose the "evil influences" on youth by government officials who flagrantly broke the law and got away with it. Later, incidentally, in 1947, Jack Warner denounced Wexley before the House Committee on Un-American Activities.[31]

In Reagan's *Angels Wash Their Faces,* the heroine's younger brother, released from reform school and determined to become a law-abiding citizen, is falsely accused of arson and murder. Because of his record the boy is convicted and sent back to prison; the movie uses his predicament to dramatize unfairness. At the conclusion of the trial, Sheridan's character indicts the judicial process. "In this city of graft and corruption," she says to the district attorney, "you've overlooked a thousand lawbreakers to convict one innocent boy."[32]

The movie implies that only by extralegal means can the system work. Moreover, it encourages skepticism about government. Reagan's character and his father, the district attorney, sympathize with the boy and are ready to stretch the law in the interest of justice. Reagan's character uses illegal means to obtain the city's books, which prove the youth's innocence and show the extent of corruption. The district attorney suspects an arson plot but lacks sufficient evidence, and orders police to enter a warehouse illegally. The Dead End Kids also learn to manipulate the law. In addition to encouraging extralegal means, the movie ends on a cynical note, suggesting that while urban reforms might be instituted, politicians cannot be trusted to initiate them without public pressure.

With such films Warner Bros. used its publicity apparatus to promote community participation in activities related to its movies' themes. At this time studios such as Warner Bros. controlled large theater networks across the country and abroad. Warner offices in Burbank and New York sent pressbooks to theater managers offering instructions about how to promote each film. There were suggestions for community betterment through citizen involvement. For *Angels Wash Their Faces* the studio's publicity department urged theater managers to exploit "How to Improve Our City" contests to emphasize how environmental and other factors caused crime, and the "necessity for abolition of slums." It urged them to get in touch with newspaper editors, Big Brother clubs, the Boy Scouts, and adult groups, as well as civic and business leaders. It suggested essay contests for schoolchildren, "What the City Needs Most" or "What Would You Do to Improve the City," awards for the best photographs that showed tenement slums, and prizes for the best rehousing projects that would involve local real estate, construction firms, and city planning groups. The studio encouraged efforts to rehabilitate juvenile offenders. It asked local authorities to make better citizens of young people who had been in trouble by giving them jobs.[33]

Even in dealing with rather tepid social themes, Warner Bros. encountered opposition from the Hays Office. In *Angels Wash Their Faces*, Breen cautioned Jack Warner to "avoid presenting a false and unfair social or political philosophy." If the studio wished to deal with political corruption, he insisted that it refer to a "specific locale" rather than to "general conditions." He wanted the mayor's characterization in *Angels* so modified that it did not suggest that inefficient, hypocritical, or opportunistic politicians could easily gain high office. In the same picture he objected to Reagan and the Dead End Kids using illegal means to obtain evidence. For him and Hays it was important to avoid suggesting that the legal system as a whole was unjust or otherwise inadequate. That the Dead End Kids were on the side of law and order was a "healthy twist," he felt, but he reminded Warner about a recent amendment to the Production Code (December 20, 1938) that forbade movies from showing minors engaged in wrongdoing in such fashion as to "incite demoralizing imitation." And, as was usual in crime films, he emphasized that everyone involved in criminal acts had to be captured and punished by due process.[34]

Because reviewers in the PCA – as well as on local and state censorship boards – assumed that criminal activity shown on the screen would be imitated, criminals could not be role models and excessive violence was forbidden. Breen rejected the first script for *Hell's Kitchen*, in part because a former gangster (played by Stanley Fields) was heroic. He befriended the reform school boys, took charge of their institution (replacing a sadistic headmaster), and escaped unpunished for his part in a brawl that violated his parole. Warner Bros. eventually consented to change the ending so that Fields' character returned to prison for his parole violation. Violence became an issue in about half of the PCA's critiques of Reagan movie scripts between 1937 and 1942. Breen eliminated violent scenes from *Love Is on the Air, Girls on Probation,* and *Nine Lives Are Not Enough.*[35]

The PCA naturally discouraged crimes against property or business. In *Hell's Kitchen* and *Angels Wash Their Faces*, arson scenes upset Breen and Hays. Arson fell into a special category at the PCA and was considered too dangerous ever to be the main theme of a film. During production of *Acci-*

dents Will Happen, Breen advised Jack Warner to distinguish clearly between racketeers and legal loan companies to avoid objections from the latter.[36]

If PCA pressure – reinforced by threats of Legion of Decency boycotts and censorship from state and local authorities – was not enough to dissuade the Warners from pushing social criticism, reaction of foreign censors drove home the need for caution. Even after Reagan's films passed the PCA, some encountered trouble abroad. Japan and Australia accepted *Angels* only after deletions, and the British Board of Film Censors certified *Hell's Kitchen* but insisted on many cuts. France, the Netherlands, and Trinidad rejected *Angels.* France, Australia, Denmark, Hungary, and British Columbia banned *Hell's Kitchen.*[37]

Juke Girl created a great controversy over whether to show it abroad. At a time when most people believed national unity was essential, just after Pearl Harbor, viewers criticized Warner Bros. for stirring class hatred. Ulric Bell of the Office of War Information, and Nelson A. Rockefeller, head of the Office of the Coordinator of Inter-America Affairs (OCIAA), believed this film should not appear in theaters outside the United States. Bell felt the picture inappropriate for Latin America because it portrayed Americans as imperialistic and would play into the hands of Nazi propaganda. Although Warner Bros. prepared Portuguese and Spanish prints, it withdrew them from Latin American distribution on advice of the Motion Picture Society for the Americas, an unofficial organization associated with the OCIAA. Given the picture's lynch-mob scenes, Warner executives conceded that the movie might create a bad impression of North Americans.[38]

In *Juke Girl,* Reagan played a migrant farmer displaced with his father when forced to leave their Kansas farm during the Dust Bowl era. Although Reagan's character was near the bottom of the established social structure, he became a champion for the downtrodden by opposing a powerful packer and shipper in northern Florida. The villain controlled growers in his region, forcing them to take low prices for their crops, his brutal foreman played by the left-wing activist Howard Da Silva. When a local farmer (a first-generation Greek immigrant) challenged the villain, Reagan's character came to his aid and later took a job farming with him. After the villain killed the local farmer, people blamed Reagan's character for the murder. Ann Sheridan, who recently had finished *Kings Row* with Reagan, played his love interest as a juke girl who had become a drifter after a bank foreclosed on her family's Nebraska farm.[39]

In *Juke Girl,* Warner Bros. transformed an exposé of rural poverty into mass entertainment. The idea for the screenplay began with Theodore Pratt's story "Jook Girl" and his *Saturday Evening Post* article "Land of the Jook," which publicized conditions of Florida's migrant farmers. Here, Pratt wrote, was the last American frontier, where men practiced "the most dramatic and outrageous kind of farming in the world." "Jook," later spelled "juke," referred to coin-operated music boxes that provided escape for the people who lived in the area's deplorable poverty. "Jook girls" were employed by taverns to "dance and make love with the patrons."[40] What happened to Pratt's story when Warner Bros. picked it up reveals a good deal about the studio's dynamics. The story initially interested executive producer Hal Wallis, who circulated it. The idea reminded associate producer Jerry Wald of *They Drive by Night* (1940), a successful film starring Bogart and George Raft. Wald wanted more violence and recommended A. I. Bezzerides, who had written the original story for *They Drive by Night*. Bezzerides and Kenneth Gamet adapted Pratt's ideas and the studio added the Reagan character.[41]

As with most Warner Bros. A pictures during this period, Wallis was a force influencing the film. He was among the studio's New Deal liberals who saw motion pictures and modern science united in creating one world. Attracted by topical themes, unafraid of controversy, he "wanted to tell the truth." He took an interest in virtually every aspect of filmmaking.[42]

As mentioned, however, it was not merely *Juke Girl*'s depiction of American society divided along class lines that caused problems with the censors. It was the movie's portrayal of mob violence. Hollywood treated mobs with ambivalence during the 1930s, and PCA handling of lynchings and vigilantism took its cue from political censor boards at the state and local level as well as abroad.[43] The mob was an instrument of rough justice in three of Reagan's pictures. In 1939, in *Angels Wash Their Faces* and *Hell's Kitchen,* it was a vehicle for indignation. Three years later the mob in *Juke Girl* had become a tool for wrongdoing, manipulated by one of the story's villains, its wrath misguided. The film did end with a suggestion that the mob might administer justice to the story's villain. PCA files for *Angels Wash Their Faces* or *Hell's Kitchen* offer little evidence that Breen or his associates objected to the mob scenes. By the filming of *Juke Girl* in late 1941, however, Breen warned that censorship boards had become highly sensitive. There was a trend away from portraying mobs favorably. *Juke Girl* was not as forthright in condemnation of mobs as was Reagan's anti–Ku Klux Klan film, *Storm Warning,* which appeared in 1950.[44]

How does one explain such treatment of crime and other social issues? Social consciousness can best be understood in the political and economic context in which Warner Bros. operated. Behind the public idealism, apparent desire to educate, and social commentary lay a minefield of government antitrust suits, anti-Semitism, Hays Office edicts, threatened public boycotts, and precarious overseas markets, any one of which could threaten the studio's existence. Add to these factors the publicity that a publisher such as Hearst could bring, and one can understand the need for caution. The Warners understood what Hearst had discovered: humanitarianism and sensationalism could be profitable. The two, though, had to be mixed carefully.

If liberalism stirred such people as Reagan, Wallis, Wexley, and perhaps even Jack Warner, political and economic reality drove the films of the era.

All this may explain why Reagan's early crime pictures sometimes reflected ambivalence for social themes. His movies with the Dead End Kids implied that poverty and urban slums produced crime. But when local authorities began to clean up the slums at the end of *Angels Wash Their Faces,* the movie was cynical about the mayor's motives – hardly a ringing endorsement of government reform. *Juke Girl* drew a society torn by class tensions. Efforts by the federal government to help the migrants discussed in Pratt's *Saturday Evening Post* article were absent. Such films are perhaps best described as offering a "pervasive mood of optimistic pessimism, which conveyed the message that as things can't get worse, they must get better."[45]

Although most of the stories endorsed law enforcement (criminals were caught and punished), they were cynical about the American social structure. Even the Production Code Administration could not completely disguise this fact. The seemingly respectable citizen – city official, businessman, advertiser, headmaster – stood behind the gangster or used him. The pillar of society became an enemy within. Justice appeared impersonal, unresponsive, and easily manipulated. Violence (which would have been even more gratuitous had not the PCA intervened), corruption, and incompetence abounded. Extralegal activities, mob violence, and vigilante justice were occasionally necessary to prod the legal system.

The more deeply one looks into how Warner Bros. put its pictures together, the fainter is the trail of reform. All these films were set in the present, many designed to exploit contemporary curiosity about events or issues. Themes came from newspaper headlines, or as in the case of *Love Is on the Air, Accidents Will Happen, Angels Wash Their Faces,* and *Hell's Kitchen,* from formulas that had worked in earlier films. In *Juke Girl,* once Wallis had chosen the story, there is little evidence that studio executives or directors discussed reform. The question was how to create entertainment, and one necessary ingredient, at least in the opinion of associate producer Wald, was violence. *Angels Wash Their Faces* and *Accidents Will Happen* showed the perils of swindling insurance companies (advertising for *Accidents* asked patrons to report unsafe drivers), and Reagan portrayed a lawyer for an insurance company at the beginning of *Girls on Probation.* Such developments probably owed as much to Warner Bros.' desire to please its creditors as to any other factor.[46]

Through the cynicism of these films, Reagan's characters emerge as optimistic about society in depression America. The system was flawed but could work if the individual retained faith in the nation's institutions. Reagan's persona, widely publicized by the studio, began to appear: attractive, courageous, compassionate, a champion of the underdog. With the help of these films, which tentatively touched social themes, the youthful actor gained a reputation as a liberal.

5

STEREOTYPES AND TABOOS

> . . . the United States is hardly more than a nation of pagans. Most peo-
> ple in the United States no longer profess even Protestant Christian-
> ity. . . . Add to this the fact that motion pictures made in the United
> States have what amounts to a *virtual monopoly* on world markets and it
> will readily be seen how *imperative* it is that some drastic action . . . *be
> launched immediately,* if we are to stem the tide of immorality which is
> rapidly engulfing the world.
>
> Joseph Breen, 1937[1]

Warner Bros.' commitment to reform never went beyond a certain timidity. It
was not deep enough to give proportion to the liberal themes found in the
studio's movies. This reluctance to push for reform was especially noticeable
in the treatment of blacks, ethnic groups, and women. Sexual conventions,
though, were a different matter: the producers knew that sex could make
money.

   Stereotyping of blacks was commonplace at the time, and any departure
from the norm, ever so slight, could provoke an immediate response. During
the summer of 1937 the comedian Jack Benny appeared with Ida Lupino and
Martha Raye in *Artists and Models,* produced by Adolph Zukor. The movie
proved controversial, especially in the South, because of a segment in which
Raye danced with black performers. Why the scene had slipped by the Production Code Administration is unclear. Even though the script had not
indicated the dancers would be black, Breen or someone from his office
almost always viewed the film before issuing a certificate.[2]

   Reaction to this film spoke volumes about race relations in Hollywood
when Reagan began making motion pictures. When censors reviewed the
picture in Atlanta, they demanded excision of the scene. "For a white woman
to act with negroes," wrote a female member of the City of Atlanta Board of
Review, "is a most certain offense to the South," where "women can't act

53

with negroes . . . on the same plane." She quoted "a very disgusted reviewer" who said Raye "out niggers the niggers," and she predicted the performance would end the actress' career. The complaint echoed a protest a few days earlier by the managing editor of the *Shreveport Journal,* who objected to "the social equality tone in the picture." Hays, Breen, and studio executives were all eager to appease such critics. One suspects that they shared the preconceptions of this period, although surely they would have been able to surmount them had black moviegoers provided a sufficiently lucrative market.[3]

Racial discrimination pervaded the studios during Reagan's first years. Black performers had difficulty getting parts unless they were willing to accept menial roles – servants, Sambos, or musicians. The baritone Paul Robeson denounced studio executives in 1942 for stereotyping blacks as "child-like and innocent" or as "plantation hallelujah shouters." He and other blacks were offended by simple-minded scenarios that seemed always to have the black "solving his problem by singing his way to glory."[4]

Nor were theaters exempt from discrimination, for they often segregated blacks from whites. In Washington, blacks picketed a whites-only theater in 1940 because they could not attend the premiere of *Abe Lincoln in Illinois.*[5]

Other ethnic groups likewise were not credited with much imagination – at least in scripts for many movies. Nevertheless, the Warners' background made it fairly easy for appeals in this regard to get a hearing. Moreover, the Hays Office managed to catch most ethnic stereotypes before they reached the screen, especially if the group in question attended the movies in large numbers.

Nor were women treated realistically. Females in Reagan's prewar movies were usually glamorous, submissive, or both. Beauty and sex were commodities. Here Warner Bros. tested the limits of the Production Code by exploiting nudity, promiscuity, incest, and abortion. Reagan's best picture from this era, *Kings Row,* went the furthest in challenging the code.

★★★

The Warners were no strangers to discrimination. Jack Warner allegedly had been denied membership in the Lakeside Country Club because he was a Jew. They were both enraged and frightened by what was happening in Europe. They condemned bigotry, promoting an Americanism that would unify Jews, Protestants, and Catholics. Many of their films encouraged Americans to think of themselves as a single people. Screenwriter Crane Wilbur's first draft of *Hell's Kitchen* described the "melting pot of a great city, where peoples of all races are fused into one nationality." The idea of the United States as a melting pot was a theme in *Knute Rockne – All American.*[6]

But racial and ethnic prejudice undercut the Warners' desire to promote tolerance and unity. Such bias took many forms. It manifested itself in Jack Warner's sometimes embarrassingly crude humor, and was pronounced in the scripts of the low-budget B movies the studio often threw together. The younger Warner had a fondness for ethnic jokes, a form of humor he had taken for granted when he worked as a youthful vaudevillian in Youngstown, Ohio, under the name of Leon Zuardo. He had learned half a dozen dialects to poke fun at Jews, Germans, Italians, Greeks, and the Irish. As studio head the temptation to indulge such humor was occasionally too much. Once, while entertaining Mme. Chiang Kai-shek at a studio dinner, he gazed "over a line-up of dead-pan oriental faces at the head table," and, at a pause in Mme. Chiang's talk, he turned to someone and said loudly, "Holy cow, I forgot to pick up my laundry."[7]

The early scripts of several Reagan pictures reveal disparaging stereotypes. *The Code of the Secret Service,* one of the Brass Bancroft movies supposedly set in Mexico, proved potentially insulting to Mexicans. When Warner Bros. released the picture, publicity noted that "hundreds of Mexicans were used in the production, some of them in featured roles, most in atmosphere bits," and "there was not a 'heavy' or villain among them." The criminals were all Americans, and Mexican authorities were shown cooperating with Reagan to bring them to justice. But if scriptwriters Lee Katz and Dean Franklin had prevailed, the story would have been different. They originally described Mexicans in uncomplimentary terms. Consider their suggestions for Mexican characters: "*Police Officer* – An intelligent, unbelieving Mexican gentleman . . . on the indolent side. . . . *Estrellita* – . . . She is extremely fat, dark and very possessive. She has a deep love for small men and large onions. *Papa* – . . . He is typically Latin in his love for his daughters, music and the great importance he attaches to his calling – garbage man."[8] In the original script that Theodore Pratt prepared for *Juke Girl,* the villain was an Italian truck operator, Dominic, described as "fat, jolly, but totally unscrupulous." He was a man to whom virtually everything was amusing, "especially his own criminal acts." Screenwriters dropped Dominic's character when they revised Pratt's story, and added a new, sympathetic figure, a Greek farmer named Nick.[9]

Breen intervened to protect the portrayals of ethnic and national groups in Reagan's films. He feared that an early version of *Code of the Secret Service* would prompt embarrassing objections from Mexico. He insisted that Warner Bros. remove all scenes showing Mexicans as "lazy, slovenly, inefficient or comedy characters" and to portray them instead as "effective, dignified, efficient," and cooperative with American officials.[10] For *Juke Girl* he urged caution in handling the new character to avoid offending Greek-Americans. (Indeed, Hal Wallis gave instructions to eliminate the word "Greek" from the script.) In other pictures, Breen interceded to eliminate material possibly offensive to Italians and German-Americans.[11]

During the late 1930s and early 1940s, blacks did not have any way to obtain respect from either producers or the Hays Office.[12] The Production Code Administration files for Reagan's early films offer little evidence that the Hays Office made any effort to improve the screen representation of blacks, who were consistently shown in unflattering or patronizing ways. Blacks appeared in several of Reagan's early pictures including *Hollywood Hotel, Going Places, Accidents Will Happen, Sergeant Murphy, Santa Fe Trail,* and *Juke Girl.* Invariably they played simpletons or persons of dubious social status. Sometimes they were the butt of openly racial humor. *Hollywood Hotel,* in which Reagan appeared briefly, featured racial jokes, whites made up in blackface, and demeaning behavior toward black characters. The film opens with Dick Powell arriving in Hollywood and being greeted by photographers at the airport. As pictures are taken, a black porter passes between the actor and the cameras. "Say," one cameraman tells another, "they better use light makeup on that guy. He photographs pretty dark."[13]

Later in the same film, the script calls for a humorous interlude that involves making a mock movie with a plantation setting during the Civil War. Slaves gather on the lawn and porch "softly singing some familiar negro . . . spiritual" and chanting "Hallelujah! Hallelujah!"[14] A black butler named Uncle Tom, kneeling before a Southern gentleman dressed in Confederate uniform, vows to protect "Missy Lucy":

"Yas, suh, Massa Robert. I'll protect her with evah drop of blood dere is in dis ol' black body o' mine!"

The Southern gentleman replies, "Ah know you will, Tom," as he cuffs the servant on his bald head.

In this appalling film, a white actor dressed in blackface pleads, "Oh, Missy, Missy, don't let 'em sen' me down the river. Don' let Simon Legree beat me no more. Ah picks mah cotton by de bale – by de bale. Don' let 'em sen' me down the river. Oh, no. Oh, no. Oh no."[15]

Films associated blacks with animals. In *Hollywood Hotel* a character asks the comedian in blackface: "Who is that monkey over there?"

"Uncle Tom," the comedian replies.[16]

A more elaborate correlation between blacks and animals appeared in *Going Places,* a picture that also starred Dick Powell and featured Louis Armstrong and Maureen Sullivan as well as an appearance by Eddie Anderson, better known as Rochester. Reagan again had only a minor part in this comedy about a racehorse that would run fast only when Armstrong played his trumpet. In the film, blacks and animals came together in several ways. First, Armstrong's character was the only one able to communicate – through music – with the horse. Additionally, in a lengthy musical interlude that featured Sullivan, Armstrong, and his band, Powell and Ellen Parker sang the following ditty, neatly linking the then-controversial swing music with blacks and the animal kingdom:

Oh, they sang a song of sixpence,
Pocketful of rye.

Four and twenty black birds
Baked in a pie.
When the pie was brought in,
Opened by the king,
All the blackbirds flew around
And started in to swing.[17]

The link had visual reinforcement. Late in *Going Places* a scene dissolved from a black groom sleeping on straw to the racehorse awakening in its stable. The two images of man and horse arc briefly superimposed, suggesting intentional association.[18]

It is clear that Reagan's early pictures utterly failed to show blacks in a decent light. During this period in his filmmaking, from 1937 until he entered military service in 1942, the two pictures that had the greatest opportunity to comment on black Americans were *Santa Fe Trail* and *Juke Girl*. During the production of the former, Breen warned Jack Warner that "discussions of slavery" could bring "adverse reaction" from the South. The film presented the abolitionist John Brown from a Southern perspective, equated him with Hitler, and all but ignored the issue of black freedom. Theodore Pratt's *Saturday Evening Post* exposé of a Florida county, which had been the inspiration for *Juke Girl,* revealed that five out of six migrant workers were black and that their living conditions were deplorable. Yet in the studio's adaptation all the main characters were white, and blacks had minor roles, usually as wide-eyed Sambos.[19]

There is little to indicate that Reagan condoned the bigotry that permeated Hollywood at this time. Certainly his earlier home environment had condemned racial and ethnic prejudice. His father, an Irish Catholic, had experienced intolerance firsthand in the predominantly Protestant Dixon, where the Ku Klux Klan was a presence. Ronald sometimes fought with schoolmates who made an issue of his father's religion. The mere fact of being Catholic made Jack – and his son – "something of an outcast." Jack Reagan "believed literally that all men were created equal," his son recalled, "and that the man's own ambition determined what happened to him after that." Reagan's father had prevented him and Neil from attending D. W. Griffith's *Birth of a Nation.* "It deals with the Ku Klux Klan against the colored folks," Jack declared, "and I'm damned if anyone in this family will go see it." In 1943, *Modern Screen* noted the elder Reagan's hostility toward the KKK. "The Klan's the Klan, and a sheet's a sheet," Jack reputedly had said about *The Birth of a Nation,* "and any man who wears one over his head is a bum." His loathing for what the Klan represented "went down to his roots," according to this account. After World War II his son, the actor, would participate in efforts to discredit the Klan on both radio and film.[20]

Significantly, Reagan's screen characters, even in the pre–World War II pictures, did not reflect the customary condescension toward minorities.

They were supportive of blacks. Reagan's George Custer, for example, emerges in *Santa Fe Trail* as the single person in pursuit of John Brown who is understanding of, if not sympathetic to, to the abolitionist's cause. On several occasions Custer speaks in Brown's defense. When Brown's son is badly injured, Jeb Stuart blames it on the senior Brown's madness. Custer, however, reminds Stuart that there is "a purpose behind that madness." After Brown's execution, Stuart boasts that Brown's cause had been "broken for good." Again, Custer speaks for Brown: "Nothing will ever break the force of John Brown, Jeb, not even death."[21]

★★★

Women found only a limited range of understanding for their problems when they watched motion pictures. In general they were pieces of furniture in a man's world. In Reagan's early films, women usually appeared in passive, supporting roles. Often portrayed as creatures of emotion, and treated with condescension, they were normally dependent on men. They frequently promoted images of beauty. With few exceptions, strong women were villainous, untrustworthy, and calculating.[22]

The quietly supportive female was one of the most popular images, and was perhaps best exemplified in Gale Page's role as Bonnie Rockne in *Knute Rockne – All American,* and by Olivia De Havilland as the Eastern-educated Kit Carson Halliday in *Santa Fe Trail.* They played opposite O'Brien and Flynn. Reagan's characters found comfort from supportive women in such pictures as *Accidents Will Happen* (Gloria Blondell), *Kings Row* (Ann Sheridan), and *This Is the Army* (1943) (Joan Leslie).

In some Reagan pictures, women were treacherous or deceptive or at least calculating. Hilda Ryker (Lya Lys) exposed Brass Bancroft's cover in *Murder in the Air.* The wife of Reagan's character in *Accidents Will Happen* betrayed him. A woman led the heroine astray in *Girls on Probation.* Ann Sheridan in *Juke Girl* scarcely inspired confidence that she would remain with Reagan on a tomato farm. Earlier she had told him: "Hear that juke in there? That's my racket. That kind of noise will always stand between you and me. . . . Stayin' on the farm was your idea, not mine." In the comedy *An Angel From Texas* (1940), Jane Wyman played Reagan's wife and easily outwitted him and another con artist portrayed by Wayne Morris, demonstrating that women were not only sometimes smarter than males but more calculating.

In other early Reagan films women appeared emotional or dependent on – and intellectually inferior to – men. In *Girls on Probation,* the heroine's fate hinged on Reagan's sense of justice, and when he presented her with an engagement ring her reaction suggested it had been a lifelong dream. The character of Mary Lou Carruthers (Mary Maguire) in *Sergeant Murphy* was to speak dialogue either "frigidly," "impulsively," "sweetly," or "excitedly." In *Tugboat Annie Sails Again* (1940), Marjorie Rambeau played a strong woman denied a salvage contract because she was "very apt to lose control of emotions and . . . temper in moments of excitement." In *Nine Lives Are*

Not Enough, when Jane Abbott (Joan Perry) was overcome by emotion, Reagan comforted her. When she attempted to help with a murder investigation, he told her to "forget it! . . . That's . . . no kind of job for you to tackle." In *Secret Service of the Air,* the character of Pamela was "adorable in a summer sports outfit" and later she and another woman left Brass and his navy associates on the patio so they could "talk clothes." In *Million Dollar Baby,* Reagan fell in love with a wealthy woman (Priscilla Lane) but hesitated to marry her. "I'm not a conventional guy," he said, "but I guess I got the good old American prejudice [against] sitting on my bustle and getting my groceries from some dame."[23]

Often women were sex objects. Few if any starlets escaped being promoted in this fashion. Ann Sheridan, Jane Wyman, and Bette Davis were no exceptions. Warner Bros.' publicity department had dubbed Sheridan the Oomph Girl and the Ideal Redhead. In addition to *Angels Wash Their Faces* and *Juke Girl,* she appeared with Reagan in such films as *Cowboy From Brooklyn* (1938), *Naughty But Nice* (1939), and *Kings Row* (1942). Publicity gave the public her measurements (36–26–36), provided articles on her clothes, and encouraged young women to emulate her. "Announce that certain 'Miss Oomph' will be somewhere in the shopping district," the pressbook for *Naughty But Nice* told promoters. "She will be a very shapely lass wearing such and such." The idea was "for contestants to identify 'Miss Oomph' simply by walking up to her and saying so."[24]

In a poster for this movie Sheridan told women "how to be popular with men. Lesson No. 1: Not too much fire. . . . Not too much ice . . . It's best to be just a bit . . . 'Naughty but Nice.'" Sheridan was "a man's woman but . . . equally popular with women. . . . She is capable of sitting up half the night playing red dog with her husband . . . and his friends (usually coming out the heavy winner and still retaining her popularity) – and taking her crocheting to join a group of women in a gabfest the next day." According to the studio, Sheridan had a prescription for saving marriages: "The mere fact that I like to do the things my husband likes doesn't strike me as anything unusual. I think there would be a lot more happy marriages if women tried to be companions more than wives."[25]

Although Wyman was a gifted actress, she too was exploited for sex appeal. She appeared with Reagan in *Brother Rat* and its sequel, *Brother Rat and a Baby,* as well as in *An Angel From Texas* and *Tugboat Annie Sails Again.* In *Brother Rat,* the studio fitted her with glasses, hoping to make her look bookish. When the attempt failed, Warner Bros. moved to capitalize on her beauty. She provided advice to bespectacled females. "Girls Can Be Glamorous in Glasses," a publicity release assured; they needed only to look at Wyman. But there was more to success, she claimed. Her break came when she dyed her hair platinum. "When I changed my hair I actually changed my whole personality," she confided. "Before I became a blonde, I had tried everything to get a start as an actress but no one in Hollywood gave me a tumble." As with Sheridan, Warner Bros. suggested that Wyman and her husband had a formula "for ideal domestic bliss." Reagan was not hard to please, and the couple did not "believe in rules."[26]

Perhaps the strongest female character in any of the pre–World War II Reagan pictures was played by Bette Davis in *Dark Victory*. This was one of the best films Reagan appeared in during this period, although his performance as a wealthy, ne'er-do-well lush was wooden. George Brent and Humphrey Bogart performed in this tearjerker about a young socialite dying of a brain tumor. Davis had earlier won Academy Awards for her performances in *Jezebel* and *The Sisters* and gave another powerful performance.

Despite the film's subject, the studio attempted to exploit Davis's sexuality, apparently with the actress's blessing. Publicity said that she would undergo "a complete metamorphosis" as a result of love. Audiences would glimpse this "up-to-the-year-and-minute girl" as her "tousled head" emerged "from coverlets and pillows." Davis's costumes, some provided by fashion designer Orry-Kelly, would launch a new trend, and the studio stressed women's attire in addition to beauty tips to admirers. Davis participated in creating a few of the fashions and asked for "a very naked dress." She "practically designed it herself," Orry-Kelly told Wallis.[27]

Reagan's films did little to challenge conventional notions about women's place. They perpetuated images found in many other pictures (it should be remembered that not only men came to theaters to see female stars but also women). Studios wanted women to be packaged trifles and accessories. They were expected to be decorative and simpleminded; if they were strong – and not diabolical – they should at least be supportive.

Breen and associates in the PCA worried so much about Hollywood's treatment of sex that they did little to change female stereotypes. In *Dark Victory* they did not object so much to revealing costumes as to implied sexual activity between Bogart, who played a stablehand, and Davis, the wealthy socialite. Breen's response to this film and to other Reagan pictures shows that he never questioned the idea that women should be subordinate. Breen and his office merely insisted that heroines conform to the morality set down by the Production Code.[28]

While Breen was apprehensive about the depiction of sex in *Dark Victory*, his concern about this film paled by comparison to his reaction to *Kings Row*, the movie that helped take Reagan to stardom in 1942 and was arguably his best film. *Kings Row* was one of an increasing number of films during the 1940s that explored psychological topics. It dealt with a galaxy of controversial themes – incest, suicide, insanity, premarital sex, nymphomania, homosexuality, sadism, and mercy killing – that one might not ordinarily associate with Reagan films. In many respects *Kings Row* was an anomaly among the pictures Reagan finished before the attack on Pearl Harbor, and had more in common with several of his post–World War II movies. Why Warner Bros. made this kind of film, one easily guesses, had much to do with money. The Warners knew full well that sex had always sold tickets, and they also sensed that the war had aroused interest in the dark side of human nature. The problem was how to get such scenes past Breen.[29]

In explaining Reagan's films, and Warner Bros.' guarded approach to treacherous topics (sex excepted), it is interesting that the picture many regard as Reagan's best began almost accidentally. In 1940, Warner Bros.' screenwriter Casey Robinson and his wife left for a vacation to the Philippines and the Orient. Before he left, Hal Wallis gave him an advance copy of Henry Bellamann's novel *Kings Row*. The novel was destined to become a bestseller and Wallis wondered if a movie could be made.

But when Robinson read Bellamann's narrative he despaired of making a movie. At the center was an incestuous affair between a doctor and his daughter. Several other characters engaged in premarital sex. One was a nymphomaniac, and others experimented with or had tendencies toward homosexuality. Another, the character of Drake McHugh, whom Reagan portrayed in the movie, had his legs amputated by a sadistic surgeon. Euthanasia was practiced on an elderly woman terminally ill. What a cornucopia of indecency, the censors would say!

As the sun set on the screenwriter's ship, sailing through the Sulu Sea toward Bali, Robinson pitched the manuscript into the water. "Nobody else is going to see this bunch of trash!" he muttered. But just as the book hit the water, an idea came about how he could avoid the censors. He would change the theme from incest to inherited insanity. He cabled Wallis: "Buy it."[30]

Even though other Reagan films exploited sex, none approached the controversies stirred by Bellamann's *Kings Row*. In the other pictures, producers met the industry's censorship requirements set down in the code by trimming scenes or dialogue. *Kings Row* was far more complicated.

To understand the furor this film caused it is necessary to know the background of the 1930 code. Sex had long been one of the most inflammatory issues in Hollywood. Just as many industry critics believed movie theaters breeding grounds for criminals, so did people believe films encouraged sexual permissiveness and undermined the family. For that reason the architect of the Production Code, Jesuit priest Daniel A. Lord, attempted to fit it to Judeo-Christian ethics. The code sought to uphold the "institution of marriage and the home" and prohibit movies from implying that "low forms of sex relationship are the accepted or common thing." Illicit sex could be treated in pictures if necessary to the plot but never shown in a way that made it appear attractive or justifiable. The code discouraged films handling sexual hygiene and venereal disease and banned the word "abortion." Passionate scenes necessary to a story had to be regulated so as not to excite the "lower and baser emotions." The code also sought to eliminate nudity, noting "that the nude or semi-nude body may be *beautiful* does not make its use in the films moral."[31]

Enforcement of the code had been strengthened in 1934 by actions of the Legion of Decency and the Production Code Administration. J. Dennis Cardinal Dougherty of Philadelphia launched an assault on the movies in May of that year after seeing an offensive billboard near his office advertising a Warner Bros. film. He forbade members of his diocese to attend pictures. He called motion picture theaters "the greatest menace to faith and morals in America today" and maintained that they presented a "false philosophy of life." He claimed movies were a "vicious and insidious attack . . . on the very foundations of our Christian civilization" what with their emphasis on "divorce, free love, marital infidelity." They undermined "marriage, the purity of womanhood, the sanctity of the home, and obedience to lawful authority," and they had an especially bad influence on children and teenagers. He declared that "one hour spent in the darkened recesses of a movie theater" could undo "years of careful training on the part of the school, the church, and the home."[32]

Harry Warner's studio at the time was struggling back from huge early depression losses and he was stunned. He and the other producers hastily met in New York. Breen, not yet head of the PCA, recalled the meeting: "There was Harry Warner, standing up at the head of the table, shedding tears the size of horse turds, and pleading for someone to get him off the hook. And well he should, for you could fire a cannon down the center aisle of any theater in Philadelphia, without danger of hitting anyone!"[33]

Hays and Breen of course essentially agreed with Cardinal Dougherty's view of sex and films. When it came to sex and the code, many people conjured a prudish Hays, photographed "in his high starched collar and wearing a mole-tooth grin, strangely evocative of the cartoons of Mr. Prohibition." This image served the Presbyterian Hays and the movie moguls who wanted the public to believe they were serious about cleaning up entertainment. For that matter, it may have captured part of Hays's personality.[34]

But the man who interpreted the code most frequently and wrestled daily with the studios was Breen, whom Samuel Goldwyn once called "Hollywood's benevolent conscience." Breen was in charge of the PCA and it was hard to imagine a more self-assured monitor. "I am the Code!" he once told PCA staff member Morris Murphy. A producer once confronted Breen about rejection of a script and suggested it might be more profitable for the studios to sell milk than to make movies. "Maybe that would be a goddam good idea," Breen responded. "If people like you would get out of the way and sell milk, maybe it would free the screen of a lot of its whorehouse crap, and decent people could sit down and enjoy themselves in a theater without blushing." By his own description the colorful Breen "stood like a man on the seashore, trying to hurl back the tides of the ocean with a pitchfork." As one of his associates noted, "the mainspring of his vitality was the fact that he nurtured not the slightest seed of self-doubt regarding his mission or his rectitude."[35]

Breen believed that a "tide of immorality" was "rapidly engulfing the world." He sometimes privately blamed Hollywood's sexual indulgence on Jewish control of the industry. After he became head of the PCA, he despaired that damage to values had been done. During Reagan's first year in Hollywood, Breen told a friend in the church hierarchy in Rome that the United States had become "hardly more than a nation of pagans," which no longer professed "even Protestant Christianity." Divorce was so accepted, he maintained, that "to attempt . . . reform, by organized protests, or otherwise, . . . would be futile." The frequency with which motion pictures mistreated the issue of marriage and divorce could not help but have a "most devastating effect."[36]

None of Reagan's Warner Bros. films, no matter how innocent or lurid their stories, escaped alteration by Breen. Bigamy, illegitimacy, childbirth, and even abortion became problems in *Boy Meets Girl* (1938), one of the first movies in which Reagan appeared (he had a small part near the end). Breen became upset because one of the characters was a pregnant waitress. The play on which this film was based suggested the woman was pregnant because of a bigamous relationship and that she gave birth to an illegitimate child. Early versions of the script insinuated that the woman might be unwed and called for her to experience labor pains. Breen also believed this story dealt unacceptably with abortion and miscarriage, and forbade any discussion of those topics. State and local censorship boards usually cut such scenes anyway.[37]

Nudity, promiscuity, the treatment of marriage, and sexual innuendo all became issues in Reagan movies. Breen cautioned about nudity when Reagan dressed in *Love Is on the Air* and when he undressed in front of Jane Wyman in *Tugboat Annie Sails Again;* much of the latter scene with Wyman was left in the final print. Promiscuity became a problem in *Juke Girl* and *International Squadron.* The "juke girls" were probably prostitutes although this angle was camouflaged. In *International Squadron,* Breen interceded to make Reagan's character less of a womanizer. An early version of *Secret Service of the Air* took a poke at the institution of marriage. Even in such a patriotic movie as *This Is the Army,* Breen condemned some of the film's lyrics as too suggestive.[38]

Breen and Hays believed it was impossible to eliminate sin from the screen because it was basic to human nature and thus a necessary part of a realistic story. Nevertheless, they were determined to control its presentation. Films involving sin were to have "compensating moral values," which included "good characters, the voice of morality, a lesson, regeneration of the transgressor, suffering and punishment."[39]

With this background, one comes to *Kings Row.* Bellamann's novel is set in a small Midwestern community at the turn of the century and tells the story of two boyhood friends, Parris Mitchell and Drake McHugh. In the novel, Parris (played in the movie by Robert Cummings) has been raised by his grandmother and is a sensitive, intelligent youth. After his grandmother dies of cancer (euthanasia ends her suffering), Parris goes to Vienna to study psychiatry and becomes a doctor. Drake's parents are also dead; he is a playboy who stands to inherit wealth when he comes of age. When a local banker embezzles his inheritance, he is reduced to poverty.

In the novel, Parris and Drake have varying relationships with the town's elite. Parris is well-bred and studies for a time with a local physician, Dr. Alexander Tower, who is "an arrogant and intrepid intelligence," contemptuous of Kings Row inhabitants. Parris is attracted to Dr. Tower's daughter, Cassandra, and the two carry on an affair, which ends when Dr. Tower kills Cassandra and then himself. Later it is discovered that there had been an incestuous affair between father and daughter. It seems that Cassandra may have been a nymphomaniac and was pregnant at the time of her death.[40]

Drake is a ladies' man and falls in love with Louise, daughter of another Kings Row physician, the sadistic Dr. Henry Gordon. But Drake also carries on with other girls, including Randy Monoghan (played in the film by Ann Sheridan), who is of a lower class than the Gordons. Dr. Gordon disapproves of Drake, and when the latter loses his money and is injured in a railyard accident, Gordon needlessly amputates both his legs. Although Randy takes care of him, he later dies of cancer. In 1940, undoubtedly many people would have considered Reagan's later description of the novel as a "slightly sordid but moving yarn" as understatement.[41]

Because Bellamann's novel achieved bestseller status, part of the public was aware of the story's sticky moral issues. At first reluctant to attempt adaptation, Warner Bros. paid Bellamann $35,000 for story rights, then agonized over how to alter the plot. Censors in the Hays Office, who understood the story and how much at odds it was with the code, reacted with alarm.

Warner Bros. turned to screenwriter Robinson to give the story a more optimistic tone. In addition to eliminating the incest by making Cassandra a victim of inherited insanity, he altered Drake's fate. In the film, Reagan's character triumphs over misfortune. Instead of succumbing to cancer, Drake recovers and sells real estate.

As Drake, Reagan gave one of his best performances. His most famous line, delivered when he awoke to discover in horror that his legs were gone, was, "Where's the rest of me?" These words he considered the most challenging of his movie career. It was, he said, the kind of "acting chore that got down inside and kind of wrung me out." He rehearsed for hours before a mirror and consulted doctors and psychiatrists. When the time came to shoot, he uttered his lines so well that no retake was required. Later he admitted that he "never did quite as well again in a single shot." The explanation, he said, "was that I had put myself, as best I could, in the body of another fellow."[42]

But this scene almost failed to appear in the final version of the film. Some thought it too depressing at a time when men and women were being mutilated in war. One recommendation called for Dr. Gordon only to fracture the legs and for Parris to perform surgery so Drake regained use of them. Jack Warner thought it better to cut off only one of Drake's legs than "to make an audience suffer with a poor sucker lying in bed throughout the picture with both legs amputated." Director Sam Wood, whom Reagan trusted, liked the original ending and argued to save it lest the conclusion have to be rewritten.[43]

Such studio qualms were minor compared with the uncertainties of Breen and his staff. They read Bellamann's book and when the studio submitted the script in April 1941, they rejected it. Breen objected to the illicit relations between Parris and Cassandra, and between Drake and Randy; to Drake's liaisons with other women; to Cassandra's characterization, with its implication of "gross sexual abnormality"; and to the mercy killing of Parris's grandmother. All these elements would have to be changed or eliminated. Breen reminded Jack Warner that British censors almost always cut any suggestion of insanity. Moreover, even if the novel could be rewritten to fit the code, there was a question of whether it was in the film industry's interest to translate a book identified publicly as repugnant.[44]

But the day after Breen offered his objections to Warner Bros., he and Geoffrey Shurlock of the PCA met with Wallis, Robinson, and Warner Bros. producer David Lewis, and came to an understanding. Breen agreed to production of *Kings Row* provided the studio added a "voice for morality." To make the movie acceptable, he stressed, it must have "compensating moral values." The changes meant not only further rewriting of Bellamann's story but a change in tone and philosophy. Breen wanted the film to condemn and penalize evil. There were many ways to punish sin, and the code allowed for the "possibility of *internal* suffering as retribution." Parris would be the voice for morality. Breen insisted on adding a scene between Parris and Drake in which Parris would "definitely condemn himself" for his affair with Cassandra. In acknowledging that the affair had been wrong, the scene would indicate Parris's "feeling of impending tragedy," which would tie in with the subsequent discovery that Dr. Tower had killed Cassandra and himself. Later, Breen insisted that Parris make a statement that he felt himself "morally responsible" for the deaths of Cassandra and her father, and that this was "to be his punishment for his immoral relations with her."[45]

Breen went over the script line by line and insisted on other changes. The film could not imply that Cassandra was a nymphomaniac. There would be only one sexual liaison between her and Parris, and no hint of an affair between Drake and Randy, or between Drake and any of the other female characters in Bellamann's novel. A scene suggesting that children were bathing nude would have to go. The mercy killing was eliminated as well as many lines of dialogue.[46]

In Warner Bros.' treatment of *Kings Row*, homosexuality all but disappeared. The studio had as much or more to do with this fact than did Breen. Homosexuality was perhaps as taboo in Hollywood films as any theme. Although homosexual characters did appear in scripts of other early Reagan films, they were treated in stereotypical fashion. By contrast, Bellamann's *Kings Row* tried to deal with the subject realistically.[47] Bellamann's tale included a gay adolescent named Jamie Wakefield, who did not appear in the movie. The novel suggested an attraction between Drake and Parris. In the movie Parris asks to spend the night in Drake's house so he would have an alibi to deny he had been with Cassandra. Reagan delivered the line, "Of course you'll have to bunk with me. I hope you won't mind, Mr. Mitchell." Originally the script called for Reagan to say, "Of course you'll have to bunk with me. I hope you won't mind the change, Mr. Mitchell." Breen objected and Hal Wallis issued instructions to create a new soundtrack. This was about as far as the studio dared – or wanted – to go with the topic.[48]

Thus did Ronald Reagan, from Dixon via Des Moines, enter a world that misrepresented and exploited ethnic groups, blacks, women, and especially sex. Moviemakers generally were unwilling to challenge the prejudices of their era – unless, of course, a profit could be turned. Even the liberal-minded Warners, who comprehended the threat of Nazism and anti-Semitism, displayed limited enthusiasm when it came to striking blows against the appalling depiction of blacks. Ethnic and national groups that went to the movies in large numbers could at least count on the Hays Office to protect their image. Blacks, however, found few defenders in the PCA, where censors were more concerned with appeasing Southern audiences than with defending black dignity. Fortunately, these circumstances were beginning to change. Reagan's early screen image stood as a refreshing contrast to the crude stereotyping of African-Americans. World War II would accelerate efforts to bring blacks into mainstream films and to give them a more respectable screen presence.

When it came to sex there were powerful pressures to take the lid off the Production Code. The strongest of these forces was financial. Hollywood knew that sex was an almost irresistible attraction that sold tickets. From the beginning, there also had been widespread dissatisfaction with the code on creative grounds. Filmmakers considered the guidelines too restrictive. Breen thus had a formidable task forcing such movies as *Kings Row* to conform. It is interesting that the young Reagan should have done his best work in this movie. In the years ahead the themes that emerged in this film would grow commonplace and it would become all but impossible to keep motion pictures within the bounds of the code.

6

THE INERTIA PROJECTOR

The Fifth Column and Trojan Horse are being discussed wherever you go – and I am so afraid that in our industry we may not take that seriously enough, that I want to be sure that I have you face to face with me, so that at least in days to come, if you don't take heed, I can feel I have done my duty and have told you that the danger is here.

Harry M. Warner in speech to
Warner Bros. employees, June 5, 1940

. . . join *Ronald Reagan* battling 20,000 unseen enemies to protect . . . the most deadly weapon ever known to man . . . a death ray projector . . . the greatest force for peace ever discovered.

Trailer for *Murder in the Air* (1940)

Within days after the outbreak of World War II in 1939, Reagan began working on a new motion picture called *The Enemy Within*. In the following weeks its name would change to *Uncle Sam Awakens* and then to the more sensational *Murder in the Air*. The film favorably portrayed the fledgling House Committee on Un-American Activities, warned of subversion from spies and saboteurs, and contained veiled criticism of those who would hinder American preparedness. Reagan played a Secret Service agent, Brass Bancroft, whose mission included defense of a new super weapon, a "death ray projector" that could stop enemy aircraft and make the United States "invincible in war," thus promising to become "the greatest force for world peace ever discovered."

Murder in the Air (1940) was one of four Brass Bancroft films that Reagan completed in 1938 and 1939. In these pictures a youthful, heroic Reagan combated counterfeiters, illegal aliens, spies, and saboteurs. The films reflected several movie industry concerns of the late 1930s. They treated federal agents in an attractive manner. For years controversy had raged over what many people considered the often all-too-favorable portrayal of crime and criminals. The Brass Bancroft series constituted part of the industry's

67

effort to improve public understanding of government agents and law enforcement. These movies also reveal how Hollywood, especially the Warner
brothers, had begun to fear the possibility of Nazi espionage in America.
Finally, as might be expected from moviemakers so antifascist and dedicated
to Hitler's destruction, some of the Bancroft films promoted military preparedness.[1]

Many Warner Bros. films attempted "to record history in the making" and
capture "current happenings." Warner Bros. estimated in 1940 that it based
a fifth of its pictures on newspaper headlines. Harry Warner insisted that the
studio researched these stories and that the films showed events accurately.
Brother Jack quipped that producer Bryan Foy's "assembly-line mind" was
always "available to stretch a four-line clipping into five or six reels." Reagan's Secret Service pictures, with emphasis on timely themes, fell into this
category. Filmed hurriedly, on low budgets and with an eye for profit, their
quality was poor. "They were movies the studio didn't want good," Reagan
later said, "they wanted 'em Thursday." Still, they amplified current events,
dramatized them, and projected them to millions of people in the United
States and abroad.[2]

⭐⭐⭐

Before Reagan's arrival in Hollywood and during the depths of the depression, when confidence in the economic and social system was at low ebb, the
image of the gangster had taken on importance in popular culture. Films and
other entertainment romanticized the outlaw. Alarmed, many people viewed
such Warner Bros. movies as *Little Caesar* (1931) and *Public Enemy* (1931)
as well as Howard Hughes's *Scarface* (1932) as part of a trend toward
disrespect for law and order.[3] Attorney General Homer S. Cummings believed that crime had become a "national problem of the first magnitude."
Among the objectives of the Conference on Crime he set up in late 1934 was
to restore respect for law enforcement, and to create a "universal abhor-
rence" of illegal activity and a "fixed determination to eradicate it." Resent-
ful of movie stereotypes of policemen, Cummings sought to improve the
image of federal agents so their work would appear in a "dignified and
technically accurate" manner. He wrote Will Hays and discussed the matter
with FBI director J. Edgar Hoover. Hays got in touch with Harry Warner and
explained the FBI's desire to cooperate with the industry. He urged Warner to
exercise care in portraying federal agents, and suggested the studio follow the
procedure it used in dealing with the army and navy so that government
agents were depicted as "thoroughly intelligent, courageous, honorable."[4]

Warner Bros. changed its approach to gangster movies. The studio that
had produced *Little Caesar* and *Public Enemy* turned out another James
Cagney film, *G-Men,* which premiered in 1935, showing a highly efficient
FBI that needed bright, well-educated, well-armed agents.

Interestingly, the FBI neither cooperated with nor endorsed this film because Hoover believed the picture portrayed the bureau incorrectly. The Warners did receive support from William Randolph Hearst, who promoted the film. Representatives from the San Francisco *Examiner* and *Call-Bulletin* met with FBI officials in late April 1935 to obtain bureau approval. But when an endorsement was not forthcoming, the papers ran stories indicating "enthusiastic approval" from law enforcement authorities who had previewed the picture. Hoover eventually praised the Warners, writing Harry that the movie industry was a leading factor in creating "public consciousness for law enforcement."[5]

G-Men marked a turning point. Thereafter movies made heroes of government agents and other lawmen. Breen congratulated Jack Warner for "so cleverly and artistically" characterizing federal operatives. With Breen and the Legion of Decency exerting pressure on the studios, sympathetic treatment of criminals all but disappeared from Warner Bros. films and from virtually all Hollywood movies during the 1930s.[6]

Reagan's four Secret Service films were part of the campaign to restore the integrity of law enforcement. In all four pictures, Reagan played a Treasury Department agent. *Secret Service of the Air* began production in September 1938 and appeared in theaters the next year. Reagan infiltrated a ring of criminals who smuggled illegal aliens from Mexico into the United States. *Code of the Secret Service* (1939) and *Smashing the Money Ring* (1939) followed and dealt with counterfeiting. The fourth film, *Murder in the Air*, contained a veiled warning about Nazi saboteurs and featured the death ray weapon called the Inertia Projector.

Studio publicity was nothing if not straightforward. *Secret Service of the Air* had been made to restore "dignity and public confidence" in the police and in other law enforcement agencies. An article, accompanied by a picture of Reagan, revealed that behind the effort to glorify G-men was an intention similar to that which moved the studio's patriotic shorts, namely to entertain while instilling patriotism. Publicity noted that at Warner Bros. a small group regularly scanned stories to insure that they gave a favorable slant to law enforcement.[7]

Warner Bros. attempted to give the Secret Service films authenticity, explaining that the stories were "but thinly disguised dramatizations of actual adventures," taken from the files of William H. Moran, former chief of the Secret Service. The studio engaged Moran as a consultant for $250 a week and hired ex–FBI special agent William L. Guthrie to head its location department. Guthrie served as liaison between Warner Bros. and the government; he praised the Reagan films, saying that the effectiveness of the Secret Service and similar organizations resulted from the "fear and respect they inspire in the hearts of law-breakers and would-be law-breakers." Guthrie urged an "international attempt, among friendly nations, to glorify their police organizations by way of films."[8]

The studio's strategy for promoting the Secret Service films called for community participation. One approach involved collaborating with law enforcement agencies. The Bancroft films were not exceptional in this regard. To publicize *Love Is on the Air,* the studio had suggested newspaper interviews with local police commissioners who would recommend "methods for ridding the country of its public enemies." If anything, though, advertising for the Secret Service movies emphasized cooperation with local authorities even more. Promotion of *Smashing the Money Ring* called for setting up "crime clue boxes" in theater lobbies in which patrons could turn in names of suspicious neighbors, as well as fingerprint booths and wanted posters. Another approach to gain community involvement endorsed Junior Secret Service Clubs, popular in the late 1930s. Warner Bros. publicized Reagan as "commander" of the Junior Secret Service, and members received a card bearing his signature. The studio suggested ways clubs could attract recruits. One recommendation was for local school rifle squads to hold marksmanship contests.[9]

Meanwhile, Warner Bros. worked on a heroic persona for Reagan. In addition to the formidable influence of the Production Code Administration, the studio system exercised virtual total control over actors. Executives selected Reagan's films, picked roles, and scheduled appearances. Producers, directors, and writers combined to create a screen personality. The code of the Secret Service was "to be dauntless in the face of danger . . . to be fearless in the face of death!" The studio tried to fit Reagan into the mold. Brass Bancroft, and therefore the actor who played him, was handsome, athletic, and rugged, a crack pilot ready to fight at the drop of a hat. Above all, Reagan's character was a patriot with a strong sense of duty. In advertising *Secret Service of the Air,* the studio maintained that Reagan "as a type" was ideal, for he was "both in appearance and personality, the representative of all that is admirable in young American manhood. While he is tall and handsome, there is nothing of the pretty boy about him, for virility is his outstanding characteristic."[10]

The attempt to develop an image for Reagan had much to do with the way the studio saw the public. Creating a male star in Hollywood, as critic Bosley Crowther observed, involved considerable trial and error. An actor had to be more than handsome. "Whereas an actress is largely exploited on the undisguised strength of her allure," he maintained, "too much or too obvious emphasis upon an actor's physical charm is malefic. The patrons invariably snicker at the blatantly romantic type as witness the embarrassing tribulations of Robert Taylor when he was just a 'pretty boy.'" Often the newcomer would start in a small role, supporting a star, "but in a part which provides that he must take a certain amount of rigorous abuse. . . . Anything namby-pamby, either in performance or characterization, will rule him out." For customers, "mettle" counted for more than "profile."[11]

Emphasis on the virile blended with that of an individual with "smashing fists . . . when guns are not handy!" Reagan was pleased not to be a "candidate for glamour roles" because he did not care to have his "hair curled." Warner Bros. let it be known that to prepare for fight scenes he had spent a couple of weeks of intensive training with the former junior welterweight world champion Mushy Callahan. Upon arrival on the set of *Code of the Secret Service,* and after shaking hands with director Noel Smith, he reportedly asked, "When do I fight – and whom?" Within an hour, the studio said, the actor "had five skinned knuckles, a bruised knee, and a lump half the size of an egg on his head." It was during the Bancroft series that Reagan's hearing difficulties began. On the set of *Secret Service of the Air* someone fired a blank .38 caliber cartridge too close to the actor's right ear, creating a permanent hearing problem.[12]

Part of Reagan's guise was that of a courageous pilot. The air hero, which blended man and machine, had been part of American folklore at least since Lindbergh's transatlantic flight in 1927.[13] Reagan appeared as a pilot in *Secret Service of the Air* and *Murder in the Air,* and in such films as *International Squadron* (1941) and *Desperate Journey* (1942). During World War II he made training films for the Army Air Corps. Although biographers maintain that he flew only once before World War II and had not liked the experience (he did not fly for years thereafter), publicity sought to give him credibility. For *Secret Service of the Air,* the studio announced that as a reserve officer he "made many training jumps from planes." Warner Bros. advised theater managers to post stills of Reagan in lobbies along with the Wright brothers, Eddie Rickenbacker, Lindbergh, and Amelia Earhart.[14]

The studio surrounded Bancroft with patriotic symbols. Films began or ended with views of national monuments such as the White House and the Capitol. They cut to the Treasury and the office of Bancroft's superior, decorated with an American flag and a picture of George Washington. Brass Bancroft fulfilled patriotic expectations, placing duty and honor above everything. He was willing to sacrifice his life. Interrupted during a vacation to take a dangerous assignment, he responded, "Aw, that's all right. That vacation was killing me anyway." In *Murder in the Air,* Brass learned his work would be extremely dangerous with no glory or monetary reward, and also that if it became necessary for him to break the law he would do so at his own risk. But as studio posters explained, agents "don't take the glory . . . they take the risks! Uncle Sam's daring undercover men get no medals . . . they get results."[15]

Bancroft's adventures resembled a genre, the action detective hero, that dated to the mid–nineteenth century. Such stories depended on constant and violent action. Warner Bros. announced that in *Secret Service of the Air,* Brass "sets off a cafe brawl that is an all-time high for the rough and tumble." *Film Daily* promised fans that *Code of the Secret Service* was a "rip-roaring thriller of bare-fisted walloping action," which had "the red meat that the thrill fans go for." The studio estimated that in the first three Bancroft pictures their hero averaged "one fight for every thousand feet of film."[16]

Of the many factors that went into the creation of Reagan's screen image, not the least of them was his acting technique. Warner Bros. admittedly selected Reagan for parts he seemed suited to play. His credibility owed much to his style, which was playing himself, or as one student has speculated, a "distillation of himself." Whereas Laurence Olivier sought to hide in an "alien character" and "avoid anything so embarrassing as self-representation," Reagan usually did not so much assume a mask or become someone different as he attempted to mold a part to fit his personality. Soon after he arrived in Hollywood, the playwright and actor Frank Craven told him: "If you're going to stand out, you've got to do things the way it comes naturally to you." Reagan considered this good counsel and the government agent films did not present a challenge. Studio literature noted in 1940 that Secret Service roles were parts that "Reagan feels he can do best and which he thoroughly enjoys playing."[17]

The Hays Office made sure that Reagan's characters operated in circumstances that fitted established patterns of behavior. None of his Secret Service pictures escaped alteration by the PCA. The violence troubled Breen, as it did in many Reagan films. Breen also worried about the depiction of drug trafficking and the punishment of criminals. *Secret Service of the Air* would have dealt with opium smuggling had Breen not intervened.[18] Treatment of criminals became an issue because the British Board of Film Censors preferred criminals captured and punished rather than killed. Breen agreed with this approach and attempted to push the storyline for *Code of the Secret Service* in this direction. The studio had to take his recommendation seriously if for no other reason than that during the late 1930s Britain was Warner Bros.' most important foreign market.[19] The Bancroft film that caused the greatest difficulty was *Smashing the Money Ring*. Originally entitled "Queer Money," it depicted a counterfeiting ring that operated behind prison walls. Breen rejected the script not only because it showed criminals with illegal weapons shooting prison guards but also because it called for a federal agent to help a prisoner escape. Warner Bros. revised the story and negotiated with the PCA for three months before receiving a certificate.[20]

Through such entertainment the studio established its anticrime credentials and Reagan emerged with an image as a crimefighter. Censors and government officials approved of the stand taken against lawlessness. The Warners also had wanted to sound an alarm about another danger facing America, but on this matter they found opposition from both Hays Office reviewers and Washington politicians.

And what was the principal threat that Brass Bancroft confronted? *Murder in the Air* suggested the peril. Raymond Schrock wrote the screenplay, completing the script on September 1, 1939, and made revisions during the next two weeks – the first days of World War II. This film took but twelve days to shoot and revealed Warner Bros.' concern not only with the representation of crime and federal agents, but with the international situation. It warned audiences about subversive activities.

The studio's worry about saboteurs was likely to have been Reagan's too, although his concern about sabotage probably did not originate in Hollywood. Interestingly, his first recollection of reading in 1916, at age five, involved newspaper accounts of sabotage. "I proudly recited," he recalled, "such events as the aftermath of a bomb that had exploded in San Francisco during a parade and the exciting details of the $40,000,000, two-dead Black Tom explosion in New Jersey."[21]

By the late 1930s the Roosevelt administration was apprehensive about Nazi spies. Fear had grown due to the deteriorating international situation in Europe and Hitler's persecution of the Jews. President Roosevelt ordered military intelligence and the FBI in 1936 to investigate subversion in the United States, and to pay attention to fascism and communism. A "Brown Scare occurred simultaneously with a muted Red Scare," one historian has observed, and it received notice in *Life,* the March of Time newsreels, newspaper columns by Drew Pearson, and radio broadcasts by Walter Winchell. In Hollywood, the Warners were already persuaded that the country faced grave danger. Even before *Confessions of a Nazi Spy* (1939), they had called attention to domestic fascism in their 1936 film, *Black Legion,* starring Humphrey Bogart.[22]

Riding a wave of public sentiment against spies, the studio publicized *Secret Service of the Air* and especially *Murder in the Air* as espionage films. Reagan's picture appeared with the publicity, reinforcing his image as a counterespionage agent. For *Secret Service of the Air,* Warner Bros. recommended that theater managers capitalize on the "recent spy scare in New York City," which had inspired numerous newspaper stories. A montage of headlines from those stories could be displayed in the lobby. "NOW," the studio announced, "you can see the amazing, inside story of how Uncle Sam's Secret Service smashes international air spies!" Such publicity could connect with newspaper stories that advertised the film and commented on "how to help your law enforcement agencies." The studio described *Murder in the Air* as having "many parallels in the daily headlines." It promised an account of a "fierce battle against the 'enemy within'" and called "its delineation of subversive activity gnawing at the roots of American democracy . . . extremely timely." It urged school essay contests such as, "What steps do you think our government must take to combat sabotage and spying?"[23]

Such sensationalism occurred amidst an already volatile atmosphere in which "belief that a Trojan horse was being readied by Hitler's supposed agents was not considered far-fetched." Suspicion abounded throughout the United States, especially as Nazi Germany conquered territories from Norway to France in the spring and summer of 1940. Whereas the FBI had investigated an average of 35 cases of possible espionage and sabotage in 1938, in 1939 it received 1,651 complaints, and apparently on one day in May 1940 it received almost 2,900. "'Fifth Column,'" the *New York World Telegram* noted, had become a "phrase on every tongue." These fears occasionally took on an anti-Semitic character as some Americans saw Jews among the potential traitors.[24]

Few individuals were more alarmed about fifth columnists than Harry Warner. He had become deeply troubled, even obsessed, by reports of subversion in the United States. In his impassioned speech before the American Legion in September 1938, he called on legionnaires to fight "unwelcome, un-American forces. . . . Drive them from their secret meeting places, destroy their insidious propaganda machines, drive out their 'Bunds' and their leagues, their clans and Black Legions, the Silver Shirts, the Black Shirts and the Dirty Shirts." So intense was his concern that it affected his health, and Jack instructed employees to stop talking with Harry about such matters.[25]

In May and June of 1940 fear of subversive activity reached high levels when Hitler's divisions slipped around the end of the Maginot line, overran Belgium, and nearly trapped the British at Dunkirk. Only an evacuation saved a third of a million British soldiers. In early June, shortly after Dunkirk, Harry Warner told six thousand assembled employees and their wives that the "danger is here." "Why, if they took the entire F.B.I. and brought them just to this one studio," he alleged, "they couldn't protect you." The only way peace could be achieved was to be "so strong in arms and defense that we can command peace." That ideal would never be realized "until we have ejected from our midst those enemies who are boring from within, who are undermining our national security and who are planning to sabotage our great country."[26]

The studio had already taken measures to safeguard security. At least twenty people at Warner Bros. were giving information to the Office of Naval Intelligence. The Warners hired several former policemen and detectives. Yet even with this network, Warner claimed, subversive literature had been distributed within his own gates, on automobiles parked in the studio's lot.[27]

Blaney F. Matthews, in a book entitled *The Specter of Sabotage* (1941), provided a sense of how fear affected Warner Bros. Reputedly a former FBI agent and chief investigator for the Los Angeles County district attorney, he was hired to manage studio security. In a dedication he described Harry, Jack, and Albert Warner as "courageous and far-seeing Americans, who were among the first of the Country's industrialists to recognize the menace of the

Fifth Column, and to engage in a relentless fight against subversive elements." He believed there were a "million Nazis in the Western Hemisphere ready for an invisible invasion of the United States." He warned that aliens were concentrated in industrial centers, that enemy agents would take advantage of "untold thousands" of foreign nationals who nursed deep hatreds for America, "even though they live and prosper here." Although Japanese-Americans were few in number and "their very racial characteristics" made it difficult for them to operate undetected as saboteurs, they could not be ignored. More dangerous were the "Quislings in our midst" who were "employed by enemy agents to assist in the consummation of the master plan to destroy America from within when the signal is flashed from Berlin to inaugurate Hitler's program of death, destruction, and terror."[28]

Although it was not always clear in the Bancroft films where the villains came from, the early scripts left little doubt. In *Secret Service of the Air,* among the illegal aliens being smuggled into the United States – some of whom were obviously saboteurs – Orientals were in evidence. In one draft of *Murder in the Air,* the film was to open with a "group of six rough looking men, obviously German and Russian types," tearing up railroad track in order to wreck an oncoming train. In the final script, however, the scene called for the men to be only of "mixed nationalities." What accounts for these script changes? Why did studios hold back even in 1939 and 1940 when they warned about spies and fascist aggression?[29]

Any studio that wanted to take a stand against Nazi Germany during the 1930s confronted resistance from censors in the Hays Office and abroad, from German-Americans, Irish-Americans, and others who opposed aiding Britain, and from isolationist senators who accused the industry of warmongering. If a studio were too obvious or heavy-handed, it risked censorship and condemnation. Breen usually rejected scripts that treated anti-Semitism or indicted Hitler on grounds they were "provocative and inflammatory" and would alienate audiences.[30]

Why did the Hays Office react this way? One explanation was economic. The movie industry depended on revenues it received from foreign distribution, and treatment of Hitler and fascism usually provoked controversy in Europe. Even the British Board of Film Censors rejected anti-Nazi films until after the outbreak of war with Germany in September 1939. Sensitive to opinion abroad and eager to protect the industry's markets there, the PCA tried to anticipate the reactions of foreign censors.[31]

Anxieties about anti-Nazi or pro-preparedness films were also grounded in a sense that American opinion was unpredictable during this period. As late as 1940 and 1941, audience analyses indicated reactions of theatergoers to war-related topics were "extremely fluid." It was difficult to predict what changes might occur between the time a studio decided to make a movie and when it was released. The Audience Research Institute at Princeton, N.J., found that the public wanted films about the war, but it also found opinion

too unstable to predict if studios could "perform a patriotic service by man-
ufacturing partisan pictures."[32]

Even after acknowledging the legitimate worries of those who counseled
the industry during a volatile time, questions still arise as to whether members of the Hays Office were either anti-Semitic or profascist and, if so, to
what extent. Some censors were unenthusiastic about the antifascist pictures
produced by Warner Bros. and other studios. As late as 1936, Hays himself
believed that Mussolini had done "constructive things" for his country and
that the Italian dictator did not intend to export fascism. At least one person
on Breen's staff remained impressed by Hitler's accomplishments in early
1939. Before he became head of the PCA, Breen bluntly criticized Hollywood Jews in correspondence with other Catholics.[33] He discouraged such
anti-Hitler films as *The Mad Dog of Europe* (1936), and when the German
consul in Los Angeles objected to production of Warner Bros.' *Confessions
of a Nazi Spy* and Charlie Chaplin's anti-Hitler film, *The Great Dictator,* he
urged reconsideration. Breen objected to the anti-Hitler tone of the script for
Warner Bros.' *Underground* (1941) and apparently succeeded in delaying
production more than a year.[34]

To note Breen's attitude is not to argue that he or the PCA approved
Hitler's anti-Semitic policies, especially once the consequences of Nazism
became obvious. He did, in fact, become involved in the industry's antifascist
movement during the late 1930s. Nor was he hostile to all "preparedness"
films. If one looks at PCA files for movies singled out as prowar propaganda
by Senator D. Worth Clark's subcommittee in September 1941, one finds
that Breen had few objections to the political themes in most of them.[35]

It was in the midst of such confusion that *Murder in the Air* opened in New
York and Hollywood in mid-July 1940. In an early draft of Schrock's story,
an opening scene (later cut) showed a map of Europe with territory dominated by the Rome–Berlin Axis. This sequence cut to stock shots of goose-
stepping Nazis, Mussolini's troops, a Soviet military parade in Red Square,
and gathering troops in Britain, France, and Poland. The voice of the Secret
Service chief accompanied these scenes and said that "once again the world
was rushing headlong into a maelstrom of death and destruction, which
would wipe civilization from the face of the earth." Then came scenes of a
peaceful United States: "While in the United States, a peace loving nation
was going about its daily pursuits, feeling secure in its traditional policy of
isolation from foreign quarrels and entanglements . . . there was destined to
occur a number of unrelated and unexplainable incidents which were to
arouse suspicions of SABOTAGE – and the presence in this country of INTER-
NATIONAL TERRORISTS." Explosions and fires followed, with the narrator
saying that "paid agents of destruction were seeking to paralyze industry,
obstruct commerce and destroy natural resources. . . . The failure of tested
machinery to properly function gave rise to the belief that alien saboteurs

were also infesting our airplane and ammunition factories, even our Navy Yards, seeking to cripple our program for National Defense."[36]

Much of this opening disappeared in the final print. The film, however, did start with fires and explosions, followed by headlines that conveyed urgency: "Government Believes Dock Fire Work of Saboteurs!" "Spies Paralyze Industry Claim Secret Service," and "President Plans Nationwide Drive of Spies and Saboteurs."

Murder in the Air centered around "the most terrifying weapon ever invented," one that discharged electrical beams capable of stopping internal combustion engines. It could knock down planes within four miles. According to the movie, it was the ultimate instrument of war.[37]

The Inertia Projector story begins with the Rice Committee – modeled after the House Committee on Un-American Activities, then chaired by Representative Martin Dies – investigating espionage. Members question Joe Garvey, who with his thin mustache, well-tailored clothes, and cosmopolitan manner projects the archetypal image of the late-1930s screen villain. Part of his villainy lies in an attempt to keep the United States out of war. He speaks in a noticeable accent and heads an allegedly patriotic society "to preserve American neutrality at any cost." The Rice Committee suspects him of promoting labor unrest and industrial sabotage. He is possibly anticapitalist, as well. The committee has difficulty pinning anything on Garvey, although it suspects a connection with Federal Enemy Number 1, Steve Swenko, the most dangerous saboteur in the United States. A break comes when a train wreck kills a hobo carrying $50,000. Suspecting the money is counterfeit, authorities call in Treasury agents Bancroft and Waters, who discover that the hobo was the infamous criminal, and was on his way to Los Angeles with a coded letter of introduction to Garvey. A tattoo identifies him as part of an international spy ring.[38]

On orders from Saxby, his superior, Brass assumes Swenko's identity and goes on to meet Garvey. Garvey plans to ruin a test of the Inertia Projector aboard the dirigible *Mason* (the name was similar to the *Macon*, a Navy dirigible that crashed off the California coast near Point Sur in February 1935). On board the *Mason* are the projector's inventor, George Hayden, and Dr. Burton Finchley, chairman of a League of Nations Committee to Outlaw War. Here Brass makes contact with Garvey's man Rumford, who is Finchley's secretary. Before Brass can carry out his mission, a powerful storm forces the *Mason* into the Pacific (it was said that producer Bryan Foy liked to have his adventures in a strong wind). Although Rumford escapes with blueprints for the weapon, Brass saves the Inertia Projector and later, with the mechanism mounted on a plane, helps shoot down the craft carrying Garvey and Rumford as they attempt to flee. With Brass at the plane's controls and the projector's inventor aiming the weapon, Brass shouts: "All right, Hayden – focus that Inertia Projector on 'em and let 'em have it!"[39]

The original script called for Finchley to be undersecretary to the British war minister, and for saboteurs to blow up the Panama Canal while Finchley watched maneuvers of the combined U.S. Atlantic and Pacific fleets. In this first version the Inertia Projector appeared almost as an afterthought. In the final print, Warner Bros. hailed the weapon as "the greatest peace argument ever invented," an instrument for peaceful ends, the "hope and prayer of all thinking people regardless of race, creed, or government." The idea undoubtedly owed much to popular culture of the time, and Warner publicity acknowledged that there had been considerable speculation on the radio and in comic strips about the possibility of a death ray device.[40]

Indeed, by 1940 death rays or ray guns were common in popular entertainment. Orson Welles's radio dramatization of H. G. Wells's *War of the Worlds* in 1938 had told of Martians using such weapons. Ray weapons appeared in more than twenty films and movie serials during the 1930s including those of Flash Gordon, Buck Rogers, and Dick Tracy, and in Gene Autry's *Phantom Empire* (1935), and *The Invisible Ray* (1936) starring Boris Karloff and Bela Lugosi. In some films the ray was used against airplane bombers, a much-dreaded menace of the time. John Wayne appeared in *Shadow of the Eagle* (1932), the first science fiction talking serial, playing an aviator opposing an enemy who had invented an antiaircraft ray gun. Laurence Olivier starred in a British film, *Q Planes* (1939) (released in the United States as *Clouds Over Europe*), in which a ray device stopped airplane engines in midair, an effect similar to that of the Inertia Projector.[41]

The fascination with death rays had a foundation in reality. Rumor circulated in Europe and the United States in 1935 that the inventor of the wireless, Guglielmo Marconi, was experimenting with an electromagnetic beam that could stop automobile and airplane engines. The *New York Times* reported that Marconi's invention had been tested by the Italian military in Ethiopia. Stories suggested that the Germans had developed a death ray that could be used against aircraft four miles away. As the British became fearful of Hitler's air superiority, Winston Churchill and his adviser Frederick Lindemann searched for ways to protect Britain from air raids. One device considered in early 1935 would have released a "sufficiently strong beam of electromagnetic waves which would heat up anything in their path to the point where living tissue would be destroyed or bombs automatically exploded." A few years later British authorities worried that Hitler had devised such a weapon. Some believed German television towers could emit transmissions to "paralyse internal combustion engines."[42]

Marconi failed to build his death ray – he died in 1937 – and British scientists, whose research ultimately produced radar, rejected the death ray as impractical. But the media kept the dream alive. The Olivier movie mentioned Marconi as creator of the weapon. Reagan in *Murder in the Air* described the Inertia Projector as a "device for throwing electrical waves capable of paralyzing alternate and direct current at their source. Do you remember," he asked his sidekick Gabby, "that news story that broke some time ago and then was hushed up about the amateur radio operator . . . who was stopping automobiles . . . for miles around with some sort of radio beam? Well, a large-scale model of that device has been installed on the dirigible." Throughout World War II, a British diplomatic officer in Los Angeles recalled, his office was besieged with ideas for ray weapons. "These inventors," he wrote, "could not be dismissed as lightly as their contrivances seemed to justify as we had been asked by the Inventions Board in Washington to pass on to them all but the most obviously insane ideas."[43]

Warner Bros. played up the idea: "If during a war you invented a death ray machine, would you turn the plans over to the government even though it meant death for hundreds of people?" They invited the public to "join *Ronald Reagan* battling 20,000 unseen enemies to protect its amazing secret!" They promised "the most deadly weapon ever known to man . . . in action!" The film was translated, shown abroad, and apparently revived for television during the late 1950s.[44]

Reagan afterward observed that these films made him the "Errol Flynn of the B's. I was as brave as Errol," he said, tongue in cheek, "but in a low-budget fashion." So rushed were the scripts that he, director Smith, Eddie Foy, Jr., and the latter's brother, Charlie, would sometimes rewrite them on the set to plug the most obvious inconsistencies.[45] Reviewers panned the stories as "uninspired," although *Variety* noted that *Murder in the Air* was "strong on novelty in the Buck Rogers vein."[46]

While reviewers did not care for the "hocus-pocus" of the Secret Service films, they usually liked Reagan's portrayal of a "heroic youngster" and the way he played Bancroft with "vigorous conviction," facing danger "with an air of 'think nothing of it.'" They approved his "charm and vitality" and his "ingratiating efforts." Here were films, the *New York Tribune* observed, with a "dashing hero" for "two-fisted he-men." The actor had struck a chord with the public. His career was on the rise. By 1941 only Flynn's fan mail surpassed his own at Warner Bros.[47]

The historical significance of these films must be measured against the Warners' concern about national security. After one considers the factors that go into creating a motion picture – economics, dispositions of writers and directors and producers, wishes of owners – such films surely revealed a studio attuned to politics. Whatever Reagan's political ideas in 1938 and 1939, his early motion picture career was part of an effort to promote respect for law and order, enhance the public's respect for government agents and the House Committee on Un-American Activities, and to alert people to subversive activities. On these issues, Reagan's character in the Bancroft films was remarkably consistent with positions taken by the real-life Reagan during his post–World War II career.

Did these events later incline Reagan as president to accept proposals for the Strategic Defense Initiative? It would not be the first time that the creations of science fiction moved toward fact. But this is speculation and one should be careful about projecting events from 1939–40. Too often when the past looks to the present its meaning distorts, if not disappears. Innumerable factors, many of which still lie hidden, touched Reagan's life in the more than forty years between *Murder in the Air* and his presidency. Still, Reagan made *Murder in the Air* when fears about Fifth Column activity in America were widespread, when death rays had become a staple of science fiction, and when rumors had circulated that such rays were a reality and their possibilities for defense intrigued some leaders. Indeed, the future president helped to dramatize that such a weapon, an instrument that would make America impregnable, would help secure world peace.

7

LESSONS FROM THE PAST

Our real home is in the past, in the silent place of memory – itself a shadow, and ourselves but shadows moving amid the uncertain ghosts of imperfectly remembered events.[1]

I don't give . . . a damn about "strict historical accuracy" if it hamstrings a story.

Writer Robert Buckner

Ronald Reagan appeared in two films with historic themes during 1940, and they helped make him a star. The better-known of these was *Knute Rockne – All American,* in which he played the ill-fated football great George Gipp. It was in this picture that Reagan as the dying Gipp uttered his well-known line, "Win one for the Gipper." The other movie, perhaps less remembered, was *Santa Fe Trail,* in which he portrayed military leader George Custer. What both pictures had in common was that they presented values out of the American past to fortify the United States at a time when the country was drifting toward the war then enveloping Europe. The Warners believed the nation's survival was in danger, and they used their studio production, including Reagan's films, to promote national unity, patriotism, and military service, and to warn about foreign aggression.[2]

Using the past to speak to the present was not new, of course. The tactic seemed attractive, given the unpredictable nature of public opinion and the opposition of censors. The Warners denied they were producing propaganda. They argued – and probably believed – that history was capable of being re-created on film "realistically and accurately." When Harry testified before the Senate subcommittee that investigated Hollywood warmongering in 1941 he said that the "only sin of which Warner Bros. is guilty is that of accurately recording on the screen the world as it is or as it has been."[3]

But re-creating the "world as it is or as it has been" is difficult under the best of circumstances and nearly impossible in a Hollywood studio. If the

Warners set the tone for their movies, they did not completely control the resultant historical interpretation; other people intervened, including producers, directors, writers, and actors. Pressure came from families and institutions whose stories were being told, from censors, and from likely audience reaction. In all of Reagan's films – indeed on the set of any picture – before the studio projected an interpretation of history, it had to reach agreement among many forces.

Reagan, one may speculate, absorbed something about history on the sets of these two films. He obtained information about the lives of the characters, to be sure, but more important, he was exposed to a way of relating the past to the present. This was a history that emphasized ambience, myth, and moral instruction, but which often showed less regard for facts.

Many years later in 1981, when Reagan was president, he returned to Notre Dame to deliver the commencement address and recalled his role in *Knute Rockne – All American*. He wanted to enlist the 1981 graduates in a cause that would "transcend communism." The film, he said, had been about more than an athlete in a "uniquely American" sport, about more than a coach who taught young men "how to play a game." It was about values, Reagan said. Rockne's greatness lay in the belief that the "noblest work of man was molding the character of man." He was a symbol of American virtues.[4]

Reagan's presidential speech revealed that he knew a good deal about the origins of the Rockne film more than forty years earlier. The Warners and Notre Dame officials had had political purposes in mind. Similarly, in 1940 the studio had hoped *Santa Fe Trail*, with its depiction of military life as glamorous and exciting, would deliver a message, too.

Knute Rockne – All American treated such themes as the plight of immigrants, assimilation into a new society, and the importance of work. In their attempt to rekindle national pride the Warners urged audiences not to think of themselves as members of ethnic, racial, or religious groups but as Americans. The movie tried to provide values around which everyone – especially the nation's youth – could unite. It portrayed Rockne as an example of the "finest ideals of courage, character and sportsmanship for all the world." It tried to show a "great and vital force in molding the spirit of modern America." The screen Rockne testified to success through work and dedication to the American way. The studio promoted a "morale-boosting . . . Americanism."[5]

The film begins with the Rockne family leaving Norway to join "millions like themselves, simple, hard-working people from the old countries, following the new road of equality." They settle in the "Great Melting-Pot of Chicago" where Knute learns the "most wonderful game in the world." The sport became important to assimilation. "Talk American," Knute urges his father. "We're all Americans now – especially me. I'm left end." As the film reveals Rockne's youth, it intersperses a montage of patriotic symbols – pictures of the Statue of Liberty and of George Washington. A job in a post office underscores commitment to work. Upon arrival at Notre Dame, Rockne explains to his roommate that he has spent six years earning money to go to college.

The film not only presented a philosophy of sport and education, but also attempted to promote values. Rockne expects his players to maintain grades. "The Notre Dame system," he says, is "based on teamwork which is a combination of self-sacrifice, brains, and sweat. And the brains come first." So, too, does winning. Squads he coaches are made up of a spectrum of young men – a "team of all nations," Reagan called them – unified by a goal of winning.[6]

At the picture's climax, an investigation has opened into charges of professionalism in college athletics. Not long before the real Rockne's death in 1931, the Carnegie Foundation probed college athletics and issued a report of scandal. The movie, however, stressed the positive qualities of football. Rockne testified before the investigating panel, as did other well-known coaches including Alonzo Stagg, Howard Jones, William (Bill) Spaulding, and Pop Warner. Warner Bros. portrayed Rockne as an honorable man, dedicated to family and football. The studio establishes his honesty in the picture when he throws a gambler out of his office. "This is one game that is clean and it's going to stay clean," he says within earshot of reporters.[7]

Rockne's testimony affords opportunity for a theory of education compatible with what the Warners believed Americans needed in 1940. It extolls a physically and morally vigorous life. Football is "more than merely helpful to boys," Rockne speculates. It, and other such games, were an "absolute necessity to the nation's best interests." Limiting an education "to books, classrooms and laboratories," he argues, would give "education too narrow a meaning for modern times." The fitness of youth is at stake. "The most dangerous thing in American life today is we're getting soft, inside and out," the Warner Bros.' Rockne says. "We're losing that forceful heritage of mind and body that was once our most precious possession."

The movie implicitly indicts pacifism and underscores the difference between America and the Old World. Sports such as football, Rockne continues, expunge the "flaccid philosophy" that makes men ill prepared to meet the perils of the real world. Athletics build "courage, initiative, tolerance, and persistence, without which the most educated brain of man is not worth very much." All "red-blooded" young men in no matter what country were "filled with what we might call the natural spirit of combat," Rockne explains. "In many parts of Europe and elsewhere in the world this spirit manifests itself in continuous wars and revolutions." But, he argues, "we have tried to make competitive sports act as a safer outlet for this spirit of combat and I think we've succeeded."[8]

The gospel of sports as a developer of character was not new to Reagan.

He had heard it from high school days. He had linked football to the biblical story of spiritual anguish found in Mark 14:32–42. His story about "Gethsemane" in the high school yearbook warned of the perils of being a quitter. It is likely that Reagan's work as a sports reporter in Des Moines reinforced ideas about the relation between sports and character.[9]

Moreover, Reagan had long admired Gipp and as a radio announcer had extolled his exploits. He relished the opportunity to play the all-American. When the movie premiered in South Bend in early October, the film's stars paid solemn homage to their characters. No one, the *South Bend Tribune* reported, was "more sincere" than the young "Donald" Reagan. With "his voice about to break," Reagan told about playing football at a small school in Illinois, and then how later, as a sports announcer, he had read a poem that had been written in tribute to Gipp. "I ask your charity when you see the picture," he requested. "I did my best and I wanted so much to do better. There are other actors who could have done better, but none wanted to do the part more than I."[10]

Reagan had almost missed the role. He received a screen test only after he managed to produce a photograph of himself in football uniform, and even then Warner Bros. tested Dennis Morgan. Screenwriter Robert Buckner wanted a comparatively unknown actor named Donald Woods. What the part required, he argued, was "a clean-cut, likable face" but "certainly not a juvenile matinee idol." Judging from performance, he doubted that Reagan could play Gipp, whom he described as "quiet, reserved, casual, laconic, relaxed." Critics who were football fans but unaware Reagan had been a lineman at Dixon and Eureka asked why someone without athletic experience had been chosen.[11]

Reagan's Gipp is a self-effacing individual who eschews publicity. He loves children. If Gipp is aloof – "I don't like people to get too close to me," he explains to the coach's wife – teammates respect his ability. Reagan's Gipp endorses Rockne's leadership: "Rock's the rare one, not me," because "he's given us something they don't teach in school, something clean and strong inside – not just courage but a right way of living that none of us will ever forget."[12]

The performance lay not only in lines Reagan delivered but in visual image. Director Lloyd Bacon and executive producer Hal Wallis refined Reagan's scenes. Wallis liked low camera angles that captured background clouds in the football frames. He urged more closeups and asked Bacon to give the actor's scenes with Bonnie Rockne more intimacy.[13]

The movie also owed much to collaboration between Buckner, Notre Dame officials, and the coach's widow, Bonnie. Buckner was an amateur historian and also wrote the screenplay for *Santa Fe Trail,* in addition to other Warner Bros. films. He had been a sports writer and had known Rockne slightly. Writing about the coach was a "labor of love." He saw a hero, a "man of action with ideals." He did not try for a psychological profile

or to draw Rockne "warts and all." He preferred a straightforward dramatization that emphasized the high points and captured what he believed was
the "full flavor" of Rockne's life.[14]

Constructing a movie version raised questions about what to include. All
histories abridge the past, but abridgment became particularly important in a
film. Buckner found it necessary to alter the record to make a more forceful
story. When he completed his work it ran seventy-seven pages, longer than
most studio treatments of historical figures. It became necessary to rearrange
information "into more compact form." Such changes did not make the
movie's scenes "fictional in a true sense," but he admitted they would "not be
recognizable to readers who come upon them cold."[15]

Buckner's fictionalization of episodes in Rockne's life, and his willingness
to ignore aspects of the coach's career that would cast the subject in an
unfavorable light, affected the movie. Rockne's friend, Father Callahan
(played by Donald Crisp), became a composite of two real priests, Father
John J. Cavanaugh and Father Charles O'Donnell. Cavanaugh had been
close to the coach, and O'Donnell spoke at Rockne's funeral. Buckner
wanted the screen version of Cavanaugh to deliver the funeral oration, to
avoid confusing audiences. Mrs. Rockne objected and a compromise was
reached with the creation of Father Callahan. Rockne's testimony before
American educational leaders was to be the climax of the picture, in which
Rockne would set out his philosophy of education. An adversarial relation
between Rockne and the panel, in Buckner's view, added an edge to the story.
The problem, he recognized, was that the scene was static. He gave Rockne
dialogue "taken entirely from his own statements, but at various times in his
life." In doing this both the letter and spirit of the scene remained "literally
true," Buckner argued.[16]

More serious were the omissions. The studio molded Rockne and Gipp
into models for the young, and ignored or glossed unflattering traits. The real
Gipp often came late to practice, rarely took part in scrimmage, and seldom
was in top physical condition. He cut classes, liked to gamble, and was
removed from the university for several weeks in 1919. But to show Gipp's
gambling, Buckner thought, would be in "questionable taste."[17]

Buckner chose to ignore some of Rockne's business affairs, as well. Rockne
had delivered "inspirational" speeches to Graham-Paige Motor Car Company dealers in 1928. The following year he signed the first of three personal
service contracts with the Studebaker Company. Buckner considered this
aspect of Rockne's life of "very little dramatic interest." It was "the one
phase of Rockne's life" that Buckner thought detracted from Rockne's stature. He regarded Rockne's exploitation of fame a "minor facet" of his
account. To "lay too strong an emphasis on the fact that he commercialized
his position to make big money," would not be a "very good ideology for our
story," Buckner said.[18]

Buckner discovered allies who virtually assured favorable treatment of his heroes. Warner Bros. signed an agreement giving Notre Dame and Mrs. Rockne the right of approval over the script. The agreement stipulated that the film had "to conform to the standards, dignity, decorum, truth and traditions of the school," and that the university's name could not appear in the title and was to be used only where "absolutely essential because of the individual relationship between the University and Rockne." Notre Dame could not appear as a football school or "otherwise a wealthy institution." Advertising was to emphasize "Rockne's interest in the youth of the nation and his ideals and . . . the true spiritual ideals and philosophy of education taught at Notre Dame."[19]

Mrs. Rockne acted through her lawyers and was on the set each day. She suggested many changes, although most were minor and dealt with inaccuracies. She insisted that Rockne's intellectual abilities be stressed and was disappointed when the picture appeared more of a football movie than originally contemplated. Before she would approve the script, the film Rockne had to become not only a "football coach and a great player, but a man of education and extraordinary memory," whose "ability to teach" and "his influence on students in the classroom was equally as great as his influence on the field." Buckner rewrote and added scenes to emphasize Rockne's intelligence.[20]

The university similarly influenced the film; indeed, the movie was in a real sense a Catholic picture. Buckner had wanted James Cagney to play Rockne, and the studio would have been happy with that choice because Cagney's box-office appeal in early 1940, many believed, was much greater than O'Brien's. But Cagney had antagonized the church not only with screen roles as a gangster but also by his outspoken opposition to the forces of General Francisco Franco during the Spanish Civil War. Between 1936 and 1939, Franco – backed by a powerful coalition of Roman Catholics, industrialists, and landowners – had overthrown the liberal government in Madrid. Many theatergoers believed Cagney a Communist. He had alienated so many Catholics that Notre Dame officials warned Warner Bros. they would not risk their reputation by letting Cagney have the part. The university preferred Spencer Tracy, perhaps the top box office draw in the country, and failing him, O'Brien. Warner Bros. tried to get Tracy, then under contract to MGM, but he was not available. O'Brien's performances as a priest had pleased Notre Dame alumni and officials who considered him a "family man of high character." Harry and Jack Warner were in no mood to cross the church, which had mobilized millions of its followers in the Legion of Decency. "You cannot make a picture of this kind and have the Catholic Church fight you," Harry wrote Wallis in early August 1939. "I can understand their point of view and you should understand it likewise."[21]

The premier in South Bend, October 4 and 5, 1940, illustrated how sports, radio, film, and patriotism could come together. Warner Bros. invested heavily in the opening. It persuaded Indiana Governor M. Clifford Townsend to

declare a Knute Rockne Week. Several states followed with similar procla-
mations. It spent $50,000 engaging special trains to bring in reporters,
celebrities, and movie officials. Reagan, Jane Wyman, and the Pat O'Brien
family were on hand. So were Rudy Vallee, Bob Hope, and Franklin D.
Roosevelt, Jr., representing his father. Tens of thousands of people doubled
and perhaps tripled South Bend's population. Using the Mutual radio hookup, alumni clubs put on fifty dinners simultaneously with Hope as master of
ceremonies. Kate Smith brought to South Bend her weekly radio program:
before several thousand people in the auditorium of John Adams High
School, Reagan and O'Brien reenacted scenes from the film that the Columbia network carried coast-to-coast. Reagan, the *South Bend Tribune* recounted, "said his lines from memory and the entire performance held the
. . . audience enthralled." Later Smith, assisted by the Notre Dame Glee
Club, sang "God Bless America."[22]

On Saturday, Reagan, O'Brien, and other members of the cast attended
ceremonies at Rockne's grave. The entourage went to Notre Dame's game
against the College of the Pacific, then coached by Alonzo Stagg. Reagan
broadcast one quarter of the contest. During halftime, before a crowd of
55,000 people and a radio audience of perhaps millions, Notre Dame's band
played "Ave Maria" as a skywriting plane spelled out "Rockne."[23]

Reagan later called his part in *Knute Rockne – All American* the "role I
liked best." It served as a "springboard" into better films, away from the
low-budget B movies. The picture's message "that all of us need so much
today: the warning that all of us must harden ourselves morally, physically,
and intellectually," supplemented Warner Bros. campaign for national preparedness. The movie surely was along the lines of what Will Hays had urged
in June 1939, when, speaking at the World's Fair, he called for a revival of the
American spirit. It was "that spirit, solemn and consecrated," he said, that
would move the United States "forward to new heights of progress and
prosperity without sacrificing the principles of individual freedom that made
us a great nation."[24]

★★★

Santa Fe Trail was the only film set in the Old West that Reagan made for
Warner Bros. He played the young George Custer, then still an American folk
hero. Reagan admired military heroes and enjoyed making outdoor pictures;
he liked this movie because it was about the frontier. *Santa Fe Trail* carried a
message to audiences, this time about honor and duty. There were other
themes, too, dear to producers, actors, and especially screenwriter Robert
Buckner.[25]

Buckner's status at the studio was far from secure in 1940, but as with
Knute Rockne he managed to leave a mark on *Santa Fe Trail*. Most writers
generally "swallowed their pride and rolled with the punches." Wilson
Mizner compared working for Warner Bros. to having intercourse with a

porcupine: "It's a hundred pricks against one," he said. Jack Warner apparently distrusted writers and reputedly could not fathom how "they could remain chained to their typewriters." That Buckner had been able to convey so much of his interpretation of Rockne was remarkable in an industry where authors became mere employees producing a commodity bought and sold on an open market.[26]

Of Scottish and English descent, Buckner's family had been prominent in the South since before the American Revolution. Born in 1906, he grew up on a plantation near Richmond, Va. He planned to become a physician and spent three years at the University of Virginia in a premedical program, where he also took courses in American history and edited the student publication, *Virginia Reel*. Traveling to Europe, he received a Bachelor of Science degree from Edinburgh University and did graduate work there in medicine. Before coming to Warner Bros. he had been a scenarist for Columbia Studios, and before that a correspondent for the *London Daily Mail* and the *New York World*. As a journalist with the *Mail*, he had traveled to the USSR and Africa. He had contributed fiction to such British publications as *Pearson's, Punch,* and *Bystander*.[27]

Buckner wrote more than fifty screenplays, at least eighty-five short stories, and produced two dozen movies during his career. He had been attracted to Rockne, one might speculate, because of the coach's ideas of honor, manliness, and physical fitness. Earlier, Warner Bros. had hired Buckner to work on another Reagan movie, *Brother Rat,* because he had briefly attended Virginia Military Institute. Later, he produced the controversial Warner Bros. film *Mission to Moscow* (1943).[28]

Set in pre–Civil War Kansas, *Santa Fe Trail* was one of three western screenplays Buckner wrote during this period. Several stories ran through the picture, one of which was the struggle to construct the Santa Fe Railroad across the frontier. That idea became lost, however, in a larger plot about pursuit of the abolitionist leader John Brown in the Kansas Territory.[29] The picture paraded an array of historical figures. In addition to Custer (played by Reagan) and Brown (Raymond Massey), it included Jefferson Davis, as well as generals Robert E. Lee, James Longstreet, and Philip Sheridan. It starred Errol Flynn as Jeb Stuart, and Olivia De Havilland as the daughter of Cyrus K. Halliday, founder and first president of the Santa Fe Railroad. The picture also featured Van Heflin as Carl Raider. Reagan's Custer was a supporting role to Flynn's Jeb Stuart.

The picture was riddled with historical inaccuracies. Buckner and others at the studio were more interested in capturing the "spirit" of the old West than in faithfully reproducing the past. Buckner had read several books about the West and an assistant, Elaine Wilmont, read others, but they missed or ignored a great deal of history. In the film, Stuart, Custer, Sheridan, and Longstreet are all shown graduating from the West Point class of 1854 (the year Stuart graduated) when, in fact, their graduations were spread over almost twenty years. When questions arose about early versions of the script connecting Henry Ward Beecher with Brown at Harpers Ferry, the studio dropped Beecher. Warner Bros.' publicity implied that Buckner's characterization of Brown was not unlike the one in Leonard Ehrlich's *God's Angry Man,* which attributed Brown's failure to fanaticism. Such disclaimers did not appease Brown's descendants, including a granddaughter, Nell Brown Groves, who brought suit against the studio.[30]

Buckner wanted to recreate only the flavor of the frontier. "I don't give . . . a damn about 'strict historical accuracy,'" he confided to Wallis, "if it hamstrings a story." What was required to make a hit movie was "eight parts entertainment to two parts fact." The Hungarian-born director Michael Curtiz, who had directed *Casablanca, Yankee Doodle Dandy, This Is the Army, Dodge City,* and *Charge of the Light Brigade,* expressed the matter perhaps more colorfully. "Vell, Jock," he once told Warner, "the scenario isn't the exact truth but ve haff the facts to prove it."[31]

Buckner's story, which commented on military honor and abolitionism, was another appeal for national unity. *Santa Fe Trail* opens with cadets at West Point, where Commandant Robert E. Lee is "already building for the defense of the newly won nation in a new world." It shows Heflin's Raider as a Brown supporter and a divisive presence among Stuart, Custer, and the others. It treats Brown and his cause as traitorous. In the barracks, with Stuart and Custer listening, Raider quotes Brown:

The breaking up of the American Union as it now exists is the basis of my plan. And that destruction must be made upon the issue of Negro slavery and on no other. . . . This object is vast in its compass, terrifying in its prospects, but sublime and beautiful in its issue. A life devoted to it would be nobly spent or sacrificed. If the federal government and its constitution are opposed to my way of thinking the fault is not mine but theirs and I shall continue to oppose them with every means and every weapon at my disposal.

Brown's cause established, Raider assures Stuart and others he has taken a lot of grief from "Southern snobs," and that the time is approaching when the "rest of us are going to wipe you and your kind off the face of the earth." The importance of a code of honor then appears, as cadets fight over Raider's words. Brought before Lee, Stuart and Custer decline to inform on Raider, each accepting responsibility.[32]

The movie emphasizes duty, honor, and country. Lee expels Raider, who joins forces with Brown. He gives Stuart and Custer the most dangerous assignments, but for the characters played by Flynn and Reagan, such assignments could hardly have been punishment. They are ecstatic to learn they will go to Kansas, where combat, excitement, and promotion await. At graduation Jefferson Davis (played by Erville Alderson) addresses the cadets about unity and responsibility. "Just eighty years ago we were fighting desperately for our freedom and we're still fighting to keep it," he says. "We are not yet a wealthy nation except in spirit. And that unity of spirit is our greatest strength. You men have but one duty, one alone, America. With your unswerving loyalty and the grace of God our nation shall have no fears for the future. And your lives will have been spent in the noblest of all causes, the defense of the rights of man."33

The rest of *Santa Fe Trail* revolves around efforts by Stuart and Custer to bring Brown to justice. The movie shows Brown as not only deranged but deceitful. He smuggles weapons into Kansas in crates marked "Bibles." His sons become casualties to fanaticism. His capture at Harpers Ferry occurs partly as a result of information provided by Raider, who too late realizes his error in supporting the abolitionist.

Santa Fe Trail uses history in other ways. The story celebrates the pioneering and entrepreneurial spirit of the frontier. De Havilland's character's father is building the Santa Fe, and Brown imperils this "bright steel highway," with its "fingers of progress." After Brown's capture and execution, the movie attempts to end on an upbeat note: Flynn and De Havilland head west to complete the railroad.

The Warners' ideas about Americanism associated progress with a pioneering spirit and the growth of business. Harry Warner had expressed these ideas in 1937, saying, "America was carved out of the wilderness by initiative – an initiative forged in lonely pioneer fires and tempered on the expanding hearths of industry." Publicity took the form of feature stories and full-page ads in newspapers hailing the Santa Fe as the "most romantic of all old trails." It credited the railroad with transforming the Southwest from a "sage-studded wasteland" into a "thriving" region with rich agricultural, industrial, and leisure opportunities. Little wonder that when the studio decided to promote this movie with an extravaganza, engaging two trains with stars and other passengers to travel to New Mexico, the Santa Fe Railway paid half the cost.34

The film also offered an interpretation of Brown and abolitionism. Buckner insisted that *Santa Fe Trail* had to be written by a "native Southerner." His scenario makes Brown the villain. Blacks, again, are wide-eyed, simple-minded Sambos. The issue of freedom all but disappears. The movie labels Palmyra, part of the underground railroad for slaves, the "cancer of Kansas," and a former slave tells Stuart, "Shuckins, if this here Kansas is freedom, then I ain't got no use for it."35

Buckner did agree, apparently after pressure from director Curtiz and studio executive Robert Fellows, to make Reagan's character, Custer, sympathetic to Brown's cause. The studio made the change to add tension between Custer and Stuart. But the picture emphasized Southern heroes, the reasonableness of opposition to Brown. Publicity proclaimed that if Lincoln would end slavery "by due process of law," Brown attempted to end it "by violence." Stuart knew "the truth" of slavery better than Brown. Warner Bros. tried to promote the movie among schoolchildren by encouraging an essay contest in which Stuart and Brown held an imaginary conversation. What would Brown, who insisted that "the sins of the nation can be wiped out only by the shedding of blood," have said "to his enemies represented by an officer in the United States Army? . . . On his side is the strength of his feeling against slavery. On the side of Jeb Stuart is law and order, and his duty as an officer in the United States Army."[36]

The studio decided on the upbeat ending, cutting a scene that would have shown Brown's execution. "*We must see the end of John Brown,*" Buckner complained in an effort to keep the scene. At the end of Brown's hanging, audiences did hear Lee (played by Moroni Olsen) proclaim, "And so perish all such enemies of the Union – all such foes of the human race."[37]

Warner Bros. intended another, perhaps more subtle message, that involved Raymond Massey's portrayal of Brown as a maniacal leader so convinced of his cause he was willing to sacrifice family, union, anything in his way. "We recognize no law but the law of God," Brown tells his son in the movie. "You will do as I command." Massey's Brown was a 1940 Warner Bros. version of Adolf Hitler. Massey already had portrayed Robert E. Sherwood's Lincoln, who was the "very epitome of the ideals for which the democracies are now struggling," the Canadian-born actor said. "There really isn't much difference between Lincoln's fight and ours. . . . if you substitute the word dictatorship for the word slavery throughout Sherwood's script, it becomes electric with meaning for our own time." He attempted something similar with his character in *Santa Fe Trail*. After completing the picture he equated Brown with Hitler. "John Brown was the embodiment of the single-tracked mind and he had the same kind of tremendous urge for physical action and blind refusal to see anything on the other side of his point of view which are characteristic of dictators today. He was an embryonic Hitler," Massey said, "the end-justifies-the-means man, and as such he was a frightening type." He contrasted Hitler with Lincoln, the former as a punitive Old Testament figure, the latter compassionate. Drawing the parallel between the Fuehrer and Brown, he described the abolitionist as the "most undemocratic character one could play."[38]

Massey's striking physical appearance in this film owed much to Jack Warner, who monitored the makeup. But even more than Warner, Wallis set the tone of Massey's performance. He instructed Curtiz to make certain that Massey's eyes had a "fanatical gleam." Massey's Brown conveyed a convincing, if sometimes poignant, aura of madness, a version of how some people may have seen Hitler in 1940.[39]

For Reagan, the opportunity to play Custer proved another break. He later noted that as the film's second lead, behind Flynn, a "new door had been opened," that people who had been oblivious to his existence at Warner Bros. began to take notice. The role came at a time in his career when he took the parts assigned to him "gratefully" and did not first ask to read the scripts. He initially was not even considered for the role, and it was only because

John Wayne had looked at the script and rejected it that he received the part. (Wayne turned down the part because he would have had to play a secondary role to Flynn.)[40]

It probably was Jack Warner who decided to have Reagan play Custer. Some people at the studio, including associate producer Robert Fellows, expressed surprise. Reagan at the time was not even among the top 100 box office attractions.[41] But, Fellows observed, he had just finished playing Gipp and had not been one of the Four Horsemen. Warner pushed Reagan because his studio needed male leads and was willing to gamble that the actor would become a star. Reagan was filmed in flattering terms. Publicity called Custer "one of the most valiant soldiers of all time" and Reagan led a cavalry charge to Flynn's rescue. As in *Brother Rat,* Reagan assumed "another great role," dashing in military uniform, living "real adventures that real Americans . . . still thrill to," this time "as gallant Custer."[42]

In portraying these two legendary figures – Gipp and Custer – Reagan the actor gave poignancy to one and compassion to the other. And in these two roles he received a history lesson. Ever since D. W. Griffith's powerful re-creation of the Civil War and Reconstruction in *Birth of a Nation* (1915), Hollywood had changed the American people's relation with the past. Film made the past seem more accessible. Moving pictures sustained audience attention and gave a sense of participation. Studios spent lavishly on sets to create an illusion of authenticity while they distorted the record to make a more interesting story. But such alterations went unnoticed by most viewers, who saw the movie's version of history not as an "interpretation" but a "final statement of the truth about its subject, driven home with all the force of visual demonstration."[43]

It is tempting to argue – as other writers have done – that Reagan was among those who confused Hollywood's versions of history with reality.[44] By the time he became president of the United States, wrote Lou Cannon, one of the most astute observers of Reagan's later career, his "mind was filled with movie scenes more vivid to him than many actual events." Cannon believed, though, that while Reagan judged stories "by their impact rather than their accuracy," he "recognized at some level that he told stories without regard for factual accuracy."[45] It is likely that he grasped that many people turned to popular entertainment to learn about the past (as he surely did), and that film history, even if not always authentic, provided a common language for them. What Hollywood provided was ample opportunity to see firsthand how history could be popularized. *Knute Rockne – All American* and *Santa Fe Trail* had been classrooms in which the past served a cause. Warner Bros.' history reveled in ambience, heroes, and spectacles, an amalgam of fact and entertainment, all combined to fit the needs of the present. It mattered little if Hollywood's history lessons ignored unpleasantness and fudged the truth, so long as the message was uplifting.

8

WARMONGERING

The movies have ceased to be an instrument of entertainment. They have become the most gigantic engines of propaganda in existence to rouse the war fever in America and plunge this nation to destruction.

Senator Gerald P. Nye, August 1, 1941

In early August 1941, only a few months before the Japanese attack on Pearl Harbor, Senator Gerald P. Nye of North Dakota launched an attack on Hollywood. In a speech before a sympathetic audience of twenty-six hundred in St. Louis, he said that movies had "ceased to be an instrument of entertainment" and had become "the most gigantic engines of propaganda in existence to rouse . . . war fever in America and plunge the nation to destruction." Pictures had been produced to "drug the reason of the American people, to set aflame their emotions, to fill them with fear Hitler will come over and capture them." As he called out the name of each Jewish producer and director – Harry and Jack Cohn, Adolph Zukor, Murray Silverstone, Sam Goldwyn, Louis B. Mayer, the three Warner brothers – a "storm of boos" arose through the auditorium. Many studio executives had come "from Russia, Hungary, Germany and the Balkan countries." These men "with motion picture films in their hands," he charged, could "address 80,000,000 people a week." So similar were their movies, he said, that it was "as if they were being operated from a central agency."[1]

The senator had allies, such as Senators Burton K. Wheeler of Montana and D. Worth Clark of Idaho. Between September 9 and 26, a subcommittee on Wheeler's Interstate Commerce Committee, chaired by Clark, conducted an investigation. Clark's staff compiled a list of about fifty films that contained war propaganda. It singled out Warner Bros. and Metro-Goldwyn-Mayer as the most prowar studios, followed by Twentieth Century Fox, United Artists, and March of Time. Eight Warner Bros. feature pictures, more than from any other studio, appeared on the list.[2]

Two films that Clark said were examples of Hollywood warmongering – *Murder in the Air* and *International Squadron* – starred Reagan. The timing of *International Squadron* made it conspicuous because it premiered in Dixon during the Louella Parsons Day celebration in September. Clark could have named other Reagan films, including *Secret Service of the Air,* which dealt with spies and saboteurs smuggled into the United States, and *Code of the Secret Service,* which spoke of patriotic duty while making a veiled reference to the crisis in Europe. The latter film ended with a call to arms. Brass Bancroft's superior, Saxby, says, "You know, a great poet once put it something like this: 'There are not leaders to lead us to honor and yet without leaders we rally. . . . '" As the film cuts to an American flag, Saxby continues: " . . . Each man reporting for duty alone out of sight and out of reach of his fellows."[3]

Nye's charges that the movie industry was anti-German and had attempted to mobilize support against Hitler were well founded. Indeed, a relationship existed between the Hollywood of Reagan's early years and the War Department; many pictures had been made with the cooperation and support of the armed forces. Long before the United States entered the war, studios had tried to warn about subversive activities, to kindle Americanism, to enhance the image of the military, and to promote the British cause.[4]

★★★

Warner Bros. frequently dressed Reagan in military attire. Even before *Santa Fe Trail,* he had performed in movies about the navy, cavalry, and the Virginia Military Institute – *Submarine D-1* (1937), *Sergeant Murphy* (1938), and *Brother Rat* (1938). Made in cooperation with military authorities, they portrayed the services in a manner designed to instill respect.

Given the history of collaboration between the studios and the military, Reagan would probably have appeared in this kind of picture even had he worked for any of the other studios. But few outdid the Warners in display of loyalty. In World War I the studio promoted patriotism by making an anti-German movie from Ambassador James W. Gerard's *My Four Years in Germany.* Its success proved to Jack Warner the possibility of making pictures with "serious purpose." *My Four Years in Germany* had set a standard, he claimed after World War II. The movies he most prized, he maintained, were those that "performed some public service in addition to being entertaining." But it did not escape his attention that patriotic movies could be financially rewarding.[5]

The Warners consistently promoted American military strength. In 1933, Jack Warner hosted a luncheon for members of Congress at which he urged a naval presence off California and read a letter from William Randolph Hearst that said an "ounce of timely preparedness will be found to be worth a pound of impotent pacifism."[6] By the mid-1930s the studio was showcasing men in uniform. Sometimes they were comedies or love stories, such as

Flirtation Walk (1934), *Shipmates Forever* (1935), or such Reagan movies as *Sergeant Murphy* and *Brother Rat.* Others – *Submarine D-1* and *Dive Bomber* (1941) – were more serious, showing training and dangerous missions. *Dive Bomber* typified this genre, showing an America on the verge of war. In the film, cadets are instructed to "fly and fight" in "the main event . . . about to start." Pictures like these, that associated military life with dignity, heroism, and romance, supported the War Department's attempts to increase enlistments.[7]

One of the first Reagan movies during the summer of 1937 (although his part was cut from the final print) was *Submarine D-1,* based on the ideas of a retired naval officer turned writer, Lieutenant Commander Frank Wead. Wead wrote Hal Wallis that he wanted to "capture the spirit" of the submarine service. Naval officers, he said, were enthusiastic. His suggestion moved forward when Jack Warner told Wallis to line up another service film that would star James Cagney or Pat O'Brien. Wallis wrote the Navy Department requesting permission to send a writer to the submarine base at San Diego and promised cooperation in every way. He sent William Guthrie to Washington to help make arrangements.[8]

Reagan worked on *Submarine D-1* enthusiastically. He told friends in Iowa that Warner Bros. was rushing the film "to take advantage of all the submarine excitement over in the Mediterranean." He was supposed to come into the picture at the end as the fiancé of the female lead, but the studio dropped that idea, preferring the woman to remain faithful to her husband, killed earlier in a submarine accident. This ending emphasized the dedication of naval officers and their families, and pleased the navy as well as Wallis, who was looking for a way to trim $150,000 from the budget. The studio deemed Reagan's part expendable.[9]

Meanwhile Reagan made *Sergeant Murphy,* a B picture filmed at the Presidio in San Francisco to show the "most picturesque" branch of the service, the cavalry. It provided his second starring role (the studio had first considered Cagney for the part in an A film) and gave Reagan another role with which he was familiar. He played an army private who becomes fond of a horse named Sergeant Murphy. The animal is a cut above the other cavalry mounts, so much so that the base commander (Donald Crisp) wants it. In the story the private convinces his superiors that Sergeant Murphy is untrainable, but unfortunately the military, rather than releasing the animal, sells it to a meat factory. The private manages to save the horse, then trains it and smuggles it into England, where it wins the Grand Nationals. Warner Bros. based this rags-to-riches story on the exploits of a real horse named Sergeant Murphy who ran in the Grand Nationals in 1925.[10]

As Reagan traveled up then-unpaved Highway 1 from Hollywood to the Presidio, he was thrilled by this opportunity. The film was "pretty much down my alley," he told the readers of the *Des Moines Sunday Register,* and recommended they see it. For those "who like action," he said, "there's nothing more thrilling than to see a battery of artillery gallop into position and get down to business – unless it is a cavalry charge." In Iowa he had been a second lieutenant in the cavalry reserves. The studio explained that he was expected to drill with California's 323rd Cavalry Regiment. Publicity noted that he was one of the best horsemen in Hollywood, and preferred to do his own riding in pictures rather than relying on stunt men. "I'm no hero," he said modestly, but "if you're 'yellow' and refuse to risk a few bruises and occasionally . . . something more serious, you might as well . . . leave Hollywood."[11]

Warner Bros. wanted to glorify the cavalry in this picture. It sent the script to the War Department, which made only minor changes in dialogue. The Army supervised scenes of base life, including the raising of the Stars and Stripes at sunrise. The publicity department promised "spectacular cavalry charges and artillery drills over rough terrain," assured viewers that real soldiers had conducted all maneuvers, and related that the artillery commander who reviewed troops was as "handsome a he-man as any movie hero ever dared to be." The studio launched a mail campaign to reserve and national guard officers, encouraging them to attend, and urged theater managers to use local armories to promote the film.[12]

The movie provoked controversy because the studio used military personnel as extras. This practice was not uncommon at other studios, but such groups as the Screen Actors Guild and the Hollywood Riding Actors Association objected. When their protests reached the White House, Jack Warner defended his actions. "For many years," he related to Roosevelt's secretary, Marvin H. McIntyre, "we have produced important pictures placing the army, navy and all other branches before the entire world in a most important light." McIntyre took the matter to the War Department, which approved troops for *Sergeant Murphy*. Secretary of War Harry Woodring said it was essential to see a "true picture of the army rather than one based upon the producer's or director's imagination."[13]

Sergeant Murphy helped convince studio executives that Reagan was improving as an actor. Bert Harlan of the *Hollywood Spectator* noted he had "gained noticeably in ease, in sureness of gesture, and in ability to get his thoughts and emotions into the cameras." Audiences liked him, Harlan said, in a comment typical of other early reviews, because he handled scenes with an "engaging spirit and conviction."[14]

Brother Rat, which appeared in late 1938, attracted more attention. It dealt with cadet life at the Virginia Military Institute and helped launch Eddie Albert's screen career. It featured Reagan and Jane Wyman in their first film together. Based on a hit stage play by two V.M.I. graduates, John Monks, Jr., and Fred F. Finklehoffe, it was in the tradition of such earlier Warner Bros. films as *Flirtation Walk* (about West Point) and *Shipmates Forever* (about Annapolis). These pictures used a lighthearted approach to show the trials and tribulations of cadets. The authors of *Brother Rat* had started the story as an English thesis while cadets at V.M.I. in 1932. They wanted to show that the institute's intense training and discipline did not "prevent a normal development of youthful high spirits."[15]

The picture made the cadets' life seem appealing. The studio first considered calling the film "Present Arms," and then "Call to Arms." But Wallis's assistant Walter MacEwen expressed reservations. "Call to Arms," he feared, would be too obviously a preparedness or war story. This problem solved, he agreed that "brave lads in uniform . . . embracing beauteous maidens" would serve as a useful advertising strategy. Publicity promoted the idea that one sure way to attract women was to wear a military uniform. Indeed, both the on-screen and off-screen romance between Reagan and Wyman seemed ideal for this strategy.[16]

Filming at V.M.I. required concessions to the institute's superintendent, Major General C. E. Kilbourne, who set out a list of conditions. He insisted on approving the film. He required Warner Bros. to accept his representative as a technical adviser. He wanted the studio to contribute $20,000 to the institute, although he eventually asked for half that amount and settled for considerably less. He hoped Monks and Finklehoffe would write the screenplay and he asked to write a foreword. He warned that if the film embarrassed V.M.I. there would be retaliation.[17]

The movie emphasized the honor code and military heroes of the Old South. Kilbourne's foreword traced V.M.I.'s history to the "sons of many aristocratic families" who left their mark on the institute through "ideals and unbending honor." Richard Macaulay and Jerry Wald wrote the screen story from the Monks-Finkelhoffe play and sought to remain faithful to Kilbourne's creed. They turned to Robert Buckner, who was sympathetic to Kilbourne and the V.M.I. tradition.[18]

The studio associated Reagan's screen image with Confederate military heroes. The pressbook urged theater managers to get in touch with Confederate veterans for reminiscences about Stonewall Jackson. It recommended that managers place pictures of famous V.M.I. graduates, including Jackson, in lobbies beside stills of Reagan and other stars from the movie. It suggested advertising copy to read: "Brother Rats today. Generals tomorrow!"[19]

Brother Rat, by Reagan's account, angered some V.M.I. graduates, but it proved so successful that the studio tried a sequel, *Brother Rat and a Baby,* which followed the characters a year after graduation. This movie, which was a pale reflection of the original, eliminated references to V.M.I.[20]

Patrons may not have connected *Submarine D-1, Sergeant Murphy,* and *Brother Rat* with the international situation, in part because the Hays Office muffled obvious commentary. Most people were not aware of the behind-the-scenes cooperation between Hollywood and the military. But the historians Charles and Mary Beard commented on the industry's willingness to be an "abject servant of propaganda from Washington." After President Roosevelt's quarantine speech in early October 1937, and subsequent efforts to improve the United States Navy, such films as *Submarine D-1*, they argued, overshadowed pictures that leaned "in the direction of peace."[21]

In the tense atmosphere before Pearl Harbor, talk about Jewish influence in Hollywood pushing the country into war took on an understandably ugly tone. The possibility of the nation's going to war was at the front of public discussion. The issue of Jewish influence was volatile at a time when Nazi Germany had stirred racial animosities in all the countries of Europe.

Senator Nye did not hesitate to raise the question. In St. Louis he claimed that East European Jews controlled any film treatment of the international situation, and that the industry had turned to pro-preparedness, anti-Nazi themes to protect investments abroad. If Britain were defeated, Nye said, it would mean that American films would lose their British market, which for most companies was their margin of profit.[22]

Of course, Jews did control most American movies, and many individuals in the motion picture colony (Jewish and non-Jewish) had come from Central or Eastern Europe.[23] The Warners had emigrated from a Polish village near the German border. Jack Warner recalled how the Russians had barred his family from attending school. Harry equated Hitler's policies with the anti-Semitic pogroms his parents had endured. Wallis's mother, also Jewish, was a native of Kobno, Russia. Edward G. Robinson, star of *Confessions of a Nazi Spy*, had come with his family from Romania. Michael Curtiz had fled Hungary after the Bolshevik revolution, and his mother and brothers lived outside Budapest until the late 1930s, when Jack Warner convinced them to emigrate. Max Reinhardt, who directed for Warner Bros., abandoned his family estate in Austria shortly before the Nazis turned it into a military headquarters.[24]

There was evidence to support Nye's assertions about the British market. When Harry Warner testified before Senator Clark's subcommittee, he played down Warner Bros.' investment, saying his company netted only $5 million from Britain each year. "If we were to stop receiving this revenue, we would continue to operate, just as we did in 1932 through 1934, when our gross revenue declined by $50 million. If we were able to adjust our affairs to offset this loss in revenue, then I certainly am not worried about a drop of $5 million."[25]

But two years earlier Warner had not been so cavalier in dismissing either that market or the industry's other foreign investments. In early 1939 a worried Warner, fearful the government's antitrust litigation would mean loss of the studio's theaters, provided an assessment of Hollywood's overseas investments. He wrote privately to Harry Hopkins that they accounted for an annual $150 million. American films occupied 70 percent of screen time worldwide; they had a "far-reaching effect . . . upon the social, political, and economic life" of other nations, and promised to Americanize the world.

They advertised American goods ("our films fairly shriek 'Buy American' ") and were "America's world Ambassador." Now more than twenty countries had imposed quotas, censorship worldwide restricted distribution, a dozen countries restricted export revenues, and Justice Department litigation sought to divorce studios from their theaters, jeopardizing domestic distribution revenues. Warner phrased his problems in terms of national interest: not only would loss of the industry's exports devastate film quality, it would have "destructive consequences upon our domestic economy."[26]

After two weeks in Europe reorganizing the studio's interests in September 1939, Warner wrote President Roosevelt pleading for help. At stake, he said, was not only film distribution abroad but the studio itself. Foreign receipts were crucial because money from distribution in the United States was insufficient. Will Hays estimated that under normal circumstances Hollywood derived 35 to 40 percent of its income from abroad. "We depend upon a world market to support our production costs," Warner explained.[27]

Britain and France had become especially important to Warner Bros. by 1939. A fourth of the company's gross receipts came from these markets. Without them the company would "operate at a large loss," and Warner refused to "forecast the length of time either our company or any other company will be able to absorb these losses." Forfeiture of part of these revenues appeared unavoidable with war. Civilians were being evacuated from industrial and metropolitan areas and blackouts imposed. Warner reported that virtually all theaters had been shut down.[28]

Loans from British banks complicated the situation. Warner Bros. had secured them with film receipts in England. With the closing of theaters, the probability that British banks would call their loans, and the unlikelihood that American institutions would lend money, Warner Bros.' situation seemed precarious. Warner likened the crisis to the early 1930s.[29]

Warner's immediate concern, though, was the federal government's antitrust proceedings and the "multitude of private suits which have been brought against us, based upon the Federal litigation." The suits could drain studio finances. He asked the president to free the company from the litigation so it could work its way out of the problems inflicted by the war.[30]

Critics who accused Hollywood of pushing the United States into war could also have pointed to activities that went beyond filmmaking and the desire to save markets. When Harry Warner testified before the subcommittee he said that the "freedom which this country fought England to obtain, we may have to fight with England to retain." He favored giving Britain and allies "all the supplies which our country can spare," but was uncertain whether the United States "should enter the war in its own defense at the present time." He had "always been in accord with President Roosevelt's foreign policy." But Harry and Jack had been ahead of the president in urging aid for the British.[31] They opposed the "cash and carry" program. Harry suggested troops. In May 1940 the brothers telegraphed Roosevelt that "cash and carry" worked "too great a hardship on these brave, unfortunate nations who are, in a way, fighting our battle for us. The least we can do," they argued, "is to supply all the material help we can command, short of actual troops and so help destroy the barbarian gang that is overrunning the world today." They wanted to use motion pictures to show Americans the "worthiness of the cause for which the free peoples of Europe" were making such tremendous sacrifices. "We cannot stand by and watch others die for the civilization which is ours as much as theirs," they said. "We cannot contentedly sit still out here and do nothing while the whole world echoes with the march of the savages to destroy everything we all hold dear. We would rather die in an effort to be helpful than live to see barbarism triumph."[32]

The Warners contributed $25,000 to the American Red Cross to purchase ambulances in June 1940, and in December sent more ambulances in the name of Harry's son, Lewis. They distributed the British Ministry of Information's film, *London Can Take It* (1940), and Jack informed the president early in 1941 that the studio had donated proceeds from the picture, shown in the United States, Canada, and South America, to the British Spitfire Fund. A few months later Harry wrote that Britain was part of America's "life-line." "What fault could anyone find if we undertook to man the Island to protect it from invasion, so as to allow the English Army to go wherever they may be needed." The Warners let the White House know they had donated two planes, one named the "President Roosevelt," the other the "Cordell Hull."[33]

As allegations of propaganda peaked in late summer 1941, Hays contended that Hollywood had consistently opposed hate films and called Senator Clark's attacks "unjustified . . . false and shameful." Motion pictures, Hays said at this time, simply mirrored the national defense efforts already under way in the United States. To ask filmmakers to "ignore the fact that we live in an era of destruction and tyranny that surpasses the blackest period of barbarism" not only aided the country's enemies, Hays added, but challenged free expression. Harry Warner sounded a similar theme before Senator Clark's panel: "Shortly after Hitler came to power in Germany I became convinced that Hitlerism was an evil force designed to destroy free people, whether they were Catholics, Protestants, or Jews," he said. "In September, 1939, when the Second World War began, I believed, and I believe today, that the world struggle for freedom was in its final stage." Such films as *Confessions of a Nazi Spy* and *Sergeant York* had been "carefully prepared on the basis of factual happenings" and had tried to capture history as it happened – or, as Hays said, to "show history white-hot from the pouring; rough in the mould."[34]

The Hollywood executives wanted to take the offensive against their critics and they became impatient with Hays. Warner, whose name had been booed during Nye's St. Louis speech, reproached Hays. "I don't mind being cheered or booed with you," he wrote, but "I don't think it's fair that we of the Industry are being booed while you are being cheered." Dissatisfied with Hays's "appeasements," film executives hired Wendell Willkie to defend them. As the *Hollywood Reporter* pointed out, his appointment was an "invitation to fight." Noting that the Senate had not authorized any probe of the industry, Willkie labeled the Clark proceedings a "sneak" investigation. He acknowledged that the producers opposed Hitler and that "the industry gladly, and with great pride," admitted that it had done everything within its power to inform the public about the American armed forces. The industry intended to continue doing the same because movies had offered only a "pale portrayal" of Hitler's atrocities, he said.[35]

The Senate investigation came to a close when Clark postponed hearings indefinitely on the ground that too many committee members were away from Washington. Isolationists knew they had lost. Nye, Clark, and Wheeler had been correct about the pro-preparedness, anti-Nazi character of Hollywood films but lost credibility when they admitted they had not seen many of the movies under investigation.[36]

The December 1941 attack on Pearl Harbor ended any further controversy over whether America should fight.

As the international situation deteriorated, then, the youthful Reagan rose to stardom. In the short span since arriving in Hollywood, he had made few mistakes. Greater opportunities were on the horizon. The times had been right for a handsome young man to play military, heroic figures, to champion patriotic virtues, and to represent the nation's history to other Americans who were perplexed about the connection between past and present.

For a man with such a large future, however, Reagan was a political innocent. Issues of war and peace seem hardly to have touched him, save for what they might mean to his acting. And even in this respect, one could never be certain whether he sketched his career (or the studio sketched it for him) for patriotic reasons or to take advantage of patriotism. When he did become more aware politically and commented on events, he often appeared superficial. He saw the Senate investigation of 1941 as part of an internationally inspired plot by German fascists. Writing in early 1946 as a guest columnist for the American Veterans Committee's *Bulletin,* he commented on events leading up to American entry into World War II:

It soon became apparent that every time Goebbels called the turn and emphasized one of his particular points, a certain group of publishers, columnists and political figures in this country took up on their own hook the same cry. For example, just prior to Pearl Harbor, Hitler broadcast internationally a speech in which he said something should be done about the Jewish-communist influence in Hollywood. A few days later, Senator Clark . . . demanded that the Senate Interstate Commerce Committee investigate the motion picture industry.[37]

In the months before Pearl Harbor, Reagan participated in the Warners' quest
for preparedness with gusto. Both his on-screen image and his off-screen
activities endorsed the British, as illustrated by the ceremony surrounding
the opening of *International Squadron.* During the Louella Parsons Day
festivities in Dixon in September 1941, Reagan joined the company of the
columnist's friend, actress Bebe Daniels, her husband Ben Lyon, and their
infant son. This "clever and courageous couple," the *Chicago Herald-
American* reported, had for two years presented weekly radio shows from
London, "sleeping in their clothes many nights in British broadcasting companies, going on the air even when the radio station was bombed during the
program." "I'm no heroine," Bebe explained in a local interview. "I was
scared stiff during the bad raids and many times my stomach felt as if it were
falling out. . . . Sleep is so topsy-turvy often from sheer exhaustion you sleep
through the alarm and are awakened by the all clear."[38]

For Dixon's citizens as well as movie audiences across the United States,
Bebe Daniels's description of air raids was dramatized by *International
Squadron,* in which Reagan portrayed an irresponsible American pilot who
joined the Royal Air Force and ultimately sacrificed his life. The movie
emphasized support for Britain, stressing duty, the perils of individualism in
wartime, and the necessity of teamwork. The picture opened with a map of
the United States; as the titles rolled, planes crossed the Atlantic. Then,
superimposed over the RAF symbol, were words telling the audience that the
movie was dedicated to men of the RAF. Viewers were reminded of
Churchill's stirring acknowledgment that "never before in the field of human
conflict have so many owed so much to so few."

Producer Brian Foy had recommended the story to Jack Warner in late
1940. The movie drew on the exploits of American pilots who flew in the
Lafayette Escadrille during World War I, experiences of American volunteers
in the RAF's Eagle Squadron in 1939–40, and a play called *Ceiling Zero.*[39]

International Squadron was only one of several Hollywood stories about
the RAF. In 1941, Darryl Zanuck produced *A Yank in the RAF* (Twentieth
Century Fox), that starred Tyrone Power and Betty Grable, and Walter
Wanger made *Eagle Squadron.* Warner Bros. also made *Captains of the
Clouds* (1942) which was about the Canadian Air Force. Such films were
popular, an audience survey suggested, because they presented Americans
with the "unaccustomed opportunity to project themselves into war."[40]

In *International Squadron,* audiences first saw Reagan's character, Jimmy
Grant, power-diving a plane. "The way I'm going to come down, I'll make
my own wind," Grant proclaims as the film opens and as the plane appears
to dive at an almost ninety-degree angle. "I'm going to get this baby to six
hundred [mph] if I have to get out and push." As screenwriter Norman Reilly
Raine told Wallis, Grant was a "cocky trouble-maker . . . son of a bitch." Of
his ability with airplanes, Grant boasts, "I can fly the crates they come in."[41]

The film quickly turns to politics. Grant comes to see the necessity of defeating the Nazis. At first uninterested in Britain's fight, he agrees to fly to England a bomber purchased by French sympathizers. As in earlier pictures, *International Squadron* shows a fictitious newspaper picture and headline ("Jimmy Grant to Fly Bomber to Europe") to herald the hero's exploits. After witnessing a German air raid, Grant agrees to fly missions for a unit made up of pilots from several countries including Czechoslovakia, Poland, and Belgium. "Sounds like the Notre Dame backfield," Reagan's character quips. "Seems funny, all those fellas of different nationalities in the same uniform."

Reagan's character is a playboy and a loner, full of bravado. But this is a foil so the film can turn serious. "It is wrong to think of ourselves," explains a French girl whom Grant tries to charm. "There is so much to be done." When Grant shoots down a German plane only to discover that his unorthodox style has cost the life of another RAF pilot, his commanding officer reprimands him: "You don't understand. There are no more individual fliers, no more aces. Only squadrons . . . as a part of a very carefully designed plan." When irresponsibility costs another pilot's life, this time a friend, Grant flies a suicide mission behind German lines to atone for his errors. The picture ends with other RAF fliers, who had resented Grant's nonconformity, acknowledging his bravery.

Warner Bros. associated Reagan's heroic character with support for the Allied cause in both this picture and in *Desperate Journey* (1942), in which he costarred with Errol Flynn. In *International Squadron,* the Production Code Administration helped mold Reagan's image, making it more wholesome than the studio intended. Breen and staff had few complaints about the political message, but they at first rejected the script because Grant appeared as a womanizer. The final version downplayed the sexual adventures so well that the Hays Office declared the movie to have "inspirational value." After the war, when Jack Warner testified before the House Committee on Un-American Activities, he cited *International Squadron* as one of half a dozen Reagan films that promoted Americanism.[42]

In *International Squadron,* fans thus saw Reagan portray an intrepid pilot, "unconquerable," one of the "avenging 'angels' hurtling out of the heavens," a man who lived only for today because he "might be a hole in the ground tomorrow." Dixon's *Evening Telegraph* ran three pictures of the actor replete in aviator's paraphernalia under the heading, "At Home in Skies."[43] Yet there was something incongruous about the bold and adventuresome image in *International Squadron* and later in *Desperate Journey,* in which Reagan again was an American in the RAF – incongruous because the actor was barely more than an actor. His appeal during this era, as noted, was strongest among moviegoers under age eighteen. Whether they or others who attended movies distinguished between Reagan the private citizen (who did not like to fly) and the image they saw on screen is uncertain, but by late 1941, few Americans were more visibly associated with military valor.[44]

9

FLYING A DESK FOR THE ARMY AIR CORPS

It is unlikely that a nation such as ours can maintain its integrity and
continue existence at its present way of living unless it establishes and
maintains the world's strongest air force.
General H. H. Arnold, 1941

The fortunes of Ronald Reagan and the American air force joined during
World War II in the First Motion Picture Unit (FMPU). General Henry H.
("Hap") Arnold, who commanded the Army Air Corps (later known as the
Army Air Force), created the FMPU in 1942 at the urging of Jack Warner.
Reagan transferred into the unit, based in Culver City, soon after he entered
active duty and remained there throughout the war, never leaving the United
States. He held a variety of jobs that included recruiting and public relations,
and eventually became post adjutant. He was most widely known for either
narrating or appearing in several of the unit's pictures. It is unclear how many
he appeared in or narrated, but the FMPU probably made at least two
hundred films, most of which ran for a half hour or less and cost only a few
thousand dollars.

Reagan thought of the FMPU as the "Signal Corps for Hap Arnold's new
air force," which was much worth celebrating. The war marked a turning
point in the development of American air power. The Air Corps in 1938 had
fewer than 22,000 men and 3,900 planes. By late 1944, when victory was in
sight and air force strength peaked, Arnold commanded 2.5 million men,
and factories were turning out 145,000 planes a year.[1]

To be sure, this buildup grew out of the necessity of war. But Arnold
argued that America's future depended on air power and had advanced this
idea long before the crisis in Europe and the Far East. When he took over as
chief of the Air Corps in 1938 he realized that a profound change in public
attitude would have to occur. Air power would depend on a comprehensive
national program and require "the cleverest use of . . . propaganda." His

104

strategy called for coordinating "every phase of the air industry," and "every phase of civil life relating to aviation." Such a plan would integrate flying into the fabric of American life and unite every citizen with a "common purpose."[2]

The war also marked a turning point of sorts for Reagan. It interrupted his acting career, yet it gave him experience as a military propagandist and increased his fascination with politics. Never again was he able to devote undivided attention to films or to regain his former momentum as a movie actor.

That he wound up in Arnold's unit and remained stateside was no accident. Strings had been pulled, although there was no hint of such maneuvering in Reagan's version of his war service. At the time of Pearl Harbor he confessed, "I hadn't given a thought to possible active duty." Why? Because the military had approved him for only "limited service" because of his poor eyesight. It later assigned him to Culver City, he said, because the FMPU needed men with film experience. All this was true, but Reagan's account of his induction obscures the fact that before he reported to Fort Mason more than four months after Pearl Harbor, Warner Bros.' employees attempted to defer him. The effort began as early as September 1941, shortly after he negotiated a new contract and still was working on *Kings Row*.[3]

Reagan's new contract in 1941 almost tripled his salary. Its mastermind was his agent, Lew Wasserman of the Music Corporation of American Artists, Inc. By his own account, Reagan wanted to wait until the release of *Kings Row* to negotiate. Wasserman reminded him he was a reserve officer, that war was likely, and that other actors such as Jimmy Stewart had been drafted. "We don't know how much time you have," he warned, "let's get what we can while we can."[4]

Wasserman judged the situation correctly. With weeks of work remaining on *Desperate Journey* in March 1942, Reagan "received a letter that didn't even need opening: on the outside, stamped in red, were the words, 'Immediate Action Active Duty.' The inside informed me I would report to Fort Mason in San Francisco in fourteen days." Reagan had been drawing his new salary for less than three months, and the studio still had not yet released *Kings Row*.[5]

When he first learned he would be called is unclear. The *South Bend Tribune* reported in October 1940 that he had "just received another letter from the government asking him how long it would take him to wind up his affairs in case of a call to act." During the summer of 1941 he was notified he would have to report.[6]

On August 29, 1941, Warner Bros.' general counsel, Roy Obringer, believed the call would come within two weeks and turned his attention to securing an extension. *Kings Row* was a major production, its budget exceeding $1,082,000, surpassing that of any previous Reagan film. To have changed actors in midproduction would have been costly. Wasserman drafted the "type of letter which should go off immediately in connection with the Ronald Reagan matter" and on September 3 sent it to Jack Warner's executive assistant, Steve Trilling. He recommended it go to the assistant secretary of war, that it detail movie properties purchased for Reagan and emphasize that induction would bring a significant financial loss. The letter asked the army to transfer him from the cavalry reserve to the reserve pool, which, as Obringer pointed out, "would more or less make his deferment permanent." In the event the War Department would not place Reagan in the pool, Wasserman recommended he go in a "deferred class" for a "reasonable period" to allow the studio to readjust its plans. Wasserman emphasized he had been advised "by high ranking officials of the Reserve Corps" that it was "vitally important" that either Warner or Wallis sign the letter.[7]

Obringer sent a letter to the assistant secretary of war along lines suggested by Wasserman. It was forwarded to the adjutant general's office and then to Ninth Corps headquarters at the Presidio, where Second Lieutenant F. K. Eberhart wrote Obringer on September 25 that the request had not been approved. Reagan was on a priority list and would be called whenever his name was reached on that list. While every effort would be made to minimize inconvenience, the letter said, national defense took priority.[8]

Under normal circumstances this letter might have discouraged attempts for deferment, but Warner Bros. had contacts in the military and in the Roosevelt administration. One of them, the adjutant general, Major General Emory S. Adams, had worked with Obringer and Jack Warner to promote enlistment through such films as *Service With the Colors* and *The Tanks Are Coming*.[9] Obringer wrote Adams. Reagan had been deferred temporarily until October 10 to complete *Kings Row*. Obringer explored the possibility of extending deferment so he could work on *Juke Girl*, scheduled to begin shooting immediately after. When response was not forthcoming, Obringer asked for an extension, stating that Reagan would be needed for another eight to nine weeks. A few days later he heard from Adams, possibly by telephone, that the correspondence had gone to General Peak, commander at the Presidio.[10]

Wishing to leave as little as possible to chance, Obringer got in touch with William Guthrie, a proven liaison between the studio and military as well as an adviser on Reagan's Brass Bancroft films. Guthrie advertised himself as a former FBI agent who had investigated spies after World War I. He had left the bureau, he claimed, because of the pay. In fact he was with the FBI two years but dismissed in 1920 "because of conduct unbecoming an Agent." An internal investigation concluded that he was "entirely dishonest"; had used "his official position to further his own ends; was not above accepting gratuities or graft; that he took cases to his friends . . . ; and that he depended very much on influential friends submitting communications in his behalf to the Department."[11] Whether Warner knew of Guthrie's past is uncertain. Guthrie was one of several men the studio used during the late 1930s to provide security, a job that likely entailed more than watching for thieves and spies. Like "Pops" Johnson in Jack Warner, Jr.'s semiautobiographical novel *Bijou Dream,* Guthrie "dealt in people with power and instinctively knew how to get from them whatever was theirs to give." He was a "fixer," in position to gather information on troublesome employees and help the studio with embarrassing problems.[12]

Guthrie suggested contacting retired Lieutenant Colonel James G. Taylor, who had been a technical adviser for Warner Bros. Taylor had been in General Peak's class at West Point. Obringer told Warner it might be possible to defer Reagan beyond *Juke Girl.* All this would cost little more than Taylor's transportation to San Francisco. Wallis agreed to the plan, telling Obringer to handle "the Ronald Reagan matter . . . as you think best," although he attempted to distance himself by saying that "I have had no part in this so far, and I don't want to become involved in it now."[13]

The efforts for deferment proved successful, and Reagan received an extension until December 1. Soon Obringer received a letter from the Presidio stating that as a result of Taylor's visit "in behalf of Warner Brothers [*sic*] and his explanation of the case," deferment was extended to January 1. Obringer learned, however, that this was the "final concession" and that Reagan could be called "any time after that date."[14]

Physical disability, it should be noted, now became a problem. Reagan later explained his poor eyesight, recounting an exam at Fort Mason after he had reported for duty. One doctor said that "if we sent you overseas, you'd shoot a general." "Yes," said another doctor, "and you'd miss him." Less than a month before Pearl Harbor he was examined at Fort MacArthur. Guthrie informed Trilling of the results and passed them to Warner and Wallis. Guthrie was "advised by his army friend," Trilling wrote, "that due to Reagan's poor eyesight, he is being permanently deferred." The news, he said, was "more or less official" and to be treated with utmost secrecy. "As we unquestionably will want no publicity, I am telling Reagan and Guthrie not to discuss it with anyone." At this time about a tenth of those called in the Ninth Corps Area were rejected for physical reasons.[15]

In addition to eyesight, another factor worked to delay induction. Although need for military manpower was becoming critical, the director of Selective Service, Colonel Lewis B. Hershey, issued a ruling in early February 1942 that the film industry was "an activity essential in certain instances to the national health, safety and interest, and in other instances to war production." He instructed California officials to defer "actors, directors, writers, producers, camera men, sound engineers and other technicians" who could not be replaced or whose drafting "would cause a serious loss of effectiveness."[16]

People in Hollywood believed Hershey's ruling ill advised at a time when the industry was under pressure to minimize deferments. A veteran producer, William A. Brady, observed that actors had not been considered essential during World War I nor were they then exempt in England. The Screen Actors Guild went on record to say that the industry should be subjected to the "same rules for the draft as the rest of the country."[17]

Yet in early 1942 less than 3 percent of Hollywood was in the service. Of thirty thousand movie industry employees only about seven hundred were on active duty. Most were technicians and craftsmen, but several well-known actors and directors were in the service including Stewart, Robert Montgomery, Wayne Morris, John Ford, Eugene Zukor, and Darryl F. Zanuck.[18]

Orders came from the War Department making it more difficult for reserve officers and men with handicaps to gain deferment. Reagan was re-tested on January 17; doctors noted vision of 7/200 bilateral correctable to 20/20. The adjutant general informed the Ninth Corps Area on March 10 that Reagan would be "retained in the cavalry reserve with eligibility for limited service with War Department overhead or corps service only."[19]

Near the end of March 1942 Reagan received orders giving him fourteen days to wind up personal affairs. By this time the actor had started *Desperate Journey,* in which Warner Bros. had invested more than $1 million, and even at this point the studio did not hesitate to ask a thirty-day postponement. Obringer argued that the studio had a "tremendous investment" and Reagan's part would require twenty-five days. His request was turned down, but Reagan's orders were amended to report April 19, a week later. On April 1 he wired he would report. Warner Bros. agreed to suspend his contract with the understanding that he would return to the studio within ten days after discharge.[20]

For Reagan service came at an awkward time, as it did for millions of other Americans. The war put his career in jeopardy. It threatened to disrupt his family. His daughter, Maureen, was then hardly more than a year old. The Reagans had just built a new house above Sunset Boulevard with a spectacular view of Los Angeles and the ocean. They moved in two weeks before Reagan left for duty. There were other worries, as well. Reagan's father had died the previous May after a series of heart attacks. Reagan had deeded a small house to his parents and had been giving his mother $175 a week. At first Nelle wanted to be alone, but later she lived with her sister. He worked out an agreement to have her handle his fan mail while he was in the service, and Warner Bros. paid her $75 a week for about a year, to be taken out of his salary when he returned.[21]

For people who read fan magazines after Pearl Harbor, Reagan, the reserve cavalry lieutenant, simply "rode away" – he went "off to war!" Stories and photographs of him in uniform with family gave devotees details about his departure and the "grim task before him." Button Nose, as Wyman was called, threw a surprise farewell party – attended by, among others, Jack Benny and his wife, Barbara Stanwyck, Ann Sheridan, and studio publicity director Charlie Einfeld. There was a tearful farewell as Reagan boarded a train for Fort Mason.

Magazines left the impression that the Reagans experienced pretty much what the average GI and his relatives did. They lived frugally, rarely entertained, and took no trips in either his 1938 LaSalle or her 1941 Cadillac. According to Wyman, her husband would "probably have enlisted after Pearl Harbor if he hadn't been a member of the Cavalry Reserve. . . . After the war broke out, they both knew it was only a question of time. Exams came from Washington, Ronnie toted books to and from the studio and boned up between shots. His papers were returned by the War Office, marked excellent." Accounts acknowledged he would be closer to home after orders transferred him to Culver City but implied he was dismayed to leave the cavalry. "It broke him up to have to put his boots and riding breeches into mothballs," one fan magazine reported.[22]

But as the actor prepared to report to Fort Mason, more behind-the-scenes maneuvering was already underway. Jack Warner and Guthrie were attempting to persuade Washington to create an Army Air Corps (AAC) motion picture unit. It is possible that even before Reagan left the set of *Desperate Journey*, they hoped to secure his services. On April 14, four days before he was to leave, Obringer wrote Guthrie: "appreciate greatly if you would see me immediately . . . as I want to talk to you relative to Ronald Reagan and have you talk to him before he leaves for Camp Mason." That Reagan knew about this possibility seems likely. The same day Obringer asked to see Guthrie he wrote the actor. "Just to let you know that I am not forgetting the Guthrie situation," he said, "will advise that it is my understanding that Guthrie will return to Hollywood Thursday, and if possible I will arrange for him to have a talk with you before you leave so that he can get your views and will do whatever is possible even after you get to camp."[23]

Obringer's optimism derived from the knowledge that Jack Warner himself would soon receive a commission to create the film unit. In fact, negotiation with Army Air Corps leaders was proceeding even as work concluded on *Desperate Journey*.

The day before Reagan left for camp, April 17, Warner became a lieutenant colonel. As he told it, during the spring of 1942 he knew he was too old for frontline duty but was frustrated watching others join the military. While he was in Washington to discuss the production of *Air Force*, General Arnold approached him. "Jack, I think it would be better all around if you got into a uniform while you're making these service pictures," Arnold said. Warner was enthusiastic.

"I agree with you," I said gaily. "Especially if you start me off as a one-star general." . . .

I could see it was the wrong time and place for a gag. General Arnold knew I was kidding around. He also knew – and I knew – that I would have signed up as a private.

"Well, Jack," he said, and his warm smile melted the icicles around the room, "you've got to have some authority on the job. How about it if we start you as a lieutenant colonel?"

"Yes, sir," I said.

I flew back to California, dug up an Army manual, and learned how and when to salute. On April 17, 1942, I was sworn in at March Field, and a couple of days later, wearing my uniform.[24]

Warner's self-serving account concealed that he had lobbied in Washington for more than six weeks before being commissioned. He began pushing for a picture unit in early 1942 that would convince parents their sons should "join the Air Corps and be proud of doing so." He understood how film could help General Arnold's plans to expand America's air force. Authority to create the unit came in late February, but the idea probably appeared in a telephone conversation in which Warner assured Arnold a propaganda section would be of immense value. Arnold was on the verge of becoming commanding general of the AAC, and he invited Warner to Washington in early March. Before going to Washington, Warner discussed his strategy with producer-director Howard Hawks. He would use Guthrie, who already knew Arnold, as a go-between to work out details.[25]

Warner's presentation to Arnold emphasized immediate needs and long-range advantages. He stressed his studio's work for national defense, his "close contact with the President," his ability to attract the best people in the movie industry. He offered to place Warner Bros.' publicity and distribution apparatus – more than four hundred theaters – at War Department disposal. Every day millions of people entered these movie houses, Warner explained, and each Army Air Corps film could be publicized the way *Sergeant York* and *Captains of the Clouds* had been. When people saw billboards for these pictures, "they will subconsciously think of the Air Corps," he predicted. Looking to the postwar period, he said the AAC would "need large appropriations to conduct experiments, make tests, and for further research." If the Air Corps had an "effective propaganda department," the government later would be more inclined to spend large sums of money.[26]

Warner flattered Arnold, predicting that the Air Corps would win the war, telling the general he would appear in inspirational pictures, filmed in color, "pinning wings on his men," addressing them "before an important armada of planes." The "men, planes, and glamour of real fighting equipment," he instructed Guthrie to tell Arnold, would sell the general's ideas.[27]

Warner anticipated that the general would be receptive to his plan. A gracious man who surrounded himself with able assistants, Arnold was respected by almost everyone who knew him. He had a reputation for being "conservative" and "slow to adopt modern air equipment and methods," an ironic assessment considering that his *Airmen and Aircraft* (1926) began by quoting Rudyard Kipling: "We are at the opening verse of the opening page of the chapter of endless possibilities." The next war, he wrote, "will start with a host of aircraft arriving unheralded over strategic points. . . . No town or city that manufactures military supplies, no matter if at a considerable distance from the frontiers, can consider itself immune from aerial attack." The only means of stopping air attacks was to have "more and better aircraft."[28]

It is worth digressing briefly to consider Arnold's ideas about air power, as they are in many ways consistent with the views Reagan came to hold on the subject. As the international situation worsened during the 1930s, Arnold became convinced that the industrial powers had locked themselves into a race for air armament and that any country that fell behind did so at its peril. "It is unlikely," he argued in 1941, "that a nation such as ours can maintain its integrity and continue existence in its present way of living unless it establishes and maintains the world's strongest air force."[29]

Arnold's vision extended into the postwar era. "Air power is the weapon with which the aggressor in this war first struck and with which future aggressors will strike," he wrote after victory. The field was subject to such "revolutionary advances" that "we can only dimly visualize the possibilities of such sudden action in the future." By neglecting "a strong peacetime military organization," the United States would neither avoid confrontations nor deter others from waging war. Arnold called for increased cooperation among the military, industry, and the nation's universities, and for the development of a global intelligence network.[30]

From the beginning Arnold understood that film could publicize the advantages of flight. He had developed a friendship with the Warners and Guthrie well before Pearl Harbor and supported the studio's campaign for preparedness by offering advice about picture projects involving pilots. The Warners, in turn, helped when asked to make a short recruiting film that would "inspire youths to forget vacations and join up." *Winning Your Wings* (1941), featuring Lieutenant Jimmy Stewart, so impressed Arnold he asked for it to be shown in as many American theaters as possible. Enlistments in the Air Corps increased dramatically (although Arnold's staff surely exaggerated when it claimed the film helped recruit more than half a million cadets).[31]

After Pearl Harbor, Jack Warner had his own purposes in approaching Arnold. He wanted to carve out a niche for himself in the production of military films. He insisted on being commissioned an "active service Colonel" and that the new unit be permanently located in the Los Angeles area. He hoped to control not only Army Air Corps film projects but those of the Signal Corps, where rival producer Darryl Zanuck was trying to expand his influence. After the War Department authorized the First Motion Picture Unit, Warner continued to argue for centralization of film activities, complaining about loss of manpower to other units and proliferation of projects.

Everything, he said, should be centered in one photographic unit and "under the control of one responsible person." There was logic to the argument, because by early 1943 the army had eleven picture units, the navy ten, and at least eight other government departments were making movies.[32]

Warner, much to his dismay, proved not to be the person to lead the centralization of military filmmaking, but he did get his way about having the First Motion Picture Unit located in southern California. Warner Bros.' Vitagraph Studios in Los Angeles housed the unit until it outgrew the premises and transferred to Hal Roach Studios in Culver City. Fort Roach or Fort Wacky, as it became known, served as its home after October 1942.[33]

At first, personnel seemed a problem. Fortunately for Warner, the War Department gave the Air Corps preferential treatment in requisitioning people during the first half of 1942. Part of Guthrie's job was to procure men for Warner's unit.[34]

At this juncture Reagan came into the picture, so to speak. In his autobiography he left the impression that he first learned of the AAC's unit when Colonel Phillip Booker at Fort Mason told him that orders had arrived transferring him to a base in the Los Angeles area. "I thought I should at least bring to the Colonel's attention the fact that this assignment meant shipping me back home – something the Army does not normally do," Reagan recounted. "Colonel Booker said he didn't think that was of any importance, and then he said, 'To tell you the truth, whether you're willing or not, you're going – because in thirty-four years, this is the first time I've ever seen the Army make sense. This is putting a square peg in a square hole.' "[35]

Reagan spent little more than five weeks as a liaison officer at Fort Mason, helping load troops headed for Australia, before transferring to Warner's unit in late May 1942. Wasserman may have helped. Warner learned from Wallis that Reagan would be joining his outfit: "I received word today that Reagan's agent has notified Trilling that Reagan's Commanding General had approved his transfer to the Air Force and that the transfer papers had been sent to Washington."[36]

And so Reagan headed home to Los Angeles. "I'm as surprised as you are," he told a writer for a fan magazine. It may have all been the luck of the draw. It was true that the Air Corps branch needed qualified men. But it did not hurt to have a persistent agent and backing of a major studio with an executive who had friends in Washington. Reagan's first job involved interviewing and processing applicants for commissions, giving studio tours to recruits, and working as a public relations officer. Warner soon recommended him for promotion to first lieutenant.[37]

★★★

General Arnold's headquarters used its films to several ends: to increase enlistments, train servicemen, build morale, define the enemy, create unity, and promote air power. Recruitment was the immediate problem. Arnold estimated the nation needed fifty thousand combat pilots. One object of the films was therefore enlistment, and plans called for films for high school and college students, with others for draft board officials. Although wartime flying was a "grim and dangerous business," Arnold admitted, early films glorified aviation and sought to give young men the "full inspirational splendor of roaring engines, of tight bomber formations gliding through the clouds."[38]

Arnold realized it would be necessary to reinterpret heroic ideals. His air hero connected the solitary gladiator with advanced technology. "In modern warfare," he had written in 1926, "it is only the air pilots who have the opportunity for engaging in individual combat comparable to the epics of past ages. This fact alone is sufficient for American youths to become absorbed in this new art." His staff supplied Warner with names of courageous fliers, and stories about American aces became a staple of AAC propaganda. Reagan seemed an appropriate choice to narrate and appear in the FMPU's films, even if in reality he did not like to fly. Warner Bros. had already created an image for him as a pilot-hero skilled at using aviation technology in *Secret Service of the Air, Murder in the Air, International Squadron,* and *Desperate Journey.* Heroic pilots appeared in several of the World War II training films that Reagan either appeared in or narrated including *Rear Gunner, Beyond the Line of Duty, Jap Zero, Target Tokyo,* and *Fight for the Sky.*[39]

One of the first pictures was *Rear Gunner,* a sequel to *Winning Your Wings.* "We've got enough pilots to fly every plane in the world," Arnold told Warner, but "we need rear gunners. . . . Can you put something together in a hurry?" And, he asked, can you "give it some romantic appeal?" Warner later claimed that *Rear Gunner* convinced thousands of men to enlist.[40]

Rear Gunner was about the making of a "modern knight of fire." Filmed in July 1942, at the Las Vegas Gunnery School and in Tucson, Arizona, it featured Burgess Meredith, who played a backward youth from Kansas transformed from a "timid farm hand into an expert marksman." Reagan played the lieutenant who gave Meredith his chance. The film follows Meredith's character from the time he is drafted, through gunnery training and into combat, where he wins the Distinguished Service Medal. Merely graduating from gunnery school builds his confidence, earns him respect from fellow cadets, and provides a "passport into the vistas of victory." Leaders know the importance of rear gunners, an instructor tells Meredith. "They know that the fire from your guns is the fire of freedom."[41]

As enlistment quotas filled, the First Motion Picture Unit turned toward instructional pictures. Arnold believed movies could teach servicemen in a fraction of the time and expense previously required. The biggest part of the FMPU's work focused on training films that helped to make the Army Air Force the "largest single educational organization in existence," Arnold claimed.[42]

Reagan appeared in some of these instructional pictures, such as *Jap Zero,* which spent much of its fewer than four hundred feet telling servicemen how to distinguish enemy planes from friendly craft. He simulated a pilot somewhere in the Pacific who defeated a Zero because he learned to recognize the enemy. His devil-may-care demeanor in *Jap Zero* was similar to the character he played in *International Squadron.*

More often, though, he narrated. In *Beyond the Line of Duty* (1942), the only movie to feature the voices of both Reagan and President Roosevelt, he explained how to conduct a successful mission, occasionally interrupting Roosevelt's narration to remind pilots of techniques learned in flight school. In the B-29 briefing films, especially important during the last months of the war as the United States prepared to attack the Japanese mainland, he informed pilots about what to expect over enemy territory.

The problem for the briefing films involved giving bombing missions some idea of targets and terrain. Because the services knew little about mainland Japan, Hollywood special effects people built a miniature set of select areas including Tokyo. The plan took most of the floor of a sound stage and was so secret that the military posted a twenty-four-hour guard. Constructing a miniature that would resemble the Japan seen from the air posed a challenge for even the best special effects experts. Eventually, matchsticks built the Emperor's stables, airfoam from mattresses became forests, piano wire made railroad tracks, and plaster sprayed by an air gun onto composition board served as the ocean. Cameramen blended film of the model with real scenes from flights over Japan. With each raid over Japan, the miniature became more accurate. Film was flown from Saipan to Culver City, where the set was redesigned to incorporate bomb damage. So skillful was the deception that even Washington officers alerted to what had been done were fooled. The military's skepticism changed to enthusiasm. Reagan too was impressed. "Only an outfit like ours could have accomplished this task. Here was the true magic of motion picture making, the climax of years of miracle-making that had made Hollywood the film capital of the world," he recounted.[43]

Improving morale after Pearl Harbor also was a purpose of the films. *Beyond the Line of Duty* was about a real hero, Captain Hewitt T. Wheless, who won the Distinguished Service Cross for valor in an Army flying fortress in the western Pacific. The picture won an Academy Award. It conveyed several messages. Like *Rear Gunner,* it said that the military services transformed boys into men. Although Wheless was "just pint sized," Reagan narrated, the uniform worked "miracles" for any cadet's self-assurance. *Beyond the Line of Duty* followed the cadets into gunnery practice where, Reagan said, "It's shooting like this that will knock them on their axis." It showed soldiers from diverse backgrounds united. In the film, Wheless became part of an eight-man combat crew, an "all-American team from every quarter of America." By focusing on courage the picture tried to build morale when the United States was only beginning to repel the Japanese in the

Pacific. After Reagan introduced the crew and their mission, the narration cut to President Roosevelt, who described their exploits.[44]

Reagan narrated another film about war in the Pacific called *Westward Bataan,* which portrayed General Douglas MacArthur as an exceptional strategist who was also a friendly and well-liked commander. It showed the island-hopping strategy used to isolate Japanese troops on New Britain and New Ireland. With supplies cut off, the Japanese could "surrender or they can rot," Reagan declared. *Westward Bataan* used maps to show American progress and helped persuade audiences the Allies were winning.[45]

Target Tokyo, one of the most widely distributed films, conveyed the message that victory was only a matter of time. This documentary followed the crew of a superfortress from the United States to Pearl Harbor to Saipan and then the final thousand miles to Tokyo. Although Japan's high command had boasted that the Japanese home islands were beyond American bombers, Reagan described the "triumphant feeling of being the first" to carry out a successful B-29 raid over Tokyo and with it the "grim satisfaction of making the Nipponese high command eat its words." As the B-29 passes over a factory in suburban Tokyo, Reagan's narration asks the pilot: "Well, bud, what are you waiting for?"[46]

Some Army Air Force pictures may have helped make viewers receptive to massive bombing; showing American dead and wounded possibly convinced audiences that drastic action was required to end the war. *Westward Bataan* was more graphic than many earlier pictures. Air raids over Japan shown in *Target Tokyo,* said one of the Air Corps chroniclers, softened the "Nippon for atomizing." Arnold, it should be noted, advocated not only the use of the atomic bomb on Japan but its offensive deployment in the postwar world.[47]

The manner in which the pictures portrayed the enemy – as fanatical, even inhuman – also prepared audiences for the American bombing. To reinforce the idea that the Japanese would fight to the last man, an American officer in *Target Tokyo* tells troops that even though they were better equipped, they should not take the enemy "too lightly because he had that fanaticism which makes him think that his mission is to die for the emperor." *Westward Bataan* declared that the Japanese government was "prepared to lose ten million in its war with America." How many was the United States prepared to sacrifice? "Well, life isn't cheap in America," Reagan responds, and as a Japanese mother picks up a box apparently with the ashes of her son, he says, "We don't raise our boys to be gods in little white boxes."[48]

Metaphors from the animal kingdom described the enemy. The officer in *Target Tokyo* tells his men to watch the enemy "as you would a rattlesnake." Before becoming a cadet in *Rear Gunner,* Meredith's character practices shooting crows or "black killers." When he shoots down any enemy plane, an early version of the script called for him to say it was just like those "black killers only this time they're yellow." A more subtle, visual metaphor appeared in *Beyond the Line of Duty.* By the time Wheless's plane arrives at its target, President Roosevelt says, the other bombers have "stirred up a hornet's nest of Japanese Zero planes." Indeed, as Japanese Zeroes encircle Wheless, they appeared on screen (having been filmed from a distance) not unlike swarming wasps. Similar characterizations appeared in other films, photographs, and literature.[49]

Yet another theme, the promotion of unity, appeared in the films. *Westward Bataan, The Fight for the Sky, Target Tokyo, Beyond the Line of Duty,* and *Rear Gunner* tried to do so by commemorating heroes and inspiring confidence in air power. Other pictures promoted religious, economic, and racial harmony. Filmmakers stressed a bond between Protestants, Catholics, Jews, Native Americans, and blacks.[50] Among Reagan's war films, *For God and Country* (1944) most strongly encouraged religious unity. Duty and sacrifice to comrades were themes in this film dedicated to army chaplains. Reagan portrayed a Catholic priest, a scholar-athlete, an "almost all-American" quarterback at Loyola. He twice appeared conducting Catholic services. Reagan's character refused to carry a weapon and died a heroic death while trying to save a comrade, an American Indian. *For God and Country* blended Judeo-Christianity and patriotism, the "province of the spirit, of life everlasting" with America's fate in the war. In the Army, the narrator said, Protestants, Catholics, and Jews were "unified by a service in the same chapel." The two best friends of Reagan's character – one a Protestant, the other a Jew – were "united in devotion to God," pastors "to all men, regardless of classification, color, or creed." Visually the picture underscored the idea that the American flag protected three faiths.[51]

A final goal of Reagan's World War II unit was to show that air power was essential to national defense. Many films celebrated American technology as they hailed the nation's air heroes. The B-29, Reagan said in *Target Tokyo,* could "carry more destruction and carry it higher and faster and farther than any bomber ever built before." No territory within the Japanese empire, however remote, could escape. At the end of *Beyond the Line of Duty,* Captain Wheless thanks Boeing workers at the giant factory in Seattle. "With these planes, we can outfight them," and, he predicts, "when we start heading over Berlin and Tokyo it's really going to be a picnic." *Fight for the Sky* followed bombing raids into Germany. Leaving from the English coast, Thunderbolts (B-47s), Lightnings (P-38s), and Mustangs (P-51s) overwhelmed the enemy's planes in "fantastic numbers," smashing German resistance. "Into these three great fighters," Reagan said, "America poured its genius," and "no American fighter ever failed because of enemy odds, however great." As pictures of pilots killed in combat were superimposed over scenes of bombs falling on Germany, he paid tribute to the men "who in the decisive hour smashed the Luftwaffe and gave us freedom of the air in Europe."[52]

Reagan's wartime filmmaking was not confined to the First Motion Picture Base Unit. His best-known World War II picture was, of course, *This Is the Army* (1943), made outside the auspices of the Army Air Corps. Warner Bros. made this movie and the War Department gave Reagan permission to take part. It grossed more than $5 million in its first year. *This Is the Army* was based on two Irving Berlin stage plays, *Yip, Yip, Yaphand,* which appeared in 1917, and *This Is the Army,* a success on Broadway in 1942. The movie added a backstage story and argued that the job started in World War I had to be finished this time. The inspirational value lay in Berlin's music, Kate Smith's singing, and the choreography. Americans from diverse backgrounds united in common purpose was an important theme, as was duty and sacrifice. A mother tearfully confided to her son: "I just want you to know its all right – I mean about the Army. . . . This is what I raised you for, to be a credit to your country and to yourself. . . . So don't worry any more, son, just take care of yourself, if you can. And . . . give it to 'em."[53]

Reagan's active duty ended on September 10, 1945, soon after Japan surrendered, and more than three years after Reagan entered Fort Mason. By this time he was a captain. William Guthrie was instrumental in obtaining the discharge. He told the Army about a plan for a feature film about a pilot, saying that Warner Bros. was producing several pictures of "vital interest to the war effort" and intended to use Reagan in them if he was released from duty. Guthrie learned in July that Reagan's discharge had been approved. In what pictures Warner Bros. had scheduled Reagan was unclear.[54]

Reagan's war service, one must conclude, was more credible than that of some people from Hollywood but less impressive than that of others. Jack Warner, who managed to retain his civilian salary of $3,500 per week while on active duty, had resigned his commission and returned to civilian life in late 1942 after being replaced as commanding officer of the FMPU and receiving orders transferring him to Chanute Field in Illinois. President Truman later awarded him the Medal for Merit (Arnold presented him the award in early 1947).[55] Errol Flynn and Cary Grant managed to avoid service. David Niven returned to England and volunteered. When Lew Ayres, who had once starred in the antiwar film *All Quiet on the Western Front,* became a conscientious objector in the spring of 1942, many theaters banned his films. Clark Gable, whose wife Carole Lombard died in a plane crash returning from an Indiana war bond rally, became Major Gable and worked with the First Motion Picture Unit, as well as flying overseas with a bomber squadron. James Stewart became a colonel and flew combat missions, a dangerous experience. Bob Hope drove five thousand miles by automobile in England to entertain servicemen. Pat O'Brien, who was forty-one at the time of Pearl Harbor, let his agent talk him out of reenlisting but traveled worldwide – often under hazardous conditions – to entertain troops. Real war was not like Hollywood showed it, he concluded. "It was more earnest, monotonous and reasonless."[56]

Although Reagan stayed in the United States and never heard a "shot fired in anger," his screen persona remained associated with courage under fire. In

Rear Gunner, Jap Zero, and *For God and Country* audiences saw his charac-
ters confront the enemy in combat. In *Beyond the Line of Duty, Fight for the
Sky,* and *Westward Bataan* he commemorated heroes. Publicity for *Rear
Gunner* emphasized Reagan's part in America's defense. Here were Burgess
Meredith and Reagan in "a new role – and a role they love: the saga of
America's men doing their part to make the world safe for democracy!"
What "greater proof of their sincerity" could be given than "to say that at
present both Meredith and Reagan are lieutenants in our armed forces?
Perhaps they were more than acting their parts in the film – perhaps they
were living them?"[57]

Reagan's service received wide publicity. If people missed his training
pictures, millions saw him in *This Is the Army* or in magazines. No
twentieth-century president, with the exception of Dwight D. Eisenhower,
had been seen in uniform by more people.

PART TWO

THE MAKING OF AN ANTICOMMUNIST

10

A FALSE START:
HICCASP

... I became an easy mark for speechmaking on the rubber-chicken and glass-tinkling circuits. It fed my ego, since I had been so long away from the screen. I loved it. But though I did not realize it then, both my material and my audience were hand-picked, or at least I was being spoon-fed and steered more than a little bit. ... I commenced to back off from speaking engagements. I had been shooting off my mouth without knowing my real target. I determined to do my own research, find out my own facts.

Ronald Reagan, 1965[1]

Three months after the bombing of Hiroshima and Nagasaki, Ronald Reagan warned Americans about the dangers of nuclear power. The scene was a dinner to honor the Harvard astronomer Harlow Shapley. Reagan's contribution to the program was a dramatic reading of Norman Corwin's poem "Set Your Clock at U-235." It preceded speeches by Congresswoman Helen Gahagan Douglas, Shapley, and the novelist Thomas Mann, and set the tone for the evening. The dinner and subsequent meeting were sponsored by the Hollywood Independent Citizens Committee of the Arts, Sciences and Professions (HICCASP), "pronounced like the cough of a dying man," Reagan later said, "a noble-spoken organization" that supported left-of-center causes.[2]

Reagan's participation was interesting in that he associated himself with calls for world unity and international control of nuclear weapons. At the time, December 1945, only a few atomic weapons existed and the United States had a monopoly. The message of December 10 was sobering and, for some, controversial, because it challenged two ideas many Americans accepted as articles of faith: nationalism and capitalism. Speakers argued that survival required changes in the way people thought and lived. Douglas believed atomic weapons were the "most revolutionary development" in history, that there was no defense against them, and that it was impossible to

121

keep the technology secret. She emphasized cooperation among the United States, Britain, and the Soviet Union, and warned that unless Congress embraced a more enlightened policy, a nuclear arms race of unprecedented proportions would follow.[3] Shapley asserted that hope lay in internationalism. "The atomic bomb was not so much over Hiroshima as it was under all of us – and still is," he said. "The world has shrunk too much for us to strut around and be nationalistic. We must be international or supernational in our thinking."[4] Mann said that free enterprise had "lost its meaning in an economy fettered by trusts and monopolies." Progress in the nuclear age required struggle against reactionaries who would hinder the development of "economic democracy, planned economy, democratic socialism." He called on America to renounce imperialism and urged "the unity of mankind, . . . economic cooperation among nations, . . . an economic and political world federation, . . . [and] the fusion of the national cultures into a world civilization."[5]

Using Corwin's words, Reagan also endorsed the quest for one world:

> The secrets of the earth have been peeled, one by one, until the core is
>   bare:
> The latest recipe is private, in a guarded book, but the stink of death is
>   public on the wind from Nagasaki: . . .
> Unless we work at it together, at a single earth,
> Then do not bother to lay wreaths for sailors who went down burning in
>   winter seas. . . .
> Oneness is our destination: has long been: is far the best of places to ar-
>   rive at. . . .[6]

The dinner was only a prelude to a much larger meeting, "Atomic Power and Foreign Policy," scheduled two nights later in the Hollywood Legion Stadium. But when Warner Bros. officials learned Reagan would perform Corwin's work again at HICCASP's mass rally, they objected, saying that it would violate his contract. Through his agent, Lew Wasserman, Reagan notified the studio he would abide by their wishes.[7]

★★★

The Hollywood Independent Citizens Committee of the Arts, Sciences and Professions had had a promising beginning in 1938, when the motion picture industry helped elect Culbert L. Olsen governor of California. Four years later its supporters reassembled to help Olsen in his unsuccessful bid for reelection. In March 1943, the group took the name of Hollywood Democratic Committee (HDC) and by 1944, united by loyalty to President Roosevelt, boasted a thousand members. Arthur Schlesinger, Jr. attacked the organization in 1946 (its name had then been changed to HICCASP), but described its inception as a "brilliant contribution" by Hollywood actors and writers to Roosevelt's 1944 campaign. Marc Connelly, HDC's chairman, told a group of Roosevelt supporters in 1944 that the organization had the support of "every liberal thinking person" in the area. When Roosevelt died, HDC supported his successor.[8]

The HDC grew under direction of its executive secretary, George Pepper, an erstwhile violinist, forced by arthritis to abandon his instrument. Pepper was a member of the Communist Party. An able leader, he "put together the HDC like a watch," Ellenore Bogigian observed, "and polished it like a jewel." HDC began cooperating with the New York–based Independent Citizens Committee of the Arts, Sciences and Professions (ICCASP) in 1945. It changed its name to the Hollywood Independent Citizens Committee of the Arts, Sciences, and Professions and affiliated with ICCASP, becoming ICCASP's Hollywood chapter in early 1946. HICCASP thus included not only actors but members of the other arts and sciences.[9]

HICCASP owed much of its growth to ICCASP's executive director, Hannah Dorner, a public relations counsel and newspaperwoman, and to its chairman, the sculptor Jo Davidson, born in Manhattan's lower East Side and the son of Russian Jewish immigrants. James Roosevelt, the late president's son, joined in early 1946 and became national director. Harold L. Ickes, former secretary of the interior, became executive chairman.[10]

A gallery of talent ranging from Albert Einstein and Max Weber to Orson Welles and Frank Sinatra lent their names to the group. A few were brilliant intellects, some were ideologues, others were idealistic, still others were fuzzy-headed – as in the case of actor Sterling Hayden, who confessed that while members discussed profound issues all he could do was "drink three to their one and try to look intelligent." It was this melange of the serious-minded and the celebrated that gave HICCASP leverage on American voters.[11]

Communists and fellow travelers were on HICCASP's executive council. In early 1946 they were in the minority compared to the liberals. Although the organization's agenda in late 1945 and 1946 coincided in some points with the Communist Party line, it would be simplistic to argue that Communists dominated HICCASP. Dorner was probably correct – if blasé – when she argued that "if the ICCASP program is like the Communist line," it was "purely coincidental."[12]

By the autumn of 1946, after the exodus of many liberals, HICCASP took positions on a range of issues. In foreign affairs it supported the United Nations. It advocated "universal disarmament." It urged lifting of secrecy on atomic energy research and supported a "system of international cooperation and control of atomic energy" under the auspices of the United Nations. It sought to prevent the unraveling of the wartime alliance and endorsed Henry A. Wallace's view that war with the USSR was not inevitable. It deplored the Truman administration's "get tough" policy with the Soviets. It attacked colonialism and called for "immediate withdrawal" of troops from China.[13]

On the domestic front, HICCASP had equally interesting ideas. It asked for "realization of Roosevelt's Economic Bill of Rights" and stronger price controls. It desired full employment, unemployment compensation, a minimum wage, improved housing, and health care. It endorsed federal aid to education, a National Science Foundation, and "more extensive use of science and technology" to stimulate production. It championed civil liberties and defended academic freedom against California's Committee on Un-American Activities, known as the Tenney Committee. It sought abolition of poll taxes, lynching, and segregation. It monitored antilabor legislation and was sympathetic to workers' unions.[14]

Although most of these ideas eventually found their way into legislation, many politicians considered as liabilities the organization's "undergraduate enthusiasm" and "leftist"-tinged "vehemence." HICCASP-supported candidates were largely unsuccessful in congressional races of 1946. The Hollywood membership concluded that the organization had dissipated its energies.[15]

HICCASP came under attack for allowing Communists into its membership. Schlesinger criticized it in *Life* magazine, claiming that "its celebrities maintained their membership but not their vigilance." If local chapters managed to stay free of communist domination, Schlesinger said, the national organization on most foreign policy issues "backed the Russians or kept quiet." *Time* raised the possibility that HICCASP was a front. "The Commies are boring in like weevils in a biscuit," it quoted one member as saying. No one refuted the charges that there were Communists in HICCASP, but Davidson argued that their numbers were exaggerated. His defense left critics unimpressed. The Tenney Committee proclaimed HICCASP one of the state's "key Communist fronts."[16]

Reagan's association with HICCASP began as early as the 1944 presidential campaign, while he was still serving with the Army Air Force in California. The Hollywood for Roosevelt Committee, chaired by Jack Warner, Samuel Goldwyn, and Katharine Hepburn, persuaded Ickes to speak at a Hollywood rally. His address at the Ambassador Hotel, titled "Don't Change to a Trojan Horse in the Middle of a War!" attacked the Republican candidate Thomas E. Dewey and was carried on a nationwide radio hookup. Several hundred movie stars, including Reagan, attended. Reagan contributed $100 to the Hollywood Democratic Committee, and his picture in captain's uniform appeared in local papers along with those of Edward G. Robinson, Gene Kelly, and Judy Garland.[17]

When asked to fill a vacancy on the organization's executive council in the summer of 1946, Reagan "felt honored." His participation on the council, though, lasted less than a month. He appeared at his first council meeting on July 2, 1946; it was a stormy, divisive session that led to several resignations. About sixty people attended, including fifty council members. Reagan sat beside RKO executive Dore Schary, and was surprised by those who attended. "Lots of people here I didn't think I'd see," he told Schary. He began to make connections with other events such as the Hollywood strikes. He sensed something was afoot.[18]

What disrupted the July 2 meeting was an attempt to quiet allegations that HICCASP was "controlled by the left." Reagan had heard the charges but believed them "Republican propaganda." When James Roosevelt suggested a statement repudiating communism, what followed was described charitably in council minutes as a "frank discussion." Reagan characterized it as "a Kilkenny brawl":

A well-known musician [Artie Shaw] sprang to his feet. He offered to recite the USSR constitution from memory, yelling that it was a lot more democratic than that of the United States. A prominent movie writer leaped upward. He said that if there was ever a war between the United States and Russia, he would volunteer for Russia.[19]

Reagan endorsed Roosevelt's proposal and found himself "waist-high in epithets such as 'Fascist' and 'capitalist scum' and 'enemy of the proletariat' and 'witch-hunter' and 'Red-baiter.'" Linus Pauling, the activist scientist, was "very quiet," the writer Dalton Trumbo "very vociferous," he recalled. "Most vehement of all" was John Howard Lawson, who, Reagan said, "persisted in waving a long finger under my nose and telling me off."[20]

Debate concluded with the chairman appointing a committee of seven to draw up a policy statement. The radio writer True Boardman headed this group. It included Reagan, Roosevelt, the writer Don Hartman, and Pauling. Trumbo and Lawson, later members of the Hollywood Ten, represented HICCASP's radical left.[21]

Reagan's account leaves little doubt that he was part of a plan to divide HICCASP. As he left the meeting, Schary invited him to Olivia De Havilland's apartment, where he met Roosevelt, Hartman, the writer Eddie Knopf, and composer Johnny Green, all pleased with the council meeting because "the whole thing had been a preconceived plot to smoke out the 'others.'" The group sought to manufacture a disagreement so that they would have a pretext to resign from HICCASP. De Havilland asked a grinning Reagan what was so funny. "Nothing," he said, explaining that he thought she was a Communist. "I thought *you* were one," she smiled back. "Until tonight, that is."[22]

The pretext for resigning came in the form of a "disinfecting resolution" that Roosevelt and De Havilland drew up and presented to HICCASP's leadership. The matter of a statement also loomed. "I started – Lincoln and I," Reagan recalled, "to scribble one on the back of an envelope." The group in the apartment reworked the statement. "It was deliberately a very innocuous document (for purposes of entrapment) until the last phrases," Reagan said. "These read: 'We reaffirm our belief in free enterprise and the democratic system and repudiate Communism as desirable for the United States.'"[23]

If the actor oversimplified the events of July 1946, he at least understood he was confronting people with different ideas. Lawson and Trumbo were contemptuous of capitalism and bourgeois culture. Others on HICCASP's executive council (as well as in the national organization, ICCASP) were sympathetic to their views.[24]

Lawson was one of the most formidable foes Reagan encountered on the policy committee and probably on the executive council.[25] In his early fifties, he possessed a "very commanding presence," Nancy Schwartz noted. "He had a slight limp that most people didn't notice, a booming voice, and the habit of smashing his fist into his open palm as he made a point." Alvah Bessie liked him because he was the "permanent bête noire of every reactionary in Hollywood" and Lester Cole considered him a "brilliant intellect and fearless activist." He began as a cable editor for Reuters in 1914, then joined the volunteer American ambulance unit in Italy and France during World War I, where he served with John Dos Passos, Ernest Hemingway, and e. e. cummings. With "bright brown eyes peering out over a hawklike nose, . . . and his dark, unruly hair" behaving "as though it had never encountered a brush," it seemed that he "had a drastic idea about every subject that surfaced." A modestly talented writer, Lawson achieved stature as a left-wing playwright during the 1920s and early 1930s, and became a screenwriter, theorist, historian, and acknowledged "high lama" of Hollywood's Communist Party. Reagan came to see him as a link in communism's international chain-of-command.[26]

Lawson was influential in the Hollywood Democratic Committee and HICCASP. He had presented HDC's policy statement in 1944, a document that urged support for Roosevelt. He called for "stamping out the sources of native fascism" and endorsed greater support for labor, minority rights, and international cooperation. In 1945 he condemned American foreign policy and praised the Soviet Union for its "peaceful" approach to other countries. Following his speech, HICCASP's membership passed a resolution opposing intervention in China's internal affairs.[27] In the months before the 1946 policy dispute, Lawson regularly attended HICCASP's executive council meetings. He tried to line up support for political candidates and chaired a committee that cooperated with the Railroad Brotherhood and the CIO, opposing antilabor legislation. He attacked racial injustice. "Racism is not a natural tendency of human beings," he asserted, but "something which is developed artificially in the interest of certain powerful groups because it benefits these groups and returns a profit to them."[28]

Lawson wanted to change Hollywood's economic structure. He gained the enmity of producers for supporting the strikes at Warner Bros. and other studios in 1945 and 1946. He believed it essential "to break down the separation between the more highly skilled professional workers, who necessarily function mainly in the commercial media, and the somewhat less experienced artists who are engaged in amateur or semiprofessional activities."[29]

Lawson considered motion pictures important in the postwar ideological struggle between the United States and the Soviet Union. "The film is ideology," he wrote, and crucial in the "battle of ideas." He called members of the film industry "'cultural' servants of Wall Street . . . monopolists" and Hollywood films propaganda for an "imperialism" that promoted the "cult of war, racism and the 'superiority' of an elite class."[30]

Trumbo was an almost equal force within HICCASP. He was a gifted writer, later blacklisted and imprisoned after the 1947 HUAC hearings.[31] A "waspish, feisty man," he complained that photographers too often made him "look like a werewolf in pansy dress." Unafraid of controversy or of aligning "himself on the side of the angels at a time when it was neither profitable nor popular to do so," he possessed an "engaging personality, a brilliantly sharp mind and an offbeat, marvelous wit." Albert Maltz remembered him as "completely intolerant of dullness." He "loved to live in a very grand style," made possible by a contract with MGM that was the envy of other writers. He had a $100,000 house in Beverly Hills but often wrote at his ranch in the Tehachapi Mountains, where, flanked by an enormous cup of coffee, he sat cross-legged in a bathtub specially fitted with a writing table. A steady stream of water ran in and out of the tub to maintain a constant temperature.[32]

When it came to political and social issues, Trumbo and Lawson were kindred spirits. Trumbo considered the Warners "perfectly normal, healthy, intelligent American capitalists – economic brothers to the Fords, . . . and the Morgans," who were "directly responsible to the great banking houses of Wall Street." He favored strong unions and supported the studio strikes in 1945 and 1946. "The fight for the freer use of the screen as a weapon for human decency," he wrote, rested "fundamentally upon an organizational basis." Free expression in Hollywood was inseparably bound with the "fight for economic security."[33]

Many of Trumbo's ideas found their way into speeches he wrote for such stars as Robinson, Hepburn, and De Havilland. Some of his talks supported Roosevelt. After FDR's death, he often invoked Roosevelt's name on behalf of labor and minorities. He attacked red-baiting and would endorse Henry A. Wallace in 1948.[34]

The addresses Trumbo prepared for De Havilland to deliver in Seattle in June 1946, however, angered HICCASP liberals, provoking their resignations. De Havilland was one of HICCASP's vice chairs, along with Linus Pauling, Lena Horne, Frank Sinatra, and Dore Schary. De Havilland had been asked to speak twice in Seattle. The programs – billed as "rededication" to the values of FDR and Wendell Willkie – were advertised on behalf of "jobs, peace, and freedom."[35]

De Havilland undoubtedly joined HICCASP for idealistic reasons and was a willing speaker. Born of English parents in Japan, she had come to America in 1919 with her younger sister, who later took the name Joan Fontaine. In

1958, living abroad but hoping to retain her American citizenship, De Havilland testified secretly before the House Committee on Un-American Activities and claimed she had been "duped" into joining HICCASP. Gradually, she said, she became suspicious of the group. She thought a minority had disproportionate influence. Members would filibuster and meetings run so late that many who had early morning calls would leave. A vote would be taken and the minority would win. She became upset by HICCASP's uncritical attitude toward labor and the Soviet Union. The organization was "not independent," but had two policies, one "pro-labor," the other "automatically pro-Russian." She realized that the "communists [were] the only ones who would automatically endorse flatly, without question, these points of view," she told HUAC.[36]

Trumbo wrote two speeches for her to give in Seattle and her reaction to them opened the revolt of HICCASP liberals. Trumbo indicted not only American racism and antiunionism, but nationalism, drawing analogies to fascist Germany. He argued that "racial bigotry, union-busting and isolationism – another word for it is nationalism – are closely related," part of the same reactionary pattern that achieved "terrible finality" in Hitler's Third Reich. "The destruction of each one is necessary for the destruction of the other two." He linked anti-Semitism with acquisition of wealth, accusing vested interests of seeking war against the USSR. He associated his position on labor with Abraham Lincoln, Roosevelt, and Wendell Willkie. He called for "vigilant protection" of labor and "full democratic rights for the Negro people."[37]

For De Havilland, Trumbo had gone too far. According to Reagan, the two talks were "so full of Communist-oriented tidbits" that the actress refused them. Apparently present when Trumbo drafted them, she was troubled. She was reevaluating her affiliation, and Trumbo's ideas convinced her she could no longer speak for the organization. But she did not want to withdraw from or force cancellation of the Seattle programs, so she turned to HICCASP's treasurer, Ernest Pascal, and to James Roosevelt. Together the three changed what Trumbo had written.[38]

The speeches that De Havilland delivered denounced communism and dissociated it from liberalism:

The adroit generals of the ultra-conservative forces of our country, have tried to confuse and divide the liberal forces by making it appear that the great liberal movement is controlled by those who are more interested in taking orders from Moscow, and following the so-called party line, than they are in making democracy work. There is only one way to answer the charge – and bury it once and for all. The overwhelming majority of people who make up the liberal and progressive groups of this country believe in democracy, and *not* in communism. We believe that the two cannot be reconciled here in the United States, and we believe that every effort should be exerted to make democracy work, and to extend its benefits to every person in every community throughout our land.[39]

Trumbo was indignant. "My dear Miss De Havilland," he wrote on June 24, "I am informed, somewhat after the fact, that the material I prepared with you for your Seattle trip failed to meet your standards and was not used. Writers customarily are informed of the rejection of their work by its return to them." He saved his worst criticism for Pascal, whom he castigated along with Roosevelt for adding denunciations of communism while deleting condemnations of fascism. "I think I understand your motives, Ernest; and to understand is, in some degree, to forgive. But don't you occasionally wonder, alone and late at night, who butchered the women of Europe and buried their living children and burned their men?" He threatened legal action if such episodes recurred.[40]

Meanwhile the Screen Actors Guild had adopted a position on communism. The issue had grown out of an effort to create an alliance between members of the actors, writers, and directors guilds. A tri-guild council would have given the groups a united front to meet problems. But the wording of a statement of purpose was an obstacle in the spring of 1946. In SAG, Robert Montgomery and George Murphy wanted a condemnation of fascism *and* communism.[41]

About a fourth of SAG's board members objected to an anticommunist declaration. Anne Revere, a member of HICCASP, was among SAG's liberal dissenters, and at a meeting in late May (from which Reagan was absent and indeed which only fifteen members attended) she convinced the board to postpone the anticommunist proclamation. Two weeks later, with two dozen board members present (including Reagan but not Revere), Montgomery and Murphy had enough support to pass a resolution denying that SAG had become a platform for "ideologies inimical to the American way of life" and opposing "any Fascist or Communist influence in the motion picture industry or the ranks of labor."[42]

Reagan had joined the debate on the tri-guild council in the early spring of 1946. When he returned to SAG's board of directors after the war, he at first was "very popular with the liberals," Revere recalled. But he disappointed her. After talking with members of the other guilds, he concluded that the writers and probably some of the directors possessed "rather exotic political beliefs." One frailty of many "progressive" organizations, he told SAG's board in April, was unwillingness to take a position on "communism and the other extreme ideologies."[43]

Like De Havilland, Reagan had started to reevaluate his political associations. A "crack" in his "staunch liberalism" had appeared during the war, when he had become disenchanted with government bureaucracy at his military base.[44] But after the war he had "blindly and busily" joined every organization he could find "that would guarantee to save the world," he recalled. "I was not sharp about communism," he said. His name became linked to at least a half dozen groups, all under surveillance by the FBI, which at one time or another were labeled communist fronts during the late 1940s. The bureau suspected that he might be a communist sympathizer.[45] One evening in the spring of 1946 he spoke to the Hollywood–Beverly Christian Church's men's club. He had made his "usual energetic pitch to howls of applause," he recounted, only to be approached afterwards by the minister, most likely the Reverend Cleveland Kleihauer, who suggested that in addition to condemning fascism, he should also denounce communism. Reagan agreed. In his next public appearance, he followed Kleihauer's advice. "I got riotous applause more than twenty times," he recalled; but then came the denunciation of communism. "The silence was ghastly." A few days later he received a letter. "I'm sure you were aware of the reaction to your last paragraph," wrote a woman who had been in the audience. "I hope you recognize what it means." Reagan was unsure of what it meant, but he began to cut back on his speaking schedule. "I determined to do my own research, find out my own facts," he disclosed.[46]

The more Reagan learned about HICCASP, the more leery he became. His brother, Neil, who then "lay in the bushes" and took license plate numbers for the FBI, warned him about the organization. "There are people in there who can cause you real trouble. They're more than suspect on the part of the government."[47]

Was Ronald Reagan acting as an informant and provocateur for the FBI or some other agency? He acknowledged under oath in 1955 that while he attempted to influence HICCASP he received confidential government information.

"Did you at that time, Mr. Reagan, have any special access to investigative facilities of the government, either national or state, with respect to Communist activity?" an attorney asked during the *Jeffers* v. *Screen Extras Guild* trial.

"Well, unofficially someone dropped in to my living room a few times and made information available to me, but told me at the time that if I ever got in trouble from using it they would deny that they had done so," he answered.[48]

That he received such information was not surprising. The government had informers at Warner Bros. dating back at least to 1940, and Director Hoover had asked an agent to see Reagan as early as September 1941. During the war the bureau interviewed him at Culver City. Certainly by 1947 Reagan was providing information about HICCASP and other Hollywood activities, and he had received the code name T-10.[49]

Armed with the resolution and a draft statement assembled in De Havilland's apartment, Reagan, Roosevelt, and Hartman attended the July 5 policy committee meeting at Roosevelt's Beverly Hills house. Reagan remembered the gathering (which was under surveillance) as stormy.

We got the floor and read what we had composed. Again, the howls and denunciations; again the finger of Lawson under my nose. "This organization," he shouted, "will never adopt a statement which endorses free enterprise and repudiates Communism!" . . . Then he hastily assured me he was not personally a Communist.[50]

Reagan suggested the issue go before the HICCASP membership in a secret ballot, a plan Lawson reputedly rejected because he felt members lacked political sophistication.[51]

Reagan's description of the policy committee meeting, while colorful, was one-sided. One observer recalled that Reagan contributed little and "seemed bored with it all." Reagan was misleading when he implied (by quoting Lawson) that the policy committee and HICCASP's council as a whole would not endorse free enterprise. The five-page statement HICCASP adopted said that "in respect to domestic policy, we believe with Franklin Roosevelt that our country can 'sustain a national income which will assure full production and full employment under our democratic system of free enterprise, with government encouragement and aid whenever and wherever it is necessary.'" But Reagan was accurate in recollecting that the committee's proclamation "hardly touched on the question of Communism."[52]

The Roosevelt–De Havilland resolution was specific, repudiating communism as a "desirable form of government for the U.S.A." although it did profess a "belief that Communist nations such as Soviet Russia" could "live together in peace and good will" with such "capitalist democratic nations" as the United States. It endorsed a different definition of free enterprise, one linked to "private ownership."[53]

When De Havilland presented the resolution to the council there was pandemonium. "We didn't get to the membership – we didn't even get back to the board," Reagan recalled. "It seems HICCASP had an even more exclusive intellectual elite – an executive committee – and somehow it was decided to settle the issue in this rarefied atmosphere. Olivia was our only representative on this group. She presented our resolution and dutifully phoned each one of us that she was the only 'aye' vote."[54]

Even so, at its July 10 meeting the council adopted with amendments the statement from the seven-person committee of which Reagan was a member. At the next board meeting De Havilland indicated dissatisfaction and proposed a resolution (presumably the one she and Roosevelt had written) for inclusion in HICCASP's policy proclamation. The following day, July 17, ICCASP's national executive committee voted to accept Roosevelt's resignation. (He had tendered it on July 9, pleading poor health.) At HICCASP's next executive council meeting on July 23, Roosevelt's resignation was discussed and De Havilland's letter severing ties with the organization read. Policy committee members decided to reconvene to consider a stronger statement that would indicate "independence from any political organization." Schary replaced Roosevelt.[55]

At the July 30 executive council meeting Boardman reported committee agreement on a change in the statement's last paragraph (it is unclear if Reagan was on the committee at this time, although minutes do not indicate his resignation). The new statement did make an effort to separate HICCASP from the Communist Party. HICCASP, it read,

has no affiliation with any political party or organization, Republican, Democratic, Communist, Socialist or other. Its policies are determined solely by the majority will of its membership. The Committee stands on issues and principles. It believes that only by careful analysis and determined action on each issue as it arises, on each candidate as he bids for election, may we hope that these United States and the world can attain the destiny envisaged and struggled for by Franklin D. Roosevelt.[56]

The amendment came too late to satisfy many of the liberals who had abandoned HICCASP. In addition to resignations by Roosevelt and De Havilland, others followed. "Very shortly HICCASP gave its last groan and expired," Reagan remembered.[57]

At what point Reagan left HICCASP is unclear. He said he sent his resignation by telegram the same evening the executive council turned down De Havilland's resolution. But De Havilland recalled that Reagan, who seemed to relate to HICCASP primarily as an "observer," remained with the organization another three months after her resignation. HICCASP's minutes do not indicate when Reagan resigned, and a list of standing committees shows that more than a month after this crisis the executive council ratified him for membership on its labor committee.[58]

Many of HICCASP's proposals achieved wider acceptance in later years and found their way into Democratic Party platforms. But by mid-1946, Hollywood had begun to turn against such programs. The division within HICCASP marked only an early phase of an era hostile to left-wing politics.

For the time, Reagan remained a Democrat, but he considered mid-1946 a turning point in his thinking about liberalism and communism. "Light was dawning in some obscure region in my head," he remembered. "I was beginning to see the seamy side of liberalism. Too many of the patches on the progressive coat were of a color I didn't personally care for." He later condemned liberals for an "ideological myopia" that prevented them from seeing the Communists as they really were.[59]

The confrontation with HICCASP members – Reagan called it "philosophical combat" – hence confirmed that the Communists actually existed. Those developments, though, did not occur in a vacuum. They were surrounded by a long period of labor violence.[60]

11

LABOR AND THE RISE TO POWER

Ronnie Reagan . . . has turned out to be a tower of strength, not only for the actors but for the whole industry and he is to be highly complimented for his efforts on behalf of everyone working in our business.

Jack L. Warner, October, 1946

The alienation of . . . fellow employees . . . may not seem important now, but such seeds of hatred have a way of sprouting into a forest of enemies.[1]

The crisis that Ronald Reagan helped create in HICCASP came at a time of intense labor unrest in the United States. In Hollywood the first of a series of strikes had begun in March 1945 and did not end until late October. A threat of walkouts continued into 1946. After a two-day stoppage in early July, another strike started in September and continued for three years.[2]

The Hollywood trouble involved rivalry between the International Alliance of Theatrical and Stage Employees (IATSE) and the Conference of Studio Unions (CSU). Their differences had a complicated history that involved a jurisdictional dispute over the division of work on movie sets, the nature of unionism, and the distribution of money. Producers lined up with the International Alliance because it controlled projectionists and therefore could shut down theaters. HICCASP and the Screen Writers Guild supported the Conference of Studio Unions.[3]

When the CSU called the first strike, Reagan had been sympathetic – at that time he had known "little and cared less about the rumors about communists." But the strikes became part of a "series of hard-nosed happenings" that altered his thinking about threats to America and forced him into decisions that challenged his oratorical skills, tested his courage, and won the enmity of Hollywood's left wing.[4]

It was in this era of labor turmoil that he became president of the Screen Actors Guild. He returned to the board of directors in February 1946. Later that year he became a member of the guild's emergency committee that tried to resolve the strikes of the summer and fall. The membership elected him third vice-president in September. The following March, when Robert Montgomery resigned as president, he filled the remainder of Montgomery's term. In November 1947 the members elected him to the first of what proved to be five consecutive one-year terms.[5]

The rivalry between the two unions predated Reagan's arrival in Hollywood. IATSE had affiliated with the American Federation of Labor. It was one of the oldest international unions in the AFL and had been in the Los Angeles area since the late nineteenth century. It had become a power in the industry by organizing workers in production and exhibition, and by combining local craft unions connected to the building trades together with projectionists, grips, and property people. The projectionists gave the union a powerful means of organizing production employees and getting the attention of producers.[6]

The International Alliance of Theatrical and Stage Employees had entered jurisdictional disputes with carpenters, painters, electricians, and other workers dating back at least to World War I. It compromised with several of these groups and in 1926 signed what became known as the Studio Basic Agreement. This agreement was sometimes confused with another accord known as the "1926 agreement" signed the year before. The latter understanding, which divided work between carpenters and IATSE members, had been made between IATSE and a local union (No. 1692) of the United Brotherhood of Carpenters and Joiners of America in the Los Angeles area. It became the basis for arbitration in 1945–6, although people did not widely understand that William (Big Bill) Hutcheson, the carpenters' general president, had not endorsed the 1925 agreement. In fact Hutcheson had repudiated it, and when Local 1692 refused to disown the arrangement he revoked the group's charter.[7]

During the depression IATSE gained a reputation for being corrupt. It came under the control of George E. Browne, who became its international president in 1934. Browne's West Coast representative was a Chicago gangster named William (Willie) Bioff. After threatening to close theaters, Browne and Bioff, "Hollywood pimps . . . , suburban, wearing chocolate double-breasted suits," made a closed shop arrangement with the studios in late 1935. They assessed IATSE members 2 percent of their salaries, which they then used as they pleased. Members had no say in local affairs. There were neither meetings nor elections.[8]

By threatening strikes and violence, Browne and Bioff coerced tens of thousands of dollars from producers. Albert Warner testified that Bioff demanded $50,000 a year and that he, personally, paid $80,000 in 1936–7. Bioff did not look frightening. "A paunchy little guy," George Murphy recalled, "his most outstanding characteristic was a pair of hard, pig-like eyes gleaming from behind thick glasses." He reputedly told producers that "anyone who resigns from this operation goes out feet first," and executives thereupon "paid through the nose." Browne and Bioff were convicted of extortion in 1941 and received ten-year prison sentences. Bioff died in 1955 in a car-bomb explosion.[9]

A progressive faction within IATSE attempted to increase the power of local unions, but when IATSE divided the reformers, many of them joined Herbert K. Sorrell's painters' union to create the United Studio Technicians Guild in early 1939. The Congress of Industrial Organizations supported the USTG, but enemies charged it with being a communist front, and its challenge to IATSE proved unsuccessful.[10]

Sorrell organized an independent union, the Screen Cartoonists Guild, that after a strike in 1941 allowed four other unions – painters, film technicians, office workers, and machinists – to gain recognition from Walt Disney Studios. The five unions, joined by carpenters, electrical workers, and others, then formed the Conference of Studio Unions. Painters and carpenters held most of the power in the CSU, which offered an alternative to the corruption of Bioff and Browne. By 1945 its membership had reached between nine and ten thousand.[11]

IATSE had, meanwhile, remained a power in the industry under the leadership of Richard Walsh. Roy M. Brewer became IATSE's international representative in early 1945. At that time IATSE had a membership of between sixteen and seventeen thousand.[12]

The jurisdictional dispute between IATSE and the CSU appeared in early 1945 when interior decorators went on strike – despite the fact that the AFL had given a no-strike pledge for the duration of the war. Strikers overturned automobiles at the gates of Warner Bros. The strike ended in October when the AFL's executive council meeting in Cincinnati ordered workers to return, set aside a thirty-day period for parties to resolve differences, and empowered a three-person committee to arbitrate remaining issues (within an additional thirty days).[13]

In the way of such matters, small problems became large. At issue was which workers would build new structures on sound stages. The arbitrators, who became known as the Three Wise Men, sought to settle the issue according to the 1925 division of work, not knowing that Hutcheson had repudiated it. In late December they awarded "construction work on exterior sets" to the carpenters' union. IATSE received jurisdiction over "erection of sets on stages, except trim and millwork on sets and stages." As the producers' labor liaison, Pat Casey, interpreted this decision, the studios fired more than three hundred carpenters and gave their jobs to members of a recently created IATSE union of "set erectors." Hutcheson protested, although the carpenters went along with this arrangement temporarily. He threatened to raise the matter at the AFL national convention, where he likely had enough votes to win. All three arbitrators later agreed that Casey's interpretation had violated their intent.[14]

At this juncture the AFL executive council directed the committee to interpret their ruling, and in August 1946, the Wise Men issued a clarification that became a source of even more controversy.[15]

Matters became complicated almost beyond comprehension. While both the CSU and IATSE vied for support of the Screen Actors Guild, Sorrell backed the Screen Players Union. It had tried to organize extras outside of SAG control, which would have weakened the guild. Sorrell threatened to boycott movies made by performers who crossed picket lines. The tactic antagonized Murphy, Montgomery, and eventually Reagan. Other matters caused Sorrell to lose support, including the CSU's message and the campaign mounted by Brewer and IATSE.[16]

During the strikes the actors held a good deal of power, because if they honored the picket lines they could close the studios and force a settlement favorable to the strikers. Had they done so, the issue "would have been settled in twenty-four hours," said Father George H. Dunne, one of the CSU's vocal supporters. American Federation of Labor rules expected affiliated unions not involved in a strike to honor lines if the matter involved a dispute over benefits between labor and management. They did not have to observe them in a jurisdictional conflict.[17]

From the outset SAG's leaders took the position that the conflict was jurisdictional. They had adopted this policy under Murphy's leadership while Reagan was in the military. It owed much to the guild's attorney, William Berger, who concluded that under SAG's contract with the producers, the guild had a legal obligation to order members to work. He advised the board to avoid taking sides. He suggested the wording of the strike ballot the board sent to the membership, and SAG members voted overwhelmingly not to honor picket lines. Throughout 1945 and much of 1946, SAG remained formally neutral and urged the AFL to set up machinery for arbitration.[18]

SAG differed from the activist organizations Reagan joined after the war and from rank-and-file unions, and that difference helps explain its position during the strikes. Where HICCASP had an agenda for reform, SAG avoided controversial issues except where they directly affected performers, and then calculated participation either to minimize damage to the profession or to enhance its image. "We were very conservative actually, when you look back on it," SAG's longtime executive secretary, John Dales, explained. Many of SAG's leaders eschewed the term "union," preferring "guild," because the name "harked back to medieval associations of artisans." "I never originally really associated it too much with the labor movement, nor did many actors," Dales said. Members "just felt they were on their own, separate and apart." One reason for this feeling involved salaries. While most SAG members made marginal incomes from acting, leaders usually had substantial salaries. *Variety* reported Reagan earning $169,750 in 1946, while Montgomery made $250,000.[19]

Up to this time Reagan's view of labor issues had been to favor cooperation and compromise. He had joined SAG in 1937 and had become a member of the board thanks to a recommendation from his wife.[20] He resigned during World War II. But while in service he helped the guild negotiate an understanding with Warner Bros. over payments to performers who appeared in the film *Hollywood Canteen* (1944).[21] The Army Air Corps kept him in touch with labor issues because it was producing films that attempted to bolster worker morale. They emphasized patriotism ("every worker is a warrior") and harmony between labor and management.[22]

The conservative nature of SAG's leadership under Murphy and Montgomery, and later Reagan, naturally produced tension between the actors and the Screen Writers Guild. The latter divided over supporting Sorrell and the CSU, with leftist members endorsing the strike. In October 1945, John Howard Lawson, Dalton Trumbo, Adrian Scott, and Albert Maltz joined John Garfield, Artie Shaw, Carey McWilliams, and other directors, actors, and musicians as observers during picketing of Warner Bros. Lawson was one of the pickets. Trumbo wrote speeches for Sorrell. The group blamed the Warners for using "hired thugs and police" to provoke "outrageous violence" that violated civil liberties.[23]

The message of Sorrell and his supporters did not win over SAG's conservatives. The leftists went on radio, gave speeches, held rallies, organized marches, prepared an array of publications, tried to enlist foreign correspondents, and appealed to union and government leaders in Europe and Latin America. They recalled IATSE's unsavory past, its "Hitlerian methods," as one backer claimed, and argued that its leaders had been chosen by Browne and Bioff.[24] They denounced the producers for union busting and red-baiting. They maintained the dispute was about wages and hours, not jurisdiction. Edward G. Robinson saw "more to life than just struggling for a livelihood." Those who worked, whether "in overalls or white collars," deserved a "life in which there is time for education and recreation." These rights were as "inalienable a part of the American heritage as the right to a job and a decent wage."[25]

Sorrell – a former boxer – had come up the hard way. At age twelve he had worked an eleven-hour day in an Oakland sewer pipe factory and was often so tired after work that he had to rest before the two-mile walk home. He advocated "rights of all people regardless of religion or race or color or creed. . . . No matter whether they were office workers, painters, ditch diggers or what they were." He believed they were "entitled to being treated alike."[26]

But suspicion that Sorrell was hostile to capitalism doomed any chance of his winning large-scale support. Enemies claimed that the CSU had been infiltrated and that he had a plan to destroy AFL unions in Hollywood. The Tenney Committee accused him of being a party member under the name of Herbert Stewart and produced an alleged membership card and handwriting experts to prove it. When a "man writes with his left hand, brushes his teeth with his left hand and eats with his left hand, it is idiotic to conclude that such an individual is right handed," the committee declared. Sorrell admitted taking money from Communists in 1945 (as during a strike in 1937) and endorsing organizations thought to be fronts. He denied belonging to the party. He acknowledged that he might have joined if different people had approached him, but said he had not trusted those who tried to recruit him. He did not believe a real Communist could be a labor leader because communism flourished in poverty.[27]

Brewer was quick to exploit the leftist character of his opponents. Where the CSU's message was many-sided, he stressed Americanism and anticommunism. A short man with a reserved demeanor, he was a former projectionist who had become president of the state federation of labor in Nebraska at age twenty-three. He believed in a conspiracy to destroy America, considered the IATSE in a "war" for survival, and blamed the Communists. He linked the CSU to the Communist Party, part of a worldwide plot to destroy the American movie industry. He called the 1945 strike a "vicious attack" on "AMERICAN labor traditions." He helped arrange for the Tenney Committee to receive the membership card linking Sorrell to the Communist Party.[28]

It was clear that many guild leaders had little patience with the CSU. When Sorrell threatened a strike in early 1946, SAG supported the producers when they vowed to keep the studios "open at all costs," even if it meant hiring non-CSU workers. During the strike in July, SAG condemned Sorrell for bypassing the AFL's central labor council, and some board members concluded that the CSU was a threat to the AFL. SAG's board appointed an emergency committee to help resolve the dispute, which included Reagan, Montgomery, and Murphy. The strike ended in an agreement known as the Treaty of Beverly Hills, which gave CSU workers a 25 percent pay increase, retroactive to the first of the year.[29]

The clarification that the Three Wise Men issued in August set in motion events that again threatened to close the studios. Hutcheson and Sorrell read it as a victory for the carpenters. IATSE objected. Hutcheson would not be satisfied, Brewer told Reagan, "until everyone who worked with wood or wood substitutes" was taken away from IATSE. Hutcheson's representative, Joseph Cambiano, seemed to confirm Brewer's fears. Walsh told the producers that if any of them changed the original interpretation of the December 1945 directive, he would "have all work stopped in the studios, exchanges, and theaters."[30]

The producers, fearing Walsh, schemed with IATSE to break the CSU. Cambiano had warned the executives that if they did not abide by the August 1946 ruling, sets would be "declared hot" and carpenters would not work on them. The producers seized this point and devised a plan whereby IATSE men started work on sets. When the studios asked CSU carpenters and painters to replace them, they refused because the sets were "hot." Under the Treaty of Beverly Hills, in which painters and carpenters agreed to abstain from work stoppages in matters relating to allocation of work, this gave the studios the right to dismiss them. By September 24, the major studios had ousted 1,200 CSU painters and carpenters. Warner Bros. fired more than any other studio. Respecting picket lines of painters and carpenters, CSU members went on strike.[31]

How much Reagan knew of this plan is unclear, although he attended at least one of the Producers Labor Committee's secret meetings in September.[32] By late summer, despite claims of impartiality, he and other SAG leaders had chosen sides. Publicly they linked themselves with IATSE and the producers. On Labor Day, Reagan, Murphy, Montgomery, Wyman, and William Holden formed part of the "Magic Circle of Movie Stars" that celebrated AFL achievements in the Los Angeles Central Labor Council's "Spectacle of Progress." The IATSE and SAG entered floats in the parade. Once a strike appeared likely, SAG leaders were careful not to alienate IATSE membership. Their concern was to keep the studios open. As Montgomery explained, the guild was "not interested in the merits of the case," but felt "that all possible steps should be taken to prevent a strike which would throw thirty thousand people out of work because of three hundred jobs."[33]

In late September 1946 several hundred pickets appeared at Warner Bros.' Burbank studio, where they listened to Sorrell shout orders through a megaphone. "There may be men hurt, there may be men killed before this is over," he reportedly warned newsmen, "but we're in no mood to be pushed around any more!" Although the strike involved many studios, he wanted to concentrate on Warner Bros. and give it a good pounding. He knew the studio's chief of security, Blaney Matthews, whose ribs he once had broken. Matthews would confront the strikers head-on, he anticipated. He assumed Matthews would react recklessly.[34]

The situation turned ugly. Someone stabbed a picket at Universal. The Hollywood chapter of the American Veterans Committee marched in uniform on behalf of the strikers, and police sent twenty-eight of the veterans to the hospital. At MGM demonstrators overturned automobiles. At Warners they smashed windshields. A worker testified that someone threw acid in his face. Warner employees crawled to their jobs through a storm drain that led from the nearby Los Angeles River. When Burbank police fired shots, the Epstein brothers – Julius and his twin, Philip – suggested that the studio change its slogan from "Combining good picture making with good citizenship" to "Combining good picture making with good marksmanship."[35]

The Warners brought in employees in buses. Reagan rode through the picket lines while working on *Night Unto Night.* Studio security wanted him to lie down to avoid rocks and Coke bottles. "I couldn't do that," he said. "So instead they made me sit by myself. They figured that if I was going to get it nobody else would be hurt."[36]

In the struggle to control SAG policy, Murphy, Montgomery, and Reagan now outmaneuvered the CSU.[37] At his last meeting as SAG president in early September, Murphy supported a change in the bylaws making it mandatory that a majority of members in a secret mail ballot had to vote for matters involving guild policy. Although board members such as Franchot Tone objected, Reagan was enthusiastic: "Adopt this in every union and see how many faults of labor would disappear," he said.[38] Reagan had little trouble convincing the board to adopt several other resolutions. One urged members to cross picket lines. Another called for a roundtable discussion between parties in the dispute. A third authorized an emergency meeting of SAG members. At a meeting on October 2, Tone explained the guild's efforts at mediation and Reagan gave a history of the controversy.[39]

Before Reagan made his presentation on October 2, he and William Holden dropped in at a meeting in the house of actress Ida Lupino, where several dozen performers led by Sterling Hayden discussed the guild's part in the strike. His party cell, Hayden later testified, had instructed him to get SAG support behind the CSU. Reagan shifted uncomfortably in his seat but Holden held him back "like a jockey going into the stretch." Finally he received the floor and talked for several minutes before submitting to questions that verged on heckling. He impressed Hayden. John Garfield encouraged the audience to listen. Howard Da Silva pulled Garfield from the room; Reagan watched as Da Silva lectured him, "shaking his finger under [Garfield's] nose for quite some time."[40]

The following day, while doing a beach scene for *Night Unto Night,* Reagan received an anonymous telephone call. If he made his report to the SAG membership, the caller said, a "squad" would disfigure his face so he could never make films again. When he reported this conversation to the studio, Matthews gave him a permit for a .32 Smith and Wesson. "I mounted the holstered gun religiously every morning and took it off the last thing at night," he said.[41]

The guild's October 2 meeting took place in an intimidating atmosphere. Two thousand of Sorrell's followers distributed literature outside the Hollywood Legion Stadium. They formed lines through which Reagan and other board members had to pass.[42]

Charges now abounded. Hutcheson's carpenters took out an ad in *Variety* challenging SAG's interpretation of the strike. It convinced the board to mail a strike ballot. Matthew Woll, vice-president of the AFL, described Hollywood as the "third largest Communist center" in America, maligned well-known performers by name, and threatened the industry with a "league for political decency."[43]

Woll's attack made an impression on guild leaders, who concluded that SAG representation at the AFL convention in Chicago was imperative. The board authorized Montgomery to attend. Reagan's committee recommended a larger delegation that included himself, Murphy, Wyman, and Edward Arnold. Reagan became the spokesman. In addition, the board hired a Chicago public relations firm.[44]

The delegation traveled to Chicago ostensibly to persuade the AFL to establish arbitral machinery and clarify issues in the strike. It visited with the three AFL arbitrators. Reagan claimed he and the actors entered the discussion "completely neutral," and that the Wise Men told them the August clarification had been a mistake, written because Hutcheson had pressed them for a "basket of words over which he could haggle." They had carried "written resignations in their pockets," Reagan said, to tender if the AFL executive council changed their December 1945 decision. In later congressional testimony, incidentally, the Three Wise Men contradicted much of Reagan's account.[45]

The actors told AFL president William Green of this meeting and threatened to send movie stars to every major city to publicize the violence at the studios if something was not done about Hutcheson. They met the latter in a late-night, five-hour session where Reagan attempted to convince him that the Three Wise Men had intended to give construction to IATSE. Hutcheson's "jolly, Santa-like presence" eventually turned indignant: "Tell Walsh that if he'll give in on the August directive, I'll run Sorrell out of Hollywood and break up the CSU in five minutes," Reagan recalled him saying. He would "do the same to the Commies." The delegation relayed these terms to Walsh, and Somerset told Sorrell what Hutcheson said.[46]

Reagan went back to Hollywood convinced that Hutcheson was an "arrogant man completely wrapped in the cloak of his own power." Jack Warner was impressed that the actor had so irritated Hutcheson and had gotten Green's attention. Reagan "turned out to be a tower of strength," Warner told his son, "not only for the actors but for the whole industry."[47]

About this time one of IATSE's locals broke ranks to support the CSU. The film technicians of Local 683 voted to honor picket lines in mid-October and without them the studios would have been hard pressed to process film. The air conditioning technicians, CSU members, were already on the lines, and film needed refrigeration to protect its sound track. Over the CSU's objection and with Brewer's blessing, Reagan spoke to Local 683 about what had happened in Chicago. During the unrest Walsh had received emergency power to cancel, suspend, or amend IATSE's constitution. He suspended the technicians' local and directed Brewer to take control.[48]

Reagan became involved in another effort at mediation when in late October he proposed and SAG arranged a roundtable discussion for representatives from forty-three local unions at the Knickerbocker Hotel in Hollywood. He, Murphy, and Arnold reported on the meetings in Chicago; but disagreements remained about what the Wise Men had said, and the next day a telephone hookup was arranged between SAG members, CSU representatives including Sorrell, and two of the arbitrators, William C. Birthright and Felix H. Knight. Birthright read from an early version of the August clarification that differed from the one the studios received. Although he telegraphed a correction the next day indicating the arbitrators intended to give "construction work" on sets to Hutcheson, Reagan ignored this emendation and argued that the August clarification favorable to the carpenters was a "deliberate fraud" concocted by Hutcheson's people.[49]

At the Knickerbocker, Brewer and Sorrell agreed to accept as an arbitrator the secretary of the Chicago Federation of Labor, Joseph Keenan. But the latter faced an impossible task. Hutcheson, IATSE, and SAG were intransigent, and the carpenters demanded a 20 percent pay increase over what they had received in July. When two thousand strikers demonstrated in late October, police arrested more than a hundred. In mid-November the houses of nonstrikers were bombed. When studios obtained injunctions limiting picketing to eight people at each gate, police took nearly seven hundred strikers into custody, the largest mass arrest since the strikes began. Sorrell was among those seized, and a grand jury indicted him. Keenan concluded that he could not settle the controversy at the local level and returned to Chicago.[50]

Reagan and SAG now abandoned even the pretense of impartiality. "I am no longer neutral," he told a group of veterans. "The CSU has proved itself unreliable. Its leadership does not want settlement of the strike. It stands to gain by continued disorder and disruption in Hollywood." The board appointed him together with Revere, Murphy, and Kelly to compose a statement condemning the CSU.[51]

The struggle for SAG's support intensified in mid-November. A pro-CSU faction made up of Hayden and others who had been at the Lupino house the night Reagan spoke came to SAG to argue that the guild was reinforcing an "anti-union, anti-labor, anti-democratic" policy. The group wanted the guild to help close the studios. "We were scared to death of their ability to do just this," Reagan recalled. He hoped to forestall another membership meeting, but when more than three hundred performers signed a petition it was not possible.[52]

The board now unanimously selected Reagan to speak for them. When he took the rostrum at the Hollywood Legion Stadium on December 19 he faced an audience of eighteen hundred. Speakers attacked him for siding with the producers. Katharine Hepburn spoke on behalf of Local 683, and Robinson for the CSU. Alexander Knox, who had portrayed Woodrow Wilson in Darryl Zanuck's movie, ridiculed the Chicago trip and mocked Reagan's presentation. "Reagan spoke very fast . . . so that he could talk out of both sides of his mouth at once," he said. The speech infuriated Reagan. Brewer vowed to run Knox out of the movies.[53]

SAG's board rebuffed Sorrell's supporters. They asked members not to vote on a strike but to show confidence in the board. Members responded more than ten to one in the affirmative. The board also blunted an offer of mediation from the Los Angeles Interfaith Council.[54]

The strike continued for many months. Sorrell charged that SAG and IATSE were in league and asked European and Latin American union leaders to publicize this "conspiracy" and to expose the American film cartel's "drive for monopoly control of foreign markets." He called for boycotts of movies made by actors who crossed picket lines. Reagan's name was high on the list of those to be shunned.[55] Father Dunne criticized the guild at a meeting of strikers and on the radio, "absolutely convinced of the moral rectitude and justice" of the CSU's cause. He called SAG's neutrality "immoral." Reagan tried to change Dunne's mind. He, Murphy, Dales, and Wyman descended on the priest at Loyola. Reagan attempted to persuade him that he had been duped by the Communists. It was all to no avail.[56]

The strike consumed a great deal of Reagan's time after he became guild president. In March 1947 more than three thousand people remained on strike. By that time the work stoppage had cost millions of dollars; but without SAG support, the CSU gradually "dissolved like sugar in hot water."[57]

Reagan's participation in postwar labor unrest helped separate him from Hollywood's left wing. Supporters of the CSU viewed him as management's man. Embittered by his willingness to cross picket lines, they called him a scab and considered him opportunistic. AFL arbitrators challenged his recollection of the Chicago convention. Karen Morley labeled his behavior as "opportunism, pure and simple." Dunne found him "handsome in an Arrow-Collar-ad" kind of way, "very articulate," but ill-informed and "obsessed" with communism – a "dangerous man." For still others he simply became that "sonofabitching bastard."[58]

Such assessments left a mark. Reagan recalled meeting two actors during the strike. "My smile was already forming and I had just started to greet them when one of the two thrust his face close to mine, his eyes burning with hatred. 'Fascist!' he hissed, literally spitting the word at me."[59]

Nevertheless, most SAG members liked Reagan's position. He kept actors working. Dales considered the December 19 meeting an "overwhelming performance" that a few months later helped Reagan win the presidency of SAG over Murphy and Gene Kelly. Reagan aligned with conservatives and middle-of-the-roaders. Montgomery thought his "heart and mind" were in the right place. Hedda Hopper wrote with some exaggeration that he handled meetings in a way that "commanded the respect of his most bitter opponents." Brewer described a "fearless foe" of communist infiltration in the American labor movement.[60]

The strikes of course increased suspicion of the studio writers. Like Hollywood's left-wing labor leaders, many would soon have to leave the industry. Reagan met with them several times, Ring Lardner, Jr., recalled, and "we argued rather sharply about the CSU." But Jack Warner considered writers expendable. Accompanied by Blaney Matthews, who "carried a thick, heavy briefcase of documents," Warner testified secretly before the House Committee on Un-American Activities in Los Angeles in May 1947 and supplied names he considered "un-American." Ninety-five percent of the effort to inject communist propaganda into movies came from writers, he claimed. The wealthy were their targets. At the studio Matthews investigated writers "very rigidly" and Warner fired anyone he believed a Communist.[61]

Ronald Reagan and his mother, Nelle, receiving the keys to the city from Dixon
mayor J. Fred Hoffman, August 1950.
Photo courtesy of the *Dixon Telegraph*, Dixon, Ill.

Dr. Cleveland Kleihauer.
Photo courtesy of the Hollywood–Beverly
Christian Church, Hollywood, Calif.

Ben Hill Cleaver.
Photo courtesy of the Disciples of Christ
Historical Society, Nashville, Tenn.

Left to right: Will H. Hays, Mrs. Jesse Hays, and Joseph I. Breen in Pasadena, Calif., June 1947.
Photo courtesy of the Indiana State Library, Indianapolis.

Poster for *Code of the Secret Service* (Warner Bros., 1939).

Don't Forget Your Jr. Secret Service Club

Make A Drive For New Members!

Announce Drive

1. Contact the youngsters of your Junior Secret Service Club of which Ronald Reagan is commander, via announcements posted in lobby and distributed in schools, boys' clubs, playgrounds, etc. Award prizes to youngster bringing in most new members.

Issue Cards

2. Issue membership cards to new members (illustrated below). Reverse side of card shows key to secret code. Special announcements written in code are mailed to members of club telling them of intended drive for new members.

Special Shows

3. Conduct special Saturday morning show for club members. Speakers from police and safety bureaus address club. Fingerprint new members under the supervision of local police officials. Issue membership cards at this time.

Club Paper

4. Distribute special issue of club paper (mimeographed) featuring club activities, publicity stories on "Smashing the Money Ring" and explanation of membership drive contest and prizes to be awarded. Include gossip column edited by youngsters.

This is to certify that

_____ is a member of the _____

The owner of this card promises to be on the lookout for dangerous spies and to follow the thrilling exploits of the secret service on the screen at the [THEATRE IMPRINT]

JR SECRET SERVICE

OPERATIVE No. 666

Ronald Reagan
Chief of Jr. Secret Service

(FRONT)

Membership card same size as shown above is available in mat form to be printed locally with theatre imprint. Order Mat No. 211—30c.

KEY TO SECRET CODE

A — g	J — r	S — x
B — t	K — w	T — e
C — d	L — s	U — m
D — k	M — c	V — p
E — b	N — z	W — i
F — a	O — f	X — v
G — l	P — y	Y — n
H — o	Q — h	Z — u
I — q	R — j	

(BACK)

Reverse side of membership card could carry ad plugging picture or made up to carry key to secret code as shown above.

Promotion for Junior Secret Service Club, Ronald Reagan, commander.
From *Smashing the Money Ring* (Warner Bros., 1939) pressbook.

Poster for *Murder in the Air* (Warner Bros., 1940).

Left to right: Unidentified pilot, Owen King, the "Inertia Projector," John Litel, Ronald Reagan, and Eddie Foy, Jr. Publicity still, *Murder in the Air.*
Photo courtesy of the Wisconsin Center for Film and Theater Research, Madison.

Harry Warner (*left*) and Jack Warner (*right*) at luncheon for the American Legion, 1938.
Photo courtesy of the USC Cinema–Television Library and Archives of Performing Arts, Los Angeles.

Errol Flynn (as Jeb Stuart) and Ronald Reagan (as George Custer) in *Santa Fe Trail* (Warner Bros., 1940).

Ronald Reagan as he appeared in the *Dixon Evening Telegraph* during Louella
Parsons Day celebration (September 1941). Publicity still for *International
Squadron*.
Photo courtesy of the Wisconsin Center for Film and Theater Research, Madison.

On the second day of their visit to Dixon for Louella Parsons Day (September 1941), movie celebrities were entertained at Hazelwood, the Charles W. Walgreen estate. Pictured left to right are Bebe Daniels, Ben Lyon, Joe E. Brown, Mrs. Charles (Myrtle) Walgreen, Mrs. Mabel Shaw (publisher of the *Dixon Evening Telegraph,* partially obscured), Louella Parsons, Ann Rutherford, Ronald Reagan, and George Montgomery.
Photo courtesy of the *Dixon Telegraph*.

(*Opposite*) Poster for *International Squadron* (Warner Bros., 1941).
Photo courtesy of the Wisconsin Center for Film and Theater Research, Madison.

THE WHOLE HEROIC STORY OF THE

INTERNATIONAL
SQUADRON

The
FOREIGN
LEGION
of the
R.A.F.

AVENGING 'ANGELS'
HURTLING OUT OF THE
HEAVENS! COURAGE
UNCONQUERABLE!
THRILLS INCOMPARABLE!

RONALD REAGAN

OLYMPE BRADNA · WILLIAM LUNDIGAN · JOAN PERRY · REGINALD DENNY

Directed by
LEWIS SEILER ·

Presented by
WARNER BROS.

Ronald Reagan

Father in khaki: Ronald Reagan, husband of Jane Wyman, father of Maureen Elizabeth

Ronald Reagan as he appeared in a fan magazine during World War II.
Photo courtesy of the Wisconsin Center for Film and Theater Research, Madison.

(*Opposite*) General Henry (Hap) Arnold and Jack Warner, 1945.
Photo courtesy of the USC Cinema–Television Library and Archives of Performing Arts, Los Angeles.

"Studio Scab (Ronald Reagan)," by Hans Burkhardt, from the post–World War
II studio strikes.
Courtesy of Jack Rutberg Fine Arts, Los Angeles.

Ronald Reagan as Screen Actors Guild president (1947).
Photo courtesy of Screen Actors Guild, Hollywood, Calif.

(*Opposite, top*) Demonstrators outside the House Committee on Un-American Activities hearings.
Photo courtesy of the Wisconsin Center for Film and Theater Research, Madison.

(*Opposite, bottom*) Dore Schary (*left*) and Melvyn Douglas with Eleanor Roosevelt.
Photo courtesy of the Wisconsin Center for Film and Theater Research, Madison.

Members of the Hollywood Ten and supporters.
Photo courtesy of the Wisconsin Center for Film and Theater Research, Madison.

(*Opposite*) Eric Johnston addressing a banquet in the Soviet Union, 1944.
Photo courtesy of the Eastern Washington State Historical Society, Spokane.

Ronald Reagan and Lauren Bacall on stage with President Harry S Truman at a campaign rally in Hollywood, September 23, 1948.
Photo courtesy of the Regional History Center, University of Southern California, Los Angeles.

Raymond Massey as John Brown in *Santa Fe Trail*.

Ronald Reagan with Ginger Rogers (*center*) and Doris Day in the anti-KKK film
Storm Warning (Warner Bros., 1951).
Photo courtesy of the Wisconsin Center for Film and Theater Research, Madison.

Poster for *That Hagen Girl* (Warner Bros., 1947), a film based on a novel that dealt with incest.
Photo courtesy of the Wisconsin Center for Film and Theater Research, Madison.

(*Opposite*) Ronald Reagan as a Western hero. Advertisement for *Law and Order* (Universal-International, 1953) as it appeared in Hollywood trade publications.

The moment at which Drake McHugh (Ronald Reagan) awakes to discover that his legs have been amputated by a sadistic doctor in *Kings Row* (Warner Bros., 1942). Reagan considered this his finest movie scene.

Jane Wyman, 1942.
Photo courtesy of the Wisconsin Center for
Film and Theater Research, Madison.

Ronald Reagan, around 1952.
Photo courtesy of the Wisconsin Center for Film and
Theater Research, Madison.

12

THE "UN-AMERICANS"

The fight for the conscience, for the soul, of the American film, is not ended.

John Howard Lawson[1]

I would say in opposing those people that the best thing to do is to make democracy work. . . . I believe that, as Thomas Jefferson put it, if all the American people know all of the facts they will never make a mistake.

Ronald Reagan[2]

The congressional investigation of Hollywood in October 1947, at which Ronald Reagan testified as a friendly witness, had a major effect not only on reputations and careers but on the direction of American cinema. Members of the House Committee on Un-American Activities (HUAC) and their supporters framed the issue simply: to expose communist propaganda. The committee's chief investigator, Robert E. Stripling, argued that Hollywood was at the center of a plan to "communize the country." He and the committee made no systematic analysis but concluded that writers were trying to destroy the public's faith in American institutions and leaders. He detected what he described as a trend in writing: "The rich were grasping, greedy exploiters of the poor, who were always honest and down-trodden. Bankers were generally despotic; landlords cruel, and tenants noble. Judges and political figures were either crooked or fatuous fools." How far the communists had gone was not as important, he said, as was their potential effect on opinion.[3]

As hearings approached, HUAC compiled a list of witnesses and issued subpoenas.[4] Some people became known as "friendly" witnesses. The committee identified nineteen who were "unfriendly," of whom eleven testified: John Howard Lawson, Dalton Trumbo, Albert Maltz, Alvah Bessie, Samuel Ornitz, Herbert Biberman, Edward Dmytryk, Adrian Scott, Ring Lardner, Jr., Lester Cole, and Bertolt Brecht – the Hollywood Ten, as they became known (Brecht left the country after his testimony). HUAC cited them for contempt, the House of Representatives overwhelmingly approved, and after court convictions, they received sentences ranging from six months to a year. The movie industry blacklisted them.[5]

Communism was of course at issue in the hearings. The Hollywood Ten were, or had been, Marxist-Leninists and pro-Soviet. But their cases were more complicated. Their appearance in the hearings stimulated thinking about the First Amendment. Their work sought to change popular attitudes toward working people, the poor, and minorities, and attacked racism and discrimination. Some of the Hollywood Ten condemned American foreign policy. Others sought to recast the past, and one went so far as to call for a full-scale reinterpretation of American history. All saw film as a means of changing society, insofar as Hollywood's economic and political realities permitted. Outcasts at the time, they would find their ideas widely accepted two decades later.[6]

In all of this Reagan was no extremist. He handled himself adeptly, although he hardly covered himself in glory. He cooperated with HUAC and the FBI but referred to Thomas Jefferson and hoped it would not be necessary to outlaw any organization such as the Communist Party on the basis of ideology. He later questioned the blacklist and criticized producers who adopted it. When his stand gained little support from the board of the Screen Actors Guild, he sought to compromise, to find a solution acceptable to the American public and, especially, to studio executives.

★★★

As the hearings began in Washington, observers squeezed into the corridors of the old House Office Building hoping to catch a glimpse of such movie stars as Robert Montgomery, George Murphy, and Gary Cooper. "There was a long drawn-out 'ooooh' from the jam-packed, predominantly feminine audience," the *New York Times* reported, "as the tall Mr. Reagan, clad in a tan gabardine suit, a blue knitted tie and a white shirt," made his way through the throng. Later, surrounded by fans, he smiled and waved for pictures with Montgomery and Murphy.[7]

Representatives of the Hollywood Committee for the First Amendment were present: Humphrey Bogart, Lauren Bacall, John Garfield, Sterling Hayden, Philip Dunne, and John Huston. They believed that HUAC jeopardized freedom. "There was no talk of Communism – from our point of view," Bacall remembered. "It had to do with the Hitlerian tactics being employed. I was up in arms – fervent. . . . My reaction was based on emotion."[8]

The House committee had its share of personalities, including California's freshman Congressman Richard M. Nixon, soon to come to prominence because of the Alger Hiss case. Unfriendly witnesses especially detested Mississippi Congressman John E. Rankin, whom they rightly considered bigoted. Rankin took little part in the Hollywood phase of the hearings. More active in confronting witnesses was Stripling, a soft-spoken Texan who was then in his mid-thirties. A pale, slim, deliberate man, he seemed aloof, even cold, and he rarely lost his temper. When Maltz called him Mr. Quisling, he "merely sipped water until the jumps in his jaw muscles quieted down."[9]

The plump, ruddy J. Parnell Thomas of New Jersey chaired the committee. When seated he was too short for the television cameras, so he sat atop a telephone directory discreetly placed beneath a cushion. As a tactician he lacked savoir faire. He turned the color of a plum when frustrated. With "one eye on witnesses, another on his press clippings," he used his chairmanship to make headlines and tarnish reputations. After the hearings concluded he was convicted of padding his payroll and entered the same prison as two of the Ten, Cole and Lardner.[10]

The hearings opened with a procession of witnesses who offered testimony about the menace of communism in Hollywood. Jack Warner spoke of "un-Americans" whom he likened to insects or disease-bearing microorganisms, "ideological termites" that had penetrated American institutions or "subversive germs" that bred in "dark corners." The antidote was publicity and Americanism. Louis B. Mayer, the writer Ayn Rand, and the director Sam Wood followed. If "you wanted to drop their rompers," the balding Wood said of the Communists, "you would find the hammer and sickle on their rear ends." In the days that followed, other friendly witnesses appeared. Actor Adolphe Menjou, who testified behind a "rich glow of sartorial splendor" (and through a haze of cigarette smoke), claimed to know many people who acted like Communists. Writer Richard Macaulay was "morally certain" he could identify more than two dozen writers who were Communists. Montgomery talked of a "lunatic fringe," while Murphy told the committee that Communists used decent-minded liberals for their ends. Cooper said, somewhat more sensibly, that he did not take any "pinko mouthing very seriously."[11]

Reagan testified on the fourth day and managed a defense of Hollywood. A small faction had regularly opposed guild policies, he said, and he suspected it of following the Communist Party line. Ninety-nine percent of SAG's members realized what was happening and had managed to prevent communist propaganda from reaching the screen. In curtailing this clique, he maintained, the guild had never once violated democratic procedure. He offered to match Hollywood's social contributions against those of any other industry. The best way to fight communism was to "make democracy work." He was confident about democracy, although concerned that fear of communism might erode liberty. As a citizen, he did not want to see the country "compromise . . . democratic principles." He hesitated to advocate outlawing the Communist Party, or any organization for that matter, on ideological grounds. "We have spent 170 years in this country on the basis that democracy is strong enough to stand up and fight against the inroads of any ideology. . . . I believe that, as Thomas Jefferson put it, if all the American people know all of the facts they will never make a mistake."[12]

Some reporters treated Reagan and other actors with condescension. The "pink-cheeked and sandy-haired Ronald Reagan looked . . . boyish . . . when he arose to speak," *Newsweek* said. Quentin Reynolds observed that Reagan made onlookers happy by sitting among the spectators. The stars who belonged to the Committee for the First Amendment received the harshest treatment, though. *Life* magazine portrayed them as dupes. "They descended on Washington by plane, breathlessly watched the hearings, signed innumerable autographs and told everybody who would listen that they thought the Thomas committee was violating civil rights." These "lost liberals," who felt "only a kind of melancholy leftishness," had recently awakened politically and were "without political moorings or orientation to anything real," according to the magazine.[13]

Reagan received substantial coverage and for the most part emerged with a positive image. He did not name names – at least publicly – and did not associate with the Committee for the First Amendment (which was, he later said, "for suckers only").[14] He gave a "decidedly creditable" performance, the *Motion Picture Daily* concluded, and "created something of a stir" with his "affirmation of . . . American democracy, in and out of Hollywood." Reynolds was even more complimentary. As anticipated, he wrote, "intelligent Ronald Reagan stole the show from his better known colleagues. Reagan, it was obvious, had done a great deal of thinking on the subject in question." The *Washington Post* quoted him to the effect that the nation should not let fear of communism compromise its commitment to democracy.[15]

By this time, it should be remembered, Reagan was an FBI informer (the bureau had given him the code name T-10). Agents had interviewed him and his wife about communist activity the previous April, and although he had not testified at HUAC's closed hearings in May it was clear by August that he would be a friendly witness. He later felt that he could have given a more favorable picture of Hollywood. On the evening before his testimony, Stripling had come to his hotel room and asked questions that gave him an opportunity to defend the movie industry. But when he took the stand, Stripling's queries took a different direction; this diminished Reagan's respect for the committee.[16]

★★★

The Hollywood Ten had prepared for their testimony in an atmosphere of suspicion. Realizing that the committee probably had arranged to tap their telephones, they resorted to bizarre precautions. "Sometime during our first stay in Washington," Dmytryk recalled, "we had learned that listening devices could be frustrated by sharp sounds. Now, few conversations were held without the constant noise of snapping fingers. It must have been a funny scene, but it was all deadly serious to us then."[17]

Confrontation overshadowed the testimony of the unfriendly witnesses. Not until the sixth day did the first of them, Lawson, testify. "I am not on trial here, Mr. Chairman," he declared. "This committee is on trial here before the American people. . . . It is unfortunate and tragic that I have to teach this committee the basic principles of American————" Before he could finish, Congressman Thomas, pounding his gavel, ordered Lawson from the stand and officers removed him from the room, to a mixture of boos and applause. When Stripling asked Trumbo if he was or had been a member of the Communist Party, there was a hush and for a few moments one could hear only the whirring of cameras and Trumbo's breathing. He evaded the question, and flashbulbs popped. He, too, was dismissed. A committee investigator then took the stand and presented evidence that Lawson and Trumbo were party members.[18]

The Ten, one must say, were controversial for several reasons. It was clear at the least that their views were pro-Soviet.[19] Lawson earned a reputation as a defender of the party line. He had been a cofounder and first president of the Screen Writers Guild, and joined the New York Communist Party in 1934. He had approached Earl Browder, whom he considered a "profoundly original and patriotic thinker," about creating a party unit in Hollywood, and became leader of a group studying Marxism with V. J. Jerome. His support for the Soviet Union (and opposition to fascism) occasionally had come through in such scripts as *Blockade* (1938) and *Action in the North Atlantic* (1943). Together with Trumbo, Bessie, and Maltz, he helped start the Marxist literary quarterly, *Mainstream,* in 1946. It was a time of "decisive struggle," he said, when "still powerful forces of imperialism and reaction" in America jeopardized "democratic victories" obtained during the war. "The ideological struggle must be waged nationally," he told an audience in August 1947, "in the whole field of culture." He denied that artists had more freedom under capitalism than socialism and argued that the USSR had "democratized" art to an extent unimaginable in the United States.[20]

Trumbo said he had joined the party in 1943 and abandoned it in 1948 "on the ground that I should in future be far too busy to attend its meetings, which were, in any event, dull beyond description." Nevertheless, when he had actually joined and quit was unclear. Paul Jarrico claimed to have recruited Trumbo during the era of the Soviet–Nazi pact, and the communist press serialized Trumbo's novels during this time.[21]

Biberman was an imposing, energetic figure who at forty-seven was still muscular and big-shouldered. He was married to actress Gale Sondergaard, who herself would be blacklisted after invoking the Fifth Amendment before HUAC in 1951. He always dressed impeccably, with a flower in his lapel and a handkerchief in his coat pocket. "He wore at least one very large ring on his large and powerful hands," Maltz recalled, and "unabashedly used perfumed

toilet water many years before it became the habit for men to do that."
Possessing a deep, resonant baritone, he spoke "with such authority and
conviction that it was impossible not to believe him." People responded to
his "contagious enthusiasm," a Unitarian minister recalled. "He was en-
dowed with an Old Testament righteous indignation. . . . His very presence
was impressive and could be formidable. He was ardent and earnest, a cru-
sader in a hurry, and he brooked resistance reluctantly." Biberman could be
"domineering and pompous," Cole remembered. "No one would ever
dream of calling him Herb or even Bert," said Bessie, who served with him in
the same Texas penitentiary. Ever the proselytizer, Biberman lectured the
federal marshals on world history and constitutional law as they drove him
across the country to prison. Bessie could never think of him without recalling a phrase that a compatriot in the Spanish Civil War once had uttered: "I
would die in pieces for what I believe."[22]

Bessie, a self-taught Marxist, was also doctrinaire. In early 1946, when
Maltz attacked the party's philosophy that art should be a weapon in the
class conflict, he (and Lawson) had denounced him as un-Marxist. "We need
more than 'free' artists," Bessie declared. "We need *Party* artists."[23]

Maltz believed that a writer should be the public's conscience, but re-
tracted his criticism after being attacked. He had studied philosophy at
Columbia University and served in prison with Dmytryk. When the latter
broke with the party in 1951, Maltz sought to discredit the director. Maltz
adhered to the party line until 1956, when Nikita Khrushchev disclosed some
of Stalin's atrocities.[24]

Dmytryk claimed he had been disillusioned with the party well before
the HUAC hearings, after a disagreement with Lawson over the script for
Cornered (1945). Others said that he attended party meetings faithfully
between 1947 and 1950. His renunciation of the party after leaving prison,
they argued, was to rehabilitate his career. Reagan and others who helped
Dmytryk reestablish himself believed the director's change of heart was
sincere.[25]

Whereas Dmytryk, Maltz, and Trumbo left the party, Lardner and Cole
remained. Lardner considered himself a "socialist, with the conviction that
for Russia at least, the Communist variety of that doctrine was the most
appropriate." Although he later admitted he had deluded himself about several issues, as late as 1976 he considered the basic beliefs of socialism as
credible as he had when younger. Cole had joined the party in 1934 and
remained into the 1980s. Staunchly anticapitalist, he believed Western industrial society was "not just *in*human but *pre*human."[26]

It was not surprising that the Hollywood Ten supported the right of workers to organize and strike. Lawson urged massive pressure against the
"monopoly-controlled media of communication." Reagan recalled how
Lawson was visible at organizational meetings and on picket lines. The

writer's activism so irked Warner that he gave HUAC a picture of him with the strikers.[27]

The Ten had championed the impoverished by portraying the "heartache of hope and daily living." Some of them sought to combine Marxism with realism, patriotism, the Constitution, and the work ethic. Trumbo wrote screenplays about the disadvantaged; the scripts' "heavies were always the rich who oppressed them." For *The Underground Stream* (1940), Maltz went to Detroit to investigate CIO-organized sit-down strikes in the automobile industry.[28] Cole tried to put "reality" into such pictures as *The President's Mystery* (1936). He believed his prosocialist views came through in the characters he created. In the screenplay for Universal's adaptation of *The House of the Seven Gables,* he changed one of Hawthorne's characters from a radical who held only a vague philosophy to an "active abolitionist" and "showed Northern capitalists of 1850 engaged in illegal slave trade." He hoped the movie would be a "radical bombshell."[29] When Biberman directed *Salt of the Earth* (1954), a film about striking New Mexico miners, he employed real mine workers and their families.[30]

The Ten wanted to end discrimination. That six of the Ten were Jewish – Lawson, Biberman, Cole, Bessie, Maltz, and Ornitz – helps account for their sensitivity to racial and ethnic prejudice.[31] Lawson considered racism a "dangerous cancer" that killed creativity. He dedicated himself to ending white Anglo-Saxon Protestant dominance. Twice jailed for efforts on behalf of Southern blacks during the 1930s, he found discrimination a catalyst for activism.[32] Convinced of the dignity and accomplishments of African-Americans, he sought to recover their past. "The monstrous myth of racism is rejected by social science," he wrote in 1947, but it was "propagated shamelessly by every American official historian." In *The Hidden Heritage* he attacked "Anglo-Saxon superiority," condemning the slave trade as "the base upon which the structure of capitalism was built." The roots of racism lay in capitalist culture. While in prison he wrote anonymously the screenplay for *Cry, the Beloved Country* (1952), filmed in South Africa, a poignant movie about racial intolerance. (Alan Paton's novel by the same title had appeared in 1948.)[33]

Virtually all the Ten hoped to eliminate intolerance and stereotypes. *Crossfire* (1947), the first full-scale postwar assault on anti-Semitism in a Hollywood film, had been the inspiration of Scott and championed by Dmytryk.[34] Maltz had earlier treated anti-Semitism in *The Pride of the Marines* (1945) and also sought to expose bigotry in *The House I Live In* (1945). Lardner's *Brotherhood of Man* (1947) urged tolerance. The black press considered Biberman's production of *New Orleans* (1947) an astute treatment of blacks. Cole tried to show Nazi cruelty toward Jews in *None Shall Escape* (1944). Trumbo denounced movies for making "tarts of the Negro's daughters, crapshooters of his sons, obsequious Uncle Toms of his fathers, superstitious and grotesque crones of his mothers, strutting peacocks of his successful men, . . . and a Barnum and Bailey sideshow of his religion."[35]

Most of the Ten saw American foreign policy as a manifestation of Western imperialism. History became a weapon. After the Soviet–Nazi pact, Maltz and Biberman argued that imperialism was perhaps more the enemy of Jews and civilization than was Hitler. Cole turned to Finnish history to explain the Soviet invasion of Finland.[36] Trumbo allowed those who opposed American involvement in the Second World War to exploit his novels, *Johnny Got His Gun* (1939) and *The Remarkable Andrew* (1941). The former was an antiwar tale told through the thoughts of a World War I veteran who had lost legs, arms, face, hearing, and sight, "without a single ray of hope to lighten his sufferings." In early 1940, Trumbo permitted its serialization in *The Daily Worker*, which announced a "passionate indictment of imperialist war," describing Johnny as "one of many courageous young Americans out of whose bodies Wall Street built a barricade behind which they guarded their profits." *The Remarkable Andrew* used the ghost of Andrew Jackson to criticize the British people as undemocratic and ask whether America should try to stop German aggression.[37] After World War II, Trumbo protested nuclear testing on Bikini Island and military exercises in the Arctic. A few years later, several of the Hollywood Ten opposed American involvement in the Korean War.[38]

Of the Ten, Lawson made the most sustained indictment of imperialism, the most extensive effort to reinterpret the past. He declared that contemporary writers faced "literally – the task of *making history*." At no other time, he told a New York audience shortly after his HUAC appearance, was there such need for "fundamental exploration of our American ideals and traditions." The people's struggle against the privileged few who controlled the state was the central theme of history. Nothing so captured American culture, he wrote in *Hidden Heritage*, as did the "revelatory phrase, *imperial democracy*."[39]

The Ten based their defense on the First Amendment and challenged the constitutionality of the Thomas committee. Lawson and Trumbo refused to affirm or deny membership in the party on the grounds that the question violated the Bill of Rights. (Each time Chairman Thomas's "gavel struck," Humphrey Bogart later told a radio audience, "it hit the First Amendment.") Shortly after the hearings Lawson "declared a fight to the finish" and said that "the great political issue of freedom for all is interwoven with the equally vital issue of artistic freedom."[40] That he should have championed free expression was ironic, given his dogmatic insistence that writers should adhere to the party line. Once an artist became committed to the working class, Lawson said, his work had a logic and purpose. He was "no longer concerned with timeless achievement," because he had "real work to do in the real world." Lawson admitted there had been "violations of democracy and over-zealous application of dogma." He did not believe that dissent was an "absolute right, irrespective of the purpose of the dissenter."[41]

The result of the HUAC hearings was the so-called Waldorf Declaration, announced not by the House committee but by producers, led by Motion Picture Association of America president Eric Johnston. At first Johnston had thought the hearings un-American. But he was most troubled by the bad publicity that had come to Hollywood. On November 24, when industry leaders assembled at the Waldorf Astoria in New York, the same day Congress voted contempt charges against the Hollywood Ten, Johnston told seventy or eighty executives that it was time to "fish or cut bait." Earlier he had advocated blacklisting known Communists who might influence films, but backed away from the idea when the producers, who feared the plan would entangle the industry in litigation, balked.[42] Now he proposed, and the producers agreed, that studios would either dismiss or suspend the Ten without pay until they resolved the contempt charges and declared under oath that they were not Communists. The industry would not hire Communists or anyone else who advocated overthrowing the government by force or by unconstitutional means. The producers wanted Congress to outlaw the Communist Party. Although Johnston talked about due process, not hurting the innocent, and avoiding a "concentration camp of suspicion," critics saw the declaration as capitulation to pressure.[43]

Studio heads looked coldly at the problem of the Hollywood Ten. They knew the Waldorf statement would be controversial. Representatives from the writers, directors, and actors guilds had met with members of the Association of Motion Picture Producers on December 3, and Mayer and other executives had explained that the problem was not a moral issue but one of getting back to business as usual. They had expelled the Ten not because of qualms about communism but because of the public's reaction. When asked if the declaration came from a desire to fight communism or protect business, Mayer admitted that the producers' first obligation was "to protect the industry and to draw the greatest possible number of people into the theaters." The problem demanded immediate action because of inflamed opinion. He did not know if the Ten were guilty and would welcome them back if they took a loyalty oath, but he would not risk offending the American public. Other executives agreed with Mayer. Nicholas Schenck of Loew's was against communism but did not consider it proper to take action until the Communists hurt his business. Schary noted that the discharged men had not been let go because they were considered Communists but because their actions made them a liability to the studios. Walter Wanger asked the guilds not to criticize the blacklist, because such a course would surely have raised more questions about Hollywood's loyalty.[44]

At this session Reagan asked several interesting questions. What procedure would determine who was a Communist – and if someone denied such an accusation, would his word suffice? No screening procedure had been or would be set up, Mayer said. The matter would be up to the discretion of each producer who would be guided "only by what they know themselves" and not "by what anyone *tells* them."

What was the difference between firing the Hollywood Ten and creating a blacklist, Reagan asked? Schary said only that the studios had dismissed the Ten because their usefulness had ended and that the courts would test the decision.

Reagan wanted to know what the industry would do if the Thomas or Tenney committees branded someone a Communist or un-American because he or she belonged to a front, but the person, while admitting membership, denied communist sympathies? It would take more than a committee to prove someone was a Communist, Schenck declared. Nevertheless, if a congressional committee called a studio employee and that person refused to say if he or she was a Communist, then Schenck would dismiss the suspect.

Reagan noted that producers had been unwilling to fire Communists before the October hearings unless the accused were proven subversives. Why the change, he wondered? Because, Schary told him, the studios faced intense public pressure.[45]

Reagan reported to SAG about the December 3 meeting, presenting a statement he hoped the board would adopt. The statement was consistent with his position before HUAC. It criticized producers for inquiring into the politics of employees or discriminating against them on the basis of ideas. Liberty could not be "held in water tight compartments," he said. "Once suppression, backed by the pressure of fear, breaks down one bulkhead, the other compartments are soon flooded." The problem involved more than the Ten; it involved the future of the guild, and SAG had a duty to protect performers. The guild was in an untenable position. "We are urged to make ourselves lawmaker, judge and jury and to take punitive measures in direct contravention of the law." SAG would cooperate with officers of the law, he said, but not assume their powers, for to do so would be to adopt communist tactics. He defined a position on communism: The guild rejected not only the theory but the Communist Party's tactics, which ignored majority rule and fair play. While SAG could not legally deny membership on the basis of belief, he said, it could keep Communists from power by requiring officers to sign the noncommunist affidavit required by the Taft-Hartley Act, recently passed by Congress to prevent, among other things, communist infiltration of labor unions.[46]

A majority of SAG's directors would not support this proposed statement, and some argued that it might appear to be a defense of communism. Several directors feared that a statement would risk further adverse publicity. When a nonbinding vote was taken on Reagan's statement, the board defeated it by a two-to-one margin.[47]

Reagan now had to compromise, and here George Murphy proved helpful. "I owe a great deal to this cool, dapper guy who had to deal with me in my early white-eyed liberal daze," Reagan recalled. "There were some of our associates, I'm sure, who believed I was red as Moscow, but Murph never wavered in his defense of me even though I ranted and railed at him as an arch-reactionary." At a special board meeting on December 12, Reagan again read a statement and Murphy at first moved its adoption but withdrew it when Walter Pidgeon recommended that the board express its views privately to the producers. Murphy submitted a motion incorporating Pidgeon's suggestion and it passed unanimously. He and Reagan withdrew to draft a letter that softened Reagan's criticism of the producers. It promised cooperation with the executives and concluded that Congress should decide the Communist Party's fate.[48]

All the while Reagan was providing the FBI with information about SAG members. The bureau had several informers in the guild and one, "Source T-9, a well-known motion picture actress," told an agent in early December that Reagan had "seen the light" and was trying to bar radicals from power. When interviewed, Reagan told the bureau he had been named to a committee, headed by Mayer, to eliminate Communists. He thought Mayer's committee was unsound because no one person or group had either the ability or the authority to determine unerringly who should be discharged. "Do they expect us to constitute ourselves as a little FBI of our own and determine just who is a Commie and who isn't?" he asked the agent.[49]

By the end of 1947, Reagan had thus moved from the position he had taken when he had opposed banning the Communist Party. In testifying before HUAC in October, he had not wanted to see any party proscribed on the basis of ideology. Now in December, he agreed with Johnston and the producers. He told the FBI that he was firmly convinced that Congress should declare the Communist Party illegal. He wanted Congress to designate what organizations were communist-controlled, so that membership could be, ipso facto, proof of "disloyalty."[50]

After the Waldorf Declaration, the Hollywood Ten sought public support. Years of litigation followed. For a while many expected that the Supreme Court would reverse their convictions. However, the Court's makeup changed in 1949. Justices Frank Murphy and Wiley Rutledge died, and more conservative justices replaced them. The Hollywood Ten recognized that prison was unavoidable.[51]

The hearings created a climate of fear and devastated Hollywood's Marxist left. Almost any effort to use film for social experimentation became suspect. The producers, who feared anything that might alienate the ticket-buying public, sought to avoid controversy and to make their films accord with whatever beliefs seemed safe at the moment.

Yet the ideas of the Ten did not disappear. In many respects their notions of justice for all Americans looked forward to the civil rights and antiwar movements of the 1960s and to the social history of the 1970s and 1980s. Lawson, who felt that the studio system prevented Marxist writers from accomplishing much, nevertheless predicted that the fight against Wall Street "art" would intensify. Trumbo believed that although pictures remained under capitalist control, the record was "better than bad." Films had changed during the 1930s. The very fact that Congress investigated Hollywood suggested progress, he said. The blacklists would be transitory defeats, victory lay in the future. Cole agreed. "Over the years, yesterday's 'subversion,'" he said, became "accepted reality."[52]

The future also lay with those who opposed the Ten. Reagan had managed himself adroitly during the 1947 hearings. As he sampled opinion in the Screen Actors Guild, he realized that liberalism was becoming a liability.

13

THE ECLIPSE OF LIBERALISM

I realized that in times just like these it is difficult to raise the standard of liberalism and collect yourself a crowd of followers.

Dore Schary, September 22, 1946

Believe me, the dilemma of the big box-office star has been considerable. No matter what his convictions, he risked his entire career by liberal activity.

Robert Ardrey, December 7, 1948

As his train pulled into the Los Angeles station in late September 1948, President Truman appeared to have little chance to win the election against New York Governor Thomas E. Dewey. The president was on a campaign swing through the state, and southern California Democrats had arranged a rally in Gilmore Stadium. Perhaps thirty thousand people came, and many more listened over the radio. The president's reception was best described by the master of ceremonies, who provided commentary for CBS radio: "Overhead, multicolored searchlights are turning the night sky into a gigantic rainbow. We have just concluded a tremendous program with ten bands, choruses, color guards, motion picture stars, and everything. The applause that you can hear indicates the tremendous response the President's address has received." As the president shook hands and prepared to leave, searchlights zigzagged over the sky. The commentator continued: "It's a tremendously thrilling sight . . . people have risen to their feet cheering . . . that boom you heard was a large rocket, and I think it is the first of what is going to be a sort of twenty-one-gun salute . . . and there it is . . . no one could have asked for a greater expression of support than here this evening . . . it has been one of the greatest campaign meetings ever held in California."[1]

If the announcer exaggerated, the excitement was understandable. Ronald Reagan helped arrange the rally and mobilize the film colony. "Truman can credit me with at least one assist," he said later, "but never thereafter."[2]

157

That autumn Reagan campaigned for other Democrats, including Minnesota's senatorial candidate, Hubert H. Humphrey. He praised the Minneapolis mayor's program for "adequate low-cost housing, for civil rights, for prices people can afford to pay, and for a labor movement free of the Taft-Hartley Law," all this in a broadcast sponsored by the International Ladies' Garment Workers Union. Humphrey's adversary was, according to Reagan, a "banner carrier for Wall Street." Reagan blamed Standard Oil for inflation. "High prices," he said, "have not been caused by higher wages, but by bigger and bigger profits."[3]

Reagan in 1950 would support Helen Gahagan Douglas against Richard M. Nixon for the Senate. He was one of a dozen Hollywood performers listed as Douglas sponsors, and he delivered several radio spots. One Douglas supporter feared Reagan would hurt the campaign because he was too radical. "He had a reputation as a far-out liberal," Lionel Van Derlin recalled.[4]

But even by the 1948 campaign Reagan was becoming more conservative. During the late 1940s he had followed a course similar to Helen Douglas's husband, Melvyn. Both had enrolled in the progressive American Veteras Committee. They joined Americans for Democratic Action along with such other anticommunist Hollywood liberals as Walter Wanger, Allen Rivkin, Roy Brewer, Art Arthur, Philip Dunne, and Howard Green.[5] Yet Reagan never felt comfortable with the AVC and the ADA. The AVC was full of dissension, and the ADA failed to develop a strong presence in Hollywood after the HUAC hearings. As both came under attack, he pulled back. The 1948 campaign marked the height of his liberalism. By 1950 he and the Douglases were going different ways.

★★★

Liberals divided after the war, and the issue that divided them was communism. Many believed the administration's get-tough poicy was extreme and for a while turned to Henry A. Wallace, the former vice-president, then secretary of commerce. He had attacked Truman's foreign policy at Madison Square Garden in September 1946; in 1948 he ran for president. But for other liberals, including Reagan, Wallace became a symbol of misguided idealism, even naïveté.[6] Reagan in 1948 organized and chaired the Labor League of Hollywood Voters in the president's behalf. Created to support anticommunist candidates, the Labor League reportedly had backing from twenty-one AFL unions. Its members wanted Truman to reject "compromise with communists or a third party," and endorse the League's anti-Wallace liberalism.[7]

Divisions, of course, weakened Hollywood liberals before the 1948 campaign. It was "difficult to raise the standard of liberalism and collect yourself a crowd of followers," producer Dore Schary observed in 1946. Reagan's employer, Jack Warner, was among those who retreated from liberalism. He began to reassess his politics soon after the war. After strikers picketed his studio, he claimed that he was the "victim of a gigantic communist conspiracy" and vowed never to make another "liberal" movie, "since liberalism was just a disguise for communist propaganda." From then on, he said, he would vote for Republicans.[8]

What happened with liberalism in Hollywood was thoroughly important in the case of the proposed movie, "Up Till Now." Warner let it be known in early 1947 that he was considering stories by anticommunist writers and announced that Reagan and Viveca Lindfors, his costar from the recently completed *Night Unto Night*, would team up with Claude Rains to star in "Up Till Now." Rains would play a confused father with two sons, one of whom (Reagan) would join the Communist Party whereas the other aligned with a fascist group. Lindfors, portraying a naturalized American, would explain the value of democracy and the "necessity for vigorous democratic action as the alternative to apathy . . . and meaningless antagonisms."[9]

The author of the story, David Goodis, seemed to believe in what he was doing. He found support in early 1947 from Warner Bros. producer Jerry Wald, who saw a message that would invigorate democracy and repudiate communism. "I am at present convinced," Wald said, "that communism can only spread once the soul is dead." Wald and Goodis beheld "Up Till Now" as a return to the big political picture Warner Bros. had produced during the 1930s. "We affirm by our story that the ills of the world can be cured – not around the negotiating table or by scholars, philosophers, or statesmen – but rather in the spirit of each individual," Goodis said. He went into detail: "Although it is not properly speaking a religious story, the message that it contains represents religion in its purest form, emphasizing the need for a spiritual renaissance in the heart of every man." He believed his story had a message for liberalism because it presented "regenerated democracy" as a solution. Between February and May 1947, Goodis put his story through more than a dozen revisions.[10]

In secret testimony before HUAC in 1947, Warner used "Up Till Now" to defend the studio's reputation. Warner was on the defensive by this time. He was never above suspicion even during the war. FBI reports hinted that he might be too friendly with the Soviets. Testimony at closed HUAC hearings in 1945 had been highly critical of the pro-Russian film *Mission to Moscow* and of the studio's New Deal films. Warner claimed that "Up Till Now" was part of a "militant intensification" of the industry's "fight against un-American ideologies," and that it would unmask unworthy citizens and foreign enemies. He would not tolerate "backslid Americans and wishy-washy concepts of Americanism." Democracy had no "middle lanes, left detours or right alleys," Warner said. "The great highway of American liberty is sufficiently broad and straight for all to travel in peace, prosperity and happiness." "Up Till Now" would reflect the "positive Americanism" in the Declaration of Independence, Constitution, and Bill of Rights. Americans needed "awakening" to the "dangerous tides" engulfing the country.[11]

But the movie was never produced. Warner feared antagonizing the public with a political picture and abruptly dropped the project in late 1947. It was one of many casualties of the post-HUAC climate.[12]

Other Hollywood liberals were more committed to liberalism. Melvyn Douglas, an uncommonly thoughtful actor, tried to clarify liberalism in June 1947, citing the philosopher Morris R. Cohen, whose *Faith of a Liberal* had appeared the previous year. "Liberalism is too often misconceived as a new set of dogmas taught by a newer and better set of priests called 'liberals,'" he said quoting Cohen. "Liberalism is an attitude rather than a set of dogmas – an attitude that insists upon questioning all plausible and self-evident propositions, seeking not to reject them but to find out what evidence there is to support them rather than their possible alternatives. This open eye for possible alternatives . . . is profoundly disconcerting to all conservatives and to almost all revolutionaries."[13]

The liberal's voice, Douglas said, using his own words, contrasted with the "laissez-faire reactionary capitalist," with the "voice of his economic opposite, the Marxist communist," and with the "voices of the religionists" – Catholic, Protestant, and Jewish fundamentalists. The liberal supported the proposition that

men are part of a world of nature, that there is a common denominator to all things in nature which gives them a certain equality – that slowly and painfully we are learning to control or to regulate the forces of nature and that, if we approach man's problems with the open mind of science and with the open heart of humanism, there is the possibility of creating a society in which men can (to some degree) solve their common problems and not be afraid of one another.

Liberals believed society should provide the necessities for survival and make good medical treatment available to all citizens. The right of labor to organize was essential and every resource should be employed to ensure full employment. Society, Douglas believed, was "like the proverbial chain – no stronger than its weakest link." He endorsed representative government, free speech, access to information, and a society predicated on sound understanding of human nature. He also provided a rationale for participation in international affairs.[14]

Although Reagan may have shared positions in common with Melvyn Douglas in 1947, it is also likely that he moved in circles with people who held sharply different views. Douglas's liberalism (and that of the New Deal) assumed the government would play a role in helping the disadvantaged, and this contrasted with the position taken by Reagan's pastor, Reverend Kleihauer. Reagan knew Kleihauer well, considered him a good man, and held membership in his congregation at the Hollywood–Beverly Christian

Church. A "Christian society is under sacred obligation so to organize itself that everyone willing and able to work may be guaranteed meaningful occupation," Kleihauer argued. Nevertheless, he counseled skepticism about those who claimed to be in need. "Bums are social parasites and should not be tolerated nor encouraged." Help to the needy was often necessary, he acknowledged, but it should always be given in a way that did not undermine self-respect, enterprise, and responsibility. After the war, Kleihauer advocated that the church "restudy the whole program of social service," and castigated "promiscuous charity" which encouraged "dishonesty and unscrupulous beggary." He was suspicious of social workers, many of whom, he maintained, "haven't religion enough to fill a thimble, and are just scientific machines, dealing with human integers." Large churches needed someone to handle charity who would be a "happy combination of the Good Samaritan and a cold-blooded banker." How much Reagan may have absorbed from Kleihauer is speculation.[15]

About the time Douglas was defining his views on liberalism, Reagan aired his opinions in an interview with Hedda Hopper. Unlike Douglas, he did not speak of critical inquiry or endorse government's role in a fairer society. "Our highest aim should be the cultivation of freedom of the individual," he said, "for therein lies the highest dignity of man. Tyranny is tyranny, and whether it comes from right, left, or center, it's evil." He worried most about infiltration and warned progressives about being used. "Right now the liberal movement in this country is taking the brunt of the communist attack," he claimed. "The Reds know that if we can make America a decent living place for all of our people their cause is lost here. So they seek to infiltrate liberal organizations just to smear and discredit them."[16]

A few weeks later Reagan emphasized the communist threat in a guest column for Victor Riesel. He and past SAG presidents opposed "indiscriminate Red-baiting," he insisted, but every union should be on guard.[17]

But how to combat the infiltration of the Screen Actors Guild became a matter of practical concern for Reagan during the summer and fall of 1947. The Taft-Hartley Act required union officials to sign affidavits declaring that they were not Communists. Most board members of SAG disliked Taft-Hartley, and many particularly resented the affidavit provision, but they disagreed over how to proceed until the law could be repealed. By mid-August, several members had not signed, including Anne Revere, who thought Taft-Hartley ill-conceived and the affidavit an encroachment on civil liberties. In early September she urged the guild to delay, reasoning that because officers of the AFL, SAG's parent union, had not signed, it made little difference what guild officers did. On September 15 she resigned as SAG treasurer rather than sign.[18]

Under Reagan's leadership, SAG's board was more tentative in opposing Taft-Hartley than were many AFL leaders. It would not support United Mine Workers president John L. Lewis when he rejected the affidavit, and it instructed guild representatives to the AFL national convention to support any resolution that required him to sign.[19] In November, after returning from the HUAC hearings, Reagan worried about the legality of denying employment on basis of belief or membership, given that Congress had not outlawed the Communist Party. Nevertheless, he opposed letting Communists become board members, arguing that they had a prior allegiance. In taking this stand he adopted a position consistent with that of Melvyn Douglas and MPAA president Eric Johnston. Following Reagan's advice, the board recommended – and SAG members endorsed – a resolution that required guild officers to sign an affidavit.[20]

Reagan participated in the American Veterans Committee, one of the most liberal of postwar veterans organizations. Like HICCASP, it advocated reform. Reagan found it attractive because it asked members to be "citizens first and veterans afterward." He "expected great things" from it, helped form one of its Hollywood chapters, and became a "large wheel" in its affairs.[21]

During World War II servicemen took seriously the talk about saving democracy and securing the four freedoms. They returned expecting a better world and believing they had a right to improve postwar society. As Louis Harris wrote in May 1945, "We feel that as a part of this world-wide struggle, we have a right to take a stand in building the world we will live in." Charles G. Bolte, one of the AVC's architects, put it more succinctly when he said, "We fight for what we fought for."[22]

Bolte was dissatisfied with such groups as the American Legion. The serviceman wanted two things, he wrote in *The New Veteran* (1945): the status he would have held had he not gone to war, and "something concrete to assure him that he and his countrymen will cash in the dividend of victory, so that he will not have to send his sons off to another war in 20 years." "Having known the fear of sudden and painful death," the new veteran was "afraid of none of the usual bogeys of civilian life." Initially Bolte felt an affinity for Wallace, and undoubtedly other AVC members shared similar sentiments.[23]

What to do about selective service divided AVC members. Bolte opposed ending peacetime conscription, a stand Reagan also took. Both thought conscription essential for national defense. Bolte, though, had an additional reason: universal military training was the best way to prevent militarism and a professional "ruling military caste." He believed a split had already developed between civilians and veterans, which he called the "most dangerous division in America today."[24]

Bolte and Melvyn Douglas endorsed the United Nations. Bolte urged amending the U.N. charter to compel national disarmament. He wanted the United Nations to have unfettered power to inspect and control atomic energy.[25]

In supporting international control of nuclear energy, AVC leaders took a position similar to that of HICCASP in late 1945. Some members wanted to share nuclear technology with the Soviets. "Scientists advise us that there is no exclusive franchise for the use of the atom," Douglas told Santa Monica veterans. "*There is* but one simple, undeniable conclusion – to share atomic power means to make it a weapon for peace, to hoard it means to make it a weapon for war." AVC members feared nuclear war. "World War III will vaporize civilization and leave a smoking crematory, filled with desolation and ghostly echoes which will have no one to hear them," Douglas predicted.[26] Philip Wylie, who wrote the novel on which Reagan's movie *Night Unto Night* was based, warned that "around the corner are enough dead American men and women and children, disintegrated and burned crispy black, to pave the streets of hell a hundred corpses deep."[27]

The AVC opposed colonialism abroad and discrimination at home (Bolte co-wrote the pamphlet *Our Negro Veteran*). It called for a "job for every veteran, with private enterprise and government working together to provide full employment for the nation," and championed "thorough social security." It became a strong critic of Taft-Hartley.[28]

The AVC grew rapidly. It attracted many liberals, such as Franklin D. Roosevelt, Jr., liberal theologian Reinhold Niebuhr, cartoonist Bill Mauldin, and journalist Tom Braden. Congressional Medal of Honor winner Audie Murphy became a member, as did General Arnold. In February 1946 the AVC claimed 108 chapters in the United States and 24 overseas. By the following October the organization boasted more than seven hundred American chapters.[29]

Reagan lent his name to the local AVC, the state organization, and also participated at the national level. At the first state convention, held in Los Angeles in late April 1946, he introduced Langdon W. Post, regional director of the Federal Public Housing Authority, who talked about how business and government might cooperate. "The sum and substance is that private enterprise and government must work for the people as a whole and not merely for private enterprise," Post said. Industry would build houses but government would guarantee material and fair profits. His "first evangelism" for the national AVC "came in the form of being hell-bent on saving the world from neo-Fascism." He believed there were "visible dangers" that fascism had taken root in America, especially among new veterans organizations. In early 1946 he used the *AVC Bulletin* to attack the Houston-based American Order of Patriots, which restricted membership to white Gentiles and required sidearms. He suggested that an international conspiracy supported neofascism in America, that even after defeat the German high command desired world conquest. He accused neofascists of dividing the United States, Britain, and the USSR; criticized assertions that war with Russia was inevitable; condemned efforts to widen racial and class divisions; denounced anti-Semitism; and castigated those who opposed price and labor controls. He did not ignore the "menace of the complete left," fellow travelers who would use liberals "to force something unwanted" on Americans.[30]

The AVC became a liability for Reagan when it came under attack for its program. The Hearst papers assailed it for supporting the Full Employment Bill and described Bolte as a "Dartmouth-bred radical" who founded "an inconsequential organization which is the left-wing effort to marshal veterans for left-wing purposes." Westbrook Pegler labeled it "red," and the American Legion, Veterans of Foreign Wars, and the Catholic War Veterans made similar accusations. The national commander of the Disabled American Veterans claimed it was made up of "4-Fs and draft dodgers." Hollywood joined the attack. William R. (Billy) Wilkerson of the *Hollywood Reporter* accused it of harboring publicity seekers, "outsiders," and "fronters." The FBI became suspicious; an agent reported that Reagan introduced a speaker at an AVC luncheon in Los Angeles in June 1946, whose talk was in "complete conformity" with the "Communist Party line."[31]

AVC members tried to refute these charges, and between 1946 and 1948 AVC anticommunist liberals managed to defeat left-wing efforts to control the national leadership. At the Des Moines convention in June 1946 moderates turned back left-wing challenges. In November the national planning committee denounced communism as a "conspiratorial" movement that would nullify the organization's goals. At the 1947 national convention in Milwaukee the organization elected Chat Patterson, Bolte's choice, as national chairman. Patterson repudiated communism "unequivocally." In 1948 the noncommunist majority rejected support of Henry A. Wallace for president of the United States, gravitated toward the Americans for Democratic Action, and "plunged the AVC into a turmoil of purification." The purge of alleged Communists and Wallaceite progressives had started as early as April and continued throughout the year.[32]

Dissension plagued the AVC in California, where a pro-Wallace faction and an Americans for Democratic Action contingent developed. In the wake of the Des Moines meeting, left-wing state leaders proposed a referendum for recalling national officers. They favored admitting citizens who fought against Franco in the Spanish Civil War. Divisions widened further in September 1947, when the area council in Los Angeles called for repeal of the county's loyalty ordinance.[33]

Such actions appalled Reagan and Douglas. They most likely joined with anticommunists in fifteen southern California chapters who formed the Progressive Caucus in early 1947 to oppose the state leadership. Believing liberalism was "on a desperate defensive everywhere," its members insisted the state AVC support the national planning committee's resolution condemning fascism *and* communism, advocated eliminating "endless debate" and "doctrinaire approaches to information," and urged a return of meetings to members for "their enjoyment, education and social activity."[34]

Through the first half of 1947 Reagan and Douglas seemed determined to remain AVC members. Rumors circulated in June that they were possible candidates for the national planning committee. In July, the *AVC Bulletin* ran a picture of Reagan (with James Roosevelt) indicating he was a charter member of the recently created Hollywood Chapter Number 2. But the division within the California AVC worsened at the state convention in Santa Barbara in early 1948. There delegates adopted resolutions calling for abolition of the Tenney and Thomas un-American activities committees, abandonment of government loyalty checks and subversive listings, repeal of Taft-Hartley, and distribution of aid to war-ravaged nations through the United Nations rather than the Marshall Plan. They criticized universal military training. Some of the Santa Barbara resolutions were not at odds with the AVC's national leadership, but taken as a whole they were controversial. The Tenney committee categorized them as straight "Communist line resolutions." By late March, celebrities began to leave the AVC. Will Rogers, Jr., charged that the California branch was "nothing but a Communist front."[35]

Reagan endeavored to move the AVC away from extremism of both left and right. In April, his Hollywood chapter voted to withdraw support from both the state and Los Angeles area councils. Its leaders accused the state leadership of remaining aloof within "cloistered monasteries uttering wails and cries of woe . . . curiously similar to the party line emanating from the Kremlin." By June, a California Committee for a National AVC had superseded the Progressive Caucus. Reagan and Douglas signed the committee's declaration condemning "totalitarian doctrines, both Fascist and Communist" and opposing communist efforts to influence the AVC. "As we are unafraid of the 'Communist' label accorded us by reactionaries, we are unafraid of the 'Redbaiter' label thrown at us by Communists." The California Committee's members characterized themselves as "non-extremists," endorsed the Marshall Plan, and opposed Wallace's presidential bid.[36]

At the 1948 national convention in Cleveland, many California delegates joined the East Wing of the AVC and tried, unsuccessfully, to prevent an anticommunist resolution. By early 1950, five of the East Wing chapters including the Hollywood Chapter Number 1 and the Wilshire Chapter had voted to end affiliation with the AVC. Consequently, the Los Angeles Area Council disbanded. Many who had been in the East Wing organized the Progressive Veterans of America. The national headquarters of the AVC confiscated the property of former southern California chapters.[37]

At what point Reagan severed ties with the AVC is unclear. He became more disenchanted when the AVC asked him to picket a studio in Army Air Force uniform. The decision to picket, made by a tiny minority, was canceled after he threatened to denounce the plan in full-page ads, he claimed. He came to believe the AVC a "hotbed" of Hollywood Communists, concerned with issues that contributed to a "Big Brother type of government," no longer a possible platform from which citizen-servicemen could work to create a better world. Nevertheless, he continued to count himself a member of its national organization. He was part of the 1953 Convention Committee in Atlantic City and belonged to the national AVC when he testified in the *Jeffers* v. *Screen Extras Guild* trial in 1955. He was a member of the AVC's National Advisory Council during the 1950s, a position he held at least until 1960.[38]

Although the movie industry had been hurt by the 1947 HUAC investigations, Reagan emerged unscathed. Many liberals even liked his performance. In late October, James Loeb, the executive secretary of the Americans for Democratic Action, considered his testimony "by all odds, the most honest and forthright from a decent liberal point of view," and called his closing statement "really magnificent." After spending two hours talking with him, Loeb came away "really impressed." Reagan had recounted to Loeb how he had spoken for HICCASP, the hostile reception accorded his criticism of Soviet policy, and his break with the organization. Although Loeb later realized Reagan was then "in mid-passage from moderate left to far right," at the time he considered him "the hero" of the Washington hearings. He hoped Reagan would "win over the liberals of the stage and screen" to the ADA's position that opposed "party-liners and . . . witch hunts."[39]

Liberals had established the national ADA in early 1947 as an alternative to Wallace's Progressive Citizens of America, and it became a magnet for anticommunist progressives. The names of ADA organizers read like a Who's Who of liberalism – Hubert Humphrey, Walter P. Reuther, Charles Bolte, Eleanor Roosevelt, Walter White, Reinhold Niebuhr, Franklin D. Roosevelt, Jr., Elmer Davis, Stewart and Joseph Alsop, and John Kenneth Galbraith all were on the list. The ADA recruited Reagan in 1947. While the ADA's leadership was diverse, most members came from similar circumstances. Most were college-educated, white, middle- or upper-middle-class Jewish men. Although the organization supported labor concerns and civil rights, it drew little support from either rank-and-file union members or blacks.[40]

Members often disagreed over objectives and tactics but stood behind the New Deal. Most supported expansion of the welfare state, safeguards for civil liberties, civil rights for blacks, strengthening of the United Nations, and the United States's plan for international regulation of atomic energy. Many championed the "vital center" liberalism advocated by one of its members, Arthur M. Schlesinger, Jr. The ADA united such New Dealers as Mrs. Roosevelt and Leon Henderson with "moderate pessimists" like Niebuhr and Davis. Its "principled liberalism" rejected millennialism and recognized that humans were imperfect. Belief in a free society and opposition to totalitarianism gave it a bond with businessmen. Its promotion of the "spirit of human decency" led it to oppose extremism.[41]

The ADA parted company with Wallace, praised Truman's veto of Taft-Hartley, and endorsed the Marshall Plan. Above all, it was anticommunist. It rejected coalitions with Communists, condemned the USSR's expansionism, and labeled the Soviet Union the primary menace to world peace. Loeb urged liberals to deny Communists membership in progressive organizations and decide whether the "*sole* objective of the progressive movement is economic security, or whether human freedom, which has historically been a co-equal dynamic of progressivism, is still a commendable objective." No movement that maintained a "double standard on the issue of human liberty can lay claim to the American liberal tradition," Loeb said. Yet he tried to separate the ADA from Russophobia. The USSR "should be viewed neither as the perennial villain . . . nor as the fixed point of international virtue," he said.[42]

Although Reagan worked for Truman's reelection in 1948, many other ADA members doubted the president's ability to hold the New Deal coalition. The ADA's national board called for an open Democratic convention, and suggested Dwight D. Eisenhower or Supreme Court justice William O. Douglas for president.[43]

The organization considered Reagan one of its "key persons" in California. When Melvyn Douglas became state chairman in early 1947, Reagan, Dunne, Wanger, and Rivkin were among those who formed the organizing committee for Southern California. Reagan attended conferences and assisted in recruiting. When Hubert Humphrey came to Los Angeles in early October 1947, Reagan was among fifty Hollywood liberals who attended a cocktail party at Douglas's house. There Humphrey spoke to performers, screenwriters, and studio attorneys who knew little about the organization. Helen Douglas (who did not join) poured tea and assured guests the group was truly progressive and not another "red-baiting outfit."[44]

The California ADA condemned the activities of the House Committee on Un-American Activities. At Melvyn Douglas's suggestion, the organizing committee took out full-page ads asking Congressman Thomas not to aid communism through shoddy procedures. The ads appealed for due process and "cultural freedom," and blamed HUAC for an atmosphere that impaired creativity. They also said that irresponsible attacks on liberals strengthened claims that democracy was a "frail and frightened thing."[45]

If Reagan found the ADA appealing, at least some ADA leaders found him attractive. The nominating committee elected him to the national board as a member-at-large in the spring of 1948. Loeb occasionally asked him to speak on behalf of causes and candidates.[46]

Reagan was not an active member of the national board – he never attended a meeting, according to Loeb – but he did offer advice. Shortly after the government of Czechoslovakia succumbed to a communist coup in early 1948, the ADA polled board members on the advisability of selective service. The ADA's national convention had come out against universal military training, and pressure built to have the organization testify before the Senate Armed Services Committee. Officers and other members were reluctant to testify unless they could support a reasonable system of selective service.

Reagan argued opposition to universal military training should be secondary to national defense. "It seems to me," he wrote national chairman Henderson, "that changing events have made the mandate of the convention less important than a reconsideration of military needs today." He urged the ADA to "make plain a belief in the necessity for some form of selective service."[47]

Reagan's tenure on the national board lasted only a year, although he maintained membership in the ADA at least until mid-1950. When he missed the board's Chicago meeting in August 1948, he explained that negotiations between SAG and producers required his presence in California. "I realize I have been of little use to the ADA since my appointment," he told Henderson, "but I want to assure you this is not caused by lack of interest. I'm convinced the ADA offers the only voice for real liberals and I look forward to the time when I can be of more help."[48]

That Reagan did not participate more may be explained by the fact the ADA's left-of-center (though staunchly anticommunist) stance made it suspect among jittery Hollywood executives. Liberals found joining the organization risky, especially after the Thomas committee hearings. Melvyn Douglas and Humphrey tried to recruit Dore Schary. But Douglas told Loeb that Schary, then under pressure from his board at RKO, had decided to limit himself to the Democratic Party.[49]

Other factors contributed to the ADA's woes in Hollywood. Writer Robert Ardrey believed the organization's "essential political maturity" made it difficult to sell to unsophisticated performers. "Show people are emotional. You'll find very few in this business who participate in politics on an intellectual level. Slam-bang convictions, violent loyalties, passionate enmities, purple principals [sic], and utter naïveté – these are the ingredients of political action in show business," he told Loeb.[50]

The ADA in southern California was also divided over what to do about Roy Brewer's application for membership. At the time – early 1948 – Brewer was a liberal Democrat, but he had been a friendly witness for the Thomas committee, was rumored to be on Tenney's advisory committee, and was a member of the conservative Motion Picture Alliance for the Preservation of American Ideals that had "helped goose" HUAC into action. He was an outspoken critic of the Douglases. "It's always been my position that we could not sell ADA in Hollywood with Melvyn Douglas at the head of it," he said. "He's made too many mistakes here, he's led too many Communist-front organizations. It would not be too serious if it were not for the antics of Douglas' wife," he declared. "We just can't swallow what she's done." He tried unsuccessfully to nominate Reagan for ADA chairman. Such ADA members as Howard Green, Emmet Lavery, and Robert Ardrey opposed Brewer's application. Green and Lavery considered him too conservative and Ardrey thought his presence would make recruiting such liberals as Gregory

Peck more difficult. Lavery, incidentally, was also unhappy about Reagan's election to the national board.[51]

During the following months the ADA did not become more acceptable to film leaders. It protested the government's loyalty program. In March 1949 it joined with the American Civil Liberties Union to demand a Senate investigation of FBI wiretapping. By autumn, syndicated columnist Westbrook Pegler attacked it for following the communist line and proclaimed Marx and Engels the source of its proposals. Senator Karl Mundt made similar accusations. By early 1950 J. Edgar Hoover believed the ADA was "becoming more and more a champion of communist causes" and asked for a report on its activities.[52]

Loeb's ambition to establish a robust branch in Hollywood never materialized, in part because of the growing anticommunist, antiliberal climate. The ADA's national office looked to Hollywood and New York for donations to cover expenses. But during the ADA's first ten months it managed to collect only $400 from the Los Angeles area. The fund-raising that Loeb expected Douglas, Reagan, and other Hollywood liberals to lead amounted to nothing. In the aftermath of the Thomas committee hearings, Douglas told the ADA that there was no money – most of what was available for liberal causes had gone to the Committee for the First Amendment. He recommended against pressing Reagan on "money matters" because it would harm the latter's relationship with the ADA.[53]

Loeb was disappointed. "There are in California in the ADA some marvelous liberals," he wrote. "Individually, they seem to have all that it takes to form a fighting liberal organization. But, for some reason, the organization there has never really lived up to its possibilities."[54]

The atmosphere created by HUAC, the industry's precarious economy, and world tensions crippled not only Hollywood's Marxist left but "vital center" liberalism too. The liberalism of the Douglases, the AVC, and the ADA troubled people of conservative natures, and it is unlikely Reagan felt at ease with it. Although it promised to make America a place of intellectual and technological creativity, that purpose was not for everyone, especially in times of economic and political confusion. Social conservatives equated it with the welfare state and the undermining of rugged individualism. Philosophical and religious conservatives feared that the spirit of inquiry dissolved not only economic principles but other beliefs ultimately grounded in faith.

Reagan confronted the problem on a more secular level. Given his upbringing in the Christian Church, the emphasis of Douglas (and Cohen) on the "dark side of religion" should have given him pause. Nevertheless, if public utterances are any indication, he rarely if ever thought about liberalism in these terms. Merely surviving in Hollywood in the anticommunist atmosphere of the late 1940s strained his liberalism. His box office appeal seemed in doubt. His employers, intent on demonstrating their anticommunism, had become squeamish about movies with liberal themes. Small wonder that Reagan chose to keep the ADA at arm's length and to side with such individuals as Brewer, Harry Warner, Cecil B. DeMille, and Y. Frank Freeman. Screenwriter Robert Ardrey captured his predicament: "Believe me," he told Loeb in 1948, "the dilemma of the big box-office star has been considerable. No matter what his convictions, he risked his entire career by liberal activity."[55]

14

BLACK DIGNITY

We asked that the warm humor of the Negro be shown, but presented in such a manner that he will be laughed with – and not laughed at.
William Walker, 1952

Neofascism seemed on the rise in the United States during the summer of 1946, press reports about antiblack and anti-Semitic agitation increased noticeably over the previous year, and the FBI stepped up investigation of the Ku Klux Klan. In southern California the state attorney general, Robert Kenny, received reports of violence: "Negroes have been beaten, fiery crosses have been burned, synagogues have been defaced, signs and symbols of the Klan have appeared in minority group neighborhoods."[1] Troubled, Reagan agreed to participate in a radio program, supported by Kenny and sponsored by the Mobilization for Democracy, called "Operation Terror," part of a series about the Klan called "It's Happening Here." It aired on station KLAC in September 1946 and chronicled more than two dozen alleged incidents in southern California as well as the lynching of blacks in Georgia. Here, reportedly, was the truth about Klan terrorism, "no guess-work, no if's, but's, or maybe's, but the plain facts, witnessed and recorded."

Reagan saw a conspiracy. "Are these just isolated cases of mob hysteria? Not on your life. There is a plan behind all this," he declared, "a capably organized systematic campaign of fascist violence and intimidation and horror. . . . The mobs are being stirred up; hopped up by racial hatred that is deadlier than marijuana." The violence was the work of a lunatic fringe, he said, "the kind of crackpots that became Reich Fuehrer; the kind of crackpots that became El Duce; the kind of crackpots who know that 'divide' comes before 'conquer.'" Terrorism, Reagan said, had to be stopped. "I have to stand and speak," he said, "to lift my face and shout that this must end, to fill my lungs to bursting with clean air, and so cry out 'stop the flogging, stop the terror, stop the murder!'"[2]

The program proved controversial. The Communist Party and the Hollywood Independent Citizens Committee for the Arts, Sciences, and Professions applauded. Los Angeles authorities, however, claimed they found little evidence of Klan activity. The violence had been perpetrated by "juveniles . . . the work of pranksters," according to Mayor Fletcher Bowron. He denounced the radio program as the work of "misguided leftist motion picture actors," and called for a grand jury investigation of the Mobilization for Democracy. The California Committee on Un-American Activities also condemned the program, proclaiming the Klan "dead" since 1941 and called the Mobilization for Democracy a "vicious, potentially dangerous Communist front" made up of "leftwing" movie people dedicated to "fomenting racial prejudice."[3]

It had been natural – given his father's hatred of the Klan – for Reagan to take part in the radio broadcast. During the 1940s and early 1950s he had connections with several organizations that attacked discrimination.[4] Nevertheless, as he gradually disassociated himself from left-wing groups, he pulled back from such organizations as HICCASP, Mobilization for Democracy, and the American Veterans Committee that pushed aggressively for civil rights. By the late 1940s he was working for black Hollywood performers mainly through the Screen Actors Guild. He remained a liberal within the context of SAG, to be sure, but when placed against the activities of the civil rights movement during this period he was at best a moderate.

The National Association for the Advancement of Colored People had long advocated better Hollywood jobs and more respectable screen images for African-Americans. During the late 1920s the association's executive secretary, Walter White, had challenged producers to use black actors more intelligently. During the war and after, the association stepped up its campaign to have blacks presented "as human beings instead of as clowns, heavies, moronic servants or as superstitious individuals scared of ghosts." Because White had helped Wendell Willkie during the Senate investigations in September 1941, Willkie agreed to appear with him before Hollywood executives at a luncheon the next year, and White again urged producers to conquer "fears and taboos." By abandoning stereotypes, he told them, "you can lessen the load of misunderstanding from which the Negro is suffering." Willkie reminded them that they belonged to groups persecuted by Hitler and should not be guilty of hurting another minority.[5]

To all appearances the meeting made an impression. The Warners (who did not attend the luncheon) and other film leaders said their studios would improve. Nevertheless, White was sensitive enough to understand that in Hollywood appearances could be deceptive. The industry "acquired a new enthusiasm whenever a protagonist for a cause came to the film capital, only to lose it and acquire another as soon as a new protagonist arrived." Executives gave lip service to racial relations but their actions suggested they were, at best, lukewarm.[6]

Progress did come, however, and the monopoly of Southern perspectives in Hollywood ended. The war proved a catalyst. Propagandists defined it as a struggle against a racist enemy. A million black Americans either were drafted or enlisted, and although segregated, fought well for their country.[7] Jack Warner cooperated with efforts to promote tolerance. After the war he had his staff compile a list of almost forty feature films made during the 1930s and early 1940s that contained "one or more powerful examples and pleas for tolerance among men." At a luncheon in 1944 for the army's first black general, Brigadier General Benjamin O. Davis, he endorsed interracial understanding. In Warner Bros.' *Hollywood Canteen* (1944) a black quartet sang the following lyrics:

> The General had a groovy crew,
> a million lads and I'm tellin' you
> there were white men, black men on the beam,
> a real, solid, all-American team.
> He had tall men, small men, fat and lean,
> the fightin'est crew you've ever seen.
> Every creed and color and every belief
> from an Eskimo to an Indian chief.[8]

Reagan's best-known World War II film, Irving Berlin's *This Is the Army* (1943), gave heavyweight boxing champion Joe Louis a small but prominent part. "I stopped worryin' the day I got into uniform," the Brown Bomber said. "All I know is that I'm in Uncle Sam's Army and we are on God's side." Another black in uniform followed by saying, "And we're right behind you, Joe." Then came a musical number, "That's What the Well-Dressed Man in Harlem Will Wear" (army khaki), which featured Louis punching the speedbag; at the end the champ marched to the front of the stage and saluted.

Nevertheless, stereotypes died hard on the Warner lot. In the same film a minstrel number ("Mandy") featured whites in blackface. It was one thing for the government to decree that black images be improved and another for the studios to make real changes. The problem lay in ingrained attitudes and is well illustrated by a story involving the Austrian-born, Hungarian-raised director Michael Curtiz. As he positioned singers and dancers in *This Is the Army,* he shouted: "Bring on the white soldiers!" After they had come on stage he roared: "Bring on the nigger troops!"

George Murphy approached the director. "Hold everything," he said.

"What's wrong?" Curtiz asked.

Murphy explained that "nigger" was offensive and suggested "colored troops."

Curtiz tried again. "Bring on the white soldiers," he instructed. Then in a bellow: "Bring on the colored niggers!"[9]

Discrimination was also entrenched in the military. The Army Air Force only reluctantly used black soldiers, and trained them in "separate but equal" facilities. General Arnold approached war pragmatically, backing away from controversy, fearing it would affect victory. He was unenthusiastic about black officers, believing that if they commanded whites serious social problems would be created. Moreover, opposition existed within the chain of command. Air force officers often were unwilling to treat black Americans with equality.[10]

The War Department endeavored to change this situation in 1943, a year marked by race riots, and part of the effort involved giving blacks a better screen image. Little foot-dragging existed in Reagan's AAF unit when it came to War Department racial policies. Reagan took part in the attempt to improve the portrayal of black soldiers. Toward the close of the war he narrated an AAF film, *Wings for This Man,* about black fighter pilots trained at the Tuskegee Army Air Field. The field lay in southeastern Alabama near a small town with Jim Crow laws, where tension often ran high between black soldiers and local whites. The base had two wartime commanders, both white. Colonel Frederick Kimble, who had doubts about the ability of blacks to fly in combat, increased segregation. His replacement, Colonel Noel Parrish, came in December 1942 and remained until after the war. Parrish was a student of psychology and anthropology. He enforced War Department policy concerning equality and sought to improve relations between the base and the local community.[11]

Wings for This Man, started in October 1944 and completed the following April, was intended for black theaters. It opened with fighter planes leaving to engage the enemy somewhere in Italy. "These are American boys going to work," Reagan narrated, noting similar missions flown over Burma, China, the Netherlands, Germany. The picture cut to a black officer who explained how his mission fulfilled a long-standing ambition. The picture underscored the effectiveness of black aviators. Of the 750 men graduated from Tuskegee, half were in combat, and of the first class only a few survived the war. That black pilots often had a three-to-one kill ratio refuted claims that they lacked aggressiveness. The film placed blacks in the mainstream of American life. To Tuskegee came students, dock workers, and "just plain citizens from everywhere U.S.A. They changed jobs, they changed clothes," Reagan explained, and "took a train into the future." Molding this "group of average Americans" into a fighting team was not easy. But there was a "new world up there." These men were "learning how high and how fast and how far" they had to go to "reach the enemy." The black pilot was "getting muscles in his mind – hard, keen, quick. . . . You can't judge a man here by the color of his eyes, the shape of his nose," Reagan said, and he concluded that in combat a person was judged by the way he performed. "Here's the answer to Adolph and Hirohito," Reagan said, as a white officer decorated a pilot. "Wings for this man. Here's the answer, wings for these Americans."[12]

Wings for This Man appealed for a united war, for acceptance of African-Americans, and suggested that the federal government could help achieve these goals. A "new road" was being carved out by these pilots, Reagan explained, "broad enough for thousands and ten thousands." It was a "road for our country." In constructing the Tuskegee airfield, government workers had removed more than timber and brush, Reagan said. They had worked to clear away "misunderstanding and mistrust and prejudice." The film implied that the new path would follow the course laid out by Booker T. Washington, who had stressed vocational training, economic self-sufficiency, and accommodation. Reagan quoted the words on Washington's gravestone: "He lifted the veil of ignorance from his people and pointed the way to progress through education and industry."[13]

Reagan's enthusiasm for black uplift at this time was consistent with the message delivered by his friend Reverend Cleveland Kleihauer of the Hollywood–Beverly Christian Church. At one time the minister had wanted to be an actor. He had an uncommon speaking voice and ability to quote Scripture from memory. A compelling presence in the pulpit, he opposed discrimination. "Democracy does not function racially in our country," he said in 1942. "Negroes, Mexicans, Indians, Orientals, could hardly with any sincerity repeat that noble expression, 'with liberty and justice for all.'" Democracy, he said, demanded that Americans be "willing to extend its privileges to all within our borders." "Proximity of races and nations is here to stay," he wrote the following year. Kleihauer condemned anti-Semitism, anti-Catholicism, and anti-Protestantism, as well as the "plague called race prejudice." He denounced the Ku Klux Klan. Racism was neither "American nor democratic nor Christian"; it was not only "damnably sinful" but "criminal" as well, a "cancer" threatening society.[14]

Black Americans disagreed over strategy in the postwar years. Activist organizations such as the NAACP wanted an aggressive campaign against stereotypes in film and other forms of entertainment. Hollywood blacks, who felt themselves a "threatened species," feared that elimination of stereotypical roles would mean the end of employment. They often opposed the NAACP as well as other organized efforts by African-Americans. Unable to present a unified front against the studios, blacks frequently had to depend on support from white liberals to improve their status within the industry.[15]

The Screen Actors Guild became a focal point in this debate, and Reagan proved important in defining its policy. During his terms as president between 1947 and 1952, conservative and middle-of-the-road actors dominated SAG.[16] Under his leadership the guild supported black demands for more dignified parts. Although unwilling to go as far as White and the NAACP in advocating elimination of roles as butlers and maids, the guild insisted that such parts respect African-Americans. Several black SAG members who were troubled by calls to abolish stereotypical roles agreed with this approach.

Before Reagan's presidency, SAG had treated black grievances with a politeness that bordered on indifference. Whereas many of the left-of-center groups Reagan associated with after the war (e.g., HICCASP and the AVC) voiced strong opposition to Jim Crow laws, poll taxes, lynchings, and segregation, SAG remained largely silent on such issues. Most guild leaders were cautious, unwilling to offend either producers or the public to advance African-Americans.[17] When the Negro Players Association asked the studios in 1941 to include more blacks in street and crowd scenes, the response was tepid. Nor were guild leaders enthusiastic in 1942 when White called for more realistic characters.[18]

The following spring the guild formed a committee, chaired by actor Franchot Tone, that met with black members upset by White's stand. Led by Hattie McDaniel, whose screen roles epitomized the stereotypical black maid (she won an Oscar for her performance in *Gone With the Wind*), the members feared that if the menial roles were lost, African-American employment would suffer. McDaniel and the veteran black actor Clarence Muse denounced White's involvement in Hollywood.[19]

The rift widened after the war. When White sought to create an NAACP Hollywood bureau in 1946 to give advice to scriptwriters, directors, and producers, he was again rebuked by McDaniel, Muse, Louise Beavers, and others. White believed his plan would eventually eliminate "Uncle Tom and Aunt Jemima" from the screen. Beavers called his scheme a "new type of streamlined gangsterism."[20]

As blacks disagreed among themselves, a more supportive attitude from the industry's white leaders became evident. When the city of Memphis attempted to ban *Curley* (Roach, 1946) because it showed black and white children playing together, MPAA president Eric Johnston criticized the censors, saying their actions could not be "tolerated if we expect American democracy to last." The directors of the Screen Actors Guild unanimously condemned the Memphis censorship board, calling its action un-American. Although Reagan was not present when the leadership passed this resolution, as guild president he likely endorsed its sentiments.[21]

Reagan meanwhile had become an active participant in guild issues involving black players. In September 1946 members adopted a resolution opposing discrimination and proposed a committee to work with screenwriters, directors, and producers to ensure that African-American characters would be presented on screen in a way that corresponded with the reality of American life. After the guild's membership passed this resolution overwhelmingly, Reagan moved to fill the committee with the resolution's three sponsors, together with four members from the board of directors: Gregory Peck (chair), George Murphy, Jeffrey Sayre, and Jane Wyman.[22]

The guild's Anti-Discrimination Committee proved divisive. Under Peck's leadership it did virtually nothing, and the directors dissolved it at a meeting in March 1947. Boris Karloff moved that in lieu of an Anti-Discrimination Committee, a black be placed on the guild's Negotiating Committee. When black members protested, however, the Anti-Discrimination Committee was revived and Warner Anderson replaced Peck. Anderson reported progress after his committee met with producers. The producers agreed that parts written for blacks would be played by blacks (not whites in blackface), that they would consider hiring more African-Americans for crowd scenes and for other unspecified roles that appeared in scripts, and that blacks henceforth would appear on screen as ordinary people rather than as caricatures.[23]

The debate among the guild's directors over whether to continue the Anti-Discrimination Committee resurfaced while Reagan was away in Washington testifying before HUAC in autumn 1947. Gene Kelly and Edward Arnold were apparently satisfied that the guild had done its duty. They and like-minded board members pointed to statistics that showed more blacks working in Hollywood than in the previous year and argued that African-Americans would be hurt if the guild persisted in approaching the producers with repetitive pleas. When Kelly moved that the board recommend a "no" vote on a new resolution to reestablish the Anti-Discrimination Committee, his motion carried unanimously. After Reagan returned from Washington, the board also defeated other proposals in late 1947 that would have set up a group to monitor discrimination.[24]

Between late 1947 and early 1952 the guild initiated little activity on behalf of blacks. The Thomas committee hearings as well as economic retrenchment created a hostile environment. Reagan continued to be identified with attacks on discrimination, although his denunciations were aimed more at anti-Semitism than at prejudice against blacks. His Hollywood chapter of the American Veterans Committee saluted *Crossfire* as "an outstanding contribution to the ideals for which we fought."[25]

A notable assault on the Klan came shortly thereafter, *Storm Warning*, released in 1950. The story centers on a young New York fashion model, Marsha Mitchell (Ginger Rogers), who upon arrival in a small Southern town witnesses the Klan's killing of a newspaper editor.[26] Reagan's character, Burt Rainey, is the county's prosecuting attorney who, despite pressure, opposes the Klan as "a bunch of hoodlums dressed up in sheets." At the climax, the Klan assembles in front of a burning cross and listens to Rainey's (Reagan's) denunciation: "It will take more than these sheets you're wearing to hide the fact that you're mean, frightened little people or you wouldn't be here desecrating the cross." To promote the picture, Reagan and Rogers toured Miami and Jacksonville. The movie unfortunately said little about civil rights and did nothing to enhance the image of African-Americans; in fact, there were no black characters in it.[27]

Reagan and other guild officials met with black members in early 1952 to consider ways to stimulate employment, and suggested pressing studio executives, writers, and directors. SAG leaders later appointed a committee that included Reagan, Murphy, and Walter Pidgeon, that asked the producers for a hearing. Such black actors as William ("Bill") Walker believed the guild had taken a "real and honest step" toward solving the "appalling case of the Negro actor."[28]

As the proposed meeting neared, a cloud hung over SAG's black performers. An informer had told the FBI that some were Communists. The charges came as the House Committee on Un-American Activities announced it would renew hearings on communist infiltration in Hollywood and issued subpoenas to thirty people. The American Legion also was pummeling Hollywood for harboring "reds." Hoping to place the employment issue above suspicion, sixteen of the guild's black performers issued a statement in mid-June 1952 disavowing communism and denouncing a conference sponsored by the Arts, Sciences and Professions Council that was to deal with equal rights in the entertainment industry. Signed by Walker, McDaniel, Beavers, and presumably approved by Reagan, it claimed that the conference was communist-inspired, that Communists exploited blacks to overthrow the government and to turn the United States into a "slave state under the whip of the Kremlin."[29]

Several studio executives – Joseph Schenck, Dore Schary, William Goetz, Y. Frank Freeman – thereupon attended the meeting held in late July. "Knowing many people's hearts can only be found in their pocketbooks," Walker recounted, the box office became "our first line of attack." The delegation pointed out that blacks comprised a tenth of the American population and had made inroads in professional sports and some industries because as a group they had developed economic importance. They argued that film could do more to cement friendship among people than any other medium. They called for more blacks in street scenes but not to the exclusion of roles as cooks, maids, butlers, and laborers, who should be shown as industrious and intelligent. "We asked," Walker said of the meeting, "that the warm humor of the Negro be shown, but presented in such a manner that he will be laughed with – and not laughed at!"[30]

★★★

White meanwhile had carried his campaign against stereotypes to television, and in 1951 threw support behind a code drafted by Henry Lee Moon, who handled public relations for the NAACP. Moon's code sought to regulate treatment of minorities by applying standards of ethics grounded in the nation's "democratic ideals." It attempted to eliminate clichés, derogatory group names ("nigger," "darky"), and distorted dialect. It urged impartial hiring procedures, casting opportunities beyond "servants, buffoons or criminals," and the presentation of public service programs unrestricted by regional prejudice. Many of SAG's black performers and most of the guild's white leadership, including Reagan, remained unimpressed. They were apprehensive about White and the NAACP. Black members disavowed White's approach and told the guild's board they did not want special attention or more than their fair share of work. Subsequently Reagan endorsed a motion that rejected a request for the guild to subscribe to a contributing membership in the NAACP.[31]

In the controversy over television Bill Walker became an important figure. He came onto SAG's board as an alternate for Robert Preston in late 1952. He had endeared himself to the board earlier when he supported the guild against its rival, Television Authority, which had adopted a resolution that called for television programs to represent blacks as they appeared in ordinary life and urged the creation of new programs to realize this goal.[32] Both groups had fought over who would be the bargaining agency for actors in the *Amos 'n' Andy* films as well as other pictures made by the Columbia Broadcasting System on the West Coast. In an election conducted by the National Labor Relations Board in early 1952 to determine who would be the representative, the Screen Actors Guild won by a two-to-one margin.[33]

Walker endorsed the television version of *Amos 'n' Andy*, a comedy that had been on radio for twenty years and was brought to television by CBS in 1951. The NAACP had attacked the program, arguing that it slandered the black middle class. But many black Americans rejected this assessment. The performers in the show, according to one recent study, considered NAACP leaders a "naive bunch of do-gooders" who were three thousand miles removed from the problem and far too eager to jeopardize actors' jobs for the "sake of a questionable principle." Many blacks agreed with Clarence Muse that the program depicted "real Negroes you and I know." Viewers did occasionally glimpse African-Americans playing educated professionals. Walker thought the program the only production that showed blacks realistically.[34]

Walker hoped the July meeting had made a positive impression, though he was aware the producers had been tepid. He was heartened when SAG's board of directors endorsed a statement on "Integration and Employment of Negro Performers," which called upon writers, directors, producers, and casting agents to recognize black artists primarily as artists and to give them parts reflecting their position in society, which then extended "from the kitchen to the United Nations." However, his optimism was tempered by realization that action was more important than words. When he addressed the guild's annual membership meeting in November 1952 he said progress had stalled. When SAG's black employment committee asked to meet with the Screen Producers Guild, they were put off for months.[35]

Walter Pidgeon replaced Reagan as guild president in 1953, but Reagan remained on the board and continued to be interested in problems of black performers. He thought the guild was on the right track in approaching the employment issue face-to-face with producers, directors, and writers, and was pleased that the Producers Guild asked to hear a spokesperson for black performers. Pidgeon asked Reagan and Walker to appear before the Producers Guild meeting in May. Reagan believed the employment committee had made the "opening wedge" with producers and that SAG should take advantage of this opportunity.[36]

It should be noted parenthetically that the board also tried to strengthen its hand in this matter by seeking support from Joseph Breen. John Dales, then the guild's executive secretary, extracted a promise from the Production Code Administration chief for prompt cooperation.[37]

When Reagan and Walker spoke to the Producers Guild, Reagan reminded them that few recent pictures had featured well-known black actors, and connected this trend with declining box office receipts. He and Walker made a plea for more roles that showed blacks in everyday life. Eager to give the impression of cooperation, the Screen Producers Guild voted unanimously to accept the recommendations.[38]

How successful was this effort to bring dignity to the black performer? There was temporary improvement, White believed. He wrote Dore Schary in 1949 that his campaign was "now happily showing results." Improvement, in White's view, lasted for only briefly between 1948 and 1951. Pressure from Southern audiences together with competition from television and loss of foreign markets combined to make progress short-lived. The "continued picturization of Negroes, Asians, Africans, and Latin Americans as either savages, criminals, or mental incompetents was doing . . . incalculable harm," White concluded, "both abroad and in the United States." Critics continued to condemn Hollywood. Shortly after Reagan and Walker had spoken to the Screen Producers Guild, Langston Hughes compared treatment of black performers in America with that in Europe and concluded that "Hollywood's ridiculous stereotype program" allowed enormous black talent to remain unused. The black man was still caricatured.[39]

Within his studio during the late 1930s and early 1940s, the Army Air Force during World War II, and the Screen Actors Guild during the late 1940s and early 1950s, one may conclude, Reagan was a liberal on racial matters. His screen image stood in contrast to the bias of Hollywood. *Wings for This Man* and "Operation Terror" reflected a liberal conscience. Insofar as the Screen Actors Guild attempted to improve the standing of black performers, Reagan was a force.

What we know from his actions and words suggest that opposition to discrimination derived from family background, and to a lesser extent from the church. He saw sports (such as the Eureka College football program, where blacks and whites played together) as a possible solution to racial problems. There is little evidence that he had any clear theory about the origin or economic underpinnings of racism, unlike John Howard Lawson, who tied bigotry to wealth and society's economic structure.[40]

Perhaps little progress could have been expected from a strategy that so relied on the benevolence of producers and censors. Hollywood executives saw equal rights, one suspects, as they did communism, that is, as an economic rather than a moral issue. They were at best cautious about proposals that might hurt the box office. Nor were the Screen Actors Guild's tactics designed to bring about major changes in Hollywood's apparatus of censorship. Breen's promise notwithstanding, it is unlikely that Reagan, black performers, or anyone else from the guild changed the attitude of the PCA's chief, who in 1948 insisted on eliminating physical contact between blacks and whites in the movie *Pinky*. In Reagan's case, good intentions were not coupled with a willingness sufficient to challenge prevailing power. Walker recalled that during these years Reagan "wore two hats all the time" and tended to go "where the money was."[41]

The fear of communist infiltration cast a "Red shadow" over efforts to improve the plight of black actors, as it did other forms of liberal activity. Reagan's efforts for African-Americans were secondary to his desire to combat communism and to build a wholesome image for the film industry. As he sought to avoid controversy and suspicions of subversion, his strategy called upon blacks to accommodate themselves to Hollywood's existing political and economic framework. It was appropriate that *Wings for This Man* paid homage to Booker T. Washington because Washington, perhaps more than any other black leader, best symbolized Reagan's stand on civil rights during his Warner Bros. years.[42]

15

SELLING HOLLYWOOD

Most of us are tired of living in a gold-fish bowl. . . . I'm perfectly aware
that we out here depend on publicity. . . . But why must it all be so one-
sided? Why not bring out the fact that the community consists in the
main of hard-working, church-going family men and women who rarely
if ever break into the headlines and who proportionately are engaged in
more charitable activities than any other group in the nation.

Ronald Reagan, 1949

Ronald Reagan campaigned for Harry Truman and Hubert Humphrey in
1948 and for Helen Douglas in 1950, retained membership in the American
Veterans Committee and the Americans for Democratic Action, and continued into the 1950s to identify himself as a liberal and a Democrat. Nevertheless, he had developed interests that moved him in a different direction.
As has been seen, holding office in the Screen Actors Guild forced him to
adopt a more conservative stance. So too did his work with the Motion
Picture Industry Council, a new organization whose goal was to improve
Hollywood's reputation. It emerged in the months following the Thomas
committee hearings, and Reagan became involved by virtue of his guild
presidency. In the Motion Picture Industry Council he joined other anticommunist liberals: Walter Wanger, Dore Schary, Allen Rivkin, Roy Brewer, Art
Arthur. They worked with conservatives like Cecil B. DeMille and Y. Frank
Freeman. Whereas the Americans for Democratic Action had an agenda to
reform society, the MPIC worked primarily to strengthen the motion picture
industry.[1]

Both the guild and the MPIC vastly assisted Reagan's development as a
politician. The former gave him a national profile and leadership in a large
organization. The latter provided proximity to producers and other industry
executives. Reagan participated not only in racial and labor issues, but also
in foreign policy and constitutional questions. Many of these matters

182

brought him in contact with the federal government. He defended Hollywood, combated communism at home and abroad, and helped create and carry out a loyalty program. He emerged as one of the industry's most effective spokesmen.

In the process he became increasingly conservative, which owed something to the circumstances of his private and professional life. In many respects it was a troubled period. If his reputation as an industry leader rose after the congressional hearings, his marriage and acting career deteriorated. "I arrived home from the Washington hearing to be told I was leaving [home]. I suppose there had been warning signs, if only I hadn't been so busy," he later said. In his career, too, he was not encouraged by reviews of *That Hagen Girl* and *Voice of the Turtle,* which appeared in late 1947. Acting was hardly a secure profession in the best of times, and as he began his first full term as guild president he was in trouble professionally, bogged down in a "never-never land between anonymity and success."[2]

All this occurred, as noted, in a time when fears about Communists multiplied and liberals became suspect. In the following months, the public would become more preoccupied with national security, what with the fall of China in 1949, the first Soviet atomic bomb, a series of sensational espionage trials, the rise of Wisconsin Senator Joseph McCarthy, and the Korean War. Even had these developments not occurred, had there been no Cold War, Reagan would have found his environment hostile to political risk-taking. Declining movie attendance, the breakup of studio theater chains, and the reimposition of foreign quotas led to layoffs and talk of even more drastic cutbacks. Hollywood had always been filled with uncertainties, but during the late 1940s it became much more so.

★★★

The Motion Picture Industry Council, so its founders hoped, would provide a large-scale, continuous public relations offensive that would unite Hollywood against its critics.[3] The idea likely originated in the December 3, 1947, meeting (where Reagan had questioned the producers about blacklisting suspected Communists), when Wanger recommended forming a public relations committee. Everyone present, including Reagan, was enthusiastic. Eric Johnston recognized the need for better publicity, and liked the notion of an all-industry council of representatives from management as well as from talent and labor unions. As SAG representatives, Reagan and Gene Kelly attended a planning session in early 1948. Schary became temporary chair of the Motion Picture Industry Council and the council opened an office. A few months later, in July, members arranged its organizational structure.[4]

Johnston attended an organizational meeting in the Screen Actors Guild's boardroom, and although he talked to the group about industry problems, he disappointed members when he thereupon resigned from the MPIC, preferring to stay in the background. Nevertheless, he brought his labor and public relations adviser, Edward Cheyfitz, to the meeting, and said he hoped he could work with the council until it was operating. The red-haired, nattily attired, seemingly indefatigable Cheyfitz enjoyed the infighting of negotiations. Controversial, he once had been a Communist. Most of his public relations clients were employers, which did little to dispel the impression that he was most interested in helping producers, although he sought the confidence of labor and management. Suspecting he would not be impartial, the Screen Writers Guild opposed his participation.[5]

The MPIC claimed to be an industrywide committee representing every element in filmmaking. In reality producers contributed two-thirds of its operating revenue. More than half the receipts came from the Association of Motion Picture Producers.[6]

Johnston's hope that the MPIC would establish unity almost came to naught. The council adopted a system of rotating chairpersons selected at random every six months. Schary reputedly chose his successor by pulling DeMille's name from a hat. The action appalled the council's labor interests because DeMille, an advocate of the open shop, had been engaged in a bitter legal controversy with the American Federation of Radio Artists, an affiliate of the AFL. Although the Radio Artists did not belong to the MPIC, two AFL affiliates, the Hollywood Film Council and Screen Actors Guild, were members. Brewer, head of the Film Council, quit the MPIC in early 1949. The Screen Actors Guild, then led by Reagan, continued membership. Brewer's Film Council agreed to rejoin after SAG insisted that the Motion Picture Industry Council change its election procedure. When Reagan, who was DeMille's cochair, became MPIC chairman in July 1949, Brewer was elected his cochair, thereby becoming Reagan's successor.[7]

After stepping down as MPIC chairman, Reagan stayed on the executive board and participated in policy. He remained as secretary long after leaving his post as Screen Actors Guild president in 1952.[8]

What sort of individuals belonged to the MPIC? Art Arthur, the executive secretary, described the organization as a "virtual Senate of the Cinema" because members included only the leading officers of Hollywood's guilds, unions, or management groups. All were anticommunists. DeMille talked about the "world conflict . . . between the individual and organized power," the "war for the survival" of individualism and free enterprise. He believed America was being undermined by "three dangerous 'isms' . . . : communism, political unionism, and socialism." They led "down to the same pit where liberty, as we know it, will die in the darkness." Freeman, the Paramount executive who once had been head of the Pepsi Cola Corporation in Atlanta, represented the Association of Motion Picture Producers. He willingly cooperated with the American Legion to eliminate Communists from Hollywood. (Freeman's studio, it should be noted, produced three of Reagan's films during the early 1950s.)[9]

The MPIC attracted men who considered themselves liberals. Like Reagan,

Arthur, Brewer, and Schary had supported Truman in 1948. Others, like Reagan, had belonged to the Hollywood Independent Citizens Committee for the Arts, Sciences, and Professions. Screenwriter Allen Rivkin of Metro-Goldwyn-Mayer, who became treasurer, resigned from HICCASP (as did Schary and Wanger) after the attempt to pass an anticommunist resolution in 1946. Like Reagan, Schary and Wanger were opponents of racism and initial critics of the Waldorf Statement. Reagan, Brewer, Wanger, and Rivkin were members of the Americans for Democratic Action.[10]

These liberals were for the most part financially successful, and they gravitated toward Hollywood executive positions: Schary had started as a writer and became a producer at RKO and MGM. Wanger was a major independent producer. The "mad and unpredictable" Arthur, who managed much of the MPIC's daily business and was an "encyclopedia of information," was a public relations specialist who later handled publicity for DeMille's *The Ten Commandments*. Brewer became a studio executive with Allied Artists. Reagan had achieved a substantial income in the years after the war in addition to rising in the Screen Actors Guild and the MPIC.[11]

The mild-mannered Schary looked for a bond to hold the Motion Picture Industry Council together, and thought that ideally the answer lay with "sound public relations" and better movies. A "public-spirited, socially conscious and civic minded" liberal, he was embattled over his political beliefs at the time of the MPIC's creation. He described himself as a "straight New Deal Democrat." Although he shied away from the ADA, he was executive producer of *Crossfire* (RKO, 1947), which attacked anti-Semitism and was produced by Adrian Scott and directed by Edward Dmytryk. He disagreed with RKO's decision to fire Scott and Dmytryk and refused, so he said, to carry out the board's decree. His liberalism brought difficulties at RKO after Howard Hughes took over, so he left to become second in command at MGM, where earlier he had been a writer and executive producer.[12]

Schary was suspect to both Hollywood's right and left. Learning about his move to MGM, Hedda Hopper wrote that the studio henceforth would be called "Metro-Goldwyn-Moscow." Mayer distrusted Schary's politics while the two were at MGM. He also became a pariah for many on Hollywood's left. As a former writer and member of the Screen Writers Guild, he defended the SWG in 1946, saying that its members would not "turn America into a group of Bolsheviks." He deplored the Thomas committee and claimed he had angered Johnston by opposing the Waldorf Statement. He tempered the latter, he said, by convincing producers to suspend, rather than fire, the unfriendly witnesses then employed. Supporters of the Hollywood Ten, noting that the Waldorf Statement had been adopted unanimously and that Schary had been present, were unimpressed.[13]

It fell to Schary to explain the Waldorf declaration to the Writers Guild. The producers, he said, had three goals. The first was to dismiss the unfriendly witnesses. Second was to avoid hiring anyone thought to be a Communist. "We do not ask you to condone this," he told the writers. The third was to restore Hollywood's honor by a public relations campaign.[14]

Seven of the Hollywood Ten sat in the audience as Schary spoke, and following his departure Dalton Trumbo made a "delightfully obscene" speech and the four hundred guild members present voted overwhelmingly to reaffirm opposition to the blacklist. Nevertheless, in a larger sense Schary had been persuasive, because the Writers Guild joined the Motion Picture Industry Council even if it became one of its most recalcitrant members.[15]

Schary reconciled his liberalism with the HUAC investigations, a reconciliation facilitated by the fact that he had opposed communism since before the Second World War. He had resigned from the communist-led League of American Writers in 1938 rather than sign a petition circulated by John Howard Lawson that attacked President Roosevelt's Latin American policy. By early 1952 he could tell a supporter of Adrian Scott (one of the Hollywood Ten) that although the Thomas committee's tactics had been alarming in 1947, the need for some similar investigating body was undeniable. Communists no less than fascists were freedom's enemies, he said. The way of the "true, constructive liberal" was difficult, he acknowledged, but people of good will would defeat subversion.[16]

In mid-1948 Johnston and Freeman invited Walter Wanger to join the Motion Picture Industry Council. Like Reagan and Schary, the courteous, urbane Wanger (né Walter Feuchtwanger) was a Roosevelt Democrat who had been associated with Hollywood's left wing. He had a reputation for trying "off-beat" topics and for being "world-minded."[17] In his pictures he often combined politics and entertainment. He won the National Peace Conference citation for *Blockade* (United Artists, 1938), produced during the Spanish Civil War; its screenplay was written by Lawson. In filming crowd scenes, director William Dieterle had "consciously followed Soviet examples." The Catholic church attacked the movie and Spanish fascists labeled Wanger a Communist. But if *Blockade* had made him controversial abroad, he was no stranger to controversy in the United States. He was active in 1946 in organizing a Los Angeles chapter of Americans United for World Government, a group the *Chicago Tribune* claimed was made up of "radicals and men of wealth" dedicated not only to world organization but to defeat of such isolationist leaders as Senator Burton K. Wheeler. As a member of the Committee for the First Amendment he supported the Hollywood Nineteen and protested the tactics of the Thomas committee.[18]

Wanger was no Communist. In asking him to work with the MPIC, Johnston chose an individual who would articulate views about film and free enterprise that coincided with his own. Wanger was thinking about how cinema could counter the Soviets. "I feel that if we will only organize our communications properly it will do a great deal toward winning the Cold War and not leave us vulnerable to psychological warfare," he told James Reston of the *New York Times* in 1947. He advocated strengthening the

British film industry to facilitate Anglo-American harmony and allow "projection of our civilization" to the rest of the world.[19]

Wanger and Reagan agreed that Hollywood needed better press relations. Both believed the industry had financed its own "blackmailing" and that "untold harm" resulted from "catering to irresponsible people in the press and on the radio. . . . If we compare our public relations to other industry [sic], such as radio," so Wanger admonished the MPIC, "we realize how short-sighted we have been and what a long view the other industries have adopted in developing good-will." In Schary's absence at the July meeting (he was on vacation, between jobs at RKO and MGM), Wanger assumed the chair and made recommendations for publicity. Reagan had asked Brewer to speak in his place. From Reagan's perspective there was little with which to disagree. He, Wanger, Schary, and Johnston were in harmony in their hopes for the Motion Picture Industry Council.[20]

Reagan became involved in many activities through the Motion Picture Industry Council. His work brought favorable publicity not merely for Hollywood but for himself. The council provided a school in public relations. He became more than a passive recipient of studio promotions – he learned to use publicity.

The council tried to keep its endeavors confidential. As executive secretary, Art Arthur took care of the "steady undercurrent" of activities that flowed "beneath the larger problems." He summarized the council's work, revealing the extent of its enterprise. In late 1950, for example, the council mailed a letter to a "high Washington official" urging that Al Jolson receive the Medal of Merit posthumously, prepared a guest column in *Weekly Variety* attacking the theory that Hollywood news had to be derogatory to be read, tried to use United Nations agencies to disseminate publicity favorable to Hollywood, discouraged Canadian censors from cutting American films, suggested themes for editorials in trade papers, placed articles about church-going performers in the *Christian Herald,* gave the State Department names of film personalities active in public service so the Voice of America could produce a program about American humanitarianism, and promoted a BBC broadcast by Alistair Cooke to contradict "malarkey about Hollywood abroad." Council members sought to confirm the "loyalty and patriotism of American films" by scanning *People's World* and *Counter-Attack*. The MPIC arranged for *Photoplay* magazine to publish an unsolicited letter to Reagan mailed by a young woman from Brooklyn who provided a testimonial to Hollywood. Scholarly criticism did not escape attention. Arthur considered anthropologist Hortense Powdermaker's *Hollywood, the Dream Factory* "lopsided" and hoped to discredit it.[21]

The council used Reagan's motion pictures to further its goals; in turn, the films benefited from council publicity. The council claimed that *The Hasty*

Heart – praised for promoting "cooperation between nations and religions" – demonstrated Hollywood's positive effect abroad. When *Storm Warning* opened in Miami, a local paper assailed Hollywood for exposing domestic fascism while neglecting the "equally ugly and dangerous other extreme – Soviet-directed Communism." Working through a local exhibitor, the MPIC persuaded the paper to run another editorial publicizing Hollywood's anticommunist endeavors. In league with the Council of Motion Picture Organizations (COMPO), it often repeated this strategy of using local exhibitors to counter critics.[22]

Reagan and the Motion Picture Industry Council tackled several problems. Elevating the esteem of the acting profession was one, as was finding solutions to declining attendance, the breakup of theater chains, high taxes, employment cuts, and low wages. Some of the issues were of an international nature, such as the imposition of foreign restrictions on American films and the spread of communism. Reagan and other industry leaders remained sensitive to charges that Hollywood had been infiltrated, and they attempted to set in motion a loyalty program. Movie censorship, in some respects unrelated to communism, proved troubling not only from abroad but in several states and more than two hundred cities.[23]

Enhancing the status of actors was an important part of Reagan's job. It became, one might say, almost a crusade. Defending his profession was a theme in many of his speeches during the late 1940s and 1950s.

The House Committee on Un-American Activities hearings had heightened suspicion of Hollywood performers. "Perhaps part of it was the thought of shelling out money at the box office to support some bum and his swimming pool while he plotted the country's destruction," Reagan said. But he also knew that public respect had been a problem before the blacklists. Even fortunate performers found themselves resented for their fame and wealth – "mocking affronts to the common man, vaguely wicked and unnatural manifestations of social inequity," Leo C. Rosten had written in 1941. Americans had long viewed actors with misgiving, considering them descendants of "rogues and vagabonds," attractive but at best amoral. "Like the whore," actors were "held in contempt but secretly envied." Even though this image was changing, Powdermaker observed in 1950 that prejudice remained: "The cliché that there are three kinds of people – men, women, and actors – is heard over and over again." Performers were considered out-of-the-ordinary, "looked down upon as a kind of subhuman species. No one respects them." They were often thought of as "children . . . , immature, irresponsible, completely self-centered, egotistical, exhibitionistic, nitwits, and utterly stupid." Psychological profiles characterized them as driven by "inner fears" or as "neurotic, unstable and asocial," and as prone to homosexuality.[24]

Leaders of the Motion Picture Industry Council believed that "drastic and affirmative action from within" was necessary. Soon after he became chair,

Reagan presided over a meeting that resolved to cooperate with law enforcement officials to rid Hollywood of its "scum fringe." The council pledged to assist with "gumshoe activities of its own to help expose predacious elements that seek to invade the industry or to fasten upon the unwary among its members."[25]

The MPIC turned to the personal conduct of Hollywood's "young and impressionable newcomers." It urged producers to be more vigilant and recommended that studios offer courses in behavior so novice performers would be "more thoroughly schooled in their responsibilities as individuals both to the public and to the industry." Deportment was important. Any crime or misconduct, even of a purely local nature, was seen as injurious to the industry.[26]

Reagan thought part of Hollywood's problem came from irresponsible reporters and overly enthusiastic press agents. Reporting stressed the unpleasant, ignoring the industry's constructive side. He was critical of gossip columnists (Louella Parsons and Hedda Hopper had reported his breakup with Jane Wyman). "Most of us are tired of living in a gold-fish bowl," he complained in 1949. "I'm perfectly aware that we out here depend on publicity and that, in a sense, it is our bread and butter. But why must it all be so one-sided?" Reagan wanted the press to emphasize that the movie community consisted mainly of "hard-working, church-going family men and women" who rarely made headlines, and who "engaged in more charitable activities than any other group" of comparable size. As for the people who fell by the roadside, "don't blame Hollywood," he said. "No one goes Hollywood – they were that way before they came here. Hollywood just exposed it."[27]

In early 1951 he again attacked the "irresponsible" press. "Certain elements in the press, the kind addicted to yellow journalism, . . . decided they could attract more readers and sell more papers and get more listeners," he said, if they emphasized the "more *flamboyant, more colorful, exaggerated* side of things and in most cases the messy side of things." Adults were offended by the movies, he noted, placing blame for that attitude on reporters whom he accused of "carelessness regarding our rights and rights of private industry. . . . They have made us look ridiculous," he charged. At a *Photoplay* dinner he stunned reporters by ticking off the names of Hopper, *Modern Screen,* and two Los Angeles dailies. Taking on the press corps was risky, *Time* cautioned. Either Reagan was a "very brave man – or a very foolish one." Unfazed, Reagan repeated his accusations, telling the 1951 Kiwanis International convention in St. Louis that Hollywood attracted reporters who lacked "journalistic integrity."[28]

Before the Kiwanis members and elsewhere Reagan defended actors, arguing that they were no longer the "troubadours, the strolling players who used to come into . . . town and live out of a trunk for a week and then pass on." They stood among the community's best citizens – public spirited and well

educated – who divorced less often than most Americans. Because performers were so maligned, "certain enemies of ours – enemies of democracy
and our way of life – think they have found a leak in the dike." He liked the
novelist Irvin S. Cobb, who he said had written,

When the curtain goes up on eternity, all men must approach the gates bearing in their
arms that which they have given to life, then the people of show business will march in
the procession, carrying in their arms the pure pearls of tears, the gold of laughter and
the diamonds of the stardust they spread on what might have otherwise been a mighty
dreary world, and I'm sure when all at last stand before the final stage door, the keeper
will say: "Open – let my children in."[29]

Even Reagan's appearance on screen mirrored his work for the Motion
Picture Industry Council. *She's Working Her Way Through College* (1952)
was one of his last movies for Warner Bros.; it nicely symbolized, it should be
noted, the retreat that he and the studio had made from defending controversial ideas. The film was a remake of a more important picture, *The Male
Animal,* that Warner Bros. had produced a decade earlier. *The Male Animal,*
a comic love story that had appeared in 1942, starred Henry Fonda and
Olivia De Havilland, and was based on a Broadway play by James Thurber
and Elliott Nugent. Fonda played a mild-mannered professor who in the
picture's climactic scene risks his job and marriage to read from a letter
written by Bartolomeo Vanzetti, the anarchist, who along with Nicola Sacco,
had been electrocuted for allegedly murdering a paymaster in Massachusetts.
Afterward Fonda utters the line, "You can't suppress ideas because you don't
like them – not in this country – not yet. . . . We're holding the last fortress of
free thought, and if we surrender to prejudice and dictation, we're
cowards."[30]

In *She's Working Her Way Through College,* Reagan assumed Fonda's
role as the professor, and Virginia Mayo portrayed a burlesque dancer who
decides to go to college and become a writer. When an administrator learns
of her previous work, he demands expulsion. At issue is not liberty to express
unpopular ideas but rather the right of a woman with a dubious background
to take part in campus activities. In the scene that Fonda's professor had used
to defend academic freedom, Reagan's character defends entertainers and the
acting profession.

There have always been those who believe . . . that the people in show business are
different from the rest of us. In a way, I guess they are, which is probably why we pay
admission to see them. . . . We are asked to believe that her previous occupation is
sufficient reason to risk the establishment here and now of a precedent which may
lead tomorrow to the barring of students because they go to the wrong church, come
from the wrong side of the tracks, or were born in the wrong country. . . . I cannot
participate in this injustice.[31]

When *She's Working Her Way Through College* played in Oregon, Reagan traveled to Portland, where the American Newspaper Guild praised him for leading the fight against communism in Hollywood. In his talk to the journalists, he praised the highly paid stars with little or nothing to gain who fought infiltration. They had beaten the Communists, he said, "by making democracy work."[32]

By the late 1940s Hollywood found itself not only on the defensive but in decline, and members of the Motion Picture Industry Council had to face unpleasant realities. Uncertainty became the watchword. As one commentator remarked with understatement, earning a living in pictures was a "highly speculative business." Changes were altering the industry and threatening stability. Producers looked for ways to cut liabilities.[33]

Reagan knew a good deal about uncertainties, because as SAG president he had to confront some of them. Moreover, they touched him personally as his acting career stalled. They threatened his standing at Warner Bros.

Attendance declined markedly, until by 1953 it was about half what it had been at its peak in 1946. Television was a factor. The baby boom contributed, as families devoted leisure time and money to building homes and enjoying other forms of entertainment such as radio. Attacks on Hollywood by the House Committee on Un-American Activities, as well as by the Legion of Decency and the American Legion did little to help.[34]

The 1947 HUAC investigation took place just prior to the Supreme Court's ruling, in *U.S. v. Paramount Pictures* (1948), that studio control of production, distribution, and exhibition violated the Sherman Act. This forced Warner Bros., Paramount, and other studios to give up theater chains and forbade them from engaging in block booking. The decision ended the industry's traditional structure. The Court's opinion, written by Justice William O. Douglas, weakened studio control over film content as exercised through the Production Code.[35]

Hollywood leaders became disillusioned with the Truman administration. The president hardly endeared himself to Reagan and producers when he urged Congress in early 1950 to eliminate a variety of tax loopholes, one of which involved filmmaking. Executives and stars had escaped "as much as two-thirds of the tax they should pay" by forming temporary corporations, Truman charged.[36]

By this time Reagan had become unhappy with the tax structure and had personal reasons for withholding support from the administration. Although earning a six-figure income and accustomed to an affluent style of life, he was experiencing financial difficulties. "True, I'd been making handsome money ever since World War II, but that handsome money lost a lot of its beauty and substance going through the 91 per cent bracket of the income tax," he complained. "The tragic fact of life in this evil day of progressive taxation is that, once behind, it is well-nigh impossible to earn your way out." He took to speaking against taxes, a theme that would continue throughout his political career. He told the Kiwanis International in 1951 that although the Communists had been beaten, there were "other more insidious and less obvious inroads being made at our democratic institutions by way of the motion picture industry." No other industry had been picked for "such discriminatory taxes." If the government could levy against people in Hollywood this way it would surely aim next at "your pocketbook."[37]

Because of the economic climate, studios began dropping large numbers of contract players. Warner Bros. announced in early 1950 that it might cut personnel by half, a move that could have affected one thousand individuals. This news combined with stories about Paramount's retrenchment could hardly have been comforting to Reagan, the star of *That Hagen Girl*, who then was feuding with Jack Warner. Roy Obringer made clear that the studio would not be unhappy if Reagan tore up the remainder of his contract.[38]

Reagan reported to the Screen Actors Guild that he was aware of the precarious situation. Of the guild's seven thousand members, only slightly more than three hundred had the security of contracts. He later told Senator Hubert Humphrey that most of the remaining 6,700 players were freelance performers who worked only a few days at a time. The overwhelming majority, he explained, made less than $5,000 a year (more than a fourth earned less than $3,000) and faced a constant struggle.[39]

Performers had been hurt by the thirty-day clause of the Taft-Hartley Act that allowed a union-shop employer to hire a nonunion worker for a short period without the employee being required to apply for union membership. Reagan appealed to the Senate subcommittee on labor–management relations to exempt the movie industry. Between 1948 and 1951 this clause had denied more than twenty-five hundred jobs to Screen Actors Guild members because studios hired nonprofessionals for bit parts. Surely, Reagan said, the authors of Taft-Hartley had not intended to discriminate against professional performers.[40]

The dire economic circumstances in Hollywood, combined with the atmosphere created by the HUAC hearings, generated enormous pressure for conformity. The anthropologist Powdermaker was not far off the mark when she wrote about an environment of "crises and continuous anxiety" that produced a "kind of hysteria," a form of "economic . . . totalitarianism" that canceled freedom of choice. The high salaries paid to leading performers, she observed, made it virtually impossible for them "to do other than the bidding of the studio heads."[41]

It was not surprising, therefore, that many of the producers' opinions came to seem reasonable to Reagan, whose movie career was headed downward. He readily incorporated their views into his own thinking. In particular, his ideas moved closer to those of Johnston. In promoting Hollywood, he and the industry's president sometimes spoke together, as when they addressed media executives at a Connecticut symposium sponsored by the *Hartford Times* in 1952. Both appealed for support. The movie theater, Johnston said, was an "important economic and social core of the community," generating business and bringing patronage to the restaurants, shops, and gas stations that sprung up around it – businesses whose success was "importantly linked to the prosperity of the newspaper itself." The time had come for cooperation. "What's good for newspapers is good for motion pictures. What's good for motion pictures is good for newspapers. What's good for both of us is good for America," Johnston declared. The industry needed more balanced press coverage, Reagan argued. "It was time we started talking to and not about each other."[42]

Reagan thus began the long transition from Democrat to Republican. If he disappointed liberals, he made a favorable impression on Johnston, who quoted him when he talked about the Motion Picture Industry Council's "remarkable progress" in promoting industrial democracy. "When you get people talking to each other, not about each other," the actor had said, "you've scored."[43]

16

"TO CAPTURE THE MINDS OF MEN"

We are pretty proud of the fact that our Government says, that in the ideological struggle that is going on on the screens of the world, it is the American motion picture, not with its message picture, just showing our store windows in the street scenes with things that Americans can buy, our parking lots, our streets with automobiles, our shots of American working men driving these automobiles, that is holding back the flood of propaganda from the other side of the Iron Curtain.

Ronald Reagan, 1951

"Today the battle of the world is to capture the minds of men," Walter Wanger declared to a group of businessmen and political leaders in 1949. Reagan agreed and similarly saw the United States – and Hollywood – engaged in a "great ideological struggle" with communism. As he became vocally anticommunist, his speeches also turned toward celebrating America as part of a divine plan, "the last best hope of man on earth."[1]

The rationale for speaking about the nation in this way was multifaceted. The idea that God favored America traced back to the Puritans. It had roots in the Christian Church and the Midwestern culture of Reagan's youth. That he came to proclaim this conviction in the early 1950s also owed much to Hollywood, where American exceptionalism had been a strong theme in his movies. Moreover, in his work with the Screen Actors Guild and the Motion Picture Industry Council he confronted problems in international relations. Two things preoccupied him and other film executives. One was expansion of the market for American movies abroad at a time of increasing restrictions. The other, thrust upon Hollywood by the congressional hearings in 1947 – and given urgency by the fall of China in 1949 and the outbreak of hostilities in Korea the following year – involved what part the industry would take in the Cold War. Here, as was often the case in Hollywood (and in Reagan's career), patriotism and self-interest converged.

194

Reagan's involvement in international affairs had developed in an interesting way. As noted, in 1945 he had lent his voice to calls for world unity and control of atomic weapons. He had pulled back when his studio objected and as he learned more about the Hollywood Citizens Committee for the Arts, Sciences and Professions. He came to take many of his cues on global issues from such Industry Council members as Wanger, as well as from others such as the Warners, and especially from Eric Johnston. In choosing Johnston to replace Hays as head of the Motion Picture Association, movie executives and financial backers selected a man in touch with their aspirations. To study Johnston is to learn a good deal about Hollywood's part in the Cold War. Johnston's world view was remarkably similar to that later held by Reagan. Johnston defined an optimistic vision but not one for the unassertive or ambivalent.

Foreign audiences had accounted for more than a third of Hollywood's revenue before the war, and with Germany's defeat studio heads saw renewed possibilities. Shortly after the collapse of the Third Reich the War Department invited several producers, including Jack Warner, to tour Europe and the Mediterranean. They arrived in London in June 1945, visited areas devastated by enemy attacks, and then flew to Germany, over the "vast ruin that was once Cologne," along the Rhine, above the Ruhr, and on to Hamburg. There they saw "miles of gaunt smokestacks, acres of twisted steel and jagged factory walls, hundreds of collapsed bridges, thousands of burned and battered freight cars scattered in broken strings among the bomb-pitted marshalling yards, mountains of rubble and canyons of fire-gutted buildings." The group inspected the concentration camp at Dachau, then went on to Paris, then to the French Riviera. The tour ended with a five-day visit to Italy.[2]

The producers informed the War Department of their eagerness to assist postwar reconstruction. Hollywood had a twelve-year supply of feature pictures that had never been shown in Germany, where in the Allied zones of occupation were now more than fifteen hundred theaters. There were forty-five hundred theaters in Italy. Beyond these outlets was France, and Hollywood's most lucrative foreign market, Britain. The movies could bolster America's prestige in the liberated countries, the producers said, as well as "cleanse the minds, change the attitudes and ultimately win the cooperation of the German people." They could also prepare American servicemen as "front line fighters in the first phase of psychological warfare," making them "well armed intellectually for a war of ideas."[3]

Expectations for Europe seemed realistic for a time; Italy imported close to six hundred American films each year, and the State Department convinced France to drop its prewar quotas. But hopes faded. The military in occupied Germany opposed Hollywood's effort to control German filmmaking, and as 1946 drew to a close it had approved fewer than fifty American movies. As France and Italy sought to build their film industries, they reimposed quotas. Samuel Goldwyn told President Truman in 1947 that the foreign receipts lost could total one fifth of gross revenues from film production. "This means more than financial disaster, it means a definite deterioration in the quality of pictures which will represent the American way of life not only at home but abroad."[4]

The most serious loss was in Britain. To rebuild their movie industry and redress a balance of payments deficit, the British required American companies to pay customs officials 75 percent of a film's anticipated theater earnings in Great Britain. Then Britons boycotted American films. The government lifted the embargo in 1948 but insisted that Americans could take out of the country only $17 million in earnings each year. It required 40 percent of screen time for British films and demanded that United States companies making movies in Britain limit the American cast to a director and leading performers.[5]

Reagan experienced production in Britain firsthand during the making of *The Hasty Heart*. He had traveled to England – his first time abroad, the trip coming in late 1948 and lasting until early 1949. After he returned to the United States, he went with a small group to the White House to appeal for help in unfreezing revenue and loosening British quotas. President Truman found the interview "very pleasant." Reagan left believing the State Department would come to Hollywood's aid.[6]

When he and his delegation visited the White House, however, they had not had a clear plan. After returning to California, and together with Jack Dales and Kenneth Thomson, Reagan proposed to make recovery assistance to Britain contingent on the relaxation of quotas. The State Department would have authority to withhold relief to any nation that "unreasonably" impeded "free interchange of ideas" by restricting movies and other forms of communication. The three argued that films were ambassadors and that Hollywood contributed to the nation's well-being. "I need not stress to you the important part played in the spread of Americanism and all it stands for by our motion pictures," Dales wrote to the White House; but the Department of State did not defend the industry as vigorously as Reagan had hoped. Government officials argued that the plan would stir resentment because it would give Hollywood a special status.[7]

This attempt to associate movies with the national interest was not new in Hollywood. During the Great Depression, it will be remembered, Hays had defended movies as "animated catalogs," and Harry Warner had proclaimed that "our films fairly shriek 'Buy American.'" After the war, studio heads equated pictures with American civilization and international harmony. Goldwyn told Truman that movies were "our greatest ambassadors at large to the whole world." Jack Warner claimed they would bring "mutual understanding between peoples." His brother, Harry, maintained they could carry

Alfred Nobel's vision of " 'one world' to the far corners of the earth," and fulfill the nation's "destiny" to spread its spirit and ideals to places in which America was "only a distant fable."[8]

But Johnston most completely identified the film industry with economic growth and the national interest. The undertaking fitted with his previous work as a four-time president of the United States Chamber of Commerce.[9] He had advocated a "people's capitalism" dominated neither by government nor private interests. He talked about a "partnership capitalism" with other countries, which would make possible the "never-ending expansion" of "dynamic Capitalism" not only in the United States but worldwide. Americans did not want " 'outposts of empire' in the form of regiments in garrisons," he had insisted, but "outposts of industry which breathe the spirit of our free society." He assumed that most Americans shared his faith and considered himself a "medium" for a "whole community of men."[10]

Johnston believed cinema should promote this economic system worldwide. Economically, Hollywood thought "in terms of an expanding world market," he said. Movies could help American business fill the economic void in countries devastated by the war. He described movies as "global showcases for American techniques, products and merchandise." It was impossible, he said, to gauge how much American exports "profited through the demand for American merchandise initially observed by foreign moviegoers in American films." Culturally, film was the "greatest conveyor of ideas – the most revolutionary force in the world today." It knew no international boundaries.[11] "The American motion picture will carry the ideas of Canton, Ohio, to Canton, China," he was reported to have said, "the point of view of Paris, Maine, to Paris, France." When he replaced Hays in 1945 Johnston made the opening of the world to American films a top priority.[12]

It is worth delving a bit deeper into Johnston's ideas, because they illuminated the controversy that surrounded the Hollywood Ten, and also because they paralleled those that Reagan advocated. The Ten had worried about Johnston. Allegedly they had been warned about him before the Waldorf Statement by White House assistant David Niles, who told them through a friend that Johnston had been made industry president by financial interests that wished "to turn Hollywood into a blurb factory for the political era based on the bomb." Before World War II ended, so Herbert Biberman claimed, "big business had begun preparations to create an American world" and looked to Hollywood to promote a "tough-minded Americanism."[13]

Johnston was forty-nine when he succeeded Hays. He was a "trim, athletic figure with a narrow, youthful face, steely blue eyes and a flashing smile." He was given to "quick, chopping chirps of laughter" that to Dore Schary "seldom seemed genuine." When required he could be an eloquent speaker, but preferred talking to small groups. He wanted the studios to be aggressive. At Paramount in mid-1947 he reportedly revealed an agreement with President Truman and Secretary of State George Marshall for using movies as American emissaries. At RKO he argued that Soviet influence in underdeveloped countries could be countered if Hollywood depicted American life constructively. At Warner Bros. he said that scenes of American gluttony could provoke resentment abroad. To screenwriters he prescribed scenarios to make communism appear ludicrous as well as treasonous.[14]

Johnston opposed government handouts. Troubled by the Great Depression because it fed "ideologies of despair," he criticized the New Deal for defeatism, a "spirit of vendetta and class warfare," and for disdain of democracy. He accused it of harboring "collectivists, socialists, communists, super-planners who looked upon business as an enemy to be destroyed." He liked the rags-to-riches parable, considered it a necessary part of American folklore, and thought of his own career in Horatio Alger terms. He preferred optimism: "Americans have not yet become accustomed to looking upon poverty as an insuperable, or even serious, obstacle." During World War II, he wrote of a "fateful duel" between individualism and statism which was worldwide and took place not so much between nations as within them. He sounded much like a latter-day Reagan when he argued that the American political system rested on belief that governmental authority derived from consent of the governed and that "every power vested in the state is a privilege conferred, and those powers not explicitly given to officialdom belong to the people." He advocated "aggressive citizenship" to counter the welfare state. "Wherever the government is small, the people are big," he proclaimed.[15]

He had profound misgivings about the Soviet Union. Before becoming MPAA president, he had twice visited the USSR, once with the U.S. Marines, who landed in Siberia after World War I, and again for six weeks in 1944 at Stalin's invitation. He had met with Soviet leaders and toured factories, and was appalled by lack of worker incentives. "In economic ideology and practice my country is not only different from yours," he told his hosts. "It is *more* different from yours than is any other country in the world. You are the most state-minded and the most collective-minded people in existence. We are the most private-minded and the most individual-minded; and gentlemen, make no mistake: *we are determined to remain so* – and even to become more so." He left convinced that Stalin knew virtually nothing about America or its people; nor, he believed, could Americans rely on cooperation or friendship with the Soviets. "Communism, militant, messianic and conspiratorial, isn't standing still," he later warned. "It swashbuckles into power where it can; where it can't it sends missionaries of its atheistic gospel, plotting and contriving for power everywhere."[16]

Confident about American science, technology, and industry, he counseled boldness and strength. He recommended enlarging the United States military. "What is necessary – absolutely necessary – is power," he said in 1948. Americans had to be on guard constantly, he later told a commencement audience at the University of Oklahoma. "That is why we are caching a stockpile of arms so ample – and developing a defense production capacity so huge that an aggressor anywhere will count ten before he speaks – and then bite his tongue before he speaks at all." He adopted a position similar to that of Henry R. Luce, who spoke of an American Century. Convinced that the nation's interest lay in "exercising world leadership to the utmost," he argued that in a shrunken world the United States had "grown too big to stay out of other people's wars." Even if the Soviet Union ceased to exist, he said, Americans would have world leadership thrust upon them. Either America would "organize the world" or it would be "organized without us and against us."[17]

Nevertheless, Johnston found the American people at midcentury "truly ... besieged" – not by foreign armies, but by "frustration, materialism and cynicism." Americans stood at a critical juncture, and the path they chose to travel would "transcend" other decisions for many lifetimes. Civilization, he said, wavered "between a life of living death or a better life than it has ever known." He resolved "to wash the Red stain out of the industry's fabric" and hoped for a "long-lasting spiritual rebirth." To him, film was an instrument in this renaissance, and Hollywood stood on the "threshold of a decisive decade."[18]

★★★

Such arguments appealed to Reagan. A "Russian–American Bund set out to capture every field of communications," he said, and the motion picture industry was particularly critical. If the Communists and their sympathizers managed a "magnificent coup," they would have gained an enormous advantage. For him the issue assumed historic proportions. No less than a "weekly audience of about 500,000,000 souls" hung in the balance.[19]

How could cinema work to the United States' advantage? Johnston was certain that movies would be subversive to communist regimes, but subtlety was critical. The average person who attended movies abroad respected American films, he believed, because Hollywood had not tried to portray American democracy in utopian terms. "Our pictures avoid deliberate, tubthumping propaganda but they exude the spirit of democracy." People who lived in the communist-controlled countries were "quick to catch the idea." The most effective movies entertained, told a good story, enlightened. "It would be a grave blunder to use the screen deliberately as a weapon of political propaganda," he warned. The purpose behind such films was "always transparent," their message "universally resented," and "always self-defeating."[20]

Johnston related to Reagan an experience in Poland. He had been trying to get the Polish government to accept more American films. One of the pictures was produced by Warner Bros. during World War II, part of it filmed against the backdrop of a Lockheed parking lot. When the scene came on, the Polish minister took Johnston's arm.

"There, Mr. Johnston, there's what we don't like, that propaganda."

At first, he had no idea of what the minister was speaking. "What do you mean propaganda?" he asked.

"All those cars in the background," the minister answered. "Are you trying to make us poor Poles believe that the workers in a factory in America drive those automobiles to work?"

Try as he might, Johnston could not persuade the minister that most American workers owned cars.[21]

Members of the Motion Picture Industry Council developed the idea that movies offered messages independent of their story lines. Wanger believed that motion pictures could advance free enterprise and to this end made the movie *Tulsa* (1949), a film not only about the oil business but more broadly a celebration of private industry. The future depended upon American industry expanding and prospering worldwide, Wanger said to an audience that included the governor of Oklahoma and president of Skelly Oil Company. A campaign should sell the American dream in India, Africa, and Latin America. Movies could accomplish more than all the academicians, scientists, and theorists combined. "Even in our gangster pictures (which many highbrows criticize and say should not be sent abroad) when we show Mr. Bogart walking down Fifth Avenue with Miss Bacall, the audiences abroad are made aware of the beautiful buildings, the well-dressed people, the automobiles, the shops full of attractive merchandise and many other things which are far more convincing than the propaganda speeches heard from the leaders of their countries."[22]

He developed this theme at the University of Chicago in early 1950 when he gave a speech entitled "Donald Duck and World Diplomacy." Hollywood had created personalities that could lead any civic movement and arouse opinion anywhere, he maintained, and "we have done a great service in not only selling America but also American products." He told businessmen in Los Angeles that the standard of living in America was the "most powerful antidote to Communism." History was "full of the sound of wooden shoes going upstairs and the patter of silken slippers coming downstairs."[23]

Reagan liked this message. "We are pretty proud of the fact that our government says, that in the ideological struggle that is going on on the screens of the world," he told Kiwanis International, that American motion pictures by "just showing our store windows in the street scenes with things that Americans can buy, our parking lots, our streets with automobiles," held "back the flood of propaganda from the other side of the Iron Curtain."[24]

How to use film became a pressing concern during the Korean War. In early September 1950 a delegation of actors and producers assembled in the White House Rose Garden, where President Truman urged them to enlist in a "campaign of truth." The industry was working on a strategy to make pictures more effective propaganda through the Motion Picture Industry Council and the Council of Motion Picture Organizations (a large umbrella association that included the MPIC). Reagan participated in forming a plan with the Department of State to make cinema a "vital weapon" in the ideological war against communism.[25]

COMPO, organized in late 1949 and early 1950 and financed by voluntary contributions from theater owners and distributors, counted among its members the Motion Picture Association of America. Created to fight communism and to publicize Hollywood's civic contributions, COMPO tried to increase movie attendance. Frustrated by being on the defensive, its leaders "longed to take the offensive and assert the affirmative values." Fearful that the government would relegate the industry to a status inferior to radio and press, they wanted Hollywood to become a full-fledged partner with the government in defeating totalitarianism.[26]

Ned E. Depinet, then RKO and COMPO president, chaired the committee that drafted the plan. Most of the work fell to the Motion Picture Industry Council's planning committee, which included Reagan and Wanger. Eager to take part in the "war of ideas," they and the other committee members had a recommendation when COMPO's representatives met with President Truman in September.[27] The proposal went through several drafts. Reagan was interested in having the government use manpower more effectively than in World War II. Committee members agreed they were most qualified to coordinate activities and determine what specialists were appropriate for film-related war work. The committee wanted Washington to tell Hollywood of projects needed and then to leave everything to the industry.[28]

Reagan and the committee wanted to establish the importance of entertainment pictures, which, they believed, had an important role to play in any war and were in no sense "superfluous" or a "readily-dispensable luxury." Feature-length movies were the "lifeblood of morale," serving as "two-hour furloughs" for men in uniform. They attracted audiences that also saw newsreels and information shorts important to the government. They carried messages against communism, their ideas veiled in amusement. The MPIC took as its "bedrock principle" that the entertainment film "should be allowed to go its natural way." Blatant messages were ill-advised, as evidenced by communist pictures that failed because their propaganda was heavy-handed. Reagan rejected the notion that what they did was even remotely similar to the work of Soviet propagandists. "We scorn the nonsense about 'aggressive imperialism,'" the group declared.[29]

Members of the Council of Motion Picture Organizations liked the plan if for no other reason than cooperation with the government seemed to win over one of the industry's most troublesome pressure groups, the California American Legion. By the end of October all of COMPO's affiliated groups had approved, except the Motion Picture Association of America. Johnston, however, threatened a veto unless it stressed private industry, called for less government involvement in filmmaking, and urged a larger role for Hollywood in planning government pictures. Not until he met with the Motion Picture Industry Council in late November and the planning committee incorporated revisions did the MPAA give its blessing.[30]

The plan covered three phases. The first dealt with stopgap measures. The second presented a strategy for the "period short of war in which the nation must remain adequately mobilized," a time, the authors admitted, that could last indefinitely. Much attention went to this phase, in which the nation would engage in a vastly expanded "truth campaign." A newly created Office of Government Films would coordinate matters and deal with government and industrial leaders. Finally, the plan considered possibilities in case of full-scale war. In that event, the power of the coordinator-director would be increased. In addition, the Office of Government Films would have authority to judge whether a film's presentation was "sound," to requisition assistance, and to supervise "incentive films" for war workers.[31]

These efforts had mixed results. Skepticism about Hollywood remained. Edward W. Barrett, the assistant secretary of state in 1950, was involved with the Campaign of Truth. He wrote in 1953 that "American films have given millions overseas a badly distorted picture of American softness, gangsterism, inhumanity, and materialism." A few pictures had so poorly judged "foreign tastes that the Communists have actually acquired and distributed extra prints of them." Still, from Hollywood's plan the State Department gained support from the movie industry. The industry apparently benefited as well. Reagan and Arthur noted that the State Department soon was doing a series of constructive stories about the industry that would refute alleged communist propaganda about Hollywood movies and personalities.[32]

★★★

If one side of Reagan's advocacy was anticommunism, another during these years exalted America. He assembled stories and developed themes that he would use in speeches for decades. Patriotism, of course, had been a staple of Reagan's life beginning in Dixon; it continued into his movie career with a studio that frequently celebrated Americana. Patriotism played well in Hollywood during the early 1950s, when even the Motion Picture Industry Council stood accused of having been infiltrated.[33]

At Warner Bros., where rumors of payroll cuts circulated, the mood was not unlike that in the months before Pearl Harbor. Harry Warner wanted a more aggressive campaign to weed out subversives and to that end tried to organize motion picture executives in the autumn of 1950. He believed that Hollywood should not wait for the FBI to ask for information but should point out people who might be disloyal. He suggested to J. Edgar Hoover that the studio's films could be used to track down fugitive Communists.[34] A week before Truman's Rose Garden talk to Hollywood representatives,

Warner summoned two thousand stars, executives, and other workers to a stage in Burbank, where he made plain that he would retain no one who belonged "to any Communist, Fascist or other un-American organization." Be strong, he told employees, "don't allow these bullies to bully you. Get rid of them." He concluded by showing *Teddy, the Rough Rider*, the pre–World War II patriotic short that had been made to warn about subversion in America. (He sent copies of the film to the White House and to Hoover.) The Warners tightened studio security. No one could be employed, Jack Warner announced, until they obtained a clearance from the plant protection and personnel director, Blaney Matthews.[35]

Hollywood found other ways to press for conformity. The conservative Motion Picture Alliance for the Preservation of American Values and the Crusade for Freedom endorsed unqualified loyalty, their message militantly anticommunist. By the end of September 1950 every major studio echoed with speeches. Most of the meetings, held in connection with the Crusade for Freedom, took place in the open air, with replicas of the freedom bell providing the backdrop. Harry Warner, Mayer, Wanger, Freeman, and DeMille spoke at many meetings, as did the actor John Wayne, then president of the Motion Picture Alliance. Warner recommended helping people behind the Iron Curtain by giving them solid evidence of American friendship. Mayer urged meeting the "big lie with the big truth." Wanger headed the Crusade for Freedom in Los Angeles County. Reagan appeared at the rallies and embraced the anticommunist oratory. At one gathering he denied that Hollywood was a "welcome haven" for Communists.[36]

Reagan was especially effective when he advocated Americanism, a theme he emphasized in speeches around the country. He spoke extemporaneously in Dixon at a dinner for him and his mother in the summer of 1950. "I'll never forget the effect the proceedings left upon me," wrote a listener who attended the dinner. "I was lost in moments of sentimental reminiscing, found myself but seconds later in gales of hearty laughter."

The listener continued:

You loved the people he spoke about because he did; you saw the places he described because they meant so much to him; you understood his wonderful sense of humor because you also knew how his early environment influenced his later life and you appreciated it. All of it helped you to know Ron as he was outside a movie projection booth and it was wonderful! He made you feel like shouting from the roof-tops that you too were privileged to be an American – because RONALD REAGAN loved America and the people who have made it the melting pot it is today![37]

Reagan talked about "America the Beautiful" to a class of graduating women at William Woods College in Fulton, Missouri, in 1952. America was "less of a place than an idea," he said, an "idea that has been deep in the souls of man ever since man started his long trail from the swamps." It was "nothing but the inherent love of freedom in each one of us." It was, he said, "simply the idea, the basis of this country and of our religion, the idea of the dignity of man, the idea that deep within the heart of each one of us is something so God-like and precious that no individual or group has a right to impose his or its will upon the people, that no group can decide for the people what is good for the people so well as they can decide for themselves."

He continued:

I, in my own mind, have thought of America as a place in the divine scheme of things that was set aside as a promised land. . . . Any place in the world and any person from those places; any person with the courage, and the desire to tear up the roots, to strive for freedom, to attempt and dare to live in a strange and foreign place, to travel half across the world was welcome here. . . . I believe that God in shedding his grace on this country has always in this divine scheme of things kept an eye on our land and guided it as a promised land for these people.[38]

That Reagan was so identified with anticommunism and patriotism made him attractive to the United World Federalists. Started after World War II, the UWF supported a system "based on a democratic, federal type of world organization" that would offer protection against wars, which national governments could no longer provide. It called for a stronger United Nations to bring about universal disarmament, but it opposed any structure that failed to deter aggression or which destroyed or weakened the rights of Americans or any other peoples. It sought "not a world super-state," but rather "strictly limited world government." It had a diverse membership that included Alan Cranston, Norman Cousins, and Malcolm Forbes, but it never had effective leadership in Hollywood where in 1952 it counted fewer than three dozen members.[39]

Initially Reagan was unenthusiastic. California leaders in early 1952 considered him to emcee their state convention but declined to ask him because he had "been quite cool and non-cooperative" toward the organization on past occasions. However, UWF state president Luther M. Carr decided to approach him after a *Newsweek* story alarmed members. It had said that "loyalty investigators" were now asking prospective government employees if they had ever been members of the UWF. Inquiries to the departments of State and Justice, as well as to Hoover, failed to turn up an investigation. Most likely, UWF leaders believed, the accusations had come from the Veterans of Foreign Wars. Because Reagan was in good standing with the Veterans of Foreign Wars, he seemed an astute choice for the UWF's state advisory board. Carr said that the organization needed his "mature wisdom and judgment." Because he was held in such high regard, he could arouse Californians to support a stronger United Nations. Reagan agreed to serve, his name appearing on UWF stationery in 1953. Little suggests, though, that he was active in the association's affairs thereafter.[40]

By the time Reagan left Warner Bros. he had experience in speaking about international affairs and had become an accomplished propagandist; he emerged as a patriotic orator. His work brought him into contact not only with powerful people in Hollywood but with government leaders. He had been to the White House and worked on a plan for the State Department that considered cinema's relation to ideology. He had access to, benefited from, and presumably exercised influence over the Motion Picture Industry Council. He operated in a world defined by Johnston, Wanger, and the Warners.

He found many of Johnston's ideas especially attractive: defense of individualism and free enterprise, opposition to communism and statism, the Horatio Alger parable, enthusiasm for science and technology, and optimism and insistence on the positive. He liked the idea of film as a weapon against communism, as a campaign to spread the American way. Johnston seemed to have a strategy for countering critics, a prescription for helping Hollywood. Reagan still called himself a "liberal," but was attracted to the optimistic, anticommunist, expansive liberalism of Johnston, which offered a secular version of the American mission and fused democracy with free enterprise. He had, as well, moved away from the liberalism of Dore Schary and Melvyn Douglas, which emphasized tolerance for diversity.

17

LOYALTY

> . . . this mixed-up approach to the problem is inspired by the Reds them-
> selves. They have deliberately taken advantage of our constitutional
> freedom to plot the death of that constitution.
>
> Ronald Reagan, 1951

Reagan's role in the Screen Actors Guild and the Motion Picture Industry
Council required him to take a stand on freedom of expression during the
early 1950s. Defending the public's right to decide what would be shown in
theaters was, as will be seen, one part of his activity. Loyalty programs,
support for resumption of congressional hearings, and rehabilitating former
Communist Party members was another.

Reagan's attitude toward blacklisting hardened after the 1947 congressional hearings. He had been skeptical about the Thomas Committee's methods
and the Waldorf Statement. By 1950, however, he willingly participated in
preparing an oath for new film industry employees. He criticized "confused"
liberals who fronted for the far left or hesitated to "smoke out" Communists.
He desired to show "misguided actors and actresses the road back to America." Fighting communism required oaths, giving former party members the
opportunity to purge themselves, and a Motion Picture Industry Council
committee to help freelance artists defend their reputations. He stood ready
to help those who would recant. Any citizen who had been a party member
but who had "now changed his mind and is loyal to our country should be
willing to stand up and be counted, admit 'I was wrong' and give all the
information he has to the government agencies who are combatting the Red
plotters," Reagan said. When the House Committee on Un-American Activities resumed its investigation of Hollywood in 1951, Reagan was among
the committee's strongest supporters. He eventually concluded that blacklists were necessary. Many of their victims were "actually working members
of a conspiracy directed by Soviet Russia against the United States."[1]

The loyalty issue proved an extraordinarily difficult problem. Reagan had dealt with it in the Screen Actors Guild after passage of the Taft-Hartley Act in 1947; but that controversy was a mere harbinger of things to come. The "fireworks," as he explained, took place after the Thomas Committee investigations and during the Korean War. The latter heightened apprehension about Hollywood and pressure for a loyalty program. "If the agents of Moscow had conceived and executed a major stratagem to unsettle Hollywood," Thomas F. Brady observed in late 1950, "they could not possibly have produced such . . . dissension and mutual distrust among motion picture makers."[2]

Reagan championed a loyalty program because he detested blacklists and wanted to help those falsely accused, his supporters believed. (His second wife, Nancy Davis, was briefly suspected.) Correcting such errors became "almost a career," Jack Dales maintained. Critics, however, described him as the "industry's watch-dog" and claimed that his loyalty crusade was simply an opportunistic way to salvage a flagging career.[3]

The Korean War created pressure to conform. The right to dissent, to criticize, became secondary to the need to protect security, and more than a few anticommunist liberals became informers. Even the American Civil Liberties Union preferred to temper its "liberalism with Cold War 'realism.'"[4]

After the war began, accusations that Hollywood had not done enough to repudiate communism alarmed SAG leaders and studio executives during the summer and fall of 1950. The American Legion, Veterans of Foreign Wars, Catholic War Veterans, Wage Earners Committee, *Red Channels,* and the Tenney committee all compiled lists of alleged Communists, called for boycotts, or otherwise tried to apply pressure. "It was open season for self-appointed guardians of Americanism," Dore Schary recalled. How could persons clear themselves if accusers denied opportunity for refutation?[5]

The worries of the time were well founded. "When the legion began its rather short reign of troublemaking," Schary remembered, Freeman, Harry Warner, and DeMille "chose that time to revive the question of loyalty oaths." Freeman said he would sign a loyalty pledge presented by anyone. Harry Warner announced that while "he loved his brother Jack, he'd put a rope around his neck and drag him to the nearest police station if he learned he was a Communist. Jack got the only laugh of the evening," Schary recalled of one meeting, "when he said, 'Harry, that would be very uncomfortable.'" When Schary argued against an oath at a Motion Picture Industry Council meeting, DeMille took notes that he allegedly threatened to give to Senator Joseph McCarthy.[6]

Reagan had a double responsibility at this time, one in the Screen Actors Guild, the other in the MPIC, and saw the matter as an industrywide problem. He supported Freeman, Warner, and DeMille, and told the guild in

September 1950 that the Motion Picture Industry Council was working out a plan with the State Department. Although some guild members had reservations, he convinced the board of directors to give the council a chance to resolve the problem.[7]

He returned to the Screen Actors Guild the next month with a plan devised by the MPIC and the conservative Motion Picture Alliance for the Preservation of American Ideals. He recommended a voluntary pledge and emphasized that the Motion Picture Industry Council had decided against a mandatory program because Communists, by nature deceitful, would willingly take an oath. The design was not perfect, Reagan admitted, but might save innocent people already blacklisted.

The oath held the Soviet Union responsible for the Korean War, endorsed American and United Nations action, and rejected Stalinism:

In support of our soldiers as they take their oath upon induction, I affirm that I will bear true faith and allegiance to the United States of America and that I will serve the United States honestly and faithfully against all its enemies.

I hold Stalin and the Soviet Union responsible for the war in Korea. I support the resistance of the United States and the United Nations against this act of imperialist aggression.

History having proved that Stalinism is totalitarianism, I repudiate its teachings and program, as I do those of every other form of dictatorship.

Reagan suggested a passage in which the signer would volunteer to participate in such Americanism programs as those supported by the Crusade for Freedom. He gained the Screen Actors Guild's support for this idea.[8]

Not everyone in the industry was amenable to this pledge. The Screen Directors Guild divided over the issue. In the wake of such controversy, the Motion Picture Industry Council decided to scrap the oath and referred the matter to a committee that refined the program. Reagan presented a revised version to the Screen Actors Guild in mid-December. This time board members expressed more serious reservations, most feeling that the program set up the Motion Picture Industry Council as a tribunal and made members judges.[9]

By this time Reagan had formed ideas about communism and how to combat it. Communists hid behind the Bill of Rights, taking "advantage of our constitutional freedom to plot the death of that constitution," he believed. "They are trying to operate on a 'can't lose' basis. For example, if we get so frightened that we suspend our traditional democratic freedoms in order to fight them – they still have won. They have shown that the democracy won't work when the going gets tough."[10]

The fight belonged to the "forces of liberal democracy," and could be waged without forfeiting liberties, he argued. Democracy guaranteed the right to think, to advocate beliefs. The law enforcement system could handle treason without sacrificing freedom, he said; no new laws were required.[11]

"If we must fight, make the enemy be properly uniformed," he urged. He compared communism to Nazi totalitarianism, called Communists "fifth columnists," and described the American Communist Party as a "Russian-American bund" that supported Russian plans for world conquest. Call these subversives "pro-Russian and take away the screen," he urged. Exposing Communists made them impotent, he said, but he warned against red-baiting. "We play right into their hands when we go around calling everybody a Communist."[12]

Reagan believed that Communists were purveyors of a false faith that hid emotional and intellectual barrenness. He undoubtedly agreed with Morris Ernst, who called them "damaged souls." "Scratch a Hollywood Communist – especially the 'intellectual' – and you'll find a person afflicted with some kind of neurosis," he told a reporter in 1951. "These people might otherwise have gone in for some kind of phony religion to ease their personal pressures. For them, communism filled that need. It let them blame their failures on something besides their own inabilities."[13]

Reagan was quick to believe in conspiracy and inclined to think the Party duped or seduced people. One could never be certain Communists had been eradicated, he said. "We learned in our fight that the party will never allow its top men to get too far into the limelight." Even after society purged party members, Reagan believed, they left a small, clandestine group that waited for democracy to let down its guard. No institution was safe. Indeed, Reagan claimed that "several elected members of Congress" were "known Communists," and "even the most conservative newspapers" employed critics who praised the "creative efforts of their little 'red brothers' while panning the works of all non-Communists."[14]

The House Committee on Un-American Activities started new hearings about Hollywood in the spring of 1951 and temporarily overshadowed efforts to create an industrywide loyalty program. The Motion Picture Industry Council cooperated with the government. Convinced of a "clear and present danger," the council offered to back any legal agency that tried to expose and destroy the international communist conspiracy. It warned those subpoenaed not to stand on constitutional rights or refuse to recognize Congress's authority. As it later put the matter in a letter to a congressman, "This country is engaged in a war with Communism. 87,000 American casualties leave little room for witnesses to stand on the first and fifth amendments; and for those who do, we have no sympathy."[15]

The council did offer hope to persons who had consorted with communist organizations. If they would confess previous associations and prove conclusively they had truly repudiated such relations, it would help. Simply to renounce earlier deeds or affiliations was not enough, though. These people would be judged by subsequent actions.[16]

Reagan assumed a central role in carrying out this policy. For those such as actresses Gale Sondergaard and Anne Revere, who would not acknowledge associations and name names, choosing the Fifth Amendment instead, black-listing awaited. For those such as the actor Sterling Hayden and director Edward Dmytryk, who confessed their affiliations, recanted ties to the party, and named other members, rehabilitated careers lay ahead.

When the House Committee on Un-American Activities subpoenaed the actress Gale Sondergaard, she approached the Screen Actors Guild, realizing that an appearance before Congress could mean the end of her career. She considered herself a "deeply loyal American" but planned to take the Fifth Amendment and wanted the guild to defend her right to do so. She suspected producers could not be trusted, that they had given the House committee carte blanche in order to save their own skins. The industry's blacklist, she predicted, would "include any freedom-loving non-conformist or any member of a particular race or any member of a union – or anyone" for that matter. Why, she asked, should she have to think about "severing . . . the main artery of my life – my career as a performer" for holding views that had won her esteem during World War II? *Daily Variety* published her appeal to the guild.[17]

The actress had enjoyed a distinguished career. Between 1936 and 1947 she appeared in more than forty films including *The Life of Emile Zola* (1937), *Juarez* (1939), and *Road to Rio* (1947). She won an Academy Award for her work in *Anthony Adverse* (1936) and a nomination for *Anna and the King of Siam* (1946). She had a reputation as an outstanding character actress who played sinister women in such pictures as *The Letter* (1940) and *Sherlock Holmes and the Spider Woman* (1944). But after her husband, Herbert Biberman, appeared before the Thomas committee in 1947, and she defended him, things changed. She received only one more movie role. After she took the Fifth Amendment before HUAC in 1951 and testimony linked her to the Communist Party before and during World War II, she received no further offers.[18]

One senses her concern, as she told the Screen Actors Guild, for the welfare of her "countrymen and all humanity," but she was not at home in the world of politics. "When the competitive spirit had been parceled out among humans she had been off on a holiday," her husband said. "She wished to 'best' no one. . . . Making a speech, participating in argument, were anathema to her. She was happy when, as an artist, behind the veil of character, she could search for expression of human emotion and the juices of life could flow freely through her."[19]

Because she had gone public and because the hearings were approaching, the directors of the Screen Actors Guild met in special session to consider her appeal. John Dales read a letter that he helped draft in reply and the board discussed whether it should be mailed. Sondergaard found little comfort in this meeting, as Reagan recounted his experience with HICCASP and how, once he had discovered it was a front, he resigned. What she wanted, he said, was for SAG to take responsibility for her decisions and activities outside of the guild. He rejected her call for SAG to condemn HUAC, arguing that its investigation had not even begun. He endorsed Dales' letter.[20]

Daily Variety published the guild's reply to Sondergaard the same day that she went before HUAC and the same day the Motion Picture Industry Council endorsed the hearings. Dales' letter noted that she had called the hearings an "inquisition" – a typical description, Dales said, by the Communist Party to discredit HUAC and the nation's form of government. It was no time for "dialectic fencing," he said, but one of compelling danger for America. SAG would continue to oppose secret blacklisting, but if a performer by her own actions outside of guild activities had so offended the American public that she had made herself unpopular at the box office, the guild could not and would not try to persuade any employer to hire her.[21]

HUAC subpoenaed Anne Revere and scheduled her testimony for mid-April. She had long been at odds with the Screen Actors Guild's conservative wing. When Reagan discussed cliques sympathetic to the communist line with the FBI, Revere's name may have come up. In April 1947 he maintained that a group of radicals on the Board met before meetings to coordinate strategy. In court testimony years later he named her as a leader of the guild's left-wing faction during the strikes of 1945 and 1946. Others implicated her with the Communist Party. Larry Parks and Lee J. Cobb told HUAC she had been a party member during the early 1940s. Roy Brewer claimed she had been among those people on the guild's board who opposed Reagan's effort to eliminate Communists from the industry. Like Sondergaard, she was blacklisted.[22]

Revere was a thoughtful person, a woman of courage and integrity. She had resigned as SAG treasurer in 1947 rather than sign the noncommunist affidavit required by Taft-Hartley, and was the lone guild officer to do so. She had not been a member of the Communist Party in 1948, she claimed, nor was she a member when she appeared before the House committee in 1951. She feared her earlier associations in a "happier climate" would destroy her career. Undecided how to respond, she asked the guild's board for advice. She received little encouragement from listening to members discuss Sondergaard's appeal.[23]

Revere made up her mind. After listening to the hearings in Washington, she decided that what the committee wanted was names. "I would not hesitate to go to the FBI and repeat the names of any people who had indicated to me that they were disloyal, or would do harm to the country," she later said. Nevertheless, because she had "never known among these people a person disloyal in word or deed," she could not in conscience give names.[24]

Unwilling to inform, understanding that a recent Supreme Court ruling made her vulnerable to contempt charges and prison if she answered some committee questions but not others, she took the Fifth and First amendments. She made a brief statement charging the committee with sabotaging the American political system. The Communist Party was still not illegal, and she told the committee that she considered any questioning of one's political or religious beliefs to be a violation of rights guaranteed under the Constitution. If she answered such questions, she said, she would be "contributing to the overthrow of our form of government as I understand it. . . ."[25]

Revere had won an Academy Award in 1945 for best supporting actress in *National Velvet*. She had been nominated for Academy Awards for *The Song of Bernadette* (1943) and *Gentleman's Agreement* (1947), an exposé against anti-Semitism produced by Darryl F. Zanuck at Twentieth Century Fox. After she refused to testify, her agent told her she was "dead" as an actress. Actually, her career had started to decline after the Tenney Committee listed the Hollywood Independent Citizens Committee for the Arts, Sciences and Professions as a front. She had worked only eight weeks in 1949. After her name appeared in *Red Channels* in 1950 her agent discovered that Paramount and Warner Bros. considered her too controversial. Aware of her changed status in the industry, she resigned from the Screen Actors Guild's Board in late May 1951.[26]

Not everyone who appeared before HUAC found the experience harmful. Sterling Hayden was rehabilitated. A former marine, he had been decorated for parachuting behind enemy lines in Yugoslavia during World War II. After the war he joined the Communist Party, and during the Conference of Studio Unions strike he opposed Reagan and the Screen Actors Guild. In 1950 he engaged attorney Martin Gang and approached the FBI for assistance. Reagan and others presumably in the Motion Picture Industry Council had told Hayden to go to the bureau to rectify his mistake. When he testified before the House committee in 1951, he named individuals he believed were Communists. The actress Karen Morley had recruited him, he said. Joining the Party was the "stupidest, most ignorant thing I have ever done," he contended. He praised Reagan. Communism had not made headway in the Screen Actors Guild largely because of him. He was "very vocal and clear-thinking . . . a one-man battalion against this thing."[27]

How deep Hayden's commitment to the Party was, or how genuine his repentance, was open to speculation. "You know, I don't know why I got out of the Party any more than I know why I joined," he said. "I could say a lot of things about those people I knew in the Party – and you know something? It would all be good. I never heard anything that was subversive." At the time of his testimony, though, Republican Congressman Morgan M. Moulder called him an "intensely loyal American citizen" and this pronouncement, together with press reaction, convinced Twentieth Century Fox that the public was on Hayden's side. The studio welcomed him back to the set of *Skid Row*.[28]

Director Edward Dmytryk, who had served a prison sentence for contempt as one of the Hollywood Ten, was also commended for his "forthright, refreshing" testimony. He agreed that anyone who failed to answer the committee's questions was a Communist. Skeptics such as his one-time cellmate Albert Maltz believed Dmytryk's conversion occurred only "after the jail doors closed shut."[29]

The director needed help to convince conservatives his rehabilitation was not a scheme to regain employment, and in this regard the Motion Picture Industry Council proved helpful. "He was in deep," Reagan said. Dmytryk realized he had only one way to get off the blacklist: "I had to purge myself." Shortly after he left prison in 1950 he allegedly asked for a meeting with the "toughest anti-Communists in town." His attorney, Bartley Crum, approached the Motion Picture Industry Council, and Reagan called together as many "cynical anti-Communists" as he could. Soon Dmytryk began meeting with a "rehabilitation" committee from the MPIC that included Reagan, Brewer, Dales, and others. Reagan and Brewer took special interest in rehabilitation. When former party members came to Brewer's office, he often turned them over to the ex-Communist Howard Costigan, who demanded that the person go to the FBI. At the heart of rehabilitation lay public repentance. The ex-member would testify and usually name names. He or she would denounce the Communist Party at union meetings and make a statement – perhaps a magazine article – renouncing his position. Brewer managed to throw the influence of the Motion Picture Alliance behind this program.[30]

If the confession and rehabilitation satisfied the Motion Picture Industry Council, an employer could be certain that most conservatives would not oppose rehiring. Dmytryk followed this route. He knew many people on the council. "All were interested in putting the whole business behind them," he recalled, "but it had to be done *their* way." They had several requisites, "some merely suggested as desirable, some absolute." The principal "absolute" was a second appearance before the House Committee on Un-American Activities.[31] After this testimony the *Saturday Evening Post* published a sympathetic article about Dmytryk. When Maltz attempted to discredit his story with a full-page advertisement in the *Hollywood Reporter,* the Motion Picture Industry Council took out an ad signed by Reagan, Brewer, Dales, and others; it was a full-page letter entitled "You Can Be Free Men Again!" Reagan and the others said they had questioned Dmytryk in great detail to find out if he wanted "to escape the Communist trap," to break free of its "unholy conspiracy," or if he only wanted his job back. "In meeting after meeting with Dmytryk, we watched . . . as, with his intellectual blinders removed, he slowly realized with growing anger the truth and the enormity of the Communist conspiracy against our land."[32]

After testifying before the House committee, Dmytryk said he felt "free of guilt"; Reagan also noticed that the director seemed to feel much better. Shortly after the *Saturday Evening Post* piece, he received a contract to direct a King Brothers movie, *Mutiny.* The following year he signed a four-year contract with Columbia. Thereafter he found steady employment.[33]

Producers wanted assurances about whom they hired, and Reagan and other members of the Motion Picture Industry Council believed a voluntary program that used the Council's Patriotic Services Committee as a screening depot would solve the problem; but this plan encountered difficulties. It required unanimous support before it could become council policy, and the Screen Writers Guild objected.

The plan was to appease conservative groups pressing Hollywood, the most feared of which was the American Legion. In the aftermath of World War II and during the Korean War, the legion was a force to be reckoned with. *American Legion Magazine* ran an article in late 1951 titled, "Did the Movies Really Clean House?" No more than three hundred card-carrying Communists were in the film industry, the author said, but if one added the "longer list of Hollywood 'big names' who have collaborated with communist party organizations and enterprises without ever formally joining the party, we have a story of communist penetration . . . which is truly shocking." The article named sympathizers and listed movies worked on by "recently-exposed communists and collaborators."[34]

The attack upset MPIC members. Art Arthur, eager to pacify such critics, drafted a refutation over Brewer's signature, to go in *American Legion Magazine.* The Writers Guild vetoed the idea because many of its members thought it was a mistake to publish under the Motion Picture Industry Council name. The writers had a suit pending against the Motion Picture Association of America challenging the Waldorf Statement and feared that an endorsement of the Arthur-Brewer article would compromise their case.[35]

But more than legal technicalities troubled the writers. They were wary of any loyalty program originating with the MPIC because of the power likely to be given the producers. They assumed that Eric Johnston and the studio heads were too willing to accept lists from the American Legion and to make other compromises for the sake of conformity. They discussed whether the Screen Writers Guild should retain council membership in early 1952. Some believed the council kept a blacklist that it gave to executives. Others argued that the Writers Guild should remain in the MPIC if for no other reason than to keep its veto over council actions.[36]

Reagan and most MPIC members did not share these misgivings. They worried about criticism that the industry was not doing enough to stop communism. Coming after the American Legion's attack was a HUAC report released in early 1952 concluding that Hollywood continued as one of the major sources of money for the American Communist Party and that the real extent of communist influence in the industry was astounding. Reagan mounted a campaign to repair the damage. He moved that the council coop-

erate with COMPO to produce newsreels to refute HUAC. Nationwide the
MPIC encouraged exhibitors to approach local editors for favorable edi-
torials. The council supplied rebuttals to Washington sources, and even some
HUAC members agreed the committee's conclusions were unfair.[37]

The American Legion persisted, telling members to use the HUAC report
in attacks on Hollywood. Reagan and MPIC officials discussed how to respond to these tactics in April. Freeman pointed out that a recent meeting
had taken place between American Legion heads and representatives from
the Motion Picture Alliance, and that he believed the industry could work
with the legion in an amicable way. Determined to end vigilante assaults,
boycotts, and picket lines, council members wanted anyone under suspicion
"to affirm their one hundred percent Americanism and their hatred of Communism." They favored a committee that would, upon request, screen job
applicants for possible communist affiliations or other activities that might
bring Hollywood into ill repute. Reagan endorsed these ideas, believed the
MPIC had never been more needed, and urged industry unity.[38]

In May, Reagan, Freeman, and Brewer (who, incidentally, had been pushing Reagan for the COMPO presidency) reviewed the recommendations that
had been made by the Patriotic Service Committee the previous December.
Freeman wanted to increase council control over releasing statements prepared by people under suspicion, as he and Brewer believed the legion "really
honest and sincere" in wanting to help. Reagan felt the problem could be
attacked by a stronger public relations effort highlighting the industry's
anticommunist record.[39] In June, Reagan moved to make the Patriotic Services Committee a permanent clearing house for prospective employees. His
plan was for freelance talent wanting jobs and wishing to know what was
"being said about them," to get in touch with their guild, which would
obtain any lists that existed from the Motion Picture Industry Council. The
council would keep on file information, reliable or otherwise, about the person, including material from the American Legion. The would-be employee
could write the council, which would use the letter to correct mistakes. The
plan was voluntary and the MPIC, Reagan explained, would not pass judgment on any claims of innocence. Art Arthur, who like Reagan was mindful
of the importance of public relations, insisted this agency should "NOT" be
called a "Loyalty Board" but rather a "Services Committee."[40]

When Reagan presented the plan to the Screen Actors Guild in June, he
emphasized pressure by local American Legion posts that compiled their
own lists of suspicious people and mailed them to legion headquarters.
Legion leaders wanted studios to give information on who should be boycotted. Reagan argued that his plan, while not perfect, would placate the legion
and be more helpful than harmful.[41]

Freeman now demonstrated how far MPIC members would go to appease
the legion. He acknowledged that it exercised power over Paramount decisions, that letters by studio employees written in self-defense were passed to

the national commander of the legion and to the editor of *American Legion Magazine*. Asked if an explanatory letter would ensure employment if the legion continued to apply pressure, his answer was a terse "no."[42]

When Screen Writers Guild president Mary McCall heard Freeman make this admission and listened to Reagan talk about a Services Committee, she was troubled. A strong-minded liberal, she disliked basing membership in the Writers Guild on politics. She objected to expelling or disciplining members on the basis of their beliefs. Not an ideologue, nor one to shrink from controversy, she had been willing to oppose both SWG's left wing and such anticommunists as Howard Hughes. Most MPIC members considered her an obstructionist. With the exception of the SWG, virtually all the council's constituent groups supported a loyalty program, with Reagan and the Screen Actors Guild among its most enthusiastic backers.[43]

In many respects, the stand McCall took within the Motion Picture Industry Council during the spring and summer of 1952 was reminiscent of the position Reagan had assumed at the meeting of studio executives in early December 1947. How did one determine who was a Communist, she asked? To accept a person's refusal to answer questions as proof of guilt turned justice upside down. An innocent person should be able to plead the Fifth Amendment on principle and not be condemned for doing so. She urged the Writers Guild not to contribute to "increasing contempt for due process." If a clearing procedure had only a 1 percent error, by "what moral right has the [Writers] Guild to pillory the innocent even in so small a percent?" The guild could gain a "clear conscience" by not setting up a court.[44]

McCall was confused by the answers that Reagan and his supporters gave. How could one find out if one's name was on a list? How could one find out where the list originated? She believed Reagan's plan flawed, doubted the MPIC intended to forgo judging letters, and reminded Reagan at an MPIC executive committee meeting that he had once said that if someone's statement seemed unconvincing, he would not hesitate to say, "This does not establish innocence." Brewer particularly alarmed her because he seemed willing to go beyond the vigilance even of the American Legion in his desire to unmask "traitors."[45]

She worried about people not Communists who nevertheless "felt no need to apologize for their lives." Such persons, Reagan reportedly told the writers, would be "on their own." As Arthur remarked, if the accused chose to treat attacks as "beneath contempt," that was their prerogative, but they could hardly claim later that the industry should have defended them more vigorously.[46]

McCall believed the plan bad union policy. It amounted to having employees tell employers about what organizations they had joined, in effect apologizing for their affiliations. Moreover, because each American Legion post was independent, if members of a post or any other pressure group decided to slander the innocent or to picket the MPIC could not offer protection. She called on executives to be more courageous.[47]

The Screen Writers Guild invited Reagan to defend the MPIC plan, and in late June board members received written arguments for and against the proposal, with Rivkin taking the affirmative, McCall the negative. Reagan and Rivkin failed to make a case, and SWG's membership later vetoed the Services Committee. McCall later delivered the results to a disappointed Reagan, who wanted to know if she had a better plan and accused the writers of "confused thinking." "There seems to be a new breed around town, the anti-anti-Communists," the *Daily Worker* reported him saying. "These are the non-Communists who denounce anyone out to get the Communists. Lots of people in our community don't realize their thinking is dictated, in that it was implanted by the Communists a few years ago. Their minds need reconditioning. . . . If the guilty themselves stand exposed, that's just too bad. . . . A committee such as was proposed would have brought the records up to date."[48]

Reagan and the Motion Picture Industry Council continued to make efforts to win over veterans groups. When the Veterans of Foreign Wars appeared on the verge of passing a resolution condemning Hollywood in August 1952, the council arranged for Reagan to speak to their national encampment at Los Angeles. Convinced that the VFW lacked the facts, he persuaded the organization to adopt a resolution praising the industry for anticommunist activities. For Reagan, this episode exemplified perfectly what the MPIC had been established to do. It had prevented "something that might have taken two years to undo – and then won credit, not criticism for the industry."[49]

Reagan's family was not unscathed by the accusations that circulated during this period. When Columbia Pictures considered Nancy Davis for a film in late 1952, the studio engaged an investigating firm in New York that confused Reagan's wife with another actress, Nancy Lee Davis, who earlier had signed an amicus curiae brief in behalf of the Hollywood Ten. Reagan's wife protested the agency's "slovenly and inaccurate report," and after her husband and Dales got in touch with Columbia, vice president B. B. Kahane apologized. "Of course, we could have taken it for granted that the wife of Ronald Reagan could not possibly be of questionable loyalty," he said.[50]

In looking back on this era, which had seen so much accusation leading people of goodwill into such personal hardship, Reagan felt proud of what had been accomplished. Hollywood, he thought, could be a model for other industries. He told SAG members that their guild had done more than any union in the country to rid itself of Communists, and had done so without allowing them access to the press. He remained critical of producers who hired people thought to have communist sympathies and lamented public apathy about the industry's work. The guild's rank and file endorsed his endeavors and in 1953 adopted a bylaw that barred Communists from membership and required new members to pledge they had never been party members or part of any group that sought to overthrow the government.[51]

Some individuals who participated in the loyalty program had second thoughts, however. Schary regretted his part. Screenwriter Leonard Spigelgass confessed, "It was the most wrongheaded thing I did in my whole life. We did it because we thought we could help people who were accused of being Communists." Dales also had reservations. "What I have debated about since," he said in 1979, "is that so many people were tarred by that brush who I don't think should have been now. . . . Even at the time, I'm saying my doubts came to the fore. I was not Ronnie Reagan or Roy Brewer. . . . I would argue about how far we were going, particularly when it got to be this clearing depot, you know, for work." People who had differed from the majority in SAG and the MPIC had been treated unjustly, he said. They had not been Communists but simply "strong liberal people who took their lumps." Someone should have prevented the producers from pushing matters to "ridiculous extremes," Dales conceded. "A line should have been called."[52]

18

A TROUBLED TIME: MOVIES AND DIVORCE

Far from being a hotbed of radicalism and immorality, the motion picture industry is truly American in its love for individualism and family unity.

Summary of Reagan speech, *Kiwanis Magazine,* 1951

During the late 1940s Reagan encountered two major difficulties in his life – a life that had known few setbacks since he left Dixon and rose from small-town anonymity to movie stardom. To top it all he had married one of the most glamorous actresses in Hollywood and seemed to have – if gossip columnists and fan magazines were to be believed – an ideal marriage. But all this turned downward when after World War II Warner Bros. placed him in a series of undistinguished films. *Stallion Road* (1947), *The Voice of the Turtle* (1947), *That Hagen Girl* (1947), *Night Unto Night* (1949), and *John Loves Mary* (1949) brought neither critical acclaim nor box office success. Reagan considered them "unfortunate"; indeed, his instinct had told him to avoid them.[1]

The second misfortune involved his marriage to Jane Wyman. What lay behind the divorce, which left him "shattered and ashamed," is necessarily open to conjecture as neither of the principals has given a full explanation. The unsteadiness in Reagan's screen career may have contributed to the breakup. As his marquee value wavered, that of his wife soared, complicating an already strained relationship.[2]

Reagan's private life thus became as problem-plagued as the lives of the characters that populated his postwar movies. The tone of Reagan's late 1940s films was different from those earlier pictures that had promoted Americanism and national defense. The postwar movies resembled *Kings Row* in their attitude about sex and family, and in their emphasis on psychological and philosophic problems. Here one returns full circle to the values of Judeo-Christianity. The Production Code had attempted to hold the line on such matters but it had few supporters in the studios. Changes were taking

219

place in American society and in Hollywood that weakened the Production Code Administration and liberalized the content of motion pictures. Reagan's movies reflected these changes, and the creators of his films sometimes hoped to hasten the demise of values they considered obsolete.

If Reagan was uncomfortable with his movies and demoralized by his family situation, he seemed untroubled by developments involving the code. He applauded the trend toward greater freedom and advocated letting the public decide what it would see.

★★★

When Reagan returned to Warner Bros. after World War II he discovered that moviemakers were themselves not sure what kind of films they should produce. "Cocktail parties were given over to guessing what kinds of pictures people wanted," he recalled. Uncertainty turned toward panic when movie attendance started to decline.[3]

Many people in Hollywood believed that the Production Code stood in the way of finding an entertainment formula that would fill movie theaters. For years Hollywood had been chafing under the code. Those who had written it preferred pictures consistent with the morality of Judeo-Christianity. They believed in the family, considered sex outside of marriage "impure love . . . banned by divine law," and objected to nudity because of its "immoral" effect on the immature. Most producers had been unenthusiastic about binding movies to this standard of morality. They wanted audiences to act as final arbiters of what could be shown. While studio executives saw the issue in terms of dollars and cents, many writers simply believed the code's morality antiquated. For them the code was "a Victorian hemline, defining an erogenous zone." To get material past Joseph Breen and the PCA, they sought – as a character in Reagan's movie *Louisa* (Universal, 1950) put it – to be "just modern enough to be interesting and not so modern as it scares 'em."[4]

To be sure, the code had been under siege from its inception, but during and after World War II many factors helped weaken its enforcement. Audience tastes were changing, and in this regard the war was surely a catalyst, helping make the narrowness of the past unacceptable. The war was a time of hardship and danger for millions of Americans but it had also allowed many of them to travel widely for the first time. GI's went all over the world, not only to Europe, as had been the case in World War I, but to the Far East. Wartime industry compelled workers to move about the country as it brought women into the workplace. While it is difficult to gauge what effect these developments had on attitudes, they may have made Americans more permissive about sexual behavior. The divorce rate increased during the war and peaked in 1946. Marriages rose rapidly toward the end of the war, followed by the baby boom. Births out of wedlock increased. New approaches to child rearing (different, certainly, from those in Reagan's Dixon church), reflected in Benjamin Spock's immensely popular *Baby and Child*

Care (1946) and in the work of the behaviorial psychologist B. F. Skinner (his 1948 utopian novel, *Walden Two,* was a bestseller), sought to create a generation of guiltless, well-adjusted, happy adults. After the war women continued to work outside the home, despite advertising and popular literature that suggested they would be happiest as homemakers, and in so doing changed the dynamics of family life. Alfred Kinsey's widely discussed *Sexual Behavior in the Human Male* (1948) challenged the idea of a single moral standard. Efforts to promote birth control and planned parenthood increased as did marriage counseling and family therapy, the latter encouraged by the psychiatrist William C. Menninger.[5]

Further developments wore away the code's authority. Hays retired in 1945. The breakup of the large theater chains during the late 1940s made it more difficult to control what was shown. Prosperity made boycotts less intimidating. Changes occurred in the way the industry applied the code. Even Breen compromised as a series of notable films challenged the code. *Dr. Ehrlich's Magic Bullet* (Warner Bros., 1940), discussed venereal disease (syphilis). *The Outlaw* (Hughes, 1941) tested the limit on nudity. *The Postman Always Rings Twice* (MGM, 1946) mixed adultery and murder. *Detective Story* (Paramount, 1951) dealt with abortion, while *A Streetcar Named Desire* (Warner Bros., 1951) treated rape, homosexuality, nymphomania, and suicide. Such foreign imports as Vittorio De Sica's *The Bicycle Thief* (P.D.S./Mayer-Burstyn, 1949) and Roberto Rossellini's *The Miracle* (Italy, 1948; U.S., 1950) posed major difficulties. The latter, written by Federico Fellini, was a tale of seduction that paralleled the biblical account of Christ's birth and led to *Burstyn v. Wilson,* a 1952 case in which the Supreme Court gave films protection under the First Amendment. Perhaps realizing that he belonged to another era, Breen retired in 1954 and his successor, Geoffrey Shurlock, was more inclined to let public opinion determine movie content.[6]

Studios were eager to capitalize on new ways of doing things. Jack Warner sensed that audiences preferred "more mature" themes and would be tolerant of bedroom comedies, nudity, and films that explored the dark side of human nature. Other studio executives made similar calculations. Psychological dramas and films noir became popular. What was remarkable about the movies of this period, one film historian has written, was "how much they shifted the focus of screen drama from an outer to an inner world."[7]

Reagan, however, disagreed with Warner over what audiences wanted and over the kinds of films in which he should appear. Warner made him into a romantic lead, hoping that if he could not be Errol Flynn he might follow Cary Grant. The actor had no objection but doubted that theatergoers wanted "parlor, bedroom, and bath." The public, he thought, craved "adventure and excitement." He liked Western or outdoor pictures ("in which I can move"), preferably with a historical flavor ("with thought and lots of action"). He was a "cavalry–Indian buff" who believed that the post–Civil War years when "our blue-clad cavalry stayed on a wartime footing against the plains and desert Indians was a phase of Americana rivaling the Kipling era for color and romance." He beheld such stories as a ticket to success. "John Wayne, saber in hand, rode right into the number one box-office spot. Ray Milland took sword in hand; so did Gregory Peck. Everyone rode into the sunset behind fluttering cavalry guidons."[8]

Reagan also saw a connection between such stories and the values he had grown up with, a point he made on Louella Parsons's radio program in 1947. It was not Western films alone that he considered important. "They might even be athletic pictures, football or baseball or whatever, to show the principles America lives by; the pioneer spirit, the sportsmanship, the health and courage." Still, Westerns fascinated him. "I think the heritage of our country is based a great deal on those early days of violence here in the West," he told a Senate committee eight years later. His personal life had gravitated toward the outdoors. He purchased Baby, the black thoroughbred filly used in *Stallion Road,* and bought an eight-acre horse farm. Later he moved to a three-hundred-plus–acre ranch in the Malibu hills, where he could ride unencumbered.[9]

Not surprisingly, he had approached his first postwar film, *Stallion Road,* with enthusiasm. Production was not completed until March 1947, almost four years after he appeared in *This Is the Army.* The studio based the story on Stephen Longstreet's novel, and William Faulkner prepared an early version of the script. Humphrey Bogart was to star, and Reagan believed Bogart's popularity would carry the movie, taking pressure off his return to Hollywood. Production would be outdoors and allow him to work with a "whole herd of beautiful horses."[10]

Nevertheless, *Stallion Road* proved disappointing. A week before filming, Bogart backed out and was replaced by Zachary Scott. Reagan enjoyed Scott as well as costar Alexis Smith, but his free ride was gone and the studio filmed the story in black and white, thus failing to capture the beauty of the California landscape. Moreover, the film hardly endorsed the outdoor values he liked, even if Warners attempted to add an upbeat ending. His character, a veterinarian, contracted anthrax, and the only hope lay in injecting himself with an untested serum. Although he recovered (in the novel the veterinarian died), Scott's character set the tone for the conclusion. As Reagan lay between life and death, Scott, a writer, discussed life's meaning:

SCOTT: Why should he die? Give me one reasonable answer.
THE DOCTOR: Why should he live? Who decides?
SCOTT: I don't know.
THE DOCTOR: Sometimes I almost have the answer. . . . We aren't saying anything, are we? . . . Why are we saying nothing?
SCOTT: All my life I've been hearing people talk, even very wise people. In the end they all said nothing. Then one day you wake up and you know what talk is – saying nothing. You say it witty, or bitter, or hard, shout it, sing it and it's all nothing,

nothing. Then after awhile you don't mind because you label the nothing something very fancy – art, philosophy, literature – it's almost bearable.[11]

Reagan hoped for more outdoor pictures. He wanted to work with John Huston in *The Treasure of the Sierra Madre* (1948), but Warner insisted he make *The Voice of the Turtle*. When he brought Alan Le May's *Ghost Mountain* to the studio (about a Confederate cavalry detachment sent into California by General Robert E. Lee on a secret mission), he assumed that Warner would cast him in it. To his dismay, Flynn obtained the role. The studio eventually gave Reagan another outdoor film, *The Winning Team,* but of the forty-one pictures he made for Warner Bros., only one, *Santa Fe Trail,* was set in the Old West. He did, of course, achieve a reputation as a cowboy hero when he made Westerns, but they came later, for other studios and for television.[12]

Instead of other outdoor films, after *Stallion Road* there followed *Night Unto Night* at Warner Bros. Although completed in early 1947 (it was the second film Reagan made after the war), it was not released until 1949. Philip Wylie's novel by the same title formed the basis for Reagan's film. Wylie thought of himself as a moral philosopher. "For . . . all of my adult life," he wrote in 1942, "I have yearned far more to contribute to thought than to mere entertainment." The book, published in 1944, was part of a series he wrote to describe the "present chaos of our world" and "disclose a science of philosophy."[13]

Wylie was perhaps an odd duck. Raised on the teachings of the Presbyterian church, he moved to "pragmatic atheism" after delving into physics, chemistry, and biology. Psychology, especially his reading of Carl Gustav Jung, led him to a philosophy that rejected human divinity and began with the recognition "that man is an animal . . . governed by instinct." He believed neither science, religion, nor ideology sufficed: "The scientific method and the Christian church have failed to lift man out of savagery. . . . All religions and all patriotisms are mental epidemics."[14] He believed religious dogma debilitating and inappropriate in matters of sex, marriage, and family. The American "sex life, . . . the family, the home, and life in all pertinent institutions" was "very close to ruin." It seemed to him "inevitable that in about ten years marriage will be regarded as a 'trial' – with an even chance of failure." The problem, he said, lay with institutions that sought to regulate behavior: "The viruses have come mainly from the church and somewhat from patriotism." He excoriated taboos surrounding sex in the United States. "Vermin have better morals," he said. "The men and women and children of broken homes, the whores and homosexuals and murderers and drunkards and drug addicts, are the true church martyrs – human beings who paid out of ignorance the price which the churches exact to keep the reins of biology in their proud, merciless grasp."[15]

The movie *Night Unto Night* did not do well. Peverell Marley's black-and-white photography captured a dark, somber tone not unlike the films noir of the period. Reagan's character was a biochemist suffering from epilepsy and trying to discover the meaning of life. The Swedish actress Viveca Lindfors portrayed a war widow haunted by the ghost of her husband. During a hurricane, Reagan withdraws to his room, ready to commit suicide. "Death isn't the worst thing in a man's life. Only the last," he says. "It's not the end," Lindfors's character counters, continuing, "I don't know the reason for death and pain but I do know that life is its own reason and it isn't ours to end." Encouraged by her love, Reagan's character decides not to kill himself. This is admittedly a more optimistic ending than the novel's, in which the protagonist steps from a curb in front of a truck.[16]

Night Unto Night was an embarrassment in more than one way. Reagan had found Wylie's novel difficult to decipher. "It was an unusual story, as most of his are, and I'm not sure we got the most out of his book," Reagan said. The film marked Lindfors's Hollywood debut. She was unenthusiastic about working with Reagan, whom she did not consider a big enough star. Apparently, however, she found Hollywood to her liking. Married with two small children, she began an affair with the picture's director Don Siegel, whose smile suggested to some at the time that "he had a pleasant secret." When work on the film began, she later divulged, "I had not had sex with a man for several months. I was hot and hungry."[17]

Before the studio released *Night Unto Night*, Reagan appeared in two other unsuccessful films, *The Voice of the Turtle* and *That Hagen Girl*. The former, made from John Van Druten's popular but controversial stage play, concerned a soldier on leave who spent the night in an unmarried woman's apartment. The latter, based on Edith Roberts's novel, treated incest, condoned marriages of convenience, and compared "old morals and old ways" to a "decaying mansion." Reagan argued in vain with Jack Warner to release him from both pictures.[18]

These films simply did not get off the ground. *The Voice of the Turtle* seemed a good gamble because the play had been a hit in New York and was even chosen for a presidential performance in Washington. Warner had marked the film for Reagan while the actor was in the Army Air Force. On stage Van Druten's three-person comedy with its "uninhibited dialogue" was considered risqué. Audiences often made up of GI's had watched the heroine's (Margaret Sullavan) "artless worries about promiscuity" and sat in hushed silence as Elliott Nugent took her into his arms as the stage went dark. "It goes over the heads of lots of them," an usher was heard to comment about the soldiers' reactions. "They just can't believe their ears sometimes so they don't get it. They're used to movies."[19] Warner Bros. then made the story into an eight-person production, with Eleanor Parker playing Sullavan's role and Reagan assuming Nugent's lead. The movie's blandness and Reagan's performance disappointed critics. Where the play had been "pleasantly candid," *Time* said, the film was "coyly prurient" as Reagan and Parker spent "most of their time gracelessly, unbelievably" demonstrating how they would not to go to bed together. The film deprived the characters of "their chief motives, their honesty, and their essential innocence," relieving them of charm and reality. Reagan played his part "as if he were trying to tone down an off-color joke for a child of eight." Reagan and Parker exacted a "studied sexlessness," the *Motion Picture Herald* observed, which "could have exploded in mentionable other hands." Reagan's serviceman was "much less worldly" than Nugent's and exhibited an "offhand manner of reading lines, which makes you wonder occasionally if his mind is on the job."[20]

That Hagen Girl proved an even greater disappointment. At first Reagan refused the role but agreed after Warner led him to believe the studio would put him in an outdoor film if he found a story. In *That Hagen Girl* he played a lawyer and war hero. Shirley Temple, by this time a teenager, portrayed Mary Hagen. The one-time child star viewed the script as a "lip-smacking . . . opportunity," but her mother was unenthusiastic about her working with Reagan, whom she considered "long on quips" and "short on talent."[21]

That Hagen Girl admittedly encountered unusual problems. Dismayed that she was gaining weight, Temple undertook a daily program of pushups, squats, steam baths, and massages before learning she was pregnant. Reagan missed several weeks when he contracted pneumonia.[22]

Beyond that, however, the plot was weak in the extreme. The picture called for Temple, as Mary Hagen, to exhibit a range of moods. Set in a small town, the plot involves a rumor that Mary is the illegitimate daughter of Reagan's character, Tom Bates. Rory Calhoun plays a young man who has courted Mary, but it is Bates who falls in love and saves her from suicide. After rescuing Mary from a river, Bates professes his love, which restores her will to live. "From suicide to exaltation in the time it takes to dry off would be tricky," Temple admitted, but added that "played right, it had high dramatic potential."[23]

The story repelled Reagan. He argued with director Peter Godfrey that Calhoun's character should win Mary, and that Bates should fall in love with an older schoolteacher. "You know, people sort of frown on men marrying girls young enough to be their daughters," he told Godfrey, not realizing that Godfrey had married a younger woman. At a sneak preview Reagan watched himself tell Mary, "I love you," and cringed as the audience moaned en masse, "Oh, no!" The studio removed the line before release and the picture ended ambiguously with Reagan and Temple leaving town by train. The audience was left to speculate, Reagan explained, whether they were "married, just traveling together, or did I adopt her."[24]

Roberts's story, incidentally, did not endorse the code's view of marriage. As envisioned by the author, Bates did not believe in traditional matrimony. For him the "watchword" was not "till death do us part" but "while happiness holds us together." In the novel he had "no sense of permanency, but a very strong sense of transience, and he held expediency in the highest esteem."[25]

Reviewers confirmed Reagan's fears. *Time* said the movie that began as a "sociological case history" ended as a "soap opera." "After reels of behaving like Shirley's father, Reagan suddenly exhibits unpaternal passion, explains breathlessly that he isn't really her father, and marries her. Moviegoers with very strong stomachs may be able to view an appearance of rebated incest as a romantic situation." (Temple had better memories. "As movie kissers go, Reagan was good," she revealed.)[26]

All this was a prelude to the breakup of the marriage that Hollywood observers – if not the principals – had believed was one of the more idyllic matches of its time. Speculating on just what caused this tragedy runs the risk of guessing at an imponderable. What seems certain was that it caught Reagan unprepared. "The plain truth was that such a thing was so far from even being imagined by me that I had no resources to call upon."[27]

The divorce was surely the result of many pressures. One was that both he and Wyman were absorbed in their careers. Their daughter, Maureen, has speculated that during World War II their "family dynamic was irrevocably changed." Wyman's career moved ahead while Reagan brought home an officer's salary of less than $300 a month. In this "apparent role reversal," Wyman made "more than her share of family decisions, financial and otherwise."[28]

The experience was not uncommon during the war, when women assumed a larger place in the work force as men entered the military. Women also received conflicting messages. Reagan's own Army Air Force film unit had tried to convince women that they should go into defense work through its labor-incentive films. While men destroyed the enemy "viciously and ruthlessly with guns and bombs," women could join the Women's Army Corps or replace men in factories. *Missing in Action* told of a mother in Akron whose son died carrying out his mission "with utter disregard for his own life." She accepted his medal and then went to work in a factory, where she took over the equipment her son had operated. *Are You Jane Doe* urged women to continue in the Douglas aircraft factories in Los Angeles so men "over there" could come home sooner. *A Message to Mothers* promoted child care; children should be properly fed as they were taught fair play and courtesy. *Ladies Day* told women in ball bearing factories that they were not "helpless" and no longer needed to be shy because they could work in a factory and still hold "down a place in the home." American boys needed these women to "roll 'em to Victory! The greatest combination in the world" would be "pistol packin' papas and ball-bearing makin' mamas."[29]

At the same time that the government delivered these messages, more conservative community leaders such as Reagan's minister in the Hollywood–Beverly Christian Church openly condemned women who left home to work. Cleveland Kleihauer believed the family the cornerstone of civilization, essential to Christianity and democracy, and Reagan respected Kleihauer.[30] If the Reagans listened to him, they found little to suggest they had a formula for a successful marriage. No institution had "so miserably failed in recent times" as had the family, Kleihauer declared in 1942. He traced juvenile delinquency to selfish parents. He indicted American homes as "cesspools of moral lawlessness and utter godlessness" where "things – automobiles, furniture, clothes, success, good times" – took priority. Although the war and government had something to do with family deterioration, in Kleihauer's view women bore a major share of the blame. Mothers were the "key" to the family's moral purity, but they had abandoned the home to work. "Under the guise of patriotism," Kleihauer said, women had "gone into the war industries, some to swell the family income, some to carry on extra-marital flirtations, and some to escape domestic drudgeries, all of which adds up to the tragic fact that both the government and big business are allowing mothers to desert their nobler and more imperative responsibilities of maintaining a wholesome, sane, inspiring home life for their children." No war work could compare to the good women did "for humanity, for country, and for God in the home." Reagan apparently agreed. It was a "man's world," he said, and woman's charge was to marry and then "teach and heal and mother their sons."[31]

Jane Wyman hardly fitted Kleihauer's definition of the ideal mother. By Reagan's account she was a "wonderful wife" but "very intense" and took "her work too seriously." She immersed herself in roles, often staying in character after she returned home from the studio. "In fact," Maureen recalled, "she lived through every role to such an extent that it was hard to recognize her when she came home." Her characters in her movies "consisted of mostly one depressingly serious part after another," which meant subjecting the family to "wide personality swings for months at a time." She won acclaim for several roles, including an Academy Award in 1948 for portraying a deaf-mute in *Johnny Belinda*. From Reagan's point of view, she never "learned to separate her work from her personal life."[32]

One might guess the extent to which Reagan brought home his own problems as he became troubled with his films and ever more involved in the guild, where he spent several evenings a week. As his wife won praise for a series of roles, he must have been perplexed by the downward course of his career – a career which had risen in a straight line before the war. It would have been natural for him to convey these worries to his family.

Moreover, his wife did not share his enthusiasm for politics and found it "exasperating to awake in the middle of the night, prepare for work, and have someone at the breakfast table, newspaper in hand, expounding on the far right, the conservative right, the conservative middle, the middle of the road." Although Reagan wanted her to discuss issues and attend meetings, she found the exchanges "far above me," and felt her own views were never taken seriously.[33]

To these strains was added a devastating episode during the filming of *That Hagen Girl*. While recovering from pneumonia Reagan learned that his wife had suffered a miscarriage. An infant girl, three months premature, survived for a few hours in an incubator. Wyman went through the experience alone as her husband recuperated in a nearby hospital. He returned home and to the set of *That Hagen Girl* haggard and seventeen pounds lighter.[34]

For such reasons the marriage that Louella Parsons had predicted would last at least thirty years and called a "wholesome and happy and utterly completely American" family came apart. "Jane and Ronnie have always stood for so much that is right in Hollywood," she lamented. The couple separated in December 1947. The following February they entered into a written property settlement and attempted a reconciliation. They separated again in May, and Wyman filed for divorce. Columnists and fan magazines blamed her for being a "moody person, temperamental, ambitious, restless, and seeking."[35]

The children suffered. By their accounts, their father often had been an absent if loving parent. Before the separation Maureen and Michael had not seen much of their parents except on weekends, a nanny providing daily care. "Oh, we were well taken care of, don't misunderstand me," Maureen recalled, "but as an adult I now realize that there's a distinct difference between the care provided by a parent and the care provided by a paid caretaker. . . . It was simply one of the prices all of us had to pay for their success." Michael had similar memories. "Like so many children of busy parents we missed having a normal relationship with ours because we saw each of them only a couple of days a month. Speaking for myself, I never really found out who they were, and I don't think they ever really knew me." His dad, he felt, had been "too busy to be an attentive father."[36]

Wyman retained custody, with Reagan relegated to Saturday visits. Maureen and Michael shuttled between boarding schools and camps. "There is no easy way to break up a home," Reagan acknowledged, "and I don't think there is any way to ease the bewildered pain of children at such times." Maureen, then seven, cried as her father attempted to explain. "For some reason I seem to remember looking out the car window as he was struggling through his explanation," she remembered, "and gazing into the clear, black night, thinking I was looking into a dark, empty hole. . . . I felt completely, and desperately, alone. . . . I had no house to go home to; in a way I had no family to go home to; and I was left behind to get along in a place where I had no friends, no roots, nothing. I felt deserted by my parents." For Michael the divorce turned life into a "daily nightmare." As a first grader forced to live part of the week in a dormitory at Chadwick, he recalled crying himself to sleep at night "wishing I could be home with Mom." When he was eight a camp counselor took nude photographs and molested him, an episode he did not reveal to his parents until thirty-five years later.[37]

Nelle – "Gramsie," the children called her – "filled much of the void," Maureen acknowledged. The children often would stay at Nelle's house on Saturday nights, and she saw to it that they attended Sunday school at the Hollywood–Beverly Christian Church. She was a "constant" in their world, a "steadying influence."[38]

Reagan continued to make pictures for Warner Bros. In 1949 he starred in two comedies, *John Loves Mary* and *The Girl from Jones Beach*. Unenthusiastic about the former, he believed the returning serviceman theme had become stale. The story about John and Mary ran into problems with censors who felt it treated marriage frivolously and lacked a voice for morality. He was more enthusiastic about *The Girl from Jones Beach,* in which he played a commercial artist seeking a woman with an ideal figure. The movie, he said, eased his "social problems," and he delivered a good comic performance. But the Jones Beach film was little more than an exhibition of curvaceous young women and hardly a great acting success. Ill luck continued to afflict his life. He became injury prone, fracturing his coccyx when making *The Girl from Jones Beach*. A few months later he broke his right leg in a charity baseball game.[39]

He left for England in November 1948 to make *The Hasty Heart* (1950) with Patricia Neal and Richard Todd. It was one of his best films, in which he portrayed a strong but compassionate American soldier recuperating from malaria in a Burmese hospital. But again there was a problem. He was the second male lead, paired with the newcomer, Todd. The trip began with a rail journey through Canada, then continued with passage on the *Britannica*. He was away four months, a time that was meant to be therapeutic and to allow him to come to grips with his "lonely inner world." To friends he seemed dejected. He found London disagreeable – thick fog, cold drizzle, drab food, dreary exteriors, high taxes and frozen revenue. He visited with Jack Warner, Jr., recently married and in London representing his father. "He was in a depressed state," the younger Warner recalled. "We discussed his personal situation. He was like the elder statesman giving advice. He talked about having to work things out." Neal remembered him in tears at a New Year's Eve party. "It was sad," she said, "because he did not want a divorce."[40]

The excursion did have justifying moments. It was "a grand adventure to be savored, swallowed, and digested . . . like a gourmet feast," Reagan recalled. He had steaks flown in from "21" in New York. "I was delighted one evening," Neal recounted, "when he invited me to share his precious treasure, but when he asked for the steaks he was told that they had 'gone bad.' Ronnie was furious," she recalled. The experience of working with Neal may have helped his loneliness. Here perhaps gossip entered the scene, for when

Jane Wyman had acted in *Johnny Belinda,* rumor had circulated during filming that she was often in the company of her costar Lew Ayres. Reagan had "haunted the set" and later reportedly told Hedda Hopper that in regard to the divorce, "I think I'll name *Johnny Belinda* as the co-respondent." Now, in London, he was making a movie with an actress who recently had ended a much-publicized affair with the married Gary Cooper. Reagan and Neal often dined together in London.[41]

The late 1940s was a confusing period for many Americans and especially so for Reagan. As he rose to leadership in the Screen Actors Guild, his film career traveled a different trajectory. None of his postwar movies was well known and they essentially amounted to a string of disasters. The divorce added to his professional setbacks. By his own admission, he was at this time unusually innocent.[42]

As to the larger issue of Hollywood's movement away from the Production Code, Reagan showed neither understanding nor concern. Kleihauer had touched on the issue during the war by condemning writers who encouraged permissiveness and steeped life in a "sense of futility and frustration."[43] But if Reagan heard this message, he apparently never associated it with motion pictures. Whatever reservations he might have had about Hollywood's impact on Judeo-Christianity he kept to himself. Instead, he embraced the position of the studio executives who wanted the public to determine film content and he argued that actors, as a group, were no less moral than most other Americans. While on the set of *The Voice of the Turtle* Reagan said he was "particularly gratified" at the "trend to realism on the screen." A "happy medium" between realism and escapism best represented the "American way." He saw little wrong with increased nudity. The flap over Jane Russell's breasts in *The Outlaw* he found more humorous than harmful. In 1949 when he chaired the Motion Picture Industry Council, the MPIC instituted a Flagpole of the Month award, given cinema's most preposterous critic. The first recipient was Lady Astor, who had reviled Hollywood for flooding the world with "wretched pictures of naked women and girls." *Kiwanis Magazine* summarized his position in 1951: "Far from being a hotbed of radicalism and immorality, the motion picture industry is truly American in its love for individualism and family unity." He warned that a whole generation was being raised to accept someone else telling them what they could see in movie theaters. From there it was a short step to controlling what people read, said, or thought. After the *Burstyn* v. *Wilson* decision Reagan told a symposium of media leaders that as a father he agreed children should be protected from obscenity, but he was "more concerned with the destruction of freedom than with vulgarity." "In the final analysis," he later said to the Kefauver committee, "isn't the American citizen, with his money at the box office, the best judge of what he wants to see?"[44]

19

"A FORK IN THE RIVER"

For me, there was a fork in the river and it was right in the middle of my life. I never meant to go into politics, it wasn't my intention when I was young. . . . I ultimately went into politics because I wanted to protect something precious.

Ronald Reagan, 1989[1]

As Reagan's movie career and personal life fell into disarray during the late 1940s, his relationship with Warner Bros. similarly deteriorated. Having reached middle age he found it difficult to compete with younger stars as a matinee idol. Because his range as an actor was limited, he found little success with more sophisticated roles. "He was just a pleasant fellow," one observer wrote, "a bit on the colorless side, lacking fire or whatever you call that 'something' which really big stars have." Warner executives had come to doubt his box office appeal. Reagan himself believed the studio treated him unfairly; he felt typecast and almost betrayed. He was unhappy to be second lead in *The Hasty Heart* (1950). He thought Jack Warner had reneged on a promise to star him in Alan Le May's *Ghost Mountain*. He took further offense when no one from the studio bothered to visit him for several weeks after he broke his leg in a charity baseball game. The situation worsened in early 1950; in an interview he said that from then on he would pick his own pictures because he could do at least as good a job as the studio. "With the parts I've had, I could telephone in my lines, and it wouldn't make any difference."[2] "Here I am playing lawyers and dying to play in westerns," he said a few months later, adding, if Warner Bros. "ever got around to putting me in a western, they'd cast me as a lawyer from the east."[3]

A compromise settled matters temporarily: Lew Wasserman negotiated a deal with Warner Bros. whereby during the remainder of his contract Reagan would make only one picture a year instead of three. For that picture he would be paid half his yearly salary. He could freelance with other companies. Wasserman lined up a multipicture arrangement with Universal that would pay $75,000 per film. His first two movies for that studio were *Louisa* (1950) and *Bedtime for Bonzo* (1951). He made three pictures with Paramount. "You could hardly see my wounded ego under all those $75,000 plasters," he remembered. Meanwhile he ended his feud with Jack Warner. On the set of *She's Working Her Way Through College,* he called to make amends, Warner matched Reagan "regret for regret, apology for apology," and afterward, somewhere beneath the studio phone booth lay a "deeply buried hatchet."[4]

Despite this arrangement his movie career was largely behind him. He discovered that freelancing was not without pitfalls. When a couple of his early script choices turned out to be flops, the feeling he experienced during *That Hagen Girl* and many of his B films returned. He refused several stories, as well as offers to go to Broadway. He was wary of working in television, fearing it would lessen his chances to make movies. A low point came in early 1954 when he was reduced to emceeing a Las Vegas nightclub act.[5]

Reagan's stock as a movie actor waned, one senses, in part because he could no longer give acting his undivided attention. As his interest had turned to more serious matters, being just a Hollywood star was no longer enough. One perceptive commentator wrote in 1947 that he noticed a change in Reagan during World War II when, as an air corps officer, he would appear before propaganda films "wearing heavy, horn-rimmed glasses and with a wider chin than . . . before," to deliver an official briefing to the press. He had gained weight, "his shoulders broadened out and the boyish air gave way to a stronger, more manly presence." His real preoccupation, the writer speculated, lay in public service, perhaps politics.[6]

Although he would never completely shed the label of being "only an actor," Reagan's future did lie in politics.[7] He acquired important assets in Hollywood that helped him in this arena. For one thing, movie stardom brought fame and name recognition with it. Moreover, the image that Hollywood created for him was surely of importance for his career outside of films. The studio molded much of it to his personality, and if part of it did not square, it likely reflected characteristics he would have liked to possess. From the start, his movie career had been bound up in all-American virtues. By the early 1950s he had a public persona often equated with athleticism, military valor, government service, aviation, compassion for the disadvantaged, opposition to bigotry, and professional success. He was as "typically American as apple pie," one publication said. Put him in any town, wrote another, and he would be one of its "solid citizens." It may well be that Reagan's limitations as an actor actually helped him politically. The fact that he most often seemed to be playing himself rather than assuming another character's identity conceivably made his screen image seem all the more real to audiences.[8]

Of course he was also a Western star, which embodied its own set of American virtues (virility, honesty, and rugged self-reliance), but this image was not so much created by Warner Bros. films as by other studios in such pictures as *The Last Outpost* (Paramount, 1951), *Law and Order* (Universal, 1953), *Cattle Queen of Montana* (RKO, 1954), and *Tennessee's Partner* (RKO, 1955). Those films, along with the later General Electric Theater and Death Valley Days television programs, helped build the persona Reagan wanted to project at Warner Bros. The effort to construct the "new Ronald Reagan" began with *The Last Outpost,* in which he played a Confederate cavalry officer. For *Law and Order,* Paramount billed him as the "last of the great shooting marshals! He lived by the gun . . . killed by the law . . . and loved a woman even his bullets couldn't tame."[9]

His virile screen image helped overcome what could have been a political liability – that he spent World War II in California. His military service was unique among presidents, and it is curious that it has not attracted more attention. His time in the Army Air Force was well publicized, although maneuvering went into arranging a date for him to report. Even then, he hardly left home. His work – publicity, making training films – was only slightly removed from what he had been doing before the war. His contacts in Hollywood continued. He associated with his studio chief, Warner. After the war he was viciously attacked in an anonymous letter, published in the *Hollywood Reporter,* as a "cutting room commando" who had "fought the war from the polished nightclub floors of Hollywood."[10]

It is interesting to consider what effect World War II might have had on his later life. He experienced the war vicariously. A large quantity of raw film, uncensored scenes of battle and of Nazi death camps, passed through his unit. "We saw the shots that were edited out before the film could be viewed by the public," he recalled. "A fighter plane cracked up on landing, in flames, the pilot vainly trying to get out of the cockpit and dying before your eyes. His comrades rushing into the flames, vainly trying to save him, until they were pulled back with their own clothing on fire." Frontline footage gave him an "almost reverent feeling for men who did face the enemy." Veneration would be part of his postwar career.[11]

The deference that Reagan paid to servicemen partially explains why remaining stateside did not have a more detrimental effect on his political career. That his screen persona remained associated with military valor throughout the war and afterward was also significant. Then, too, Hollywood stars were quick to come to his defense.[12] Poor eyesight provided a plausible reason for restricted duty and Reagan recounted the story of his vision in amusing fashion in his autobiography, never mentioning his deferments.

During his years in radio and film Reagan discovered a great deal about using the media. These lessons he carried into television, and they proved of inestimable benefit to his political career. He mastered performing before microphones, cameras, and audiences, as well as how to dramatize events. He gained training in propaganda and public relations. His experience in this regard had begun innocently as a performer in pre–World War II films designed by the studio to promote patriotism and preparedness. During the war he was base public relations officer for a unit eventually located at Hal Roach Studios. He appeared in or narrated training films and *This Is the Army*. After the war his endeavors with the Motion Picture Industry Council, many of which were hidden from public view, amounted to selling Hollywood. During the Korean War he was introduced to the techniques and tactics of making films into ideological weapons against communism. He not only learned timing and delivery; he learned how to create and control publicity behind the scenes.

Reagan demonstrated exceptional ability as a forceful, sought-after speaker. Over the years he emceed dozens, perhaps hundreds, of benefits, and gave speeches on behalf of the Screen Actors Guild and the Motion Picture Industry Council. In private, one-to-one sessions, he was not necessarily impressive; Bill McGoogan, Jr., observed, when interviewing Reagan on a St. Louis–bound train in 1951, that he "didn't give the impression of a dynamic leader." Nevertheless, when addressing an audience, Reagan was an "excellent speaker," as a columnist for the *Hartford Times* wrote in 1952. "If the motion picture industry wants an ambassador of good will, and it seems to need many, it would do well to enlist his service." These sentiments were echoed a few days later in the *Dallas Morning News,* which described him as a "dynamic" orator.[13]

Much of Reagan's speechmaking initially defended the movie industry and entertainers. Actors had long been on the margins of respectability in American society. At Warner Bros., moviemaking was entwined with political and social life, but the studio, and more generally Hollywood, were never completely above suspicion by either the public or the government. Few opinion makers, though, doubted the screen's power to transform opinion, and in the struggles to control the content of motion pictures, industry leaders mounted a largely successful campaign to convince people that the movies were a force for patriotism and anticommunism. Reagan came to the fore of this effort. Through the Screen Actors Guild and the Motion Picture Industry Council he did much to make Hollywood respectable. If actors did not enjoy the status he believed they deserved in 1952, they at least stood on the threshold of an era when they would achieve new levels of prestige and influence, and when entertainment and politics would be united as never before.

In at least one other way Reagan's later career benefited from Hollywood. He gained executive experience and political friends. Leadership in the Screen Actors Guild and the Motion Picture Industry Council impressed observers. "It was at the MPIC that many of us realized for the first time the great promise in your leadership talents," Art Arthur told him. During the Hollywood strikes he demonstrated he had the courage to take a controversial stand and defend it. After the House Committee on Un-American Activities hearings he showed himself remarkably adaptable in a treacherous political terrain. He made enemies, but he also made allies, especially among the wealthy, powerful, and conservative. Jack Dales, who worked with him in the guild, saw a decisive, popular leader, "not a deep intellectual, but a very honest man," who was surprisingly "pragmatic." Some saw potential for public office. Art Arthur, Dore Schary, Allen Rivkin, and Roy Brewer urged him to run for the United States Senate as a Democrat. California businessmen, led by the automobile dealer Holmes Tuttle, encouraged him. Reagan declined.[14]

In these ways, then, the movie career assisted the later political career. There was yet another link with Hollywood that requires a somewhat more involved explanation. The principles that Reagan came to champion in his political career (capitalism, patriotism, Judeo-Christianity versus godless communism) combined religion, small-town America, the entertainment world, and the modern industrial state. In some manner they derived from his upbringing in Illinois, yet his experience in Hollywood transformed them. He was born and raised in the Midwest, where religion, community, and belief in America were strong. Such men as Reverend Ben Cleaver denounced communism, emphasized individual responsibility, advocated Christian character, and stressed the family as the cornerstone of civilization. Reagan's family was comparatively liberal, what with his father a New Deal Democrat and both parents opposing racial and religious discrimination. In the Midwest he lived and worked in communities where admiration for heroes and boosterism for business was widespread, and where community leaders faced the future with a robust optimism. Few people doubted the uniqueness of America or questioned patriotism.

In his film career Reagan encountered a more complicated world. With the exception of a few individuals such as Reverend Cleveland Kleihauer, he found little that encouraged the church's view of the proper life. The movie industry exploited sex. Many people in Hollywood wanted to undermine the Production Code that had been designed to ensure that motion pictures sanctioned the family. Reagan had little grasp of the forces at play, or of the larger issues, and championed greater freedom for the screen. Warner Bros., with its emphasis on rags-to-riches stories and its enthusiasm for Americanism, did promote a sense of community. Yet the studio and Hollywood generally lacked a lasting commitment to liberal reform. This was poor soil in which to nurture any such sentiments that Reagan might have brought from the Midwest. From the beginning, the Warners, who had been Hoover Republicans, were willing to give in to the Legion of Decency and the American Legion, and to such political conservatives as Hearst, Hays, and Breen.

Americanism, though, was another matter. It connected Dixon and Hollywood and, eventually, politics. It was not controversial. Such films as *Knute Rockne* showed a nation of immigrants, assimilated around common ideals. It celebrated the American spirit. The congressional investigations into communism after the war and the economic instability of the industry brought renewed pressures. Jack Warner, Eric Johnston (who replaced Will Hays as head of the MPAA), and Reagan himself turned toward an Americanism that emphasized anticommunism, capitalism, technology and progress, and military strength. They resolved to spread the American way worldwide and oppose those who objected. When Congresswoman Helen Gahagan Douglas warned about the nuclear arms race, Reagan's voice fell silent. Where such liberals as Dore Schary talked about tolerance and Melvyn Douglas championed a spirit of inquiry, Reagan was outspoken in support of loyalty. Where the Hollywood Ten stressed America's diverse racial and ethnic heritage, arguing that discrimination was rooted in capitalism, and condemned Western imperialism, Reagan spoke of how the nation united "all the bloodstreams of all the national origins in the world" into a distinctive "American personality."[15]

When Reagan and the Warners spoke of Americanism they used the term synonymously with patriotism. It was alloyed with money and opportunism. Patriotism played extremely well at the box office throughout Reagan's career at Warner Bros. Still, this patriotism had a spiritual dimension. It could become a civil religion that united the nation and traditional religious faith, a union of the secular and the sacred. Harry Warner joined Americanism with religion when he called for unity between Protestants, Catholics, and Jews. Reagan helped deliver this message in the Army Air Force film, *For God and Country*. Later he said that America was part of a divine plan. God had intended it to be a "promised land," the "last best hope of man on earth."[16]

Americanism was bound up with national security and military strength. As the threat from Nazi Germany increased, the Warners had become obsessed with spies. They promoted preparedness and the uniform. They recreated history to serve their goals. For them – and for Reagan – heroes, especially military heroes, had helped build America. It was not surprising that after Pearl Harbor, Jack Warner lobbied for a film unit that publicized air power, nor that Reagan worked in this unit that General Arnold, an apostle of American air superiority, sponsored.

The year 1952 marked the end of the first phase of Reagan's life, and a beginning of the second. He remarried, in what would prove an enduring and supportive union. He ended his association with Warner Bros. and stepped down as Screen Actors Guild president after five terms, although he remained on its board of directors and continued as secretary of the Motion Picture Industry Council. He moved toward a career in television. As guild president he signed a blanket waiver in July 1952 that gave the agency that represented him, Music Corporation of America, the right to produce television programs. The arrangement, later investigated by the Justice Department, strengthened MCA's power and proved advantageous to Reagan. In 1954 he became host of one of the agency's early productions, the General Electric Theater. His political identity would further unfold in the years that followed, first as a GE spokesperson and on Death Valley Days, then as California governor, and finally in national politics.[17]

Reagan, one might conclude, came to Hollywood at a time when motion pictures were reaching a peak of popularity, threatening to change the very nature of American civilization in the process. He flourished in this world that manufactured dreams, where politics and entertainment converged. For most people, the movies provided only an escape from everyday life. For him, however, Hollywood turned dreams into reality.

ABBREVIATIONS

The following abbreviations are used in the Notes and the References.

AAC: Army Air Corps, later Army Air Force (AAF)
AAF: Army Air Force
ACA: Archdiocese of Chicago Archives, Chicago
ADA: Americans for Democratic Action
AFI-LA: American Film Institute, Los Angeles
AFL: American Federation of Labor
AMPASL: Academy of Motion Picture Arts and Sciences Library, Beverly Hills, Calif.
AUND: Archives of the University of Notre Dame, South Bend, Ind.
AVC: American Veterans Committee
AVCB: *AVC Bulletin* or *Bulletin of the American Veterans Committee*
BD: Board of Directors, Screen Actors Guild
BL-UCB: Bancroft Library, University of California, Berkeley
BLCU-NY: Butler Library, Columbia University, New York
BYUA-P: Harold B. Lee Library, Brigham Young University, Provo, Utah
CDT: *Chicago Daily Tribune*
CHA: *Chicago Herald-American*
CHE: *Chicago Herald and Examiner*
COMPO: Council of Motion Picture Organizations
CP: Communist Party
CSCAC: Culver-Stockton College Archive, Canton, Mo.
CSU: Conference of Studio Unions
DCHSN: Disciples of Christ Historical Society, Nashville, Tenn.
DET: *Dixon Evening Telegraph*
DETA: Dixon Evening Telegraph Archive, Dixon, Ill.
DL-USC: Doheny Library, University of Southern California, Los Angeles
DMSR: *Des Moines Sunday Register*
DPLD: Dixon Public Library, Dixon, Ill.
EB: Executive Board, Screen Actors Guild
EBM: Executive Board Meeting, HICCASP
EB-SWG: Executive Board, Screen Writers Guild
ECAE: Eureka College Archive, Eureka, Ill.
ECM: Executive Council Meeting, HICCASP

238

FBI-FOIA: Federal Bureau of Investigation Records, Washington, D.C.
FDRL: Franklin D. Roosevelt Library, Hyde Park, N.Y.
FMPU: First Motion Picture Unit, Army Air Force, later known as 18th Army Air Forces Base Unit (Motion Picture Unit)
HBCCL: Hollywood–Beverly Christian Church Library, Hollywood, Calif.
HCN: Hollywood Citizen-News
HDC: Hollywood Democratic Committee (later known as HICCASP)
HHPL-WB: Herbert Hoover Presidential Library, West Branch, Iowa
HICCASP: Hollywood Independent Citizens Committee of the Arts, Sciences, and Professions
HIWP-S: Hoover Institute of War and Peace, Stanford University, Stanford, Calif.
HL-SM: Huntington Library, San Marino, Calif.
HSSC: Hollywood Studio Strike Collection, University Research Library, University of California, Los Angeles
HSTLI: Harry S Truman Library, Independence, Mo.
HUAC: House Committee on Un-American Activities
IATSE: International Alliance of Theatrical and Stage Employees
ICCASP: Independent Citizens Committee of the Arts, Sciences, and Professions
JHL-SIU: John Howard Lawson Papers, Southern Illinois University, Carbondale, Ill.
JLW-USC: Jack L. Warner Collection, University of Southern California, Los Angeles
JMPA-STL: Jesuit Missouri Province Archives, St. Louis, Mo.
KIHI: Kiwanis International Headquarters, Indianapolis, Ind.
LAC: Los Angeles Citizen
LACCHR: Los Angeles County Court House Records, Los Angeles
LADN: Los Angeles Daily News
LAE: Los Angeles Examiner
LAEHE: Los Angeles Evening Herald and Express
LAMN: Los Angeles Mirror News
LAT: Los Angeles Times
LC: Library of Congress, Washington, D.C.
LL-GU: Lauinger Library, Georgetown University, Washington, D.C.
LLHV: Labor League of Hollywood Voters
LLIUB: Lilly Library, Indiana University, Bloomington
MAFB: Maxwell Air Force Base
MGM: Metro-Goldwyn-Mayer
MPAA: Motion Picture Association of America (successor in 1945 to the MPPDA)
MPAPAV: Motion Picture Alliance for the Preservation of American Values
MPBRSD-LC: Motion Picture, Broadcasting, and Recorded Sound Division, Library of Congress, Washington, D. C.
MPIC: Motion Picture Industry Council
MPIC-EC: Motion Picture Industry Council, Executive Committee
MPPDA: Motion Picture Producers and Distributors of America
NA: National Archives and Records Administration, Washington, D.C.
NAACP: National Association for the Advancement of Colored People
NAS: National Archives and Records Administration, Suitland, Md.
NIHS-SB: Northern Indiana Historical Society, South Bend
NLRB: National Labor Relations Board
NNSM: National Archives and Records Service, Motion Picture, Sound and Video Branch
NYDM: New York Daily Mirror
NYDN: New York Daily News
NYHT: New York Herald Tribune

NYJA: New York Journal American
NYPL: New York Public Library, New York
NYPL-SCRBC: New York Public Library, Schomburg Center for Research in Black
    Culture, New York
NYPLA: New York Public Library Annex, New York
NYPLLC: New York Public Library, Lincoln Center, New York
NYT: New York Times
PCA: Production Code Administration
PSCD: Palmer School of Chiropractic, Davenport, Iowa
PULP: Princeton University Library, Princeton, N.J.
QCTM-D: Quad City Times Morgue, Davenport, Iowa
RAAF-FMPU-MAFB: Records of Army Air Force, First Motion Picture Unit, Max-
    well Air Force Base, Alabama
RFCCD: Records of the First Christian Church, Dixon, Ill.
RKO: Radio-Keith-Orpheum Corporation
RR: Ronald Reagan
SAG: Screen Actors Guild
SAGA: Screen Actors Guild Archive, Hollywood, Calif.
SBPL: South Bend Public Library, South Bend, Ind.
SBT: South Bend Tribune
SBTM: *South Bend Tribune* Morgue, South Bend, Ind.
SCCA-SAD: State of California, Court of Appeal, Second Appellate District
SCLSSR-LA: Southern California Library for Social Studies and Research, Los
    Angeles
SDG: Screen Directors Guild
SEG: Screen Extras Guild
SFCB: San Francisco Call-Bulletin
SFE: San Francisco Examiner
SHSWM: State Historical Society of Wisconsin, Madison
STLGD: St. Louis Globe-Democrat
SWG: Screen Writers Guild
UA: United Artists
UA-SHSWM: United Artists Collection, State Historical Society of Wisconsin,
    Madison
UNDRB: University of Notre Dame Religious Bulletin
URL-UCLA: University Research Library, University of California, Los Angeles
USNWR: U.S. News & World Report
USTG: United Studio Technicians Guild
UWF Mss.: United World Federalist Manuscripts, Lilly Library, Indiana University,
    Bloomington
WBAHP-P: Warner Bros. Archive of Historical Papers, Princeton University, Prince-
    ton, N.J.
WBAHP-USC: Warner Bros. Archive of Historical Papers, University of Southern
    California, Los Angeles
WHHPI: Will H. Hays Papers, Indiana State Library, Indianapolis, Ind.
WSJ: Wisconsin State Journal (Madison)

NOTES

Preface

1. Quotations, Lawson, *Film in the Battle of Ideas*; RR, *Where's*, 140, 162; RR, "America the Beautiful," 9; and ("capture"), Wanger, "Tulsa Speech," 1.
2. In addition, between 1937 and 1952, Reagan appeared in one film for Metro-Goldwyn-Mayer, two for Universal, and two for Paramount.

1. Dixon

1. Quotations, *Springfield Leader and Press*, June 7, 1952, p. 3; and *Springfield Sunday News Leader*, June 8, 1952, p. B4.
2. Quotation, Truman's longhand notes, President's secretary's files, Harry S Truman Papers, HSTLI.
3. Reagan was a "Democrat for Eisenhower" during 1952. See Leuchtenburg, "Reagan's Secret Liberal Past," 20.
4. Quotation, Ronald Reagan, "America the Beautiful," 8. See also McArthur, *Actors*, 123.
5. Quotation, *Springfield Leader and Press*, June 7, 1952, p. 3.
6. Quotation, Hulston oral history, 1988, HSTLI.
7. The nickname "Dutch" reputedly came from his father, who, after Ronald's birth, said that his new son looked "like a fat little Dutchman." RR, *American Life*, 21; and Neil Reagan, "Private Dimensions and Public Images," 10.
8. Quotations, RR, *Where's*, 17, 18.
9. See Ida Zeitlin, "Ronald Reagan," *Modern Screen* (March 1943), p. 31, in "Reagan Scrap Book," Audrey Dixsan, comp., 1942 (hereafter cited as Reagan Scrapbook), ECAE; RR to O. Dallas Baillio, Jan. 19, 1977, reprinted in *A.L.A.* (American Library Assoc.), Feb. 1981, p. 61, DPLD; and RR, *American Life*, 25.
10. Quotations, RR to Helen P. Miller, Sept. 3, 1981, DPLD; and RR to Baillio, Jan. 19, 1977, ibid. Also RR, *American Life*, 31.
11. The Dixon library housed other authors – Tolstoi, Balzac, Dickens, Hugo – whose works might have taken a boy's imagination, but there is no record that Reagan read them. When works were checked out of the Dixon Public Library, the borrower's card number was recorded in the book. A search in 1986 of all fiction books in the library with authors' last names starting from A through L failed to uncover a single work with Reagan's number. It should be noted,

though, that many pre-1930 editions of popular authors (Zane Grey, Edgar Rice Burroughs, Mark Twain) were discarded when they wore out.

Reagan's reading while in Hollywood included Thorne Smith (*Turnabout*), Sinclair Lewis (*Babbitt*), Mark Twain (*Adventures of Tom Sawyer* and *Huckleberry Finn*), Pearl Buck, H. G. Wells, Damon Runyon, and Erich Remarque. See RR to Miller, Sept. 1, 1981, DPLD; RR to Baillio, Jan. 1977, ibid.; RR, *American Life,* 31–2; and RR, "How To Make Yourself Important."

12. See *DET,* Aug. 20, 1927, pp. 1–2; and RR interview with author, Oct. 16, 1989. On Reagan's fascination with heroes, see Griswold, "I'm a sucker," 11, 21.

13. E.g., see *DET,* June 2, 1928, p. 3.

14. Quotations, *DET,* Feb. 22, 1928, p. 4. See also "Being from the Sky," ibid., Feb. 24, 1928, p. 4.

Among Shaw's friends and one of the area's best-known residents was drugstore magnate Charles Walgreen. He and his wife purchased an estate on Rock River known as Hazelwood in 1928. Reagan was often there during his college years as a caddie for Walgreen, and he became friends with the family. See Walgreen, *Never a Dull Day,* 212–13, 217–18, 227–9, 242, 298–9; and Edwards, *Early Reagan,* 73–4, 117–18, 249–50.

15. As a high school senior, he also started as center for the town's YMCA basketball team. Quotations, RR, *American Life,* 35 (also ibid., 34–7, 39); and RR, *Where's,* 18. See also *DET,* Dec. 17, 1927, p. 9.

16. See *DET,* Oct. 10, 1927, p. 8; ibid., Oct. 17, 1927, p. 7; Nov. 23, 1927, p. 10; and Nov. 25, 1927, p. 5.

17. Quotation, RR, *Where's,* 63. See also ibid., 64; *Woodford County Journal,* Oct. 16, 1980, p. 1; and Gordon interview with author, June 8, 1988.

18. Quotation, *DET,* Aug. 3, 1928, p. 1. See also ibid., June 18, 1931, p. 1; July 23, 1932, p. 2; Sept. 4, 1928, p. 2; and RR, *Where's,* 21. One former Dixon resident remembered Reagan as a "conscientious" lifeguard. Potterveld interview with author, Feb. 7, 1987. See also RR, "Meditations of a Lifeguard," *Dixonian: 1928 (Cinema Number)* (Dixon: The Senior Class, Dixon High School, 1928), 103.

19. This chapter is based on sources largely untapped by Reagan biographers. They include Ben Hill Cleaver's papers in the DCHSN; the Reagan-Cleaver family correspondence at CSCAC; and church records from Cleaver's ministry in Dixon. This chapter is also based on a thorough reading of the *Dixon Evening Telegraph (DET)* between 1926 and 1928 as well as on interviews with Reagan and Cleaver's daughters, Helen and Margaret. For works that deal with Reagan and the First Christian Church, see Wills, *Reagan's America,* 16–26, 33, 35, 56–7, 59, 102, 112; Wills, "Nelle's Boy," 1002–06; Cannon, *President Reagan,* 39, 211, 212, 216, 288; Cannon, *Reagan,* 24, 34; and Edwards, *Early Reagan,* 33–6, 39, 56–60, 65–7, 75, 92.

20. Quotations, Michael Reagan, *Outside,* 20 (also 50, 270); and RR, *American Life,* 20, 22 (also 32, 56).

21. Ronald Reagan was baptized on June 21, 1922, by Reverend David Franklin Seyter, a pastor from Pine Creek, and not, as Garry Wills suggests, by Ben Cleaver. Cleaver did not assume the Dixon ministry until August 22, 1922. The previous pastor, Harvey Waggoner, died June 1, 1922. Reagan's brother, Neil, apparently had been baptized in the Catholic church as an infant, but his mother felt uncomfortable with that arrangement. Neil left the Dixon Christian Church in 1927. For Reagan's baptism, I am indebted to Ron Marlow, historian of the Dixon First Christian Church (telephone interview with author, Dec. 14, 1992). See also "History of First Christian Church . . . ," Johnson comp., pp. 2, 4,

RFCCD; Standard Church Register and Record, pp. 82–3, ibid.; and Wills, *Reagan's America*, 21.

22. See Standard Church Register and Record, p. 82, RFCCD; Gardiner, "Nelle Reagan," 3–4; RR, *Where's,* 10–13; Margaret (Cleaver) Gordon interview with author, June 8, 1988; and RR, *American Life,* 22, 31.

23. Quotations, RR, *Where's,* 55. Nelle's donations to the church were small. For example, she pledged five dollars on May 30, 1926; on June 24, 1927, she pledged two dollars, and had paid one dollar a month later. "Ledger," p. 123, RFCCD.

24. For Nelle's other church activities, see "Business Meetings of the Church," Jan. 13, 1926, Standard Church Register and Record, 237, RFCCD; May 20, 1926, ibid., 238; "Meetings of Church Officers," Jan. 2, 1929, p. 204; "Other Records of Interest," Jan. 16, 1929; Dec. 11, 1929; Jan. 14, 1930, ibid., 250–2. See also *DET,* Nov. 9, 1927, p. 12; Dec. 2, 1927, p. 3; Dec. 20, 1927, p. 12; Jan. 13, 1928, p. 6; Feb. 17, 1928, p. 5; March 19, 1928, p. 2; April 6, 1928, p. 5; April 10, 1928, p. 10; April 26, 1928, p. 2; and Sept. 1, 1937, p. 3. See also Gardiner, "Nelle Reagan," 5; Evelyn Carpenter's observations in Lorraine Rutkowski's "Lorrie's Lookout," 25 (publication of the Ronald Reagan fan club, c. 1950), in DETA; "Report of Building Fund Treasurer For the Year Ending Dec. 31, 1926," Jan. 7, 1927, p. 1, RFCCD; "Report of Parsonage Building Fund Secretary, Jan. 11, 1928, "List of Parsonage Pledges and Payments," in *Annual Reports,* ibid.; and RR, *American Life,* 35.

25. Quotations, Helen Cleaver to author, March 25, 1985; Gordon interview with author, June 8, 1988; Nancy Reagan, *My Turn,* 107; RR, *American Life,* 22. See also ibid., 20–1; Gardiner, "Nelle Reagan," 5, 13; Potterveld interview with author, Feb. 7, 1987; and *DET,* Nov. 9, 1927, p. 2.

26. Quotation, Beverly Strouss, "Mrs. Reagan Says, 'Dixon More Beautiful Than Ever' " (undated clipping, probably published in *DET*), in DETA. See also Mrs. J. E. Reagan to Mrs. [Eleanor] Roosevelt, Oct. 10, 1939, box 2257, Eleanor Roosevelt Papers, FDRL; Secretary to Mrs. Roosevelt to Mrs. Reagan, Nov. 16, 1939, ibid.; RR, *Where's,* 10; and Gardiner, "Nelle Reagan," 6, 13.

27. Quotations, Helen Cleaver to author, March 25, 1985; RR, *American Life,* 40 (also ibid., 75–6); Wills, *Reagan's America*, 18 (also 59, 102, 112); and Dutch [RR] to Helen Cleaver, Feb. 26, 1975, Reagan-Cleaver correspondence, CSCAC. Also, Gordon interview with author, June 8, 1988; and Edwards, *Early Reagan,* 68, 75, 142–3.

28. The Disciples of Christ wanted "to simplify the doctrines of Christian faith and promote a union of all Protestant denominations." They hoped to restore "primitive Christianity," wanted members to follow the New Testament, and believed every person capable of understanding its message. The Disciples gave followers the choice to decide for themselves any remaining "doubtful and inferential matters." They exalted the individual's conscience about the will of the church or congregation. In 1906 the Disciples had a nationwide membership of 1,142,359 and almost 90 percent of the members lived in rural areas or towns with populations of 25,000 or less. Quotations, *DET,* March 16, 1928, p. 6; Garrison, *American Religious Movement,* 9, 10, 14; and Hatch, "Christian Movement," 567. See also ibid., 551; Garrison, *Religion Follows the Frontier,* 3–144; Harrell, *Social Sources,* 3, 5–6, 71; and Marty, *Irony,* 164.

29. About this time, Cleveland Kleihauer, who would be Reagan's pastor in California, put the matter more broadly. The Disciples promoted Christian unity for the "evangelization of the world," he said. Quotation, Kleihauer, Simpson, and Golden, "Report of the Commission to the Orient," 912; and *DET,* Dec. 9,

1927, p. 5. See also ibid., April 20, 1928, p. 9. On Cleaver's efforts to improve cooperation between Protestant churches, see Ben Hill Cleaver, "Christ Among the Candlesticks" (hereafter cited as "Candlesticks") (a paper for the 1934 Illinois ministers' retreat concerning the present welfare of local churches), 1934, p. 6, DCHSN. See also B. H. Cleaver to Brethren, Jan. 13, 1926, "Annual Reports for Year Ending Dec. 31, 1925," RFCCD; and *DET,* Jan. 13, 1928, p. 6; April 5, 1928, p. 10; and March 16, 1928, p. 6.

The local church in the Disciples of Christ was sometimes referred to as a "Christian Church" or "Church of Christ," and less frequently as a "Church of Disciples of Christ." In 1906, the Disciples movement separated and a more conservative branch became known as the "Churches of Christ" (plural).

30. Many Disciples were also active in post–Civil War politics; one, James Garfield, reached the White House. Quotation, Harrell, *Social Sources,* 25; also 3, 29–31.

Ben Cleaver attended Christian University, a Disciples school in Canton, Missouri, later renamed Culver-Stockton College. He graduated in 1902.

31. "Impressed as they were by the power of wealth, few church leaders questioned the Christianization of hard work and acquisitiveness." Quotation, Harrell, *Social Sources,* 34; also 33, 36–7, 39, 43, 46, 49.

32. Cleaver attended the University of Chicago between October, 1911, and March, 1912. Quotation, Thomas Israel to author, May 17, 1988. See also Gordon interview with author, June 8, 1988; Thomas Israel interview with author, May 10, 1988; and Fred Goodwin conversation with author, May 7, 1988.

33. Garrison, *An American Religious Movement,* 9. For Cleaver's view of salvation, see "Who Are Condemned?" 1904, in "Sermons: When and Where Delivered," Cleaver File, DCHSN.

34. Cleaver, who thought that poorly educated ministers also threatened the church, advocated better training. See Ben Hill Cleaver, "A Brief Sketch of the Christian Churches of Ralls County, Missouri, and the Ministers Therefrom," 1966, p. 9, in personal papers file, Ben Hill Cleaver, DCHSN (hereafter cited as "A Brief Sketch"). See also Ben H. Cleaver, "*Lectures* On the Last Twenty-two Books of The New Testament" (hereafter cited as "*Lectures*") (prepared and presented during the spring of 1908), pp. 1, 14, 45, Cleaver File, DCHSN; Cleaver, "Candlesticks," 1, 2, 3, 4, 5, 7, 8; and "From B. H. Cleaver," *Christian-Evangelist,* Jan. 29, 1931, p. 162. For the Disciples' disagreement on how to respond to urban problems, see Harrell, *Social Sources,* 5–6, 71, 72, 75, 83; and Marty, *Irony,* 164.

35. Cleaver came to Dixon from Streator, Illinois, where he had been pastor for three years. Most of his appointments had been three to four years in length. Cleaver had three daughters, Elizabeth, Helen, and Margaret. A fourth child, Carolyn, died in infancy. See "Record of Ministerial Service," Cleaver File, DCHSN; B. H. Cleaver to Frederick D. Kershner, *Christian Evangelist,* July 26, 1928, p. 950; and Howard, *Ralls County,* 362.

36. Quotation, Dorothy (Bovey) Potterveld, interview with author, Feb. 7, 1987. Also Gordon interview with author, June 8, 1988; Cleaver to Dear Brethren, Jan. 13, 1926, "Annual Reports for Year Ending Dec. 31, 1925," RFCCD; *DET,* March 16, 1928, p. 6; "History of First Christian Church (Disciples of Christ), Dixon, Illinois, From 1895 to September, 1966," from the daily diaries of Charles W. and Frank M. Johnson, compiled by Bess Johnson, Jan., 1958, pp. 4–5, RFCCD; Standard Church Register and Record: Meetings of Church Officers, [April 2?, 1931], [p. 230?], RFCCD; [Cleaver], "A Brief Sketch," p. 1, DCHSN; and Burrus Dickinson interview with author, May 11, 1988.

37. Quotations, RR, *American Life,* 30, 52. On opposition to race hatred in the

church's Women's Missionary Society, see *DET,* Nov. 4, 1927, p. 3. See also ibid., Sept. 9, 1927, p. 3; Feb. 3, 1928, p. 3; and Nancy Reagan, *My Turn,* 106–7. For Jack Reagan's opposition to discrimination, see this volume, Chapter 5.
38. Quotation and on the number of blacks in Dixon, Gordon interview with author, June 8, 1988. Also Dorothy Bovey Potterveld to author, May 31, 1988; Crain, *Development of Social Ideas,* 178–87; McAllister and Tucker, *Journey in Faith,* 357; and Harrell, *Social Sources,* 161, 206, 207.
39. Or they heard about the "great, wonderful and backward land" called India. Quotations, *DET,* April 20, 1928, p. 3; March 3, 1928, p. 3; and Feb. 21, 1928, p. 2. Also Margaret Cleaver Gordon, telephone interview with author, July 13, 1988; and Marty, *Irony,* 162.

    Anti-Catholicism was the most pronounced form of nativism in the Disciples' thought, although anti-Semitism and antiradicalism also appeared. Cleaver occasionally criticized Catholicism and Judaism, but was neither strongly nativistic nor sympathetic to the KKK. His early lectures indicate that he considered elements of Judaism unfriendly to Christianity, yet thought it possible for Jews and Christians to unite. See Cleaver, *"Lectures,"* 10, 11, 18, 23, 34–5, 38, 54, 59, 60; and Cleaver, "Candlesticks," 6. Also Lessner, "The Imagined Enemy," v–vi, 347–79.
40. Quotations, Cleaver, "A Brief Sketch," 5, DCHSN. On the New Testament and slavery, see Cleaver, *"Lectures,"* 41. On Cleaver and the NAACP, Israel interview with author, May 10, 1988; and Gordon interview with author, June 8, 1988. See also Howard, *Ralls County,* 57.
41. Cleaver helped organize the Benevolence Institute to help the disadvantaged. See *DET,* Dec. 5, 1927, p. 2; also Dec. 6, 1927, p. 10. For Nelle's work for the Institute and the needy, see ibid., Dec. 5, 1927, p. 2; Dec. 13, 1927, p. 9; Dec. 14, 1927, p. 3; Dec. 16, 1927, p. 3. See also ibid., Nov. 22, 1927, p. 4; Nov. 28, 1927, p. 2; Dec. 20, 1927, p. 12; Dec. 23, 1927, p. 10; and Jan. 7, 1928, p. 2. On the Disciples and charity, see Harrell, *Social Sources,* 40–2, 50, 62, 69.
42. See *DET,* Nov. 15, 1927, p. 5; and Feb. 6, 1928, p. 3. The church offered a variation on the Golden Rule: "Do to other salesmen as you would want them to do to yours." See *Hostess Reference Book* (Dixon, Ill.: Ladies' Aid Society, First Christian Church, [1928]), 9, 11, in RFCCD. On Reagan and the Hi-Y Club, see *DET,* Jan. 26, 1928, p. 2; Feb. 16, 1928, p. 9; and March 16, 1928, p. 7.
43. Text quotations, Cleaver to Brethren, Jan. 13, 1926, RFCCD. Cleaver taught his family that there were "lots of things more important than money." Note quotation, Gordon interview with author, June 8, 1988.
44. Disciples were occasionally sympathetic to the complaints of organized labor, but many were suspicious of unions, equating them with radicalism. Cleaver urged frugality and fair wages for workers. See *DET,* Oct. 7, 1927, p. 3. Quotation, Lessner, "The Imagined Enemy," 355. See also ibid., 347; and Harrell, *Social Sources,* 105, 108, 125.
45. Quotations, "Some Memories of John Stephen Cleaver . . . ," 4. Disciples talked about the implications of the Bolshevik revolution.
46. Quotations, RR to Cleaver Family, Dec. 16, 1974, Reagan-Cleaver correspondence, CSCAC. Reagan was recalling Cleaver's sentiments, not his exact words. In Eureka, Cleaver was not inclined to "stir up things" over social causes. Burrus Dickinson, interview with author, May 11, 1988.
47. On Missionary Society, see *DET,* Nov. 9, 1927, p. 7. Margaret Cleaver was president of the Girls Hi-Y Club at this time. See ibid., Dec. 15, 1927, p. 6; Jan. 26, 1928, p. 2; Feb. 23, 1928, p. 2; Feb. 25, 1928, p. 2; April 4, 1928, p. 3; and May 29, 1928, p. 8; Marty, *Irony,* 299, 309; and *Hostess Reference Book,* 5, RFCCD.

48. Margaret Cleaver Gordon emphasized her father's admiration for Gandhi. Her father hated war, she said, but "perhaps thought it inevitable." Cleaver recognized that many Disciples sympathized with Gandhi's beliefs, but reminded them the Indian leader was a Hindu, not a Christian. Gandhi quotations, Cleaver quoting a Disciple missionary who had been to India in Cleaver, "Candlesticks," 4. Also Gordon interview with author, June 8, 1988. On Christian Endeavor, see *DET,* Nov. 9, 1927, p. 12. On religion and power, see remarks at Reagan's baccalaureate service in 1928. *DET,* May 28, 1928, pp. 1, 5.

49. Quotations, RR, *Where's,* 7, 8, 9. See also RR, *American Life,* 25, 33. In part because many Disciples believed pauperism resulted from drunkenness, most church members supported prohibition. Some who viewed drink as a cause of poverty had little compassion for the poor. See Harrell, *Social Sources,* 41 and 208–42.

50. Quotation (Nancy Reagan's words, not RR's), Nancy Reagan, *My Turn,* 105. The most plausible assessments of the influence of Jack Reagan's alcoholism have been provided by Lou Cannon, whose own father was an alcoholic, and by Nancy Reagan. See ibid., 105–7; and Cannon, *President Reagan,* 206–31. Also on this topic, see Dallek, *Politics of Symbolism,* 15–16, 52–3, 86, 140, 194; Wills, *Reagan's America,* 33–5; Cannon, *Reagan,* 26; and RR, *American Life,* 31.

51. Quotation, RR, "Life" (poem), *Dixonian: 1928 (Cinema Number),* 15 (Dixon: Senior Class, Dixon High School [1928]), 95.

52. Quotations, Gordon interview with author, June 8, 1988. See also RR, *American Life,* 41. On Nelle's opposition to divorce, see Gardiner, "Nelle Reagan," 5.

    Temperance had widespread support in Dixon and in Reagan's Christian Church in California. The Dixon newspaper linked drinking to crime, and local politicians endorsed temperance, associating it with good citizenship. Cleaver preached against drinking, was a member of the Women's Christian Temperance Union, and aligned his church with the Illinois Anti-Saloon League. On Dixon and temperance, see *DET,* April 25, 1928, p. 7. Also ibid., April 10, 1928, p. 10. For Cleaver and temperance, see ibid., Dec. 14, 1927, p. 11; Jan. 13, 1928, p. 5; Feb. 10, 1928, p. 5; April 20, 1928, p. 9; Sept. 24, 1928, p. 5; and Cleaver to Frederick D. Kershner, *Christian Evangelist,* July 26, 1928, p. 950. On Cleaver's membership in the WCTU, see *DET,* Jan. 24, 1928. On the Illinois Anti-Saloon League, see Cleaver to Brethren of the Congregation, Jan. 14, 1925, "Annual Reports for Year Ending Dec. 31, 1924," RFCCD. Teachings about alcohol (and drugs) were later reinforced by Reagan's California Christian Church. See, for example, C. K. [Cleveland Kleihauer], "The Peace Terms of Evil," *Christian Challenger,* 6 (July 20, 1947), 1, HBCCL; and "The High Cost of Experience," ibid., 6 (Oct. 12, 1947), 1, HBCCL.

53. Quotation, RR, *An American Life,* 53. See also RR, *Where's,* 56, 61; Neil Reagan, "Private Dimensions and Public Images," 13–14; Michael Reagan, *Outside,* 183; and Nancy Reagan, *My Turn,* 119.

54. Quotation, Lears, "From Salvation to Self-Realization," 8. Also RR, *Where's,* 18.

    For the contrast between the child-rearing practices recommended by the Dixon church of Reagan's youth and those suggested by the Hollywood–Beverly Christian Church of Reagan's young adulthood, see *Christian Challenger,* 4 (May 20, 1945), 1; and ibid. (June 17, 1945), 1, both HBCCL.

55. Quotations, *Hostess Reference Book,* 3, 4, 5, 13, RFCCD.

56. Quotations, Margaret (Cleaver) Gordon to author, May 25, 1988; and Helen Cleaver to author, March 25, 1985. Both sisters noted Reagan's lack of regular church attendance as president. "Even Nixon held services in the White House," Margaret noted. Gordon interview with author, June 8, 1988. Also Don Little-

john interview with author, March 19, 1985. Before Reagan became president, observers also commented on his casual church attendance. See Marjorie Hyer, "Reagans Likely to Attend Several Churches," *Washington Post*, Jan. 18, 1981, p. A18.

57. Quotations, RR, *Where's*, 22; and RR to The Reverend and Mrs. Ben H. Cleaver, Jan. 4, 1973, Reagan-Cleaver Correspondence, CSCAC. Also, Roberts, "A Mighty Russian Pulpit for Reagan," p. 7.

58. Cleaver and Reagan disagreed over Vietnam, China, and the United Nations. Quotations, RR interview with author, Oct. 16, 1989. See also Gordon interview with author, June 8, 1988; and Michael Reagan, *Outside*, 186.

2. Learning to Communicate

1. From Margaret Cleaver's graduation address, "A Chair for the New Home," reprinted in *DET*, June 4, 1928, p. 5.

2. About thirty young people (usually eight to ten attended) belonged to Christian Endeavor. It provided experience in public speaking and leading meetings, according to one of its members. Reagan led discussions on such topics as "What Would Happen if All Church Members Were Really Christians?" and "What Difference Does It Make What We Do on Sundays?" See *DET*, Sept. 23, 1927, p. 12; ibid., Jan. 20, 1928, p. 5; and Gordon interview with author, June 8, 1988. See also program for "Easter Week Services," RFCCD; and RR, *Where's*, 15. For Reagan as toastmaster, see *DET*, April 16, 1928, p. 2.

3. Quotations, RR, *Where's*, 37; and RR, *American Life*, 42. Also ibid., 35, 41–3.

4. Quotation, Potterveld to author, May 31, 1988. "A gentleman should never ask a lady to dance with him if he has removed his coat," the Ladies Aid Society told young men. Quotation, *Hostess Reference Book*, 5, in RFCCD.

5. See *DET*, Dec. 24, 1927, p. 16; RR, *American Life*, 30; and RR, *Where's*, 17–18.

6. Quotations, *DET*, Sept. 16, 1927, p. 5; Gordon interview with author, June 8, 1988. On church members' opposition to Sunday night movies, see Potterveld to author, May 31, 1988. Also Cleaver to Brethren of the Congregation, Jan. 14, 1925, RFCCD.

7. The theme for this meeting was "The World – My Neighborhood." Quotations from summary of meeting in *DET*, Sept. 9, 1927, p. 3.

8. Quotations from Margaret Cleaver's graduation address, "A Chair for the New Home," reprinted in *DET*, June 4, 1928, p. 5.

9. Quotations, RR, *Where's*, 15. Also Neil Reagan, "Private Dimensions and Public Images," 11; RR, *American Life*, 35; and Gordon interview with author, June 8, 1988.

10. Quotation, Gordon telephone interview with author, July 13, 1988. See also RR, *Where's*, 37–8; RR, *American Life*, 41–2, and "One Remembers Reagan," *Reagan's Dixon* (Dixon, Ill.: The Official Dixon Press, 1980), in QCTM-D. On Frazer's likely influence on Reagan, Gordon interview with author, June 8, 1988.

11. *DET*, Feb. 19, 1928, p. 3. Quotation, RR, *Where's*, 38. Also *Dixonian: 1928*, 47, 65, 67. The yearbook's motif was a motion picture.

12. See RR's letter "To My Lady Fair and Her Sister," Nov. 21, 1922, DETA; RR, *Where's*, 23–4; and RR, *American Life*, 44–5.

13. Quotations, RR, *American Life*, 57; and RR, *Where's*, 29.

14. Quotation, *The 1932 Prism* (Eureka College yearbook), 120, ECAE. See also *Prism 1931*, 112, 114; RR, *Where's*, 38, 43–4; and RR, *American Life*, 57–8. Occasionally Reagan performed outside college auspices, as in a play arranged by Ben Cleaver in which Reagan portrayed a mid-nineteenth-century minister. See

Episode 2, "The New Meeting House – 1848" (a play in five episodes), Cleaver Files, DCHSN.

15. Quotations, Gordon interview with author, June 8, 1988; and RR, *American Life*, 76. See also ibid., 75; and RR, *Where's*, 45.

16. *Peoria Evening Star*, Nov. 26, 1928, p. 1; and Bert Wilson's statement of resignation to the Eureka College board of trustees, reprinted in *Eureka Pegasus*, Nov. 26, 1928, pp. 1, 3.

17. *Peoria Evening Star*, Nov. 23, 1928, section 4, p. 10; *DET*, Nov. 24, 1928, p. 1. See also *Eureka Pegasus*, Nov. 19, 1928, pp. 1, 3; *Peoria Journal*, Nov. 22, 1928, p. 1; *Daily Pantagraph* (Bloomington, Ill.), Nov. 22, 1928, p. 2; Nov. 23, 1928, p. 2; and *Peoria Evening Star*, Nov. 23, 1928, p. 22.

18. Quotation, RR, *Where's*, 28. Also *Peoria Journal*, Nov. 25, 1928, section 1, p. 2; Nov. 27, 1928, p. 4; *Peoria Evening Star*, Nov. 26, 1928, p. 1; and Wills, *Reagan's America*, 41, 47–8.

19. Quotations, RR, *Where's*, 28 (see also 27); and Howard Short, quoted in Wills, *Reagan's America*, 48 (also 43).

20. Burris Dickinson quoted in Wills, *Reagan's America*, 43. Wills argues that Reagan oversimplified and distorted the issues of the strike (see 51–2). During the strike, Dickinson's uncle, then head of the board of trustees, became acting president when Wilson resigned. Burris Dickinson became president of Eureka College in 1939. See also RR, *Where's*, 26, 30.

21. Quotation, RR, *Where's*, 28–9. See also RR, *American Life*, 47–8.

22. RR, *Where's*, 30.

23. Quotations, anonymous source, interview with author; and Zeitlin, "Ronald Reagan," 91, Reagan Scrapbook, ECAE.

24. Quotations, RR interview with Tom Brokaw, Jan. 18, 1989, NBC television; *Eureka Pegasus*, Dec. 18, 1928, p. 1. For course offerings, see *Eureka College Bulletin: General Catalogue, 1933–1934*, 32 (May 1933), 48–9. Also RR, *American Life*, 49; RR, *Where's*, 31; and RR interview with author, Oct. 16, 1989.

25. Quotations, *Prism 1931*, 67 (also 78); and *1932 Prism*, 70 (also 111). See also RR, *Where's*, 25, 30–2, 35–57; Gordon interview with author, June 8, 1988; RR interview with author, Oct. 16, 1989; Dickinson interview with author, May 11, 1988; *DET*, March 11, 1932, p. 3; *Woodford County Journal*, Oct. 16, 1980, p. 7; and *Eureka Pegasus*, Dec. 11, 1928, p. 1.

26. Quotations, anonymous source, interview with author; and *1932 Prism*, 43.

27. Quotation, RR, *Where's*, 41 (also 52); and RR, *American Life*, 54–5.

28. Quotations, RR, *American Life*, 55 (also 22, 62); and RR, *Where's*, 41.

29. Quotations, Potterveld interview with author, Feb. 7, 1987; RR, *Where's*, 44–5; and unlabeled clipping, Reagan Scrapbook, ECAE.

30. RR, *Where's*, 42, 44–5; and RR, *American Life*, 19–20.

31. Quotations, RR, *Where's*, 50 (also 55); *Davenport [Iowa] Democrat and Leader*, quoted in *DET*, Oct. 28, 1932, p. 12. The Dixon paper reported often on Reagan's progress as an announcer in Iowa. See *DET*, Oct. 7, 1932, p. 2; Oct. 26, 1932, p. 2; Jan. 28, 1933, pp. 1–2; and Feb. 10, 1933, p. 2. Also RR, *American Life*, 63–6.

32. Palmer, *Palmers*, 107–8; and RR, *Where's*, 47.

33. Quotations, *Interesting Sidelights of Broadcasting Station WOC, Davenport, Iowa* [192?], p. 6, in B. J. Palmer files, PSCD. Also p. 7.

34. Palmer mesmerized audiences in small towns, holding them in complete silence as he talked about alternatives to surgery and drugs. He thought that a spirit called INNATE existed within everyone and was a component of the "Universal Intelli-

gence." The chiropractor's manipulations released what he referred to as the "Power Within." Quotations, Palmer, *Palmers*, 156–7. Also 89, 93, 95, 139, 142, 154; and *Kokomo [Indiana] Tribune*, quoted in *The P.S.C. Lecture Bureau*, revised Jan. 1, 1920 (Davenport, Iowa: The Palmer School of Chiropractic, 1920), 24–5.

35. Quotations, Palmer, *Palmers*, 88, 92, 98 (also 137–8, 140); and Palmer, *Radio Salesmanship*, 4, in B. J. Palmer files, PSCD.

36. Edwards, *Early Reagan*, 132; Wills, *Reagan's America*, 103–4; and RR, *American Life*, 69.

37. Quotation, *Program Dedication Week*, 1, no. 27 (Oct. 8–14, 1922) (Davenport, Iowa: The Palmer School of Chiropractic, 1922), p. 37, in B. J. Palmer files, PSCD.

38. Quotation, Palmer, *Palmers*, 112. Also 110.

39. Quotation, *DET*, Aug. 21, 1934, p. 1. See also Oct. 19, 1933; March 8, 1934, p. 1; Sept. 4, 1934, p. 1; and Jan. 21, 1936, p. 2. *Radio Stars* had named Reagan one of the leading announcers.

40. See RR, *Where's*, 58–9; *DET*, Feb. 26, 1936, p. 1; and Wills, *Reagan's America*, 110, 410 (n. 1).

41. Quotations, RR, *Where's*, 59. Also ibid., 65–7.
    Reagan covered sports as a newspaper reporter, as well. As a columnist, Wills contends he adopted a muckraking style that offered the "facts behind the sham" in a world where "athletic innocence and aspiration" verged on the "religious." Wills's conclusion apparently is based on only one Reagan column. Wills, *Reagan's America*, 115, 126; for Reagan as a journalist, see also 115–31, 410 (n. 1).

42. For Leslie Howard interview, see RR, "'Dutch' Got That Date After All," *DMSR*, July 18, 1937, p. 8. See also RR, *Where's*, 58–60; and Wills, *Reagan's America*, 107, 108, 132.

43. Reagan resembled actor Ross Alexander, who had taken his life earlier at age twenty-nine. George Ward, quoted in Edwards, *Early Reagan*, 154; also 155. See also RR, "The Making of a Movie Star," *DMSR*, June 13, 1937, p. 6.

44. Quotation, RR, *Where's*, 74 (also 73).

45. Quotations, *DET*, May 20, 1937, p. 11 (also p. 1); and Herb Plambeck, quoted in Edwards, *Early Reagan*, 157; see also 151–7; and RR, *American Life*, 78–81.

3. From Rags to Riches

1. Quotations, RR, "The Making of a Movie Star," *DMSR*, June 13, 1937, p. 6. See also RR, *Where's*, 76.

2. Quotations, Rosten, *Hollywood*, 133.

3. Quotations, Schwartz, *Hollywood Writers' Wars*, 84; and Mary McCall, quoted in Rivkin, HELLO HOLLYWOOD!, 448.

4. Quotations, RR, *Where's*, 75. See also RR, *American Life*, 84.

5. Quotation, O'Brien, *Wind*, 240.

6. Warner Bros. also used Reagan's announcing abilities in *Sergeant Murphy* for a racing scene. See pressbook for *Sergeant Murphy*, pp. 6–7, reel 8, UA-SHSWM. Quotations, RR, "'Dutch' Tells What Happens," *DMSR*, Sept. 5, 1937, p. 5. See also review from *Hollywood Reporter*, quoted in *DMSR*, Aug. 22, 1937, p. 10; and RR, *American Life*, 81–7.

7. Quotations, RR, "'Dutch' Does First Scene Over Again," *DMSR*, July 4, 1937, p. 3; and RR, "'Dutch' Makes His First Scene," ibid., June 27, 1937, p. 6.

8. Quotations, Will H. Hays, radio address for the Cinematograph Trade Benev-

olent Fund of London, p. 3, for release March 16, 1944, WHHPI; and from lyrics of "Hooray for Hollywood," in *Hollywood Hotel.*

9. Pressbook for *An Angel From Texas,* 7, UA-SHSWM.

10. Quotation, Curtis Bernhardt to David Lewis, folder 4, Ronald Reagan contract files, WBAHP-USC. See pressbook for *Million Dollar Baby,* 13, UA-SHSWM. In *Cowboy From Brooklyn,* Reagan was an associate of a glib promoter played by Pat O'Brien; in *Going Places,* the son of a wealthy horse owner; in *Naughty But Nice,* a music publisher; and in *An Angel From Texas,* Wyman's husband, a shady promoter.

11. RR, "'Dutch' Tells How Movie Horse," *DMSR,* Aug. 29, 1937, p. 8.

12. Quotations, RR, "'Dutch' Got That Date After All," ibid., July 18, 1937, p. 8; and RR, "'Dutch' Pulls a Couple of Boners," July 11, 1937, p. 6.

13. Quotations, RR, "'Dutch' Tells How Movie Horse," ibid., Aug. 29, 1937, p. 8.

14. Quotations, RR, "'Dutch' Starts New Picture," ibid., Aug. 8, 1937, p. 8; and RR, "Glamorous Hollywood?" Aug. 22, 1937, p. 10.

15. Although Reagan's contract bound him to the studio for seven years, the Warners had the option every six months to drop him. Quotations, pressbook for *Sergeant Murphy,* 7, UA-SHSWM; and RR, "The Making of a Movie Star," *DMSR,* June 13, 1937, p. 6. See also pressbook for *Cowboy From Brooklyn,* UA-SHSWM; and RR, "Four Pictures Finished," *DMSR,* Oct. 3, 1937, p. 8. When *Accidents Will Happen* premiered in 1938, Iowa theater managers were told to promote Reagan as the local boy who made good. Pressbook for *Accidents Will Happen,* 6, UA-SHSWM.

16. Quotations, RR, "Pretty Margaret Lindsay," *DMSR,* Sept. 12, 1937, p. 8; and RR, "Bosses Change Their Minds," Aug. 1, 1937, p. 8.

17. Roddick, *New Deal in Entertainment,* 7–8; RR, *American Life,* 118; and Alicoate, ed., *1941 Film Daily Year Book of Motion Pictures,* 580. Charles Einfeld and Robert Taplinger headed studio public relations at this time.

18. Quotations, Niven, *Empty Horses,* 82; and Dmytryk, *It's a Hell of a Life,* 102. See also Parsons, *Gay Illiterate,* 149; and Robins, *Alien Ink,* 121–4.

19. Quotations, pressbook for *Brother Rat and a Baby,* 5, UA-SHSWM. See also Parsons, *Gay Illiterate,* 158–9; Steve Trilling to Mr. Wilder, Dec. 5, 1939, folder 4, Reagan contract files, WBAHP-USC; Trilling to Mr. De Patie, Dec. 20, 1939, ibid.; Louella Parsons Scrapbook, AMPASL; and Cannon, *Reagan,* 60–2.

20. Quotations, Parsons, *Gay Illiterate,* 159; and *Variety,* Nov. 22, 1939, quoted in Edwards, *Early Reagan,* 199 (also 200); and *Eureka College Pegasus,* Jan. 12, 1940.

21. Quotation, Maureen Reagan, *First Father,* 27.

22. Quotations, RR, "'Dutch' Tells What Happens," *DMSR,* Sept. 5, 1937, p. 5.

23. Jarrico quoted in Schwartz, *Hollywood Writers' Wars,* 103. Will Hays, always eager to accentuate the positive qualities of cinema, hailed such pictures as "vital social documents" that were "notable for their educational value." Such entertainment, Hays maintained, could also be used by educational leaders to "illustrate and emphasize social problems." Quotations, Hays, "Fifteen Years," 2. Also Hays, "Enlarging," 2. For Warner Bros. and reform, see this volume, Chapters 4 and 5.

24. See Carlisle Jones, "Biography of Harry M. Warner," undated, folder: "Harry M. Warner – Biography," box 56, JLW-USC. On the Warners' support of Franklin Roosevelt in 1932, see Jack Warner, *My First Hundred Years,* 207–8. On the significance of Czar Alexander II's assassination for east European Jews, see Howe, *World of Our Fathers,* 5–7. Between 1870 and 1914, approximately two

million Jews, 80 percent of whom came from Russia or the Austro-Hungarian Empire, migrated to the United States. Herberg, *Protestant – Catholic – Jew*, 178.

25. Quotations, "Warner Brothers," *Fortune*, 16 (Dec. 1937), 208; Van Ryn, "Warner Brother Number One," 14; O'Brien, *Wind*, 254; and Gabler, *Empire*, 193 (also 192).

26. After the actor Phil Regan. RR interview with author, Oct. 16, 1989. Quotations, "Notes on Harry M. Warner", undated, pp. 9–10, folder: "Harry M. Warner – Clips Prior to 1943," box 56, JLW-USC; and Van Ryn, "Warner Brother Number One," p. 15. See also Gabler, *Empire*, 292.

A sense of the dynamics between Jack and Harry Warner can be found in Jack Warner Jr.'s semiautobiographical novel, *Bijou Dream*, e.g., 282–3, 324–5, 365–75. The novel's story is in many ways consistent with the picture of the Warners that emerges from family correspondence in JLW-USC.

27. According to the Warners, this motto came from a story about the studio in the *New York Times*. See address given by Jack L. Warner, Sept. 21, [1945?], p. 7, Biography File, Jack Warner, AMPASL. Harry Warner quoted in *Jewish Advocate*, June 29, 1944; in *Cleveland Plain Dealer*, July 10, 1944; and in Jones, "Biography of Harry M. Warner," 2, 3.

28. Quotations, Jack Warner, *My First Hundred Years*, 122, 223; O'Brien, *Wind*, 254–5; Milton Sperling quoted in Gabler, *Empire*, 193; and Bacall, *By Myself*, 177, 253.

29. Quotations, [Jack L. Warner], "Notes for Washington Talk," [March? 1942], folder 6, box 60, JLW-USC; and Jack Warner, Jr. quoted in Gabler, *Empire*, 293.

30. On Hollywood and anti-Semitism, see Vaughn, "Morality and Entertainment," 46, 57, 62–3. On anti-Semitism in the United States during the 1930s, see Higham, "American Anti-Semitism Historically Reconsidered," in Stember et al., *Jews in the Mind of America*, 246, 248; Keller, "Jews and the Character of American Life since 1930," in ibid., 260–5; and Strong, *Organized Anti-Semitism*.

31. See Colgan, "Warner Bros.' Crusade," (doctoral thesis, 1985), 34–8, 40–1. The Warners offered different explanations for closing their German theaters. Jack maintained it was because the Nazis murdered one of their employees – an explanation Colgan doubts. During World War II, Harry told government investigators that Warner Bros., in its effort to develop sound pictures during the 1920s, invested several million dollars in German patents. Warner traveled to Germany frequently to attend to the company's interests and became convinced after Hitler's rise that "the Germans under no circumstances could be trusted." Presumably these experiences led to the decision to close operations. See Jack Warner, *My First Hundred Years*, 249. Quotation, summary of Warner's remarks, in statement by Harry Warner, Nov. 27, 1942, box 1164, RG 159, NAS.

32. After the death of the Warners' father in 1935, the United States government also sued the brothers to collect taxes connected with the sale of their father's stock in early 1936. See Colgan, "Warner Bros.' Crusade," 69–70; and Steele, *Propaganda*, 155–6.

33. Harry M. Warner to Mr. President, Sept. 5, 1939, box 4, OF 73, Franklin D. Roosevelt Papers (hereafter cited as FDR Papers), FDRL. Warner had just returned from Europe, where air raid precautions necessitated blackouts and threatened a total loss of revenue from British and French theaters.

34. See Jack Warner, *My First Hundred Years*, 275; and Colgan, "Warner Bros.' Crusade," 246.

35. The influx of political refugees from Europe into Hollywood predated the Third

Reich. Hitler's rise accelerated this migration. The Warners hoped to persuade and bring to the United States "all the great leaders, unappreciated and unwanted in their native lands." With this flood of new arrivals during the 1930s, "Hollywood became a kind of Athens," S. N. Behrman wrote. "It was as crowded with artists as Renaissance Florence. It was a Golden Era." Quotations, Gladys Lloyd Robinson, "Thomas Mann in Hollywood," [April 9, 1938], in "Scrapbook – 1938," JLW-USC; and Behrman, *Tribulations,* 163. See also Ceplair and Englund, *Inquisition in Hollywood,* 94–8; and Erika and Klaus Mann, *Escape to Life,* 265–81.

36. Quotations, Robinson reporting Mann's description to her, in Robinson, "Thomas Mann in Hollywood." See also Erika and Klaus Mann, *Escape to Life,* 266; *Thomas Mann Diaries, 1918–1939,* 297; and Barnouw, *Weimar Intellectuals,* 140–1.

37. Mann quoted in Robinson, "Thomas Mann in Hollywood." Mann, who was suspected of being sympathetic to communism, was under surveillance by the FBI in 1938. See Mitgang, *Dangerous Dossiers,* 80–4.

38. Colgan, "Warner Bros.' Crusade," 42, 49–50, 53.

39. Quotations, "Warner Brothers," *Fortune* (Dec. 1937), 220; Harry M. Warner, address to the American Legion, Sept. 19, 1938, FDRL (emphasis in the original text); Jack Warner to Doc Salomon, Feb. 10, 1939, box 59, folder 10, JLW-USC. See also Colgan, "Warner Bros.' Crusade," 50–1. For other members of the Hollywood Committee of Fifty-Six, chaired by Melvyn Douglas, see box 1, Melvyn Douglas Papers, SHSWM.

40. Quotations, Harry M. Warner, address to the American Legion, Sept. 19, 1938, pp. 2–3, 6–8, box 4, OF 73, FDR Papers, FDRL; and Harry M. Warner, "United We Survive, Divided We Fall!" p. 13, Address made June 5, 1940, to six thousand Warner Bros. employees and their wives; folder: "Harry M. Warner – Speeches & Interviews," box 56, JLW-USC.

41. Quotations, Jack Warner in *NYT,* Jan. 15, 1939, section 9, p. 5; Harry M. Warner, "Hollywood's Obligations"; Harry Warner quoted in Colgan, "Warner Bros.' Crusade," 25; and Harry Warner, Address to the American Legion, Sept. 19, 1938, p. 7, box 4, OF 73, FDR Papers, FDRL.

42. For Reagan's social commentary pictures see this volume, Chapter 4.

43. The studio's best-known and most controversial picture in this regard was *Confessions of a Nazi Spy* (1938). For a list of spy films compiled by the Hays Office, see Will H. Hays to A. D. Lasker, Dec. 10, 1938, and Roger Albright to Hays, May 13, 1942, WHHPI. See also Dick, *Star-Spangled Screen,* 95–6.

44. Jack Warner quoted in *NYT,* Jan. 15, 1939, section 9, p. 5.
   Warner Bros. used history in action films, full-length features (see this volume, Chapters 6 and 7), and patriotic shorts. Harry Warner defended the accuracy of the latter, but many of them spoke to contemporary concerns. They carried titles such as *The Declaration of Independence* (1938), *The Bill of Rights* (1939), and *The Monroe Doctrine* (1939). They portrayed such personalities as Patrick Henry (*Give Me Liberty,* 1936), Stonewall Jackson (*Under Southern Stars,* 1936), Abraham Lincoln (*Lincoln in the White House,* 1939), and Theodore Roosevelt (*Teddy the Rough Rider,* 1937). *Sons of Liberty* (1939) told the story of Haym Salomon, a merchant and banker from Poland who was of Jewish–Portuguese ancestry, and who helped finance the American Revolution.

45. See this volume, Chapters 6–8.

46. This survey ranked Reagan tenth among the newcomers, ahead of Jane Wyman (twelfth), John Wayne (thirteenth), and Lucille Ball (forty-fourth) but behind

Jeffrey Lynn (first), Lana Turner (fifth), George Murphy (sixth), and Ingrid Bergman (eighth). In April 1941, a survey of "dark horses" who showed the "greatest promise of becoming big marquee names before 1944," ranked Reagan fourth. See Audience Research Institute, Report 20, "Dark Horses" (June 1940), [p. 4], in *Gallup Looks at the Movies*, microfilm reel 4; and Audience Research Institute, Report 78 (April 24, 1941), in ibid.

47. Quotation, Jane and Ronald [Reagan] to Jack [Warner], Sept. 5, 1941, folder 3, Reagan contract file, WBAHP-USC. For Reagan's contracts, see folder: "Ronald Reagan – Artist," ibid. On his elevation to stardom, see *DET*, Jan. 23, 1941, p. 1.

48. See *Seventh Audit of Marquee Value* (July 1941), and *Eighth Audit of Marquee Value* (Oct. 1941), in *Gallup Looks at the Movies*, microfilm reel 1; and *Ninth Audit of Marquee Value* (Jan. 1942), ibid., reel 2.

49. See, for example, *Ninth Audit of Marquee Value* (Jan. 1942), "Analysis by Sex, Age, Income," in *Gallup Looks at the Movies*, reel 2. Quotation, *Third Audit of Marquee Value* (Oct. 1940), ibid., reel 1.

50. Quotations, from fan magazine (unnamed, undated), Reagan Scrapbook, ECAE; and "Command Performance," in fan magazine (unnamed, undated), ibid.

51. Quotations, RR, "How To Make Yourself Important," ECAE.

52. Quotations, pressbook for *Love Is on the Air*, 3, 5, UA-SHSWM. See also pressbook for *Code of the Secret Service*, 9, ibid. Other pre–World War II films in which Reagan was given an athletic background included *Hell's Kitchen* (hockey) and *Brother Rat* (baseball).

53. Quotations, "Command Performance," unnamed, undated fan magazine, Reagan Scrapbook, ECAE. On Reagan as government agent and military man, see this volume, Chapters 6–9.

54. This evaluation was made by Warner Bros. general counsel, Roy Obringer, in 1944, as the studio anticipated Reagan's return from military service. Quotation, R. J. Obringer to Ralph Lewis, Sept. 20, 1944, folder 3, Reagan contract file, WBAHP-USC.

55. *DET*, Sept. 11, 1941, p. 5.

56. Quotations, Parsons, *Gay Illiterate*, 162 (also 161); and *CHA*, Sept. 16, 1941, copy in Parsons Scrapbook, AMPASL. See also Walgreen, *Never a Dull Day*, 298.

57. Quotations, *CHA*, Sept. 16, 1941, Parsons Scrapbook, AMPASL.

58. Quotation, ibid. See also *DET*, Sept. 15, 1941, p. 2; Parsons, *Gay Illiterate*, 150–60; and Louella Parsons to W. R. Hearst, Sept. 18, 1941, folder: "Louella Parsons," carton 35, W. R. Hearst Papers, BL-UCB.

4. Reform

1. Other writers have discussed Warner Bros.' social consciousness films during the 1930s but none have used the Warner Bros. archives, the PCA files, or analyzed Reagan's movies. On Warner Bros. and the New Deal, see Roddick, *New Deal in Entertainment*, 12, 65, 73, 119–20, 173–4, 249, 252; Roffman and Purdy, *Hollywood Social Problem Film*, 84–8; Bergman, *We're in the Money*, 92–109; Higham, *Warner Brothers* 2, 138 (Higham maintained that Warner Bros. sought not only to entertain but also "to instruct," ibid., 1); and Jack Warner, *My First Hundred Years*, 218–24.

2. Quotation, Jack Warner, *My First Hundred Years*, 208. Also ibid., 207–8, 216; "Warner Brothers," *Fortune* (Dec. 1937), 212; Harry Warner to Roosevelt, June 20, 1932, Papers of the Democratic National Committee, FDRL; H. Warner to Roosevelt, Aug. 8, 1932, ibid.; *LAE*, undated clipping in ibid.; and Roffman and Purdy, *Hollywood Social Problem Film*, 84.

3. Quotation, Hugh S. Johnson to Jack Warner, Feb. 13, 1934, "Scrapbook – 1929–1934," JLW-USC. See copy of letter, probably Will Hays to Jack Warner [July 6, 1933], WHHPI; and *NYT,* Feb. 16, 1933, p. 2.
4. Gabler, *Empire,* 318; Colgan, "Warner Bros.' Crusade," 69–71; and *Variety* (March 10, 1937), 5. On Harry Warner's disenchantment with the New Deal, see "Warner Brothers," 212.
5. Quotations, RR, *Where's,* 139.
6. Harry Warner quoted in *LAE,* Feb. 10, 1936, in Harry Warner Scrapbook, JLW-USC.
7. Quotations, David Todd to Stephen Early, Oct. 14, 1933, box 2, OF 73, FDR Papers, FDRL; and Payne Fund Studies, quoted in de Grazia and Newman, *Banned Films,* 38 (also 36–9). See also Mitchell, *Children and Movies,* 147–8.
8. Quotation, Forman, *Our Movie Made Children,* 196 (also 4, 196–213). For the Payne Fund Studies, and for social science research dealing with film and children, see Martin, *Hollywood's Movie Commandments,* 25; Jowett, *Film,* 210–32 (esp., 220–9); Sklar, *Movie-Made America,* 122–40, 173, 324–5; Considine, "Depiction of Adolescent Sexuality" (doctoral thesis, 1981), 25–41; and Wartella and Reeves, "Historical Trends," 118–33. At the national level, the Brookhart Bill, which would have outlawed block booking, was introduced in early 1928, but never passed. Vaughn, "Morality and Entertainment," 44–5.
9. Facey, *Legion of Decency,* 58.
10. Hays, *Memoirs,* 459. For other authorities, in addition to Adler, to whom Hays turned, see "Authoritative Statements Concerning the Screen and Behavior," MPPDA, comp. [Dec. 1934], 13–19, WHHPI; "Rotary Interviews Will H. Hays," 11–12; and Milliken, "Memorandum on the Question," Dec. 11, 1933. On Warner Bros. economic status, see Warner Bros. Pictures, Inc., "A Financial Review and Brief History, 1923–1945" (Jan. 15, 1946), 28, WBAHP-P.
11. Quotations, *LAE,* Feb. 10, 1936, copy in Harry Warner Scrapbook, JLW-USC. See also this volume, Chapter 6.
12. Quotations, *Hollywood Reporter,* April 15, 1937, p. 7. For Reagan's signing, see ibid., p. 2. Also Colgan, "Warner Bros.' Crusade," 47.
13. For the view that Flynn was acting as a German agent, see Higham, *Errol Flynn,* 19, 135–40. Flynn claimed that Hearst had commissioned him to write articles. See Flynn, *My Wicked, Wicked Ways,* 217, 231. Also Vice Consul Clifton P. English to Consul General [Monnett Davis], Buenos Aires, Feb. 11, 1940, Errol Flynn FBI file, FBI-FOIA, SHSWM; George H. Adams to Secretary of State, Feb. 10, 1940, ibid.; FBI report, file no. 65–31, March 28, 1940, ibid.; and FBI report, "Dr. Hermann Frederick Erben with aliases," March 18, 1940 [?], p. 10, NY file no. 65–1715, ibid.
14. Quotations, Jack Warner to Charlie Einfeld, April 15 and 16, 1937, folder 12, box 58, JLW-USC.
15. Quotations, Warner to Einfeld, April 15, 1937, ibid.; and Grad Sears to Warner, April 22, 1937, folder 1, box 59, ibid.
16. Quotation, Hearst to Jack Warner, April 22, 1937, folder 1, box 59, JLW-USC. See also "Fight Red Movies," *CHE,* April 20, 1937, p. 16; Warner to W. R. [Hearst], April 22, 1937, folder 1, box 59, JLW-USC; and Colgan, "Warner Bros.' Crusade," 177–8.
17. Quotations, memorandum, "Compensating Moral Values" [June 13, 1934], [pp. 1, 2], WHHPI.
18. Quotations, memorandum attached to Breen to Lord, Dec. 5, 1937, pp. 3 (emphasis in original text), 4, unmarked folder, Daniel A. Lord Papers, JMPA-STL.

19. Breen quoting encyclical "Atheistic Communism," memorandum attached to Breen to Lord, Dec. 5, 1937, p. 6, ibid.
20. J. D. Battle to Will Hays, Aug. 29, 1934, PCA file for *Black Fury,* AMPASL; Hays to Battle, Sept. 4, 1934, ibid.; Hays to H. M. Warner, Sept. 4, 1934, ibid.; Breen to Jack Warner, Sept. 12, 1934, ibid. The Hays Office eliminated references to communism and changed the "radical" tone in other pictures too. See, for example, PCA files for *Heroes for Sale* (Warner Bros., 1933) and *Winterset* (RKO, 1936), AMPASL.
21. The PCA charted how each movie portrayed lawyers, judges, doctors, bankers, police, and legislators. This effort to control the portrayal of authority figures helps to explain the tone of the decade's social-problem pictures. Students of Warner Bros.' pictures have indicted the studio for not providing a more penetrating critique of American society during the depression, arguing that the movies blamed the 1930s crisis simply on individual evil. Films were given "contemporary relevance by injecting occasional scenes or comments about the Depression in a story that was otherwise asocial." Quotation, Roffman and Purdy, *Hollywood Social Problem Film,* 82. See also ibid., 109–10; and Bergman, *We're in the Money,* 101, 103–4, 107–8.
22. Quotations, RR, *Where's,* 53–4; also 42, 52; and RR, *American Life,* 66–9.
23. Quotations, RR, *American Life,* 66; RR, *Where's,* 139; and Maureen Reagan, *First Father,* 117. See also Edwards, *Early Reagan,* 149; and Wills, *Reagan's America,* 108.
24. Quotations, Edward G. Robinson to D. R. Taft, Dec. 22, 1938, box 29, Edward G. Robinson Papers, DL-USC.
25. Reporter films such as *Love Is on the Air* (a remake of Paul Muni's 1934 film *Hi Nellie*) and *Nine Lives Are Not Enough* (based on Jerome Odlum's novel of the same title) related both to the era's social consciousness and gangster films. See Roy Chanslor, "Hi Nellie," *Liberty Magazine* (Sept. 16, 1933); and Roffman and Purdy, *Hollywood Social Problem Film,* 40–5.
26. Reagan's character also combated crime in four films in which he played a treasury agent. See this volume, Chapter 6. Reagan played in only one contemporary crime film for Warner Bros. after World War II, *Storm Warning* (1951).
27. Fictitious headlines or magazine stories with Reagan's picture appeared in *Love Is on the Air, Nine Lives Are Not Enough, Knute Rockne – All American* (1940), *International Squadron* (1941), and *That Hagen Girl* (1947). Quotations, "Temporary Script," by [Fred] Niblo [,Jr.], May, 1941, for *Nine Lives Are Not Enough,* folder 3, box 286, series 1.2, UA-SHSWM.
28. See minutes, Warner Bros. board of directors meetings, Sept. 27, 1938; April 27, 1939; Sept. 8, 1939; April 30, 1940; Aug. 20, 1940; Nov. 13, 1940; and Jan. 29, 1941, WBAHP-P.
29. Quotation, from film, SHSWM. Reagan earned $600 for *Girls on Probation,* which took scarcely more than a month to make. Critics thought he had done "well enough" with a "routine role" as a "sympathetic hero." Quotations, *NYJA,* Oct. 20, 1938, in PCA file for *Girls on Probation,* AMPASL.
30. Roffman and Purdy, *Hollywood Social Problem Film,* 136–7, 141–2; Bergman, *We're in the Money,* 160; Pells, *Radical Visions,* 273; and Roddick, *New Deal in Entertainment,* 131–2. Also Breen to J. L. Warner, Jan. 19, 1938, and Walter MacEwen to [Hal] Wallis, April 4, 1938, reprinted in Behlmer, ed., *Inside Warner Bros.,* 66–7.
31. Quotations from opening scene of *Angels With Dirty Faces,* "Final" script, May 27, 1938, iii [p. 1], John Wexley Papers, SHSWM.

32. Quotations, from film, SHSWM.
33. Quotations, pressbook for *Angels Wash Their Faces*, 17, ibid.
34. Quotations, Breen to Jack Warner, Sept. 15, 1938, and Feb. 10, 1939, PCA file for *Angels Wash Their Faces*, AMPASL.
35. See "Rev. Temporary" script for *Hell's Kitchen*, by [Crane] Wilbur, Nov. 26, 1938, folder 5, box 177, series 1.2, pp. 121–4, UA-SHSWM; Breen to Jack Warner, Dec. 14, 1938, PCA file for *Hell's Kitchen*, AMPASL; Breen to Jack Warner, May 27, 1937, PCA file for *Love Is on the Air*, ibid.; and Breen to Jack Warner, June 3 and 10, 1941, PCA file for *Nine Lives Are Not Enough*, ibid. See also Breen reaction to Reagan's Brass Bancroft films, this volume, Chapter 6. If Reagan's films were representative, the PCA worked to limit violence to women. See Breen to Jack Warner, April 29 and May 31, 1938, PCA file for *Girls on Probation*, ibid.; Breen to Warner, Nov. 8, 1949; and Breen to Warner, Jan. 11, 1950, PCA file for *Storm Warning*, ibid.
36. On arson, see Martin, *Hollywood's Movie Commandments*, 126. See also Breen to Jack Warner, Dec. 14, 1938, and memo from G. S. [Geoffrey Shurlock], Dec. 15, 1938, PCA file for *Hell's Kitchen*, AMPASL; Breen to Warner, Feb. 10, 1939, PCA file for *Angels Wash Their Faces*, ibid.; Breen to Warner, Oct. 7, 1941, PCA file for *Juke Girl*, ibid.; and Breen to Warner, Aug. 27, 1937, PCA file for *Accidents Will Happen*, ibid. Occasionally, a movie such as *Accidents Will Happen* would pass Breen's office only to be condemned by state officials. New York educational leaders denounced this film because it showed a successful scheme to swindle an insurance company.
37. See PCA files for *Hell's Kitchen* and *Angels Wash Their Faces*, AMPASL.
38. See Estell Watson to Warner Bros., June 18, 1942, story file for *Juke Girl*, WBAHP-USC; Charles Einfeld to Jack Warner, Dec. 21, 1942, ibid.; Ulric Bell to Einfeld, Dec. 26, 1942, ibid.; Einfeld or Owen Jones [?] to Warner, Dec. 28, 1942, ibid.; and *NYT*, Aug. 23, 1942, section 8, p. 3. For other films pulled from distribution or altered to avoid offending Latin American audiences, see ibid.
39. Da Silva also appeared with Reagan in *Nine Lives Are Not Enough*.
40. Pratt said that few farmers benefited from the federal government's effort to improve living conditions and housing in the area defined the "absolute low in America's rural slums." See "Temporary, 'Jook Girl,'" by Pratt, May 1, 1941, folder 4, box 210, series 1.2, pp. 1–3, 6, UA-SHSWM. Quotation (John Becher quoted), Pratt, "Land of the Jook," 40 (see also 20–1).
41. Jerry Wald to Hal Wallis, April 30, 1941; Bob Fellows to Wallis, May 2, 1941; Bill Cagney to Wallis, May 8, 1941; Richard Macaulay to Wallis, May 2, 1941; R. J. Obringer to Wallis, Sept. 29, Oct. 1, and Oct. 2, 1941; Wallis to Obringer, Oct. 2, 1941, story file for *Juke Girl*, WBAHP-USC.
42. Quotation, Wallis and Higham, *Starmaker*, 29. See also ibid., 40; and Wallis, "Modern Science and the Motion Picture," 2.
43. Between 1930 and 1934 the number of lynchings in the United States peaked and efforts to outlaw such activity increased. Hollywood's depictions of mob activity during the 1930s and early 1940s varied. Movies like *The Secret Six* (1932) and *This Day and Age* (1933) favorably portrayed vigilantism and protofascist justice. By the middle of the decade, such films as *Fury* (1936), *Legion of Terror* (1936), *Black Legion* (1936), and *They Won't Forget* (1937) pointed out the naïveté of vigilante groups and condemned the mob as a subverter of law and order. Later such movies as Frank Capra's *Mr. Smith Goes to Washington* (1939) and *Meet John Doe* (1941) warned the public of dictators.
44. Reagan's pictures suggest that the changes in the portrayals of mobs in 1930s films may not have been as clear-cut as other writers have suggested. See Roffman

and Purdy, *Hollywood Social Problem Film*, 66–8, 165–78; and Bergman, *We're in the Money*, 110–22. On worries about the reaction of Mexican censors to lynch scenes, see Breen to Jack Warner, Nov. 4, 1941; Breen to Warner, Oct. 17, 1941, PCA file for *Juke Girl*, AMPASL; and unsigned [Harry M. Warner] to Charles Einfeld, Dec. 16, 1942, story file for *Juke Girl*, WBAHP-USC.

45. Quotation, Erens, *Jew in American Cinema*, 126 (Erens commenting on a recurring theme in Jewish cinema and theater during the early 1930s).
46. See pressbook for *Accidents Will Happen*, 6, ibid.

5. Stereotypes and Taboos

1. Quotation (emphasis in original text), from memorandum attached to Breen to Lord, Dec. 5, 1937, pp. 1, 3, unmarked folder, Lord Papers, JMPA-STL.
2. Breen to Maurice McKenzie, Sept. 16, 1937, PCA file for *Artists and Models*, AMPASL.
3. Quotations, Mrs. Alonzo Richardson to Breen, Aug. 31, 1937, PCA file for *Artists and Models*, ibid.; and Dolph Frantz to Adolph Zukor, Aug. 25, 1937, ibid. On Hays and Breen, see Hays to Breen, Sept. 27, 1937, PCA file for *Artists and Models*, ibid.; Breen to Hammell, Sept. 6, 1937, ibid.; and Breen to Hammell, Oct. 15, 1937, PCA file for *The Big Broadcast of 1938*, ibid.
4. Robeson quotations, *NYT*, Sept. 23, 1942, p. 28. Robeson was an exception among black actors, the only one to have starred in a prominent film produced by a major studio. In 1938, one study estimated that he earned between $2,000 and $3,000 per week. See Chapter 12 of *Motion Pictures and Negro Actors* [Research Study Compiled by Workers of the Writers Program of the Works Projects Administration in New York City for "Negroes in New York," 1936–41], microfilm reel 3, NYPL-SCRBC.
5. *NYT*, Jan. 23, 1940, p. 16.
6. Quotation, "Hell's Kitchen," screenplay by Crane Wilbur, folder 3, box 177, series 1.2, UA-SHSWM. Also Edwards, *Early Reagan*, 203.
7. Warner was not the only individual at the studio who made ethnic or racial slurs. When Reagan arrived in Hollywood and went to see casting director Max Arnow, he wore a new white sport coat and blue pants. "Where the hell did you get that coat?" inquired Arnow, who told Reagan that he looked "like a Filipino." Reagan recounted this episode to newspaper readers in Iowa. Text quotations, Jack Warner, *My First Hundred Years*, 9. Also ibid., 40, 62–3 (on blacks); and Flynn, *My Wicked, Wicked Ways*, 295. Note quotation, RR, "The Making of a Movie Star," *DMSR*, June 13, 1937, p. 6.
8. Quotations, pressbook, *Code of the Secret Service*, 10, UA-SHSWM; and "Final Script" [by Lee Katz and Dean Franklin], folder 6, box 68, RG 1, UA-SHSWM. Similar portrayals of Mexican police and merchants were made in the final script. For Reagan's embarrassment over the film, see RR, *Where's*, 83–4.
9. Quotations, "Temporary, 'Jook Girl,'" by Pratt, May 1, 1941, pp. 16, 4, 9, folder 4, box 210, series 1.2, UA-SHSWM. See also "Revised temporary, 'Jook Girl,'" Gamet and Bezzerides, Aug. 26, 1941, folder 7, box 210, series 1.2, ibid.
10. Quotations, Breen to Jack Warner, Dec. 7, 1938, PCA file for *Code of the Secret Service*, AMPASL. In Reagan's film *Stallion Road* (1947), Breen insisted the Mexican characters speak normally rather than in broken English to avoid offending Mexican audiences. See Breen to Warner, Nov. 5, 1945; and Breen to Warner, Feb. 12, 1946, PCA file for *Stallion Road*, ibid.
11. For *Accidents Will Happen*, Breen insisted that a lawyer in the film "not be characterized as a Jew." Quotation, Breen to Jack Warner, Aug. 31, 1937, PCA

file for *Accidents Will Happen,* AMPASL. See also Breen to Warner, Aug. 27, 1937, ibid.; Breen to Warner, May 27, 1937, PCA file for *Love Is on the Air,* ibid.; Breen to Warner, Oct. 7, 1941, PCA file for *Juke Girl,* ibid., and this volume, Chapter 6 for *Murder in the Air.*

12. The lack of black influence in Hollywood, one might speculate, resulted from the fact that African-Americans did not buy large numbers of movie tickets during the late 1930s. Theaters oriented to black audiences existed, to be sure, and they would become more important economically later. In addition, a potentially noteworthy African market, still largely under colonial control, existed by 1944, with almost a thousand theaters capable of seating more than a half million people. See Golden, comp., *Motion Picture Markets – 1944: Africa,* NYPL-SCRBC.

13. Quotation, script for *Hollywood Hotel,* "Second Revised Final," by Wald, Leo, Macauley, Aug. 8 to Nov. 4, 1937, p. 11, folder 9, box 183, series 1.2, UA-SHSWM. See also film, reel 1. Blacks also had brief appearances as either maids or doormen in such Reagan films as *Brother Rat* (1938) and *Naughty But Nice* (1939).

14. Quotations, *Hollywood Hotel* script, "Revised Final," "Hollywood Bandwagon," by Wald, Leo, Macaulay (July 21 to Aug. 16, 1937), p. 132, folder 8, box 183, series 1.2, UA-SHSWM.

15. Quotations, *Hollywood Hotel,* dialogue transcript (1938), pp. 4, 5, reel 5-A, box 32, series 1.3, UA-SHSWM.

16. Quotations from film, SHSWM.

17. Quotation, *Going Places,* dialogue transcript, 77–8, reel 7, series 1.3, UA-SHSWM. See also the film, SHSWM. This film, in which Armstrong played a stablehand, featured Armstrong's jazz band and several black singers, including Sullivan, in a maid's uniform. It perpetuated images of blacks in menial jobs, showed them as childlike and perhaps licentious, and emphasized a fondness for controversial music (in this case, swing). During Armstrong's first appearance in the picture, two white males addressed him as "Uncle Tom."

18. In addition to *Going Places,* such other prewar Reagan movies as *Sergeant Murphy* and *Accidents Will Happen* disparaged the intelligence of African-Americans.

19. Quotations, Breen to Jack Warner, July 6, 1940, story file for *Santa Fe Trail,* WBAHP-USC. Also, this volume, Chapter 7; and Pratt, "Land of the Jook," 40.

20. Quotations, RR, *American Life,* 31 (also 22, 30–1); RR, *Where's,* 8 (also 9); and Jack Reagan quoted in Zeitlin, "Ronald Reagan," 27 (also 91), Reagan Scrapbook, ECAE.

21. Quotations from film, SHSWM. In *Sergeant Murphy,* Reagan's character was sympathetic to a black stablehand.

22. Reagan's characters had little or no romantic interests in *Knute Rockne – All American* and *Desperate Journey.* In the first of the Brass Bancroft films, *Secret Service of the Air,* he had a girlfriend, but in later films the romantic interest either disappeared or, as in the case of *Code of the Secret Service,* went undeveloped. "Looks like farewell to romance," Brass told Saxby in *Secret Service of the Air,* as duty to country took precedence over female companionship. In the Bancroft pictures, Reagan's sidekick, Gabby, was more likely to become involved with women, as in *Murder in the Air.*

23. Reagan's character in *Dark Victory* was supposed to be "as full of chatter as a parrot or a woman." Quotations, dialogue script, *Sergeant Murphy,* 13, 16, 15, 17, UA-SHSWM; "Revised Final" of "The Murder Plane," by Raymond Schrock, Sept. 12, 1938, p. 11a, folder 6, box 344, RG 1, series 1.2; and from early draft of "The Murder Plane," by Schrock, p. 18, folder 4, box 344, ibid.;

from the film *Million Dollar Baby*, ibid.; and from *Dark Victory* screenplay by Robinson, July 1, 1938 (unfinished script), folder 6, box 89, series 1.2, ibid.

24. Quotations, pressbook for *Naughty But Nice*, 7, UA-SHSWM; see also 21, 24.
25. *Naughty But Nice* also promoted music (jitterbug and swing) in which "inhibitions were cast to the four corners of the sound stage." Quotations, ibid., 14, 21 (also 19); and pressbook for *Cowboy from Brooklyn*, 12, UA-SHSWM.
26. Quotations, pressbook for *Brother Rat and a Baby*, 9, UA-SHSWM; "Jane Wyman's Hair Brings Luck," in pressbook for *An Angel from Texas*, 10, ibid.; and "Ronald Reagan Easy to Please," ibid. See also pressbook for *Brother Rat*, 16, ibid.
27. Quotations, pressbook for *Dark Victory*, 10, 12, 13, 14, 16, 21, ibid.; and Orry-Kelly to Hal Wallis, Oct. 17, 1938, story file for *Dark Victory*, WBAHP-USC.
28. Breen to Jack Warner, Oct. 17, 1938, PCA file for *Dark Victory*, AMPASL.
29. After World War II, Reagan appeared in *Stallion Road, That Hagen Girl, Voice of the Turtle, John Loves Mary*, and *Night Unto Night*. Incest, premarital sex, suicide, and the depiction of marriage were at issue in one or more of these films. See this volume, Chapter 18. On Hollywood films and psychoanalysis or psychiatry, see Donald Ogden Stewart, "Watch Out for a Trend," *NYT*, May 4, 1941, section 10, p. 4.
30. Quotations, Robinson's reminiscences, McGilligan, ed., *Backstory*, 305. See also Friedrich, *City of Nets*, 86.
31. Quotations from Production Code.
32. Quotations, open letter to editor, unnamed publication, May 25, 1934, copy in office minutes, Warner Bros. board of directors minutes, volume 3, WBAHP-P.
33. Breen quoted in Vizzard, *See No Evil*, 50.
34. Quotation, ibid., 36.
35. Quotations, ibid., 104, 103, 52, 55, 75.
36. Quotations, memorandum attached to Breen to Lord, Dec. 5, 1937, Lord Papers, JMPA-STL.
37. The story (a caricature of Hollywood studios), based on a successful Broadway play written by Sam and Bella Spewack, allowed Reagan to work with James Cagney and Pat O'Brien. See Breen to Francis Harmon, Dec. 31, 1937, PCA file for *Boy Meets Girl*, AMPASL. See also additional correspondence in this file; and temporary script for *Boy Meets Girl*, March 25, 1937, pp. 35–8, folder 3, box 4, series 1.2, UA-SHSWM.
    The code prohibited scenes of childbirth, and Breen rarely permitted discussion of that topic. As for pregnancy, he allowed reference where necessary to a plot but usually prohibited extended commentary about it.
38. See Breen to Jack Warner, June 1, 1937, PCA file for *Love Is on the Air*, AMPASL; Breen to Warner, June 17, 1940, PCA file for *Tugboat Annie Sails Again*, ibid.; Breen to Warner, Dec. 4, 1942, and Breen to Warner, Feb. 25, 1943, PCA file for *This Is the Army*; and "Second Revised Script," 121–2, Oct. 6, 1938, of Schrock's "The Murder Plane" [*Secret Service of the Air*], folder 5, box 344, RG 1, series 1.2, UA-SHSWM. Breen rejected the initial script of *Million Dollar Baby* because the female lead was shown drunk. See Breen to Hays, March 29, 1941, PCA file for *Million Dollar Baby*, AMPASL; and Breen to Hays, March 31, 1941, ibid.
39. Quotations, "Compensating Moral Values" [June 13, 1934], WHHPI.
40. Quotation, Bellamann, *Kings Row*, 337; also 276. Although the code discouraged treatment of suicide, it appeared in several films in addition to *Kings Row*, including *Night Unto Night* and *That Hagen Girl*. It was most thoroughly discussed in the PCA for Reagan's movie *Santa Fe Trail*, in which John Brown's teenage son, in an early version of the script, kills himself. Breen, fearful of possible influence on young viewers, called the scene "shockingly offensive," and

"anti-social." Breen to Jack Warner, July 11, 1940, PCA file for *Santa Fe Trail*, AMPASL.

41. Quotation, RR, *Where's*, 4.
42. Quotations, ibid., 6, 103.
43. Quotation, Jack [Warner] to Mr. Wallis, May 23, 1941, picture file for *Kings Row*, folder 5, WBAHP-USC. See also David Lewis to Hal Wallis, Sept. 4, 1941, ibid.; memorandum to Jack L. Warner, Jan. 19 [1941], ibid.; and RR, *Where's*, 103.
44. Quotation, Breen to Jack Warner, April 22, 1941, PCA file for *Kings Row*, AMPASL.
45. Quotations, from "Reasons Underlying The General Principles," Production Code; from a statement prepared on the PCA's action on *Kings Row*, undated, p. 4, in PCA file for *Kings Row*, AMPASL; Breen to Warner, April 24, 1941, ibid.; and PCA to J. Warner, July 18, 1941, ibid.
46. Breen to J. L. Warner, April 24, 1941, picture file for *Kings Row*, folder 5, WBAHP-USC.
47. *Hollywood Hotel* featured a male dress designer, and in *Angels Wash Their Faces*, the mayor had an effeminate secretary named Gildersleeve. In both films, Breen warned Jack Warner against characterizing these figures as "pansies." In *Boy Meets Girl*, Breen required the studio to eliminate the word "fairies." Breen also objected to portraying a character in *Tugboat Annie Sails Again* as a "pansy." Breen to Jack Warner, July 23, 1937, PCA file of *Hollywood Hotel*, AMPASL; Breen to Warner, Feb. 10, 1939, PCA file for *Angels Wash Their Faces*, ibid.; Breen to Warner, March 30, 1937, PCA file for *Boy Meets Girl*, ibid.; and Breen to Warner, June 17, 1940, PCA file for *Tugboat Annie Sails Again*, ibid.
48. The novel suggested that Drake McHugh had bisexual tendencies, having perhaps had a sexual relationship with Jamie when the two were boys. Jamie continued to hold a physical attraction for Drake later although Drake came to believe such feelings abnormal, if not perverse. See Bellamann, *Kings Row*, 7–8, 175, 383, 386, 396. Quotations from film, SHSWM. See also Breen to J. L. Warner, April 24, 1941, picture file for *Kings Row*, folder 5, WBAHP-USC; and Wallis to [David] Lewis, Sept. 23, 1941, ibid.

6. The Inertia Projector

1. For additional literature related to this chapter, see Vaughn, "Spies," 355–80.
2. Quotations, testimony of Harry M. Warner, Sept. 25, 1941, 343, Clark *Hearings* (also ibid., 340); Jack Warner quotations, Warner, *My First Hundred Years*, 259; and RR, *American Life*, 89. See also pressbook for *Murder in the Air*, 6, UA-SHSWM. Other early Reagan films based in part on newspaper stories included *Sergeant Murphy* and *Accidents Will Happen*.
3. Gangster movies date back at least to D. W. Griffith's *The Musketeers of Pig Alley* (Biograph, 1912), but they became prominent with Paramount's *Underworld* (1927) and *The Racket* (1928). See Tuska, *Dark Cinema*, 131–6; Bergman, *We're in the Money*, 4–13; Roffman and Purdy, *Hollywood Social Problem Film*, 15–20; Jowett, *Film*, 206; Jowett, "Bullets, Beer and the Hays Office," 57–75.
4. Quotations, Cummings, "A Twelve Point Program," 24; Cummings, "Law Enforcement as a Profession," 55; Cummings, "The Lessons of the Crime Conference," 59; and WHH [Will H. Hays] to Harry Warner, March 1935, story file, *G-Men*, folder 2057, WBAHP-USC. See also Cummings to Hays, March 1, 1935, ibid.; Powers, *G-Men*, xvi; Hays, *Memoirs*, 457; Powers, "One G-Man's Family," 474–7; and Powers, "The Attorney General and the G-Man," 329–46.

5. Quotations, *SFE*, April 25, 1935, copy in Warner Bros. FBI file: "'See' References," FBI-FOIA, SHSWM; and Hoover to H. M. Warner, Sept. 29, 1935, Warner Bros. FBI file, ibid. See also Hoover to John G. Bradley, April 17, 1935, ibid.; E. P. Guinane to Director, April 25, 1935, ibid.; clippings from *SFE* and *SFCB* for April 23–5, 1935, in ibid.; and File Memo, W. L. M., March 28, 1935, box 2, OF 73, FDR Papers, FDRL.

6. Quotation, Breen to Jack Warner, Feb. 14, 1935, PCA file for *G-Men*, AMPASL. See also Powers, *G-Men*, xvii–xviii, 74; Roddick, *New Deal in Entertainment*, 108–10; Bergman, *We're in the Money*, 83–8; and Reilly, "A New Deal for the FBI," 644–5.

7. Quotation, pressbook for *Secret Service of the Air*, 10, UA-SHSWM.

8. Quotations, *Code of the Secret Service*, folder 371, box 13, RG 1, ibid.; and pressbook for *Secret Service of the Air*, 9, ibid.

9. Quotations, pressbook for *Love Is on the Air*, [6], ibid.; and pressbook for *Smashing the Money Ring*, 7, ibid. See also Powers, *G-Men*, 188–206.

10. Quotations, pressbook for *Code of the Secret Service*, 10, UA-SHSWM; and pressbook for *Secret Service of the Air*, 10, ibid. Also on Reagan's image, see pressbook for *Smashing the Money Ring*, ibid.; and this volume, Chapter 3.

11. Quotations, Crowther, "Movies Without Gables," 14.

12. Quotations, pressbook for *Code of the Secret Service*, 3, 8, UA-SHSWM; pressbook for *Smashing the Money Ring*, 2, ibid.; also 3; Gordon Casson, "Hollywood's Fighting Stars," *Progressive Weekly (People's Daily World)*, Aug. 12, 1939, p. 6; and "Reagan's Hearing Problem," *Newsweek* (Sept. 19, 1983), 91.

13. Ward, "Meaning of Lindbergh's Flight," 3–16.

14. Quotation, pressbook for *Secret Service of the Air*, 10, UA-SHSWM. Also pressbook for *Murder in the Air*, ibid.; and this volume, Chapter 8. Biographers note that Reagan had flown in a plane only once before World War II, and that for many years thereafter he would not fly; they disagree, however, on when and where that single flight occurred. Nevertheless, Reagan later claimed that as a radio sports announcer he occasionally flew to events "in an open-cockpit biplane wearing a leather helmet and goggles, and . . . loved it." Only after a series of airline crashes in the early 1950s did he stop flying, he maintained. Quotation, RR, *American Life*, 128. See also Wills, *Reagan's America*, 114, 237, 283, 293, 297; and Edwards, *Early Reagan*, 199–200. For additional evidence of Reagan's dislike of flying, see testimony of Ronald Reagan, Aug. 18, 1947, "Jurisdictional Disputes," *Hearings*, 248; and Michael Reagan, *Outside*, 93.

15. Quotations, opening scene, *Code of the Secret Service*, SHSWM; and pressbook for *Code of the Secret Service*, 3, UA-SHSWM. See also first version of "Uncle Sam Awakens," folder 5, box 270, RG 1, UA-SHSWM.

16. Quotations, trailer, folder: "Secret Service of the Air," box 63, series 1.3 (Warner dialogues), UA-SHSWM; pressbook for *Code of the Secret Service*, 2, UA-SHSWM; and pressbook for *Smashing the Money Ring*, 3, ibid. On the action detective genre, see Vaughn, "Spies," 362–3.

17. Quotations, Jonathan Marks in *NYT*, Oct. 9, 1984, p. 35; Olivier, *Confessions*, 38; RR, "'Dutch' Meets Some Movie Stars," *DMSR*, June 20, 1937, p. 4; and pressbook for *Murder in the Air*, 6, UA-SHSWM. Also on Reagan's acting style, see Maureen Reagan, *First Father*, 43–5.

18. Breen to Jack Warner, Sept. 1938, PCA file for *Secret Service of the Air*, AMPASL. The Production Code forbade showing the drug trade in any way, although it was amended in 1946 to allow a more liberal treatment of the topic.

19. Breen to Jack Warner, Sept. 17, 1938, PCA file for *Secret Service of the Air*, AMPASL; Breen to Warner, Feb. 3, 1939, PCA file for *Code of the Secret Service*,

ibid.; Street, "The Hays Office and the Defense of the British Market," 37–55; and Low, *Film Making in 1930s Britain*, 54–72. About 18 percent of the total United States film market came from Britain during the 1930s. See Colgan, "Warner Bros.' Crusade," 64.

20. See Breen to Jack Warner, June 19, 1939, June 22, 1939, June 26, 1939, Aug. 18, 1939, and Sept. 13, 1939; "Memorandum for the Files," June 23, 1939; Hays to Harry Warner, June 30, 1939; and H. J. McCord to Breen, Sept. 22, 1939, PCA file for *Smashing the Money Ring*, AMPASL.

21. Quotation, RR, *Where's*, 12.

22. Quotation, Ribuffo, *Old Christian Right*, 182; also 178–9. President Roosevelt directed the FBI to investigate the American Nazi movement in America as early as 1934, and Warner Bros. began making antifascist films a year earlier. See Colgan, "Warner Bros.' Crusade," 88–110; and Vaughn, "Spies," 378 (n. 55).

23. Quotations, pressbook for *Secret Service of the Air*, 7, UA-SHSWM; and pressbook for *Murder in the Air*, 5, 6, ibid.

24. Quotation, Diamond, *Nazi Movement in the United States*, 21. Statistics for fiscal year 1939. See *New York World Telegram*, June 6, 1940. See also Shepardson and Scroggs, *United States in World Affairs*, 327. The FBI had between two thousand and twenty-five hundred agents to combat fifth column activities. On the equation of Jews with fifth columnists, see Friedman, *No Haven*, 113–14; on fear of fifth columnists in America, see ibid., 105–28. On Nazi propaganda in the Western Hemisphere and the presence of German spies, which was undoubtedly exaggerated, see Vaughn, "Spies," 379 (n. 62).

25. Harry suffered from ulcers. See Jack Warner to Joseph Hazen, Jan. 25, 1939, folder 17, box 58, JLW-USC; Hazen to Warner, Jan. 10, 1939, and Jan. 27, 1939, ibid.; and Colgan, "Warner Bros.' Crusade," 241, 248. Quotation, Harry Warner, Address to the American Legion, Sept. 19, 1938, pp. 3, 6, box 4, OF 73, FDR Papers, FDRL.

26. Quotations, Harry Warner, "United We Survive, Divided We Fall!" June 5, 1940, pp. 4, 7, 13–14, JLW-USC. Also ibid., 6.

27. Arthur Cornelius, Jr. to Director [J. Edgar Hoover], June 7, 1940, Warner Bros. FBI file HQ 94–1-17015, section 1, FBI-FOIA, SHSWM; and Hoover to Special Agent in Charge, July 18, 1940, ibid. Throughout the 1930s, most studios maintained close contacts with local police, if only to keep their stars' transgressions out of the newspapers. It is likely that several of these contacts made their way onto studio payrolls when they retired – if not before. Niven, *Empty Horses*, 22, 87.

28. Quotations, Matthews, *Specter of Sabotage* [5], 29, 41, 37, 43.

29. Quotations, *Murder in the Air*, script (Sept. 13, 1939), folder 7, box 270, RG 1, series 1.2, UA-SHSWM.

30. Quotation, Breen as quoted in Colgan, "Warner Bros.' Crusade," 114.

31. Maltby, *Harmless Entertainment*, 10; Richards, "The British Board of Film Censors," 39; and Robertson, *British Board of Film Censors*, 91–101.

32. Quotations, Audience Research Institute, Report 16, "The Audience Acceptance Value of War Pictures" (June 21, 1940), in *Gallup Looks at the Movies*, microfilm reel 4; and Audience Research Institute, Report 117, "Audience Acceptance of War Subjects" (Oct. 30, 1941), in ibid.

33. Quotation, Hays, *Memoirs*, 517; also 517–19. For a four-page summary of *Confessions of a Nazi Spy*, protesting the film because it treated Germany and Hitler unfairly by ignoring the Nazi dictator's "spectacular" political achievements, see Summary, K. L., Jan. 22, 1939, PCA file for *Confessions of a Nazi Spy*,

AMPASL. Also Breen to Wilfrid Parsons, Oct. 10, 1932, box 3, Wilfrid Parsons Papers, LL-GU; and Colgan, "Warner Bros.' Crusade," 44–5.

34. Breen objected to the anti-Nazi character of other films, including Twentieth Century Fox's *The Man I Married* (1940) and *Man Hunt* (1941), and Columbia Pictures' *The Phantom Submarine* (1940). See PCA files for these films, AMPASL.

35. This conclusion about the films mentioned in the 1941 Senate investigation is based on the author's examination of the PCA files for each picture on the committee's list. On the hearings, see this volume, Chapter 8. See also Colgan, "Warner Bros.' Crusade," 61.

36. Quotations, first version of "Uncle Sam Awakens," folder 5, box 270, RG 1, UA-SHSWM.

37. Quotation, dialogue script, *Murder in the Air*, reel 2-B, pp. 3, 4, box 49, RG 1, UA-SHSWM.

38. Quotation from working script and film, SHSWM. That the Dies Committee was the model for the film's Rice Committee, see research file, *Murder in the Air*, WBAHP-USC. Most likely Harry insisted that the film portray the Dies Committee. Jack opposed the idea, fearing unfavorable publicity. Jack Warner to Harry Warner, Oct. 5, 1939, folder 17, box 58, JLW-USC.

39. Quotation, script for *Murder in the Air*, p. 101, folder 8, box 270, RG 1, UA-SHSWM. See also Vizzard, *See No Evil*, 53. Suspicions existed at the time that sabotage caused the crash of the *Macon*. The dirigible's remains were located in 1991. See *NYT*, Feb. 13–20, 22, 26, 1935. Also *WSJ*, April 28, 1991, pp. 1F, 4F.

40. Quotations from film, SHSWM. See also dialogue script, 4, box 49, series 1.3, RG 1, UA-SHSWM; script for *Murder in the Air*, pp. 59–61, folder 5, box 270, RG 1, ibid.; also script for "Enemy Within," Sept. 1, 1939 (compare with subsequent script dated Sept. 13, 1939, ibid.); and pressbook for *Murder in the Air*, UA-SHSWM.

41. See Vaughn, "Spies," 370–1, 379 (n 72).

42. *NYT*, Oct. 18, 1935, p. 17 and March 15, 1935, p. 1. Quotations, Jones, *Most Secret War*, 16, 50 (also 63–4, 84). See also Hyde, *British Air Policy*, 323, 329; and Rowe, *One Story of Radar*, 6–7.

43. Quotations, from film, SHSWM; and Cleugh, *Without Let or Hindrance*, 132. See also Weart, *Nuclear Fear*, 41–7.

44. Quotations, pressbook for *Murder in the Air*, 4, UA-SHSWM (see also posters for this film, ibid.); and trailer, p. 1, *Murder in the Air*, box 49, Warner dialogues, series 1.3, RG 1, ibid.

45. Quotation, RR, *Where's*, 83. It is clear that the Inertia Projector had been written into the script of *Murder in the Air* before filming began, September 18, 1939. See production file, *Murder in the Air*, WBAHP-USC.

46. Quotations, review of *Secret Service of the Air*, by T. M. P., *NYT*, March 2, 1939; review of *Murder in the Air*, in *Variety* [Dec. 22, 1939?]. For reviews of *Smashing the Money Ring*, see Robert W. Dana, *NYHT*, Nov. 17, 1939, and Wanda Hale, *NYDN*, Nov. 17, 1939.

47. Quotations, review of *Code of the Secret Service*, in *Hollywood Reporter*, May 15, 1939; review of *Secret Service of the Air*, by T. M. P., *NYT*, March 2, 1939; review of *Secret Service of the Air*, in *NYDN*, March 2, 1939; review of *Smashing the Money Ring*, by Edith Werner, *NYDM*, Nov. 17, 1939; review of *Secret Service of the Air*, by Bert Harlan in *Hollywood Spectator*, Feb. 18, 1939; review of *Code of the Secret Service*, in ibid., May 15, 1939; and review of *Secret Service of the Air* in *New York Tribune*, March 2, 1939. On Reagan's fan mail, see pressbook for *Million Dollar Baby*, reel 6, UA-SHSWM. On audience reaction to

Reagan, see also this volume, Chapter 3. Unfortunately, conclusions about public reaction to Reagan are hindered by the fact that most of Warner Bros.' distribution records at the University of Southern California are not available to researchers.

7. Lessons from the Past

1. Father Donovan speaking in Bellamann, *Kings Row,* 117.
2. Two other examples of feature-length films in which Warner Bros. used the past to comment on contemporary politics were *Juarez* (1939) and *The Fighting 69th* (1940). See Vanderwood, "Introduction: A Political Barometer," 9, 19–20; Colgan, "Warner Brothers' Crusade," 279–300; Obringer to Henry L. Stimson, Jan. 28, 1941, box 18, RG 407, records of the adjutant general's office (hereafter cited as AG records), NA; Emory S. Adams to Obringer, Feb. 10, 1941, ibid.; and Isenberg, *War on Film,* 94–6.
3. Quotations, testimony of Harry Warner, Sept. 25, 1941, Clark *Hearings,* 343, 339.
4. Quotations, *NYT,* May 18, 1981, p. B7. Also ibid., 1; and Roberts, "Return to the Land of the Gipper," 14.
5. Quotations, opening scene of *Knute Rockne – All American,* SHSWM; and Roddick, *New Deal in Entertainment,* 204. Also see Harry Warner, address to the American Legion, Sept. 19, 1938, p. 8, box 4, OF 73, FDR Papers, FDRL; and *SBT,* Oct. 4, 1940, p. 10.
6. Quotations, RR, *Where's,* 94; and from the film, SHSWM.
7. Quotation, from film, SHSWM. Stagg, Jones, Spaulding, and Warner had cameo roles in the film. See also Savage, et al., *American College Athletics,* Preface, Chapters 2, 6, 8, 10–12; and Steele, *Knute Rockne,* 36, 73.
8. Quotations from film, SHSWM. Portions of this speech were also quoted in *UNDRB,* Oct. 5, 1940, copy in AUND.
9. RR, "Gethsemane," *Dixonian* (1928), 92; and this volume, Chapter 1. See also Wills, *Reagan's America,* 115–31.
10. Quotations, *SBT,* Oct. 4, 1940, p. 1.
11. Reagan asked Pat O'Brien to persuade Jack Warner and Wallis to give him the part of Gipp. See O'Brien, *Wind,* 240. Quotations, Robert Buckner to Robert Fellows, Feb. 28, 1940, story file, ibid. See also RR, *Where's,* 92; and RR, "The Role I Liked Best," 67.
12. Quotations from film, SHSWM.
13. Hal Wallis to [William K.] Howard, April 12, 1940, story file for *Knute Rockne – All American,* WBAHP-USC; and Wallis to Lloyd Bacon, May 1, 1940, ibid.
14. Quotations, Buckner to J. Arthur Haley, April 26, 1939, story file for *Knute Rockne – All American,* WBAHP-USC; Buckner's introduction to script, dated March 20, 1939, story file for ibid.; Buckner to Rev. Eugene Burke, C.S.C., March 20, 1939, ibid.; and Buckner to Haley, March 20, 1939, ibid.
15. Quotations, Buckner to Haley, April 26, 1939, ibid.
16. Quotations, Buckner to Haley, April 26, 1939, ibid. See also Buckner to Haley, May 9, 1939, ibid.; and Buckner to John J. Cavanaugh, June 22, 1939, ibid.
17. Scenes were to have shown Gipp playing pool but they did not appear in the final version. Reagan knew Gipp's shortcomings and as president related them to friends. Quotation, Buckner's research notes, ibid. See also Bonnie Rockne, ed., *Autobiography of Knute K. Rockne,* 234; and Steele, *Knute Rockne: A Bio-Bibliography,* 19–21. See Roberts, "Return to the Land of the Gipper," 14.
18. Quotations, Buckner to MacEwen, March 28, 1939, story file for *Knute Rockne – All American,* WBAHP-USC. See also Huston, *Salesman;* Steele, *Knute*

Rockne, 41–2; Buckner to MacEwen, Feb. 1 and 19, 1939, story file for *Knute Rockne – All American*, WBAHP-USC; J. L. Warner to Wallis, Feb. 15, 1939, ibid.; and [Robert] Lord to Wallis, May 4, 1939, ibid. Among the movie's falsifications was its account of how Rockne developed the Notre Dame's backfield shift, suggesting the idea came from watching a dance routine. Wills, *Reagan's America*, 122.

19. Quotations, Obringer to [Jack] Warner, Feb. 13, 1939, story file for *Knute Rockne – All American*, WBAHP-USC.

20. Quotations, Vitus G. Jones and Bonnie Rockne to Warner Bros. Pictures, Inc., June 12, 1939, legal file for *Knute Rockne – All American*, WBAHP-USC. Also Jones, Obenchain, and Butler to Warner Bros. Pictures, Inc., Feb. 16, 1940; Hugh O'Donnell to Obringer, Feb. 21, 1940; Buckner to Robert Fellows, Feb. 26, 1940; Fellows to Wallis, Feb. 29, 1940, ibid. Also see RR, *Where's*, 94.

21. Quotations, J. Arthur Haley to Bryan Foy, Aug. 2, 1939, story file for *Knute Rockne – All American*, WBAHP-USC; and H. M. Warner to Wallis, Aug. 7, 1939, ibid. On Notre Dame's rejection of Cagney, see also Haley to Buckner, July 24, 1939, and other correspondence in ibid. Catholic publications publicized Cagney's effort to raise money for the Loyalists. For opinion considering Cagney a Communist, see Audience Research Institute, Report 25, "Communism and Hollywood" (Sept. 10, 1940), [p. 1], in *Gallup Looks at the Movies*, microfilm reel 4. See also *Audit of Marquee Values* (April 1940), *Second Audit of Marquee Values* (July 1940), and *Third Audit of Marquee Values* (Oct. 1940), in *Gallup Looks at the Movies*, microfilm reel 1; and Audience Research Institute, Report 34, "Believe-It-Or-Not Equations" (Nov. 28, 1940), in *Gallup Looks at the Movies*, microfilm reel 4.

22. Kate Smith made a half dozen noontime broadcasts from South Bend during Knute Rockne Week. Quotations, *SBT*, Oct. 5, 1940, p. 12. See also ibid., Oct. 4, 5, 6, 1940; *NYT*, Oct. 5, 1940, p. 20; *CDT*, Oct. 4, 1940, p. 29; ibid., Oct. 5, 1940, p. 19.

23. See "Schedule of events," Sept. 19-Oct. 5 [1941], Hugh O'Donnell President's Papers, folder 39, box 82, AUND. See also *SBT*, Oct. 6, 1940, section 4, p. 1; *Notre Dame Scholastic*, 74 (Oct. 11, 1940), 10; ibid., 75 (Oct. 3, 1941), p. 18; and Alicoate, ed., *1941 Film Daily Year Book of Motion Pictures*, 773–4.

24. Quotations, RR, "The Role I Liked Best," 67; *UNDRB*, Oct. 5, 1940, copy in AUND; and Hays, quoted in *Motion Picture Herald* [?], June 3, 1939, in WHHPI. See also *SBT*, Oct. 6, 1940, section 4, p. 1.

25. *Stallion Road* (1947) was also filmed in the West but had a contemporary setting. In addition, Reagan appeared in *The Bad Man* (MGM, 1941).

26. Quotations, Niven, *Empty Horses*, 97, 104 (also 97–111); Jack Warner, quoted in O'Brien, *Wind*, 255. See also Rosten, *Hollywood*, 306–27; and Powdermaker, *Hollywood, the Dream Factory*, 131–49. Buckner worked on other Reagan films including *Brother Rat* and *Angels Wash Their Faces*.

27. See Biography file, Robert Buckner, AMPASL.

28. See Buckner to McEwen, March 21, 1938, story file for *Brother Rat*, WBAHP-USC.

29. In addition to *Santa Fe Trail*, Buckner was a screenwriter for *Dodge City* (1939) and *Virginia City* (1940).

30. For the research material Buckner and Wilmont used, see RB/ew to E. G. Ryder, July 2, 1940, research file, *Santa Fe Trail*, WBAHP-USC; Herman Lissauer to Buckner, Jan. 22, 1940; and other correspondence in ibid. See also Ehrlich, *God's Angry Man*; and pressbook for *Santa Fe Trail*, reel 8, p. 20, SHSWM.

31. Quotations, Buckner to Wallis, Nov. 28, 1940, story file for *Santa Fe Trail*,

WBAHP-USC; Buckner to Fellows, Dec. 22, 1939, ibid.; and Curtiz, quoted in Jack Warner, *My First Hundred Years,* 160.

32. Quotations from movie, SHSWM.
33. Quotations, ibid.
34. Quotations, from movie, SHSWM; article, "Initiative," attached to letter, Einfeld to Jack Warner, March 19, 1937, folder 12, box 58, JLW-USC; *Santa Fe New Mexican,* Dec. 12, 1940, p. 2; and advertisement in ibid. See also *NYT,* Dec. 22, 1940, section 9, p. 5.
35. Quotations, Buckner to Wallis, April 4, 1940, story file for *Santa Fe Trail,* WBAHP-USC; and from movie, SHSWM. See also Cripps, *Making Movies Black,* 67, 97–8.
36. Quotations, pressbook for *Santa Fe Trail,* 7, 18, UA-SHSWM.
37. Quotations (emphasis in original), Buckner to Wallis, Nov. 28, 1940, story file for *Santa Fe Trail,* WBAHP-USC; and from movie, SHSWM.
38. Quotations from movie, SHSWM; *NYT,* Oct. 30, 1938, section 9, p. 3; and Massey quotations, interview in M. R. Werner, *Along the Santa Fe Trail* (Np.: Warner Bros. Pictures, Inc., [1940]), 26, in publicity file for *Santa Fe Trail,* WBAHP-USC. Publicity emphasized similarities between Brown, Hitler, and Stalin. M. R. Werner, "John Brown's Part in 'Santa Fe Trail' Is Based on History," *Santa Fe New Mexican,* Dec. 12, 1940, p. 10; and pressbook for *Santa Fe Trail,* reel 8, p. 5A, SHSWM. See also Jones, *Roosevelt's Image Brokers,* 45–6, 79–80, 100.
39. Quotation, Wallis to Michael Curtiz, Aug. 19, 1940, story file for *Santa Fe Trail.* WBAHP-USC. See also Jack Warner to Robert Fellows, July 26, 1940, ibid.
40. Quotations, RR, *Where's,* 95–6. Also Trilling to Wallis, June 24, 1940, and June 26, 1940, story file for *Santa Fe Trail,* WBAHP-USC; and list of potential characters, June 2, 1940, ibid.
41. Reagan was not among the top 100 stars listed in the first six audits of marquee values published between April, 1940, and April, 1941. Errol Flynn was in the top ten film stars, and in mid-1940 ranked seventh. See *Audit of Marquee Value* (Oct. 1940, and July 1941) in *Gallup Looks at the Movies,* microfilm reel 1. See also this volume, Chapter 3.
42. Quotations, pressbook for *Santa Fe Trail,* 5A, 8A, 18, SHSWM. See also Jack Warner to Curtiz, July 17, 1940, story file, *Santa Fe Trail,* WBAHP-USC; T. C. Wright to Taplinger and Einfeld, July 25, 1940, ibid.; and Fellows to Taplinger, July 25, 1940, ibid. On Custer's changing image through history, see Hutton, "From Little Bighorn to Little Big Man," 30, 35–6.
43. Quotations, Smith, "Introduction," 11. See also Lowenthal, *Past Is a Foreign Country,* 230, 258, 367–8; and Hughes, "Evaluation of Film as Evidence," 67.
44. Wilson Carey McWilliams described Reagan's sense of the past as "strikingly disordered; his memories . . . intertwined with old fantasies and bits drawn from old movies, all recalled and related as *fact.*" His was "not an objective past but an existential creation, the product of will." Quotations, Wilson Carey McWilliams, "The Meaning of the Election," 162. See also Rogin, *Ronald Reagan, The Movie,* 7–8 (Rogin also made the point that Reagan confused movies with historical fact in an interview with CBS's "Sixty Minutes," Dec. 15, 1985).
45. Quotations, Cannon, *President Reagan,* 60, 97.

8. Warmongering

1. Quotations, Gerald Nye addressing an America First Committee rally in St. Louis, Aug. 1, 1941, quoted in *STLGD,* Aug. 2, 1941.

2. Warner Bros. films named by the committee included: *Confessions of a Nazi Spy* (1939), *British Intelligence* (1940), *Dive Bomber* (1940), *A Dispatch from Reuters* (1940), *Sergeant York* (1941), and *Underground* (1941). MGM produced six films on the list; Columbia Pictures, six; United Artists distributed five; Twentieth Century Fox produced four; Paramount, three; and March of Time made eight films, most of them short subjects. Eleven films had been distributed from England. See Gledhill, ed., *Press Clipping File*, 1941; and Clark *Hearings*, 172–85. See also Mosley, *Zanuck*, 195–7; and Dunne, *Take Two*, 139–41, 144–5.

3. Quotations, *Code of the Secret Service*, script dated Feb. 10, 1939, "Added Scene," folder 6, box 68, RG 1, UA-SHSWM. See also Breen to Jack Warner, Dec. 7, 1939, PCA file for *Code of the Secret Service*, AMPASL.

4. Cooperation between Hollywood and the military dated back at least to the production of D. W. Griffith's *Birth of a Nation* in 1915. See Suid, *Guts & Glory*, 17, 18, 24–33; and Dick, *Star-Spangled Screen*, 38, 93–7.

5. *My Four Years in Germany* cost $50,000 but grossed eight times that amount. Like the book, it indicted German militarism. Quotations, Jack Warner, address before the Screen Writers Guild, Sept. 22, [1945?], Jack Warner biography file, AMPASL. For a list of Warner Bros.' films that promoted defense and Americanism, see testimony of Jack Warner, Oct. 20, 1947, *HUAC Hearings, Oct. 1947*, 22–31. See also Isenberg, *War on Film*, 152.

6. Quotation, Hearst to Jack Warner, Oct. 3, 1933, "Scrapbook – 1929–1934," JLW-USC. See also Frank Shaw to Jack Warner, Sept. 25, 1933, ibid.; T. T. Craven to Warner, Oct. 7, 1933, ibid.; *LAE*, Oct. 7, 1933; ibid., Oct. 29, 1933; *LAT*, Oct. 7, 1933; *LAEHE*, Oct. 7, 1933; *HCN*, Oct. 7, 1933; and *Illustrated Daily News* [Oct. 7?, 1933], clippings in ibid.

7. Quotations, from film, cited in Dick, *Star-Spangled Screen*, 84. When the army attempted to expand to 375,000 men in mid-1940, the adjutant general's office enlisted the expertise of corporations, advertising firms, and movie companies. Warner Bros. cooperated with the War Department to make several short films, including *Service with the Colors* (1940), *The Tanks Are Coming* (1940), *Navy Blues* (1941), *Wings of Steel* (1941), and *Here Comes the Cavalry* (1941). See E. S. Adams to J. Walter Thompson Company, July 3, 1940; Adams to H. A. Baker, July 19, 1940; Jack Warner to W. M. Wright, Jr., July 5, 1940; Jack Warner to Adams, July 11, 1940; and Adams to Jack Warner, Aug. 15, 1940, box 2576, RG 407, AG records, NA. Also Jack Warner to Adams, June 10, 1941, box 2573, RG407, AG records, NA.

8. Quotation, Wallis to Frank Wead, Jan. 2, 1935, story file for *Submarine D-1*, WBAHP-USC. See also Jack Warner to Wallis, Sept. 17, 1935, ibid. Incidentally, Cagney's past activities made him unacceptable to naval officials. "They hate his guts," Wead told the studio. The Navy liked O'Brien, however. See Guthrie to Wallis, July 3, 1936; Edelman to Wallis, July 5, 1936; Edelman to Wallis, July 22, 1936; Wallis to W. H. Standley, Oct. 30, 1935; Lou Edelman to Wallis, Nov. 21, 1935; Wallis to Edelman, Nov. 21, 1935; Wead to Edelman, Nov. 24, 1936, ibid.

9. Reagan worked on *Submarine D-1* in late June and again in early August 1937. Quotation, RR, " 'Dutch' Sees the Sights of Movie Lot," *DMSR*, July 25, 1937, p. 8. See also RR, "Four Pictures Finished," ibid., Oct. 3, 1937, p. 8; Norman Reilly Raine to Edelman, Oct. 22, 1937, story file for *Submarine D-1*, WBAHP-USC; A. J. Bolton to Wallis, Dec. 9, 1939, ibid.; and Wallis to Edelman, May 17, 1937, ibid.; RR, *Where's*, 81.

10. Quotation, trailer, publicity file for *Sergeant Murphy*, WBAHP-USC. Reagan worked on this film from July 18 to Aug. 5, 1937.

11. Quotations, RR, " 'Dutch' Starts New Picture," *DMSR*, Aug. 8, 1937, p. 8; and

RR, " 'Glamorous Hollywood?' " ibid., Aug. 22, 1937, p. 10. See also pressbook, *Code of the Secret Service*, 8, 9, 10, UA-SHSWM; RR, " 'Dutch' Takes a 'Prince of Wales' Ride," *DMSR*, Aug. 15, 1937, p. 8; pressbook for *Sergeant Murphy*, 6, ibid.; and Herman Lissauer to Bryan Foy, May 3, 1937, story file for *Sergeant Murphy*, WBAHP-USC.

12. Quotations, trailer, publicity file for *Sergeant Murphy*, WBAHP-USC. See also Sax to Wright, July 18, 1937, story file for *Sergeant Murphy*, WBAHP-USC; Breezy Eason to Wright, Nov. 17, 1937, ibid.; memorandum, Edwin Watson to Marvin McIntyre, July 9, 1937, box 3, OF 73, FDR Papers, FDRL; and pressbook, *Sergeant Murphy*, 3, 6, 7, UA-SHSWM.

13. Quotations, Jack Warner to McIntyre, July 8, 1937, box 3, OF 73, FDR Papers, FDRL; McIntyre to Warner, July 9, 1937, ibid.; and Harry Woodring to Kenneth Thomson, Aug. 28, 1939, box 4, ibid. See also Thomson to Woodring, Aug. 22, 1939, box 4, ibid.; and Edwin Watson to McIntyre, July 9, 1937, box 3, ibid.

14. Quotations, Bert Harlan, Review, *Hollywood Spectator*, Dec. 18, 1937. Reagan earned $700 for *Sergeant Murphy*.

15. Quotation, C. E. Kilbourne's original foreword [?] to *Brother Rat*, story file for *Brother Rat*, WBAHP-USC. See also Suid, *Guts & Glory*, 36.

16. The movie centered around Albert's character who was secretly married, and whose wife was pregnant. The term "brother rat" denoted first-year cadets. Quotations, Walter MacEwen to Wallis, July 12, 1938, story file for *Brother Rat*, WBAHP-USC. See also Wallis to Robert Lord and William Keighley, June 28, 1938, ibid.; Roddick, *New Deal in Entertainment*, 280; "Uniforms Get 'Em," pressbook, *Brother Rat*, Reel 1, p. 13, UA-SHSWM. In promoting *Secret Service of the Air*, Warner Bros. also encouraged the idea that girls liked men in uniform. See "In Love With Uniform," pressbook for *Secret Service of the Air*, 10, ibid. The same theme appeared in *Rear Gunner*, made after the United States entered World War II.

17. Frank McCarthy to Jacob Wilk, Feb. 17, 1938, story file for *Brother Rat*, WBAHP-USC. Also C. E. Kilbourne to Jacob Wilk, Feb. 26 and March 11, 1938, ibid.; and related correspondence in ibid.

18. Quotations, original dedication, ibid.

19. Quotation, pressbook, *Brother Rat*, 6, UA-SHSWM. See also ibid., 7, 9.

20. RR, *Where's*, 108. For reviews of Reagan in *Brother Rat*, see *Des Moines Register*, Dec. 9, 1938; *NYT*, Nov. 5, 1938; *NYHT*, Nov. 5, 1938; *Screen and Radio Weekly*, Oct. 23, 1938; and *National Box Office Digest*, Oct. 18, 1938. See also story file for *Brother Rat and a Baby*, WPAHP-USC.

21. Quotations, Beard and Beard, *America in Midpassage*, 596. Production records from Warner Bros. tend to confirm the Beards' observation.

22. See *STLGD*, Aug. 2, 1941. Anti-Semitism doubtlessly influenced many attacks on Hollywood during this period but it is questionable that Nye was anti-Semitic. See *Cong. Record*, Oct. 7, 1941; *Variety*, Sept. 9, 1941; Cole, *Senator Gerald P. Nye*, 186–93, 218–19; Cole, *America First*, 8, 10, 105, 117, 131–40, 149–50; and Cole, *Roosevelt and the Isolationists*, 274, 345, 380, 411, 470, 476.

23. On Jewish involvement in the film industry, see Eren, *Jew in American Cinema*, 53–4, 75–7. See also Cole, *America First*, 141; Strong, *Organized Anti-Semitism*, 19; Niven, *Empty Horses*, 103; and Ceplair and Englund, *Inquisition in Hollywood*, 95–8.

24. Director William Dieterle, who was not Jewish but "loathed" National Socialism and who directed such pictures as *Juarez* and *A Dispatch from Reuters*, was brought to the United States from Germany by Warner. On the Warner family, Michael Curtiz, Max Reinhardt, and William Dieterle, see Jack Warner, *My First*

Hundred Years, 15–31, 249, 264, 275–6. See also from Harry Warner's speech, "United We Survive, Divided We Fall!" June 5, 1940, JLW-USC; Freedland, *Warner Brothers,* 3–7; obituary of Mrs. Eva Wallis, newspaper clipping in biography file of Hal Wallis, AMPASL; Robinson, *All My Yesterdays,* 1–2, 6–17; Meyer, *Warner Brothers Directors,* 12, 75–8, and 119–21. Quotation, Erika and Klaus Mann, *Escape to Life,* 266.

25. Quotation, testimony of Harry Warner, Sept. 25, 1941, Clark *Hearings,* 347.
26. Quotations, H. M. Warner to Harry Hopkins, March 6, 1939, box 117, Harry Hopkins Papers, FDRL. On quotas, see Rosenberg, *Spreading the American Dream,* 102–3.
27. Quotation, Harry Warner to Franklin D. Roosevelt, Sept. 5, 1939, box 4, OF 73, FDR Papers, FDRL. For Hays's estimate of overseas revenues, see Will H. Hays, "Motion Pictures in 1940–1941," *Film Facts* [March 12, 1941], 5, copy in WHHPI.
28. Quotations, Harry Warner to Roosevelt, Sept. 5, 1939, box 4, OF 73, FDR Papers, FDRL. Although Warner's fears were exaggerated, there was "a marked decline" in attendance in British theaters over the next year and a half. The Audience Research Institute reported that whereas 49 percent of the population went to the movies one or more times a week in November 1938, by February 1941, attendance had dropped to 39 percent. See Audience Research Institute, Report 72, "Theatre Attendance in England" (May 10, 1941) in *Gallup Looks at the Movies,* microfilm reel 4. On the American film industry's response to changed conditions in Britain after the war began, see Jarvie, *Hollywood's Overseas Campaign,* 351–60.
29. Harry Warner to Roosevelt, Sept. 5, 1939, box 4, OF 73, FDR Papers, FDRL.
30. Quotation, ibid. See also S. T. E. [Stephen Early] to Edwin M. Watson, Sept. 6, 1939, box 4, OF 73, ibid.; Watson to J. Warner, undated; and Attorney General to Watson, Sept. 14, 1939, ibid.
31. Quotations, testimony of Harry M. Warner, Sept. 25, 1941, Clark *Hearings,* 339. Colgan, who has made the most thorough treatment of Warner Bros.' efforts on behalf of national defense before Pearl Harbor, also notes that the Warners were ahead of the White House in wanting to help Britain. See Colgan, "Warner Bros.' Crusade," 71.
32. Quotations, Harry and Jack Warner to the president, May 20, 1940, box 60, JLW-USC.
33. See *NYT,* June 6, 1940, p. 15; ibid., June 12, 1940, p. 21; and ibid., Dec. 14, 1940, p. 4. See also Lord Beaverbrook to Jack and Harry Warner, Jan. 20, 1941, folder 4, box 60, JLW-USC. Also Jack Warner to Franklin Roosevelt, Jan. 22, 1941; Harry Warner to Roosevelt, July 23, 1941; Jack Warner to Roosevelt, Sept. 30, 1941; Stephen Early to Jack Warner, Oct. 8, 1941, box 4, OF 73, FDR Papers, FDRL; and Aldgate and Richards, *Britain Can Take It,* 120–2.
34. Quotations, Hays to [D. Worth] Clark, Aug. 30, 1941, reprinted in *Motion Picture Herald,* Sept. 6, 1941; and testimony of Harry M. Warner, Sept. 25, 1943, Clark *Hearings,* 338, 339; also ibid., 343. See also excerpt from statement (by Hays?), [Sept. 1941], copy in WHHPI; Will H. Hays, untitled draft, Oct. 21, 1942, ibid.; and *NYT,* Sept. 1, 1941.
35. Quotations, H. Warner to Hays, Aug. 6, 1941, WHHPI; *Hollywood Reporter,* Sept. 3 and Sept. 9, 1941; *Motion Picture Daily,* Aug. 27, 1941; *Philadelphia Inquirer,* Sept. 12, 1941. See also, Lowell Mellett to the President, memorandum, Aug. 27, 1941, box 5, OF 73, FDR Papers, FDRL; memorandum for Mrs. Dennison, Aug. 28, 1941, box 4, ibid.; and *LAE,* Sept. 9, 1941.
36. Harry Warner revealed that Nye had even praised *Confessions of a Nazi Spy* after

seeing it at a private screening. See *Film Daily*, Oct. 9, 1941; *Washington Evening Star*, Sept. 25, 1941; and testimony of Harry Warner, Sept. 25, 1941, Clark *Hearings*, 345.

37. Quotation, RR, "Fascist Ideas are Still Alive in U.S.," 6.
38. Quotations, *CHA*, Sept. 16, 1941, Parsons Scrapbook, AMPASL. Also Parsons, *Gay Illiterate*, 100–2, 156–63.
39. Frank Wead, author of *Submarine D-1*, wrote *Ceiling Zero*. Testimony of Harry Warner, Sept. 25, 1941, Clark *Hearings*, 351.
40. Quotation, Audience Research Institute, Report 117, "Audience Acceptance of War Subjects" (Oct. 30, 1941), in *Gallup Looks at the Movies*, microfilm reel 4.
41. Quotations, Raine to Wallis, March 4, 1941, story file for *International Squadron*, WBAHP-USC; and from film, SHSWM.
42. See Breen to Jack Warner, March 6, 1941, PCA file for *International Squadron*, AMPASL. Warner said his studio made about a hundred films that promoted Americanism or warned of the dangers of fascism and communism. Other Reagan movies included *Submarine D-1*, *Knute Rockne – All American*, *This Is the Army*, *Beyond the Line of Duty*, and *Rear Gunner*. See testimony of Jack Warner, Oct. 20, 1947, *HUAC Hearings, Oct. 1947*, 22–3, 30.
43. Quotations, from poster for *International Squadron*, negative in publicity stills for film, SHSWM; and *DET*, Sept. 15, 1941, p. 2. As noted, by 1941 the image of Reagan as a pilot had appeared in other films. See this volume, Chapter 6.
44. See also this volume, Chapter 3. Reagan's performance in *International Squadron* received mixed reviews. For favorable comments, see *Hollywood Reporter*, Aug. 13, 1941. See also *NYT*, Nov. 14, 1941; and *Washington Times Herald*, Nov. 15, 1941. *Variety* reported, however, that Reagan did not "jell" and his character alienated audiences. Quotation, *Variety*, Aug. 13, 1941.

9. Flying a Desk for the Army Air Corps

1. Quotation, RR, *American Life*, 98. The First Motion Picture Unit in Culver City and the Training Film Production Laboratories at Wright Field produced 600 films. The FMPU made at least a third of them. The Army Air Force also used more than a hundred other films from outside sources, primarily from such makers of military equipment as Minneapolis-Honeywell and General Electric. Scanlan, comp., *History*, 39, 51–2 (microfilm no. A2986), MAFB. World War II accelerated not only the development of modern aviation, but space and nuclear technology as well. See McDougall, *Heavens and the Earth*, 5, 41, 78, 132, 211; and Sherry, *Rise of American Air Power*.
2. Quotations, Arnold and Eaker, *Winged Warfare*, 255, 258, 259. See also Marshall, Arnold, and King, *War Reports*, 452; and Arnold, *Global Mission*, 172–3.
3. Quotation, RR, *American Life*, 97; also 96–7.
4. Quotation, RR, *Where's*, 104. Lew Wasserman became Reagan's agent after MCA purchased William Meiklejohn's agency in 1940. See Moldea, *Dark Victory*, 62; and Brownstein, *Power and the Glitter*, 179–89, 212–23.
5. Quotation, RR, *Where's*, 105.
6. Quotation, *SBT*, Oct. 3, 1940 (premiere edition for Knute Rockne Week), p. 7. See also *NYT*, Sept. 20, 1940, p. 12.
7. Quotations, Lew (on MCA stationery) to Steve Trilling, Sept. 3, 1941, folder 3, Reagan contract files, WBAHP-USC; Obringer to J. L. Warner, Sept. 22, 1941, ibid.; and draft of letter, Warner Bros. Pictures to Assistant Secretary of War, Sept., 1941, ibid. See also Obringer's memo, Aug. 29, 1941; Fort MacArthur to Obringer, Aug. 30, 1941; Obringer to Ralph Lewis, Sept. 20, 1944, ibid.; and Crowther, "Movies Without Gables," 14.

8. See Obringer to Assistant Secretary of War, Sept. 6, 1941, folder 3, Reagan contract files, WBAHP-USC; F. K. Eberhart to Obringer, Sept. 25, 1941, ibid.; and Obringer to E. S. Adams, Sept. 23, 1941, ibid.

9. See Jack Warner to Adams, July 11, 1940, box 2576, RG 407, AG records, NA; Adams to Warner, July 18, 1940, ibid.; and Adams to Warner, Aug. 20, 1940, box 2577, part 2-A, ibid.

10. See Fort MacArthur to Obringer, Aug. 30, 1941, folder 3, Reagan contract files, WBAHP-USC; Obringer to Adams, Sept. 23, 1941, ibid.; Wallis to Obringer, Oct. 3, 1941, ibid.; and Obringer to Adams, Oct. 3, 1941, ibid.

11. Quotations, memorandum regarding "William L. Guthrie," R. C. Hendon to Mr. Nichols, May 21, 1941, FBI file for William L. Guthrie, FBI-FOIA, SHSWM; and Memorandum for Mr. Tolson from W. R. Glavin, regarding Guthrie, Oct. 17, 1939, ibid. See also *Nashville Tennessean,* April 23, 1938, copy in ibid.

12. Quotation Jack Warner, Jr., *Bijou Dream,* 282; also 262–7, 273–7, 294–5, 303. Jack Warner (the father) described Guthrie as the "studio police chief." Quotation, Jack Warner, *My First Hundred Years,* 173; also ibid., 279. Guthrie helped the studio arrange filming at military bases and aircraft factories and such pictures as *Submarine D-1, Dive Bomber,* and *Captain of the Clouds,* and was a liaison with the government for *I Wanted Wings, The Tanks Are Coming,* and *Wings of Steel.* During part of 1941, according to Warner, Guthrie took leave from the studio to work undercover for the government. On Guthrie's contact with the military, see the following letters in RG 407, NA: June 8, 1940 (AG 004.5); Dec. 28, 1940 (AG 004.5); Jan. 2, 1941 (AG 341); Jan. 8, 1941 (AG 341); Jan. 31, 1941 (AG 004.5); Feb. 26, 1941 (AG 004.5); March 26, 1941 (AG 004.5); Aug. 20, 1941 (AG 004.5).

13. Quotations, Wallis to Obringer, Oct. 6, 1941, folder 3, Reagan contract files, WBAHP-USC; and Obringer to Wallis, Oct. 6, 1941 (two memos), ibid.

14. Eberhart to Obringer, Oct. 15, 1941, ibid.; Obringer to Warner, Oct. 16, 1941, ibid.; C. L. Sampson to Obringer, Oct. 17, 1941, ibid.; and Obringer to J. L. Warner, Oct. 20, 1941, ibid.

15. Quotations, RR, *Where's,* 107. Also RR, *American Life,* 97; Trilling to Warner-Wallis, Nov. 15, 1941, folder 3, Reagan contract files, WBAHP-USC; and "Report on Rejections of Selected Men," Nov. 1, 1941 and Dec. 23, 1941, folder 10, box 170, RG 394, Ninth Corps Area, AG, general administration file, 1935–43, NAS.

16. Quotations, *NYT,* Feb. 9, 1942, p. 1; also p. 9.

17. Quotation, ibid., Feb. 10, 1942, p. 24.

18. See ibid., pp. 1, 9. Also Brady, "On the Firing Line," 5.

19. Quotation, A. C. Kelly to Commanding General, Ninth Corps Area, March 10, 1942, folder 3, Reagan contract files, WBAHP-USC. Reagan provided two accounts of what service limitations his physical exam imposed. In 1965 he made no mention of being required to remain in the United States when he wrote: "... I was tagged 'Limited service – eligible for corps area service command, or War Department overhead only.'" In 1990, he wrote: "My report read: 'Confined to the continental limits, eligible for corps area service command or War Department overhead only.'" Quotations, RR, *Where's,* 105 (also 106); and RR, *American Life,* 97 (also 98).

20. G. L. Van Norman to Reagan, March 27, 1942; Obringer to Commanding General, Ninth Corps Area, March 28, 1942; Horace F. Sykes to Obringer, March 30, 1942; Bowen to Reagan, March 30, 1942, telegram; Obringer to J. L. Warner, March 31, 1942; and Reagan to Bowen, April 2, 1942, folder 3, Reagan contract files, WBAHP-USC. Also Obringer to Reagan, April 1 and 9, 1942; and

memo on Reagan, April 9, 1942, ibid. The attempt to defer Reagan was not unique. Obringer also helped Errol Flynn apply for a deferment. Higham, *Errol Flynn*, 172–4; and FBI file for Errol Flynn, FBI-FOIA, SHSWM.

21. See *Modern Screen*, (March 1943?), and ibid. (April 1943), 99–100, copies in ECAE; *Jane Wyman Reagan v. Ronald W. Reagan*, case file number D360058 (divorce), LACCHR; Maureen Reagan, *First Father*, 40–1, 59–61; Obringer to [Jack] Warner, April 2, 1942; Obringer to Reagan, April 13, 1942; and Obringer to J. L. Warner, April 13, 1943, folder 3, Reagan contract file, WBAHP-USC.

22. Cynthia Miller, "So Long, Button-Nose," *Modern Screen* (July 1942), 57–8, 84; and Jane Wyman, "My Soldier," ibid. (Jan. 1943), 25–7, 59. Also, "Destination Unknown-Lt. and Mrs. Ronald Reagan (Jane Wyman) Say, 'Live for Today – Tomorrow Takes Care of Itself,'" (unnamed, undated), copy in Reagan Scrapbook, ECAE; and Friedrich, *City of Nets*, 105–6.

23. Quotations, Obringer to Guthrie, April 14, 1941, and Obringer to Reagan, April 14, 1942, folder 3, Reagan contract files, WBAHP-USC.

24. Quotations, Jack Warner, *My First Hundred Years*, 283–4.

25. Quotation, [Warner], "Notes for Washington Talk," undated [1942], box 60, JLW-USC. Also directive from Otto Johnson regarding AAF Motion Picture Unit, Feb. 24, 1942, in "Suggested Plan for Operation for Motion Picture Activities Division, Army Air Forces," ibid.; and Arnold to Jack Warner, March 2, 1942, ibid.

26. Quotations, [Warner], "Notes for Washington Talk," ibid.

27. Quotations, "Notes on Guthrie's Trip to Washington," undated, ibid.

28. Quotations, *Report for the Business Executive*, No. 159 (March 5, 1942), 4, box 60, JLW-USC; and C. D. F. Chandler, "Editorial Preface," in Arnold, *Airmen and Aircraft*, iii; and from Arnold, *Airmen and Aircraft*, 154, 156.

29. Quotation, Arnold and Eaker, *Winged Warfare*, 260. See also Arnold and Eaker, *This Flying Game*, 279.

30. Arnold encouraged civil aviation and private piloting so that in war the nation would always have a ready reserve of people who knew how to fly. Quotations, Marshall, Arnold, King, *War Reports*, 414, 454, 457. See also 415, 417, 452.

31. See correspondence between Arnold, Guthrie, and the Warners in boxes 13 and 22, Papers of Henry H. Arnold, LC. Quotation Scanlan, comp., *History* [p. 2] (microfilm no. A2986), MAFB.

32. Quotations, Jack Warner to General [Arnold], July 10, 1942, box 60, JLW-USC. See also additional notes and correspondence in folders 6 and 11, box 60, ibid.; and Mosley, *Zanuck*, 197–8. For a list of the Army units and other government departments producing training and/or morale films during early 1943, see Schedule A, attached to Amen and Hinkel to The Inspector General, March 5, 1943, box 1160, RG 159, NAS.

33. See "Memorandum for the Adjutant General," June 27, 1942, box 295, RG 407, AG records, NA. The Culver City unit was consolidated with a Signal Corps unit (which made AAF training films) at Wright Field, and in Nov. 1943, renamed the Motion Picture Branch (MPB). In Aug. 1944, the name of Reagan's unit changed from the "1st Motion Picture Unit" to the "18th Army Air Forces Base Unit (Motion Picture Unit)." See Scanlan, comp., *History . . . January 1 through Jan. 31, 1944*, p. 1 (microfilm no. A2987), MAFB; and Scanlan, comp., *History*, 12–13, 26–7, 39, 42, 51–2, 73 (microfilm no. A2986), MAFB.

34. Scanlan, comp., *History*, 7–16 (microfilm no. A2986), MAFB; Craven and Cate, eds., *Army Air Forces In World War II*, vol. 6, 540–1; "Notes on talk with Guthrie," March 20, 1942, box 60, JLW-USC; Wallis to Warner, April 3, 1942,

ibid.; "Notes on Guthrie's call, April 3, 1942," ibid.; and Warner to Guthrie, July 13, 1942, ibid.

35. Quotation, RR, *Where's,* 112–13.
36. Quotation, Wallis to Jack Warner, May 29, 1942, box 60, JLW-USC. See also RR, *American Life,* 97.
37. Quotation, unnamed, undated fan magazine, Reagan Scrapbook, ECAE. For Reagan's defense of his service, see RR, *Where's,* 113. See also ibid., 109; Leon Schlesinger to Jack Warner, June 24, 1942; and Warner to Commanding General, AAF, Aug. 5, 1942; and Robert A. Koerper to [Jack] Warner, undated, box 60, JLW-USC. See also "Table of Organization," June, 1942, box 295, RG 407, classified decimal file 1940–1942, AG records, NA.

Others whose service Warner sought to influence included Wallis, Jerry Wald, Lou Metzger, Clark Gable, and Cary Grant. See correspondence in box 60, JLW-USC; Jack [Warner] to Arnold, June 22, 1942, box 22, Arnold Papers, LC; and Jack Warner, *My First Hundred Years,* 284.
38. Quotations, Marshall, Arnold, King, *War Reports,* 317 (also 316); and Scanlan, comp., *History* [p. 1] (microfilm no. A2986), MAFB. See also "Suggested Plan of Operation for the Motion Picture Activities Division, Army Air Forces," submitted by Jack Warner, April 24 (April 30), 1942, box 60, JLW-USC; and Jack Warner to Donald P. Phillips, April 9, 1942, ibid.; and Arnold and Eaker, *Winged Warfare,* xiii.
39. Quotation, Arnold, *Airmen and Aircraft,* vi. See Jack Warner to Arthur I. Ennis, March 26, 1942, box 60, JLW-USC; and Fred Gage and L. M. Combs to Warner, April 9, 1942, ibid.
40. Quotations, Jack Warner, *My First Hundred Years,* 281. Also ibid., 282; and Jack Warner to Minton Kaye, July 21, 1942, box 60, JLW-USC.
41. Quotations, pressbook for *Rear Gunner,* publicity file, WBAHP-USC. See also Murphy. *"Say,"* 230.
42. Quotation, Marshall, Arnold, King, *War Reports,* 313.
43. Quotation, RR, *Where's,* 120. See also ibid., 117–19; and Scanlan, comp., *History,* 64, 67, 69 (microfilm no. A2986), MAFB.
44. Quotations from film, SHSWM.
45. The Signal Corps produced the film for the War Department. Quotation from film, NNSM.
46. Quotations, RR's narration in film, NNSM. See Scanlan, comp., *History* . . . *March 1–31, 1945,* p. 8 (microfilm no. A2987), MAFB.
47. Quotation, Scanlan, comp., *History,* 64 (microfilm no. A2986), MAFB. See also Marshall, Arnold, King, *War Reports,* 463–4; and Roeder, "Note on U.S. Photo Censorship in WWII," 193.
48. Quotations from *Target Tokyo* and *Westward Bataan,* NNSM.
49. See Wallis to Hollingshead, July 13, 1942, story and production Files, *Rear Gunner,* WBAHP-USC. Quotations, script for *Rear Gunner* dated July 10, 1942, ibid.; and Roosevelt's narration in *Beyond the Line of Duty,* SHSWM. See also Dower, *War Without Mercy,* 81–107, 160–3, 302–3, 312–13.
50. For AAF films and civilian workers in defense plants, see this volume, Chapter 11. For war propaganda and blacks, see Chapter 14. AAF films also appealed to women: see Chapter 18.
51. Quotations from film, NNSM. See Scanlan, comp., *History* . . . *Jan. 1 through Jan. 31, 1944,* pp. 23–4 (microfilm no. A2987), MAFB.
52. Quotations, from RR's narration in *Target Tokyo* and *Fight for the Sky,* NNSM; and Wheless in *Beyond the Line of Duty,* SHSWM. See also Scanlan, comp.,

History . . . March 1–31, 1945, p. 8 (microfilm no. A2987), MAFB; and Scanlan, comp., *History . . . April 1–30, 1945,* p. 8A, ibid.

53. Quotations from the film, SHSWM. See also production file for *This Is the Army,* WBAHP-USC; RR, *Where's,* 121–2; and Meyer, *Warner Brothers Directors,* 107. Reagan also made a short USO film for MGM, *Mr. Gardenia Jones,* and occasionally left Culver City to participate in war loan drives. See Scanlan, comp., *History . . . Jan. 1–31, 1944* (microfilm no. A2987), MAFB.

54. Reagan became post adjutant in Dec. 1944, a position he held until the following April. RR interview with author, Oct. 16, 1989. See also Scanlan, comp., *History . . . Dec. 1–31, 1944,* p. 4 (microfilm no. A2987), MAFB; Scanlan, comp., *History . . . April 1–30, 1945,* p. 1 (microfilm no. A2987), MAFB; M. Warren, *History . . . Sept. [?] 1–30, 1945,* p. 0850 (microfilm no. A2987), MAFB; Anderson to Guthrie, July 10, 1945, folder 2, Reagan contract files, WBAHP-USC; Guthrie to Trilling, July 17, 1945, ibid.; and Guthrie to Whom It May Concern, July 23, 1945, ibid.

55. Cynics insinuated that Warner's medal was the result of a deal behind the scenes. One rumor reached FBI director Hoover claiming that Warner secured the award by paying Arnold $50,000 for his life story. See R. B. Hood to Director, FBI, Dec. 13, 1947, section 2, Warner Bros. file (HQ 94–1-17015), FBI-FOIA, SHSWM. That orders had been cut transferring Warner to Chanute AFB, and Arnold's intervention to cancel the orders is indicated in the card index of the Arnold Papers, LC.

56. Quotation, O'Brien, *Wind,* 267; see also ibid., 265–86. On Ayres, *NYT,* March 31, 1942, p. 23; April 1, 1942, p. 23; April 2, 1942, p. 23; April 3, 1942, p. 25; April 10, 1942, p. 4; Brady, May 18, 1942, p. 18; May 19, 1942, p. 23; Aug. 16, 1942, p. 38; and Brady, "Hollywood Dossier," 3. On Gable, see Dwiggins, *Hollywood Pilot,* 153, 165–6. On Niven, see *Moon's a Balloon,* 231–2, 241–3, 246–7, 252–3, 262–3, 269, 277. For other entertainers, see *USO Camp Shows,* Vol. 3, *No. 15,* p. 52; *No. 16,* pp. 27, 30; *No. 17,* pp. 14–19b; Vol. 5, *No. 18,* pp. 79–84, 104–7, 109, 111, NYPL.

57. Quotations, pressbook for *Rear Gunner,* publicity file, WBAHP-USC.

10. A False Start: HICCASP

1. Quotation, RR, *Where's,* 141, 142.
2. Quotations, ibid., 166. Norman Corwin was a well-known radio dramatist who was the first recipient of the One World Award, established in honor of Wendell Willkie. See Barnouw, *Golden Web,* 71, 88, 116–21, 151–4, 163–5, 208–14, 238–42; and Bannerman, *Norman Corwin.*
3. See minutes of meeting of executive board, HICCASP, Oct. 25, 1945, pp. 1–2, box 2, Hollywood Democratic Committee (HICCASP) Papers (hereafter cited as HICCASP Papers), SHSWM; Helen Gahagan Douglas to George Pepper, Nov. 12, 1945 (and attached "Resolution on the Use of Atomic Energy . . . ," for release Nov. 15, 1946), box 10, ibid.; Helen Douglas, *Full Life,* 217; and *LADN* [?], Dec. 11, 1945, copy in box 10, ibid.
4. Quotation, *LADN* [?], Dec. 11, 1945, in box 10, HICCASP Papers, SHSWM. On scientists and world government following World War II, see Boyer, *Bomb's Early Light,* 33–81, 173.
5. Quotations, Speech by Thomas Mann, Dec. 10, 1945, box 10, HICCASP Papers.
6. Quotation, Norman Corwin, "Set Your Clocks at U-235," in box 10, HICCASP Papers, SHSWM. See also George Pepper to RR, Dec. 18, 1945, ibid.; and Progress Report, Nov. 9 to Dec. 20, 1945, box 2, ibid.

7. Obringer to Espinosa, Dec. 6, 1945 (Wasserman's response on left-hand corner), folder 2, Reagan contract files, WBAHP-USC. "Set Your Clock at U-235" proved controversial and in 1949 led to Corwin's name appearing on an FBI list of people accused of being sympathetic to communism. See Bannerman, *Norman Corwin,* 204–5.

8. Quotations, Schlesinger, "U. S. Communist Party," 93; Connelly quotation from remarks at dinner for Harold Ickes, Oct. 8, 1944, tape recording 297A, tape no. 8, HICCASP Papers, SHSWM. See also "Hollywood Democratic Committee: Background," box 1, HICCASP Papers, ibid.; and HDC to Harry Truman, April 26, 1945, folder: "PPF 504," box 486, Harry S Truman Papers, HSTLI.

9. Bogigian quoted in Ceplair and Englund, *Inquisition in Hollywood,* 227; also ibid., 225–8. By Jan. 1945, the HDC claimed 2,700 members. See "Hollywood Democratic Committee: Background"; "Agreement of Specific Cooperation . . . ," between the HDC and ICCASP, March 29, 1945; and "National Organization Proposals . . . ," Feb. 1, 1946, box 1, HICCASP Papers, SHSWM.

10. MacDougall, *Gideon's Army,* vol. 1, 111.

11. Quotation, Hayden, *Wanderer,* 347. See also "Political Notes: Glamor Pusses," *Time,* 48 (Sept. 9, 1946), 23, 25.

12. Quotations, "Glamor Pusses," 25. See also "Semi-Annual Report of the Executive Director," to ICCASP, 17, undated [Fall 1946?], box 1, HICCASP Papers, SHSWM; and Ceplair and Englund, *Inquisition in Hollywood,* 228.

13. Quotations, "Semi-Annual Report of the Executive Director," to ICCASP, undated [Fall 1946?], box 1, HICCASP Papers, SHSWM; To the Honorable Harry Truman, Dec. 12, 1945, box 10, ibid.; Harlow Shapley quoted in speech, Dec. 10, 1945, *LADN* [?], Dec. 11, 1945, in ibid. See also "Atomic Power, An answer to Truman's Tenn. Speech," undated, ibid.; minutes of executive council meeting (hereafter cited ECM), Sept. 17, 1946, box 2, ibid.; and minutes of membership meeting, HICC, Nov. 30, 1945, p. 4, box 10, ibid.

14. Quotations, "Semi-Annual Report of the Executive Director," to ICCASP, undated [Fall 1946?], box 1, ibid. HICCASP urged abolition of the House Committee on Un-American Activities. See George Pepper to Thomas Mann, Jan. 15, 1946, box 4, ibid. See also "The Threat to Academic Freedom in California," remarks by Linus Pauling, Jan. 21, 1946, box 4; "Academic Freedom Meeting," address by Thomas Mann, Jan. 21, 1945, box 4; and "Program and Platform for 1946," ICCASP Meeting, Feb. 10, 1946, box 1, ibid. On race relations, labor, and endorsement of candidates, see minutes of executive board meeting (hereafter cited as EBM), March 18, 1946, p. 2, box 2; minutes, EBM, May 14, 1946, p. 2, box 2; minutes, EBM, May 26, 1946, [pp. 1–2], box 2; minutes, EBM, June 11, 1946, pp. 1–2, box 2; minutes, ECM, July 20, 1946, p. 2, box 2; minutes, EBM, Aug. 6, 1946, pp. 1–2, box 2; minutes, EBM, Aug. 27, 1946, p. 2, box 2, ibid.

15. Quotations, "Glamor Pusses," 24–5. See also minutes, ECM, Nov. 14, 1946, p. 1, box 2, HICCASP Papers, SHSWM.

16. Quotations, Schlesinger, "U. S. Communist Party," 93; "Glamor Pusses," 25; and Calif. HUAC, 1947, *Third Report,* 369. See also *NYT,* Oct. 8, 1946, p. 13.

17. See clippings and copy of Ickes's speech of October 8, 1944, box 6, HICCASP Papers, SHSWM.

18. Quotation, RR, *Where's,* 166. See also, "Elected at meeting of Executive Council April 30, 1946," box 2, HICCASP Papers, SHSWM (Reagan was not elected at this meeting); and minutes, ECM, July 3, 1946, ibid. (Subsequent minutes suggest this date was a misprint and should read "July 2.") See also testimony of Ronald Reagan, July 1, 1955, *Jeffers v. Screen Extras Guild,* 3399, SCCA-SAD.

19. See also testimony of RR, *Jeffers v. Screen Extras Guild*, July 1, 1955, pp. 3398–9, SCCA-SAD. Quotations, from counsel's cross examination of Reagan in ibid., 3409; and RR, *Where's*, 166.
20. Quotations, RR, *Where's*, 167. For opposition to the anticommunist statement, see also Harry Grobstein to True Boardman, July 3, 1946, box 1, HICCASP Papers, SHSWM.
21. See minutes, ECM, July 3, 1946, box 2, ibid.; and Ceplair and Englund, *Inquisition in Hollywood*, 237–8.
22. Quotations, RR, *Where's*, 167–8. Also RR, *American Life*, 111–13.
23. Quotations, RR, *Where's*, 168. Also RR, *American Life*, 113.
24. Ring Lardner, Jr., and Paul Robeson were sympathetic to Marxism. Government investigators linked other ICCASP members to front organizations. See Lardner, *Lardners*, 254–8; *NYT*, Oct. 8, 1946, p. 13; Mitgang, *Dangerous Dossiers*, 79–84; and *LAE*, Sept. 6, 1958, p. 6. See also this volume, Chapters 11 and 12.
25. Linus Pauling, who would win two Nobel Prizes, was also an imposing intellect who drove De Havilland "to the wall" over the anticommunist resolution. His main concern, though, was controlling atomic weapons. Ellenore Bogigian quoted in Schwartz, *Hollywood Writers' Wars*, 261. See also minutes of "Conference on Atomic Energy," ICCASP, Dec. 3, 1945, box 10, HICCASP Papers, SHSWM; and Pauling, *No More War!*, 9, 11.
26. See RR, *Where's*, 161–2. Quotations, Schwartz, *Hollywood Writers' Wars*, 27; testimony of Edward Dmytryk, April 25, 1951, *HUAC Hearings, 1951*, 417; Bessie, *Inquisition in Eden*, 93; Cole, *Hollywood Red*, 176; Carr, *Dos Passos*, 124; and Carr, *Left Side of Paradise*, 91. See also Lawson, "Biographical Notes," 73; Dos Passos, *Best Times*, 69; and Gardner, "International Rag," (doctoral thesis, 1977), v.
27. Quotation, "Statement of Policy, Read at Exec. Bd., Aug. 18, 1944," by Lawson, box 1, HICCASP Papers, SHSWM; and Lawson to HICCASP membership, minutes, membership meeting [Nov. 30, 1945], box 10, ibid.
28. Quotation, meeting of the science and education division of HICCASP, June 17, 1946, box 2, ibid. See also minutes, EBM, May 14 and 26, 1946; and minutes, ECM, June 11, 1946, box 2, ibid. In contrast to Lawson, De Havilland, who was on ICCASP's board of directors, attended HICCASP's executive council meetings irregularly in 1946, appearing at the Jan. 24, Feb. 8, June 11, and July meetings. Neither her name nor Reagan's appears, for example, in the minutes for Feb. 26, March 18, April 2 and 30, or May 14, 1946. See box 2, ibid.
29. Quotation, Lawson, "Introduction to Panel Discussion," Aug. 3, 1947, p. 5, box 12, JHL-SIU.
30. Quotations, Lawson, *Film in the Battle of Ideas*, from title, 10, 17; see also 11, 22.
31. Trumbo's films included *Kitty Foyle* (RKO, 1940) (nominated for an Academy Award), *The Remarkable Andrew* (Paramount, 1942) (adapted from Trumbo's novel), *Thirty Seconds Over Tokyo* (MGM, 1944) (which won a *Boxoffice* Magazine Award), and *Our Vines Have Grapes* (MGM, 1945) (a *Parents* Magazine Medal picture). After being blacklisted, Trumbo continued to work under pseudonyms while self-exiled in Mexico. He won an Academy Award in 1957 writing under Robert Rich for *The Brave One* (RKO, 1956). In 1960, he did the screenplays for *Exodus* (Preminger/UA, 1960) and *Spartacus* (BYNA/Universal, 1960).
32. Quotations, Schwartz, *Hollywood Writers' Wars*, 77 (also 269); Trumbo to Mr. DeBaise, May 28, 1948, box 2, Dalton Trumbo Papers, SHSWM; Trumbo, "On Publishing a Book," 19 (also ibid., 21); and Maltz, "Citizen Writer in Retro-

spect" (oral history), vol. 2, 692, and vol. 1, 329. See also "A Note on the Author," in Trumbo, *Harry Bridges;* Trumbo's sketch of himself in Trumbo, "Dalton Trumbo's Own Story," 7; Trumbo to W. F. K., Dec. 2, 1947, in Manfull, ed., *Additional Dialogue,* 61; Navasky, *Naming Names,* 81; Bessie, *Inquisition in Eden,* 183–6; and testimony of Louis Burt Mayer, Oct. 20, 1947, *HUAC Hearings, Oct. 1947,* p. 73.

33. Quotations, Trumbo to Sam Sillen [1946], folder: "Trumbo Correspondence (Jan. 1-Dec. 1946)," box 1, Trumbo Papers, SHSWM.

34. Schwartz, *Hollywood Writers' Wars,* 213, 255–7.

35. Quotations from program and advertisement scheduled for June 20, 1946, folder: "Trumbo Correspondence" (Jan. 1-Dec. 1946), box 1, Trumbo Papers, SHSWM. Also "Elected at meeting of Executive Council April 30, 1946," box 2, HICCASP Papers, ibid.

36. Quotation, *LAE,* Sept. 6, 1958, p. 6. Also ibid., 1; and *LAMN,* Sept. 5, 1958, section 1, pp. 1–2, in box 4, HICCASP Papers, SHSWM.

37. "The drive of certain interests toward war against the Soviet Union, the drive of certain others toward war against American labor finds a friendly force in the drive of organized bigots against our racial, religious and political minorities," Trumbo wrote. Quotations, [ICCASP speech drafts], 3, 6–7, attached to De Havilland to Trumbo, June 27, 1946, folder: "Trumbo Correspondence" (Jan. 1–Dec. 1946), box 1, Trumbo Papers, SHSWM.

38. Quotation, RR, *Where's,* 167. See also Trumbo to De Havilland, June 24, 1946; De Havilland to Trumbo, June 27, 1946; [Trumbo] to Ernest [Pascal], [June 1946]; and George Pepper to Trumbo, June 25, 1945, folder: "Trumbo Correspondence" (Jan. 1–Dec. 1946), box 1, Trumbo Papers, SHSWM.

39. Quotation, "Seattle Meeting – June 21, 1946 – Olivia De Havilland," p. 2, folder: "Trumbo Correspondence" (Jan. 1–Dec. 1946), box 1, Trumbo Papers, SHSWM.

40. Quotations, Trumbo to De Havilland, June 24, 1946; [Trumbo to Pascal], [June, 1946]; ibid. See also "Drafts and Notes for Letter by Trumbo, [c. June 1946]," ibid.

41. The denunciation of communism seemed desirable after the Research Institute of America, which supplied information to employers, claimed SAG had "left-wing tendencies." Quotation, SAG minutes, BD, April 29, 1946, p. 3000, SAGA. See also, ibid., April 1, 1946, p. 2986; and May 13, 1946, p. 3008, ibid.

42. Quotations, press release for June 17 [1946], SAG minutes, BD, 3024, SAGA. See also executive board of SWG to SAG's BD, March 20, 1946, pp. 2990–90D; SAG minutes, BD, Feb. 18, 1946, pp. 2964–6; BD, March 18, 1946, pp. 2978–9; BD, April 15, 1946, p. 2995; BD, May 27, 1946, p. 3016; June 10, 1946, pp. 3019, 3021–2; and John C. Lee to George Murphy, ibid., March 26, 1945, pp. 2781–81A, SAGA.

43. Quotations, RR, *Where's,* 178 (also 179); Revere quoted in *Oakland Tribune,* July 27, 1980, p. D-3; and SAG minutes (not necessarily Reagan's exact words), BD, April 1, 1946, p. 2986, SAGA. Reagan, Montgomery, and Murphy recommended against the tri-guild council and it never materialized. See ibid., BD, March 10, 1947, p. 3231.

44. The civil services' "inefficiency, empire building, and business-as-usual attitude" during the war appalled him, Reagan said. Quotation, RR, *American Life,* 102; and RR, *Where's,* 123.

45. Quotations, RR, *Where's,* 141. Reagan's name was associated with several organizations that California's Un-American Activities Committee claimed were fronts including HICCASP, the Committee for a Democratic Far Eastern Policy,

the Joint Anti-Fascist Refugee Committee, Mobilization for Democracy, the American Veterans Committee, and the Americans for Democratic Action.

46. Quotations, RR, *Where's*, 141–2. See also RR, *American Life*, 106–7.

47. Quotations, Neil Reagan, "Private Dimensions and Public Images," 30. See also ibid., 31; minutes, policy committee meeting, July 5, 1946, p. 2, box 1, HICCASP Papers, SHSWM; and minutes, ECM, July 10, 1946, p. 1, box 2, ibid.

48. Quotations, Testimony of Ronald Reagan, July 1, 1955, pp. 3399–3400, *Jeffers v. Screen Extras Guild*, SCCA-SAD.

49. In 1942, Blaney Matthews fingerprinted studio employees for the FBI, and the Bureau asked to use Warner Bros. as a front in Central and South America. Harry Warner agreed on condition that the arrangement be kept secret from Jack. On Warner Bros., see Confidential Report to Director, FBI, Nov. 30, 1942, section 1 of HQ64–4680; Arthur Cornelius, Jr., to Director, June 7, 1940, section 1 of HQ94-1-17015; and R. B. Hood to Director, March 4, 1942, section 2 of HQ94-1-17015, Warner Bros. FBI file, FBI-FOIA, SHSWM. On Reagan, see office memorandum, M. A. Jones to Mr. Nichols, May 23, 1951, p. 7; and FBI report, Los Angeles, Dec. 27, 1943 (100–7399), pp. 5–6, Ronald Reagan FBI file, FBI-FOIA, SHSWM.

Whether Reagan acted under FBI directives in 1946 is unclear. HICCASP's policy committee meeting of July 5 was under bureau surveillance, and De Havilland later claimed that at the time Reagan was working for the bureau. See memorandum to Mr. Nichols, May 23, 1951, p. 8; report 100–7399; and memorandum, SAC, Los Angeles to Director, April 18, 1947, bureau file 100–340327 (LA 100–21198), Reagan FBI file, ibid. Also see De Havilland interviewed in "The Real Ronald Reagan," on "Frontline," narrated by Garry Wills, PBS, Jan. 18, 1989.

50. Quotation, RR, *Where's*, 168. This recollection is consistent with Reagan's account given to FBI agents in April, 1947. See memorandum to Director, April 18, 1947 (LA 100–21198), Reagan FBI file, FBI-FOIA, SHSWM.

51. RR, *Where's*, 168.

52. Quotations, unidentified observer quoted in Ceplair and Englund, *Inquisition in Hollywood*, 238; Statement of Policy, submitted to the executive council, July 10, 1946, box 1, HICCASP Papers, SHSWM; and memorandum to Director, April 18, 1947 (LA 100–21198), Reagan FBI file, FBI-FOIA, SHSWM. See also statement of policy in "Your Future Is in *Your* Hands Now!," box 1, HICCASP Papers, SHSWM.

53. A copy of the full resolution that De Havilland wanted HICCASP to adopt was sent to the executive council by Marjorie Allen (De Havilland's secretary) and is undated, in folder: "PCA Founding," box 1, HICCASP Papers, SHSWM.

54. Quotations, RR, *Where's*, 168–9. See also *LAE*, Sept. 6, 1958, p. 6 (De Havilland's description of the meeting given later to HUAC); and Cannon, *Reagan*, 79.

55. Quotation, minutes, EBM, July 23, 1946, box 2, HICCASP Papers, SHSWM. See also minutes, ECM, July 10, 1946, box 2; minutes, EBM, July 16, 1946, p. 2, box 2; minutes, National Executive Committee (ICCASP), July 17, 1946, box 3, ibid. See also James Roosevelt to Hannah Dorner, July 5, 1946, box 3; and Roosevelt to Jo Davidson, July 9, 1946, box 3, ibid.

56. Quotation, minutes, ECM, July 30, 1946, p. 2, box 2, ibid.

57. Quotation, RR, *Where's*, 169. Joan Fontaine and Howard Green resigned at approximately the same time as did De Havilland. The point at which others who supported the anticommunist statement resigned is more difficult to ascertain, although it is clear the group did not resign en masse. Ernest Pascal's resignation was not accepted by HICCASP's executive council until November 26, 1946, and

Schary was still participating in Council affairs in late November. See minutes, EBM, July 23, 1946, and minutes, EBM, Nov. 26, 1946, box 2, HICCASP Papers, SHSWM. See also Allen Rivkin to Walter Reilly, July 11, 1952, and Dore Schary to My dear General, July 10, 1952, folder 4, box 100, Dore Schary Papers, SHSWM.

HICCASP turned toward launching a third party campaign in the 1948 elections. In late 1946 representatives from ICCASP and the National Citizens Political Action Committee met and formed the Progressive Citizens of America. By July 1948, this group had become known as the Independent Progressive Party.

58. Quotation, De Havilland in interview on "The Real Ronald Reagan." See also RR, *Where's,* 169; and "Standing Committees as ratified by Executive Council at meeting August 27, 1946," box 1, HICCASP Papers, SHSWM.

59. Quotations, RR, *Where's,* 169. See also SAG minutes, BD, March 19, 1951, p. 4057, SAGA.

60. Quotation, RR, *Where's,* 166, 169.

11. Labor and the Rise to Power

1. Quotation, from presentation by pro–Conference of Studio Unions faction to SAG, Nov. 11, 1946, SAG minutes, p. 3140A, SAGA.

2. On wartime and postwar strikes in America, see Lipsitz, *Class and Culture,* esp. 14–134.

3. For HICCASP's support of the strike, see box 9, HICCASP Papers, SHSWM. Accounts sympathetic to the CSU include "Dalton Trumbo Reports," speech by Trumbo; McWilliams, "Inside Story of the Hollywood Strike," 9; Dunne, "Christian Advocacy" (oral history, 1981); and Sorrell, "You Don't Choose Your Friends" (oral history, 1963). See also Ceplair and Englund, *Inquisition in Hollywood,* 216–25 (the CSU "represented the only hope for a democratic labor union movement in Hollywood"; ibid., 216); Moldea, *Dark Victory,* 65–72; and Wills' *Reagan's America,* 224–40. In addition, see Schwartz, *Hollywood Writers' Wars,* 221–4, 226–9, and 243–53. For an account more sympathetic to IATSE, see Dales, "Pragmatic Leadership" (oral history, 1981), 10–16, 20; Prindle, *Politics of Glamour,* 40–9. For Reagan's recollections, see *Where's,* 126–85. For the background to the dispute between IATSE and the CSU, see Perry and Perry, *History,* 332–7.

4. Quotations, RR, *Where's,* 138–9, 142; also ibid., 133.

5. Robert Montgomery resigned when he entered the production phase of the industry. See SAG minutes, BD, Feb. 11, 1946, p. 2960; minutes, BD, March 18, 1946, p. 2981; minutes of annual meeting, Sept. 15, 1946, p. 3081; and minutes, BD, March 10, 1947, pp. 3224–8, SAGA. Walter Pidgeon became SAG president in 1952, and Reagan was elected to a three-year term on the guild's board of directors. He won additional three-year terms to the board in 1955 and 1958, and was again elected president in 1959.

6. See Perry and Perry, *History,* 321.

7. For the agreement, signed Nov. 29, 1926, see "Jurisdictional Disputes" *Hearings,* 2184–6. See also testimony of William L. Hutcheson, Feb. 23, 1948, ibid., 1400, 1406–7; and Perry and Perry, *History,* 322–8.

8. Quotation, Lowell, "Memories," 58. See also Moldea, *Dark Victory,* 20–8.

9. SAG had hired private investigators, who passed damaging information about Browne and Bioff to columnist Westbrook Pegler. Quotations, Murphy, *"Say,"* 221, 223. See also ibid., 223–4; RR, *Where's,* 160; Wills, *Reagan's America,* 227; Caute, *Great Fear,* 488; Moldea, *Dark Victory,* 27, 35–40; newspaper clipping

dated Oct. 21, 1941, folder: "Harry M. Warner – Biography," box 56, JLW-USC; and newspaper clipping dated Oct. 22, 1941, ibid.

10. See Perry and Perry, *History,* 331–5.

11. Ibid., 335–7; Wills, *Reagan's America,* 228; Ceplair and Englund, *Inquisition in Hollywood,* 216–17; and Schwartz, *Hollywood Writers' Wars,* 221.

12. Walsh appointed Brewer international representative of IATSE effective Jan. 1, 1945. He was in charge of locals 44 and 683. "Jurisdictional Disputes," *Hearings,* 885–6; McWilliams, "Inside Story of the Hollywood Strike," 9; Wills, *Reagan's America,* 224–30; and Ceplair and Englund, *Inquisition in Hollywood,* 217.

13. The arbitration committee included William C. Doherty, president of the National Association of Letter Carriers, Felix Knight, head of the railway car men, and William C. Birthright, leader of the barbers' union. For the "Cincinnati Agreement," see "Jurisdictional Disputes," *Hearings,* 13, 463. See also SAG minutes, BD, Oct. 29, 1945, p. 2894, SAGA. Material on labor unrest in 1945 is in box 46, JLW-USC, and box 2734, WBAHP-USC. See also "Chronological History of Screen Set Designers, Local 1421 Dispute," folder 1A, box 1, HSSC, URL-UCLA; RR, *Where's,* 126–38; and Wills, *Reagan's America,* 228–30.

14. Quotations, "Jurisdictional Disputes," *Hearings,* 14. Also ibid., 464–5; testimony of William Hutcheson, Feb. 23, 1948, pp. 1381–7; testimony of Ronald Reagan, Aug. 18, 1947, p. 236; testimony of William Doherty, Aug. 18, 1947, p. 271 (also p. 272). On the arbitrators' view of Casey's interpretation, see ibid., 280–1; and Aug. 19, 1947, p. 302. On Doherty's view of Hutcheson's repudiation of the 1925 agreement, see Aug. 18, 1947, p. 274.

    Part of the confusion involved the meaning of "erection" and "construction." In an earlier time, many sets were miniatures built by carpenters outside the studio and then delivered to the stage, where IATSE members set them up. But increasingly, sets were created onstage inside the studio or on location, and Hutcheson wanted the carpenters to have the right to build them. He wanted "erection" – which IATSE men would handle – to mean the "assembling of sets . . . already built." Quotation, minutes, AFL executive council meeting, in testimony of William Hutcheson, Feb. 23, 1948, ibid., 1402.

15. Set erection, the arbitrators said in August, meant "assemblage of such sets on stages and locations" and belonged to IATSE. However, "construction work" on these sets belonged to the carpenters. Quotations, Aug. 16, 1946; clarification in folder 4, box 1, HSSC, URL-UCLA. See also "Jurisdictional Disputes," *Hearings,* 33.

16. By contrast, Brewer had supported the Screen Extras Guild, which eventually brought extras back into SAG's fold. For the struggle between SEG and the Screen Players Union, see Prindle, *Politics of Glamour,* 38–9, 44. Also SAG minutes, BD, Aug. 20, 1945, pp. 2853–4, and Aug. 27, 1945, p. 2859, SAGA.

17. Quotation, Dunne, "Christian Advocacy," 23.

18. The vote to observe picket lines was defeated 3,298 to 96. See "Jurisdictional Disputes," *Hearings,* 220–1. Also Berger's letter, March 15, 1945, pp. 2773–73D, in SAG minutes; SAG minutes, BD, Oct. 14, 1945, p. 2883, SAGA. Also see the conversation between Steve Trilling and Jack Dales, Oct. 17, 1945, box 2734, WBAHP-USC; and Wills, *Reagan's America,* 229–30.

19. Quotations, Prindle, *Politics of Glamour,* 22 (also 16–33); Dales, "Pragmatic Leadership," 8, 20. See also, ibid., 8, 43; SAG minutes, BD, Nov. 26, 1945, p. 5, SAGA; Powdermaker, *Hollywood, the Dream Factory,* 209; *Variety,* Feb. 9, 1949, pp. 7, 15; Perry and Perry, *History,* 337–53; and Wills, *Reagan's America,* 218–22; May, "Movie Star Politics," 133, 136.

20. SAG minutes, BD, July 14, 1941, p. 1874; and ibid., Aug. 11, 1941, p. 1887, SAGA; Dales, "Pragmatic Leadership," 4–5; Edwards, *Early Reagan,* 231; and RR, *Where's,* 132.

21. RR, *Where's,* 133; SAG minutes, BD, Dec. 20, 1943, p. 2507–8, SAGA; ibid., Jan. 10, 1944, pp. 2521, 2523; ibid., special meeting, BD, Dec. 9, 1943, pp. 2498; Jack Dales, "For the Confidential Information of Members" [Jan. 1944], in letter, H. M. Warner to SAG, Jan. 6, 1944, SAG minutes, p. 2524A (also Warner's letter, pp. 2524–24C); and press release, "There *IS* a Difference Between the War and the Warners," [Dec. 1943], SAG minutes, 2501–01A, SAGA.

22. Quotations, from film *Court Martial by Conscience,* RAAF-FMPU-MAFB (microfilm no. A0492), MAFB; and from film *Our Town Today,* ibid. See also Testimony of Ronald Reagan, Aug. 20, 1947, "Jurisdictional Disputes," *Hearings,* 356. *Beyond the Line of Duty,* which Reagan narrated, ended with Captain Wheless telling Boeing employees that their jobs could mean the difference between victory and defeat. The Army Air Corp's "labor incentive" films appealed to workers at the Douglas Aircraft factories, to ball bearing makers, and to tire manufacturers, and included such titles as *For Valor, Mud and Morale, Has Akron Been Bombed?, Planes We Never Made,* and *Tires That Were Never Made.* Narration for the films is available in the RAAF-FMPU-MAFB (microfilm no. 0492). See also Scanlan, *History . . . Jan. 1 through Jan. 31, 1944,* p. 19 (microfilm no. A2987), MAFB; and records of the 18th AAF Base Unit, p. 0935 (microfilm no. A2987), MAFB. For AAF labor films aimed at women, see this volume, Chapter 18.

23. Quotations, telegram, Lawson, Trumbo, et al. to Jack and Harry Warner, Oct. 8, 1945, box 2734, WBAHP-USC. See also Lawson, Trumbo, et al., to Jack Warner and Harry Warner, Oct. 9, 1945, box 9, HICCASP Papers, SHSWM; SAG minutes, BD, Aug. 20, 1945, p. 2854, and ibid., Aug. 27, 1945, p. 2857, SAGA; and Schwartz, *Hollywood Writers' Wars,* 226–9.

24. Seven members of Browne's executive board who sat in 1940 retained their seats in 1946. Quotation, McWilliams, "The Inside Story of the Hollywood Strike," 9. See also "Proposed Foreign Publicity Campaign for 683-CSU," folder 2, box 1, HSSC, URL-UCLA; "Dalton Trumbo Reports" (speech), Oct. 13, 1945; testimony of George Dunne, Aug. 22, 1947, "Jurisdictional Disputes," *Hearings,* 406; Caute, *Great Fear,* 488; and Moldea, *Dark Victory,* 65.

25. Quotations, proposed script for Edward G. Robinson to be used in CIO-sponsored broadcast in Nov. 1945, in telegram, Alan Reitman to George Pepper, Nov. 8, 1945, box 9, HICCASP Papers, SHSWM. See also Linus Pauling, "The Threat to Academic Freedom in California," Jan. 21, 1946, box 4, ibid.; *LAEHE,* Oct. 9, 1945, and *LAT,* 10, 1945 (copies in box 9, ibid.); and *LAE,* Feb. 18, 1946, copy in folder: "Strike Clippings," box 47, JLW-USC.

26. Sorrell, "You Don't Choose Your Friends," 86.

27. Quotation, Calif. HUAC, 1947, *Third Report,* 173 (also 169–77). See also testimony of Roy Brewer, Oct. 27, 1947, *HUAC Hearings, Oct. 1947,* 346; Sorrell, "You Don't Choose Your Friends," 3–10, 16–18, 22, 86, 134, 198–9, 208; and Ceplair and Englund, *Inquisition in Hollywood,* 217. For the Communist Party's support of the CSU, see folder: "Communist Party," file box, Hollywood Studio Strike Collection, SCLSSR-LA. For cash donations in 1946 from the Communist Party, see letters from Corresponding Secretary, Ladies Auxiliary of the Conference of Studio Unions to Emil Freed, Nov. 26, 1946, and Jan. 6, 1947, ibid.

28. Quotations, Brewer's views summarized in testimony of George Dunne, Aug. 22, 1947, "Jurisdictional Disputes," *Hearings,* 406; text of Brewer press statement,

in *Hollywood Closeup*, no. 1 (Nov. 1, 1945), [p. 4]; and Brewer to Gregory Peck, Oct. 18, 1945, box 9, HICCASP Papers, SHSWM (emphasis in original text). See also "Jurisdictional Disputes," *Hearings*, 885–6; Prindle, *Politics of Glamour*, 41, 45–6; Testimony of Roy Brewer, Oct. 28, 1947, *HUAC Hearings, Oct. 1947*, 345–6; and for copy of "Herbert Stewart" card, see IATSE, *General Bulletin* (Dec. 1946), 20, 21.

29. Other emergency committee members were Leon Ames, Franchot Tone, and Anne Revere. Quotation, SAG minutes, special meeting, BD, Feb. 18, 1946, p. 2962, SAGA. See also ibid., 2962–4 (Reagan did not attend this meeting); SAG minutes, BD, Feb. 11, 1946, p. 2955; June 24, 1946, p. 3025; and July 1, 1946, pp. 3033–4, SAGA. For the Treaty of Beverly Hills, July 2, 1946, see "Jurisdictional Disputes," *Hearings*, 1023. See also Reagan testimony, Aug. 18, 1947, ibid., 223.

30. Cambiano maintained that anything made of wood or wood substitutes belonged under the carpenters' jurisdiction. See RR, *Where's*, 146–7; and testimony of Joseph Cambiano, Aug. 25, 1947, "Jurisdictional Disputes," *Hearings*, 554–5. Quotations, Reagan quoting Brewer, testimony of Ronald Reagan, Aug. 18, 1947, ibid., 224 (also 223–4); and summary of Walsh's views (not necessarily his exact words), minutes, Producers' Labor Committee, Aug. 22, 1946, in ibid., 908. Also see testimony of William Hutcheson, Feb. 23, 1948, ibid., 1402; and Wills, *Reagan's America*, 233–4.

31. The producers also maintained that the August clarification was invalid because the AFL's arbitration committee ceased to exist after it issued the December directive, a claim rejected by the arbitrators. Testimony of William Doherty, Aug. 18, 1947, "Jurisdictional Disputes," *Hearings*, 277. Quotation, Cambiano quoted in minutes of Producers' Labor Committee meeting, Sept. 11, 1946, ibid., 909. See also ibid., 908–14; "The Situation as Interpreted by the Authors," in ibid., 528–9; *LAE*, Sept. 24, 1946, copy in Folder: "1946 – Strike Clips," box 47, JLW-USC; and Wills, *Reagan's America*, 233–6.

32. Minutes, Producers' Labor Committee, Sept. 11, 1946, "Jurisdictional Disputes," *Hearings*, 908; also ibid., Sept. 17, 1946, p. 911.

33. Quotations, SAG minutes, BD, Sept. 17, 1946, p. 3089, SAGA (not necessarily Montgomery's exact words). Reagan shared Montgomery's view of the strike. See testimony of Ronald Reagan, Aug. 20, 1947, "Jurisdictional Disputes," *Hearings*, 356; and ibid., Aug. 18, 1947, pp. 219–20, 226. See letter to "Dear Member," SAG minutes, p. 3098A, SAGA; and *LAC*, Sept. 6, 1946, pp. 1, 3.

34. Quotation, *LAT*, Sept. 27, 1946, pp. 1–2. See also Sorrell, "You Don't Choose Your Friends," 48–9, 152.

35. Quotation, Rivkin and Kerr, *Hello Hollywood!*, 411. For Universal, see Brady, "Hollywood Back to Work." On the AVC, *NYT*, Oct. 2, 1946, p. 3; *LADN*, Sept. 28, 1946, p. 1; and *People's Daily World*, Oct. 2, 1946, p. 1. For MGM, *NYT*, Sept. 29, 1946, p. 25. For Warner Bros., ibid., Sept. 28, 1946, p. 3; affidavit of Douglas Tatum, Sept. 26, 1946, affidavit of Anthony J. Characky, Sept. 27, 1946, and affidavit of Theus Doolittle, Sept. 27, 1946, box 2734, WBAHP-USC. See also testimony of Herbert Sorrell, July 13, 1955, pp. 4251–3, *Jeffers v. Screen Extras Guild*, SCCA-SAD; *HCN*, Sept. 27, 1946, and *LADN*, Sept. 28, 1946, pp. 1, 3 (copies in folder: "1946 – Strike Clips," box 47, JLW-USC).

36. Reagan quoted in McGoogan, "How the Commies Were Licked." At MGM, Mickey Rooney, Esther Williams, and Clark Gable crossed picket lines, but Bette Davis, Joan Crawford, and Claude Rains at Warner Bros., and Pat O'Brien and Ethel Barrymore at RKO, honored the lines. See Brady, "Hollywood Back to Work"; *LAT*, Sept. 27, 1946, p. 2; "Chronology of Feature Motion Pictures

Produced between Jan. 1, 1943 and Dec. 31, 1948," box 2734, WBAHP-USC; *LADN*, Sept. 28, 1946, pp. 1, 3; *NYT*, Sept. 28, 1946, p. 3; ibid., Oct. 1, 1946, p. 3; and Oct. 3, 1946, p. 3.

37. Reagan named Anne Revere, Karen Morley, Lloyd Gough, Howard Da Silva, and Howland Chamberlain as opponents of SAG's strike policy. Reagan testimony, July 1, 1955, *Jeffers* v. *Screen Extras Guild*, 3382, 3384, SCCA-SAD.

38. Before this change, a quorum of fifteen percent of the membership could transact business. Quotation, RR, *Where's*, 178. See also Murphy, *"Say,"* 296; testimony of George Murphy, Oct. 23, 1947, *HUAC Hearings, Oct. 1947*, 211; SAG minutes, BD, Sept. 9, 1946, pp. 3076–7, SAGA; ibid., Oct. 7, 1946, p. 3107; and McGoogan, "How the Commies Were Licked."

39. See resolution, SAG minutes, Sept. 23, 1946, p. 3096; SAG minutes, BD, 3095, 3098–98B; ibid., BD, Sept. 30, 1946, p. 3101; ibid., special meeting, BD, Sept. 17, 1946, pp. 3090–1, SAGA.

40. Quotations, Reagan testimony, July 1, 1955, *Jeffers* v. *Screen Extras Guild*, 3396, SCCA-SAD (also 3395); and RR, *Where's*, 171. See also ibid., 171–4; testimony of Sterling Hayden, April 10, 1951, *HUAC Hearings, 1951*, part 1, 142–3, 162; and SAG minutes, BD, Sept. 30, 1946, p. 3001, SAGA.

41. Quotations, Reagan testimony, July 1, 1955, *Jeffers* v. *Screen Extras Guild*, 3395, SCCA-SAD (also 3392–3); and RR, *Where's*, 174.

42. See *LAE*, Oct. 3, 1946, and *LADN*, Oct. 3, 1946, copies in folder: "1946 – Strike Clips," box 47, JLW-USC.

43. Members voted 2,748 to 509 not to honor picket lines. Quotations, Woll, "Warning to Hollywood," 896; and SAG minutes, BD, Sept. 30, 1946, p. 3101, SAGA. Also ibid., 3099–3102; ibid., Oct. 7, 1946, p. 3108; and "Jurisdictional Disputes," *Hearings*, 229.

44. For other members of the delegation which also met with Matthew Woll in Chicago, see SAG minutes, BD, Sept. 23, 1946, p. 3095, SAGA. See also ibid., Sept. 30, 1946, pp. 3099–3101; Oct. 7, 1946, p. 3106; Oct. 21, 1946, p. 3117; and Reagan testimony, Aug. 20, 1947, "Jurisdictional Disputes," *Hearings*, 349.

45. The arbitrators denied that Hutcheson pressured them, that they had used the phrase "basket full of words," or that they had written resignations (although Doherty said he would have resigned if either the AFL convention or executive committee had repudiated him). Quotations, Reagan testimony, Aug. 20, 1947, "Jurisdictional Disputes," *Hearings*, 349 (also 345); and Reagan testimony, Aug. 18, 1946, ibid., 234 (RR quoting arbitrators), 235. See also SAG minutes, BD, Oct. 21, 1946, p. 3118, SAGA; and testimony of Felix Knight, William Birthright, and William Doherty, Aug. 18, 1947, and Aug. 19, 1947, "Jurisdictional Disputes," *Hearings*, 278–9, 289, 293.

46. Quotations, RR, *Where's*, 150, 152 (Hutcheson quoted) (also 160). See also Hutcheson quoted, Reagan testimony, Aug. 18, 1947, "Jurisdictional Disputes," *Hearings*, 237, 240. Also see Murphy, *"Say,"* 287.

  Reagan's autobiographical account of the meeting in which Sorrell learned of Hutcheson's remarks differs from his testimony before the Kearns committee in 1947 and in the 1955 *Jeffers* v. *Screen Extras Guild* trial. See Reagan testimony, Aug. 18, 1947, "Jurisdictional Disputes," *Hearings*, 240; testimony of Pat Somerset, Aug. 18, 1947, ibid., 245; Reagan testimony, July 1, 1955, *Jeffers* v. *Screen Extras Guild*, 3391, SCCA-SAD.

47. Quotations, RR, *Where's*, 152; and Jack L. Warner to Jack M. Warner, Oct. 15, 1946, folder: "Jack M. Warner, 1946–1947," box 73, JLW-USC.

48. IATSE *General Bulletin*, no. 346 (Aug. 1946), 4; ibid., no. 368 (Dec., 1946), 8; *Hollywood Citizen*, Oct. 17, 1946, in folder: "1946 – Strike Clips," box 47,

JLW-USC; SAG minutes, BD, Oct. 21, 1946, pp. 3118–19; Reagan testimony, Aug. 18, 1947, "Jurisdictional Disputes," *Hearings*, 240; Walsh to Brewer, Oct. 22, 1946, folder 4, box 1, HSSC, URL-UCLA; Brewer to Local No. 683, Oct. 23, 1946, ibid.; and Brady, "Hollywood Unrest," 1, 3.

49. Reagan and Dales continued for many years to accept Birthright's reading of the wrong memorandum as evidence that the August clarification was bogus. Dales, "Pragmatic Leadership," 13. Quotations, RR, *Where's*, 155; and W. C. Birthright to George Murphy, Oct. 26, 1946, in "Jurisdictional Disputes," *Hearings*, 162. See also testimony of Herbert Sorrell, Aug. 14, 1947, ibid., 161–2; testimony of William Birthright, Aug. 18, 1947, ibid., 279–80; Birthright testimony, Aug. 19, 1947, ibid., 327–8; transcript of telephone call, Oct. 25, 1946, ibid., 254–5; SAG minutes, BD, Oct. 21, 1946, p. 3119.

50. See *NYT*, Oct. 27, 1946, p. 4; ibid., Nov. 13, 1946, p. 20; Nov. 14, 1946, p. 2; Nov. 16, 1946, pp. 1, 3; Nov. 20, 1946, p. 35; Nov. 23, 1946, p. 4; SAG minutes, BD, Nov. 4, 1946, pp. 3130–1, SAGA; ibid., special meeting, BD, Nov. 11, 1946, pp. 3136–8, SAGA; and special meeting, BD, Nov. 17, 1946, pp. 3143–4, ibid.

51. Reagan quoted, *LAE*, Nov. 18, 1946, copy in folder: "1946 – Strike Clips," box 47, JLW-USC. See also SAG minutes, special meeting, BD, Nov. 17, 1946, pp. 3144–5, 3147–47B, SAGA.

52. The pro-CSU faction also included Morley, Da Silva, Chamberlain, Keenan Wynn, Shimen Ruskin, Hume Cronyn, Alan Reed, Alexander Knox, and Stanley Prager. Quotations, RR, *Where's*, 173; and letter (unsigned copy) to Ladies and Gentlemen, Nov. 11, 1946, SAG minutes, p. 3140C, SAGA. See also SAG minutes, special meeting, BD, Nov. 11, 1946, pp. 3137–8; ibid., regular meeting, BD, Nov. 25, 1946, pp. 3157–8; ibid., Dec. 9, 1946, pp. 3161–2; and ibid., special meeting, BD, Dec. 16, 1946, pp. 3169–71.

53. Knox quoted in Schwartz, *Hollywood Writers' Wars*, 249–50. See also Dales, "Pragmatic Leadership," 14 (also 14–16); and *Film Technicians Daily Bulletin* [Local 683], undated [Dec. 1946?], folder 6, box 1, HSSC, URL-UCLA. See also ibid., no. 51 (Dec. 14, 1946); SAG minutes, special meeting, BD, Dec. 16, 1946, p. 3171, SAGA; and Murphy, *"Say,"* 288.

54. The vote was 873 to 75. SAG minutes, p. 3213, SAGA. See also ibid., BD, Dec. 23, 1946, p. 3177; Jan. 6, 1947, pp. 3189–90; Jan. 27, 1947, p. 3197, SAGA; and resolution passed by Interfaith Council of Los Angeles, Dec. 19, 1946, folder 8, box 1, HSSC, URL-UCLA.

55. Quotations, Sorrell to Louis Daquin, Jan. 2, 1947, folder 2, box 1, HSSC, URL-UCLA. See also "Speakers' Manual," CSU and Film Technicians' Local 683 IATSE, pp. 2–3, folder 14, box 1, ibid.; RR, *Where's*, 184; SAG minutes, BD, Jan. 27, 1947, p. 3197, SAGA; and *NYT*, Jan. 31, 1947, p. 17.

56. Quotations, "Speech of Father Dunne at the Mass Meeting of the CSU and Local 683," Feb. 2, 1947, pp. 1, 3, folder 11, box 1, HSSC, URL-UCLA. See also Dunne, "Christian Advocacy," 23–9; testimony of Father Dunne, Aug. 22, 1947, "Jurisdictional Disputes," *Hearings*, 412–13; and Wills, *Reagan's America*, 237.

57. In early March, Sorrell was found north of Los Angeles bound and severely beaten. Quotation, RR, *Where's*, 157. See also *NYT*, March 4, 1947, p. 22; ibid., March 12, 1947, p. 31; and Ceplair and Englund, *Inquisition in Hollywood*, 222–5.

58. Quotations, Morley quoted in *Oakland Tribune*, July 27, 1980, p. D3; Dunne, "Christian Advocacy," 25, 28; and RR, *Where's*, 171. Also FBI report, Los Angeles, Sept. 13, 1950, regarding "COMPIC" (100–138754–667), pp. 7–8,

Reagan file, FBI-FOIA, SHSWM; and Burkhardt, "Los Angeles Art Community" (oral history, 1977), 48.

59. Quotation, RR, *Where's*, 175.

60. Quotations, Dales, "Pragmatic Leadership," 16; Hopper, "Mr. Reagan Airs His Views," 7 (Montgomery quoted in ibid.); and Brewer, "The Full Story of Our Stand on the Coast," 6.

61. Quotations, Lardner quoted in Schwartz, *Hollywood Writers' Wars*, 248; Jack Young, "Actor, producer win Un-American 'Oscar,' " *Daily People's World*, May 16, 1947, copy in box 3, Kenny and Morris Papers, SHSWM; testimony of Jack Warner, Oct. 20, 1947, *HUAC Hearings, Oct. 1947*, 12; from Jack Warner's May 15, 1947 testimony, reprinted in testimony of Jack Warner, Oct. 20, 1947, ibid., 42 (also 13, 14, 42–3, 50, 51). For Warner's testimony of May 15, 1947, see ibid., 40–52. See also *Daily Variety*, May 16, 1947, copy in ibid.; *LAE*, May 16, 1947, p. 1; and *LAT* [?], May 16, 1947, in ibid.

12. The "Un-Americans"

1. Quotation, Lawson, "Cold War and the American Film," 4.

2. Quotation, Reagan testimony, Oct. 23, 1947, *HUAC Hearings, Oct. 1947*, 217.

3. Quotations, Stripling, *Red Plot*, 70–1. See also *NYT*, Jan. 7, 1949, p. 2; and Gabler, *Empire*, 365.

4. The groundwork for the October hearings had been laid when Eric Johnston, Jack Tenney, and J. Edgar Hoover testified before HUAC in March 1947, about infiltration. Investigators, the FBI, and informers assisted the committee. As seen, HUAC held secret sessions in May.

5. Only Lawson and Trumbo stood trial. The other eight agreed to accept the verdicts given these two. Most were sentenced to prison in 1950 for one year. Dmytryk and Biberman, who appeared before a different judge, got six-month terms. The economic status of the Ten varied in 1947. Trumbo, Lardner, Scott, and Dmytryk were making substantial salaries. Cole was close to becoming a producer. Maltz was doing well as a freelance writer. Lawson, Biberman, Bessie, and Ornitz were no longer in favor with the studios. Ceplair and Englund, *Inquisition in Hollywood*, 262–3, 268.

6. The work of the Hollywood Ten was more voluminous than this chapter can suggest. Among the best studies about the Ten are Ceplair and Englund, *Inquisition in Hollywood*, esp. 254–360; Schwartz, *Hollywood Writers' Wars*, esp. 266–80; and Andersen, "Red Hollywood," 141–96. See also Dick, *Radical Innocence*, based largely on the Ten's published work.

7. Quotation, *NYT*, Oct. 24, 1947, p. 12. See also *NYDM* [?], Oct. 24, 1947, copy in Reagan file, FBI-FOIA, SHSWM.

8. Quotations, Bacall, *By Myself*, 159. Also Olson, "Movie Hearings," 142. The SWG and the Progressive Citizens of America were also among the groups supporting the unfriendly witnesses.

9. Quotation, Olson, "Movie Hearings," 138; also 145. On Stripling's alleged white supremacist views, see Wesley, *Hate Groups*, 10.

10. Quotation, "Hollywood Goes on Trial," 41. Also see Olson, "Movie Hearings," 138, 145; and Maltz, "Citizen Writer in Retrospect," vol. 2, p. 646.

11. Quotations, testimony of Jack Warner, Oct. 20, 1947, *HUAC Hearings, Oct. 1947*, pp. 10–12; testimony of Samuel Grosvenor Wood, Oct. 20, 1947, ibid., 66; testimony of Richard Macaulay, Oct. 23, 1947, 198; testimony of Robert Montgomery, Oct. 23, 1947, 205 (also 204); testimony of Gary Cooper, Oct. 23,

1947, 221 (also 220, 224); and "Hollywood Goes on Trial," 40. See also testimony of Adolph Menjou, Oct. 21, 1947, *HUAC Hearings, Oct. 1947*, p. 94, and testimony of George Murphy, Oct. 23, 1947, ibid., 209; *Time*, Oct. 27, 1947, p. 25; "Reds: Star Witnesses," *Newsweek*, 30 (Nov. 3, 1947), 24; Olson, "Movie Hearings," 146; and *NYDM*, Oct. 24, 1947, in Reagan file, FBI-FOIA, SHSWM.

12. Quotations, Reagan testimony, Oct. 23, 1947, *HUAC Hearings, Oct. 1947*, pp. 217, 218. See also 214 and 218. At the time, Reagan thought the unfriendly witnesses should have been allowed to present their prepared statements (only Maltz and Bessie were permitted to do so). The Ten's statements appeared in Kahn, *Hollywood on Trial*. See also FBI report, Los Angeles, Dec. 19, 1947, pp. 23–4 (LA 100–15732), Reagan file, FBI-FOIA, SHSWM.

13. Quotations, "Reds: Star Witnesses," 24; "The Movie Hearing Ends," 47; and Olson, "Movie Hearings," 142. See also Reynolds, "Movie Probers Let Down"; and *NYT*, Oct. 24, 1947, p. 12.

14. Quotation, RR, *Where's*, 200. Reagan and Jane Wyman had given the FBI names of suspected Hollywood communists when a bureau agent interviewed them on April 10, 1947. See memorandum, SAC, Los Angeles to Director, FBI, April 18, 1947, regarding HICCASP (100–340327); see also report by Los Angeles agent, Aug. 4, 1947, regarding "Communist Infiltration of the Motion Picture Industry," pp. 155–7 (100–15732); report to Director, FBI, Aug. 22, 1947, regarding HUAC (100–138754); memorandum, SAC, Los Angeles to Director, FBI, Aug. 12, 1947, regarding HUAC; and FBI Report, Dec. 19, 1947, pp. 22–5, 40 (LA 100–15732), Reagan file, FBI-FOIA, SHSWM.

15. Quotations, *Motion Picture Daily*, 62 (Oct. 24, 1947), 1; Reynolds, "Movie Probers Let Down"; and "Coercing Hollywood" (editorial), *Washington Post*, Oct. 25, 1947, p. 10.

16. See Reagan testimony, Aug. 18, 1947, "Jurisdictional Disputes," *Hearings*, 220; and FBI report, Los Angeles, Dec. 19, 1947, p. 24 (100–15732), Reagan file. FBI-FOIA, SHSWM. On the FBI's use of informers, see O'Reilly, *Hoover and the Un-Americans*, 231–6.

17. Quotation, Dmytryk, *It's a Hell of a Life*, 104.

18. See ibid., 99. Quotations, testimony of John Howard Lawson, Oct. 27, 1947, *HUAC Hearings, Oct. 1947*, pp. 291, 294. See also ibid., 295–304; testimony of Dalton Trumbo, Oct. 28, 1947, 333–41; testimony of Louis Russell, Oct. 27 and 28, 1947, 296–304, 341–2; and Olson, "Movie Hearings," 138.

19. Some of the Hollywood Nineteen, such as Howard Koch, were not Communists. All of the Hollywood Ten, though, were accused of being party members by witnesses who testified before HUAC in 1951. See testimony of Richard J. Collins, April 12, 1951, *HUAC Hearings, 1951*, part 1, pp. 218–29; testimony of Meta Reis Rosenberg, April 13, 1951, ibid., part 1, pp. 286, 288; testimony of Edward Dmytryk, April 25, 1951, part 2, pp. 415, 417–19, 422–3, 429, 433; testimony of Budd Schulberg, May 23, 1951, part 3, pp. 586, 588–9, 601, 606–7; testimony of Martin Berkeley, Sept. 19, 1951, part 4, pp. 1582–3, 1587, 1590–1, 1597, 1599; and *Annual Report*, HUAC (1952), 40–56.

20. Quotations, Lawson draft attached to Joseph North to Lawson, July 9, 1943, box 10, JHL-SIU; Lawson, "Introduction to Panel Discussion," Aug. 3, 1947, p. 2, box 12, ibid.; and Lawson, "Art Is a Weapon," 18 (see also Lawson, "Art is a Weapon," pp. 896–7, folder: "Manuscripts, Autobiography"), box 99, JHL-SIU. See also Gardner, "International Rag," 391; Carr, *Left Side of Paradise*, 87; Schwartz, *Hollywood Writers' Wars*, 88; Ceplair and Englund, *Inquisition in Hollywood*, 60–5; and *Daily People's World* [S.F.], Oct. 1, 1946, p. 5. For Lawson's Marxism and pro-Soviet stance after he left prison, see Lawson, *Film in the Battle of Ideas*, 9–10, 16; and Lawson, *Film: The Creative Process*, v.

21. Trumbo quoted in Manfull, ed., *Additional Dialogue*, 435 (n. 16). See also Schwartz, *Hollywood Writers' Wars*, 185.

22. Biberman was a notable director with New York's Theatre Guild. After the hearings, he became the "motor wheel and dynamo" for the Ten as he sought to maintain their organization and support. Quotations, Maltz, "Citizen Writer in Retrospect," vol. 2, pp. 703–4 (Stephen Fritchman quoted) (also 702–3); Cole, *Hollywood Red*, 266; Bessie, *Inquisition in Eden*, 44, 115. See also ibid., 45–6; and Sondergaard speech, April 21, 1950, in *On the Eve of Prison*, 6.

23. Quotation, Bessie, "What Is Freedom for Writers?" 10 (emphasis in original text) (also 8). See also Maltz, "What Shall We Ask of Writers?" 22; Lawson, "Art Is a Weapon," 18–20; Maltz, "Citizen Writer in Retrospect," vol. 2, pp. 570–85; Bessie, *Inquisition in Eden*, 10, 12, 16, 18; Ceplair and Englund, *Inquisition in Hollywood*, 233–6; and Navasky, *Naming Names*, 287–302. Bessie fought in the Spanish Civil War and from that experience wrote *Men in Battle* (1939). For four years, he was a feature writer for the *New Masses* as well as a drama, film, and book critic. His screen credits included *The Very Thought of You* (1944), *Hotel Berlin* (1945), and *Objective Burma!* (1945).

24. See Maltz, "Writer as the Conscience," 11; Maltz, "Citizen Writer in Retrospect," vol. 1, pp. 375–7; and Ceplair and Englund, *Inquisition in Hollywood*, 236. By 1947, Maltz had probably achieved greatest respectability as an often anthologized short-story writer. His screenplays included *This Gun for Hire* (1942), *Pride of the Marines* (1945), *Destination Tokyo* (1944), and *Cloak and Dagger* (1946), the last in collaboration with Lardner.

25. Dmytryk, *It's a Hell of a Life*, 71–2; Maltz, "Citizen Writer in Retrospect," vol. 2, pp. 570–85, 798, 799; Dmytryk Interview, 1959, p. 1302, BLCU-NY; and Ceplair and Englund, *Inquisition in Hollywood*, 358.

26. Lardner, the youngest of the Ten, was the son of the well-known American humorist. He coauthored the screenplay for *Woman of the Year* (1942), which won an Academy Award. Cole became a prolific screenwriter. His movies included *The President's Mystery* (1936), *The House of Seven Gables* (1940), *Objective Burma!* (1945), and *The Romance of Rosy Ridge* (1947). He was elected to the SWG's Board in 1946 and was running for reelection when subpoenaed by HUAC. Quotations, Lardner, *Lardners*, 254 (also 256); and Cole, *Hollywood Red*, 9 (italics in original text; also 37, 138). See also *San Diego Union*, Jan. 12, 1982, p. D1; Schwartz, *Hollywood Writers' Wars*, 152, 269; Navasky, *Naming Names*, 80; Andersen, "Red Hollywood," 180–1; and Ceplair and Englund, *Inquisition in Hollywood*, 292–3. For Lardner, Ornitz, Biberman, Scott, Marxism, and the Communist Party, ibid., 47–8, 58–9, 86; and testimony of Edward Dmytryk, April 25, 1951, *HUAC Hearings, 1951*, part 2, pp. 413, 417.

27. Quotation, Lawson, "Introduction to Panel Discussions," Aug. 3, 1947, p. 4, box 12, JHL-SIU. See also ibid., 5; telegram (Lawson, et al.) to Jack Warner, Oct. 9, 1945, box 9, HICCASP Papers, SHSWM; RR, *Where's*, 161; and testimony of Jack Warner, May 15, 1947, reprinted in Warner's testimony of Oct. 20, 1947, *HUAC Hearings, Oct. 1947*, 50.

28. Quotations, Lawson, "The Cold War and the American Film"; and Trumbo to Jack [Lawson], Dec. 6, 1953, box 6, Trumbo Papers, SHSWM. See also Andersen, "Red Hollywood," 182; Greenfield, *Work and the Work Ethic*, 71–2; and Trumbo, *Harry Bridges*, 2.

29. Quotations, Cole, *Hollywood Red*, 159, 172. See also Lawson, *Film: The Creative Process*, 120; and Ceplair and Englund, *Inquisition in Hollywood*, 303.

30. The Motion Picture Industry Council attacked this film and IATSE projectionists refused to show it. See *NYT*, July 1, 1971, p. 50; Andersen, "Red Hollywood," 180; and Biberman, *Salt of the Earth*, 41–2, 245.

31. On Lawson's sensitivity about being Jewish, see Gardner, "International Rag," 9, 30–1; Brenman-Gibson, *Clifford Odets*, 223; and drafts of Lawson's autobiography, JHL-SIU. Also on the Ten, see Bessie, *Inquisition in Eden*, 10, 191; Maltz, "Citizen Writer in Retrospect," vol. 1, pp. 2–4, and vol. 2, pp. 623, 630; Cole, *Hollywood Red*, 56–7; Ceplair and Englund, *Inquisition in Hollywood*, 262, 424; Sondergaard speech of April 21, 1950, *On the Eve of Prison*, 6; Kahn, *Hollywood On Trial*, 98–9; and Navasky, *Naming Names*, 81.
32. In 1934, Lawson was part of a delegation that visited and reported on the Scottsboro Boys, seven blacks accused of raping two white girls. It was one of two trips he made to Alabama (the other investigated a steel strike and its impact on blacks); on both occasions he was jailed by local authorities. Quotation, Lawson, "The Best in the American Tradition," p. 3, literature panel, Conference on Cultural Freedom and Civil Liberties, Oct. 25–6, 1947, box 12, JHL-SIU. Also, [Lawson], "On Censorship," 3; and Lawson, *Southern Welcome*, esp. 14.
33. Lawson also wanted to rediscover the traditions of other minorities. Quotations, Lawson, "Parrington," 42; and Lawson, *Hidden Heritage*, 217, 527. See also ibid., vii, 215–17, 231–42; Lawson, "Biographical Notes," 74; and Lawson [aka Howard Jennings], "Revisionism and American History," 743, 747. For *Cry, the Beloved Country*, see box 40, JHL-SIU.
34. Neither Scott nor Dmytryk were Jewish, however. Dmytryk interview, 1959, pp. 1328–9, BLCU-NY. See also Maltz, "Citizen Writer in Retrospect," vol. 2, p. 598; Schwartz, *Hollywood Writers' Wars*, 269; Navasky, *Naming Names*, 81; and Andersen, "Red Hollywood," 181.
35. Maltz's novel, *The Cross and the Arrow*, repudiated the idea that racial characteristics made the Germans inherently war makers. The United States government helped issue 140,000 copies of this work for American servicemen abroad. While in prison, Cole and Lardner tried to undermine the institution's Jim Crow practices. Quotation, Trumbo, "Minorities and the Screen," 497. See also Trumbo to Lawson, Dec. 6, 1953, box 6, Trumbo Papers, SHSWM; statements by Maltz and Scott before HUAC in Kahn, *Hollywood on Trial*, 88, 106–9; Maltz, "Citizen Writer in Retrospect," vol. 1, pp. 181, 380–4, and vol. 2, pp. 523–4; Navasky, *Naming Names*, 81; Ceplair and Englund, *Inquisition in Hollywood*, 168–71; Schwartz, *Hollywood Writers' Wars*, 235–7; Bessie, *Inquisition in Eden*, 64; Short, "Hollywood Fights Anti-Semitism, 1945–1947," 160–3; and Cole, *Hollywood Red*, 318, 321.
36. See *People's World* (S.F.), March 14, 1941, p. 2; ibid., March 13, 1941, p. 1; Cole, *Hollywood Red*, 171–2; and Ceplair and Englund, *Inquisition in Hollywood*, 165.
37. Quotations, Trumbo, *Johnny*, 301; and advertisement, *Daily Worker* (N.Y.), March 16, 1940, p. 4. For serialization of *Johnny*, see ibid., March 17, 1940-April 29, 1940. See also Trumbo to Elsie McKeogh, March 23, 1940, box 1, Trumbo Papers, SHSWM. The Chicago *Tribune* and *People's World* (S.F.) published excerpts from *Remarkable Andrew*. E.g., *People's World*, April 5, 1941, p. 7; April 7, 1941, p. 6; April 8, 1941, p. 5; and April 9, 1941, p. 5. See also Trumbo, "On Publishing a Book," 19–21. For Trumbo's subsequent regrets over the book, see Trumbo to McKeogh, May 19, 1941, box 1, Trumbo Papers, SHSWM; Trumbo to McKeogh, [late 1945 or early 1946?], in Manfull, ed., *Additional Dialogue*, 39; and Trumbo to McKeogh, Jan. 12, 1948, ibid., 70.
38. In 1971, Lardner won an Academy Award for the screenplay of the antiwar film *M*A*S*H*, which was set in Korea. During the Vietnam War, *Johnny Got His Gun* was revived and in 1971 was made into a film, which Trumbo directed. See Bessie, *Inquisition in Eden*, 59; Cole, *Hollywood Red*, 66–9, 331; Andersen, "Red Hollywood," 169; and Olson, "Movie Hearings," 141.

39. Quotations, Lawson, "Heritage of American Culture," 13 (italics in original text); [Lawson], "On Censorship," 3; and Lawson, *Hidden Myth* (italics in original text), 530. See also ibid., 527, 531; Lawson, "Biographical Notes," 74; Lawson [aka Jennings], "Revisionism and American History," 742; and Lawson, "Parrington," 24, 25, 34.

40. Quotations, radio script, Committee on First Amendment, "Hollywood Fights Back," Nov. 2, 1947, spot 14, box 27, JHL-SIU; and Lawson, "On Censorship," 1. On the Ten's legal strategy at the hearings, see Ceplair and Englund, *Inquisition in Hollywood*, 263–71. See also Lardner, *Lardners*, 320–2; and Bessie, *Inquisition in Eden*, 6–7.

41. Left-wing writers approached Lawson to read manuscripts and he became, as Maltz noted, a censor of their ideas. Quotations, Lawson, "Art Is a Weapon," 20; Lawson, "Life and Death of a Magazine," 444, folder 3, box 99, JHL-SIU; and Lawson, "Art as a Weapon," 899, folder 9, box 99, ibid. See also Maltz, "Citizen Writer in Retrospect," vol. 1, pp. 364–8, 515; Ring Lardner, Jr. to Editor, *NYT*, Aug. 16, 1977, reprinted in *NYT*, Aug. 26, 1977, p. 20; Schwartz, *Hollywood Writers' Wars*, 152–3; Dmytryk, *It's a Hell of a Life*, 126–7; testimony of Edward Dmytryk, April 25, 1951, *HUAC Hearings, 1951*, 417–18; Cole, *Hollywood Red*, 176; and Brenman-Gibson, *Clifford Odets*, 285.

   Lawson's intolerance notwithstanding, the Ten's case encouraged others, such as Alexander Meiklejohn, to consider how the First Amendment could be used to protect unpopular ideas. See Maltz to Meiklejohn, Dec. 15, 1949, folder 7, box 20, Alexander Meiklejohn Papers, SHSWM; Meiklejohn, "Everything Worth Saying Should Be Said," 8, 32; and Meiklejohn, *Free Speech*.

42. Johnston quoted in Ceplair and Englund, *Inquisition in Hollywood*, 328. See also *Motion Picture Daily*, Oct. 30, 1947, pp. 1, 5; "The Movie Hearing Ends," 47; and Stripling, *Red Plot*, 75; Schary, *Heyday*, 164; testimony of Eric Johnston, March 27, 1947, *HUAC Hearings, March 1947*, 290, 294; testimony of Eric Johnston, Oct. 27, 1947, *HUAC Hearings, Oct. 1947*, 312–13; and *Washington Post*, Oct. 28, 1947, p. 1.

43. Those who had been under contract – Trumbo, Cole, Lardner, Scott, Dmytryk – were suspended. Johnston hoped Congress would clarify the legal status of Communists so that when producers agreed among themselves not to hire someone, they would not be open to charges of conspiracy. Quotations from Waldorf Declaration; and Johnston's statement to HUAC in Johnston's testimony, Oct. 27, 1947, *HUAC Hearings, Oct. 1947*, 308. See also ibid., 313, 323, 326–7; Ceplair and Englund, *Inquisition in Hollywood*, 328–32; and Trumbo, *Time of the Toad*, 14–15.

44. See "Report of Joint Meeting of Boards of Directors of the Three Talent Guilds with Members of the Association of Motion Picture Producers," Dec. 3, 1947, SAG minutes, pp. 3415, 3415A, 3415C, 3415D, SAGA. Quotations from report, not necessary exact words of the speaker.

45. Quotations (emphasis in original text), from "Report of Joint Meeting . . . ," Dec. 3, 1947, pp. 3415A, 3415B, ibid. See also Johnston testimony, Oct. 27, 1947, *HUAC Hearings, Oct. 1947*, 313.

46. Jack Dales and SAG's attorney Lawrence Beilenson defended Reagan's position. Dales said that the producers had failed to establish criteria for who was a Communist and that it was Congress's responsibility to set such guidelines. Beilenson believed that America experienced periodic "waves of hysteria," and that the public always disavowed such attitudes. Quotations, "Statement Proposed by Ronald Reagan, Discussed at the Board Meeting of December 8, 1947, for Further Discussion at Special Meeting December 12, 1947," SAG minutes, 3414, SAGA; and SAG minutes, BD, Dec. 8, 1947, p. 3411. Also ibid., 3410–12.

47. SAG minutes, BD, Dec. 8, 1947, pp. 3411–12, SAGA.
48. Quotations, RR, *Where's*, 179. See also board of directors, Screen Actors Guild to Motion Picture Producers Committee, Dec. 13, 1947, in SAG minutes, BD, Dec. 12, 1947, p. 3422, SAGA; and ibid., 3417–18.
49. In Feb. 1948, Reagan gave the FBI information about guild members who were part of a "clique" that "invariably followed the Communist Party line." Quotations, FBI report, Dec. 19, 1947 (LA 100–15732), pp. 22, 24, Reagan file, FBI-FOIA, SHSWM (also ibid., 40); and memorandum, Jones to Nichols, May 23, 1951 (100–351326–5), ibid.
50. Quotation, FBI report, Dec. 19, 1947, p. 24, ibid.
51. Ceplair and Englund, *Inquisition in Hollywood,* 350–4.
52. Quotations, Lawson, *Film in the Battle of Ideas,* 89; Trumbo to Lawson, Dec. 6, 1953, box 6, Trumbo Papers, SHSWM; and Cole, *Hollywood Red,* 153. See also Carr, *Left Side of Paradise,* 93; Ceplair and Englund, *Inquisition in Hollywood,* 307; and Navasky, *Naming Names,* 78.

13. The Eclipse of Liberalism

1. Quotations from RR's commentary, "President Harry Truman Reception, Sept. 23, 1948, Program," folder: "OF 200–2-H – Trip File California," box OF 751, Truman Papers, HSTLI.
2. Quotation, RR, *Where's,* 139.
3. Reagan quoted in Leuchtenburg, "Reagan's Secret Liberal Past," 20. Reagan also spoke on a program sponsored by the International Ladies' Garment Workers' Union on June 16, 1949, participating in the inaugural broadcast of WFDR-FM. See program, box 54, MSS/3/2, ADA Papers, SHSWM. See also Calif. HUAC, 1948, *Fourth Report,* 383.
4. Van Derlin quoted in Leamer, *Make-Believe,* 160. See also Leuchtenburg, "Reagan's Secret Liberal Past," 20.
   It is doubtful, as Anne Edwards argues, that Reagan switched his support from Douglas to Nixon during the 1950 campaign. Edwards cited a 1982 interview given by actor Robert Cummings in which Cummings claimed to have received a late-night telephone call from Reagan, who reportedly said: "I'm trying to help a senator get elected and we're giving a party for him tomorrow night. Can you come? . . . His name is Richard Nixon." Edwards's conclusion is questionable. Cummings did not specify a date on which he received Reagan's call. It is just as probable that Cummings was referring to the 1952 campaign, when Nixon, then already a senator, was running for vice-president. Cummings quoted in McClelland, *Hollywood on Ronald Reagan,* 229. See also Edwards, *Early Reagan,* 417–18.
5. Douglas stated his opposition to communism before Pearl Harbor and severed ties with such groups as the Motion Picture Democratic Committee and the Hollywood Anti-Nazi League. See John Lechner to FBI, May 28, 1940, box 1, Melvyn Douglas Papers, SHSWM; see also Melvyn Douglas to Lechner, June 18, 1940, ibid.; Melvyn Douglas to Martin Dies [Aug. 1940] (and attached newspaper clipping dated Aug. 20, 1940), ibid.; and Ceplair and Englund, *Inquisition in Hollywood,* 144–7.
6. On postwar liberalism, see Hamby, *Beyond the New Deal,* esp. 121–68; McAuliffe, *Crisis on the Left,* 3–74; and Pells, *Liberal Mind,* 52–182.
7. Roy Brewer was vice chair of the Labor League of Hollywood Voters. Quotations, Howard Costigan to Oscar Chapman, Nov. 8, 1948, folder: "PPF 4193,"

box P-582, Truman Papers, HSTLI. See also Truman to LLHV, Nov. 10, 1948, ibid.; *Hollywood Reporter,* Nov. 11, 1948; Memorandum, M.A. Jones [?] to Mr. Nichols, May 23, 1951 (100–138754–513), pp. 2, 4; and FBI report, Jan. 18 [?], 1949, p. 6, (LA 100–15732), p. 6, Reagan file, FBI-FOIA, SHSWM.

8. Quotations, speech by Schary, Sept. 22, 1946, p. 1, copy in box 10, Melvyn Douglas Papers, SHSWM (also ibid., 3); and Jack Warner quoted in *Daily Worker* (New York), Dec. 1, 1945, p. 11. See also memorandum, Jones to Nichols, Jan. 18, 1957 (HQ 94–33509), pp. 1, 3–4, 6, 7, Jack Warner file, FBI-FOIA, SHSWM.

9. Quotation, Brady, "Topical Hollywood," 5. See also Weiler, "By Way of Report," 5.

10. Wald quoted in Garnier, *Goodis,* 94 (trans. from the French by Beverly M. Vaughn); and Goodis quoted in ibid., 90; see also 89–98.

11. Quotations, press release for April 21 [1947], folder: "Speeches and Interviews," box 628, JLW-USC. See also Jack Warner testimony, Oct. 20, 1947, *HUAC Hearings, Oct. 1947,* 40–1; *Hollywood Reporter,* April 21, 1947; *Variety,* April 21, 1947. Brady, "Topical Hollywood," 5.

At about the time Warner considered "Up Till Now," Darryl Zanuck of Twentieth Century Fox announced plans to produce "The Iron Curtain," one of the best-known cold war movies, a film inspired by J. Edgar Hoover's speech before HUAC in March, 1947. On Warner, see George K. Killion to Matthew J. Connelly, June 13, 1945, folder: "OF 73 (1945)," box 333, OF, Truman Papers, HSTLI; and memorandum, Jones to Nichols, Jan. 18, 1957 (HQ 94–33509), Jack Warner file, FBI-FOIA, SHSWM. On Zanuck, see *Variety,* April 10, 1947, copy in Kenny-Morris Papers, box 3, SHSWM; Brady, "Contract Time in Hollywood," 5; and Leab, "'The Iron Curtain' (1948)," 153–88. On pressures on Americans to adopt a strong anticommunist line in early 1947, see Powers, *Secrecy and Power,* 286–9; and Barrett, *Tenney Committee,* 31.

12. See Jack Warner testimony, May 15, 1947, reprinted in Warner's testimony of Oct. 20, 1947, *HUAC Hearings, Oct. 1947,* 40–1; and Garnier, *Goodis,* 97.

13. Cohen quoted by Melvyn Douglas, "Liberalism," 2. See also, Cohen, *Faith of a Liberal,* 437–8; and Cohen, *Dreamer's Journey,* 6, 23, 56–76.

14. If liberalism was good for America, "we can assume that it is good for other societies," Douglas said. In an interrelated world, he added, insecurity "in Palestine, Russia or Timbuktu creates insecurity within the social structure of America." Quotations, Douglas, "Liberalism," 1–2, 4, 5, 6.

15. Quotations, "A Labor Sunday Message – 1944," *The Christian Challenger,* 3 (Sept. 10, 1944), 1; "Dr. Kleihauer Says," ibid., 2 (June 13, 1943), 1; and C. K., "Panhandlers and Preachers," ibid., 5 (Jan. 20, 1946), 1, HBCCL. See also ibid., 2 (June 6, 1943), 2; and RR interview with author, Oct. 16, 1989.

Kleihauer, a graduate of the University of Nebraska, came from Seattle to lead the Beverly Christian Church, which merged with the Hollywood Christian Church in October, 1934, to form the Hollywood–Beverly Christian Church. He commented often on social and political issues in the church newsletter, *The Christian Challenger.*

16. RR quoted in Hopper, "Mr. Reagan Airs His Views," 7.

17. RR quoted in memorandum, Jones to Nichols, May 23, 1951, p. 2, Reagan file, FBI-FOIA, SHSWM. See also *New York Post,* June 24, 1947.

18. Failure of leaders to sign the affidavit risked the guild's sanction from the National Labor Relations Board. See Resolution 1, SAG minutes, BD, p. 3377-A; ibid., BD, Aug. 18, 1947, p. 3335; Sept. 8, 1947, pp. 3353–4; Revere to SAG Board,

Sept. 15, 1947, in SAG minutes, pp. 3363; and SAG minutes, BD, Sept. 29, 1947, pp. 3359–60, SAGA.

19. In late 1947 the board adopted a stand consistent with the AFL in that it required officers to sign the affidavit so benefits from the NLRB and union shop would not be lost; it also endorsed AFL efforts to challenge the constitutionality of Taft-Hartley. But it was not prepared to go as far as the AFL in opposing congressmen who had voted for Taft-Hartley. See SAG minutes, BD, Sept. 8, 1947, p. 3354, SAGA. Also ibid., Sept. 29, 1947, pp. 3359–61; Nov. 3, 1947, p. 3387; Nov. 16, 1947, p. 3392; Resolutions 3 and 4, Nov. 4, 1947, SAG minutes, p. 3377A–77B; and press release, Jan. 15, 1948, SAG minutes, pp. 3442–42A, SAGA.

20. SAG minutes, BD, Nov. 16, 1947, pp. 3391–2, SAGA; ibid., Nov. 24, 1947, 3401; press release, Jan. 15, 1948, SAG minutes, p. 3442; Melvyn Douglas to Chat Paterson [sic], Nov. 8, 1947, box 3, Melvyn Douglas Papers, SHSWM; and testimony of Eric Johnston, Oct. 27, 1947, *HUAC Hearings, Oct. 1947*, 312.

21. Quotations, RR, *Where's*, 141, 165. At what point Reagan joined the AVC is unclear although the organization recruited the cast of *This Is the Army*. See *AVCB* (May 15, 1945), [3].

22. Quotations, Harris to editor, *AVCB* (May 15, 1945), [3]; and Bolte, *New Veteran*, 173. For information about Bolte and other early AVC leaders, see *AVCB*, 1 (July 1, 1946), 14–16; Tyler, "American Veterans Committee," 420; and FBI Report, Los Angeles, regarding AVC, June, 17, 1946 (100–22857), pp. 1, 2, section 1, American Veterans Committee file, FBI-FOIA, SHSWM.

23. Quotations, Bolte, *New Veteran*, 5, 144–5 (also 74). See also Bolte to Wallace, Aug. 5, 1944, box 10, Henry A. Wallace Papers, FDRL; *AVCB* (March 1, 1945), [1–3]; and masthead of ibid. (Aug. 1, 1944), [1].

24. Quotations, Bolte, "Conscription Between Wars," 332; and Bolte, *New Veteran*, 145.

25. See proposed national platform, 4, attached to Bolte and Gilbert Harrison to Melvyn [Douglas], May 19, 1947, box 3, Melvyn Douglas Papers, SHSWM; Melvyn Douglas speech, July 30, 1946, p. 11, box 10, ibid.; and Bolte, "Conscription Between Wars," 332.

26. Quotations (emphasis in original text), Melvyn Douglas speech, July 30, 1946, p. 12, box 10, Melvyn Douglas Papers, SHSWM. See also proposed national platform, 4, attached to Bolte and Harrison to Melvyn [Douglas], May 19, 1947, box 3, ibid.; and AVC letter to President Truman, in *AVCB* (Sept. 15, 1945), 1.

27. Quotation, Wylie, "The Atom Bomb," 4. See also Wylie, *Generation of Vipers*, 256–72; Wylie, *Essay on Morals*, 104–13; Wylie, *Tomorrow!*, 313; and Wylie, *Three to be Read*, 3–113.

28. Quotations, from "Statement of Intentions," attached to *AVCB* (Aug. 1, 1944), attached to Wallace to Bolte, Aug. 11, 1944, folder: "American," box 3, Wallace Papers, FDRL. See also Tyler, "American Veterans Committee," 422.

29. See *AVCB*, 1 (Nov. 15, 1945), [2]; ibid., 1 (Feb. 1, 1946), 1, 6; 1 (March 15, 1946), 3; 1 (May 1, 1946), 4; 1 (Sept. 1, 1946), 4; 1 (Oct. 15, 1946), 7; 2 (March 1, 1947), 1; and James, "Battle of A. V. C.," 707.

30. Quotations, Post quoted in FBI report (LA), regarding AVC, June 17, 1946 (100–22857), p. 5, Reagan file, FBI-FOIA, SHSWM; RR, *Where's*, 141; and RR, "Fascist Ideas Are Still Alive in U.S.," 6. In September 1946 Reagan was asked to talk at a conference on "The Challenge of the Post War World to the Liberal Movement," about how war veterans could be reintegrated into civilian life. In November sources informed the FBI he was a member of the National Finance Committee. See "Provisional Agenda," conference, Sept. 21–2, 1946, box 3, Melvyn Douglas Papers, SHSWM. See also FBI report (Indianapolis), Sept. 13,

1946 (100–2239); FBI report (N.Y.) April 29, 1947 (100–80087), pp. 28–9; and memorandum, Jones [?] to Nichols, May 23, 1951 (nos. 100–339008–49 and 100–339008–109), p. 3, Reagan file, FBI-FOIA, SHSWM.

31. Editorial quoted, *AVCB*, 1 (Sept. 15, 1945), 1; Pegler quoted in Tyler, "American Veterans Committee," 426; Dow Walker quoted in press release, undated, folder: "Correspondence 1946 Feb. 18–July 29," box 3, Melvyn Douglas Papers, SHSWM; and memorandum, Jones to Nichols, May 23, 1951, p. 3, Reagan file, FBI-FOIA, SHSWM. See also *NYT*, May 11, 1946, p. 7.

32. Quotations, Tyler, "American Veterans Committee," 430 (also 422–36); and *AVCB*, 3 (Nov. 1947), 2. See also press release, undated, folder: "Correspondence 1946 Feb. 18–July 29," box 3, Melvyn Douglas Papers, SHSWM; press release ("AVC Blasts Communist Party"), Nov. 10, [1946?], p. 1, box 11, ibid.; "Statement on Fascism by the National Planning Committee of the American Veterans Committee," Nov. 9–11, 1946, ibid. *AVCB*, 1 (July 15, 1946), 1; James, "Battle of A.V.C.," 706–7; *NYT*, June 16, 1946, p. 26; ibid., June 17, 1946, p. 15, and Nov. 11, 1946, p. 22.

33. See Hobert W. Burns to editor, *AVCB*, 1 (Oct. 1, 1946), 5. See also *People's Daily World* [SF], Oct. 1, 1947, p. 3.

34. Quotations, Oren Root, Jr., to editor, *AVCB*, 1 (Oct. 1, 1946), 5; Theo. Robinson to Editor, ibid., 2 (Feb. 1, 1947), 5; and Bill Morrison to Melvyn Douglas, June 4, 1947, box 3, Melvyn Douglas Papers, SHSWM.

35. E.g., Chat Patterson had called for abolition of HUAC and the AVC's national leadership opposed Taft-Hartley. Quotations, Calif. HUAC, 1948, *Fourth Report*, 387 (also 388); and Rogers, quoted in *LAT*, March 24, 1948. See also *AVCB*, 2 (July 1947), 12 (for RR's picture); ibid., 3 (Nov. 1947), 2; ibid., 3 (March 1948), 7; and *People's Daily World*, Feb. 25, 1948, p. 6.

36. Quotations, *Spotlights* (Hollywood Chapter No. 2, AVC), 1 (April 15, 1948), 1, in box 3, Melvyn Douglas Papers, SHSWM; and *AVCB*, 3 (June 1948), 3. See also ibid., 3 (July 1948), 3, 5; and Tyler, "American Veterans Committee," 434.

37. See *AVCB*, 5 (Jan. 1950), 1; ibid., 5 (Feb. 1950), 3; and Tyler, "American Veterans Committee," 434–5.

38. Quotations, RR, *Where's*, 165–6. See also Reagan Testimony, July 1, 1955, pp. 3400–2, *Jeffers v. Screen Extras Guild*, SCCA-SAD. For evidence that the Hollywood chapter of the AVC picketed in sympathy with strikers, see undated clipping, folder: "1946 – Strike Clips," box 47, JLW-USC. AVC stationery provides evidence of Reagan's membership on the 1953 convention committee and on the AVC's national advisory council at least until 1960. See folder 10, box 1, MSS/3/5, ADA Papers, SHSWM.

39. Quotations, Loeb to RR, Oct. 25, 1947, box 1, series 3, ADA Papers, SHSWM; Loeb to Charles A. Wellmann, Oct. 25, 1947, box 4, MSS/3/3, ibid.; Loeb to Mrs. Hamilton von Breton, Oct. 25, 1947, ibid.; and Loeb, "Notes, Comments and Recollections on ADA Inspired by the one-volume history written by Clifton Brock, in 1965" [undated, c. 1970?], 12 (also 13), folder 5, box 3, James I. Loeb, Jr. Papers, SHSWM. See also Loeb to RR, undated [1947?], series 3, no. 5, reel no. 57 (microfilm), ibid.; and Hamby, *Beyond the New Deal*, 148–9. Reagan also apparently made a good impression on some conservatives at the HUAC hearings. See Nixon, *In the Arena*, 190.

40. Gillon, *Politics and Vision*, ix. Reagan did not discuss the ADA in *Where's* or in *American Life*.

41. See Schlesinger, *Vital Center*, x, 166, 209, 254–6. See also press release for Jan. 6, 1947, folder 3, box 5, Loeb Papers, SHSWM. Loeb to Art Arthur, Nov. 1, 1947,

folder 1, box 6, MSS/3/3, ADA Papers, SHSWM; "Statement of Political Policy by the Board of the Americans for Democratic Action, Adopted . . . April 11, 1948," series 3, no. 16, reel no. 59 (microfilm), ibid.; and Gillon, *Politics and Vision*, viii–ix.

42. Quotations, Loeb, "Progressives and Communists," 699 (emphasis in original text); and Loeb, "Letter of the Week," *New Republic* (Jan. 27, 1947), 46. See also Pells, *Liberal Mind*, 108–9; and Hamby, *Beyond the New Deal*, 161–4, 185, 193.

43. See "Statement of Political Policy . . . [ADA], April 11, 1948." See also Hamby, *Beyond the New Deal*, 224–9, 237–9, 241–3.

44. Quotations, Jeri Despol to Loeb, Oct. 16, 1947, box 4, MSS/3/3, ADA Papers, SHSWM; and "*Key Persons – California*," series 3, no. 5, reel no. 57 (microfilm), ADA Papers, SHSWM (also "California Organizing Committee," ADA, ibid.). See also *LADN* [?], Oct. 4, 1947, clipping in box 4, MSS/3/3, ADA Papers, SHSWM; Loeb, "Notes, Comments and Recollections on ADA," 12, Loeb Papers, SHSWM; Ceplair and Englund, *Inquisition in Hollywood*, 144–7; and Ryskind, *Hubert*, 114.

45. Reagan's role in drafting the ads is unclear, but their argument was similar to the position he adopted before HUAC a few days later. Quotations, see ad, *Hollywood Reporter*, Oct. 15, 1947, box 11, Melvyn Douglas Papers, SHSWM. See also Loeb to RR, Oct. 25, 1947, box 1, MSS/3/3, ADA Papers, SHSWM; and Loeb to Arthur, Nov. 1, 1947, box 6, ibid.

46. The ADA's nominating committee named Reagan to the national board without obtaining his consent. See Loeb to RR, April 27, 1948, box 6, ibid.; and Loeb to RR, Aug. 6, 1948, box 1, series 2, ibid.

47. Quotations, RR to [Leon] Henderson, undated (handwritten note at bottom of letter, Henderson to Board Member, March 25, 1948), series 2, no. 48, reel no. 32 (microfilm), ibid. See also Loeb, "Notes, Comments and Recollections on ADA," p. 12, Loeb Papers, SHSWM.

48. Reagan's name appeared on ADA stationery as a national board member as late as June 1949, but by July 7 his name had been dropped. His membership in the ADA probably continued beyond 1950. In June 1951, national chairman Francis Biddle thanked him for his "generous response" to an ADA appeal for support. Quotations, RR to Henderson, July 15, [1948], series 2, no. 186, reel no. 45 (microfilm), ADA Papers, SHSWM; and Biddle to RR, June 11, 1951, box 4, MSS/3/3, ibid. See also membership lists Sixteenth Congressional District chapter for July 19, 1948, and for April 26 and Aug. 11, 1949, box 6, MSS/3/3, ibid. Also Loeb to RR, March 26, 1949, box 1, MSS 3/2, ibid.

49. See Melvyn Douglas to Loeb, Nov. 24, 1947, box 4, ibid.

50. Quotations, [Robert Ardrey] to Loeb, Jan. 24, 1948, box 1, MSS/3/3, ibid.

51. Quotations, Howard J. Green to Wilson W. Wyatt, Jan. 31, 1948, box 1, MSS/3/3, ADA Papers, SHSWM; and Brewer quoted in *Westwood Hills Press*, Feb. 17, 1948, p. 1, copy in ibid. See also Faith Schwarz to Loeb, Feb. 19, 1948, ibid.; Green to Wyatt, Jan. 31, 1948, box 1, MSS/3/3; Lavery to Joe Rauh, Feb. 25, 1948; [Ardrey] to Loeb, Jan. 24, 1948; Lavery to Rauh, Feb. 25, 1948; and *Daily Variety*, 58 (Feb. 24, 1948), 1.

52. Quotation, Hoover to Tolson and Ladd, (indexed Jan. 4, 1950), ADA file, FBI-FOIA, SHSWM. See also memorandum, V. P. Keay to Mr. Fletcher, Nov. 29, 1949, p. 6, ibid.; confidential FBI report on ADA, Nov. 29, 1949 (100–347196–41), pp. 79–81, 130–3, ibid.; FBI report (100–348196-A), ibid.; Pegler, "Fair Enough"; and Hamby, *Beyond the New Deal*, 389–90, 494–5.

53. Even after the HUAC hearings, Loeb hoped Hollywood would provide $40,000

to $50,000 in contributions. Quotation, Loeb to Arthur, Nov. 1, 1947, box 6, MSS/3/3, ADA Papers, SHSWM.

54. Quotations, Loeb to Arthur, ibid.; and Loeb to Esther Murray, May 4, 1948, ibid.

55. Quotations, Ardrey to Loeb, Dec. 7, 1948, box 2, MSS/3/3, ADA Papers, SHSWM; and Cohen, *Faith of a Liberal,* 337. See also ibid., 337–61, 438; Douglas, "Liberalism," 2, 6; and Nash, *Conservative Intellectual Movement,* 3–130, 364 (n. 48).

14. Black Dignity

1. The Secretary of the San Diego Branch of the NAACP made these allegations. Reagan claimed to have noticed an increase in extremist groups after the war, observing "more than forty veterans' organizations arise; most of them seemed to be highly intolerant of color, creed, and common sense." As noted (this volume, Chapter 13), he denounced the American Order of Patriots in early 1946. Quotations, Margaret James to Kinny [*sic*], Aug. 9, 1946, box 30, Robert Kenny Papers, BL-UCB; and RR, *Where's,* 141. Compare also the number of stories devoted to the KKK in the *NYT* in 1945 with the following year. For FBI investigations, which increased in seven states, see ibid., Aug. 1, 1946, p. 14; and ibid., Sept. 1, 1946, section 4, p. 4.

2. Quotations from transcript of "Operation Terror," 2, 6; and from broadcast excerpt of "Operation Terror," 1, 5, Sept. 9, 1946, attached to memorandum, SAC, Los Angeles to Director, FBI, Sept. 20, 1946 (100–343748), Reagan file, FBI-FOIA, SHSWM.

3. Quotations, *LAT,* Sept. 13, 1946, p. 2 (Bowron quoted); Fletcher Bowron to DeWitt Wallace ("misguided"), Sept. 13, 1946, box 2, Fletcher Bowron Papers, HL-SM; Calif. HUAC, 1948, *Fourth Report,* 254; and Calif. HUAC, 1947, *Third Report,* 45, 57. See also ibid., 44, 57–62; Hallenback Club Communist Party to Kenny, April 26, 1946, box 29, Kenny Papers, BL-UCB; Romona Evergreen Branch, Communist Party to Kenny, April 18, 1946, box 29, ibid.; True Boardman to Robert W. Jenny [*sic*], May 1, 1946, box 24, ibid.; and Bowron to Foreman, Los Angeles Grand Jury, Sept. 13, 1946, box 2, Bowron Papers, HL-SM.

4. These associations included HICCASP, Mobilization for Democracy, the AVC, SAG, Warner Bros., the AAF, the Hollywood–Beverly Christian Church, and the ADA.

5. Quotations, White, *Man Called White,* 201 (also 198–202); White to Mendel Silberberg, Aug. 5, 1942, box A281, group 2, NAACP records, LC; White quoted in press release by Arch Reeve [July 18, 1942], ibid. See also White to Bette Davis, July 27, 1942, ibid.; Cripps, *Slow Fade to Black,* 375–6; and *LAT,* July 20, 1942, pp. 1, 5.

6. E.g., Will Hays and the producers opposed White's suggestion to appoint a black to the MPPDA. Quotation, White, *Man Called White,* 202. See also Wanger to Wendell [Willkie], July 22, 1942, folder 6, box 31, Wanger Papers, SHSWM; White to Melvyn Douglas, March 12, 1942, box A281, group 2, NAACP records, LC (and related correspondence in ibid.); NAACP, *Annual Report for 1942,* 32; Noble, *Negro in Films,* 220–1; and Leab, *From Sambo to Superspade,* 129–30.

7. The war brought together blacks, their white allies, and government agencies whose propaganda objectives happened to coincide with the social goals of African-Americans. See Cripps, "Movies, Race, and World War II," 49–57, 60–6; Cripps, *Making Movies Black,* 27–8; Koppes and Black, "Blacks, Loyalty, and Motion-Picture Propaganda," 391, 393, 399, 404; Finkle, "Conservative Aims of

Militant Rhetoric," 692–713; Washburn, *Question of Sedition*, 54–6, 100–2, 131–2; Cripps, *Slow Fade to Black*, 388; Writers' War Board, *How Writers Perpetuate Stereotypes*, 5–6; Dalfiume, *Desegregation*; Wynn, *The Afro-American and the Second World War*; and Osur, *Blacks in the Army Air Forces*.

8. Quotations, Alex Evelove to J. L. [Warner], March 21, [1946?] (includes list of films), folder 22, box 60, JLW-USC; and from song lyrics, "The General Jumped at Dawn," by Larry Neal and Jimmy Mundy, reel 1 of *Hollywood Canteen*, SHSWM. See also Davis to Jack Warner, April 26, 1944, folder 17, box 60, JLW-USC; and Robert Benjamin to Warner, March 3, 1944, ibid.

9. Quotations, Murphy, *"Say,"* 257. *This Is the Army* served at most as a transitional film between the callous Hollywood portrayals of blacks before the war and more sympathetic postwar treatments. See Koppes and Black, "Blacks, Loyalty, and Motion-Picture Propaganda," 403.

10. See Osur, *Blacks in the Army Air Forces*, 23, also viii–ix, 9, 62–85; and Polenberg, *War and Society*, 123–6.

11. See Osur, *Blacks in the Army Air Forces*, 43–5; Capra, *Name Above the Title*, 359; Cripps and Culbert, *"The Negro Soldier* (1944)," 618–40, esp. 623; Polenberg, *War and Society*, 126–30; and Sitkoff, "Racial Militancy and Interracial Violence," 661–81.

12. Quotations and account of black sacrifices from RR's film narration, NNSM. Also Phenix, "Eagles Unsung," 26; and Scanlan, *History . . . Oct. 1–31, 1944*, pp. 8–9 (microfilm no. A2987), MAFB.

13. Quotations from RR's narration, NNSM.

14. Quotations, Kleihauer in *Christian Challenger*, 1 (July 5, 1942), 1; ibid., 2 (Aug. 15, 1943), 1; 3 (May 28, 1944), 1; 3 (March 26, 1944), 1; 3 (May 28, 1944), 1; 3 (Aug. 6, 1944), 1; Kleihauer, "Is Hitler Still Alive?" ibid., 4 (May 13, 1945), 1. See also ibid., 1 (June 14, 1942), 1; 1 (Oct. 4, 1942), 1; 3 (June 4, 1944), 1; Kleihauer, "Things We Cannot Afford," ibid., 4 (Jan. 21, 1945), 1; Kleihauer, "The Immorality of Goodness," ibid. (March 25 [?], 1945), 1; and Cole, *Christian Churches . . . of Southern California*, 187.

15. Quotation, Cripps, "Dark Spot in the Kaleidoscope," 19. See also 18–19; and Cripps, *"Amos 'n' Andy*," 33–54.

16. Prindle, *Politics of Glamour*, 44.

17. The AVC proposed that minorities should have the right to sue for slander or libel against an entire majority group. See "Platform Passed by First Constitutional Convention," June 15, 1946, p.8, in box 11, Melvyn Douglas Papers, SHSWM. For SAG, see SAG minutes, EC, Dec. 30, 1938, p. 1008; ibid., EC, Sept. 29, 1941, p. 1927; and EC, Oct. 20, 1941, p. 1946.

18. See Thomson to Bessie Marie Reed, Jan. 7, 1942, box A281, group 2, NAACP records, LC; and related correspondence in ibid. For worries among SAG leaders about bad publicity in the black press, see SAG minutes, BD, Aug. 24, 1942, p. 2136, SAGA; and ibid., Sept. 14, 1942, p. 2147, ibid.

19. White to Norman O. Huston, Sept. 10, 1943, box A281, group 2, NAACP records, LC; SAG minutes, BD, March 1, 1943, pp. 2286–7, SAGA; and ibid., May 24, 1943, pp. 2355–6; Cripps, *Slow Fade to Black*, 374; and Ashton, "Changing Image of Blacks in American Film: 1944–1973" (doctoral thesis, 1981), 33–4.

20. Quotations, White to Sterling Brown, Feb. 20, 1946, box A279, group 2, NAACP records, LC; and Herman Hill, "Hollywood Stars Rap Interference," *N.Y. Pitts Courier* [?], Feb. 2, 1946, in ibid. See also Fredi Washington, "Fredi Says," *People's Voice*, Feb. 9, 1946, copy in ibid. For White's bureau, see related correspondence in ibid.

21. Quotation, MPAA press release [Sept. 1947?], PCA file for *Curley*, AMPASL. See

also John Dales to Johnston, Oct. 1, 1947, ibid.; and SAG minutes, BD, Sept. 29, 1947, p. 3362, SAGA.

22. Reagan was elected third vice-president at the annual meeting on September 15, but the minutes are silent on his position. See Resolution 4 (submitted to SAG members Oct. 11, 1946, and passed 992 to 34), SAG minutes, annual meeting, Sept. 15, 1946, pp. 3081, 3084, 3142A, SAGA; and SAG minutes, BD, Nov. 25, 1946, pp. 3156–7, ibid.

23. SAG minutes, BD, March 10, 1947, p. 3232; ibid., March 24, 1947, p. 3240; April 21, 1947, p. 3260; May 26, 1947, p. 3284; and Aug. 4, 1947, p. 3329.

24. See ibid., Oct. 20, 1947, pp. 3367, 3372. See also Resolution 13, Nov. 4, 1947, pp. 3377E–77F, ibid.; SAG minutes, BD, Nov. 24, 1947, pp. 3399, 3401, ibid.; and press release, Jan. 15, 1948, pp. 3442–42A, ibid.

25. Quotation, *AVCB,* 3 (July, 1948), 1.

26. Roger's character had come to visit her sister, Lucy (Doris Day), only to discover that the murderer (Steve Cochran) was Lucy's husband.

27. In promoting this film, the studio encouraged theater managers to contact the local Anti-Defamation League and American Civil Liberties Union. Quotations from film. See also "Prexy Chatter," [1950?], p. 6, DETA; Richard Brooks to Jerry Wald, Feb. 3, 1948, story file for *Storm Warning,* WBAHP-USC; pressbook for *Storm Warning,* 1, 4, [8], ibid.; and Cripps, *Making Movies Black,* 270.

Reagan's character, Yank, in Warner Bros.' *Hasty Heart* (1950), it should be noted, was sympathetic to the black soldier Blossom, played by Orlando Martins. At one level, the studio gave Martins' character a dignified persona. On another level, however, he retained a pose not unlike the simpleminded stereotype in other films because he did not speak English.

28. Quotations, William Walker's presentation to SAG's annual Hollywood membership meeting, Nov. 9, 1952, SAG minutes, p. 4340A, SAGA. Also ibid., 4340; SAG minutes, BD, April 7, 1952, pp. 4221–22; June 16, 1952, p. 4255; and telephone interview with William Walker by author, March 21, 1988.

29. Quotation, "Release Friday June 13, [1952]," SAG minutes, pp. 4263–63A, SAGA. See also telephone interview with William Walker by author, March 21, 1988; *LAT,* June 13, 1952, part 1, p. 2, part 2, p. 3; *Variety* (June 11, 1952), 2; and Ceplair and Englund, *Inquisition in Hollywood,* 51, 291.

30. Quotations from Walker's presentation to SAG's annual Hollywood membership meeting, Nov. 9, 1952, SAG minutes, 4340–40A, SAGA.

31. These black performers, while critical of White, were not necessarily attacking the suggested code. Quotations, "Proposed code for television," attached to White to George Heller, May 7, 1951, box A626, group II, NAACP records, LC. See also SAG minutes, BD, July 28, 1952, p. 4281; ibid., July 14, 1952, p. 4271, SAGA; SAG minutes, EC, June 1, 1953, p. 4445, ibid.; and Cripps, *Making Movies Black,* 240.

32. Walker joined the SAG's Board on Oct. 28, 1952. See SAG minutes, BD, Jan. 28, 1952, p. 4198, SAGA; Feb. 12, 1952, p. 4202; Oct. 28, 1952, p. 4329; and Nov. 9, 1952, p. 4338. See also press release, July 16, [1951], attached to George Heller To All Networks, Television Stations, etc., Feb. 20, 1952, box A626, group 2, NAACP records, LC; and White to Heller, May 7, 1951, ibid.

33. The vote made SAG the "official representative" of all performers in 99 percent of all movies to be exhibited in the United States. Television Authority was affiliated with the AFL and represented television performers and officials of the Columbia Broadcasting System, American Broadcasting Company, National Broadcasting Company, and the Du Mont Television Network. At this time, it was made up of five labor unions, but neither SAG nor the Screen Extras Guild was part of the

setup. Television Authority hoped to merge these unions. Quotation, *Variety,* Feb. 13, 1952, p. 22. Also ibid., Jan. 23, 1952, p. 2.

34. Quotations, Ely, *Adventures,* 218 (see also 216–18); Ely, "Amos 'n' Andy" (doctoral thesis, 1985), 537 (also 511–87, esp. 521–2 for Walker); and Muse quoted in Cripp, "*Amos 'n' Andy,*" 42. See also ibid., 33–54; and "Amos 'n' Andy win friends in TV controversy," *Printer's Ink,* 236 (Aug. 17, 1951), 13.

35. Quotation from statement "Integration and Employment of Negro Performers," attached to SAG minutes, 4340B, SAGA. See also Walker's presentation to SAG's annual Hollywood membership meeting, Nov. 9, 1952, SAG minutes, 4340A, ibid.; and SAG minutes, BD, March 9, 1953, p. 4404.

36. Quotation, SAG minutes, BD, April 13, 1953, p. 4430, SAGA. See also ibid., 4427; and March 9, 1953, p. 4404.

37. See SAG minutes, BD, March 23, 1953, p. 4415, ibid.

38. See SAG minutes, BD, May 11, 1953, p. 4435, ibid.; *Hollywood Reporter,* 124 (May 5, 1953), 3; ibid. (May 8, 1953), 2; *Daily Variety,* 79 (May 5, 1953), 1, 4; and ibid. (May 8, 1953), 2.

39. Quotations, White to Schary, June 7, 1949, folder 17, box 108, Schary Papers, SHSWM; White, *How Far the Promised Land?,* 207; and Hughes, "Hollywood's Ridiculous Stereotype Program," 11. See also Hughes, "Major Differences," 11.

40. Reagan's thinking about race through the early postwar years appears consistent with the attitudes held by "conscience liberals" – individuals, Thomas Cripps noted, who were "moved by isolated outrages" but lacked a "broad view of racism and therefore a programmatic means of dealing with it." See Cripps, "Movies, Race, and World War II," 52; also 49–50, 54. Lawson's view was also limited. He assumed discrimination was rooted in Western capitalism and downplayed racism in the Soviet Union and communist China.

41. Breen made a limited effort to improve the image of blacks after World War II. In Reagan's film *Night Unto Night,* Breen insisted that the maid Josephine "be handled in such a way as not to cast disparagement on the Negro nor be in any way offensive." But Breen also concluded in early 1949 in reviewing *Pinky* that "physical contact between Negroes and whites" would be offensive "in a number of sections of this country." Text quotations, from Walker's presentation to SAG's annual Hollywood membership meeting, Nov. 9, 1952, SAG minutes, 4340A, SAGA; telephone interview with Walker by author, March 21, 1988; and telephone interview with Walker by author, Oct. 29, 1987. Note quotations, Breen to J. L. Warner, Sept. 6, 1946, PCA file, *Night Unto Night,* AMPASL (also Breen to Warner, Oct. 19, 1946, ibid.); and Breen to Jason Joy, Feb. 28, 1949, PCA file, *Pinky,* ibid.

42. Quotation, Calif. HUAC, 1947, *Third Report,* 44.

15. Selling Hollywood

1. Information about the MPIC can be obtained from the Schary, Wanger, and the Herbert Biberman-Gale Sondergaard Papers in SHSWM, from the Art Arthur Papers and Cecil B. DeMille Papers in BYUA-P, and from the Motion Picture Industry Council Papers in AMPASL. The SAG minutes reveal the interaction between that guild and the MPIC.

2. Quotations, RR, *Where's,* 201; and Black, *Child Star,* 407. For reviews, e.g., *Time,* Nov. 10, 1947, p. 104 and Dec. 15, 1947, p. 103.

3. The MPIC was but one component of this offensive. Through the Theatre Owners of America the industry supplied pro-Hollywood stories to the local press that *Variety* estimated reached twenty million readers. *Variety* (July 14, 1948), 4, 16; ibid. (July 21, 1948), 4; and Brady, "Hollywood Discord."

4. SAG minutes, BD, Jan. 5, 1948, pp. 3427–8, SAGA; and "Report of Joint Meeting of Boards of Directors of the Three Talent Guilds with Members of the Association of Motion Picture Producers," Dec. 3, 1947, SAG minutes, 3415D, ibid.
5. See MPIC minutes, July 20, 1948, pp. [1], 3, folder 23, box 13, Wanger Papers, SHSWM; Schwartz, *Hollywood Writers' Wars*, 269–70; *NYT,* May 25, 1959, p. 29; *Variety* (July 21, 1948), 4; and testimony of Eric Johnston, Oct. 27, 1947, *HUAC Hearings, Oct. 1947,* 314–21.
6. See Art Arthur to All Members of MPIC Finance Committee, Sept. 25, 1950, folder 23, box 13, Wanger Papers, SHSWM; and MPIC minutes, July 20, 1948 [p. 1], ibid.
7. DeMille had been barred from the American Federation of Radio Artists for not paying a $1 million political campaign assessment during 1944. He appealed to the U. S. Supreme Court and lost. See Schary to the editors, [Jan. 29, 1949], folder 9, box 108, Schary Papers, SHSWM. See *NYT,* Feb. 6, 1949, section 2, p. 5; ibid., Feb. 1, 1949, p. 30; March 3, 1949, p. 33; March 15, 1949, p. 35; and March 16, 1949, p. 35. For Reagan's election, see July 24, 1949, section 2, p. 3.
8. For example, see letterhead of Samuel G. Engel, Sept. 20, 1955, folder 1, box 14, Wanger Papers, SHSWM.
9. Freeman was vice-president of Paramount and chairman of the board of the Association of Motion Picture Producers. Quotations, Arthur to Kenneth Clark, Dec. 15, 1975, box 43, Arthur Papers, BYUA-P; and DeMille in *V.F. W. Magazine,* 40 (Sept. 1952), 27. See also DeMille interview (1958), 1–2, BLCU-NY; and Cole, *Hollywood Red,* 180.
10. Reagan and Brewer also belonged to the Southern California Committee of the International Rescue and Relief Committee and the LLHV. See FBI report no. 317183, Reagan file, FBI-FOIA, SHSWM; guest list in "Trip File California," OF 200-2-H, box OF 751, Truman Papers, HSTLI; Dmytryk interview (1959), 1377, BLCU-NY; Allen Rivkin to Walter Reilly, July 11, 1952, folder 4, box 100, Schary Papers, SHSWM; Schary interview (1958), 79, BLCU-NY; and Schary, *Heyday,* 164–5.
11. Arthur also had been a newspaperman, columnist, and television writer. He was a member of the SWG's Executive Board during 1947–48 and was considered among SWG's conservatives. Quotations, Rivkin, HELLO HOLLYWOOD!, 430. See also Schwartz, *Hollywood Writers' Wars,* 264, 323–4; and Bessie, *Inquisition in Eden,* 137.
12. Although Schary was the son of Jewish immigrants from Russia who came to America during the early 1890s, Dmytryk contended he had no part in the conception of *Crossfire* and had been reluctant to undertake the project. Quotations, Schary to editors, [Jan. 19, 1949], folder 9, box 108, Schary Papers, SHSWM; "Dore Schary" [Nov. 19, 1951], p. 4, folder: "Biographical Data," box 46, ibid. (also "Biography," [1957], p. 2, ibid.); Schary interview (1958), 35, BLCU-NY (also 1, 43–5, 79). See also Schary, *For Special Occasions,* 4, 7; Kahn, *Hollywood on Trial,* 187; *NYT,* Jan. 25, 1948, section 2, p. 5; Schary, *Heyday,* 166, 168–73; *Variety* (July 14, 1948), 3; ibid. (July 21, 1948), 22; Dmytryk, *It's a Hell of a Life,* 89; and Dmytryk interview (1958), 1328–30, BLCU-NY.
13. Schary maintained that he, Wanger, and Samuel Goldwyn opposed the Waldorf Statement and that a vote was never taken on it. Quotations, Schary, *Heyday,* 209 (also 164–7, 201–2, 219–20); and speech by Schary, Sept. 22, 1946, box 10, Melvyn Douglas Papers, SHSWM. See also Schary interview (1958), 79, BLCU-NY.
14. Schary quoted in Kahn, *Hollywood on Trial,* 188. Also ibid., 187; and Cole, *Hollywood Red,* 292.
15. Quotation, Bessie, *Inquisition in Eden,* 226. See also Cole, *Hollywood Red,* 292.

16. Quotations, Schary to Betty Scheyer, Feb. 20, 1952, folder: "Un-American Activities," box 59, Schary Papers, SHSWM. See also Schary interview (1958), 35–6, BLCU-NY; Schary, *Heyday,* 106; and Ceplair and Englund, *Inquisition in Hollywood,* 162–3, 165, 167.

17. Quotations, Schary interview (1958), 20, BLCU-NY. See also Freeman and Johnston to Wanger, June 11, 1948, folder 23, box 13, Wanger Papers, SHSWM; Wanger to Freeman and Johnston, June 11, 1948, ibid.; Schary to Wanger, June 16, 1948, ibid.; and Ceplair and Englund, *Inquisition in Hollywood,* 276.

18. Although the nationality of the rescue ship was not identifiable in *Blockade,* Lawson intended for it to be a Soviet vessel. Wanger's other films included *Gabriel Over the White House* (MGM, 1933), *The President Vanishes* (Paramount, 1934), *Foreign Correspondent* (UA, 1940), *Sundown* (UA, 1941), *Eagle Squadron* (Universal, 1942), and *Joan of Arc* (RKO, 1948). Quotation, Lawson, *Film: The Creative Process,* 126 (also ibid., 125); *CDT,* Aug. 6, 1946, p. 4 [?]. See also ibid., 1; and *Motion Picture Daily,* 62 (Oct. 28, 1947), 6.

19. Quotations, Wanger to Reston, Oct. 29, 1947, folder 22, box 18, Wanger Papers, SHSWM; and Wanger to C. D. Jackson, April 24, 1950, folder 37, box 10, ibid. Wanger had accompanied Schary when the latter addressed the SWG on the Waldorf Declaration. See Bessie, *Inquisition in Eden,* 226. On Wanger, see also this volume, Chapter 16.

20. Quotations, from Wanger, "Recommendations" (1948), attached to Wanger to Adolph Zukor, March 4, 1953, folder 1, box 14, Wanger Papers, SHSWM; and Wanger to Johnston, July 3, 1948, folder 37, box 10, ibid. See also MPIC minutes, July 20, 1948, pp. 2, 3, folder 23, box 13, ibid.; undated press release, ibid.; Wanger to Schary, Sept. 21, 1948, ibid.; and *Variety,* July 21, 1948, p. 3.

21. Quotations, Arthur to Edward Barrett, Aug. 27, 1951, file no. 511.00/8–2751 CS/H, box 2242, RG 59, records of the Department of State, NA (also Arthur to Barrett, Dec. 9, 1950, file no. 398.43-UNESCO/12–950 CS/H, RG 59, ibid.); and undated memorandum to MPIC member from Arthur, attached to Arthur to Dear Member, Dec. 11, 1950, folder 23, box 13, Wanger Papers, SHSWM. See also Art [Arthur] to Walter [Wanger], April 28, 1950, ibid.

22. In Virginia, for example, exhibitors repudiated charges that Hollywood was a hotbed of divorce, and tried to discredit any other criticism of the industry. Quotation, from *Miami Daily News,* quoted by Arthur in "Public Relations Team," reprinted from *Independent Film Journal* (undated), copy in folder 24, box 13, Wanger Papers, SHSWM. *Hasty Heart* won the World Students Service Fund's annual "Peace Parchment." See undated clipping, folder 1, box 14, ibid.

23. On foreign quotas and communism, see this volume, Chapter 16; on loyalty tests, see Chapter 17; on censorship, see Chapter 18.

24. Quotations, RR, *Where's,* 200; Rosten, *Hollywood,* 74; Fenichel, "On Acting," 147 ("fears"), 156 ("whore"); McArthur, *Actors and American Culture,* 123 ("rogues") (also 123–67); Powdermaker, *Hollywood, the Dream Factory,* 254 ("cliché," "children") (also 36–7, 94–9, 113, 295, 302–3, 327–8); and Taft, "A Psychological Assessment of Professional Actors," 371 (also 367). See also RR, "America the Beautiful," 8; and Prindle, *Politics of Glamour,* 8–10, 56.

25. Quotations, Hift, "Leaders Seek Fair Deal"; and Spiro, "Hollywood Acts." See also *NYT,* Oct. 14, 1949, p. 34.

26. Quotations, from MPIC, quoted in Spiro, "Hollywood Acts"; and *NYT,* Oct. 14, 1949, p. 34.

27. Schary also shared these sentiments. Quotations, RR quoted in Hift, "Leaders Seek Fair Deal"; and RR, "It's More Than a Jungle."

28. Quotations, *Variety* (March 14, 1951), 2, 18; *Time,* 57 (Feb. 26, 1951), 56; and RR, "Motion Pictures and Your Community," 25.

29. Quotations, RR, "Motion Pictures and Your Community," 25; and (RR quoting Irvin S. Cobb) RR, "Hollywood's Press Relations," *Film Daily,* undated guest column, copy in folder 24, box 13, Wanger Papers, SHSWM. See also RR, "It's More Than a Jungle."

30. Quotation, dialogue from Thurber and Nugent, *Male Animal,* Act 3, 129–30. See also Nugent, *Events,* 134–5, 260.

31. Quotation from the film.

32. RR quoted in *Oregonian,* July 9, 1952, p. 11. See also *NYT,* July 12, 1952, p. 14.

33. Quotation, Pryor, "Hollywood Digest."

34. Mayer, "'COMPO' Formed"; Sklar, *Movie-Made America,* 269–85 (esp. 272, 274); Leff and Simmons, *Dame in the Kimono,* 163–4; "The Fortune Survey," *Fortune,* 39 (March 1949), 43; and Baughman, *Republic of Mass Culture,* 35–6.

35. The antitrust litigation had been filed a decade earlier by the Roosevelt administration but was put on hold during the war. See *U.S. v. Paramount Pictures Inc.,* 334 US 131, 92 LE 1260, 68 S Ct 915 (1948). See also de Grazia and Newman, *Banned Films,* 69–70; Sklar, *Movie-Made America,* 273–4; and Izod, *Hollywood and the Box Office,* 120–5.

36. By forming a temporary corporation to make a film, individuals were taxed at the capital gains rate rather than at the higher individual rate. Quotation, *NYT,* Jan. 24, 1950, p. 16 (also p. 14).

37. Quotations, RR, *Where's,* 245 (also 139); and RR, "Motion Pictures and Your Community," 25. See also Norman, "Reagan Good Film Spokesman"; Nancy Reagan, *My Turn,* 124; and May, "Movie Star Politics," 142.

38. See Dales, "Pragmatic Leadership," 3; Obringer to J. L. Warner, Feb. 17, 1950, folder 1, Reagan contract files, WBAHP-USC; and Obringer to Warner, May 26, 1950, ibid. On Warner Bros., see *NYT,* March 2, 1950, p. 33. On Paramount, see Brady, "Hollywood Takes Stock."

39. The number of contract players at all movie studios dropped from 742 to 315 between March 1, 1947, and March 1, 1950, Reagan reported. See Brady, "Hollywood Digest"; RR to Humphrey, Aug. 17, 1951, in SAG minutes, BD, 4138–38A, SAGA; and Pryor, "Hollywood Digest."

40. See RR to Humphrey, Aug. 17, 1951, in SAG minutes, BD, 4138B, SAGA. See also Pryor, "Hollywood Digest." Richard Nixon introduced an amendment to the law that reduced the thirty-day requirement to two days.

41. Quotations, Powdermaker, *Hollywood, the Dream Factory,* 35, 327.

42. Quotations, *Hartford Times,* June 4, 1952, p. 1; and RR quoted in Norman, "Reagan Good Film Spokesman."

43. Reagan quoted by Eric Johnston, guest column for Victor Riesel, undated, *Daily News,* in box 43, Arthur Papers, BYUA-P. Other quotations from Johnston in ibid.

16. "To Capture the Minds of Men"

1. Quotations, Wanger, "Tulsa Speech"; and RR, "America the Beautiful," 13.

2. Quotations, Harmon, "Western Europe in the Wake of World War II," 13 (also 14, 25–6).

3. Quotations, suggested official statement by the producers' group to General A. D. Surles, Aug. 10, 1945, pp. 12, 16, Jack Warner, *Scrapbook – Part II, European Trip, 1945,* JLW-USC (also, ibid., 1, 5, 8, 11, 17, 20); and Harmon, "Western Europe in the Wake of World War II," [1].

4. Quotation, Goldwyn to Mr. President, Sept. 16, 1947, folder: "OF 73 (Jan.–Oct. 1947)," box 334, official files, Truman Papers, HSTLI. See also Sklar, *Movie-Made America,* 275; and Izod, *Hollywood and the Box Office,* 118.

5. See Sklar, *Movie-Made America*, 274–5; Izod, *Hollywood and the Box Office*, 117–19; Jarvie, *Hollywood's Overseas Campaign*, 213–72, 398–405, 416–25; *NYT*, April 2, 1949, p. 12; and Brady, "Hollywood Protest."

6. Roy Brewer, Kenneth Thomson, and Jack Dales accompanied Reagan to the White House in April, 1949. Quotation, Truman to DeMille, April 18, 1949, folder: "OF 73 (Jan.–June 1949)," box 334, official files, Truman Papers, HSTLI. See also DeMille to President, April 14, 1949, ibid.; Dales to John Steelman, April 28, 1949, ibid.; *NYT*, April 2, 1949, p. 12; Brady, "Hollywood Protest"; and SAG minutes, BD, April 18, 1949, p. 3701, SAGA.

7. Quotations, Dales to Steelman, April 28, 1949, folder: "OF 73 (Jan.–June 1949)," box 334, official files, Truman Papers, HSTLI. See also draft of letter, attached to memorandum, Special Assistant to the Under Secretary (of State) to Russell Andrews, June 9, 1949, ibid.; James McCullough to Russell Andrews, May 20, 1949; and M.S.B. to M. A., June 14 [?], 1949.

8. "If Americanism is to prevail within our borders, if world democracy is to be established, if civilization is to survive, such things will come about through mass feeling rather than through the will of an enlightened few," Jack Warner said in 1946. "Motion pictures can best show and tell the millions of one nation how the millions of another land live and behave." Text quotations, Goldwyn to Truman, Sept. 16, 1947, HSTLI; *[Los Angeles?] Daily Telegraph*, Dec. 12, 1934, in folder: "Harry M. Warner Clips – 1945," box 56, JLW-USC; and "Harry M. Warner Extols the Motion Picture and America," *Hollywood Reporter* (22d Anniversary Issue), 121 (Nov. 10, 1952), part 2. Note quotation, Jack Warner in ibid., 89, (Aug. 6, 1946), [3]. See also Jack Warner, "The Playbill: Films Reflect The Spirit of the Times," *NYHT*, Sept. 9, 1945, in Warner Scrapbook, JLW-USC; "Pix Must Aid in War Prevention – Warner," *Film Daily*, Dec. 17, 1945, in ibid.; *LAT*, Dec. 17, 1945, in ibid.; *Variety* (Dec. 17, 1945); and *Motion Picture Herald* (Dec. 31, 1945).

9. Johnston rose from modest beginnings to become one of Spokane's most successful businessmen. He advocated the open shop and became the first leader of the Spokane Chamber of Commerce in 1931. Between 1934 and 1941 he was director of the United States Chamber of Commerce, and between 1942 and 1946, its president. He ran unsuccessfully as a Republican candidate for the U.S. Senate in 1940. As U. S. Chamber president he dismayed members when he visited Franklin Roosevelt in the White House. See Johnston interview (1959), 895–7, BLCU-NY; and E. E. Convoy to Director, FBI, Dec. 8, 1944, section 1 (94–2-587), Will Hays file, FBI-FOIA, SHSWM.

10. Quotations, Johnston, *America Unlimited*, 2, 87 (also 3, 40, 87–98); Johnston, *We're All In It*, 183, 188, 197–8. See also ibid., 22, 215–16; Johnston, "The Motion Picture on the Threshold," 15; and Johnston, "A Talk to Russia," 639.

11. Quotations, Johnston, "A New Era In Entertainment," 11; and statement of Eric Johnston, Dec. 20, 1946, *Postwar Planning Hearings, Dec. 1946*, pp. 2522–3. See also Johnston, "The Modern Tool for Teaching," 1, 2, 5; Johnston, *America Unlimited*, 134–7, 189–202; and *NYT*, Jan. 28, 1948, p. 26.

12. Johnston quoted in S. V. R., "Movie Man's Burden," 37 (also 38). The *New Republic* may have embellished Johnston's language. In his 1946 annual report, Johnston said: "In terms of facilities and speed of communication, Canton, China, and Canton, Ohio, Paris, France and Paris, Maine, have almost as much contact as neighboring villages." Johnston, "The Motion Picture on the Threshold," 7.

On Johnston's efforts to end restrictions in Britain, see *NYT*, Nov. 14, 1946, p. 39; ibid., Nov. 24, 1946, p. 34; May 2, 1947, p. 33; March 2, 1948, p. 28; March 7, 1948, section 2, p. 5; March 19, 1948, p. 29; March 21, 1948, section 2, p. 5;

March 28, 1948, section 2, p. 5. On iron curtain countries see ibid., Oct. 5, 1948, p. 3; and Oct. 20, 1948, p. 23. See also *USNWR,* 30 (Feb. 2, 1951), 29; *Variety,* July 14, 1948, p. 3; Johnston, "After the Marshall Plan," 16; 19-F, folder 23, box 13, Wanger Papers, SHSWM; and Jarvie, *Hollywood's Overseas Campaign,* 227–37.

13. Quotations, Biberman, *Salt of the Earth,* 10. Niles dealt with civil rights and minority issues.

14. Quotations, *USNWR,* 30 (Feb. 2, 1951), 28; and Schary, *Heyday,* 160. See also S. V. R., "Movie Man's Burden," 37–8; *NYT,* Jan. 30, 1948, p. 4; and *Motion Picture Herald,* Aug. 31, 1946.

15. Quotations, Johnston, *America Unlimited,* 3, 5, 59, 61, 75, 79 (also 5–11, 72, 81); and Johnston, "Aggressive Citizenship," 633. See also ibid., 634; *USNWR,* 30 (Feb. 2, 1951), 28; and *Senior Scholastic,* 58 (Feb. 14, 1951), 7.

16. Johnston also traveled to Moscow in September 1948, hoping to sell American films to the Soviets. See Smith to Secretary of State, Sept. 17, 1948 (decimal file no. 861.4061 MP/9-1748 HH), and Kohler to Secretary of State, Sept. 21, 1948 (decimal file no. 861.4061 MP/9-2148 HH), box 6659, RG 59, records of the Department of State, NA.

    Quotations, Johnston, "A Talk to Russia," 638 (emphasis in original text) (also 639); and Johnston, "After the Marshall Plan," 69. See also Johnston "The Modern Tool for Teaching," 6; Johnston interview (1959), 893–4, BLCU-NY; and Johnston, *We're All In It,* 13, 31, 50–1, 75–121 (esp. 89), 203, 207, 211.

17. Quotations, Johnston, *We're All In It,* 35–7, 207; and Johnston, "Land of the Calculated Risk," 560.

18. Quotations, Johnston, *We're All In It,* 46 (also 64, 211, 215, 217); Johnston, "Land of Calculated Risk," 562; clipping from *Kansas City Star,* undated [early 1951?], folder: "Industry Anti-Communist Record," box 55, Schary Papers, SHSWM; and from Johnston, "The Motion Picture on the Threshold." See also Johnston, *America Unlimited,* 124, 129; Johnston, "After the Marshall Plan," 16; and Johnston, "Unexplored Continent," 7; Baughman, *Luce,* 129–57; and May, "Movie Star Politics," 125–8, 139–40, 142, 144–5, 148.

19. Quotations, RR, "Motion Pictures and Your Community," 108–9; and RR, *Where's,* 162 (also 164). See also RR interview with author, Oct. 16, 1989.

20. Quotations, 19-F, folder 23, box 13, Wanger Papers, SHSWM; and statement of Eric Johnston, Dec. 20, 1946, *Postwar Planning Hearings, Dec. 1946,* 2523.

21. Quotation, RR interview with author, Oct. 16, 1989.

22. Quotations, Wanger, "Tulsa Speech," 1. See also ibid., 2; Art Arthur to Wanger, April 27, 1949, folder 23, box 13, Wanger Papers, SHSWM; and William Hassett to Wanger, May 11, 1949, folder: "OF 73 (Jan.–June 1949)," box 334, official files, Truman Papers, HSTLI.

23. Quotations, Wanger, "Donald Duck and World Diplomacy," 6; Wanger, "Wooden Shoes and Silken Slippers," 3 (Voltaire quoted by Wanger), 5. See also Wanger's speech to National Industrial Advertisers Association [1950], [p. 2], folder 9, box 37, Wanger Papers, SHSHW.

24. Quotation, RR, "Motion Pictures and Your Community," 110. See also Arthur to Wanger, July 28, 1949, folder 23, box 13, Wanger Papers, SHSWM; and Schary, *Heyday,* 164–5.

25. Quotations, *NYT,* Sept. 9, 1950, p. 11; and "Report Prepared Prior to Any Declaration of National Emergency – A Plan for Cooperation with the U.S. Government," submitted by MPIC and COMPO, attached to Arthur to All Members of Planning Committee, Dec. 13, 1950, folder 23, box 13, Wanger Papers, SHSWM.

26. Quotation, Mayer, "'COMPO' Formed," 5. See also *NYT,* Dec. 18, 1949, section

2, p. 6; Abram Meyers to [Dallas] Halverstadt, Dec. 30, 1949, box 3, Halverstadt
files, Truman Papers, HSTLI; and Halverstadt to Steelman, Sept. 7, 1950, ibid.
For member organizations of COMPO see "A Plan for Cooperation with the U.S.
Government," submitted by COMPO and the MPIC [1950], folder 23, box 13,
Wanger Papers, SHSWM.

27. Quotation, Ned Depinet to President, Aug. 11, 1950, folder: "PPF 210 (1949–
53)," box 447, Truman Papers, HSTLI. On meeting with Truman, which Reagan
did not attend, see Steelman to Depinet, Sept. 1, 1950, ibid.; SAG minutes, BD,
Sept. 12, 1950, p. 3971, SAGA; and "Attendance" list, box 3, Halverstadt files,
Truman Papers, HSTLI. For other members of COMPO's Committee for Cooper-
ation with the U. S. Government, in addition to Reagan and Depinet, see
Halverstadt to Steelman, Sept. 7, 1950, ibid. For the MPIC's planning committee,
which also included Brewer, Arthur, Rivkin, B. B. Kahane, and Leonard
Spigelgass, see Arthur to Planning Committee, Aug. 30, 1950, folder 23, box 13,
Wanger Papers, SHSWM. Also Arthur to RR, et al. [July, 1950?], ibid.

28. "Proposed Report of the Planning Committee" (first rough draft), July 20,
[1950], folder 23, box 13, Wanger Papers, SHSWM. See also undated and untitled [July, 1950?] report on the MPIC's planning committee ideas, ibid.; "Motion Picture Industry-Federal Government Cooperation," [Sept. 5, 1950], box 3,
Halverstadt files, Truman Papers, HSTLI; memorandum, George M. Elsey, Aug.
2, 1950, folder: "OF 73 (August, 1950-May, 1951)," box 334, official files,
Truman Papers, ibid.; and Barrett, *Truth Is Our Weapon*, esp. 72–100.

29. Quotations, undated and untitled report [July, 1950?] of MPIC's planning committee ideas, folder 23, box 13, Wanger Papers, SHSWM; and "Report Prepared
Prior to Any Declaration of National Emergency" [Dec. 13, 1950], p. 12, ibid. See
also "Proposed Report," July 20, [1950], ibid.

30. See Arthur to MPIC Planning Committee, Sept. 21, 1950, folder 23, box 13,
Wanger Papers, SHSWM; Arthur to MPIC Planning Committee, Oct. 27, 1950,
ibid.; and clipping in *Variety* (Oct. 3, [1950]), copy in ibid. For changes in plan
made by Johnston's office, see "A Plan for Cooperation with the U.S. Government
in the Production of Armed Forces and Information Films . . . ," submitted by
the MPIC, 1, 4, attached to Arthur to MPIC Planning Committee, Nov. 24, 1950,
folder 23, box 13, ibid. See also Arthur's letter, ibid.

31. Quotations, "Report Prepared Prior to Any Declaration of National Emergency"
[Dec. 13, 1950], pp. 4, 7, 10, 11; also ibid., 9, folder 23, box 13, Wanger Papers,
SHSWM.

32. Quotations, Barrett, *Truth Is Our Weapon*, 287. See also agenda, MPIC membership meeting [by Art Arthur?], Aug. 20, 1952, [p. 5], box 33, Arthur Papers,
BYUA-P; and Reagan's minutes of MPIC meeting, Aug. 20, 1952, p. 7, ibid.

33. See memorandum to Mr. Nichols, May 23, 1951, regarding "Ronald Reagan,
Movie Actor," 5, Reagan file, FBI-FOIA, SHSWM.

34. In October 1949, eleven members of the American Communist Party were convicted under the Smith Act of conspiring to overthrow the government, and in
July 1951, several of them skipped bail to avoid prison. Warner wanted to help
apprehend them and Hoover, who was enthusiastic about Warner's suggestion,
forwarded pictures of the fugitives so that the studio could produce a newsreel. H.
M. Warner to Hoover, Oct. 11, 1951 (HQ 94–1-17015), section 3, Warner Bros.
file, FBI-FOIA, SHSWM; Hoover to Harry Warner, Oct. 18, 1951, ibid.; and
related correspondence in ibid. On Warner's plan to organize executives, see
memorandum, SAC, Los Angeles to Director, FBI, Nov. 9, 1950 (HQ 94–
1-1705), section 2, ibid.

35. Quotations, *NYT*, Sept. 2, 1950, p. 11. See also, ibid., Sept. 10, 1950, section 2, p.
5; Hoover to Harry Warner, Sept. 15, 1950 (HQ 94–1-17015), section 2, Warner

Bros. file, FBI-FOIA, SHSWM; related correspondence in ibid.; memorandum, July 24, 1951 (HQ 94-1-17015), section 3, ibid.; and George Dorsey to Charles Ross, Sept. 22, 1950, folder: "OF 73 (Aug. 1950-May 1951)," box 334, official files, Truman Papers, HSTLI.

36. Quotations, *NYT,* Sept. 28, 1950, p. 39; and RR in speech shown on "The Real Ronald Reagan," "Frontline," PBS-TV, Jan. 18, 1989. See also Spiro, "Anti-Communist Feeling Rising in West"; and Spiro, "Hollywood Digest." Conservative Hollywood employees concerned about communist infiltration established the Motion Picture Alliance for the Preservation of American Values in 1944. See Sklar, *Movie-Made America, 257.* For Reagan's anticommunism, see also this volume, Chapter 17.

37. Quotations, Lorraine Makler, "Everybody's Kind of Guy" [c. 1950], p. 31, in DETA.

38. Quotations, RR, "America the Beautiful," 9.

39. Quotations, Luther Carr to RR, March 17, 1953, folder: "California State Advisory Board," California file, UWF Mss., LLIUB; and "The Policy of United World Federalists, Inc." [1953], pp. 1, 3, folder: "1953 National Convention," ibid. See also "April 30/52 Membership Count," folder: "1952 National Convention-Philadelphia," ibid.; "Southern California Chapter Membership Count," Dec. 31, 1950, folder: "California Convention – 1951," ibid.; "Confidential" statement by Robert A. Keyworth [June 1950?], folder: "California," box (file drawer) 27, ibid.; and Forbes, "Smearing World Government," 12.

40. Quotations, *Newsweek,* 41 (Feb. 2, 1953), 10; Ilse Lewin to Ted Baer, Feb. 6, 1952, folder: "1952 California Convention – General," California file, UWF Mss., LLIUB; and Carr to RR, March 17, 1953, folder: "California State Advisory Board," ibid. See also RR to Carr, March 24, 1953, ibid.; "Tentative Outline for Assembly Program" [undated – probably late Jan. or early Feb., 1952], folder: "1952 California Convention – General," ibid.; Helen Shuford to Abraham Wilson, Jan. 30, 1953, folder: "1953, Jan.–Apr.," box 169, ibid.; Harley Cope to Norman Cousins, March 17, 1953, folder: "1953, Jan.–Apr.," box 169, ibid.

17. Loyalty

1. Quotations, RR, "How Do You Fight Communism?"; RR quoted in McGoogan, "How the Commies Were Licked"; RR quoted in Edwards, *Early Reagan,* 404 (n); and RR, *Where's,* 201. See also FBI report, Los Angeles, Dec. 19, 1947 (LA 100–15732), p. 24, Reagan file, FBI-FOIA, SHSWM.

2. Quotation, RR paraphrased in McGoogan, "How the Commies Were Licked"; and Brady, "Hollywood Divided."

3. Quotations, Dales, "Pragmatic Leadership," 22; and Cole, *Hollywood Red,* 326.

4. Quotation, McAuliffe, *Crisis on the Left,* 107. See also ibid., 89–107; and Navasky, *Naming Names,* 45–69.

5. Quotation, Schary, *Heyday,* 239.

6. According to Schary, actor William Holden and producers William Goetz, Nate Springold, B. B. Kahane, and Darryl Zanuck opposed appeasing the American Legion. Quotations, Schary, *Heyday,* 241; see also ibid., 238–41.

7. See SAG minutes, BD, Sept. 12, 1950, pp. 3973–4, SAGA.

8. Quotation, ibid., Oct. 9, 1950, p. 3980, SAGA. See also ibid., 3981; and Brady, "Hollywood Divided."

9. See SAG minutes, BD, Dec. 18, 1950, p. 4020, SAGA; ibid., Jan. 8, 1951, p. 4029; and Arthur to All Members, Services Committee, Dec. 6, 1950, in SAG

minutes, p. 4022. For SDG, see *NYT,* Oct. 27, 1950, p. 25. See also ibid., Oct. 14, 1950, p. 13; Oct. 16, 1950, p. 30; Oct. 19, 1950, p. 26; Oct. 24, 1950, p. 17; Brady, "Hollywood Divided"; and Brady, "Hollywood Turmoil."

10. Quotations, RR, "How Do Your Fight Communism?" See also McGoogan, "How the Commies Were Licked."
11. Quotation, RR, "How Do You Fight Communism?"
12. Quotations, RR, "How Do You Fight Communism?"; and RR quoted by McGoogan, "How the Commies Were Licked."
13. Quotations, Ernst and Loth, *Report,* 127 (also 7, 11, 64, 187–8, 190); RR, "How Do You Fight Communism?"; and RR quoted by Bassett, "Communism in Hollywood."
14. Reagan was familiar with Ernst's work. Ernst volunteered to discuss his findings with the MPIC in early 1952. See Reagan's minutes, MPIC meeting, March 26, 1952, p. 5, box 33, Arthur Papers, BYUA-P. Quotations, RR quoted by McGoogan, "How the Commies Were Licked"; RR, "How Do You Fight Communism?" Schary also liked Ernst's views. See Schary interview (1958), 79–80, BLCU-NY.
15. Quotations, "Official Statement," of the MPIC regarding HUAC Hearings, March 21, 1951, box 55, Schary Papers, SHSWM; and from letter by MPIC to Congressman John S. Wood (and HUAC), [Sept., 1951], printed in *Daily Variety,* copy in ibid.
16. "Official Statement" of the MPIC regarding HUAC, March 21, 1951, ibid.
17. Quotations, Sondergaard to SAG's BD, March 13, 1951, in SAG minutes, 4059–59A, SAGA.
18. On Sondergaard, see folder 3, box 69, Biberman–Sondergaard Papers, SHSWM; and Edwards, *Early Reagan,* 425. For testimony linking her to the Communist Party, see testimony of Larry Parks, March 21, 1951, *HUAC Hearings, 1951,* part 6, p. 2303; testimony of Elizabeth Wilson, Sept. 21, 1951, ibid., part 5, p. 1719; and testimony of Lee J. Cobb, June 2, 1953, *HUAC Hearings, 1953,* p. 2349.
19. Quotations, Sondergaard to SAG's BD, March 13, 1951, in SAG minutes, 4059, SAGA; and Biberman, *Salt of the Earth,* 24.
20. See SAG minutes, special meeting, BD, March 19, 1951, p. 4057, SAGA.
21. Quotations, [Dales] to Sondergaard, March 20, 1951, in SAG minutes, p. 4060, ibid. See also SAG minutes, BD, April 9, 1951, p. 4064, ibid.
22. See testimony of Roy M. Brewer, May 18, 1951, *HUAC Hearings, 1951,* part 2, p. 517. See also Parks testimony, March 21, 1951, ibid., part 6, p. 2303; Cobb testimony, June 2, 1953, *HUAC Hearings, 1953,* p. 2349; Reagan testimony, July 1, 1955, pp. 3382–83, *Jeffers v. Screen Extras Guild,* SHSWM; FBI report, Aug. 4, 1947 (LA 100–15732), 156, 157, Reagan file, FBI-FOIA, SHSWM; FBI report, Dec. 19, 1947 (LA 100–15732), pp. 24–5, ibid.; Jones [?] to Nichols, May 23, 1951 (100–351326–5), ibid.; and Sklar, *City Boys,* 183.
23. Revere grew up in Westfield, N.J., was baptized in the Presbyterian Church there, and graduated from Wellesley College. Her acting career began in the theater, and in 1934 she moved to Hollywood. Quotation, Revere interview (1955). Also SAG minutes, BD, March 19, 1951, p. 4057, SAGA; and ibid., May 28, 1951, p. 4095, ibid.
24. Quotations, Revere interview (1955).
25. Quotation, testimony of Anne Revere, April 17, 1951, *HUAC Hearings, 1951,* part 2, p. 319.
26. See SAG minutes, BD, May 28, 1951, p. 4095, SAGA; Revere interview (1955); and Short, "Hollywood Fights Anti-Semitism, 1945–1947," pp. 174–80.

27. Quotations, testimony of Sterling Hayden, April 10, 1951, *HUAC Hearings, 1951,* part 1, pp. 144, 162. See also ibid., 143, 148–9; Reagan testimony, July 1, 1955, p. 3394, *Jeffers* v. *Screen Extras Guild,* SHSWM; RR, *Where's,* 171–4; McGoogan, "How the Commies Were Licked"; *NYT,* April 11, 1951, p. 14; and Brady, "Hollywood Is Calm."

28. Quotations, Hayden, *Wanderer,* 371 (also 348–50, 370–91); and Hayden testimony, April 10, 1951, *HUAC Hearings, 1951,* part 1, p. 164. See also *NYT,* April 12, 1951, p. 21; ibid., April 11, 1951, pp. 1, 14; and Brady, "Hollywood Is Calm."

29. Quotation, Michigan congressman Charles Potter in testimony of Edward Dmytryk, April 25, 1951, *HUAC Hearings, 1951,* part 2, p. 438; and Maltz, quoted in Ceplair and Englund, *Inquisition in Hollywood,* 358. See also Dmytryk, *It's a Hell of a Life,* 72.

30. Reagan quoted by McGoogan, "How the Commies Were Licked"; Dmytryk, *It's a Hell of a Life,* 145; and Cogley, *Report on Blacklisting,* 83.

31. Quotations, Dmytryk, *It's a Hell of a Life,* 145 (emphasis in original text). See also Cogley, *Report on Blacklisting,* 84–5; and Ceplair and Englund, *Inquisition in Hollywood,* 359.

32. RR, et al., "You Can Be Free Men Again!" *Hollywood Reporter,* June 6, 1951, copy in box 55, Schary Papers, SHSWM. In addition, the MPIC and the U. S. Department of State considered letting Dmytryk tell his story on the Voice of America. See Motion Picture Industry Council to Department of State, April 26, 1951, and Department of State to MPIC, May 26, 1951 (decimal file nos. 811.452/4–2651 and 811.452/5–2651) (from index file cards), RG 59, records of the Department of State, NA.

33. Quotations, Dmytryk, *It's a Hell of a Life,* 147. See also McGoogan, "How the Commies Were Licked"; and Ceplair and Englund, *Inquisition in Hollywood,* 359.

34. Twentieth Century Fox released nine of these films; Columbia Pictures, eleven; MGM, eight; United Artists, nine; Universal-International, five; Warner Bros., six; and Paramount, three. Quotations, Matthews, "Did the Movies Really Clean House?" 13, 51; see also 49, 51–6.

35. See Mary McCall to Arthur, Jan. 9, 1952, box 69, Biberman–Sondergaard Papers, SHSWM; and minutes, EB-SWG, Jan. 21, 1952, ibid. See also Reagan's minutes, MPIC meeting, Jan. 16, 1952, pp. 4–5, box 33, Arthur Papers, BYUA-P.

36. See Schary, *Heyday,* 239. See minutes, EB-SWG, Jan. 21, 1952, p. 5, box 69, Biberman–Sondergaard Papers, SHSWM.

37. See Chairman's Agenda, MPIC membership meeting, March 26, 1952, pp. 4–5, box 33, Arthur Papers, BYUA-P; Reagan's minutes, MPIC meeting, Feb. 20, 1952, p. 4, ibid.; and *Annual Report,* HUAC (1951), 8.

38. Quotation, minutes, MPIC-EC, April 11, 1952, box 69, Biberman–Sondergaard Papers, SHSWM. See also "The Objectives and Purposes of M.P.I.C. Shall be as Follows," attached to Adrian McCalman to Frances Inglis, April 4, 1952, ibid.; and Chairman's Agenda, MPIC membership meeting, March 26, 1952, p. 5, box 33, Arthur Papers, BYUA-P.

39. Quotations, from Art Arthur's notes, dated May 27, 1952, of meeting of exploration subcommittee of MPIC-EC, May 20, 1952, folder 6, box 69, Biberman–Sondergaard Papers, SHSWM. See also Reagan's minutes, MPIC meeting, March 26, 1952, p. 3, box 33, Arthur Papers, BYUA-P.

40. Quotations, "MPIC Resolution" [June 2?, 1952], folder 6, box 69, Biberman–Sondergaard Papers, SHSWM; and Arthur to Howard Green (emphasis in origi-

nal text), June 9, 1952, ibid. See also Reagan's minutes, MPIC meeting, June 18, 1952, p. 3, box 33, Arthur Papers, BYUA-P.

41. Reagan suspected the SWG might veto this plan and he was willing to have SAG act on a plan of its own. See SAG minutes, BD, June 16, 1952, p. 4254, SAGA; and Reagan's minutes, MPIC meeting, June 18, 1952, p. 2, box 33, Arthur Papers, BYUA-P.

42. Mary McCall recounted Freeman's admissions to the SWG. Quotation, minutes, EB-SWG, June 2, 1952, folder 6, box 69, Biberman–Sondergaard Papers, SHSWM. For organizations compiling names, see "Attention! SWG Members," June 20, 1952, ibid.

43. Warner Bros. hired McCall during the early 1930s to help adapt her novel *Revolt* into a motion picture, later released as *Scarlet Dawn* (1932). Subsequently, she found steady employment with several studios. During World War II, she chaired Hollywood's War Activities Committee. See minutes, special meeting, EB-SWG, June 19, 1952, p. 2, folder 6, box 69, ibid.; SAG minutes, BD, June 2, 1952, p. 4245, SAGA; ibid., June 16, 1952, p. 4254; and Schwartz, *Hollywood Writers' Wars*, 100–2, 187, 211, 262.

44. Quotations, minutes, special meeting, EB-SWG, April 28, 1952, p. 3 (from minutes, not necessarily McCall's exact words), box 69, Biberman–Sondergaard Papers, SHSWM; also ibid. 4.

45. Quotations, see minutes, special meeting, EB-SWG, June 19, 1952, p. 1 (from minutes, not necessarily Brewer's exact words), ibid. See also minutes, EB-SWG, June 2, 1952 [p. 3?], ibid.; June 23, 1952, p. 5, ibid.; and SAG minutes, BD, June 16, 1952, p. 4254, SAGA.

46. Quotations, minutes, EB-SWG, June 2, 1952 [p.3?], box 69, Biberman–Sondergaard Papers, SHSWM; and Arthur to Green, June 9, 1952, ibid.

47. See "McCall Statement," July 3, 1952, ibid.; minutes, EB-SWG, June 2, 1952, p. 4, ibid.; minutes, special meeting, EB-SWG, June 19, 1952, pp. 1–2, ibid.; and minutes, EB-SWG, June 23, 1952, pp. 5–6, ibid.

48. Reagan quoted in *Daily Worker,* July 30, 1952, p. 7, in Reagan file, FBI-FOIA, SHSWM. See also minutes, EB-SWG, June 23, 1952, p. 5, box 69, Biberman–Sondergaard Papers; statements by McCall and Rivkin, dated July 3, 1952, in ibid.; and minutes, EB-SWG, July 28, 1952, p. 1, ibid.

49. Quotation, Reagan's minutes, MPIC meeting, Aug. 20, 1952, pp. 5, 6, box 33, Arthur Papers, BYUA-P. See also "Resolutions Adopted by the 53rd National Encampment," *V.F.W. Magazine,* 40 (Sept. 1952), 33.

50. Quotations, B. B. Kahane to Mrs. Ronald Reagan, Jan. 7, 1953, SAGA; and Nancy Reagan quoted in Edwards, *Early Reagan,* 403. See also ibid., 400–3, 403 (n).

51. See Los Angeles to Director, FBI, July 1, 1953 (100–157201), Screen Actors Guild (1939–1953) file, FBI-FOIA, SHSWM; Los Angeles to Director, July 29, 1953, ibid.; SAG minutes, BD, March 9, 1953, p. 4406, SAGA; and Edwards, *Early Reagan,* 404 (n).

52. Spiegelgass quoted in Leamer, *Make-Believe,* 160; and Dales quoted in May, "Movie Star Politics," 145.

18. A Troubled Time: Movies and Divorce

1. Reagan usually retained a dignified persona in his postwar films, his characters often struggling against disease or intolerance. Quotation, RR, *Where's,* 204. On Reagan's unhappiness with his roles, see ibid., 192–6, 204–5, 210, 212–13. Contrast these roles to those discussed in this volume, Chapters 6–8.

2. Quotation, Nancy Reagan, *My Turn*, 108.
3. Quotation, RR, *Where's*, 205; also 191.
4. Quotations, from Production Code of 1930; from *Louisa* (Universal International, 1950), MPBRSD-LC; and Gilbert, *Cycle of Outrage*, 169. See also Lord, *Played By Ear*, 273; and Vaughn, "Morality and Entertainment," 46–56, 64–5.
5. Such changes may have intensified fears about communism during the 1940s and 1950s. What became known as McCarthyism "was fueled, in large measure, by suspicion of the new secularism, materialism, bureaucratic collectivism, and consumerism that epitomized not only the achievement but the potential 'decadence' of New Deal liberalism." A "cosmopolitan urban culture" seemed to threaten national security no less than communism. Quotations, May, *Homeward Bound*, 10. On family culture and sexual attitudes during this period, see ibid., 19, 58–161; Gilbert, *Another Chance*, 54–75; Chafe, *Unfinished Journey*, 123–8; Gordon, *Woman's Body*, 341–90; Graebner, "The Unstable World of Benjamin Spock," 612–29; Friedan, *Feminine Mystique*; and Bérubé, *Coming Out Under Fire*, 255.
6. See de Grazia and Newman, *Banned Films*, 77, 78–83,188, 231–3; and Shurlock, *Oral History*, 82, 85–6, AFI-LA. On the code's decline, see Vaughn, "Morality and Entertainment," 64–5; and Leff and Simmons, *Dame in the Kimono*, esp. 109–240.
7. On Hollywood and changing entertainment patterns, see this volume, Chapter 15. Quotations, Jack Warner, "Films Reflect the Spirit of the Times"; and Sklar, *Movie-Made America*, 255. See also Deming, *Running Away from Myself*; Tuska, *Dark Cinema*; Gabbard and Gabbard, *Psychiatry and the Cinema*, esp. 60–74; and Leff and Simmons, *Dame in the Kimono*, 128.
8. Quotations, RR, *Where's*, 205 (also 186, 191–2); and Reagan, quoted in Redlings, "Opinions of an Actor." See also Edwards, *Early Reagan*, 322.
9. Quotations, from transcript of radio program in *Eureka College Bulletin*, 46, No. 7 (July 1947), ECAE; statement of Ronald Reagan, June 16, 1955, *Kefauver Hearings, 1955*, p. 92. See also RR, *Where's*, 187–9.
10. Quotation, RR, *Where's*, 186.
11. Quotation, from film, SHSWM. See also RR, *Where's*, 186; and Longstreet, *Stallion Road*, 301. The cynicism of Scott's character made little impression on Breen, who worried most about the treatment of marriage and passionate kissing. See Breen to Jack Warner, April 3, 1946 (and related correspondence), PCA file for *Stallion Road*, AMPASL.
12. Reagan had been loaned to MGM to appear in *The Bad Man* (1941), which was also set in the West. Warner Bros. produced *Rocky Mountain* (1950) from Alan Le May's story *Ghost Mountain*. A copy of the screenplay, which Le May helped write, is in folder 6, box 3, Winston Miller Papers, SHSWM. See also RR, *Where's*, 192; Grobel, *Hustons*, 285, 288; and Edwards, *Early Reagan*, 323.
13. Wylie's quest for a philosophic position found expression in his novel *Finnley Wren* (1934) and later in a work of social and moral criticism, *Generation of Vipers* (1942), where he attacked "momism" – the damaging influence on American males of excessive mother's love. In *Night Unto Night* (the title came from Psalms 19), "the protagonist was to think out his theory from the experience and events of his life; the reader was to learn, as it were, by the doing." Wylie's *Essay on Morals* followed three years later. Quotations, Wylie, *Essay on Morals* (1947), vii, xi (also xvi); and Wylie, *Generation of Vipers*, xvii. See also Wylie, *Night Unto Night*; and Sklar, *City Boys*, 16.
14. Wylie traveled to the Soviet Union but found communism repressive and drew parallels between it and religion. Quotations, Wylie, *Essay on Morals* (1947), ix,

153 (also 174–7); ibid. (1951), 13, vii (also 7); and Wylie, *Generation of Vipers*, x, xiv (also xxii).

15. Redefining morality, he admitted, was "a large order" and "presumptuous" too. Critics agreed. Readers failed to understand him and he felt misrepresented by reviewers. After finishing *Night Unto Night*, he acknowledged that he needed an additional ten thousand pages and another ten years to make his "important points." Quotations, Wylie, *Essay on Morals* (1951), xvii, xx (also v, xvi–xx); ibid. (1947), vii, xi, 156, 158, 164 (also x–xi, 162). See also Wylie, *Opus 21*, 17–18.

16. Quotations from film, SHSWM. See also Wylie, *Night Unto Night*, 372. Wylie's skepticism about the morality sustaining the code went unchallenged by the PCA. See Breen to Jack Warner, Sept. 6, 1946, PCA file for *Night Unto Night*, AMPASL.

17. Quotations, Lindfors, *Viveka . . . Viveca*, 151, 153–5; and RR, *Where's*, 189.

18. Quotations, Roberts, *That Hagen Girl*, 311. See also ibid., 299–306. In Wylie's novel, one character referred to marriage as a "legal adjustment." Quotation, Wylie, *Night Unto Night*, 367.

19. Quotations, from Virginia Wright's review in *Daily News*, Feb. 21, 1948, copy in PCA file for *Voice of the Turtle*, AMPASL; "How Servicemen took to 'Turtle,'" *PM*, July 2, 1944, clipping in ibid. See also Van Druten, *Voice of the Turtle* [v]; Van Druten, *Way to the Present*, 7, 16–17; Morris Ebenstein to J. Warner and J. Wilk, Nov. 20, 1946, legal file, *Voice of the Turtle*, WBAHP-USC; Spiro, "Hollywood Memos"; and Nugent, *Events*, 177–8.

20. The PCA took much of the excitement away from the story. Breen objected to Parker's having a weekend lover, pronounced the script devoid of compensating moral values, and insisted on new scenes indicating that Reagan had not spent the night in her apartment. Quotations, *Time*, Dec. 15, 1947, p. 103; *Motion Picture Herald*, Dec. 27, 1947, in PCA file for *Voice of the Turtle*, AMPASL; and review by Virginia Wright, *Daily News*, Feb. 21, 1948, ibid. Other reviewers were kinder. See *Hollywood Reporter*, Dec. 26, 1947; and *Film Daily*, Dec. 29, 1947, copies in ibid. See also RR, *Where's*, 192–3; Spiro, "Hollywood Memos"; unsigned copy of letter to Deli and John, June 4, 1946, story file, *Voice of the Turtle*, WBAHP-USC; and Breen to J. Warner, June 3, Oct. 29, Nov. 19, 1946, PCA file for *Voice of the Turtle*, AMPASL.

21. Quotations, Black, *Child Star*, 406, 407.

22. Ibid., 406–10. Reagan missed filming in June and early July 1947.

23. Quotations, ibid., 406.

24. Quotations, RR, *Where's*, 193–4. Incest was dropped from the film when Breen insisted that gossip about Mary's parentage be minimized. See Roberts, *That Hagen Girl*, 304–10; Breen to J. Warner, Aug. 29, 1946, and April 24, May 19, June 5, and June 24, 1947, PCA file for *That Hagen Girl*, AMPASL.

25. Quotations, Roberts, *That Hagen Girl*, 308.

26. Quotations, *Time* (Nov. 10, 1947), 104; and Black, *Child Star*, 412.

27. Quotation, RR, *Where's*, 201.

28. Quotations, Maureen Reagan, *First Father*, 71; also 70.

29. Quotations, from General Arnold's recruiting speech to WACS in Special Film Project 111 (Oct. 13, 1944), see FPU records (microfilm no. A0492), MAFB; and from film scripts in ibid. On government propaganda and women during World War II, see Honey, *Creating Rosie the Riveter*.

30. "Biologically speaking," Kleihauer said, "the home is the cell out of which all other types of social organisms are formed. Sociologically speaking, the home is the social unit which develops the patterns of mind, attitude and principle which

are injected into the larger social groupings of life; such as politics, industry, economics and race relations. Governmentally speaking, the home is a miniature state in which governmental policies are taught and executed. It is here that anarchy, civic indifference or real democracy is taught and practiced. Morally and spiritually speaking, the home is the school of character where we learn in the family unit what later we express in ideals, principles, and philosophies in the wider social relationships of life. It does not require the wisdom of Solomon to see how desperately important the home is in all that pertains to the well being of life, democracy, character and religion." Quotations, *Christian Challenger,* 1 (May 3, 1942), 1, HBCCL (also 3 [April 23, 1944], 1). See also RR interview with author, Oct. 16, 1989. Reagan remained a member of Hollywood–Beverly Christian Church until he married Nancy Davis.

31. Quotations, Kleihauer, "The American Home," *Christian Challenger,* 2 (May 16, 1943), 1, HBCCL; Kleihauer in ibid., 1 (May 3, 1942), 1; and RR, "America the Beautiful," 13. See also *Christian Challenger,* 3 (Dec. 5, 1943), 1; ibid., 1 (July 26, 1942), 1; and 2 (Sept. 26, 1943), 1, HBCCL.
32. Wyman was nominated for an Academy Award for Best Actress in *The Yearling* (Metro, 1946). She had also given a strong performance in *The Lost Weekend* (Paramount, 1945), which won an Academy Award for Best Picture. Quotations, RR quoted, in Cannon, *Reagan,* 63; and Maureen Reagan, *First Father,* 44–5; see also 43–5.
33. Wyman quoted in Perrella, *They Call Me,* 130–1. See also Friedrich, *City of Nets,* 327–8; Edwards, *Early Reagan,* 355; Cannon, *Reagan,* 63; and RR, *Where's,* 196.
34. See Black, *Child Star,* 408; and RR, *Where's,* 194–5.
35. Reagan did not contest the divorce which became final on July 18, 1949. He agreed to pay Wyman $500 a month and received visitation rights to see the children. Quotations, Parsons in *LAE,* July 4, 1946; and in *LAT,* undated [Feb. 9, 1948?], in Reagan clipping file, AMPASL; and from *Silver Screen,* quoted in Morella and Epstein, *Jane Wyman,* 127 (also 116–27). For Hedda Hopper, see press release, "Trouble in Paradise," Reagan clipping file, AMPASL. See also Cannon, *Reagan,* 60–5; Edwards, *Early Reagan,* 325–32, 353–5; Wills, *Reagan's America,* 161, 168, 173; and court records, *Jane Wyman Reagan* v. *Ronald W. Reagan,* case file number D360058, LACCHA.
36. Quotations, Maureen Reagan, *First Father,* 55; and Michael Reagan, *Outside,* 25–6, 149.
37. Quotations, RR, *Where's,* 202; Maureen Reagan, *First Father,* 68, 70, 79 (also 53, 76–86); and Michael Reagan, *Outside,* 10, 24. See also ibid., 41–8, 261–6; and Morella and Epstein, *Jane Wyman,* 127.
38. Quotations, Maureen Reagan, *First Father,* 59; also 62.
39. Reagan also made a cameo appearance (as did Wyman and Maureen) in *It's a Great Feeling* (1949). *John Loves Mary* was based on Norman Krasna's Broadway play and featured Patricia Neal, Jack Carson, Edward Arnold, and Wayne Morris. In *The Girl from Jones Beach,* Reagan appeared with Virginia Mayo. Quotation, RR, *Where's,* 204 (also 205, 213–14); Breen to J. Warner, Oct. 28, 1947, PCA file for *John Loves Mary,* AMPASL; memorandum for the files by J. A. V., Dec. 23, 1947, ibid.; Stephen Jackson to Warner, Jan. 9 and Jan. 28, 1948, ibid.; Jackson to Warner, April 13, April 29, and May 10, 1948, PCA file for *The Girl from Jones Beach.*
40. Quotations, RR, *Where's,* 208 (also 205–12); Jack Warner, Jr., quoted in Leamer,

Make-Believe, 149; Neal quoted in Cannon, *Reagan,* 64. See also Neal, *As I Am,* 90; and Nancy Reagan, *My Turn,* 95–6.

41. Lew Ayres had been a conscientious objector during World War II. Quotations, RR, *Where's,* 206, 208; Neal, *As I Am,* 112 (also 111); RR quoted in Cannon, *Reagan,* 63; and Hedda Hopper quoted in Morella and Epstein, *Jane Wyman,* 120. See also Leamer, *Make-Believe,* 149; and Edwards, *Early Reagan,* 327–32, 354, 371.

42. See RR, *Where's,* 140.

43. Quotation, *Christian Challenger,* 1 (Aug. 2, 1942), 1, HBCCL; and Kleihauer, "Be Good and Like It," ibid., 2 (March 7, 1943), 2.

44. When the Kefauver committee investigated the relation between movies and juvenile delinquency in 1955, Reagan argued that violence was a dramatic necessity in films and maintained that parents could counter the harmful effects of screen obscenity and brutality on children. He was more concerned about the impact of film censorship on youth. Reagan quoted in Redlings, "Opinions of an Actor." Other quotations from *NYT,* Nov. 21, 1949, p. 28; summary of RR's speech to the Kiwanis International Convention, June 21, 1951, *Kiwanis Magazine* (Aug. 1951), 25; RR quoted in Norman, "Reagan Good Film Spokesman," 16; and statement of Ronald Reagan, June 16, 1955, *Kefauver Hearings, 1955,* 94. See also ibid., 92–3, 95–6; RR, "Motion Pictures and Your Community," 54; RR, *Where's,* 140, 144, 164; *NYT,* June 17, 1955, p. 24; and Gilbert, *Cycle of Outrage,* esp. 162–95.

19. "A Fork in the River"

1. Quotation, Ronald Reagan's farewell address, Jan. 11, 1989, reprinted in Ritter and Henry, *Ronald Reagan,* 182. For text of the entire speech, see ibid., 179–85.

2. Quotations, W. H. Mooring, "Postwar Reagan," *Picturegoer,* July 19, 1947, copy in Ronald Reagan clipping file, Blum Collection, SHSWM. RR quoted in *LAM,* Jan. 6, 1950, copy in folder 1, Reagan contract files, WBAHP-USC. See also RR to Jack [Warner], May 3, [1950], ibid.

3. When Roy Obringer suggested that Reagan might wish to void his contract, Reagan pointed out that unlike Bogart or Flynn, he had "always played ball and been loyal to the company." Reagan quoted in article by Ezra Goodman, *LADN* [?], July 24, 1950, copy in Reagan clipping file, AMPASL; Reagan's remarks reported to Jack Warner in Obringer to Warner, May 26, 1950, folder 1, Reagan contract file, WBAHP-USC (see also Obringer to Warner, Feb. 17, 1950, ibid.).

4. Quotations, RR, *Where's,* 213, 217. After Wasserman worked out new terms, Reagan's remaining pictures for Warner Bros. were *Storm Warning, She's Working Her Way Through College,* and *The Winning Team.* Reagan made only one additional picture, *Law and Order* (1953), for Universal. For Paramount, Reagan made *The Last Outpost* (1951), *Hong Kong* (1952), and *Tropic Zone* (1953). Surely Reagan would not have quarrelled with Dore Schary's assessment of Wasserman as the "smartest . . . man I ever met in pictures." Schary interview (1958), 66–7, BLCU-NY.

5. Quotation, RR, *Where's,* 244. See also ibid., 241–2, 245–51; RR, *American Life,* 125; Edwards, *Early Reagan,* 445–7; and Terry Mulgannon, "When Ronnie Played Vegas," *Los Angeles Magazine* (April, 1983), 178–9, 310–11. Reagan's other pictures during the 1950s included *Prisoner of War* (MGM, 1954), *Cattle Queen of Montana* (RKO, 1954), *Tennessee's Partner* (RKO, 1955), *Hellcats of the Navy* (Columbia, 1957). His last film, *The Killers* (NBC-TV), appeared in 1964.

6. See Mooring, "Postwar Reagan."
7. For Reagan's concern about being labeled "only an actor" during the 1966 California governor's race, see RR, *American Life*, 151.
8. Quotations, Rothe, ed., *Current Biography*, 502; and "Solid Citizen," undated, unmarked clipping in Ronald Reagan clipping file, Blum Collection, SHSWM. See also Lorraine Makler, "Everybody's Kind of Guy," *Prexy Chatter* (Ronald Reagan Fan Club), Aug., 1950, *DETA*. The studio characterized Reagan in his early roles as a "combination of Tom Swift and Dick Tracy." His post–World War II image was more mature. For example, his character in *Louisa* (Universal, 1950), was an architect for an insurance company who earned a good salary, who was on the verge of being promoted, and who described himself as a "simple, hard-working citizen with a family I was proud of, and a wife who respected me." Quotations, pressbook, *Voice of the Turtle*, UA-SHSWM; and from film, *Louisa*.
9. Quotation from poster for *Law and Order*, folder 19,878, box 676, *Law and Order* file, Universal Studio Collection, DL-USC; and folder 14,206, box 479, ibid.
10. Quotations, letter from a "Wounded Marine," *Hollywood Reporter*, Aug. 20, 1946, Reagan clipping file, AMPASL.
11. Quotations, RR, *Where's*, 117. Also RR, *American Life*, 99–100.
12. See full-page ad, signed by Eddie Albert, Melvyn Douglas, Douglas Fairbanks, Jr., William Holden, John Howard, Jeffrey Lynn, Gene Markey, Wayne Morris, and Audie Murphy, defending Reagan's service, in *Hollywood Reporter* 89 (Aug. 22, 1946), 13, Reagan clipping file, AMPASL.
13. Quotations, McGoogan, "How the Commies Were Licked in Hollywood"; Anne Norman, "Reagan Good Film Spokesman," *Hartford Times*, June 5, 1952, p. 16; and Fairfax Nisbet, "Film Notables Arriving for COMPO Parley," *Dallas Morning News*, June 9, 1952, part 2, p. 4. See also RR, *Where's*, 249. On Reagan's development as an orator, see Ritter and Henry, *Ronald Reagan*.
14. Quotations, Art Arthur to RR, May 21, 1976, box 43, Arthur Papers, BYU; and Dales, "Pragmatic Leadership," 52; see also ibid., 23, 28, 29. See also Arthur to RR, March 12, 1973, box 14, Arthur Papers, BYU; and Edwards, *Early Reagan*, 331, 444.
15. Quotations, RR, "America the Beautiful," 10.
16. Quotation, ibid., 13. On Reagan's later "exaltation of American civil religion," see Pierard and Linder, *Civil Religion & the Presidency*, 257–83 (quotation, 257); and Ritter and Henry, *Ronald Reagan*, 115, 118–21.
17. The SAG-MCA agreement, and more generally Reagan's role in television, fall beyond the scope of this study. For the SAG-MCA arrangement and the Justice Department's investigation, see Wills, *Reagan's America*, 261–78; Edwards, *Early Reagan*, 435–40; and Moldea, *Dark Victory*.

REFERENCES

Archival Collections

Alabama

Maxwell Air Force Base:
   Records of the Army Air Force First Motion Picture Base Unit (later known as 18th
   Motion Picture Base Unit)

California

Berkeley:
   Bancroft Library, University of California
      Adrian J. Falk Papers   •   William Randolph Hearst Papers   •   Hiram W.
      Johnson Papers   •   Hardin B. Jones Papers   •   Robert W. Kenny Papers   •
      Leonard B. Loeb Papers   •   Thomas J. Mooney Correspondence and Papers   •
      James F. T. O'Connor Collection   •   Ronald Reagan Gubernatorial Era Region-
      al Oral History Office   •   George R. Stewart Papers   •   Thomas M. Storke
      Papers   •   August Vollmer Papers
Beverly Hills:
   Margaret Herrick Library, Academy of Motion Picture Arts and Sciences Library
      Biography files
         Joseph Breen   •   Robert Buckner   •   Michael Curtiz   •   Martin
         Quigley   •   Raymond Schrock   •   Hal Wallis   •   Jack L. Warner   •   Jane
         Wyman
      Louella Parsons Scrapbook   •   Motion Picture Industry Council Papers   •
      Production Code Administration Files
         For all Ronald Reagan feature films plus approximately 150 related motion
         pictures
      Ronald Reagan Collection   •   Jay A. Schlein Collection   •   Hal Wallis
      Collection
Hollywood:
   Hollywood–Beverly Christian Church Library
   Christian Challenger (1941–7)

Screen Actors Guild Archive
  Minutes, board of directors, Screen Actors Guild (1937–53) • Minutes, executive committee, Screen Actors Guild (1937–53) • Oral histories
    Leon Ames • Robert Montgomery • Anne Revere • Gale Sondergaard
  Screen Actor • *Intelligence Report*
Los Angeles:
American Film Institute
  Oral history (Geoffrey Shurlock) • Jack Warner clipping file
California, State of, Court of Appeals, Second Appellate District
  Testimony (*Jeffers v. Screen Extras Guild,* 1955)
    Roy Brewer • Edward Dmytryk • Buck Harris • George Murphy • Ronald Reagan • Herbert K. Sorrell
Doheny Library, School of Cinema–Television Collection, University of Southern California
  William Dieterle Collection • Donald Gledhill, ed., *Press Clipping File on the Senate Sub-Committee War Film Hearings, vol. 1* • Neal Graham Collection • Metro-Goldwyn-Mayer Papers
    Production files
      Prisoner of War file • *The Bad Man* file
  Hal Roach Collection (Hollywood Museum Collection) • Edward G. Robinson Papers • Universal Studio Collection
    Production files
      Bedtime for Bonzo file • *Louisa* file • *Law and Order* file
  Jack L. Warner Collection • Warner Bros. Archive of Historical Papers
    Contract files
      Errol Flynn • Wayne Morris • Ronald Reagan • Jane Wyman
    Production files
      Accidents Will Happen • *Angels Wash Their Faces* • *Beyond the Line of Duty* • *Boy Meets Girl* • *Brother Rat* • *Brother Rat and a Baby* • *Code of the Secret Service* • *Confessions of a Nazi Spy* • *Dark Victry* • *Desperate Journey* • *G-Men* • *Girls on Probation* • *Going Places* • *Hell's Kitchen* • *Hollywood Canteen* • *International Squadron* • *Juke Girl* • *Kings Row* • *Knute Rockne – All American* • *Love Is on the Air* • *Murder in the Air* • *Night Unto Night* • *Nine Lives Are Not Enough* • *Rear Gunner* • *Santa Fe Trail* • *Secret Service of the Air* • *Sergeant Murphy* • *Smashing the Money Ring* • *Stallion Road* • *Submarine D-1* • *Swing Your Lady* • *That Hagen Girl* • *This Is the Army* • *The Voice of the Turte*
    Warner Bros. patriotic shorts files
      Bill of Rights • *Declaration of Independence* • *Flag of Humanity* • *Lincoln in the White House* • *The Monroe Doctrine* • *Old Hickory* • *Pony Express* • *Romance in Louisiana* • *Sons of the Fighting 69th*
Los Angeles County Court House Archives
  Ronald Reagan–Jane Wyman divorce records (case file number D360058)
Southern California Library for Social Studies and Research
  Hollywood Studio Strike Collection
UCLA Film and Television Archive, Powell Library, University of California, Los Angeles
  Hearst Metrotone Newsreel Collection

University Research Library, University of California, Los Angeles
Fox Studio Collection • Adaline Guenther Papers • Stuart Heisler
Papers • Hollywood Studio Strike Collection, 1945–8 • *Los Angeles
Daily News* Photo Archive • Oral histories:
Hans Burkhardt • Jack Dales • George H. Dunne • Dorothy
Healey • Stanley Plog • Neil Reagan • Herbert K. Sorrell
Norton Air Force Base:
DAVA Motion Picture Depository, DAVCOM Division
Films
For God and Country • *Big Picture* • *Westward Bataan* • *Wings for
This Man* • *Fight for the Sky*
Stanford University:
Hoover Institute of War and Peace
America First Papers • Motion Picture Research Council Papers • Ronald
Reagan Collection • United World Federalist Msc. Records, 1945–55

District of Columbia

Washington:
Federal Bureau of Investigation files obtained under the Freedom of Information
Act
Americans for Democratic Action • American Veterans Committee • Com-
mittee for a Democratic Far Eastern Policy • Errol Flynn • William L.
Guthrie • Will H. Hays • Hollywood Independent Citizens Committee for
the Arts, Sciences and Professions • Labor League of Hollywood Voters •
Ronald Reagan • Screen Actors Guild • Harry Warner • Jack L.
Warner • Warner Bros. Pictures, Inc.
Lauinger Library, Georgetown University
Wilfrid Parsons Papers
Library of Congress
Papers of Henry H. Arnold • Motion Picture, Broadcasting, and Recorded
Sound Division – Films:
The Bad Man • *The Hasty Heart* • *Louisa* • *Q-Planes* • *She's Work-
ing Her Way Through College* • *The Winning Team*
Records of the National Association for the Advancement of Colored People
National Archives
RG18: General Services Administration records • RG59: General Records,
Department of State, decimal file 1945–54 • RG107: Office of the Secretary of
War, Central Deferment Board (CDB) • RG407: Records of the adjutant gener-
al's office • National Archives and Records Service, Motion Picture, Sound
and Video Branch (NNSM):
Films
Fight for the Sky • *For God and Country* • *Jap Zero* • *Target
Tokyo* • *Westward Bataan* • *Wings for This Man*

Illinois

Carbondale:
Morris Library, Southern Illinois University
John Howard Lawson Papers
Chicago:
Archdiocese of Chicago Archives

alphabetical file drawers
   Joseph Breen • FitzGeorge Dinneen • Fox Film Corp. • Will H. Hays • Daniel A. Lord • George Cardinal Mundelein • Martin Quigley • Harold Stuart • Warner Bros. Pictures, Inc. • Adolph Zukor
General Chancery files • George Cardinal Mundelein Papers
Illinois Regional Archives Depository, Ronald Williams Library, Northeastern Illinois University
   Cook County police censorship records
Dixon:
Records of the First Christian Church • Dixon Public Library • *Dixon Telegraph* morgue
Eureka:
Eureka College Archives
   The Pegasus • *The Prism* • Ronald Reagan World War II Scrapbook • School Catalogs

Indiana

Bloomington:
Lilly Library
   United World Federalist Manuscripts
Indianapolis:
Indiana State Library
   Will H. Hays Papers
South Bend
Archives of the University of Notre Dame, Memorial Library
   Executive Vice-Presidents: O'Donnell and Cavanaugh Papers • Hugh, C.S.C., President's Papers • *Notre Dame Scholastic* • *University of Notre Dame Religious Bulletin*
Northern Indiana Historical Society
   Knute Rockne Week file
South Bend Public Library
   Knute Rockne Week clipping file
South Bend Tribune morgue
   Knute Rockne Week file

Iowa

Davenport:
Palmer School of Chiropractic
   B. J. Palmer Papers
Quad City Times morgue
   picture file
West Branch:
Herbert Hoover Presidential Library
   Herbert Hoover Papers • James P. Goodrich Papers

Maryland

Suitland:
National Archives and Records Administration
   RG 87: U.S. Secret Service records • RG 159: Office of the Inspector General, correspondence, Boxes 1159–68 • RG 165: War Department, General Staff,

G-1 (personnel), numerical file 1921–42 • RG 208: Records of the Office of
War Information (NC-148) • RG 394: (U.S. Army Commands), Ninth Corps
Area, Adjutant General, general administration file, 1935–43 • Records of the
Ninth Service Command, Adjutant General Office, decimal file 1931–41

Missouri

Canton:
  Culver-Stockton College Archive
    Ronald Reagan–Cleaver family correspondence
Columbia:
  Lenoir Home
    Helen Cleaver (deceased) – family correspondence
Independence:
  Harry S Truman Library
    Files of Dallas S. Halberstadt • Papers of David K. Niles • Harry S Truman
    Papers, official file • Harry S Truman Papers, president's personal file •
    Truman Diary, president's secretary's files
St. Louis:
  Jesuit Missouri Province Archives
    Daniel A. Lord Papers

New Jersey

Princeton:
    Theater Collection, Princeton University Library
      Warner Bros. Archive of Historical Papers
        Minutes, board of directors, 1927–45, 1947–9 • Minutes, special meet-
        ings of the board of directors, 1950–2 • Distribution records • Ronald
        Reagan contract files
      Legal files
        Accidents Will Happen • *Angels Wash Their Faces* • *Beyond the Line
        of Duty* • *Desperate Journey* • *Murder in the Air*

New York

Hyde Park:
  Franklin D. Roosevelt Presidential Library
    Papers of Stephen Early • Papers of Harry Hopkins • Papers of Lowell
    Mellett • Papers of Eleanor Roosevelt • Papers of Franklin D. Roosevelt,
    official file • Papers of Franklin D. Roosevelt, president's personal file •
    Papers of James Roosevelt • Papers of Henry A. Wallace
New York:
  Butler Library, Columbia University
    Popular Arts Project
      See "Interviews and Oral Histories"
  New York Public Library
    American Veterans Committee Bulletin • Authors
      Philip Wylie • John Van Druten • Edith Roberts
    Camp Shows, Inc. • *Operation USO: Report of the President* • *United
    Services Organizations, Releases . . .* • *USO Bulletin*
  New York Public Library Annex

Speeches
Eric A. Johnston
Authors
John Howard Lawson • Dalton Trumbo • Philip Wylie
New York Public Library, Lincoln Center
Authors
John Howard Lawson • Lester Cole
Chamberlain and Lyman Brown Theatrical Agency Collection • Ronald Reagan clipping file, 1937–86
New York Public Library, Schomburg Center for Research in Black Culture
"Amos 'n' Andy" clipping file • *Storm Warning* clipping file

Tennessee

Nashville:
Disciples of Christ Historical Society
Ben Hill Cleaver file • Cleveland Kleihauer file

Utah

Provo:
Brigham Young University Archives
Art Arthur Papers • Cecil B. DeMille Papers

Washington

Spokane:
Eastern Washington State Historical Society
Eric Johnston Papers

Wisconsin

Madison:
State Historical Society of Wisconsin
American Federation of Labor Papers • Records of the Americans for Democratic Action • Alvah Bessie Papers • Herbert Biberman and Gale Sondergaard Papers • Daniel Blum Collection • I. A. L. Diamond Papers • Melvyn Douglas Papers • Hollywood Democratic Committee (HICCASP) Papers • Hollywood Ten Papers • Langston Hughes Papers • Gordon Kahn Papers • Robert Walker Kenny and Robert S. Morris Papers, 1940–57 • Howard E. Koch Papers • Ring Lardner, Jr., Papers • Emmet Lavery Papers • James I. Loeb, Jr. Papers • John K. McCaffery recordings, 1956–62 • Eugene Mailes Papers • Albert Maltz Papers • Groucho Marx Papers • Alexander Meiklejohn Papers • Winston Miller Papers • Dore Schary Papers • Shepard Collection
First Motion Picture Base Unit Films
Resisting Enemy Interrogation (c. 1942) • *The Memphis Belle: A Story of the Flying Fortress* (1944)
Herman E. Shumlin Papers • Stamerl Collection • Ed Sullivan Papers • Dalton Trumbo Papers • United Artists Collection:
Films
thirty-eight Ronald Reagan feature films made for Warner Bros. before 1950

Pressbooks
  Accidents Will Happen • *An Angel From Texas* • *Angels Wash Their Faces* • *Boy Meets Girl* • *Brother Rat* • *Brother Rat and a Baby* • *Code of the Secret Service* • *Cowboy From Brooklyn* • *Dark Victory* • *Love Is on the Air* • *Million Dollar Baby* • *Murder in the Air* • *Naughty But Nice* • *Night Unto Night* • *Nine Lives Are Not Enough* • *Santa Fe Trail* • *Secret Service of the Air* • *Sergeant Murphy* • *Smashing the Money Ring*
Scripts
  Accidents Will Happen • *Code of the Secret Service* • *Dark Victory* • *Going Places* • *Hollywood Hotel* • *Juke Girl* • *Love Is On the Air* • *Murder in the Air* • *Naughty But Nice* • *Night Unto Night* • *Nine Lives Are Not Enough* • *Secret Service of the Air* • *Sergeant Murphy* • *Smashing the Money Ring*
Walter F. Wanger Papers • John Wexley Papers • Wisconsin Manufacturers Association Papers

Published Documents

Behlmer, Rudy (selected, edited, and annotated). *Inside Warner Bros. (1935–1951)* (New York: Viking, 1985).
Gallup Looks at the Movies: Audience Research Report, 1940–1950 (Wilmington, Del.: American Institute of Public Opinion and Scholarly Resources, n.d.).
Gallup, George H. *The Gallup Poll: Public Opinion, 1935–1971: Volume One, 1935–1948* (New York: Random House, 1972).
Gledhill, Donald, ed. *Press Clipping File on the Senate Sub-Committee War Film Hearings: Volume 1, August 1 Through October 15, 1941* (Hollywood, Calif.: Academy of Motion Picture Arts and Sciences, 1941).
Manfull, Helen, ed. *Additional Dialogue: Letters of Dalton Trumbo, 1942–1962* (New York: Evans, 1970).
Marshall, George, H. H. Arnold, and Ernest J. King. *The War Reports of General of the Army George C. Marshall, General of the Army H. H. Arnold, [and] Fleet Admiral Ernest J. King* (Philadelphia: Lippincott, 1947).
National Association for the Advancement of Colored People. *Annual Report of 1942* (New York: NAACP, [1942]).
Swisher, Carl, ed. *Selected Papers of Homer Cummings: Attorney General of the United States, 1933–1939* (New York: Scribner, 1939).
USO. *Camp Shows Inc., New York – Reports of Activities, Etc.* Volumes 3 and 5, New York Public Library.

Government Hearings or Publications
(arranged chronologically)

Hearings Before a Subcommittee of the Committee on Interstate Commerce. United States Senate, Seventy-Seventh Congress, First Session, Pursuant to S. Res. 152 (Sept. 9–26, 1941) (Washington, D.C.: Government Printing Office, 1942) (cited as Clark *Hearings*).
Congressional Record (Sept., Oct., 1941).
"Investigation of the National Defense Program." *Hearings before a Special Committee Investigating the National Defense Program,* United States Senate, Seventy-Eighth Congress, First Session, Pursuant to S. Res. 6 (Washington, D.C.: Government Printing Office, 1943), part 17 – "Army Commissions and Military Activities of Motion Picture Personnel."

Golden, Nathan D., comp. *Motion Picture Markets – 1944: Africa* (Washington, D.C.: Bureau of Foreign and Domestic Commerce, Department of Commerce, 1944).

Report: Joint Fact-Finding Committee on Un-American Activities in California ([Sacramento]: Senate of the State of California, 1945).

"Postwar Economic Policy and Planning." *Hearings before the Special Committee on Postwar Economic Policy and Planning,* House of Representatives, Seventy-Ninth Congress, First and Second Sessions, Pursuant to H. Res. 60, Part 9 (Washington, D.C.: Government Printing Office, 1946) (cited as *Postwar Planning Hearings, Dec. 1946*).

California Legislature. *Third Report: Un-American Activities in California, 1947: Report of the Joint Fact-Finding Committee to the Fifty-Seventh California Legislature* ([Sacramento]: Senate of the State of California, 1947) (cited as Calif. HUAC, 1947, *Third Report*).

Hearings Before the Committee on Un-American Activities. March, 1947 (cited as *HUAC Hearings, March, 1947*).

"Hearings Regarding the Communist Infiltration of the Motion Picture Industry." *Hearings Before the Committee on Un-American Activities,* House of Representatives, Eightieth Congress, First Session, Public Law 601 (Washington, D.C.: Government Printing Office, 1947) (cited as *HUAC Hearings, Oct., 1947*).

"Jurisdictional Disputes in the Motion-Picture Industry." *Hearings before a Special Subcommittee of the Committee on Education and Labor,* House of Representatives, Eightieth Congress, First Session, Pursuant to H. Res. 111 (Washington, D.C.: Government Printing Office, 1948) (cited as "Jurisdictional Disputes," *Hearings*).

California Legislature. *Fourth Report of the Senate Fact-Finding Committee on Un-American Activities, 1948: Communist Front Organizations* ([Sacramento]: Senate of the State of California, [1948]) (cited as Calif. HUAC, 1948, *Fourth Report*).

California Legislature. *Fifth Report of the Senate Fact-Finding Committee on Un-American Activities, 1949* ([Sacramento]: Senate of the State of California, [1949]) (cited as Calif. HUAC, 1949, *Fifth Report*).

"Communist Infiltration of Hollywood Motion-Picture Industry." *Hearings before the Committee on Un-American Activities,* House of Representatives, Eighty-Second Congress, First Session (Washington, D.C.: Government Printing Office, 1951) (cited as *HUAC Hearings, 1951*).

California Legislature. *Sixth Report of the Senate Fact-Finding Committee on Un-American Activities, 1951* ([Sacramento]: Senate of the State of California, [1951]) (cited as Calif. HUAC, 1951, *Sixth Report*).

Annual Report of the Committee on Un-American Activities for the Year 1951 (Washington, D.C.: Committee on Un-American Activities, House of Representatives, 1952) (cited as *Annual Report,* HUAC [1951]).

Annual Report of the Committee on Un-American Activities for the Year 1952 (Washington, D.C.: Committee on Un-American Activities, House of Representatives, 1952) (cited as *Annual Report,* HUAC [1952]).

Hearings before the Committee on Un-American Activities (Washington, D.C.: Government Printing Office, 1953) (cited as *HUAC Hearings, 1953*).

"Juvenile Delinquency (Motion Pictures)." *Hearings before the Subcommittee to Investigate Juvenile Delinquency of the Committee on the Judiciary,* United States Senate, Eighty-Fourth Congress, First Session, Pursuant to S. Res. 62 (Washington, D.C.: Government Printing Office, 1955) (cited as *Kefauver Hearings, 1955*).

Interviews, Oral Histories, Autobiographies, Memoirs, and Diaries

Ames, Leon. Interview, 1979, SAGA.
Arnold, H. H. *Global Mission* (New York: Harper Bros., 1949).
Bacall, Lauren. *By Myself* (New York: Knopf, 1979).
Behrman, S. N. *Tribulations and Laughter: A Memoir by S. N. Behrman* (London: Hamish Hamilton, 1972).
Bessie, Alvah. *Inquisition in Eden* (New York: Macmillan, 1965).
Biberman, Herbert. *Salt of the Earth: The Story of a Film* (Boston: Beacon, 1965).
Black, Shirley Temple. *Child Star: An Autobiography* (New York: McGraw-Hill, 1988).
Blackmer, Sidney. Oral history, 1959 (Oral History Research Office, Popular Arts Project, BLCU-NY).
Bovey, Dorothy (Dorothy Potterveld). Interview with author, Shorewood, Wis., 1987.
Burkhardt, Hans. "Los Angeles Art Community: Group Portrait." Interviewed by Susan Einstein (Los Angeles: Regents of the University of California, 1977), URL-UCLA.
Cagney, James. *Cagney by Cagney* (Garden City, N.Y.: Doubleday, 1976).
Capra, Frank. *The Name Above the Title: An Autobiography* (New York: Macmillan, 1971).
Chaplin, Charlie. *My Autobiography* (New York: Simon & Schuster, 1964).
Cleaver, Ben H. "Some Memories of John Stephen Cleaver by His Son Ben Hill Cleaver," DCHSN.
Cleaver, Helen. Telephone interview with author, 1985.
Cleaver, Margaret (Mrs. James Gordon). Interview with author, Richmond, Va., 1988.
Cleugh, Eric. *Without Let or Hindrance: Reminiscences of a British Foreign Service Officer* (London: Cassell, 1960).
Cohen, Morris Raphael. *A Dreamer's Journey: The Autobiography of Morris Raphael Cohen* (Glencoe, Ill.: Free Press, 1949).
Cole, Lester. *Hollywood Red: The Autobiography of Lester Cole* (Palo Alto, Calif.: Ramparts, 1981).
Dales, Jack. Interview, 1979, SAGA.
Dales, Jack. "Pragmatic Leadership: Ronald Reagan as President of the Screen Actors Guild." Interviewed by Mitch Tuchman (Los Angeles: Regents of the University of California, 1981), URL-UCLA.
Davis, Loyal. *A Surgeon's Odyssey* (Garden City, N.Y.: Doubleday, 1973).
De Havilland, Olivia. *Every Frenchman Has One* (New York: Random House, 1961).
DeMille, Cecil B. Oral history, 1958 (Oral History Research Office, Popular Arts Project, BLCU-NY).
DeMille, Cecil B. *The Autobiography of Cecil B. DeMille* (Englewood Cliffs, N.J.: Prentice-Hall, 1959).
Dickinson, Burrus. Interview with author, Eureka, Ill., 1988.
Dmytryk, Edward. *It's a Hell of a Life but Not a Bad Living* (New York: Times Books, 1978).
Dmytryk, Edward. Oral histories, 1958, 1959 (Oral History Research Office, Popular Arts Project, BLCU-NY).
Dos Passos, John. *The Best Times: An Informal Memoir* (New York: New American Library, 1966).
Douglas, Helen Gahagan. *A Full Life* (Garden City, N.Y.: Doubleday, 1982).

Douglas, Helen Gahagan. "Congresswoman, Actress, and Opera Singer: Helen Gahagan Douglas." Interviewed by Amelia Fry, 1973, 1974, 1976 (Berkeley: Regents of the University of California, 1982), BL-UCB.

Douglas, Melvyn, with Tom Arthur. *See You at the Movies: The Autobiography* (New York: University Press of America, 1986).

Douglas, Melvyn. Oral history, 1958 (Oral History Research Office, Popular Arts Project, BLCU-NY).

Dunckel, Earl B. "Ronald Reagan and the General Electric Theater, 1954–1955." Interviewed by Gabrielle Morris (Berkeley: Regents of the University of California, 1982) BL-UCB.

Dunne, George H. "Christian Advocacy and Labor Strife in Hollywood." Interviewed by Mitch Tuchman (Los Angeles: Regents of the University of California, 1981), URL-UCLA.

Dunne, Philip. *Take Two: A Life in Movies and Politics* (New York: McGraw-Hill, 1980).

Flynn, Errol. *My Wicked, Wicked Ways* (New York: Putnam, 1959).

Goodwin, Fred. Interview with author, Cape Girardeau, Mo., 1988.

Hayden, Sterling. *Wanderer* (New York: Knopf, 1963).

Hays, Will H. *The Memoirs of Will H. Hays* (Garden City, N.Y.: Doubleday, 1955).

Healey, Dorothy. "Tradition's Chains Have Bound Us." Interviewed by Joel Gardner (Los Angeles: Regents of the University of California, c. 1982), URL-UCLA.

Hope, Bob, with Melville Shavelson. *Don't Shoot, It's Only Me: Bob Hope's Comedy History of the United States* (New York: Putnam, 1990).

Horne, Lena, and Richard Schickel. *Lena* (Garden City, N.Y.: Doubleday, 1965).

Horne, Lena, as told to Helen Arstein and Carlton Moss. *Lena Horne in Person* (New York: Greenberg, 1950).

Howe, Irving, with Kenneth Libo. *World of Our Fathers* (New York: Harcourt Brace Jovanovich, 1976).

Hulston, John K. Oral history interview, Jan. 11, 1988, by Niel M. Johnson, Independence, Mo., HSTLI.

Israel, Thomas. Interview with author, Cape Girardeau, Mo., 1988.

Johnston, Eric A. Oral history, 1959 (Oral History Research Office, Popular Arts Project, BLCU-NY).

Jones, R. V. *Most Secret War* (London: Hamish Hamilton, 1978).

Koch, Howard. *As Time Goes By: Memoirs of a Writer* (New York: Harcourt Brace Jovanovich, 1979).

Lardner, Ring, Jr. *The Lardners: My Family Remembered* (New York: Harper & Row, 1976).

Lawson, John Howard. Unpublished autobiography, JHL-SIU.

Lawson, John Howard. *Film: The Creative Process: The Search for an Audio-Visual Language and Structure* (New York: Hill & Wang, 1964).

Lindfors, Viveca. *Viveka . . . Viveca . . .* (New York: Everest House, 1981).

Littlejohn, Don. Interview with author, Eureka, Ill., 1985.

Loeb, James I., Jr. *Autobiography* (microfilm, 1959, SHSWM).

Lord, Daniel A. *Played by Ear: The Autobiography of Daniel A. Lord, S. J.* (Chicago: Loyola University Press, 1955).

Maltz, Albert. "The Citizen Writer in Retrospect." Interviewed by Joel Gardner (2 vols., Los Angeles: Regents of the University of California, 1983), URL-UCLA.

Mann, Eirka, and Klaus Mann. *Escape to Life* (Boston: Houghton Mifflin, 1939).

Mann, Thomas. *Thomas Mann Diaries, 1918–1939.* Translated from the German by Richard and Clara Winston (New York: Abrams, 1982).

Martin, Olga J. *Hollywood's Movie Commandments: A Handbook for Motion Picture Writers and Reviewers* (New York: Wilson, 1937).

Montgomery, Robert. Interview, 1979, SAGA.

Murphy, George, with Victor Lasky, *"Say . . . Didn't You Used to be George Murphy?"* (Edinburgh: Bartholomew House, 1970).

Neal, Patricia, with Richard DeNeut. *As I Am: An Autobiography* (New York: Simon & Schuster, 1988).

Niven, David, *The Moon's a Balloon* (New York: Putnam, 1972).

Bring On the Empty Horses (New York: Putnam, 1975).

Nixon, Richard. *In the Arena: A Memoir of Victory, Defeat, and Renewal* (New York: Simon & Schuster, 1990).

Nugent, Elliott. *Events Leading Up to the Comedy: An Autobiography* (New York: Trident, 1965).

Nugent, Elliott. Oral history, 1958 (Oral History Research Office, Popular Arts Project, BLCU-NY).

O'Brien, Pat. *The Wind at My Back: The Life and Times of Pat O'Brien* (Garden City, N.Y.: Doubleday, 1964).

Olivier, Laurence. *Confessions of an Actor: An Autobiography* (New York: Simon & Schuster, 1982).

Ornitz, Samuel Badisch. *Haunch Paunch and Jowl: An Anonymous Autobiography* (New York: Boni and Liveright, 1923).

Palmer, Dave. *The Palmers: Memoirs of David D. Palmer* (Davenport, Iowa: Bawden Bros., 1977).

Parsons, Louella O. *The Gay Illiterate* (Garden City, N.Y.: Doubleday, Doran, 1944).

Parsons, Louella O. Oral history, 1959 (Oral History Research Office, Popular Arts Project, BLCU-NY).

Plog, Stanley. "More Than Just an Actor: The Early Campaigns of Ronald Reagan." Interviewed by Stephen Stern (Los Angeles: Regents of the University of California, 1981), URL-UCLA.

Quigley, Martin. *Decency in Motion Pictures* (New York: Macmillan, 1937).

Quigley, Martin. Oral history, c. 1958 (Oral History Research Office, Popular Arts Project, BLCU-NY).

Reagan, Maureen. *First Father, First Daughter* (Boston: Little, Brown, 1989).

Reagan, Michael, with Joe Hyams. *On the Outside Looking In* (New York: Kensington, 1988).

Reagan, Nancy, with William Novak. *My Turn: Memoirs of Nancy Reagan* (New York: Random House, 1989).

Reagan, Nancy, with Bill Libby. *Nancy* (New York: William Morrow, 1980).

Reagan, Neil. "Private Dimensions and Public Images: The Early Political Campaigns of Ronald Reagan." Interviewed by Stephen Stern (Los Angeles: Regents of the University of California, 1981), URL-UCLA.

Reagan, Ronald, *An American Life* (New York: Simon & Schuster, 1990).

Reagan, Ronald, with Richard G. Hubler. *Where's the Rest of Me?* (New York: Duell, Sloan and Pearce, 1965).

Reagan, Ronald. Interview with author, Century City, Calif., 1989.

Revere, Anne. Interview, Feb. 25, 1955 (folder 3, box 69, Biberman–Sondergaard Papers, SHSWM).

Interview, 1979, SAGA.

Rivkin, Allen E. *Doubleday & Company, Inc. Presents The Rivkin–Kerr Production of HELLO HOLLYWOOD: A Book about the Movies by the People Who Make Them* ([New York: Doubleday], 1962).

Robinson, Edward G., with Leonard Spigelgass. *All My Yesterdays: An Autobiography* (New York: Hawthorn, 1973).

Rockne, Knute, with Bonnie Skiles Rockne, ed. *The Autobiography of Knute Rockne* (Indianapolis: Bobbs-Merrill, 1931).

Schary, Dore. *For Special Occasions* (New York: Random House, 1962).

Schary, Dore. *Heyday: An Autobiography* (Boston: Little, Brown, 1979).

Schary, Dore. Oral history, 1958 (Oral History Research Office, Popular Arts Project, BLCU-NY).

Scott, Zachary. Oral history, 1959 (Oral History Research Office, Popular Arts Project, BLCU-NY).

Shephard, Tom. Interview with author, Dixon, Ill., 1985.

Shurlock, Geoffrey. *Oral History with Geoffrey Shurlock* (Beverly Hills, Calif.: Center for Advanced Film Studies, 1975), AFI-LA.

Sondergaard, Gale. Interview, 1979, SAGA.

Sorrell, Herbert K. "You Don't Choose Your Friends: The Memoirs of Herbert Knott Sorrell." Oral history project (Los Angeles: Regents of the University of California, 1963), URL-UCLA.

Vizzard, Jack. *See No Evil: Life Inside a Hollywood Censor* (New York: Simon & Schuster, 1970).

Van Druten, John. *Way to the Present: A Personal Record* (London: Michael Joseph, 1938).

Walgreen, Myrtle R. *Never a Dull Day: An Autobiography* (Chicago: Regnery, 1963).

Walker, William ("Bill"). Telephone interviews with author, 1987, 1988.

Wallis, Hal. Oral history, 1958 (Oral History Research Office, Popular Arts Project, BLCU-NY).

Wallis, Hal, and Charles Higham. *Starmaker: The Autobiography of Hal Wallis* (New York: Macmillan, 1980).

Walters, Salene (Salene Walters Lamm). Telephone interview with author, Dexter, Mo., 1991.

Warner, Jack L., with Dean Jennings. *My First Hundred Years in Hollywood* (New York: Random House, 1965).

White, Walter. *A Man Called White: The Autobiography of Walter White* (New York: Viking, 1955).

How Far the Promised Land? (New York: Viking, 1955).

Zukor, Adolph, with Dale Kramer. *The Public Is Never Wrong: The Autobiography of Adolph Zukor* (New York: Putnam, 1953).

Newsletters, Newspapers, and Periodicals

American Legion Magazine
American Veterans Committee Bulletin
Baltimore Afro-American
California Eagle
Chicago Daily Tribune
Chicago Defender
Chicago Herald American
Chicago Herald and Examiner
Christian Challenger (Hollywood–Beverly Christian Church)
Christian Science Monitor
Daily Pantagraph (Bloomington, Ill.)

Daily Variety
Daily Worker
Dallas Morning News
Des Moines Dispatch
Des Moines Sunday Register
Des Moines Tribune
Dixon Evening Telegraph
Exhibitors Herald World
Film Daily
Film Technicians Daily Bulletin
Forbes Magazine of Business
Fortune

General Bulletin (IATSE)
Hartford [Conn.] Times
Hollywood Citizen-News
Hollywood Closeup: An IATSE Information Bulletin in the Public Interest
Hollywood Reporter
Hollywood Spectator
Intelligence Report (Screen Actors Guild)
Liberty Magazine
Life
Los Angeles Citizen
Los Angeles Daily News
Los Angeles Examiner
Los Angeles Herald-Express
Los Angeles Times
Modern Screen
Motion Picture Daily
Motion Picture Herald
Nashville Tennessean
Nation
New Republic
New York Daily News
New York Herald Tribune
New York Post
New York Times
New York Times Magazine
Newsweek
Notre Dame Scholastic
Oregonian [Portland]
Pegasus (Eureka College)
People's Daily World

People's Voice
Peoria Evening Star
Peoria Journal
Philadelphia Inquirer
Printer's Ink
Prism (Eureka College)
St. Louis Globe-Democrat
San Francisco Chronicle
San Francisco Examiner
Santa Fe New Mexican
Saturday Evening Post
Screen Actor
Senior Scholastic
South Bend Tribune
Spotlights (Hollywood Chapter 2, American Veterans Committee)
Springfield [Mo.] Leader and Press
Springfield [Mo.] News and Leader
University of Notre Dame Religious Bulletin
U.S. News & World Report
USO Camp Shows . . . Reports
USO Bulletin
Variety
V.F.W. Magazine
Warner Spirit (Warner Bros. Pictures, Inc.)
Washington Evening Star
Washington Post
Washington Times Herald
Woodford County Journal

Speeches, Articles, Books, Novels, and Plays

Arnold, H. H. *Airmen and Aircraft: An Introduction to Aeronautics* (New York: Ronald Press, 1926).
"General 'Hap' Arnold Joins AVC," *AVC Bulletin*, 2 (March 1, 1947), 1.
Arnold, H. H., and Ira C. Eaker, *Winged Warfare* (New York: Harper Bros., 1941).
This Flying Game (New York: Funk & Wagnalls, 1943).
Bassett, James. "Communism in Hollywood." *New York Mirror*, May 28, 1951, copy in Ronald Reagan file, FBI-FOIA, SHSWM.
Bellamann, Henry. *Kings Row* (New York: Simon & Schuster, 1940).
Bessie, Alvah. "What Is Freedom for Writers?" *New Masses*, 58 (March 12, 1946), 8–10.
Bolte, Charles G. "Conscription Between Wars," *Nation* (March 24, 1945), 332.
The New Veteran (New York: Reynal & Hitchcock, 1945).
Bolte, Charles G., and Louis Harris. *Our Negro Veteran* (New York: Public Affairs Committee, pamphlet no. 128, [c. 1947]).
Brady, Thomas F. "On the Firing Line." *New York Times*, Feb. 15, 1942, section 8, p. 5.
"Hollywood Back to Work." Undated clipping, folder titled "1946 – Strike Clips," Box 47, JLW-USC.

"Hollywood Unrest." *New York Times,* Oct. 27, 1946, section 2, pp. 1, 3.

"Contract Time in Hollywood." *New York Times,* April 13, 1947, section 2, p. 5.

"Hollywood Dossier: Fading Echoes from the Lew Ayres Case. . ." *New York Times,* April 26, 1947, section 8, p. 3.

"Topical Hollywood." *New York Times,* April 27, 1947, section 2, p. 5.

"Hollywood Discord." *New York Times,* Feb. 6, 1949, section 2, p. 5.

"Hollywood Protest." *New York Times,* April 24, 1949, section 2, p. 5.

"Hollywood Takes Stock." *New York Times,* March 12, 1950, section 2, p. 5.

"Hollywood Divided by Loyalty Pledge Issue." *New York Times,* Oct. 22, 1950, section 2, p. 5.

"Hollywood Turmoil." *New York Times,* Oct. 29, 1950, section 2, p. 5.

"Hollywood Digest." *New York Times,* Nov. 19, 1950, section 2, p. 5.

"Hollywood Is Calm." *New York Times,* April 15, 1951, section 2, p. 5.

Brewer, Roy M. "The Full Story of Our Stand on the Coast." *IATSE Official Bulletin,* 372 (May 1947), 6.

Crowther, Bosley. "Movies Without Gables." *New York Times Magazine* (Sept. 13, 1942), 14.

Cummings, Homer S. "A Twelve Point Program." Delivered before the Continental Congress of the Daughters of the American Revolution, April 19, 1934; in Swisher, ed., *Selected Papers of Homer Cummings,* 24–6, 37–8.

"The Lessons of the Crime Conference." Address at the closing session of the Attorney General's Conference on Crime, Dec. 13, 1934; in Swisher, ed., *Selected Papers of Homer Cummings,* 44–5, 53–5.

"Law Enforcement as a Profession." Address before the International Association for Identification, Sept. 30, 1937; in Swisher, ed., *Selected Papers of Homer Cummings,* 58–60.

Davis, Patti, with Maureen Strange Foster. *Home Front: A Novel* (New York: Crown, 1986).

Douglas, Melvyn. "Liberalism." Speech, June 4, 1947; box 10, Melvyn Douglas Papers, SHSWM.

Dunne, George. "Socialism and Socialism: Why Christian Democrats and Socialists Should Get Along." *The Commonweal,* 43 (Nov. 23, 1945), 134–9.

Foner, Philip S., ed. *Paul Robeson Speaks: Writings-Speeches-Interviews, 1918–1974* (New York: Brunner/Mazel, 1978).

Forbes, Malcolm. "Smearing World Government." *Forbes Magazine of Business,* 65 (March 15, 1950), 12.

Harmon, Francis. "Western Europe in the Wake of World War II (June 17–July 18, 1945)." (Unpublished report of movie producers' European trip); in Jack L. Warner *Scrapbook – Part II, European Trip 1945,* JLW-USC.

Hays, Will H. "Rotary Interviews Will H. Hays about the Movies." *The Rotarian* (April 2, 1934), 11–12.

"Fifteen Years of Motion Picture Progress: Annual Report to the Motion Picture Producers and Distributors of America, Inc." (New York: March 29, 1937).

"Enlarging Scope of the Screen: Annual Report to the Motion Picture Producers and Distributors of America, Inc." (New York: March 27, 1939).

Hift, Fred. "Leaders Seek Fair Deal for Hollywood." *New York Times,* October 30, 1949, section 2, p. 4.

"Hollywood Goes on Trial." *Life,* 23 (Nov. 3, 1947), 40–1.

Hopper, Hedda. "Mr. Reagan Airs His Views." *Chicago Sunday Tribune, Grafic,* May 18, 1947, p. 7.

Hughes, Langston. "Hollywood's Ridiculous Stereotype Program Allows Great Negro Talent to Remain Idle." *Chicago Defender,* May 16, 1953, p. 11.

"Major Differences Between Europe and America for Negro Theatrical Performers." *Chicago Defender,* May 23, 1953, p. 11.

James, Daniel. "The Battle of A.V.C." *Nation* (June 14, 1947), 707.

Johnston, Eric. "A Talk to Russia." in *International Conciliation: Documents for the Year 1944* (New York: Carnegie Endowment for International Peace, 1944), no. 404, pp. 637–46.

America Unlimited (Garden City, N.Y.: Doubleday, Doran, 1944).

"The Motion Picture on the Threshold of a Decisive Decade." *Annual Report to the Motion Picture Association of America, Inc.* (New York: MPAA, 1946).

"The Unexplored Continent." Commencement address, University of Southern California, June 15, 1946, NYPLA.

"The Modern Tool for Teaching." Radio broadcast (American Broadcasting Company), Sept. 1, 1946; files of Dallas C. Halverstadt, in Harry S Truman Papers, HSTLI.

We're All In It (New York: Dutton, 1948).

"After the Marshall Plan – What?" *Collier's,* 123 (May 21, 1949), 16.

"Aggressive Citizenship – Our Individual Responsibility: A Bill of Duties for Free Men." Speech to Kiwanis International, June 23, 1949; in *Vital Speeches,* 15 (Aug. 1, 1949), 633–4.

"The Land of the Calculated Risk." Commencement address, University of Oklahoma, Norman, June 4, 1951; in *Vital Speeches,* 17 (July 1, 1951), 559–62.

"A New Era in Entertainment: A Statement by the President." In *1952 Annual Report: Motion Picture Association of America, Inc.* (New York: MPAA, c. 1952), 5–14, 19–27.

Kleihauer, Cleveland, R. N. Simpson, and John R. Golden. "Report of the Commission to the Orient." *Christian-Evangelist,* 63 (July 22, 1926), 905–12.

Lardner, Ring, Jr. "My Life on the Blacklist." *Saturday Evening Post,* 234 (Oct. 14, 1961), 38–40, 42–4.

Lawson, John Howard. *A Southern Welcome (In Georgia and Alabama): A Report by John Howard Lawson* (Report 7, 1934), NYPLA.

Theory and Technique of Playwriting (New York: Putnam, c. 1936).

"The Heritage of American Culture." *The Clipper,* 2 (July 1941), 6–13.

"Art Is a Weapon." *New Masses* (March 19, 1946), 18–20.

[a.k.a. Howard Jennings]. "Revisionism and American History." *Political Affairs,* 25 (Aug. 1946), 742–62.

"Parrington and the Search for Tradition." *Mainstream,* 1 (Winter 1947), 23–43.

"On Censorship." Speech, Oct. 30, 1947; box 27, JHL-SIU.

"The Cold War and the American Film." Speech, March 26, c. 1949; box 12, JHL-SIU.

The Hidden Heritage: A Rediscovery of the Ideas and Forces that Link the Thought of Our Time with the Culture of the Past (New York: Citadel, 1950).

Film in the Battle of Ideas (New York: Masses & Mainstream, 1953).

"Biographical Notes." *Zeitschrift fur Anglistik und Amerikanistik,* 4, no. 1 (1956), 73–6.

Film: The Creative Process. The Search for an Audio-Visual Language and Structure (New York: Hill & Wang, 1964).

Loeb, James I., Jr. "Progressives and Communists." *New Republic* (May 13, 1946), 699.

Longstreet, Stephen. *Stallion Road* (New York: Messner, Inc., 1945).

McGoogan, Bill, Jr. "How the Commies Were Licked in Hollywood." *St. Louis Globe-Democrat,* copy in box 55, Schary Papers, SHSWM.

McWilliams, Carey. "The Inside Story of the Hollywood Strike: 'Jurisdictional Dispute,' Is Really a Lockout." *PM* (Sept. 2, 1945), 9.

Maltz, Albert. "What Shall We Ask of Writers?" *New Masses,* (Feb. 12, 1946), 19–22.

"The Writer as the Conscience of the People." Address delivered at Conference on Thought Control in the United States, under the auspices of the Arts, Sciences, and Professions, Council of the Progressive Citizens of America, Los Angeles, July 11, 1947, in Albert Maltz. *The Citizen Writer* (New York: International, 1950), 11–20.

Matthews, Blayney F. *The Specter of Sabotage* (Los Angeles: Lymanhouse, 1941).

Matthews, J. B. "Did the Movies Really Clean House?" *American Legion Magazine,* 51 (Dec. 1951), 12–13, 49–56.

Mayer, Arthur L. "'COMPO' Formed to Combat Attacks on Filmdom." *New York Times,* Oct. 29, 1950, section 2, p. 5.

Meiklejohn, Alexander. "Everything Worth Saying Should Be Said." *New York Times Magazine* (July 18, 1948), 8, 32.

Free Speech And Its Relation to Self-Government (New York: Harper & Bros., 1948).

Milliken, Carl E. "Memorandum on the Question of Scientific Findings as to the Behavioristic Influences of the Screen Particularly with Regard to Juvenile Delinquencies." Submitted to the U.S. Subcommittee on Racketeering, Dec. 11, 1933, WHHPI.

Norman, Anne. "Reagan Good Film Spokesman," *Hartford Times,* June 5, 1952, p. 16.

Odlum, Jerome. *Nine Lives Are Not Enough* (New York: Sheridan, 1940).

Olson, Sidney. "The Movie Hearings." *Life,* 23 (Nov. 24, 1947), 137–8, 141–2, 145–6, 148.

Palmer, B. J. *Radio Salesmanship: How Its Potential Sales Percentage Can Be Increased* (Davenport: Palmer School of Chiropractic[?], n.d.).

Pegler, Westbrook. "Fair Enough." *Washington Times-Herald,* Nov. 8, 1949.

Pratt, Theodore. "Land of the Jook." *Saturday Evening Post* (April 26, 1941), 20–1, 40, 43.

Pryor, Thomas M. "Hollywood Digest." *New York Times,* Sept. 2, 1951, section 2, p. 5.

Reagan, Ronald. "The Making of a Movie Star. . . ." *Des Moines Sunday Register,* June 13, 1937, p. 6 (Iowa News).

"'Dutch' Meets Some Movie Stars and Gets Good Advice." *Des Moines Sunday Register,* June 20, 1937, p. 4 (Iowa News).

"'Dutch' Makes His First Scene, He's Scared – But Thrilled!. . . ." *Des Moines Sunday Register,* June 27, 1937, p. 6 (General News).

"'Dutch' Does First Scene Over Again. . . ." *Des Moines Sunday Register,* July 4, 1937, p. 3 (General News).

"'Dutch' Pulls a Couple of Boners. . . ." *Des Moines Sunday Register,* July 11, 1937, p. 6 (General News).

"'Dutch' Got That Date After All: 'Dutch' Reagan's Own Story." *Des Moines Sunday Register,* July 18, 1937, p. 8 (General News).

"'Dutch' Sees the Sights of Movie Lot, Tries for Date, But Misses." *Des Moines Sunday Register,* July 25, 1937, p. 8 (General News).

"'Dutch' Starts New Picture; Learns Why 'Doubles' Do Stunts. . . ." *Des Moines Sunday Register,* Aug. 8, 1937, p. 8 (General News).

"'Dutch' Takes a 'Prince of Wales' Ride on Wild Army Horse. . . ." *Des Moines Sunday Register,* Aug. 15, 1937, p.8 (General News).

"'Glamorous Hollywood?' – Phooey! – Just a Lot of Hard Work. . . ." *Des Moines Sunday Register,* Aug. 22, 1937, p. 10 (General News).

"'Dutch' Tells How Movie Horse Showed Up the Bluebloods. . . ." *Des Moines Sunday Register,* Aug. 29, 1937, p. 8 (General News).

"'Dutch' Tells What Happens at Gay Hollywood Preview. . . ." *Des Moines Sunday Register,* Sept. 5, 1937, p. 5 (General News).

"Bosses Change Their Minds So 'Dutch' Makes Part of His First Picture All Over Again. . . ." *Des Moines Sunday Register,* Sept. 12, 1937, p. 8 (General News).

"Pretty Margaret Lindsay, Iowa Screen Star, Shows 'Dutch' the Sights of Los Angeles. . . ." *Des Moines Sunday Register,* Sept. 12, 1937, p. 8 (General News).

"Four Pictures Finished, 'Dutch' Gets a Raise, Hunts for a House. . . ." *Des Moines Sunday Register,* Oct. 3, 1937, p. 8 (General News).

"How To Make Yourself Important." (As told to Gladys Hall), *Photoplay* (Aug. 1942), copy in Reagan Scrapbook, ECAE.

"Fascist Ideas Are Still Alive in U.S." *AVC Bulletin,* 1 (Feb. 15, 1946), 6.

"The Role I Liked Best." *Saturday Evening Post* (Jan. 1, 1949), 67.

"How Do You Fight Communism?" *Fortnight,* Jan. 22, 1951.

"Motion Pictures and Your Community." Speech, June 21, 1951, *Proceedings of the 1951 Kiwanis Convention,* 107–10, in KIHI (see also *Kiwanis Magazine,* 36 [Aug. 1951], 25).

"America the Beautiful." Commencement address, May 3, 1952; in *Echoes from the Woods* (Fulton, Mo.: William Woods College, 1952), 8–13.

"It's More Than a Jungle." *Variety* (Forty-eighth Anniversary Issue), Jan. 6, 1954, p. 20.

A Time for Choosing: The Speeches of Ronald Reagan, 1961–1982 (Chicago: Regnery Gateway, 1983).

Speaking My Mind: Selected Speeches (New York: Simon & Schuster, 1989).

Redlings, Lowell. "The Hollywood Scene: Opinions of an Actor." *Hollywood Citizen News,* March 25, 1947; in Reagan clipping file, AMPASL.

Reynolds, Quentin. "Movie Probers Let Down By Stars But Customers Love the Show." Unlabeled newspaper clipping, Oct. 24, 1947; Ronald Reagan file (100–138754-A), FBI-FOIA, SHSWM.

Roberts, Edith. *That Hagen Girl* (Garden City, N.Y.: Doubleday, 1946).

[Sondergaard, Gale]. *On the Eve of Prison: Two Addresses by Gale Sondergaard and Albert Maltz* (Hollywood: The Arts, Sciences and Professions Council, 1950).

Spiro, J. D. "Hollywood Memos," *New York Times,* June 29, 1947, section 2, p. 5.

"Hollywood Acts." *New York Times,* Oct. 23, 1949, section 2, p. 5.

"Anti-Communist Feeling Rising in the West." *New York Times,* Sept. 10, 1950, section 2, p. 5.

"Hollywood Digest," *New York Times,* Sept. 17, 1950, section 2, p. 5.

Stripling, Robert E. *The Red Plot Against America* (Drexel Hill, Pa.: Bell, 1949).

S. V. R. "Movie Man's Burden." *New Republic,* July 27, 1947, p. 37.

"The Movie Hearing Ends." *Life,* 23 (Nov. 10, 1947), 47.

Thurber, James, and Elliott Nugent. *The Male Animal: A Comedy in Three Acts* (New York: Samuel French, 1939).

Trumbo, Dalton. *Johnny Got His Gun* (Philadelphia: Lippincott, 1939).

"Dalton Trumbo's Own Story." *Daily Worker,* March 13, 1940, p. 7.

"On Publishing a Book." *The Clipper,* 2 (Jan. 1941), 19.

Harry Bridges: A Discussion of the Latest Effort to Deport Civil Liberties and the Rights of American Labor (Hollywood, Calif.: League of American Writers, 1941).

The Remarkable Andrew (Philadelphia: Lippincott, c. 1941).

"Minorities and the Screen." *Writers' Congress: The Proceedings of the Conference held in October 1943 under the sponsorship of the Hollywood Writers' Mobilization and the University of California* (Berkeley and Los Angeles: University of California Press, 1944).

"Dalton Trumbo Reports . . . The Real Facts Behind the Motion Picture Lockout." Speech, Oct. 13, 1945; box 9, HICCASP Papers, SHSWM.

"Confessional." [Poem] *Mainstream*, 1 (Winter 1947), 16–22.

The Time of the Toad: A Study of Inquisition in America by One of the Hollywood Ten (Hollywood, Calif.: 1949).

Van Druten, John. *The Voice of the Turtle: A Comedy in Three Acts* (New York: Random House, 1944).

Van Ryn, Frederick. "Warner Brother Number One." *Liberty Magazine,* Oct. 31, 1941, p. 14.

Wallis, Hal. "Modern Science and the Motion Picture." Address at Alfred Nobel Anniversary Dinner, Dec. 10, 1946, condensed in *Motion Picture Letter* (issued by Public Information Committee of the Motion Picture Industry), 6 (Jan. 1947).

Wanger, Walter. "Tulsa Speech." April 12, 1949; folder 4, box 37, Walter Wanger Papers, SHSWM.

"Donald Duck and World Diplomacy." Lecture delivered at the University of Chicago, March 30, 1950; folder 7, box 37, Walter Wanger Papers, SHSWM.

"Wooden Shoes and Silken Slippers." Speech delivered to National Retail Dry Goods Association, May 31, 1950; folder 8, box 37, Walter Wanger Papers, SHSWM.

Warner, Harry M. Address delivered by Harry M. Warner before officers and representatives of the American Legion, Sept. 19, 1938; box 4, OF 73, FDR Papers, FDRL.

"Hollywood's Obligations As a Producer Sees Them." *Christian Science Monitor,* March 16, 1939, copy in box 56, JLW-USC.

"United We Survive, Divided We Fall!" Speech, June 5, 1940; box 56, JLW-USC.

"Harry M. Warner Extols the Motion Picture and America." *Hollywood Reporter* (22d Anniversary Issue), 121 (Nov. 10, 1952), part 2.

Warner, Jack L., "The Playbill: Films Reflect the Spirit of the Times." *New York Herald Tribune,* Sept. 9, 1945, in *Scrapbook,* JLW-USC.

Address before the Screen Writers Guild, Sept. 22, [1945?], Warner Bros. File, AMPASL.

"Pix Must Aid in War Prevention – Warner." *Film Daily,* Dec. 17, 1945, in *Scrapbook,* JLW-USC.

Warner, Jack M., Jr. *Bijou Dream: A Novel* (New York: Crown, 1982).

"Warner Brothers." *Fortune,* 16 (Dec. 1937), 208.

Weiler, A. H. "By Way of Report." *New York Times,* April 13, 1947, section 2, p. 5.

Woll, Matthew. "Warning to Hollywood," *American Photo-Engraver,* 38 (Oct. 1946), 896.

Wylie, Philip. *Finley Wren: His Notions and Opinions, . . . A Novel in a New Manner* (New York: Farrar & Rinehart, 1934).

Generation of Vipers: A Survey of Moral Want. . . . (New York: Rinehart, 1942).

Night Unto Night (New York: Farrar & Rinehart, 1944).

"The Atom Bomb and the Veteran." *AVC Bulletin,* 1 (March 1, 1946), 4.

Essay on Morals: A Science of Philosophy and a Philosophy of Science. . . . (New York: Rinehart, 1947, 1951).

Three to be Read: Containing The Smuggled Atom Bomb, Sporting Blood, and Experiment in Crime (New York: Rinehart, 1948, 1951).

Opus 21: Descriptive Music for the Lower Kinsey Epoch of the Atomic Age. . . .
  (New York: Rinehart, 1949).
Tomorrow! (New York: Rinehart, 1954).
Wyman, Jane. "My Soldier." *Modern Screen* (Jan. 1943), copy in Reagan Scrapbook,
  ECAE.

Ph.D. and M.A. Theses

Ashton, Charlotte Ruby. "The Changing Image of Blacks in American Film: 1944–
  1973" (doctoral thesis, Princeton University, 1981).
Atwood, Dee J. "The Impact of World War I on the Agencies of the Disciples of
  Christ" (doctoral thesis, Vanderbilt University, 1978).
Brown, Richard P. "John Howard Lawson as an Activist Playwright: 1923–1937"
  (doctoral thesis, Tulane University, 1964).
Carr, Gary Lee. "The Screen Writing of John Howard Lawson, 1928–1947: Play-
  wright at Work in Hollywood" (doctoral thesis, University of Texas at Austin,
  1975).
Colgan, Christine. "Warner Bros.' Crusade Against the Third Reich: A Study of Anti-
  Nazi Activism and Film Production, 1933–1941" (doctoral thesis, University of
  Southern California, 1985).
Considine, David M. "The Depiction of Adolescent Sexuality in Motion Pictures,
  1930–1980" (doctoral thesis, University of Wisconsin, Madison, 1981).
Ely, Melvin Patrick. "*Amos 'n' Andy:* Lineage, Life, and Legacy" (doctoral thesis,
  Princeton University, 1985).
Erens, Patricia B. "The Image of the Jew in the American Cinema: A Study in Ster-
  eotyping" (doctoral thesis, Northwestern University, 1981).
Gardner, Robert Merritt. "International Rag: The Theatrical Career of John Howard
  Lawson" (doctoral thesis, University of California, Berkeley, 1977).
Gustafson, Robert. "The Buying of Ideas: Source Acquisition at Warner Brothers,
  1930–1949" (doctoral thesis, University of Wisconsin, Madison, 1983).
Jacobs, Lea. "The Production Code and Women's Films" (doctoral thesis, University
  of California, Los Angeles, 1986).
Lessner, Richard E. "The Imagined Enemy: American Nativism and the Disciples of
  Christ, 1830–1925" (doctoral thesis, Baylor University, 1981).
Linden, Kathryn B. "The Film Censorship Struggle in the United States from 1926 to
  1957, and the Social Values Involved" (doctoral thesis, New York University,
  1972).
Sargent, John A. "Self-Regulation: The Motion Picture Production Code, 1930–
  1961" (doctoral thesis, University of Michigan, 1963).
Sparr, Arnold J. "The Catholic Literary Revival in America, 1920–1960" (doctoral
  thesis, University of Wisconsin, Madison, 1985).
Turner, Jay Craig. "Public Reaction to the National Legion of Decency as Reflected in
  the Popular Press, 1934–1952" (M.A. thesis, University of Texas at Austin,
  1984).
Yeck, Joanne Louise. "The Woman's Film at Warner Brothers, 1935–1950" (doctoral
  thesis, University of Southern California, 1982).

Secondary Sources

Aldgate, Anthony & Jeffrey Richards. *Britain Can Take It: The British Cinema in the
  Second World War* (Oxford: Blackwell Publishers, 1986).
Alicoate, Jack, ed. *The 1941 Film Daily Year Book of Motion Pictures* (Hollywood
  [?]: The Film Daily, 1941).

Andersen, Thom. "Red Hollywood." In Suzanne Ferguson and Barbara Groseclose, eds., *Literature and the Visual Arts in Contemporary Society* (Columbus, Ohio: Ohio State University Press, 1985), 141–96.

Bannerman, R. LeRoy. *Norman Corwin and Radio: The Golden Years* (University, Ala.: University of Alabama Press, 1986).

Barnouw, Dagmar. *Weimar Intellectuals and the Threat of Modernity* (Bloomington: Indiana University Press, 1988).

Barnouw, Erik. *The Golden Web: A History of Broadcasting in the United States. Volume 2 – 1933 to 1953* (New York: Oxford University Press, 1968).

Barrett, Edward L., Jr. *The Tenney Committee: Legislative Investigation of Subversive Activities in California* (Ithaca, N.Y.: Cornell University Press, 1951).

Barrett, Edward W. *Truth Is Our Weapon* (New York: Funk & Wagnalls, 1953).

Barrett, Laurence I. *Gambling with History: Ronald Reagan in the White House* (Garden City, N.Y.: Doubleday, 1983).

Basinger, Jeanine. *The World War II Combat Film* (New York: Columbia University Press, 1986).

Baughman, James L. *Henry R. Luce and the Rise of the American News Media* (Boston: Twayne, 1987).

The Republic of Mass Culture: Journalism, Filmmaking, and Broadcasting in America since 1941 (Baltimore: Johns Hopkins University Press, 1992).

Beard, Charles A., and Mary R. Beard. *America in Midpassage* (New York: Macmillan, 1939).

Behrman, S. N. *Tribulations and Laughter: A Memoir by S. N. Behrman* (London: Hamish Hamilton, 1972).

Bergman, Andrew. *We're in the Money: Depression America and Its Films* (New York: Harper & Row, 1971).

Bérubé, Allan. *Coming Out Under Fire: The History of Gay Men and Women in World War Two* (New York: Free Press, 1990).

Black, Gregory. *Hollywood Censored: Morality Codes, Catholics, and the Movies* (New York: Cambridge University Press, 1994).

Boyer, Paul. *By the Bomb's Early Light: American Thought and Culture at the Dawn of the Atomic Age* (New York: Pantheon, 1985).

Brenman-Gibson, Margaret. *Clifford Odets: American Playwright, The Years from 1906–1940* (New York: Atheneum, 1981).

Brownstein, Ronald. *The Power and the Glitter: The Hollywood-Washington Connection* (New York: Pantheon, 1990).

Cannon, Lou. *Ronnie and Jesse: A Political Odyssey* (Garden City, N.Y.: Doubleday, 1969).

Reagan (New York: Perigee, 1982).

President Reagan: The Role of a Lifetime (New York: Simon & Schuster, 1991).

Caro, Robert A. *The Years of Lyndon Johnson: Means of Ascent* (New York: Knopf, 1990).

Carr, Gary. *The Left Side of Paradise: The Screenwriting of John Howard Lawson* (Ann Arbor, Mich.: UMI Research Press, 1975, 1984).

Carr, Virginia Spencer. *Dos Passos: A Life* (Garden City, N.Y.: Doubleday, 1984).

Caute, David. *The Great Fear: The Anti-Communist Purge Under Truman and Eisenhower* (New York: Simon & Schuster, 1978).

Ceplair, Larry, and Steven Englund. *The Inquisition in Hollywood: Politics in the Film Community, 1930–1960* (Garden City, N.Y.: Doubleday, 1980).

Chafe, William H. *The Unfinished Journey: America since World War II* (New York: Oxford University Press, 1986).

Cogley, John. *Report on Blacklisting: I: Movies* (New York: Arno, 1956, 1972).

Cohen, Morris R. *The Faith of a Liberal: Selected Essays* (New York: Holt, 1946).

Cole, Clifford A. *The Christian Churches (Disciples of Christ) of Southern California: A History* (St. Louis: Christian Board of Publication, 1959).

Cole, Wayne S. *America First: The Battle Against Intervention, 1940–1941* (Madison: University of Wisconsin Press, 1953).

Senator Gerald P. Nye and American Foreign Relations (Minneapolis: University of Minnesota Press, 1962).

Roosevelt and the Isolationists, 1932–45 (Lincoln: University of Nebraska Press, 1983).

Crain, James A. *The Development of Social Ideas Among the Disciples of Christ* (St. Louis: Bethany, 1969).

Craven, Wesley Frank, and James Lea Cate, eds. *The Army Air Forces in World War II: Volume Six: Men and Planes* (7 vols., Washington, D.C.: Office of Air Force History, 1983).

Cripps, Thomas. *Slow Fade to Black: The Negro in American Film, 1900–1942* (New York: Oxford University Press, 1977).

"The Dark Spot in the Kaleidoscope: Black Images in American Film." In Randall M. Miller, ed., *The Kaleidoscopic Lens: How Hollywood Views Ethnic Groups* (Englewood, N.J.: Ozer, 1980), 15–35.

"Movies, Race, and World War II: *Tennessee Johnson* as an Anticipation of the Strategies of the Civil Rights Movement." *Prologue: Journal of the National Archives,* 14 (Summer 1982), 49–67.

"*Amos 'n' Andy* and the Debate Over American Racial Integration." In John E. O'Connor, ed., *American History/American Television* (New York: Ungar, 1983), 33–54.

Making Movies Black: The Hollywood Message Movie from World War II to the Civil Rights Era (New York: Oxford University Press, 1993).

Cripps, Thomas, and David Culbert. "*The Negro Soldier* (1944): Film Propaganda in Black and White." *American Quarterly,* 31 (Winter 1979), 618–40.

Dalfiume, Richard M. *Desegregation of the U.S. Armed Forces: Fighting on Two Fronts, 1939–1953* (Columbia, Mo.: University of Missouri Press, 1969).

Dallek, Robert. *Ronald Reagan: The Politics of Symbolism* (Cambridge, Mass.: Harvard University Press, 1984).

De Grazia, Edward, and Roger K. Newman. *Banned Films: Censors and the First Amendment* (New York: Bowker, 1982).

Deming, Barbara. *Running Away from Myself: A Dream Portrait of America Drawn from the Films of the Forties* (New York: Grossman, 1969).

Diamond, Sander A. *The Nazi Movement in the United States, 1924–1941* (Ithaca, N.Y.: Cornell University Press, 1974).

Dick, Bernard F. *The Star-Spangled Screen: The American World War II Film* (Lexington: The University Press of Kentucky, 1985).

Radical Innocence: A Critical Study of the Hollywood Ten (Lexington: The University Press of Kentucky, 1989).

Dower, John W. *War Without Mercy: Race and Power in the Pacific War* (New York: Pantheon, 1986).

Dwiggins, Don. *Hollywood Pilot: The Biography of Paul Mantz* (Garden City, N.Y.: Doubleday, 1967).

Edwards, Anne. *Early Reagan* (New York: Morrow, 1987).

Ehrlich, Leonard. *God's Angry Man* (New York: Readers Club, 1932, 1941).

Ely, Melvin Patrick. *The Adventures of Amos 'n' Andy: A Social History of an American Phenomenon* (New York: Free Press, 1991).

Erens, Patricia. *The Jew in American Film* (Bloomington: Indiana University Press, 1984).

Ernst, Morris L., and David Loth. *Report on the American Communist* (New York: Holt, 1952).

Facey, Paul W. *The Legion of Decency: A Sociological Analysis of the Emergence and Development of a Social Pressure Group* (New York: Arno, 1945, 1974).

Fenichel, Otto. "On Acting." *Psychoanalytic Quarterly,* 15 (1946), 144–60.

Finkle, Lee. "The Conservative Aims of Militant Rhetoric: Black Protest during World War II." *Journal of American History,* 60 (Dec. 1973), 692–713.

Forman, Henry James. *Our Movie Made Children* (New York: Macmillan, 1933).

Freidel, Frank. *Franklin D. Roosevelt: The Apprenticeship* (Boston: Little, Brown, 1952).

Freedland, Michael. *The Warner Brothers* (New York: St. Martin's, 1983).

Friedan, Betty. *The Feminine Mystique* (New York: Dell, 1963, 1970).

Friedman, Saul S. *No Haven for the Oppressed: United States Policy Toward Jewish Refugees, 1938–1945* (Detroit: Wayne State University Press, 1973).

Friedrich, Otto. *City of Nets: A Portrait of Hollywood in the 1940's* (New York: Harper & Row, 1986).

Gabbard, Kim, and Glen O. Gabbard. *Psychiatry and the Cinema* (Chicago: University of Chicago Press, 1987, 1989).

Gabler, Neal. *An Empire of Their Own: How the Jews Invented Hollywood* (New York: Crown, 1988).

Gardiner, Gordon P. "Nelle Reagan: Mother of Ronald Reagan, President of the United States." In *Bread of Life* (May 1981) (monthly published from the Ridgewood Pentecostal Church); copy in RFCCD.

Garnier, Philippe. *Goodis le vie en noir et blanc: Biographie* (Paris: Editions du Seuil, 1984).

Garrison, Winfred Ernest. *Religion Follows the Frontier: A History of the Disciples of Christ* (New York: Harper Bros., 1931).

An American Religious Movement: A Brief History of the Disciples of Christ (St. Louis: Bethany, 1945).

Gilbert, James. *A Cycle of Outrage: America's Reaction to the Juvenile Delinquent in the 1950s* (New York: Oxford University Press, 1986).

Another Chance: Postwar America, 1945–1985 (Chicago: Dorsey, 1986).

Gillon, Steven M. *Politics and Vision: The ADA and American Liberalism, 1947–1985* (New York: Oxford University Press, 1987).

Gordon, Linda. *Woman's Body, Woman's Right: A Social History of Birth Control in America* (New York: Grossman, 1976).

Graebner, William. "The Unstable World of Benjamin Spock: Social Engineering in a Democratic Culture, 1917–1950." *Journal of American History,* 67 (Dec. 1980), 612–29.

Greenfield, Thomas Allen. *Work and the Work Ethic in American Drama, 1920–1970* (Columbia, Mo.: University of Missouri Press, 1982).

Griswold, Jerry. "'I'm a sucker for hero worship,'" *New York Times Book Review* (Aug. 30, 1980), 11, 21.

Grobel, Lawrence. *The Hustons* (New York: Scribner, 1989).

Hamby, Alonzo L. *Beyond the New Deal: Harry S. Truman and American Liberalism* (New York: Columbia University Press, 1973).

Harrell, David Edwin, Jr. *The Social Sources of Division in the Disciples of Christ, 1865–1900, Volume II: A Social History of the Disciples of Christ* (2 vols., Athens, Ga.: Publishing Systems, Inc., 1973).

Hatch, Nathan O. "The Christian Movement and the Demand for a Theology of the People." *Journal of American History,* 67 (Dec. 1980), 545–67.

Herberg, Will. *Protestant – Catholic – Jew: An Essay in American Religious Sociology* (Garden City, N.Y.: Doubleday, 1955, 1960).

Higham, Charles. *Warner Brothers* (New York: Scribner, 1975).

Errol Flynn: The Untold Story (Garden City, N.Y.: Doubleday, 1980).

Higham, John. "American Anti-Semitism Historically Reconsidered." In Charles Herbert Stember et al., *Jews in the Mind of America* (New York: Basic, 1966), 237–58.

Honey, Maureen. *Creating Rosie the Riveter: Class, Gender, and Propaganda during World War II* (Amherst: University of Massachusetts Press, 1984).

Howard, Goldena Roland. *Ralls County, Missouri* (New London, Mo.: Walsworth, 1980).

Hughes, William. "The Evaluation of Film as Evidence." In Paul Smith, ed., *The Historian and Film* (Cambridge University Press, 1976), 49–79.

Huston, McCready. *Salesman from the Sidelines* (New York: Long & Smith, 1932).

Hutton, Paul A. "From Little Bighorn to Little Big Man: The Changing Image of a Western Hero in Popular Culture." *Western Historical Quarterly,* 7 (Jan. 1976), 19–45.

Hyde, H. Montgomery. *British Air Policy Between the Wars, 1918–1939* (London: Heinemann, 1976).

Isenberg, Michael T. *War on Film: The American Cinema and World War I* (Rutherford, N.J.: Farleigh Dickinson University Press, 1981).

Izod, John. *Hollywood and the Box Office, 1895–1986* (New York: Columbia University Press, 1988).

Jacobs, Lea. *The Wages of Sin: Censorship and the Fallen Woman Film, 1928–1942* (Madison: University of Wisconsin Press, 1991).

Jarvie, Ian. *Hollywood's Overseas Campaign: The North Atlantic Movie Trade, 1920–1950* (Cambridge University Press, 1992).

Jones, Alfred Howorth. *Roosevelt's Image Brokers: Poets, Playwrights, and the Use of the Lincoln Symbol* (Port Washington, N.Y.: Kennikat, 1974).

Jones, R. V. *Most Secret War* (London: Hamish Hamilton, 1978).

Jowett, Garth. *Film: The Democratic Art* (Boston: Little, Brown, 1976).

"Bullets, Beer and the Hays Office: *Public Enemy* (1931)." In John E. O'Connor and Martin A. Jackson, *American History/American Film* (New York: Ungar, 1979), 57–75.

Kahn, Gordon. *Hollywood on Trial: The Story of the 10 Who Were Indicted* (New York: Boni & Gaer, 1948).

Keller, Morton. "Jews and the Character of American Life since 1930." In Charles Herbert Stember et al., *Jews in the Mind of America* (New York: Basic, 1966), 259–72.

Koppes, Clayton R., and Gregory D. Black. "Blacks, Loyalty, and Motion-Picture Propaganda in World War II." *Journal of American History,* 73 (Sept. 1986), 383–406.

Leab, Daniel J. *From Sambo to Superspade: The Black Experience in Motion Pictures* (Boston: Houghton Mifflin, 1975).

"'The Iron Curtain' (1948): Hollywood's First Cold War Movie." *Historical Journal of Film, Radio and Television,* 8, no. 2 (1988), 153–88.

Leamer, Laurence. *Make-Believe: The Story of Nancy & Ronald Reagan* (New York: Harper & Row, 1983).

Lears, T. J. Jackson. "From Salvation to Self-Realization: Advertising and the Therapeutic Roots of the Consumer Culture, 1880–1930." In Richard Wightman Fox and T. J. Jackson Lears, eds., *The Culture of Consumption: Critical Essays in American History, 1880–1980* (New York: Pantheon, 1983), 3–38.

Leff, Leonard J., and Jerold L. Simmons. *The Dame in the Kimono: Hollywood, Censorship, and the Production Code from the 1920s to the 1960s* (New York: Grove Weidenfeld, 1990).

Leuchtenburg, William E. *In the Shadow of FDR: From Harry Truman to Ronald Reagan* (Ithaca, N.Y.: Cornell University Press, 1983).

"Reagan's Secret Liberal Past." *New Republic,* 188 (May 23, 1983), 18–25.

Lipsitz, George. *Class and Culture in Cold War America: "A Rainbow at Midnight"* (South Hadley, Mass.: Bergin, 1981).

Lord, Daniel A. *Dare We Hate Jews?* (St. Louis: The Queen's Work, 1939).

Low, Rachael. *The History of the British Film, 1929–1939: Film Making in 1930s Britain* (London: George Allen and Unwin, 1985).

Lowell, Robert. "Memories of West Street and Lepke." In Robert Lowell, *Life Studies* (London: Faber & Faber, 1959), 58.

Lowenthal, David. *The Past Is a Foreign Country* (Cambridge University Press, 1985).

McAllister, Lester G., and William E. Tucker. *Journey in Faith: A History of the Christian Church (Disciples of Christ)* (St. Louis: Bethany, 1975).

McArthur, Benjamin. *Actors and American Culture, 1880–1920* (Philadelphia: Temple University Press, 1984).

McAuliffe, Mary Sperling. *Crisis on the Left: Cold War Politics and American Liberals, 1947–1954* (Amherst: University of Massachusetts Press, 1978).

McClelland, Doug. *Hollywood on Ronald Reagan: Friends and Enemies Discuss Our President, The Actor* (Winchester, Mass.: Faber & Faber, 1983).

MacDougall, Curtis D. *Gideon's Army, Volume I: The Components of the Decision* (3 vols., New York: Marzani & Munsell, 1965).

McDougall, Walter A. . . . *The Heavens and the Earth: A Political History of the Space Age* (New York: Basic, 1985).

McGilligan, Pat, ed. *Backstory: Interviews with Screenwriters of Hollywood's Golden Age* (Berkeley: University of California Press, 1986).

McWilliams, Wilson Carey. "The Meaning of the Election." In Marlene Michels Pomper, ed., *The Election of 1984: Reports and Interpretations* (Chatham, N.J.: Chatham House, 1984), 157–83.

Maltby, Richard. *Harmless Entertainment: Hollywood and the Ideology of Consensus* (Metuchen, N.J.: Scarecrow, 1983).

Martin, Olga J. *Hollywood's Movie Commandments: A Handbook for Motion Picture Writers and Reviewers* (New York: Wilson, 1937).

Marty, Martin E. *Modern American Religion, Volume I: The Irony of It All, 1893–1919* (Chicago: University of Chicago Press, 1986).

May, Elaine Tyler. *Homeward Bound: American Families in the Cold War* (New York: Basic, 1988).

May, Lary. "Movie Star Politics: The Screen Actors' Guild, Cultural Conversion, and the Hollywood Red Scare." In Lary May, ed., *Recasting America: Culture and Politics in the Age of Cold War* (Chicago: University of Chicago Press, 1989), 125–53.

Meyer, William R. *Warner Brothers Directors: The Hard-Boiled, the Comic, and the Weepers* (New Rochelle, N.Y.: Arlington House, 1978).

Mitchell, Alice Miller. *Children and Movies* (Chicago: University of Chicago Press, 1929).

Mitgang, Herbert. *Dangerous Dossiers: Exposing the Secret War Against America's Greatest Authors* (New York: Fine, 1988).

Moldea, Dan E. *Dark Victory: Ronald Reagan, MCA, and the Mob* (New York: Viking, 1986).

Morella, Joe, and Edward Z. Epstein. *Jane Wyman, a Biography* (New York: Delacorte, 1985).

Mosley, Leonard. *Zanuck: The Rise and Fall of Hollywood's Last Tycoon* (Boston: Little, Brown, 1984).

Nash, George H. *The Conservative Intellectual Movement in America: Since 1945* (New York: Basic, 1976).

Navasky, Victor S. *Naming Names* (New York: Viking, 1980).

Noble, Peter. *The Negro in Films* (New York: Arno, 1970).

O'Reilly, Kenneth. "A New Deal for the FBI: The Roosevelt Administration, Crime Control, and National Security." *Journal of American History*, 69 (Dec. 1982), 638–58.

  Hoover and the Un-Americans: The FBI, HUAC, and the Red Menace (Philadelphia: Temple University Press, 1983).

Osur, Alan M. *Blacks in the Army Air Forces during World War II: The Problem of Race Relations* (Washington, D.C.: Office of Air Force History, 1977; New York: Arno, 1980).

Pauling, Linus. *No More War!* (New York: Dodd, Mead, 1958).

Pells, Richard H. *Radical Visions and American Dreams: Culture and Social Thought in the Depression Years* (New York: Harper, 1973).

  The Liberal Mind in a Conservative Age: American Intellectuals in the 1940s and 1950s (New York: Harper & Row, 1985).

Perrella, Robert. *They Call Me the Showbiz Priest* (New York: Trident, 1973).

Perry, Louis B., and Richard S. Perry. *A History of the Los Angeles Labor Movement, 1911–1941* (Berkeley and Los Angeles: University of California Press, 1963).

Phenix, William. "Eagles Unsung: The Tuskegee Airmen in World War II." *Michigan History*, 71 (May–June 1987), 24–30.

Pierard, Richard V., and Robert D. Linder. *Civil Religion & the Presidency* (Grand Rapids, Mich.: Academie, 1988).

Polenberg, Richard. *War and Society: The United States, 1941–1945* (Philadelphia: Lippincott, 1972).

Powdermaker, Hortense. *Hollywood, the Dream Factory: An Anthropologist Looks at the Movie-Makers* (Boston: Little, Brown, 1950).

Powers, Richard Gid. "The Attorney General and the G-Man." *Southwest Review*, 62 (Fall 1977), 329–46.

  "One G-Man's Family: Popular Entertainment Formulas and J. Edgar Hoover's F.B.I." *American Quarterly*, 30 (Fall 1978), 471–92.

  G-Men: Hoover's FBI in American Popular Culture (Carbondale: Southern Illinois University Press, 1983).

  Secrecy and Power: The Life of J. Edgar Hoover (New York: Free Press, 1987).

Prindle, David F. *The Politics of Glamour: Ideology and Democracy in the Screen Actors Guild* (Madison: University of Wisconsin Press, 1988).

Quigley, Martin. *Decency in Motion Pictures* (New York: Macmillan, 1937).

Ribuffo, Leo P. *The Old Christian Right: The Protestant Far Right from the Great Depression to the Cold War* (Philadelphia: Temple University Press, 1983).

Richards, Jeffrey. "The British Board of Film Censors and Content Control in the 1930s: Foreign Affairs." *Historical Journal of Film, Radio and Television*, 2, no. 1 (1982), 39–48.

Ritter, Kurt, and David Henry. *Ronald Reagan: The Great Communicator* (Westport, Conn.: Greenwood, 1992).

Roberts, Steven V. "Return to the Land of the Gipper." *New York Times*, March 9, 1988, p. 14.

"A Mighty Russian Pulpit for Reagan." *New York Times*, May 31, 1988, p. 7.

Robertson, James C. *The British Board of Film Censors: Film Censorship in Britain, 1896–1950* (London: Croom Helm, 1985).

Robins, Natalie. *Alien Ink: The FBI's War on Freedom of Expression* (New York: Morrow, 1992).

Roddick, Nick. *A New Deal in Entertainment: Warner Brothers in the 1930s* (London: British Film Institute, 1983).

Roeder, George H., Jr. "A Note on U. S. Photo Censorship in WW II." *Historical Journal of Film, Radio and Television*, 5, no. 2 (1985), 191–8.

Roffman, Peter, and Jim Purdy. *The Hollywood Social Problem Film: Madness, Despair, and Politics from the Depression to the Fifties* (Bloomington: Indiana University Press, 1981).

Rogin, Michael. *Ronald Reagan, the Movie and Other Episodes in Political Demonology* (Berkeley and Los Angeles: University of California Press, 1987).

Rosenberg, Emily S. *Spreading the American Dream: American Economic and Cultural Expansion, 1890–1945* (New York: Hill & Wang, 1982).

Rosten, Leo C. *Hollywood: The Movie Colony, The Movie Makers* (New York: Harcourt, Brace, 1941).

Rothe, Anne, ed. *Current Biography: Who's News and Why* (New York: Wilson, 1950).

Rowe, A. P. *One Story of Radar* (Cambridge University Press, 1948).

Ryskind, Allan H. *Hubert: An Unauthorized Biography of the Vice President* (New York: Arlington, 1968).

Savage, Howard J., et al. *American College Athletics*, Bulletin 23 (New York: Carnegie Foundation, 1929).

Scanlan, James, comp. *History of the 18th AAF Base Unit (Motion Picture Unit) (Formerly Designated 1st Motion Picture Unit)* Historical Division, Army Air Force, 1945; microfilm no. A2986, Maxwell Air Force Base, Alabama.

Scanlan, James and M. Warren, comp. *History of the First Motion Picture Unit . . .* Historical Division, Army Air Force, c. 1945; microfilm no. A2987, Maxwell Air Force Base, Alabama.

Schlesinger, Arthur M., Jr. "The U.S. Communist Party." *Life*, 21 (July 29, 1946), 84–96.

The Vital Center: The Politics of Freedom (Boston: Houghton Mifflin, 1949).

Schwartz, Nancy Lynn (completed by Sheila Schwartz). *The Hollywood Writers' Wars* (New York: Knopf, 1982).

Scobie, Ingrid W. *Center Stage: Helen Gahagan Douglas, A Life* (New York: Oxford University Press, 1992).

Shepardson, Whitney H., and William O. Scroggs. *The United States in World Affairs: An Account of American Foreign Relations, 1940* (New York: Harper & Row, 1941).

Sherry, Michael S. *The Rise of American Air Power: The Creation of Armageddon* (New Haven, Conn.: Yale University Press, 1987).

Short, K. R. M. "Hollywood Fights Anti-Semitism, 1945–1947." In K. R. M. Short, ed., *Feature Film as History* (London: Croom Helm, 1981), 157–89.

Sitkoff, Howard. "Racial Militancy and Interracial Violence in the Second World War." *Journal of American History*, 58 (Dec. 1971), 661–81.

Skinner, James M. *The Cross and the Cinema: The Legion of Decency and the National Catholic Office for Motion Pictures, 1933–1970* (Westport, Conn.: Greenwood/Praeger, 1993).

Sklar, Robert. *Movie-Made America: A Cultural History of American Movies* (New York: Vintage, 1975).

  City Boys: Cagney, Bogart, Garfield (Princeton, N.J.: Princeton University Press, 1992).

Smith, Paul. "Introduction." In Paul Smith, ed., *The Historian and Film* (Cambridge University Press, 1976), 1–13.

Steele, Michael. *Knute Rockne: A Bio-Bibliography* (Westport, Conn.: Greenwood, 1983).

Steele, Richard W. *Propaganda in an Open Society: The Roosevelt Administration and the Media, 1933–1941* (Westport, Conn.: Greenwood, 1985).

Street, Sarah. "The Hays Office and the Defense of the British Market in the 1930s." *Historical Journal of Film, Radio and Television,* 5, no. 1 (1985), 37–55.

Strong, Donald S. *Organized Anti-Semitism in America* (Washington, D.C.: American Council on Public Affairs, 1941).

Suid, Lawrence H. *Guts & Glory: Great American War Movies* (Reading, Mass.: Addison-Wesley, 1978).

Taft, Ronald. "A Psychological Assessment of Professional Actors and Related Professions." *Genetic Psychology Monographs,* 64 (Nov. 1961), 309–83.

Tuska, Jon. *Dark Cinema: American Film Noir in Cultural Perspective* (Westport, Conn.: Greenwood, 1984).

Tyler, Robert L. "The American Veterans Committee: Out of a Hot War and Into the Cold." *American Quarterly,* 18 (Fall 1966), 419–36.

Vanderwood, Paul J. "Introduction: A Political Barometer." In Paul J. Vanderwood, ed., *Juarez* (Madison: University of Wisconsin Press, 1983), 9–41.

Vaughn, Stephen. "Spies, National Security, and the 'Inertia Projector': The Secret Service Films of Ronald Reagan." *American Quarterly,* 39 (Fall 1987), 355–80.

  "Morality and Entertainment: The Origins of the Motion Picture Production Code." *Journal of American History,* 77 (June 1990), 39–65.

Ward, John W. "The Meaning of Lindbergh's Flight." *American Quarterly,* 10 (1958), 3–16.

Wartella, Ellen, and Byron Reeves. "Historical Trends in Research on Children and the Media: 1900–1960." *Journal of Communication,* 35 (Spring 1985), 118–33.

Washburn, Patrick. *A Question of Sedition: The Federal Government's Investigation of the Black Press during World War II* (New York: Oxford University Press, 1986).

Weart, Spencer R. *Nuclear Fear: A History of Images* (Cambridge, Mass.: Harvard University Press, 1988).

Wesley, David. *Hate Groups and The Un-American Activities Committee* (New York: Emergency Civil Liberties Committee, 1962).

Wills, Garry. "Nelle's Boy: Ronald Reagan and the Disciples of Christ." *Christian Century,* 103 (Nov. 12, 1986), 1002–6.

  Reagan's America: Innocents at Home (Garden City, N.Y.: Doubleday, 1987).

Writers' War Board. *How Writers Perpetuate Stereotypes: A Digest of Data for the Writers' War Board by the Bureau of Applied Social Research of Columbia University* (New York: Writers' War Board, 1945).

Wynn, Neil A. *The Afro-American and the Second World War* (New York: Holmes & Meier, 1975).

INDEX

341